Public Administration in the New Reality

Alikhan Baimenov · Panos Liverakos
Editors

Public Administration in the New Reality

palgrave
macmillan

Editors
Alikhan Baimenov
Astana Civil Service Hub
Astana, Kazakhstan

Panos Liverakos
Astana Civil Service Hub
Astana, Kazakhstan

ISBN 978-981-96-3844-4 ISBN 978-981-96-3845-1 (eBook)
https://doi.org/10.1007/978-981-96-3845-1

This Palgrave Macmillan imprint is published by the registered company Springer Nature Singapore Pte Ltd.
The registered company address is: 152 Beach Road, #21-01/04 Gateway East, Singapore 189721, Singapore

To the guardians of the long-term interests of the People

Foreword by Kassym-Jomart Tokayev

Public administration of the twenty-first century faces immense and unique challenges that require novel approaches. These challenges are interconnected, spread beyond national borders, span across various policy domains, and happen faster and on a much bigger scale than in the past. This makes the formulation of policy responses and the effect of their implementation much harder to anticipate.

It calls for a new breed of civil servants possessing a set of skills and competencies, who are fairly compensated, and thus sufficiently capacitated to operate in the contemporary environment.

Achieving effective governance through executing government policies and regulations and providing quality services should be a top priority for public servants. The uninterrupted and flawless functioning of government institutions is largely dependent on the level of performance of civil servants.

Complex and interlinked challenges the world is facing today are an unprecedented crash test for public governance systems. This is the *new reality*, as reflected in the title of this book. It depicts an era characterised by greater volatility, uncertainty, complexity, ambiguity, brittleness, anxiety, non-linearity, and incomprehensibility—hence, a world often described as the VUCA and BANI world.

Fortunately, governments around the world are responding to these shifts, as they realise that they cannot afford to lag behind in a world of increasingly dynamic change, where pluralistic and diversified societies have higher expectations from their governments. They should quickly adapt to the ongoing changes and thus remain responsive to people's essential needs. It is vital to be innovative to keep structures and systems more citizen-oriented, flexible, responsive, and creative, while capitalising on the immense advancement of digital technologies.

Government also realise they need to attract human resources with appropriate knowledge, professional experience, competencies, and skills to effectively cope with the daunting tasks ahead. In this context, public human resource management policies and practices have become salient and prominent, as they can contribute positively to selecting and recruiting knowledgeable, skilful, and creative individuals.

Governments also increasingly employ tools that take advantage of scientific and technological developments to formulate, implement, monitor, and evaluate policies. For instance, they are gradually incorporating such technologies in such areas as health care, education social protection, and transportation. Likewise, mainstreaming of cognitive technologies (better known as AI), integrated with big data analytics allow policymakers to advance their understanding of the cost, impact, and consequences of their policy choices. Moreover, digital technologies are also used to upgrading the performance of government functions and HR management.

Kazakhstan is no exception. For the past several years, it has embarked on an ambitious transformation trajectory across the political, economic, and social domains poised to achieve its mid- and long-term development objectives and join the ranks of the fifty most developed countries by 2050. In public governance, its primary objectives are to eradicate bureaucracy and corruption, increase the level of people's trust in government, and render quality public services. The Concept for Public Administration (2021) and the Concept for Civil Service (2024) provide for a new "people-centred" model of public administration.

Kazakhstan has put into practice the concept of a "Listening State" to expand opportunities for citizens to participate in the decision-making processes. Kazakhstan has also introduced policies for the de-bureaucratisation of public administration and the digitalisation of public services and government operations. It has also laid the foundation to establish a reserve of highly qualified individuals from various sectors and backgrounds, who can serve the public interest.

Furthermore, our country also promotes public dialogue among countries aimed at learning from each other's experiences. A good example of this is the Astana Civil Service Hub, a multilateral institutional platform for knowledge and experience exchange in the field of public governance, fully supported by the Government of the Republic of Kazakhstan.

In this context, this book—a publication of the Astana Civil Service Hub—is a remarkable addition to the body of knowledge, as it casts light on how public administrators worldwide adapt to the emerging new reality as well as imparts considerable insights on specific aspects of public administration and civil service. It also highlights the significance of international cooperation and partnerships, which have become more salient and ever important in these turbulent and tumultuous times, we all live in.

Astana, Kazakhstan
November 2024

Kassym-Jomart Tokayev
President of the Republic
of Kazakhstan

Introductory Note by Larbi Djacta

The Omnipotent Role of the Civil Service

Large-scale transformative developments in technology, the environment and the economy are profoundly impacting public administration and civil service in the twenty-first century. Rapid technological advancements, such as artificial intelligence and big data analytics, are further revolutionising the delivery of public services. Pressing environmental challenges demand proactive policies, while economic changes such as automation and the rise of the knowledge economy require that public administrations implement relevant strategies to mitigate societal impacts.

In addition, increased interconnectedness necessitates international collaboration among public administrations, facilitating the exchange of ideas, best practices, and policies, thereby influencing governance approaches. In an era characterised by complex issues such as climate change, rapid technological advances, and global crises like the recent COVID-19 pandemic, the role of public administration and civil servants is critical. They must implement policies effectively, translating political decisions into tangible actions, and ensuring that government policies are executed fairly, efficiently, and transparently, meeting public expectations.

To fulfil their mission, civil servants must possess specialised knowledge and expertise spanning across various fields, including economics, public health, education, and environmental science, along with expertise in statistics, data analysis, and communication. These competencies enable them to formulate evidence-based policies and offer informed advice to policymakers. Civil servants must also embrace innovation, foster diversity, and promote inclusive policies to remain adaptable and agile. Such flexibility enhances the quality and effectiveness of governance, allowing institutions to address emerging challenges and seize opportunities for positive change.

Civil servants must adhere to codes of conduct and ethical standards to prevent corruption, nepotism, and abuse of power, while promoting accountability and transparency. Upholding these principles enhances public trust and confidence in government institutions, especially in times of instability and upheaval. Ultimately, civil servants remain indispensable for promoting good governance, fostering development, upholding democratic values, and addressing complex challenges globally in the twenty-first century.

As Chair of the International Civil Service Commission, I emphasise the vital and multifaceted role of the international civil service in the twenty-first century. This service is key for addressing global challenges and fostering international cooperation. Organisations such as the United Nations (UN) and its Development Programme (UNDP), the World Bank (WB), the International Monetary Fund (IMF), the World Health Organisation (WHO), and other organisations exemplify the international civil service's pivotal role in enhancing global governance.

These organisations provide a platform for countries to collaborate on issues ranging from peace and security to sustainable development and public health. They are at the forefront of global efforts to achieve the Sustainable Development Goals (SDGs). In this context, they offer technical assistance, financial support, and policy advice to promote sustainable development in areas such as poverty eradication, education, health care, gender equality, public administration, and environmental conservation.

International development organisations also work together to address transnational challenges such as climate change, pandemics, terrorism, human trafficking, and cybercrime. They coordinate responses, share information and expertise, and develop common strategies to mitigate these threats to global stability and prosperity.

Moreover, international civil service entities advocate for and protect human rights globally. They monitor human rights situations, investigate violations, provide support to victims, and promote adherence to international human rights standards and treaties. Most importantly, international civil servants foster cooperation and dialogue through multilateral negotiations and collaborative initiatives. They build consensus, resolve differences, and promote shared interests, fostering understanding, trust, and mutual respect.

International civil servants serve as catalysts for global cooperation, peace, and development. They work across borders and disciplines to build a more just, equitable, and sustainable world for present and future generations. In fulfilling their mandate, they must uphold principles of transparency and accountability, ensuring efficient and effective use of resources. They are accountable to member states, donors, and the global community.

The International Civil Service Commission (ICSC) fulfils its mandate by addressing all aspects of international staff employment conditions. It is actively involved in various areas under its statute, making decisions on matters such as daily subsistence allowances, cost of living, post adjustment, and hardship entitlements. In other areas, the ICSC makes recommendations to the General Assembly, which then takes relevant decisions on issues such as professional salary scales, dependency allowances, and education grants. Additionally, the Commission makes recommendations to executive heads of organisations on human resources policy issues.

The ICSC plays a crucial role in enhancing the international civil service in the twenty-first century through its key functions. It establishes policies, guidelines, and standards related to the conditions of service, salaries, allowances, and benefits for international civil servants across various international organisations. By setting these standards, the ICSC ensures fairness, transparency, and equity, which are essential for attracting and retaining talented individuals in the international civil service, thereby enhancing its effectiveness in the twenty-first century.

The Commission enhances the efficiency and effectiveness of the international civil service through its reviews and recommendations, also benefiting national civil service systems. It evaluates organisational structures, job classifications, and performance management systems to ensure alignment with the evolving needs of development organisations and the global context.

Additionally, the Commission conducts regular salary surveys and analyses to ensure that compensation packages offered to international civil servants remain competitive with those in other sectors and industries, assisting organisations in attracting and retaining top talent. The ICSC also promotes diversity and inclusion by advocating for equal opportunities for all employees, regardless of their gender, nationality, ethnicity, or background. This includes efforts to address gender parity, promote the rights of persons with disabilities, and foster cultural sensitivity.

The International Civil Service Commission (ICSC) supports capacity building and professional development initiatives within international organisations by providing guidance on training programmes, career development opportunities, and performance evaluation systems. A notable example of this effort is the collaboration with the Astana Civil Service Hub, a multilateral knowledge and information exchange platform based in Kazakhstan, which helps disseminate its professed principles and practices among participating countries. Both organisations work to enhance the skills and competencies of civil servants, building a more capable and resilient workforce at the international and national levels. They also share common values in developing civil services and promoting cooperation and dialogue among countries, fostering understanding, trust, and mutual respect.

In the rapidly changing global landscape of the twenty-first century, the Commission plays a crucial role in addressing emerging challenges facing the civil service, such as rapid technological advancement, climate change, global health crises, and geopolitical shifts. By providing guidance and support to international and other organisations, the ICSC helps ensure the continued relevance and effectiveness of the civil service. It promotes professionalism, integrity, and excellence within the international civil service, contributing to the achievement of the goals and mandates of international organisations.

Addressing these complex issues requires collective action, innovative solutions, and political will at the national, regional, and international levels. Collaboration among governments, civil society, academia, and the private sector is essential for building a more resilient, sustainable, and inclusive world in the new reality. The ICSC remains key to fostering this collaboration and driving progress in the new reality.

New York, USA
October 2024

Larbi Djacta
Chairman, International Civil
Service Commission (ICSC)

Contents

Notes on Contributors

Celine Grace Abella currently works as a Communications Specialist at the Eastern Regional Organization for Public Administration (EROPA). She is also a Master of Public Administration Student at the University of the Philippines National College of Public Administration and Governance (UP NCPAG). Previously, she worked as a Programme Manager of the Sustainable Development and Regional and Local Governance Cluster (SDRLGC) of the Development Academy of the Philippines, Graduate School of Public and Development Management (DAP-GSPDM). She oversaw several research and extension programmes mainly on futures thinking, Sustainable Development Goals (SDGs), and regional and local development. Celine is also involved in various trainings conducted by the Philippine Society for Public Administration (PSPA) and the Philippine Futures Thinking Society (Phil Futures). She obtained her Bachelor's degree in Consular and Diplomatic Affairs from De La Salle College of Saint Benilde.

Almazbek Akmataliev has been working as the Rector of the Academy of Public Administration under the President of the Kyrgyz Republic named after Zhusup Abdrakhmanov since 2018. In the civil service, he went from deputy head of the district administration to the head of the region. He has extensive experience in managing projects and development programmes on a national scale. For a long time, he worked in the educational field in various positions at the Academy of Sciences, the Ministry of Education. He stood at the origins of the creation of Naryn State University and was one of the first rectors of this university. 2022–1992. He has also worked with international institutions as ARIS; the technology park in the Kyrgyz-Turkish Manas University; European Commission Programmes TEMPUS: HONOR, TEMPUS: CANEM, TEMPUS: ISMU, TEMPUS: CANQA, TEMPUSIV: EDUCA, TEMPUS: Erasmus Mundus EACEA, TEMPUS: TOSCA, TEMPUS SCM; Soros Foundation-Kyrgyzstan; Aga Khan Foundation; Peace Nexus, etc, on different topics. He is Professor, Doctor of Political Sciences, with over 30 scientific publications. Also, author of 2 monographs and 3 textbooks for universities. Since 2009 is Honoured Worker of Education of the Kyrgyz Republic.

Demetrios Argyriades is a graduate of the London School of Economics and Political Science and the Sorbonne University. He started his career in Britain and Greece and, in 1967, joined the ranks of the international public service, working first for the Organisation for Economic Cooperation and Development (OECD) and then the United Nations Secretariat. In the past 25 years, he has served as a consultant to the EU, the Bank of Greece, the United Nations Department of Economic and Social Affairs (UNDESA), the United Nations Development Programme (UNDP), and other international organisations on human resources development, public service reform, ethics, and democratic governance. From 1975, he taught for several years at the New York University and the International Training Centre (ITC) of the International Labour Organisation (ILO) in Turin, as well as other colleges and universities in the USA and abroad. He has published very widely, in four languages, and has served as Rapporteur of the four successive Working Groups of the International Institute of Administrative Sciences (IIAS) on Global Governance, as well as Rapporteur-General of the 25th International Congress of the IIAS, in 2001. He is a Doctor *honoris causa* of the University of Athens and recipient of the American Society of Public Administration (ASPA) F. W. Riggs Award.

Alikhan Baimenov is Chairman of the Steering Committee of the Astana Civil Service Hub and a distinguished public figure, who has held leading public posts in the Government of the Republic of Kazakhstan. In his political career, he has served as the Head of the Executive Office of the President, Head of the Office of the Prime Minister, Chairman of the Agency for Civil Service Affairs, Minister of Labour and Social Protection, and a member of the Parliament of Kazakhstan. Dr Baimenov has overseen two waves of civil service reform of the Republic of Kazakhstan, as well as the Concept of Social Protection for Kazakhstan's citizens. He has graduated from the Karaganda Technical Institute (1981) and completed his post-graduate studies at the Moscow Motor-Road Institute (1985–1988). He holds a Ph.D. in Technical Sciences. He is the author of the monographs *Public Service. International Experience. Kazakhstani Model* (2000), *Civil Service in the Republic of Kazakhstan* (2000) and of a series of publications on such issues as social protection, public management and public service, management, as well as political and party building. Moreover, he is the co-editor of a book titled "Public Service Excellence in the twenty-first Century" and published by Palgrave in the early part of 2019. He was also the guiding force behind the "Review of Global and Regional Trends of Civil Service Development" a book published in 2017 under the auspices of the Astana Civil Service Hub. Dr. Baimenov is a recipient of several national and international awards, including a Special Award of the UN Office of South-South Cooperation for promoting regional and interregional cooperation in the civil service field. He is also a member of the National Academy of Natural Sciences.

Joseph Besigye Bazirake is a Post-doctoral Researcher at Nelson Mandela University's Chair for Critical Studies in Higher Education Transformation (CriSHET), South Africa. His extensive scholarly engagement spans international politics, peace and conflict studies, and higher education transformation, with notable contributions to publications and international handbooks, covering topics such as higher education and international change, the responsibility to protect principle, forced migration and asylum seeking, climate change discourse in peacebuilding, the global refugee crisis, race-based conflict, and the role of students as agents of change.

Emilia Sičáková Beblavá is Professor at the Institute of Public Policy at Comenius University in Bratislava where she conducts research and teaches courses on public governance. She was involved with Transparency International Slovakia since 1998 as its President and later as the Board Member (until 2015). Her post-graduate programmes involve Georgetown University, Yale University, and Harvard University.

Miroslav Beblavý is an Adjunct Professor at Sciences Po in Paris, the Scientific Coordinator of European Experts Network in Economics of

Education, and Public Financial Management Advisor for the International Monetary Fund. He is also former Associate Professor at the Faculty of Social and Economic Sciences of the Comenius University in Bratislava (2010–2014); a former Member of Parliament in Slovakia (2010–2020); and a former Senior Research Fellow at the Centre for European Policy in Brussels (2011–2019). He has extensive experience in anti-corruption, as well as education policy from both an academic and practical perspectives. As an academic, he published internationally on anti-corruption policies and strategies, as well as on education policy. As a politician, he was both a Chair of the Parliament's Conflict of Interest Committee and member of the Education Committee. He was directly involved in uncovering numerous cases of corruption and abuse in the education sector. He holds a Ph.D. in Economics from the University of St. Andrews in the United Kingdom.

Ieva Daniela Beinaroviča is an Auditor and a Lecturer in the Department of Political Science, University of Latvia. Her area of research is evidence-informed policy learning and change in the context of holistic emergency management. As a former practitioner of public administration, Ieva Daniela Beinaroviča gained practical experience in efficiency and quality management in the public sector, as well as policy planning and digitisation, and emergency management during the Covid-19 pandemic.

Guido Bertucci is Executive Director of "*Governance Solutions International*", an organisation which promotes the development and sharing of innovative experiences in governance. Previously, he was in charge of the United Nations Programme on Public Administration and Development, which promotes sound public policy, good governance, and efficient and competent public administration around the world. He is an alumnus of the Global Agenda Councils of the World Economic Forum. He has been responsible for advocacy activities in governance and public administration at the global level; he has directed research, has organised global meetings, and has provided technical assistance on emerging issues in public policy, governance, and public administration. He has also advised governments in formulating strategies for human resources and leadership development. He has been cooperating in the organisation of the World Government Summit held annually in the UAE. Earlier, he was responsible for the creation and management of the United Nations Public Administration Network (UNPAN) with more than thirty international and regional partners. Guido Bertucci holds a *Laurea* in Political Science and a post-graduate Diploma in Administrative Sciences from the Catholic University of Milan. He has received several honorary doctoral degrees. He speaks fluent Italian, English, French, and Spanish.

Alex Bello Brillantes Jr. is Professor Emeritus of Public Administration, former Dean of the National College of Public Administration and Governance of the University of the Philippines (2004–2010), UP Scientist (2021), and Secretary-General of the Eastern Regional Organization for Public Administration (EROPA). He served as Executive Director of the Local Government Academy (1993–1997), Commissioner (Deputy Minister) of the Commission on Higher Education (2013–2017), and President of the Asian Association for Public Administration (AAPA). He received a Distinguished Alumni award for Innovative Public Administration Education from the UP Alumni Association in 2023 and East West Center Distinguished Alumni Award in 2018. He was also a recipient of the International Publications Award from the University of the Philippines for seven times. He obtained his AB and MPA from the University of the Philippines, and M.A. and Ph.D. from the University of Hawaii at Manoa, USA.

Ainna Shariz Comia is currently the Project Officer for the USAID Urban Connect Activity implemented by the WSP USA Solutions Inc. She also serves as the Senior Researcher and Office Manager of the Eastern Regional Organization for Public Administration (EROPA). At EROPA, she oversees research projects, the quarterly online bulleting, and manages events and training programmes. Previously, she was a Project Assistant IV at the Development Academy of the Philippines (DAP), where she facilitated training for local government units. She has also worked as a Research Project Associate for the Philippines Society for Public Administration (PSPA), focusing on bureaucracy, peace, and governance research, and with the Philippines Futures Thinking Society as Programme Manager of the FT 101 Regional Futures Consortium Workshop. Ms. Comia is a *Magna Cum Laude* graduate in Consular and Diplomatic Affairs from De La Salle College of Saint Benilde.

Nelin Estocado Dulpina is a University Researcher of the Center for Leadership, Citizenship, and Democracy of the National College of Public Administration and Governance, University of the Philippines Diliman. She is a candidate for the Doctor of Public Administration degree. She holds a B.A. in Anthropology and a Master's degree in Women and Development Studies, both from the University of the Philippines Diliman.

Maia Dvalishvili is currently the Deputy Head of the Civil Service Bureau of the Republic of Georgia. Between 2010 and 2014, she served at the Ministry of Culture and Monuments Protection, first as Main Specialist of the Legal Provision Division and then Head of the Division. She holds an Executive Master Degree of Public Administration from the Hertie School, a Master's degree in International Law from the Georgian Institute of Public Affairs and a Bachelor's degree in Law from Ivane Javakhishvili Tbilisi State University. Maia is also a member of the Astana Civil Service Hub Advisory Board since 2017. She has published a guidebook on Civil Service Law of Georgia, a Practical Guide for Managers, and has co-authored a publication titled Guidebook on Management and Leadership in the Civil Service.

Rajneesh Gupta is an accomplished Indian public servant with 25 years of diverse experience, including key roles in the Ministry of Railways. As Executive Director at RDSO, Lucknow, he spearheaded in safety-signalling systems. His professorship at the National Academy of Indian Railways and diverse leadership positions underlines his deep knowledge and expertise in signalling, telecommunications, and project management. Beyond his professional achievements, Gupta is a Fullbright Scholar at Indiana University, USA, focusing on public policy. His academic journey is equally noteworthy, with credentials from IIT Roorkee and ISM Mohali, culminating in his current pursuit as a doctoral student.

Jahi Jahija is Professor of Public Administration at the University of Tetovo in North Macedonia. He has worked for many years for public institutions in North Macedonia in the field of Public Administration. From 2007 to 2011, he worked as a Coordinator (responsible) for the employment procedures of civil servants in the Republic of North Macedonia. From 2011 to 2019, he was State Secretary at the Ministry of Information and Administration in North Macedonia. During this period, he was also a member and Chairman of the Board of ReSPA (Regional School for Public Administration), Danilovgrad, Montenegro. From 2017 to 2019, he coordinated the Special Group of Public Administration Reform in North Macedonia within the EU Association and Stabilization Committee. From 2016 to date, he has been a member of the Advisory Board of ACSH (Astana Civil Service Hub).

Saltanat Janenova holds a Ph.D. degree in Social Policy from the University of Edinburgh (UK). Over the past decade, Saltanat has been active in teaching, research, and consultancy in the public policy field with a focus on the Eurasia region. Saltanat is currently a Lecturer in Public Policy at the School for Policy Studies, University of Bristol (United Kingdom), and Research Advisor at the National Analytical Centre, Nazarbayev University (Kazakhstan). Her research interests include public sector reforms, open government, citizens engagement, and public service innovations. Saltanat Janenova's research articles have been published in reputable journals: *International Review of Administrative Sciences, International Journal of Public Sector Management, Public Administration and Development, Review of Public Personnel Administration, International Review of Public Policy, and Central Asian Survey.*

Aleksis Jarockis is a Ph.D. student in Social Sciences at the University of Latvia, Riga. In 2014, he completed a professional Master's degree in Management of Organisations at the School of Business and Finance. He also studied at Duke University's Sanford School of Public Policy in 2015, specialising in public sector financing and management. Currently, Aleksis Jarockis is the Director of the Communication Department at the Ministry of Finance of the Republic of Latvia. He is an active member of the European Communication and Research Association (ECREA) and the European Association of Communication Directors (EACD). His research interests include government communication, public administration, and organisational communication.

Catherine Kardava a Doctor of Law, is currently the Director of the Georgian Parliamentary Research Centre, and Professor at the Altebridge, International University of Management and Communication, and the Shota Meskhia State Teaching University at Zugdidi. She is a professional with many years of scientific experience. In 2006, Ms. Kardava defended her dissertation of Candidate of Legal Sciences, Law at the Tbilisi State University, and in 2012, she received her Ph.D. in the field of Law on Public Service at Humboldt University of Berlin. Catherine Kardava was the Head of the Legal Provision Unit at the Legal Department of the Ministry of Culture and Monument Protection for four years and the Head of the Civil Service Bureau of Georgia for nine years. She has been actively involved in the ongoing public administration reform of the country. She has received various scholarships such as a scholarship of the Parliament of Berlin at Humboldt University, a scholarship of the Fund for Development and Reforms, and the German Academic Exchange Service (DAAD). Since 2007, Ms Kardava has been conducting trainings in the field of administrative law, administrative procedural law, ethics in public service, public administration management and leadership, etc. She is a member of the Astana Civil Service Hub Advisory Board and scientific supervisor of doctoral students at the Academy of Public Administration of Kazakhstan. Catherine Kardava has authored numerous scientific articles, manuals and legislation regulating public service, anti-corruption, etc.

Mirzokhid Karshiev is a Doctoral Researcher at the University of Helsinki, where his research has focused on administrative transformations and local governance in Uzbekistan and Central Eurasia. In his more than 15 years of professional experience, he worked in government, business, and research entities in Uzbekistan. He has also consulted international organisations such as UNDP and the World Bank on local governance, public administration, and digital transformation issues.

Bahram Khalilov is Deputy Chairperson of the State Examination Centre since 2016, when the Civil Service and the State Student Admission Commissions merged. Prior to this appointment, Mr. Khalilov was Chairman of the Civil Service Commission under the President of the Republic of Azerbaijan (2015–2016). He served as chief consultant on Legislation and Legal Expertise in the Presidential Administration—formerly the Apparatus of the President—between 1996 and 2005. Bahram Khalilov also served as the Head of Department on Law and Defence of the Ganja City Executive (1994–1996) and as a consultant, chief consultant, and Head of Law Department in different institutions (1984–1994). He has also been involved as an expert in several international and local projects. He holds a degree of Law from Odessa National University (1980). He continued his education at Moscow University graduating in 1984. Bahram Khalilov is author of approximately 20 articles published in several newspapers in Azerbaijani, Russian, and English languages.

Christine Leitner is Senior Adviser and co-founder, Centre for Economics and Public Administration Limited (CEPA, UK). Christine focuses on policy and legal frameworks in the field of digital government and public sector innovation. Since 2013, she has been a Senior Policy Advisor at the Austrian Ministry of Labour and Economy, where she is responsible for (digital) trade policy and participates in the relevant workstreams at the OECD. Prior to that she headed the Centre for European Public Administration and the Department for E-Governance and Administration at Danube University (AT) and was a Senior Lecturer at the Maastricht-based European Institute of Public Administration (NL). Between 2002 and 2010, she was the Programme Director of the European Commission's European eGovernment Awards. Christine has extensive experience working with European and international organisations, including the European Commission, the OECD and UNDP. She was a member of the Supervisory Board of the Estonian E-Governance Academy, the European Commission's Expert Group on Public Sector Innovation, and of the Selection Committee for the Bloomberg Mayors Challenge Europe. She has been a member of the expert jury in numerous international and national awards, e.g. the Sultan Qaboos Awards for Excellence in e-Government (Oman); the European Public Service Award (EU); and the World Government Summit (Dubai), and serves as an assessor in the UAE Government Excellence Programmes. Christine is a Visiting Lecturer at the University of Public Administration and Finance, Ludwigsburg, Germany, and has lectured at a wide range of academic institutions, including the Kennedy School of Government, ESADE, the European University Institute in Florence, the University of Maastricht, the University of Applied Sciences in Berne, and other schools of Public Administration in and outside Europe. She is the editor and/or author of numerous publications on digital government and service innovation and has chaired or co-chaired several academic conferences including the International Conference on the Human Side of Service Engineering (HSSE), the International Conference on Electronic Government and the Information Systems Perspective (EGOVIS/DEXA), and the Central and Eastern e-Government Days (CEEGov). She has been a keynote speaker at numerous international conferences, including EU Ministerial Conferences and the UNDP/Astana Civil Service Hub Talks.

Panos Liverakos is a governance and public administration expert, currently engaged with the Astana Civil Service Hub as a senior technical advisor. He has served for many years as a Chief Technical Advisor/ Team Leader with UNDESA and UNDP. His work covered a wide range of topics including institutional development, change management, governance assessments, public administration, and civil service reform and development. It also involved partnership building and networking with governments and public institutions in the Western Balkans, Central and Eastern Europe, the Commonwealth of Independent States, and South-East Asia. Prior to this, he worked as a freelance consultant on various assignments ranging from innovation design and implementation of change management and performance management systems. He has also worked as an analyst and researcher for the Long Island Regional Planning Board engaged in large-scale needs-assessments and forecasting projects. He holds PhD in Political Economy and Public Policy and MA in Political Science degrees from the State University of New York at Stony Brook. He also holds a first degree from Bournemouth University in business administration and institutional management. He is the editor and author of several publications on public administration and civil service reform.

Alexander Lopez holds a Ph.D. from the University of Oslo, and he is currently the Director for International Affairs of the Latin American Centre for Development Administration (CLAD) and inter-governmental organisation with 24 member states as well as Professor at the National University of Costa Rica. He is the former Director of the "Central American Institute for Public Administration" (ICAP), a regional international organisation. He has worked in several countries including Norway, Viet Nam, South Africa, India, Brazil, México, and throughout Central America on issues related to public administration and environmental international policies. Dr. López has given lectures and seminars in more than 40 countries around the world and has published extensively in Spanish and English with well-known editorial houses such as SAGE, Massachusetts Institute of Technology Press (MIT Press), Routledge, and Kluwer Academic Publishers.

Reiou Regie Manuel graduated *Magna Cum Laude* with a Bachelor of Arts in Broadcast Communication from the University of the Philippines Diliman. She also holds a Master of Public Administration from the University of the Philippines—National College of Public Administration and Governance. She currently serves as Development Management Officer III and Division Chief for the Research, Planning, and MIS Division at the City Government of Caloocan. Her expertise spans health promotion, decentralisation, public policy, ethics and accountability, and sustainable development. Ms Manuel is a member of the Philippine Society for Public Administration and Phi Kappa Phi Honor Society. She was also honoured with the Inaugural Marie Rosenberg Award for

Best Conference Paper at the 2023 EROPA Conference. She is currently working on a manuscript focused on health promotion governance and transportation ethics.

Geraldine Fraser-Moleketi served as Minister of Public Service and Administration from 1999 to 2008. She was also a member of the National Executive Committee of the African National Congress (ANC) until 2007. A strong advocate for South Africa and Africa's social and economic transformation, Fraser-Moleketi played a role in the Convention for a Democratic South Africa (CODESA), as an alternate to Joe Slovo on the Management Committee of CODESA, the multiparty negotiating forum that gave birth to South Africa's constitutional democracy in 1994. Dr. Fraser-Moleketi was also a member of the Constituent Assembly that crafted and adopted "The Constitution of the Republic of South Africa, 1996". Fraser-Moleketi served as a Member of Parliament (MP) of South Africa's first democratic parliament from 1994 to 2008 and in the Cabinet of three consecutive governments, first under President Nelson Mandela and thereafter, President Thabo Mbeki. As a member of parliament and government, Fraser-Moleketi influenced the development of transformative policies on social welfare and population development, as well as public service and administration. In her drive to make continual public contributions on issues such as youth and women empowerment, along with capacity development in education, governance, and poverty eradication, she was involved with various initiatives and structures in the African Development Bank (AfDB) and bodies of the United Nations (UN). These roles included the United Nations Development Programme (UNDP) and the Committee of Experts of Public Administration (CEPA), a subsidiary body of the United Nations Economic and Social Council (ECOSOC). Fraser-Moleketi is a former Director of Global Democratic Governance Practice of the UNDP and served as a member of the Quadrennial Comprehensive Policy Review of the United Nations Development System. She currently serves as Chair of the CEPA, a subsidiary body of ECOSOC. Fraser-Moleketi is Chancellor of the Nelson Mandela University and former Chairperson of the Advisory Council of the Mapungubwe Institute for Strategic Reflection (MISTRA). She has been appointed as Chairperson of the Thabo Mbeki Foundation as of November 2021. Her qualifications include a Master's degree in Administration (Cum Laude) from the University of Pretoria, and a qualification in "Leading Organisational Change" programme at

Wharton Business School at the University of Pennsylvania. In addition, she has been awarded "Digitally Savvy Board Member Certificate" with Sloane Executive Education, Massachusetts Institute for Technology (MIT). She is a Fellow of the Institute of Politics at the Kennedy School of Government at Harvard University. Fraser-Moleketi was awarded a D.Phil. Honoris Causa by the Nelson Mandela University in April 2017. The North-West University (NWU) conferred an Honorary Doctorate, on Dr. Geraldine Fraser-Moleketi, on 19 November 2021 for "exceptional contributions to the South African political landscape and society". During her early political career, she joined the ANC while it was banned in South Africa and served in various formations of the movement. Fraser-Moleketi also served on the national executive committee of the ANC. In preparation for the first democratic elections in 1994, she served as the national deputy elections coordinator for the African National Congress. Prior to being appointed as Minister of Public Service and Administration, she was Deputy Minister for Welfare and Population Development and subsequently the Minister for Welfare and Population Development. As such, she was responsible for the expansion of the social security safety net and specifically the inception of the child support grant. She led an inter-ministerial committee for children and young people/youth at risk and developed leading programmes on the war against poverty. As Minister of Public Service and Administration, her flagship initiative was the Government Employee Medical Aid Scheme (GEMS), which was registered in 2005 to provide health insurance cover to government employees especially lower paid employees who had no cover until that point. Further initiatives include instituting Senior Management Service for the development of a professional senior management cadre and revitalising the "Batho Pele" (People first) programme to develop a strong service delivery culture within the South African public service. Fraser-Moleketi initiated the Occupation Specific Dispensation (OSD), which sought to create a career path for professionals through a review of the remuneration structure of professionals outside of the management track within the Public Service. She, along with a team, developed and implemented the Community Development Workers Programme in an endeavour to bridge the gap between government and disadvantaged communities. She also made an exceptional public contribution to the improvement of society beyond the country's borders both while in government and later in the UNDP and the AfDB. Dr. Fraser-Moleketi served on the High-Level Panel on Fragile States, established by

Dr. Donald Kaberuka (President of the AfDB), and chaired by Liberian President Ellen Johnson Sirleaf. The High-Level Panel presented their report entitled "Ending Conflict and Building Peace in Africa: A Call to Action" to the 22nd African Union Summit in January 2014. Fraser-Moleketi was a former Special Envoy on Gender of the AFDB and served at the level of Vice-President and was, among others, involved with the finalisation and implementation of the Gender Strategy within the AfDB in an endeavour to support its policies towards inclusive economic growth in Africa. She introduced various flagship initiatives, including the conceptualisation and initial launching of the Affirmative Finance Action for Women in Africa Fund in May 2016. Geraldine J Fraser-Moleketi serves on boards across academia, think tanks, and the private sector. She was born in Cape Town in August 1960.

Nadia Mukadam is a Research Assistant and Social Media Manager at Nelson Mandela University's Engagement and Transformation Portfolio (ETP), collaborating closely with the Chair for Critical Studies in Higher Education Transformation (CriSHET). With a background in Applied Language Studies, Marketing, Business, and Communication Management, she approaches research from an interdisciplinary perspective, with a particular interest in the intersection of higher education transformation, critical pedagogies, public administration, and institutional culture.

James L. Perry is Distinguished Professor Emeritus in the Paul H. O'Neill School of Public and Environmental Affairs, Indiana University, Bloomington. From 2012 through 2017, he was Editor in Chief of *Public Administration Review* (*PAR*), the premiere global professional journal in public administration. He is currently co-editor for *Asia Pacific Journal of Public Administration*. Perry has edited three editions of the *Handbook of Public Administration,* most recently in 2015 (with Robert Christensen, Jossey-Bass). The *Handbook* is a leading comprehensive resource for public professionals. In 2020, he edited *Public Service and Good Governance for the Twenty-first Century* (U of Penn Press), in collaboration with the Volcker Alliance. His newest book is *Managing Organizations to Sustain Passion for Public Service* (Cambridge University Press, 2021). The book is a synthesis of 30 years of research on public service and prosocial motivation. It provides detailed proposals for how emerging behavioural-science knowledge can be used to reimagine motivation of public employees. The book is a blueprint for transforming civil service systems globally. Perry's leadership in public administration is exemplified by many recognitions received during his career, including the Dwight Waldo Award for career contributions to public administration, the H. George Frederickson Award for career contributions from the Public Management Research Association, the John Gaus Award from the American Political Science Association for a lifetime of exemplary scholarship in the joint tradition of political science and public administration, and the Routledge Prize for outstanding contributions to public management research from the International Research Society for Public Management. He is a Fellow of the National Academy of Public Administration. Perry received an undergraduate degree from the University of Chicago and M.P.A. and Ph.D. degrees from the Maxwell School of Citizenship and Public Affairs, Syracuse University. In addition to Indiana University, Perry has also held faculty appointments at University of California, Irvine, Chinese University of Hong Kong, University of Wisconsin, Madison, Yonsei University, Katholieke Universiteit Leuven, and University of Hong Kong.

Iveta Reinholde is Professor of Public Administration in the Department of Political Sciences of the University of Latvia. She has considerable experience in conducting policy evaluations, working in multinational teams and international settings on such areas as public administration reform, internal audit, human security and public services. In addition, fields of her research include EU public policy, public policy evaluation and analysis, public sector organisations, and organisational theory. Iveta is experienced in advising and designing policy recommendations for national and local governments. She is currently the Head of the Public Council of the National Audit Office in Latvia and since 2014, she is an independent expert for the Congress of Local and Regional Authorities of the Council of Europe. In 2019, she was awarded with the *Alena Brunovska Award for Teaching Excellence in Public Administration* by NISPAcee.

Karl Emmanuel Villanueva Ruiz graduated with a Bachelor of Library and Information Science (BLIS), University of Santo Tomas (2015). He ranked 1st in the Philippine Librarians' Licensure Examination (2016). He graduated with a degree of Master of Library and Information Science from the UP Diliman School of Library and Information Studies (2024), and he has been an NGPAG librarian since 2017. He has co-authored public administration articles with Dr. Brillantes like "Good

Practices in Collaborative Governance", "Issues and Concerns on Decentralization in Some Asian Countries", "Public Administration in the Philippines: features, trends, issues, and directions", "Open Government and Freedom of information: The Philippine Experience", and others. He has also received the international Publications Award from the University of the Philippines in 2023.

Baktybek Shamkeev works as the Director of the Institute for Public Administration Development Research at the Academy of Public Administration under the President of the Kyrgyz Republic named after Zhusup Abdrakhmanov. Prior to that, he worked as the head of various state financial institutions, such as Aiyl Bank OJSC, the State Mortgage Company and others. For a long time, he worked in the consulting business, gained invaluable experience as a consultant and trainer in strategic planning, management, financing, team building, corporate development in the field of Agro-industrial complex, and infrastructure development, and has teaching experience at the Academy of Management under the President of the Kyrgyz Republic, where he developed and taught educational courses for students of the APMCU on the following topics: "Rural Development", "Management of Development Programs and Projects", "Microfinance in Entrepreneurship". Thanks to this experience, in 2015 he received the international certificate "CMC (Certified Management Consultant)". Currently, the institute headed by him is engaged in research in the field of public administration and the development of skills and competencies of managers at various levels.

Christian M. Stiefmueller is Managing Director, Centre for Economics and Public Administration (CEPA). Christian provides advice to public sector clients and civil society organisations. He has authored numerous reports, policy statements, and commentaries on regulation and governance, with a particular emphasis on the financial sector. His research focus at present is on the legal and societal aspects of disruptive technological innovation. Christian is a regular speaker at international conferences and has worked as an expert with a variety of international organisations and institutions, including the World Bank and the International Monetary Fund (IMF), European and national governments and legislative bodies, and civil society organisations. Previously a senior investment banker, Christian has more than 20 years' first-hand experience in the financial industry and worked for major global banks advising corporate clients and financial investors on mergers, acquisitions, and capital markets transactions. He also managed two London-based corporate finance advisory firms serving clients in the technology and telecom sectors. He holds graduate degrees in Law and Applied Languages from the University of Innsbruck and an M.B.A degree from the University of California (Berkeley).

Malvīne Stučka is currently a Ph.D. candidate in the Department of Political Science of the University of Latvia. Her research is focused on political leadership in local government. She has been a participant in a number of research projects on issues of local governments, public administration human security and resilience. She has publications on political leadership, policy implementation and reforms of public administration.

Gulimzhan Suleimenova is responsible for the effective implementation of the capacity building strategy of the Hub. She has extensive experience in research and higher education and executive education systems. Her research interests focus on public servants' training, performance evaluation systems, and corruption. She has authored several research articles and book chapters. Dr. Suleimenova joined the Academy of Public Administration under the President of Kazakhstan, where she supervised research commissioned by the Presidential Administration and the Agency for Civil Service Affairs (2009–2012). Under her leadership, the Senior Executive Service Training Programmes for Kazakhstani Corps "A" administrative civil servants were developed and introduced (2013–2014). She has also been involved in many collaborative research and education projects supported by various organisations including UNFPA, EU, World Bank, Temasek Foundation, Friedrich Ebert Foundation, and Hanns-Seidel-Stiftung Foundation, as well as by different government agencies.

Aziza Umarova is an expert on the political economy of reforms and public sector performance in Central Asia. A thoughtful practitioner who brings regional insight and analysis, while engaging in a variety of roles. Since 2017, through her boutique consulting firm SmartGov, she has devised and delivered numerous projects across the region. Before that she advised on public sector innovation at the UNDP Global Centre for Public Service Excellence in Singapore. Prior to that she served with the United Nations Development Programme for a decade where she coordinated UNDP's ground-breaking multi-million governance portfolio in Uzbekistan. In 2022, she was a Visiting Fellow at the Davis Centre for Eurasian Studies at Harvard University, and in 2019 at SAIS, John Hopkins University. From March 2023, she serves as the coordinator of the newly set up Delivery Unit, at the Agency for Strategic Reforms under the President of Uzbekistan. She is also a Chatham house expert, a member of the Steering Committee of the Astana Civil Service Hub, and member of the Board of JC Uzbekistan Airports and JC Tashkent Public Transport Company. Over the years, she has rendered consulting services to UNICEF, the World Bank, UNFPA, GIZ, ADB, OECD, etc. She is the author of a chapter on Uzbekistan in the book "Public Service Evolution in 15 Post-Soviet Countries: Diversity in Transformation" (Palgrave, 2022). She holds a Master's degree in International Relations (M.A.) from St Andrews University, Chevening scholarship (2006), and a Bachelor's degree (B.A.) in International Economics from the University of World Economy and Diplomacy, Uzbekistan (2004). Aziza has worked and lived in the United Kingdom, China, and Austria. She is currently the coordinator of the Delivery Unit of the Agency for Strategic Reforms under the President of Uzbekistan.

Darkhan Zhazykbay started his career as a teacher at Almaty Law Institute and Academy of the Ministry of Internal Affairs of the Republic of Kazakhstan. He is a Candidate of Sciences in Philosophy. He has held various positions within the Ministry of Internal Affairs—from being a teacher to becoming the Head of the Personnel Department of the Academy of the Ministry of Internal Affairs of the Republic of Kazakhstan. Darkhan Zhazykbay was appointed to various posts. He became the Deputy Chief of Staff of the Senate of the Parliament of the Republic of Kazakhstan and Deputy Head of the Department of Internal Policy of the Executive Office of the President of the Republic of Kazakhstan. In 2019, he was appointed as the Deputy Chairman of the Agency of the Republic of Kazakhstan for Civil Service Affairs. In 2022 by Decree of the Head of State, he was appointed Chairman of the Agency of the Republic of Kazakhstan for Civil Service Affairs.

List of Figures

List of Tables

CHAPTER 1

Public Administration in the New Reality: Challenges, Implications, and Prospects

Alikhan Baimenov and Panos Liverakos

1.1 Introduction

From as far back as the emergence of the proto states, human civilisation advancement has consistently imposed new demands on the management of collective affairs. Periodically, governance systems face significant shocks, serving as accelerators for seeking new concepts and practices. The contemporary era is no exception, as evolution of public administration to date reflects a dual process. On the one hand, thinkers and scholars propose new ideas; on the other, rulers, politicians, and governments—whether guided by such ideas or intuition—experiment and accumulate experience. In the twenty-first century, this dual process has accelerated, driven by factors such as the exponential growth of knowledge, increased

A. Baimenov · P. Liverakos (✉)
Astana Civil Service Hub, Astana, Kazakhstan
e-mail: panos@liverakos.info

A. Baimenov
e-mail: alikhan.baimenov@undp.org

A. Baimenov and P. Liverakos (eds.), *Public Administration in the New Reality*, https://doi.org/10.1007/978-981-96-3845-1_1

citizen awareness, and advances in modern communication technologies. Within this dynamic environment, the historical quest for effective governance continues.

The COVID-19 pandemic became a powerful revealer, as it also exposed other pressing issues, thus compelling a critical reconsideration of existing governance models—at the conceptual level. Existing governance systems do not seem ready to cope with the magnitude and scope of these global challenges. In other words, national and international structures, and systems—values and norms, organisation, and rules—are not adequately geared to addressing the requirements, but instead compound these challenges. Therefore, the world must agree on new models of governance, based upon new conceptual constructs, from institutions and norms to types of governance, as well as systems of international cooperation and coordination, for coping with the multiple crises. This needs to be accomplished in the midst of rising tensions, divisions, and embedded competition among societies and countries.

Indeed, the recent COVID-19 pandemic has entailed a significant global disruption with many significant health, economic, political, and security implications, whose effects will be felt for years to come. It has been a decisive event, reminding people worldwide minds, that we live in an era of crises. It is a new reality, in which humanity is challenged with multiple crises; characterised by shared global challenges, like climate change, pandemics, financial instability, technological disruption, and others. They exert strains on our countries and societies all around the world. These challenges, moreover, are likely to become more frequent and intense with the passage of time.

Naturally, due to their very nature and complexity, these challenges span across many different policy domains. For instance, climate change and environmental degradation affect the food and water security of poor countries. They also exert considerable influence on migration flows, let alone the perilous loss of biodiversity. Similarly, digital technologies have now become ubiquitous, spreading faster and faster. They are diffusing rapidly, disrupting norms and values in communities and countries, as well as labour markets and jobs in different cascading ways that many find it difficult to anticipate.

The technological challenges are further exacerbated by other conditions present in the world, due in large part to the digital [r]evolution. One such condition is the fragmentation of communities and countries, and antagonism among them—fuelled, in large part, by geopolitical tensions motivated by the quest for hegemony—and the imbalance that exists between the capacity of structures and systems to cope with crises collectively and what is actually needed (NIC 2021). Ironically, as the world is more interconnected utilising digital communication systems, this very connectivity also creates and further exacerbates tensions in societies, divided over core values and goals.[1]

In this context, governance structures and public administration systems become extremely important as, by default, they constitute a crucial component in safeguarding the short-, medium-, and longer-term public interest (ACSH 2023). Public administration systems are critical in shaping and implementing policies that are effective and relevant to alleviating the effects of various crises, performing government functions, and dispensing basic and essential public services to citizens responsively and efficiently. Accordingly, if public administration intends to remain relevant, it must anticipate and effectively address the risks and grasp the opportunities driven by the megatrends.

This chapter begins with an analysis of some of the large-scale changes—megatrends—that are shaping our contemporary societies and economies. Understanding the dimensions and complexity of the issues that cause such unpredictable abrupt effects is imperative. We must also try to fathom the environment in which they manifest themselves deeply affecting our economies and societies. All these are crucial factors in devising policies to tackle them effectively, thus reflecting directly on the capacity of public administration to deal with them.

Later, the chapter shifts its focus on the policy and technical tools public administration disposes in order to confront priority issues, along with the skills and competencies required to operate in an uncertain environment leading to a discussion of public human resources in the new reality. It further delves into ways espoused by different countries in tackling issues of governance and public administration that are geared towards the new reality. The chapter concludes with a discussion of challenges emerging in efforts to transform public administration and face the related opportunities ahead.

[1] Utilising this connectivity people tend to gravitate to information also read by people who share similar views, reinforcing beliefs and understandings of the "truth", resulting to increased fragmentation along national, cultural, or political preferences (NIC 2021).

1.2 Global Megatrends and Their Multifaceted Effects on Public Administration

Megatrends are the macroeconomic and geostrategic forces shaping our world today. These are large-scale, transformative changes that influence how societies and economies take shape over extended periods, with profound effects on development and the direction of our world. Their implications are broad and varied with many risks to assuage and opportunities to grasp, whenever possible (Halal 2013).

Furthermore, while their separate impact is expected to be considerable, megatrends are closely inter-related, and thus cannot and should not be addressed in isolation. Inter-relationships are evident when considering, for instance, the links between the demographic shifts and climate change. With the increase in the world population and a growing middle class in the emerging economies, a 50% jump in food production to meet a rising demand can safely be predicted with a corresponding rise in both water and energy consumption (UNFAO 2012). Climate change will certainly exacerbate pressure on these resources, given the potentially devastating and irreversible effects of prolonged droughts and extreme weather events. Climate change will also impact the global megatrend of urbanisation, as the number of people displaced by climate change increases (KPMG 2014).

Naturally, such megatrends and their effects also influence future governance and public administration systems. These need to be in the forefront of the transition in ensuring human development, economic prosperity, security, social cohesion, and environmental sustainability, to just mention few. Thus, it is important for governments to grasp the major game-changing developments experienced worldwide, in order to mitigate the political, economic, and social impacts. In this context, governments are not only responsible for identifying the critical issues and place themselves into a position that they can fairly predict their impacts. They are also responsible for both shaping and implementing policies that are considered suitable for addressing those issues.

It is thus imperative for governments to intervene in remedying the impact of these megatrends by devising policies, legal frameworks, and implementation programmes. Public administration is the medium and vehicle in all three aspects as it ought to have the capacity to assist on devising policy and regulations, as well as on implementing programmes deriving from policy initiatives. For these to happen, strategies need to be devised, while also skills and competencies of public administrators must be upgraded (OECD 2019b; PMI 2022).

Several of these megatrends also affect organisational structures, work modalities, and internal operations of public administration, as well as the delivery of public services in a digital realm. Obviously, such requirements further affect the human resource capacity of public administration that now must be aligned to new ways of functioning and operating in the new global reality. This requires new modalities in the selection, recruitment, promotion, and performance monitoring in the public service, as well as novel conditions that may make the work in the public sector sufficiently attractive for prospective civil servants.

Overall, megatrends are relevant in the long term as their effects will be felt over several decades. They are also relevant worldwide, as their effects spill over countries of different sizes and levels of prosperity. Therefore, governments will need to undertake a variety of responses to properly address the issues involved, while also considering the inter-connection between causes and effects. They need to adapt whole-of-society and whole-of-government approaches to cope with the depth and complexity of the challenges posed (OECD 2019a).[2] For instance, the combination of changes in the environment, population pressures, and economic growth in developing countries already place more stress on such essential natural resources as water, food, arable land, and energy, while taxing the resilience of natural and built systems (KPMG 2014; PWC 2016).

Research on megatrends has yielded an insight on a variety of trends emerging in broad areas of human activity and the natural environment. They appear in different studies with varying labels although often overlapping and correlated, despite the different terms that are used to describe them (Naughtin et al. 2024). The following come to mind: individual empowerment, diffusion of power, demographic patterns, and a growing food, water, and energy nexus (NIC 2012); resource depletion, species decline and extinction, economic shift to the east, an ageing population, interconnectivity, and a quest for higher-end experience and social relationships (Hajkowicz et al. 2012); economic globalisation, the Internet and the WWW, shifting balance of global power, unsustainable

[2] See also https://documents1.worldbank.org/curated/en/270541555605484950/pdf/Human-Capital-Project-How-Countries-Nurture-Human-Capital-Implement-a-Whole-of-Government-Approach.pdf on the utilisation of a whole-of-government approach in human resource management.

population growth and resource consumption, technological leaps and climate change (Gore 2013); and digital disruption, climate crisis, demographic shifts, economic shifts, labour shortages, and civil and equality movements (PMI 2022).

To these we need to add demographic changes, the rise of individualism, enabling technology, economic interconnectedness, public debt, economic power shift, climate change, resource stress, and urbanisation (KPMG 2014); shifts in global economic power, demographic shifts, accelerating urbanisation, rise of technology, climate change, and resource scarcity (PWC 2016). More challenges include the growth in emerging markets, labour productivity and talent management, the global flow of goods, information, and capital, natural resource management, and the increasing role of governments (Birshan et al. 2023).[3] But we must also mention the proliferation and intensification of conflicts, AI fuelling misinformation, accelerating biodiversity loss and ecosystem degradation, increasing risk of zoonotic diseases, increasing polarisation, increasing waves of migrants, etc. (UNDP 2024b).

At the same time, a significant decline in trust, not only in politicians and political parties but also in government institutions as a whole is observed in this new reality. This erosion of trust is linked to both long-term socio-economic and environmental trends, as well as acute shocks like the pandemic and geopolitical tensions. It also reflects deeper systemic challenges within modern state institutions, including the struggle to balance long-term strategic priorities with the temptation for short-term populist wins—a dilemma even the most developed economies face. Furthermore, citizens' increased awareness, driven by global digital social networks, also contributes to this trust deficit. Indeed, with widespread Internet access and an abundance of digital social networks citizens are more than ever informed about solutions in other countries, they can compare and assess decisions of their governments utilising certain benchmarks—thus, creating a quasi-competitive environment as well.

Addressing these issues calls for further research into creating self-evolving models of governance and public administration that can adapt to changing circumstances while maintaining public trust. This global interconnectedness necessitates innovative responses to rebuild trust. One promising approach could involve blending direct democracy methods,

[3] Although more business-oriented, these trends are also closely related with those that also affect the world as a whole.

such as Switzerland's frequent referendums on key issues, with Estonia's efficient and reliable electronic systems, enabling cost-effective and trustworthy citizen participation in decision-making. Such hybrid models could address the trust gap and enhance democratic legitimacy in the face of modern challenges.

This part of the chapter is devoted to discussing several megatrends affecting the world today and how their potential impact(s) are related to public administration that needs to adapt to the new reality. In other words, how megatrends may affect the coordination of complex and interconnected policies or how they may affect its organisational structures, internal operations, work modalities, human resource capacity development, and the delivery of personalised and proactive public services. For instance, the key megatrends affecting the public service include demographics, climate change, technological advancement, and deepening social fragmentation. It is evident that the confluence of these trends has strained the capacity of public administration to respond to current challenges, let alone prepare for the future. Thus, the unfolding impacts of the megatrends point to the need for innovation, coordination, collaboration, and adaptability to address complex economic, environmental, and social challenges continually arising (Baimyrzaeva and Meyer 2020).

In other words, the multifaceted effects of megatrends on public administration call for a proactive and adaptive approach. Public administration must fully embrace digital technologies, address demographic and environmental challenges, and navigate through evolving political, economic, and social realms. Public administration needs to be geared towards developing flexible, innovative policies. It also needs to invest heavily in the continuous capacity development of its human resources so that they can better manage the complexities, which they are confronted with and thus enhance its effectiveness in serving the public.

The presentation below is focused on six core megatrends: changing demographics, climate change, global economic activity realignment including globalisation, technological evolution, empowered citizens, and increasing urbanisation.

1.2.1 Changing Demographics

Increasing life expectancy and falling birth rates are increasing the proportion of elderly people around the world, particularly in more advanced countries. This is bound to challenge the sustainability of social welfare systems, i.e., pensions and health care (UNDP 2024a: 29).[4] By contrast, other regions are facing the challenge of integrating large youth population into saturated or stagnant labour markets (KPMG 2014).

Some societies are ageing rapidly and as a result older people will constitute a larger share of the total population. This demographic shift will certainly affect national priorities for government spending. Demand for social services and health care will put severe pressure on budgetary priorities competing with other equally vital expenditures, or even crowd them out, taking also into consideration that the ability to use debt as a policy tool is limited in advanced economies, potentially resulting in higher taxes to maintain social programmes. Health systems may also need re-engineering to handle more participants. Ageing populations are also linked to the migration megatrend. It is a plausible policy choice to significantly change the demographic composition of advanced countries and thus to offset the negative effects of ageing on both social security systems and labour markets.[5]

Developing countries, by contrast, are not affected by the ageing factor but many have to confront another challenge. The rapidly growing demographic group of young men and women entering the workforce will represent a cohort of people who need to earn enough to be fed, housed, educated, and engaged in gainful employment for their productive potential to be realised. However, as many of these young women and men are confronted with limited economic opportunities at home, they most probably will boast the migration flows to the developed world. The growth, moreover, in the youth population of the developing countries, in a number of cases, could create increased radicalisation and civil unrest, with the likelihood of disruptive transnational movements taking hold in these societies. This could create both internal and external security issues that will require greater investment and innovative strategies to combat (KPMG 2014). Furthermore, an increasing population of ageing people

[4] Conversely, this ageing trend also provides opportunities for new services catering to ageing populations, such as new services in health care, neighbourhoods for ageing citizens with robotic facilities, regenerative medicine, tissue engineering, health tourism, etc. https://www.bbc.com/news/business-20003002.

[5] Many advanced countries are challenged to find workers, and thus they have sought temporary solutions by extending retirement ages and instituting easier immigration policies.

in some regions against the explosive population growth in others may contribute to shifts in economic power, resource scarcity, and changes in societal norms.

The changing demographics, including ageing populations, urbanisation, and migration, impact public administration in various ways. Governments must address the growing needs of diverse populations, including social services, infrastructure, and employment opportunities. Additionally, demographic shifts may require adjustments in policies related to health care, education, and workforce management. For instance, governments and public administration will be forced to develop policies to address the needed re-skilling of the older members of the workforce in all parts of the world, especially in ageing economies. However, this ageing workforce may have to be supplemented by migrant workers. Thus, governments need to devise policies to integrate newcomers into their economic and social life.

Furthermore, changing demographics and higher concentration of populations will require from governments and public administration sets of policies that will ensure the sustainability of welfare systems and cope with higher demand for public services in mega-cities including transportation, housing, sanitation, and health services, as well as effective urban planning and infrastructure development, ranging from new road networks to schools and hospitals. In this context, governments and public administration need to design policies and programmes that cater to these issues. These span across several areas, further highlighting the need for coordination and collaboration among government departments.

1.2.2 Climate Change

Human activity has increased greenhouse gas emissions to unprecedented levels, triggering climate change. This is causing a complex mix of unpredictable changes to the environment testing the resilience of natural and human-made systems. Nowadays, the impact of climate change represents a growing concern, as we all become witnesses to its various manifestations. It is also evident that the world's ecological habitat and biodiversity are under severe stress from human activity and the climate change, which can lead to extinction of species and pose the question whether adequate human responses can emerge in a timely fashion (Hajkowicz et al. 2012).

Increasing complexity and uncertainty throughout represent a pressing challenge for many countries that lack both the resources and competencies to address the related issues. The impact from the frequency and intensity of extreme weather conditions, rising sea levels, and coastal erosion affect existing methods of producing food, for instance. Furthermore, as sea levels rise in proportion to rising temperatures on the Earth, coastal cities may be forced to invest in fortifying their infrastructure to ensure the physical safety of their inhabitants, diverting resources from other equally important policy areas.

Climate change can be the source of tensions between nations, in disputes for water, for instance. In fact, potential conflicts are brewing already between countries that share transboundary water resources. According to the Global Policy Forum, more than fifty countries on five continents might soon be caught up in water disputes unless they move quickly to establish agreements on how to share reservoirs, rivers, and underground water aquifers. As the global population continues to grow, these disputes will become more acute and more critical to national survival particularly when it comes to such basic resources as water, food, and energy sources. This will undoubtedly lead to regional and potentially even global confrontations over water, oil, wind, fishing, hunting, and mineral rights.

This megatrend is, moreover, exacerbated by urbanisation, i.e., the concentration of expanding populations into mega-cities, putting stress on the natural resource supply chain, as governments endeavour to deliver at much higher demand levels with scarce resources available. To deal with such issues effectively it is necessary for governments and public administration to take proactive measures. Governments need to develop strategies for sustainability, resilience, and adaptation to mitigate the impacts of inevitable and imminent environmental crises. This may involve implementing regulations, promoting renewable energy, and investing in green infrastructure (PWC 2016). However, achieving the right combination of adaptation and mitigation policies may prove to be difficult for most governments to implement, considering the fact that environmental crises should be dealt at the global level to be effective, requiring seamless coordination and cooperation among countries and public authorities in general.

Manifestly, the combined pressures of population growth, economic growth, and climate change will place increased stress on essential natural resources. These will include water, food, arable land, and energy. Such issues will place sustainable resource management at the centre of the governments' agendas. Failing to do this will impact the ability of governments to deliver on core policy areas of economic prosperity, security, social cohesion, and environmental sustainability. On the other hand, the need to tackle such issues may well be at odds with the need for economic growth with a view to sustaining expected standards of the world population at large, putting pressure on governments to refrain from taking drastic measures in coping with the effects of climate change.

The profound effects of climate change require new policies and regulation to promote environmental sustainability, while ensuring that standards of living remain intact and improving. Thus, governments and public administration need to develop strategies and policies to cope with the direct and indirect effects of climate change. Hence public administration must increasingly focus on promoting sustainable development and building resilience to environmental—as well as economic and social—challenges. This includes the development and implementation of initiatives related to climate change adaptation, resource management, and disaster preparedness.

1.2.3 Global Economic Activity Realignment and Globalisation

Realignment of global economic activity led by the BRICs and other fast-developing countries is in the process of shifting the world economy from west to east and from north to south. Rapid income growth in Asia and, to a lesser extent, in South America and Africa is raising the standards of billions of people, who are gradually transitioning to the middle-income classes.[6] It is also important to note that economic growth has increased the interconnectivity of trade and investment flows among them. These are growing much faster than the traditional routes from developed-to-developing and developed-to-developed countries.

Realignment of global economic activity is also aiding multi-polarity in the world. Specifically, the shift from largely West-led global organisations to regional players is reshaping power relationships among countries. This

[6] China and India have contributed to 20% of world GDP over the past 10 years. When combined with Brazil and Russia (to form the BRIC nations), these four countries will have higher economic output than the United States by 2018 (Wilson et al. 2010). By 2030, the bulk of global GDP will be generated from non-OECD countries (OECD 2010). This will represent a major shift for the world economy.

shift also creates more powerful national economies in different regions with more abundant resources available to protect or to invest (NIC 2012; OECD 2010).

Furthermore, the interconnectivity among countries has increased, due to globalisation—a fact that has implications for public administration. Governments need to collaborate at the international level on such issues as trade and climate change. This requires greater coordination, networking, and diplomatic skills among public administrators. It also entails a need that international conventions be strengthened to achieve progress and optimal economic benefits for all. Besides, as fast-developing countries in the South and in the East exert a greater influence on the global economy leading to re-balancing power, both international institutions and national governments will need to focus more on maintaining their transparency and inclusiveness. Additionally, globalisation inevitably leads to a transfer of ideas, best practices, and policies among countries, thus exerting considerable influence on the shape of governance structures, approaches, and systems.

Other elements of economic transformation including automation and the rise of a knowledge economy also influence public administrations in terms of economic policy, taxation, and labour market regulations. Governments must adapt to changing economic realities, address income inequality, and support economic sectors afflicted by technological disruptions. They must also pay more attention to fiscal policies and budgetary allocations, as these decisions impact public service quality and infrastructure development.

However, important new challenges arise in the measure that economies are increasingly connected to risks beyond their national borders. These risks not only move quickly but also defy the scope of national regulation, demanding international cooperation. As the trend towards increased economic interconnectivity continues, governments throughout the world will need to cooperate and to ensure that they have policy frameworks in place in order to capture the benefits of trade and manage risks effectively.

Globalisation denotes that governments and public administration must navigate complex international issues and collaborate across national borders, while they still have direct responsibility for dealing with the impacts of the megatrends within their borders, as well as dealing with transnational issues like trade regulations, international security, and global pandemics. International collaboration also promotes and facilitates the exchange of knowledge and thus the adoption of policies from one another leading to eventual convergence of public administration practices. Dealing with others at the international level allows for the acquisition of new skills in managing diverse populations and understanding international cultural dynamics, especially in multi-cultural societies. In this context, governments have to strive to strengthen international cooperation and partnerships and develop flexible policies that can be adapted to local contingencies.

1.2.4 Technological Evolution

Rapid advancement, integration, and diffusion of digital technologies are transforming societies and economies at an unprecedented rate. A combination of the Internet, network capable mobile devices,[7] data analytics, machine learning capabilities (artificial intelligence), cloud computing, nanotechnology, etc., has virtually altered the landscape where societies and economies function, interact, and communicate.

In the measure that the world becomes more interconnected, people, businesses, and governments are increasingly moving into the digital world to deliver and access services, obtain information, perform transactions, shop, work, and interact with each other.[8] Furthermore, this exponential growth in the volume and speed of access to information and communication among people has numerous effects with respect to public institutions. Although this growing new wave of technological advances creates new and novel opportunities and generates new markets, it also tests government capacity to harness benefits and provide prudent oversight; however, it also challenges existing institutions and institutional structures (Marmier et al. 2022).

[7] By 2020, there were eighty billion connected devices, nine billion mobile phones, and five billion internet users, 50% of whom connect through handheld devices (UNDP 2024a).

[8] This invisible network amounts to a world without borders, where tasks can be completed at the blink of an eye and the touch of a finger, and where online video, social media, and digital imagery create an era of connectivity and convergence that will change future human interaction in every aspect of life. Conversely, the global reach of the internet and social media platforms has created a substantial propaganda and recruiting vehicle for radical groups seeking to spread their message to disaffected populations around the world (NIC 2012).

Digitalisation and the gradual expansion of artificial intelligence applications are integral to the evolution of public administration. This encompasses the utilisation of big data, changes in state machinery business processes, and, undoubtedly, advancements in delivering public services to the population. Indeed, artificial intelligence, big data analytics, and the Internet-of-Things are revolutionising how public administration operates. Together, these developments enhance labour productivity, improve the quality-of-service delivery, and provide significant support in the formulation of political decisions. However, as history demonstrates, the adoption of new technologies must come with a heightened level of responsibility, as numerous challenges are posed related to cybersecurity, privacy concerns, and the digital divide. It also predetermines the growing importance of human resource management, particularly in addressing issues of corporate culture and ethics.

Such rapid technological developments as artificial intelligence, big data analytics, and the Internet-of-Things are revolutionising how public administration operates. They enable governments to improve service delivery, enhance decision-making processes, and increase efficiency in resource allocation. However, they also pose numerous challenges related to cybersecurity,[9] privacy concerns, and the digital divide.

The widespread use of digital technologies is rapidly improving a broad range of human experience and capabilities. However—at least in the short term—these same technologies disrupt long-standing systems and societal dynamics, forcing individuals, communities, and governments to adjust and find new ways of living, working, and managing. As it happens with any disruption, some will thrive while others will struggle, eventually creating increasing inequalities and imbalances, although emerging technologies are not solely responsible for these developments, but likely to aggravate and amplify them (NIC 2012).

It is obvious that the rise of digital technologies has transformed public administration by enabling e-governance, improving service delivery, and increasing transparency. Citizens now expect online access to government services and information in real time. Governments have responded to this need by digitising public services, while they continue to improve

[9] Network vulnerabilities to such attacks creates national security vulnerabilities that extend beyond financial crime to the crippling of key infrastructure and access to classified information that could compromise critical national infrastructure.

their systems and processes. However, this also poses challenges related to data privacy and security.

Furthermore, policy decision-making is enhanced as governments and public administration utilise big data and analytics to inform their decisions and improve their service efficiency. In a similar context, the use of automation and artificial intelligence streamlines administrative processes, reduces costs, and improves accuracy—however, also requiring the acquisition of new skill sets and raising new concerns about job displacement. Thus, governments may have to invest in digital infrastructure and cybersecurity, along with providing training and development programmes to equip public servants with the necessary technical and other skills.

1.2.5 Empowered Citizens

Expanding global economic activity, rapid growth of emerging economies, and widespread advancement of new communication and other digital technologies along with advances in global education have empowered individuals like never before. This has led to increasing demands for transparency, efficiency, and accountability with participation in government and public decision-making. To this, one may add a note about worldwide increase in women's empowerment, representing a very significant social trend on its own merit.[10] This is not only the case in developed economies but also in regions and countries of the world more prone to adhering to traditional behaviours and norms.

The empowerment of individuals also implies the social transformation that includes shifts in values, lifestyles, and social norms. This is actually taking place in many societies now. The emergence of a middle class of approximately five billion people, all interconnected via the Internet, will derive unprecedented growth in the future, as they will tend to demand higher-end goods and services, as well as a better treatment throughout.

Social and cultural changes that include shifts in values, lifestyles, and social norms will influence public administration in shaping public priorities, preferences, and expectations. Governments must be responsive to evolving societal needs, including addressing such issues as social justice, diversity, and inclusion. Social changes also affect public service delivery, citizen engagement, and community development initiatives.

[10] Singh, S. Viewpoint: Megatrends that will change everyone's lives. http://www.bbc.com/news/business-20003002.

Thus, governments must navigate complex political landscapes, build consensus, and uphold democratic principles while also addressing diverse interests.

In this context, governments and public administration must navigate complex political realms and manage diverse stakeholder interests. This must include such universal issues as racial equality, gender rights, and equity that can drive public policy changes and require public administration to be more responsive and including. It is thus important for public administration to promote transparency and inclusion in the decision-making process and accountability of their actions, in order to build consensus and trust with stakeholders by engaging in the process.

1.2.6 Urbanisation

It is safe to expect that the world's population will continue growing over the coming fifty to sixty years. It is expected to reach a peak of 10.3 billion people in the mid-2080s, up from 8.2 billion in 2024. The United Nations (UN) anticipates that by 2030, 50% of the world's population, i.e., 4.9 billion, will dwell in cities.[11] The UN further estimates that, by 2025, there will be twenty-two mega-cities, each with more than ten million people; with seventeen of them located in developing economies (UNDESA Population Division 2024). These new cities will rise rapidly and require massive investments in smart infrastructure to accommodate explosive growth. Mega-projects may be required to build and consolidate needed city infrastructure, support new trade flows, i.e., airports, seaports, and road networks. They will also need to address housing, education, health, security, employment demands, etc.[12]

Ensuring that growing cities are effectively managed will likely become a priority—and a challenge forcing governments to monitor the process of urbanisation closely, and manage growth sustainably, while also ensuring

[11] The fact that the world's population is likely to peak by 2080 has important implications for the sustainability of our current way of living on this planet. In this context, it is well recognised that efforts to slow population growth, reduce poverty, achieve economic progress, improve environmental protection, and reduce unsustainable consumption and production patters are mutually reinforcing (UNFPA 1994).

[12] The rapid urbanisation trend has led to a significant decline in the quality of life in many developing countries which lack the ability to deal with pressures on utilities and services in urban centres. Growing informal housing and traffic congestion is the contemporary effect of this trend.

access to housing, water, and energy for all residents. In developed economies and older cities of the developing world, infrastructure will be strained to the utmost, as population expands. At the same time, governments will be required to manage their cities, maintain competitiveness in the face of growing global competition, as well as tackle social and service-oriented impacts flowing from urbanisation, both positive and negative. In addition, a higher concentration of people in these emerging mega-cities may enhance the impact of natural and human-caused disasters. It will require a massive holistic approach by governments to address the humanitarian, defence, and security challenges that come along with them.

Overall, megatrends profoundly impact public administration by shaping policy agendas, institutional frameworks, and administrative practices. Governments must be proactive in both anticipating and responding to these trends, effectively addressing contemporary challenges and opportunities. This requires strategic foresight, innovation, and collaboration across sectors and stakeholders. It also requires the use of practices and techniques that can assist public administration to effectively tackle matters and issues it is confronted with.

1.3 The Role of Government and Public Administration in the New Reality

The preceding analysis highlights the magnitude of global megatrends and their multifaceted impact on economies and societies. It also underscores the apparent need for governments, across the world, so as to confront the challenges and implications arising from them, and act accordingly to address them adequately. Yet, this does not imply that there is one and only path that all governments must follow. The impact of each megatrend at the national level, coupled with the idiosyncrasies of countries of varying size, different stage of development, governance model in place, culture, and a multitude of other factors, will invariably call for varying approaches. One thing is clear.

Governments cannot afford to stick to business-as-usual models for tackling the complex issues and the wicked problems of the new reality but need to adapt to new and versatile models of governance, based on novel conceptual constructs that are more suitable and apt for accomplishing their policy goals. The emerging consensus essentially suggests that governments ought to develop new approaches to governance and create the capacity needed to cope with new realities, and to adapt novel practices and new techniques in their quest to deliver what is expected of them.

Governments must become more integrated, in order to be able to achieve better policy coordination. They must also endeavour to become outward focused, making better and wider use of technology. In this context, governments and public administration also ought to take advantage of the abundant big data generated in the digital domain. These combined with data analytics can assist in devising evidence-based public policy, and to ensure better policy coordination to achieve desired policy objectives.

Furthermore, governments need to adapt to a versatile system of regulatory practices aimed at aligning regulations swiftly, in line with the rapid changes caused by the ever-accelerating technological advancement in a multitude of policy domains. These range from ethical considerations in genetics to privacy concerns over personal data. Governments, moreover, need to expand their engagement in international and regional fora to address transnational and interconnected issues, e.g., environmental degradation and migration. In doing so, governments need to minimise costs by optimising the quality of government services taking a holistic view of sustainable development systems (KPMG 2014).

Such are the major prerequisites for governments and public administration to remain relevant in the twenty-first century. Fortuitously, it seems that governments and public administration seem to have, at their disposal, an abundance of instruments in order to cope with the challenges in the new reality, and the demands that are placed upon them, in order to continue devising policies that are effective and implement programmes aimed at alleviating the negative effects of the megatrends; concurrently providing, at the same time, an environment conducive to taking full advantage of opportunities arising from emerging circumstances.

Moreover, it seems that governments have grasped that they require a diverse and adaptable workforce possessing appropriate knowhow, as well as skills and competencies, in order to cope with the salient issues of the twenty-first century. That is a workforce capable of assuming the proper roles and promptly performing their functions with a view to effectively navigating the complex challenges confronting the world. The next section of this chapter outlines the qualifications, skills, competencies, and qualities public servants should possess to face this new reality. The present section continues with a discussion of the various instruments and mechanisms that governments and public administration can deploy in order to accomplish their policy objectives.

To achieve more integration, governments and public administration may use various frameworks, mechanisms, and tools for better policy coordination and implementation; having regard especially for the fact that most issues span across several policy domains, that they are interlinked, and that they often affect one another. Consequently, it is essential to establish policy coordination mechanisms that are capable of reacting to the challenges of the new reality emerging at the national, but also at the regional and international levels. It must be borne in mind in this connection that several issues like climate change and migration require multilevel policy coordination at the multilateral level. *Reinholde et al.* provide an analysis of such policy coordination frameworks in Chapter 4. They highlight the imperative need for the alignment of actions and interactions among agencies, officials, and politicians at the national, regional, and international levels, as well as intensive collaboration and communication among respective actors and stakeholders as they endeavour to manage effectively and implement well-coordinated and integrated policies, especially during crises.

Conversely, these frameworks are complemented with various systems and methods designed to achieve optimal intergovernmental performance on strategic priorities of the various policy areas that span across multiple government agencies and require effective collaboration to meet strategic priorities in service delivery. This represents a complex challenge that also necessitates a cultural shift within government organisations in order to facilitate cohesive efforts and achieve policy objectives. *Umarova* in Chapter 5 delves into the topic of intergovernmental performance on strategic priorities with respect to the delivery of public services. She highlights a number of systems that have been deployed in various countries with some considerable success across the world, including some Central Asian countries.

As mentioned earlier, the effects of some megatrends stretch across country boundaries, due to their transnational features. Thus, cooperation is required across countries and regions, to effectively control the effects of such megatrends as migration, environmental preservation, and health crises management. Governments realise that such challenges as environmental protection require uniform approaches and common principles that apply at the international level, encompassing virtually all countries in the world. As a result, international cooperation is elevated to a more prominent role in the international system. In Chapter 8, *Kardava* explores a number of aspects of international cooperation in this new reality. She argues that, to prevent and manage the transnational and cascading crises of the current era, it is important that democratically governed countries adopt government practices intended to secure a more effective multilateral engagement in tackling issues of common interest across a spectrum of policy domains.

International cooperation in public administration entails the adoption of best practices and implementation of innovative solutions, whether by studying a specific country's overall experience, or by studying specific good practices and innovative solutions applied in a particular policy area and have been adopted by a score of countries across the globe. In this case, nuances in implementation are observed due to cultural, historical, and other country-specific factors, often emphasised in the work of institutional economists (Gwartney et al. 2024; Acemoglu and Robinson 2012; Tabellini 2010).

Undoubtedly, a megatrend that has a most significant impact across many different policy domains is technological evolution, culminating in the digital transformation of our world. Digital technologies are already a large part of our lives and revolutionising the ways we operate, communicate, socialise, and interact with one another, improving, for the most part, a broad range of human experience and capabilities. However—at least in the short term—these same technologies have disrupted long-standing and well-entrenched systems and societal dynamics, forcing individuals, communities, and governments to adjust into new ways of living, and operating, working, and managing their own affairs.[13]

Similarly, such rapid technological developments as artificial intelligence, big data analytics, and increasing digitalisation of public services are revolutionising how public administration functions and interacts with citizens and business enterprises. Such digital technologies enable governments to augment their decision-making processes, to improve service

[13] As it happens with any disruption, some will thrive while others will struggle, eventually creating increasing inequalities and imbalances, although emerging technologies are not solely responsible for these developments, but likely to aggravate and amplify them (NIC 2012).

delivery increasing their efficiency in human and financial resources allocation. Concurrently, they also pose numerous challenges related to cybersecurity, privacy concerns, and the digital divide.

Chapter 3 provides some insights on the legal and regulatory frameworks for digital technologies. *Leitner and Stiefmueller* highlight the risks and dependencies associated with the rapid and widespread progress in the digital realm, taking care not to overlook the significant benefits that digital technologies have yielded across a wide range of policy areas. They explore the principal challenges that policymakers are facing in recalibrating the role of government, while seeking to design effective policy and regulatory frameworks in this fast-changing environment. They also seek to achieve a proper balance between benefits and risks inherent in the rapid adoption and development of technology, while intervening in a timely manner and avoiding stifling innovation.

This is because rapid technological development is having a transformative impact on governments across the globe, from the ways in which they communicate with people to the development of innovative solutions enhancing public service delivery and fostering sustainable development, e.g., use of emerging technologies. However, one should also keep in mind the potential associated challenges and risks which exist, and they must also be urgently addressed, such as the persistent digital divides, data gaps, as well as security and privacy issues. There are also growing concerns about the potential disruptive changes that rapid advancements in technology may bring to societies and public administrations worldwide, with questions of adequate governance and regulation of emerging technologies, such as artificial intelligence, remaining as elaborated on by the United Nations Committee of Experts on Public Administration (CEPA) at its recently held 23rd session.[14]

It is apparent that the role of government and public administration, in this new reality, appears to be more critical than ever, as we try to navigate the complexities of contemporary governance while improving and enhancing the quality of life for citizens. It is imperative that they focus on several crucial aspects to succeed. Public administration must focus on *resilience*, ensuring that systems are in place to respond quickly and effectively to crises. It must also embrace digital governance, improving service delivery through digital innovation, enhancing transparency, and

[14] https://publicadministration.desa.un.org/intergovernmental-support/cepa/23rd-session/report-and-summary.

engaging citizens more effectively. In fact, transparency, citizen engagement, and accountability are of paramount importance in enhancing its legitimacy and foster cooperative and trustful relationships with the citizenry.

In a similar manner, public administration must focus on data collection and analysis to inform public policy decisions, monitor outcomes, and adapt strategies based on evidence, as well as cultivate a culture of innovation, encouraging creative means of problem-solving and responses to emerging needs. Last but not least, public administration must cultivate collaboration and cooperation, in addressing complex global issues, to leverage resources and expertise. Naturally, such requirements lead to discussion of human resources management, as governments and public administration need to reform, in order to adapt to new realities successfully. This is the subject of the following section.

1.4 Public Administration Human Resources for the New Reality

The magnitude, complexity, and intensity of the issues stemming from the unfolding megatrends and their effects on our world make it imperative for public administration to attract and retain a well-equipped workforce, able to cope with new realities. It requires a diverse and adaptable workforce of civil servants equipped with the appropriate knowledge, suitable skills, and competencies to navigate effectively the complex challenges of our contemporary world is faced; only thus will it be able to contribute to human development.

Contemporary civil servants must possess a broad understanding of such interdisciplinary subjects as technology, economics, analytics, sociology, environmental science, and geopolitical relations. Integrated knowledge will thus enable them to grasp the complexity of the often-multi-faceted issues and to formulate holistic solutions that incorporate multiple perspectives. Civil servants must also possess analytical skills, essential to interpreting data and other information, with a view to evaluating policy alternatives and making evidence-based policy decisions. This requires proficiency in data analysis, statistical and research methods, and methodologies to assess the impact of policies and programmes implemented.

Given the rapidly changing manifestation of challenges in this new reality, civil servants must learn to be creative and innovative in their approach to problem-solving, as well as adaptable and resilient in the face of uncertainty and fast change. Thinking out-of-the-box and exploring unconventional solutions to address emerging issue, adapting quickly to changing policy priorities and organisational structures will enable civil servants to remain effective in dynamically changing environments.

This entails that civil servants should be proficient in risk management, both methods and techniques needed to identify, assess, and mitigate risks associated with alternative policy decisions and programme implementation. To ensure that civil servants remain competent at all times, given the evolving nature of issues, continuous learning and professional development will be necessary. They need to update their knowledge constantly in the light of emerging trends and to acquire new skills as needed. This entails uninhibited access to training programmes, mentorship opportunities, leadership development initiatives, and support for further educational or professional certification.

Civil servants ought, moreover, to possess competencies to understand and respect different perspectives, values, and norms, as they often operate in a globalised setting. They must be trained to communicate effectively both complex ideas and concepts and to engage multiple stakeholders in building public support for policy initiatives. This entails that they possess interpersonal skills and the ability to build and nourish networks to facilitate collaboration, cooperation, and partnership-building across sectors and disciplines at the national, regional, and international levels.

Needless to emphasise that it is also important to nourish a culture of innovation, collaboration, and creativity within the public service. Individuals, so prepared, may thrive in dynamic and forward-thinking environment and may be adequately motivated to perform well. Thus, encouraging experimentation, fostering interdisciplinary collaboration, and empowering public servants to take initiative can help devise out-of-the-box policies and programmes that adapt well to the demands of contemporary policy issues, characterised by great complexity. In this context, exceptional performance should be recognised and rewarded, as it acts as a motivator.

Equally, attracting and retaining the “ideal” civil servant for the new reality requires offering a combination of competitive incentives that align with the values, aspirations, and expectations of prospective candidates. For instance, a competitive compensation and benefits package, including such other benefits as paid time for learning, can make the civil service an attractive career option compared to the private sector. These are all essential elements for attracting top talent in the civil service (ACSH 2016).

In their effort to attract and retain high-calibre personnel, public administration must also take account of the changes taking place in the labour market. Currently, this is witnessing dramatic changes fuelled by a number of factors. For instance, the speed of technological advancement, coupled with the introduction of artificial intelligence, has revolutionised the job profiles and the types of jobs available. *Bertucci*, in Chapter 7, delves into the contemporary labour market discussing the effects of changing economic and technological environments, including automation, and the rise of a knowledge economy on labour market [de]regulation. He also looks at the challenges faced by public administration from the policy and management perspectives, and what governments should do to remain relevant in the job market by updating their human resource management systems and their human resource planning.

In sum, government can certainly attract and retain appropriate individuals in the civil service, as it confronts new realities. It can thus build a talented and motivated workforce that is well equipped to tackle the complex challenges facing governments and public administration. To do this, governments must offer a combination of incentives, highlighted above. It seems to be the best way to develop a public service that comprises dynamic and multifaceted individuals, who are technologically proficient, data-driven, innovative, collaborative, globally minded, adaptive, ethical, culturally competent, effective communicators, as well as life-long learners. By embodying these characteristics and attributes, public servants can effectively navigate the complexities of governance and, given the new realities, contribute to building more inclusive, resilient, and sustainable societies. In Chapter 2, *Perry and Gupta* discuss the influential attributes for developing a public culture for the emerging new reality, which may motivate and empower civil servants to pursue the public good, but equally operate effectively in a complex global environment.

1.5 The Way Forward

The major challenges the world is facing nowadays make imperative the need for public administration, as a crucial component of governance to tackle the crucial issues of the new reality. Naturally, for public administration to remain relevant, it must adapt new and novel ways of thinking and of acting that depart from conventional practices. It needs to undergo strategic transformation by shifting towards ways of operation. In this context, it also ought to focus and strategically employ long-term planning in determining priorities, as most contemporary issues require long-term approaches, and often must be tackled at the international level.

Not surprisingly, a number of governments and public administrations around the world seek ways for moving forward, in this direction. Gradually, they introduce initiatives designed to cope with the effects of the megatrends and their manifestations in several policy areas. For instance, many have capitalised on the spectacular advancements of digital technologies—gathering considerable momentum because of, and during, the COVID-19 pandemic—which ended up improving public service delivery greatly. Similarly, public administration has capitalised on other scientific and technological developments by increasingly employing tools for evidence-based policy making and implementation. They have further introduced behavioural-based public policy making to encourage people to act in ways that will reduce pressures on social systems,[15] or metrics to appraise whether public funds are allocated to cost-effective policies and programmes. Furthermore, given the transnational nature of many contemporary issues, i.e., climate change, migration, etc., public administration is more internationally integrated through active engagement with counterparts in other countries with increased cooperation and coordination.

In this context, governments have realised that to increase capacity to move forward, they will require a workforce that possesses the needed, skills, knowledge, experience, and competencies. As a result, they have begun to shift their human resource management systems, utilising new tools and techniques to recruit and retain suitable individuals, apt to excel in this new and complex environment. Such people are fully aware of global trends and of their impacts. They possess deep integrated knowledge, factor such information into their decision-making processes, but

[15] For an analysis how behavioural science may be used for developing behavioural-based public policy, see Chapter 6. In that chapter, Janenova addresses two questions: (1) in what ways have governments in the post-Soviet Eurasia region experimented with behavioural insights? And (2) what are the challenges and ethical considerations related to the application of behavioural policies in the Eurasia?

also remain adaptive to unanticipated situations, and able to formulate novel policies within and across multiple domains.

It is only through integration of all these diverse elements that public administration can make the difference and remain relevant in the constant effort to adapt. The envisioned transformation is not only an institutional change, but a paradigm shift towards a more efficient, and equitable governance system, where public trust is restored, and organisational excellence becomes a norm rather than an exception (Halal 2013).

In considering the way forward, it is also crucial to recognise that public administration operates under dual pressures: the heightened expectations of citizens and the way politicians operate. It is also essential to understand that the balance between rational and irrational considerations differs for politicians and professional civil servants. While rationality tends to dominate among professional civil servants, irrationality is more common among politicians due to the nature of their activities and the dynamics of political competition. This divergence introduces additional challenges in an already complex era.

The second part of this book comprises a series of chapters exhibiting how public administration evolves across the regions and countries of the world. Using the COVID-19 pandemic period as a departure point, they explore the progress made by public administration in adapting and responding to contemporary issues in an ever-evolving international environment, which is currently trending towards a multipolar world. In general, it seems that public administration, shaped by broader historical contexts, values, and needs, is transitioning, but this transition is not clear-cut, as each era has provided departure points for the next, often carrying on the character and challenges of its preceding era (OECD 2010).

Moleketi-Fraser et al. explore the many forms that transformation of public administration in countries on the African continent has taken (Chapter 9). They argue that public administration has played a crucial role in realising transformative goals, thereby ensuring effective governance and sustainable progress in a dynamically evolving global context. They show that African countries aligned their policies, plans, and public administration practices with the SDGs, on the basis of the Agenda

2063 emphasising the need for integrated approaches, multisectoral collaboration, and evidence-based policy making.[16]

They showcase numerous examples of policies and programmes that African countries devise and implement in upgrading the performance of public administration and improving governance. South Africa's "People first" Programme—*Batho Pele*—is a noteworthy example of this. Its primary goal remains the enhancement of public service delivery through such innovative strategies as comprehensive training, active citizen engagement, and the rigorous pursuit of service quality improvement—a government policy fostering citizen-centred governance, in other words. Another noteworthy example of public administration moving forward is Rwanda's focus on institutional development and capacity building. This has signalled the intention to elevate transparency levels, foster improved governance practices, and bolster overall institutional capacity.[17] Despite such efforts, however, to upgrade public administration, challenges still persist in both implementation and monitoring. For instance, in some cases, favouritism appears to still take precedence over competence in appointment decisions.

Adoption of digital technologies is also making inroads in Africa's public administration systems. It happens through the impact of e-government initiatives in select countries, which enhance transparency and accountability fostering the engagement of citizens in the policymaking process, thus providing for improved public participation and enabling citizen oversight of government activities.[18] Furthermore,

[16] See "Agenda 2063: The Africa We Want". **It is the** master plan for transforming Africa into the global powerhouse of the future. It is the continent's strategic framework that aims to deliver on its goal for inclusive and sustainable development and is a concrete manifestation of the pan-African drive for unity, self-determination, freedom, progress, and collective prosperity pursued under Pan-Africanism and African Renaissance. The Agenda prioritises inclusive social and economic development, continental and regional integration, democratic governance and peace and security among other issues aimed at repositioning Africa to becoming a dominant player in the global arena. https://au.int/sites/default/files/documents/36204-doc-agenda2063_popular_version_en.pdf.

[17] Numerous other examples, from Ethiopia, Cameroon, Liberia, Tanzania, Ghana, etc., appear in Chapter 9.

[18] In fact, the COVID-19 pandemic has contributed to a four-per cent increase in the E-Government Development Index (EGDI) value, with 30% of African countries in the high EGDI group and 60% in the middle.

SMART analytics and inter-agency collaboration assist in improving service delivery, reduce costs, prevent corruption, and foster innovation.[19]

In contrast, several South-East Asian countries cope with contemporary challenges, the so-called polycrises, utilising multi-nodal governance approaches. *Brillantes et al.* describe such approaches in Chapter 10 as governance systems with a strong and competent central authority that prepares comprehensive long- and medium-term development plans that essentially lay out the general policy guidelines, while subordinate levels of government, in particular, local governments, are tasked with local-level policy execution and implementation; and ministries and specialised government agencies provide direction with financial and technical support.

The experience of these countries ranges from rapid centralisation to forming responsible ministries and line departments, e.g., health, interior, social welfare, emergency management, etc. Furthermore, it demonstrates experience in mobilising sub-national institutions and sub-national government with a view to implementing government policy, making sure that their efforts are aligned, coordinated, and not moving in disparate policy directions. In practice, however, when the COVID-19 pandemic broke out, these countries' governance structures employed a combination of centralised and decentralised crisis responses.

For instance, Singapore's centralised and structured COVID-19 reaction included intensive public health measures, while Indonesia's decentralised task groups incorporated public–private collaborations to tackle COVID-19. However, Thailand established a coordination authority, the CCSA,[20] which utilised a whole-of-government approach bringing together all vital government entities and empowered provincial leaders to make localised decisions within the CCSA's framework. This diversity, moreover, has demonstrated how different government frameworks handle crises (Djalante et al. 2020).

[19] However, African countries still have to confront systemic challenges. They include such issues as inadequate infrastructure, lack of technical expertise, and limited financial resources. To fully realise the benefits of digital technologies, African countries need to prioritise digital transformation and to develop frameworks that support the adoption of digital technologies in public administration further and work towards reducing the digital divide.

[20] Centre for COVID-19 Situation Administration (CCSA), that engaged government officials from various sectors to coordinate a unified response allowing for some flexibility at the local level.

In sum, in this age of polycrises, a multi-nodal approach to governance and public administration is a plausible path to follow in order to tackle poly- and inter-twined crises; ranging from disaster risk reduction, environment and climate change, or health crises like the recent pandemic. By contrast, experience in a number of South-East Asian states demonstrates that multi-nodal policy responses to polycrises ought to be centrally enabled by agile and flexible governance institutions. It is required, moreover, that national authorities and central coordinating bodies play lead roles, in order to facilitate quick and decisive action by lower levels of government during a rapidly evolving emergency.

Conversely, crisis management in public administration can be a complex challenge, especially in transboundary situations like mass refugee influxes (Nolte et al. 2020).[21] In Chapter 11, *Sičáková-Beblavá and Beblavy* profess a rationale for such complexity. It is, on the one hand, because rapid responses are required and, on the other, issues of legitimacy, transparency, and accountability are at stake. Also, it is because typically, crisis management transcends administrative levels, and ministerial domains and sectors. It is characterised by uniqueness, ambiguity, complexity, and high uncertainty (Christensen et al. 2016).[22] Hence, crisis management presents political leaders with challenging agendas. These are decisive and critical to the political order and governance processes.

In this context, crises usually serve as catalysts for institutional development, often leading to the creation of new institutional forms, structures, powers, and processes. Furthermore, as usually crises disrupt conditions that had previously resisted change, they often open windows of opportunity for changes that had previously been deemed impossible and postponed on account of (Randma-Liiv and Kickert 2017).[23] At the same time, it is observed that institutional change can become manifest as an episodic and dramatic rather than continuous and incremental process.

This is distinctly observed, in the European public administration space in which public administration structures underwent significant transformations in reaction to substantial shifts in both the domestic and

[21] Cited in *Sičáková-Beblavá and Beblavy*, Chapter 11 "When the Four Horsemen of Apocalypse get Schengen Visa: European Public Administrations and Governance in the Era of Pandemic, War, and Permanent Crisis".

[22] Ibid.

[23] Ibid.

international contexts. For instance, four external shocks examined—the Eurozone crisis; the migration crisis; the COVID-19 pandemic; and the war in Ukraine—indicate that major adjustments were made to the European public administration realm as a direct response to these external challenges. This has happened, moreover, while the European public administration space has been confronted by such numerous crises as the green transition, demographic shifts, technological advancement, skills shortages, and mounting fiscal pressures from many sources (European Commission 2021).[24]

We may conclude that, while such mounting crises have exerted pressure on the European public administration systems, they have also acted as catalysts for a transformative change. In other words, the crises have had a creative impact on administrative and governance mechanisms. They have also made the EU evolve from a chiefly norm-setting apparatus to an executive agent with a direct operational engagement.[25] This illustrates that crises have propelled the EU towards deeper integration, altering its administrative and organisational DNA in ways hitherto unimaginable.

We may also conclude that the multilayered nature of government, with its complex decision-making procedures and their inherent difficulties in taking collective action, highlights the indispensable role of coordination and collaboration. These are the subjects discussed in Chapters 4 and 5 of this book. They reveal that robust governance structures, coordination mechanisms, and integration of specialised knowledge into politically salient decisions are pivotal in effectively addressing and resolving complex issues like the crises situations already mentioned. This combination is a clear shift towards decision-making frameworks which are inherently interdisciplinary and require robust systems for the difficult task of assimilating expert knowledge.

In such other countries of the world as those in the Caucasus and Central Asia, the COVID-19 pandemic proved to be a major challenge for public administration systems. The crisis revealed that the existing development strategies and programmes did not consider such risks as those associated with the crisis; in this case of the pandemic, it also brought to light other persistent challenges, the climate change among them, as well

[24] Ibid.

[25] For example, ccollective purchases of vaccines or potential shared bids for energy resources and military support for Ukraine have become new responsibilities.

as depletion of natural resources, widespread digitalisation, etc. In this complex environment, governments had to reconsider their governance approaches to ensure sustainable development and the well-being of their population, under conditions of increasing uncertainty, turbulence, and instability. This involved the critical re-evaluation of policies and practices, so that actions may be formulated, and decisions made in such a way as to address these challenges effectively.

In a similar perspective, it is obvious that the pandemic changed the agenda of public administration reform and civil service development, especially with regard to direction and priorities. Significantly, in most cases, the new agenda includes improvements in governance and meeting expectations of citizens. Thus, they have placed an emphasis on improving strategic planning and enhancing risk management, as well as recognising that citizens are the primary drivers for reform and thus also at the forefront of the agenda for change. They have, moreover, placed considerable emphasis on digitalisation—a process initiated before the pandemic but vastly accelerated during the pandemic. It remains a priority today. Furthermore, they have embarked on another wave of civil service development, leading to an enhancement of the human resource management function.

An overall conclusion of the above analysis demonstrates that reforms in public administration and the civil service undertaken in each of these countries are characterised by diverse initiatives. However, despite their differences, all those efforts share some common goals: improving the capacity for innovation, agility, efficiency, and transparency of public administration, as well as try to ensure a fairer distribution of resources and public goods to better meet the needs and expectations of citizens.

Another emerging approach to a transformation of public administration is going beyond the nation-state and into the regional and international space, as numerous issues have an inherently transnational nature. These force public administration to adjust traditional practices in order to facilitate the management of regional and global processes. An example of this emerging pattern occurs in Latin America, where public administration faces several challenges, considered transnational threats, stemming from a variety of sources, i.e., people, digital networks, and the physical environment. The importance of these transnational issues has become more evident with each new crisis or threat. This has rendered comprehensive governance structures necessary prerequisites to ensure that decisions are made in a way that enables governments to cope with the new reality competently. Whether it is trade, capital flows, migration, or climate change, the world is far more interconnected now than previously.

Lopez's analysis, in Chapter 12, indicates that the transnational dimension of public administration is growing rapidly. For instance, in Latin America combatting drug trafficking is not an easy task and it requires efforts at the regional level through inter-institutional and inter-sectoral work, adapting an effective network logic to meet the needs of all the populations that are exposed or vulnerable to this critical threat. Another example is migration. It has evolved into a transnational issue also requiring a multilevel governance approach in a multi-dimensional manner. The countries of the region need to jointly devise dignified and effective policies, which consider alliances and collaboration as main drivers in achieving a greater degree of coordination and coherence. These are essential prerequisites in endeavouring to achieve a regional policy on migration that adjusts to the new migratory reality—also, at the global level. Climate change is another transnational issue, concerning Latin America, as much as the rest of world, which is intricately linked to economic and security aspects, thus requiring regional, as well as international cooperation.[26]

Indeed, managing transnational issues requires cooperation among countries to mitigate risks and ensure the long-term viability of policies instituted. Such issues require joint decision-making processes among the various countries and actors, and they suggest a needed adjustment in traditional practices to facilitate the effective management of global processes that, in turn, reshape the world. Even though this may entail redefinition of the powers and capacities of states, as well as their respective rights and obligations, it merits our attention in an urgent basis.

Ultimately, the search for effective responses to the challenges of the new reality is ongoing worldwide. This effort encompasses the enhancement of policy development tools, the creation of conducive

[26] Impacts of climate change, such as extreme weather events that affect economic activities worldwide, or substantial investments required for mitigation measures such as renewable energy infrastructure, and international regulations aimed at addressing climate change are needed that all require international cooperation. Similarly, climate change is increasingly recognised as a significant threat to international security due to its potential to exacerbate existing geopolitical tensions, trigger conflicts, and destabilise regions.

environments, and the implementation of certain operational, technological, and political solutions tailored to unique country-specific contexts. Importantly, this search extends beyond practices and tools to include the development of new conceptual frameworks for governance. Over the past 30–40 years, the limitations of such approaches as NPM have been thoroughly tested through practice, giving rise to the development of new models. This paradigm shift addresses broader conceptual issues in public administration, adapting to the demands of a new reality and taking on a longer-perspective.

For this, the concept of Stewardship may be a cornerstone for the public service in the new reality. In this context, stewardship plays a major role, as a necessary quality for all public servants. Even more nowadays, it highlights a staple mission of the public service: to maintain and upgrade the long-term capacity of government and public administration to act for the greater public good, to manage prudently and responsibly, an inter-generational obligation to preserve our world. Addressing the long-term concerns of fellow citizens in respect of their country will have the effect of nurturing the inherited legacies of the past, clarifying compelling alternatives, and adopting possible options to the needs of coming years (ACSH 2023).

Overall, as there is no universal model for the way forward it is crucial that public administration remains free of dogma. It should be open to innovation, in terms of both technological advancements and organisational methods for policy support. Equally, it needs to be responsive to citizens' demands, demonstrating institutional flexibility. Last but not least, public administration should prioritise flexibility in human resource management and corresponding advancement in its corporate culture.

References

Acemoglu, Daron, and James A. Robinson. 2012. *Why nations fail: The origins of power, prosperity, and poverty*. New York: Crown Business.

ACSH. 2016. Global and regional trends in civil service development. Astana: Astana Civil Service Hub. https://www.astanacivilservicehub.org/uploads/research_pdf/GlobalandRegional%20trends_in_civil_service_development.pdf.

ACSH. 2023. Stewardship and public service: An introduction. Astana: Astana Civil Service Hub. https://www.astanacivilservicehub.org/uploads/research_pdf/research%20project/Stewardship%20and%20Public%20Service%20An%20Introduction.pdf.

Baimyrzaeva, Mahabat, and Carolyn Taylor Meyer. 2020. Megatrends and the future of work for public sector leaders and educators. *International Journal of Public Leadership* 17 (2): 178–195. https://doi.org/10.1108/IJPL-07-2020-0064.

Birshan, Michael, Jan Mischke, and Olivia White. 2023. Why the path of global wealth and growth matters for strategy. McKinsley & Company Quarterly.

Christensen, T., P. Lægreid, and L.H. Rykkja. 2016. Organizing for crisis management: Building governance capacity and legitimacy. *Public Administration Review*, 76 (6): 887–897.

Djalante, R., L. Nurhidayah,, V.M. Hoang, T.N.P. Nguyen, Y. Mahendradhata, A. Trias, J. Lassa, and M.A. Millerg. 2020. COVID-19 and ASEAN responses: Comparative policy analysis. *Progress in Disaster Science* 8: 1–12. https://doi.org/10.1016/j.pdisas.2020.100129 and https://www.ncbi.nlm.nih.gov/pmc/articles/PMC7577870/.

European Commission. 2021. "Supporting Public Administrations in EU Member States to Deliver Reforms and Prepare for the Future." Commission Staff Working Document, SWD(2021) 25 final.

Gore, A. 2013. *The future: Six drivers of global change*. London: Random House.

Gwartney, James, Robert Lawson, and Ryan Murphy. 2024. Economic Freedom dataset, published in Economic Freedom of the World: 2024 annual report. Fraser Institute.

Hajkowicz, S., H. Cook, and A. Littleboy. 2012. Our future world: Global megatrends that will change the way we live. Commonwealth Scientific and Industrial Research Organisation of Australia (CSIRO) Futures Australia. https://www.csiro.au/en/research/technology-space/data/our-future-world.

Halal, W. 2013. Through the mega-crisis: The passage to global maturity. *Foresight* 15 (5): 392–404.

KPMG. 2014. Future State 2030: The global megatrends shaping governments. https://assets.kpmg.com/content/dam/kpmg/pdf/2014/02/future-state-2030-v3.pdf.

Marmier, A., M.A. Munoz-Pineiro, E. Boelman, M. Hristova, A.L. Vetere Arellano, and A. Tsakalidis. 2022. *Interlinkages for a megatrend on accelerating technological change and hyperconnectivity*. Edited by E. Boelman. Luxembourg: Publications Office of the European Union. https://publications.jrc.ec.europa.eu/repository/handle/JRC126570.

NIC. 2021. Global Trends 2040. A more contested world. https://www.dni.gov/index.php/gt2040-home

Naughtin, Claire, K., Emma Schleiger, Alexandra Bratanova, Andrew Terhorst, and Stefan Hajkowicz. 2024. Forty years in the making: A systematic review of the megatrends literature. *Futures* 157 (March). https://www.sciencedirect.com/science/article/pii/S0016328724000120.

Nolte, I.M., A.M. Bushnell, and M. Mews. 2020. Public administration entering turbulent times: A study of service quality during the refugee crisis. *International Journal of Public Administration*, 43 (16): 1345–1356.

OECD. 2010. *Perspectives on global development 2010: Shifting wealth.* Paris: Development Centre, Organisation for Economic Development and Cooperation.

OECD. 2019a. Whole-of-government coordination and policy coherence. In *Governance as an SDG accelerator: Country experiences and tools.* Paris: Organisation for Economic Development and Cooperation. https://www.oecd-ilibrary.org/docserver/7ed12bf1-en.pdf?expires=1726739005&id=id&accname=guest&checksum=BF0FD02274034A028B36A3DC16301281.

OECD. 2019b. *Skills strategy—The skills implications of megatrends.* Paris: Organisation for Economic Development and Cooperation. https://www.oecd-ilibrary.org/docserver/46a24c27-en.pdf?expires=1726827264&id=id&accname=guest&checksum=B831B536F743B7C6F22056B468C1F7EA.

PMI. 2022. Global megatrends 2022. Project Management Institute. https://www.pmi.org/-/media/pmi/documents/public/pdf/learning/thought-leadership/pmi-megatrends-2022.pdf?rev=087ea6f24b62411bb5a42dcce4a6739f&sc_lang_temp=en.

PWC. 2016. Five megatrends and their implications for global defence and security. https://www.pwc.com/gx/en/government-public-services/assets/five-megatrends-implications.pdf.

Randma-Liiv, T., and W. Kickert. 2017. The impact of the fiscal crisis on public administration reforms: Comparison of 14 European countries. *Journal of Comparative Policy Analysis: Research and Practice*, 19 (2): 155–172.

Tabellini, Guido. 2010. Culture and institutions: Economic development in the regions of Europe. *Journal of the European Economic Association* 8 (4): 677–716. https://doi.org/10.1111/j.1542-4774.2010.tb00537.x.

UNDESA, Population Division. 2024. World Population Prospects 2024: Summary of results (UNDESA/POP/2024/DC/NO. 9). https://www.un.org/development/desa/pd/sites/www.un.org.development.desa.pd/files/files/documents/2024/Jul/undesa_pd_2024_wpp_2024_advance_unedited.pdf.

UNDP. 2024a. *Human Development Report 2023/2024: Breaking the gridlock.* New York: United Nations Development Programme.

UNDP. 2024b. *2024 UNDP trends report: The landscape of development*. New York: United Nations Development Programme.

UNFAO. 2012. World agriculture towards 2030/2050, the 2012 revision. http://www.fao.org/docrep/016/ap106e/ap106e.pdf.

UNFPA. 1994. Programme of action (Adopted at the International Conference on Population and Development (ICPD)). https://www.unfpa.org/sites/default/files/event-pdf/PoA_en.pdf.

Wilson, D., A.L. Kelston, and S. Ahmed. 2010. Is this the BRICs decade? BRICs Monthly. Goldman Sachs Global Economics, Commodities, and Strategy Research.

PART I

Environment and Tools

CHAPTER 2

Cultivating Organisational Culture to Facilitate Public Service Excellence

James L. Perry and Rajneesh Gupta

2.1 Introduction

At the core of thriving democracies is an undeniable truth: good governance, characterised by efficiency, transparency, and accountability in public institutions. Equally vital is the relentless drive for high performance, which fuels progress, sparks innovation, and enhances societal well-being. Yet, this truth is frequently overshadowed by rent-seeking behaviours, where officials place personal gain above public welfare. These practices erode public trust and stifle economic development, with corrupt administrations failing to effectively mobilise sufficient levels of resources (Krueger 1974).

J. L. Perry (✉)
Paul H. O'Neill School of Public and Environmental Affairs, Indiana University, Bloomington, IN, USA
e-mail: perry@iu.edu

R. Gupta
Research Designs & Standards Organisation (RDSO), Ministry of Railways, Government of India, Lucknow, Uttar Pradesh, India

A. Baimenov and P. Liverakos (eds.), *Public Administration in the New Reality*, https://doi.org/10.1007/978-981-96-3845-1_2

The impact of rent seeking extends far beyond simple bureaucratic inefficiency. It involves the pursuit of personal gains within governance systems, leading to sub-standard public service delivery (Naim and Hasan 2018) and weakened bureaucratic functionality (Kali 2020). Furthermore, rent seeking influences economic growth and inequality, affecting firms' adoption of new technologies (Pierre-Daniel 2001; Spinesi 2009). Historical factors, such as colonial-era bureaucracies, continue to shape current governance practices. For example, in Brazil, these legacies have resulted in limited access to justice and poor public services (Naritomi et al. 2007), whereas, in East European countries, a politicised bureaucracy fosters corruption and reduces accountability (Meyer-Sahling and Mikkelsen 2016). These examples highlight the urgent need for governance reforms.

Stepping back to examine the larger context, it seems that a reciprocal relationship between high-performing organisations and good governance exists. Good governance provides the environment of reinforcing public values, which in turn strengthens performance through enhanced efficiency and accountability. Transforming bureaucracies to prioritise public interest over personal gain is paramount, especially in developing nations (Grindle 1997; McDonnell 2020). This chapter will navigate this complex terrain, proposing empirically grounded pathways for reforming public institutions. Recognising that rent seeking is a major barrier, this chapter identifies potential attributes, associated with public organisations, to deliver good governance and high performance. Moreover, it explores the process through which these attributes are ingrained in organisational cultures.

2.2 The Impact of Rent Seeking on Good Governance and High Performance

Rent seeking, initially defined by Tullock (1967) involves the pursuit of existing wealth instead of creating new wealth. Krueger (1974) characterised rent seeking as a counterproductive use of resources that distorts public policy and results in the misallocation of these resources.

2.2.1 Theoretical Bases of Rent-Seeking Behaviour

Public choice theory posits that bureaucrats often pursue self-interest, leading to rent-seeking behaviours, a tendency that is further underlined by principal-agent theory. The theory highlights the conflicts of interest between bureaucrats (agents) and the public (principals), pointing out that in the absence of proper accountability, rent seeking becomes increasingly prevalent. Building on this notion, institutional theory suggests that lax regulations and oversight create environments where rent seeking thrives. In addition, organisational culture, as defined by the shared values and norms within an institution, plays a pivotal role in shaping individual behaviours (Schein 1992). In such contexts, a culture promoting self-interest and opportunism is more likely to foster rent-seeking practices, ultimately undermining the effectiveness of public services.

2.2.2 *Economic and Political Consequences of Rent Seeking*

Rent-seeking behaviour, which is prominent in economic activity, politics, culture, and public administration, results in notable output losses and is a key driver of bureaucratic inefficiency (Vasilev 2013). This behaviour not only undermines service delivery and erodes public trust, but also stifles economic growth (Pierre-Daniel 2001; Sarte 2000). It is instrumental in creating inefficiencies in government spending and skews policymaking, where political interests often prevail over economic interests (Pierre-Daniel 2001). Furthermore, Lambsdorff (2002) emphasises that corruption, a particularly destructive type of rent seeking, severely damages welfare more than other activities, because of its widespread reach and focused interests.

2.3 Organisational Culture Attributes That Advance Good Governance and High Performance in Public Organisations

In the long run, what cultural attributes reduce rent-seeking behaviour and undermine its corrosive effects? We focus on six attributes that research and practice identify as particularly influential: mission mystique, high-performance expectations, professional integrity, leadership's strategic focus, transparency, and impartiality as fundamental public values, and empowered public servants. We now proceed to define each of these attributes and provide examples of why they matter and how they make a difference.

2.3.1 Mission Mystique

Mission mystique (Goodsell 2010, 2011) refers to the profound connection between an organisation's purpose, its culture, and the motivation of its workforce. At its core, mission mystique is about embedding a shared sense of purpose and dedication in a public organisation, thereby guiding its actions, and sustaining its identity over time. The source of this belief system is deeply rooted in the organisation's central mission—the fundamental purpose that justifies its existence and shapes its strategies and operations. This central mission, coupled with the organisation's commitment to serving societal needs, forms the bedrock of mission mystique.

Mission mystique guides the organisation through challenges and changes by fostering a distinctive reputation, intrinsic motivation among employees, and a culture of continuous renewal and learning. The societal need the organisation addresses underlines its relevance, grounding its mission in the urgent and tangible benefits it provides to the community or nation. This relevance is critical for maintaining public support and legitimacy. Furthermore, intrinsic motivation, fuelled by the alignment of personal values with the organisation's mission, ensures a resolute and passionate workforce (Perry 2021), essential for achieving long-term success.

Several key elements significantly bolster the belief system of mission mystique. First, celebrating the agency's history fosters pride and ensures continuity. Second, promoting beliefs open to debate enhances adaptability and responsiveness to change. Finally, granting qualified policy autonomy facilitates innovation within established boundaries. These components, coupled with a culture that embeds these beliefs and practices, transform mission mystique from an abstract idea into a living, breathing aspect of the organisation's identity. By fostering an environment where the mission, not just external rewards, motivates employees, organisations can surpass traditional performance measures in commitment and effectiveness.

To develop mission mystique in their cultures, organisations should prioritise clear mission statements, maintain workforce continuity, and embrace adaptability. Clearly articulating the mission ensures organisational goals deeply resonate, aligning employee and stakeholder efforts towards a shared objective. Workforce continuity builds a culture of resilience, attracting and retaining talent driven by more than compensation, fostering identity, pride, and a dedication to public service. Moreover, a genuine capacity for change highlights an organisation's dedication to innovation and flexibility, crucial for public service challenges. These strategies together foster a culture where shared values enhance performance, promoting governance that is responsive, accountable, and mission aligned. This alignment of mission clarity, employee commitment, and flexibility defines excellence in public governance.

The US National Park Service, for example, steadfastly upholds its mission, safeguarding America's natural and cultural wonders, and addressing the crucial need for environmental preservation and public enrichment. With a legacy of conservation, the National Park Service's reputable standing reflects a deep-rooted commitment to its cause, enriched by a culture that emphasises environmental ethics and honours historical milestones. Employees, driven by a shared passion for the mission, embody intrinsic motivation, nurtured by comprehensive training and a collective ethos of stewardship.[1] The agency's openness to innovative conservation strategies and its ability to autonomously navigate policy within its mandate allows for adaptive management practices. This commitment to continuous evolution and responsiveness to changing environmental and societal demands illustrates the dynamic, mission-focused culture at the heart of the National Park Service.

A second example of the influence of mission mystique is the Virginia State Police, which champions public safety, effectively responding to the critical societal needs of law enforcement and crime prevention. Renowned for its dedication and broad scope of responsibilities, the Virginia State Police's reliance on intrinsic motivation is evident in its officers, many of whom are inspired by family traditions or a profound sense of duty to serve and protect. This ethos is supported by a culture that prizes professionalism, ethical conduct, and reverence for the agency's history, fostering a strong organisational identity. The Virginia State Police encourages innovation and adaptation through open dialogue and feedback mechanisms, maintaining policy flexibility to meet emerging challenges. Its commitment to ongoing professional development ensures

[1] For an articulate discussion of the concept of stewardship in the public service, see Everest-Phillips, Max. 2003 Stewardship and public service: An introduction. Astana, KZ: Astana Civil Service Hub, https://www.astanacivilservicehub.org/uploads/research_pdf/research%20project/Stewardship%20and%20Public%20Service%20An%20Introduction.pdf.

the force remains at the forefront of modern law enforcement, showcasing a resilient and mission-aligned culture.

In Bolivia, the transformative power of mission mystique is vividly demonstrated in health sector organisations. Employees in these organisations hold a profound belief in their mission, viewing their roles as essential and impactful. This belief is not just theoretical; it translates into tangible actions and outcomes. Employees see their organisations as innovative and responsive, and this perception fuels a commitment to delivering superior services. This collective ethos of striving for excellence and responsiveness to client needs elevated their performance, setting them apart from other organisations. The health workers' deep-seated conviction about their mission and their role in fulfilling it, exemplifies how mission mystique can drive high performance and significantly enhance service quality in the public sector (Grindle 1997).

In Ghana, the impact of mission mystique is vividly evident at a poorly resourced agricultural extension institute. Despite facing considerable resource constraints, workers harboured a strong belief in the significance of their activities. They were committed to training farmers and enhancing agricultural output, viewing each individual's role as crucial to the organisation's overall success. This sense of mission, deeply ingrained in their professional identity, transcended the institute's material limitations. It reflects how mission mystique can inspire dedication and drive performance, even in challenging environments, by instilling a shared sense of purpose and responsibility among employees (Grindle 1997).

To summarise, mission mystique significantly enhances an organisation's culture and operations, driving employees to align their efforts with the organisation's core purpose and values. This deep-seated belief in the organisation's mission not only motivates employees beyond monetary incentives but also fosters a strong commitment to professionalism and service as is clear from the given examples.

2.3.2 *High-Performance Expectations*

High-performance expectations are essential for setting aspirations and standards for driving exceptional achievements and outcomes. High-performance expectations are critical for moulding operations in public organisations with strong cultures. By setting high bars for performance, these organisations create an environment where excellence is the norm. They instil a sense of purpose and urgency, ensuring that every action and decision aligns with the overarching goal of maximising public value. This approach not only enhances the effectiveness of public services, but also fosters public trust and confidence in government.

High-performance expectations are communicated by a variety of mechanisms, including competitive recruitment and performance-based career advancement across all phases of an employee's engagement with the organisation. Organisations adopt clear job descriptions, rules, and training programmes that underscore performance criteria. Furthermore, they implement probationary periods and regular periodic performance assessments to reinforce these standards. Effective management of incentives and rewards, both monetary and non-monetary, rewards high performers and sets a benchmark for others. Conversely, poor performance is addressed with appropriate measures. This approach cultivates an environment where high performance is not just expected but ingrained in the organisational culture.

An often-repeated story about a janitor at NASA conversing with President John Kennedy offers a compelling illustration of high-performance expectations (Carton 2018; Lachance 2017). When asked by President Kennedy what he did, the janitor famously replied, "I'm helping put a man on the moon". This simple yet profound statement reflects the organisational culture at NASA, where every employee, regardless of their position, understands and embraces high-performance expectations that reflect their role for the larger mission of the organisation or nation.

High-performance expectations are not confined to technical or scientific roles, but extend to all levels, fostering a sense of ownership and responsibility in each task, no matter how small. The janitor's mindset exemplifies how high-performance expectations can permeate an organisation, leading to a collective drive towards excellence as a common goal. This not only elevates individual performance but also ensures good governance by aligning every action with the organisation's overarching objectives, thus creating a cohesive and effective operation.

2.3.3 Professional Integrity

Professional integrity, characterised by steadfast adherence to ethical principles, honesty, and moral values within professional conduct, is indispensable in the public sector for ensuring good governance and high performance. It is also viewed as a virtue essential for professions that require public trust, shaping professional actions in accordance with the legitimate expectations of the society, and hence is considered a fundamental component of ethical practice (Eriksen 2015). Employees who embody professional integrity play a crucial role in enhancing trust among the public, guaranteeing transparency in decisions, and upholding accountability. Such ethical conduct is instrumental in boosting public sector organisations' efficiency, effectiveness, and credibility, marking a significant step towards achieving organisational excellence (Asmawati et al. 2019; Tannimalay et al. 2021).

Transitioning towards a culture prioritising integrity over mere compliance highlights the importance of moral mindfulness and a deep-seated commitment to ethical standards. This shift is vital in a setting where ethical conduct and public trust are paramount, as it directly impacts decision-making processes, strengthens stakeholder trust, and enhances organisational reputation. Public sector entities can prioritise integrity by creating an environment where ethical behaviour is expected and exemplified, thus fostering increased transparency, accountability, and public confidence (Verhezen 2010).

Furthermore, the essence of professional integrity is magnified in the light of public service motivation. Employees driven by a genuine desire to serve the public good are likelier to engage in ethical conduct and uphold integrity. When supported by an organisational culture that treasures integrity, this intrinsic motivation creates an ideal environment for fostering good governance and superior performance. The interplay between intrinsic motivation and an integrity-valuing climate is key to cultivating a culture of ethical excellence (Tannimalay et al. 2021; Wright and Pandey 2008).

The transformation of Nigeria's National Agency for Food and Drug Administration and Control (NAFDAC) under the leadership of Dora Akunyili is a striking example of how integrity can revolutionise public sector performance and governance. When Akunyili assumed leadership, she encountered an organisation crippled by laxity, corruption, and inefficiency. Her response was not just a reshuffling of roles but a cultural upheaval, underpinned by an unwavering commitment to integrity. She began by assembling a team skilled as well as deeply aligned with the National Agency for Food and Drug Administration and Control's mission, emphasising both competence and a strong ethical orientation. This team was instrumental in implementing a rigorous purge, a bold move that dismissed corrupt and underperforming staff, setting a new tone of zero tolerance for corruption and mediocrity.

Akunyili's leadership was characterised by an ethical stance focused on professionalism that extended to all levels of the organisation, from high-ranking officials to junior employees. Training programmes were established, both locally and internationally, fostering a culture of professional development anchored in ethical practices. In addition, a robust internal whistle-blowing mechanism was put in place, encouraging and rewarding the exposure of malpractices. This comprehensive approach to integrity reshaped the National Agency for Food and Drug Administration and Control into a formidable entity in safeguarding public health, turning it into a beacon of good governance and high performance in the public sector (McDonnell 2020).

2.3.4 *Leadership's Strategic Focus*

This attribute refers to the proactive and strategic focus of organisational leaders on driving exceptional performance while upholding principles of good governance by setting a standard for excellence and integrity. Strategic focus instils a sense of responsibility and ambition within their teams, fostering an environment where excellence is not just a goal, but a norm. This guides decision-making processes towards outcomes that are not only effective but also ethically sound and transparent, thereby enhancing accountability and trust. In public sector organisations, where the implications of actions extend to society at large, the leadership's commitment to good governance and high performance is indispensable. It not only streamlines internal processes but also significantly elevates the quality of public service.

By emphasising meritocracy and aligning organisational goals with broader national or sectoral objectives, leaders can instigate profound change. Such leadership goes beyond traditional management, cultivating a culture where performance, ethical standards, and strategic relevance are paramount. This shift towards a culture of empowerment and excellence transforms individuals, often resistant to change, into active contributors to the organisation's success. The result is an organisation that not only excels in its performance but also significantly contributes to broader developmental goals, exemplifying effective and purposeful governance.

The revitalisation of the Kenya Tea Development Agency under the leadership of Charles Karanja epitomises how focused leadership attention on good governance and high performance can profoundly transform a public sector organisation. Karanja, recognising the importance of balancing meritocracy with organisational orientation, strategically reformed the Kenya Tea Development Agency's recruitment process. This reform was not merely about hiring skilled individuals but about instilling a culture where performance and adherence to the organisational ethos were paramount.

Karanja's approach to leadership was multifaceted: he valued personal connections for initial recruitment but made final hiring decisions based on merit and organisational fit, evaluated through rigorous interviews and performance assessment during a trial employment period. Under his stewardship, the Kenya Tea Development Agency established a performance-driven culture, where officials were quickly removed if they failed to meet expectations, including those with personal ties to Karanja. This clear, merit-based approach extended to all levels of the organisation, fostering a competitive yet cooperative environment. By focusing on performance and good governance, Karanja steered the Kenya Tea Development Agency to become a global leader in tea production, showcasing how the leadership's unwavering commitment to these principles can lead to remarkable organisational success and transformation (McDonnell 2020).

2.3.5 *Transparency and Impartiality as Fundamental Public Values*

Public values like transparency and impartiality are fundamental cornerstones in the realm of public sector organisations, serving as guiding principles that shape their culture and operational framework. Transparency is the openness and clarity with which organisations conduct their activities, ensuring visibility to stakeholders. Transparency in an organisation fosters trust and credibility, leading to a culture where accountability is expected and upheld. It also enables effective monitoring and encourages responsible behaviour, as actions and decisions are visible and subject to evaluation and scrutiny. Impartiality, on the other hand, is the unbiased and fair treatment of all stakeholders, free from favouritism or prejudice. Impartiality ensures neutrality and fairness by mandating equal treatment of all parties, eliminating favouritism, and fostering decisions based on merit rather than bias. These values serve as benchmarks, setting standards for evaluating processes and outcomes, thereby fostering a culture of trust and credibility.

Transparency is the cornerstone of clear communication and trust-building, ensuring that employees are fully informed about the rationale behind organisational decisions. This clarity is instrumental in shaping perceptions of fairness, particularly in evaluations and compensation, thereby nurturing an environment of equity. Impartiality, on the other hand, is the linchpin for unbiased and equitable decision-making, a fundamental aspect of a just and balanced workplace. The synergy of these values culminates in heightened employee engagement and retention, as trust and fairness are the bedrock of employee satisfaction and performance. They guarantee that organisational management is not just effective and efficient, but also ethically aligned and public interest oriented, creating a workplace where employees are not only motivated but deeply committed to the organisation's success and integrity.

Tasso Jereissati's tenure as governor of *Ceará*, Brazil is a prime example of how transparency and impartiality can revolutionise public sector performance and governance. Focused on transforming a poor north-eastern state, Jereissati implemented policies that significantly reduced corruption, improved transparency, and promoted meritocracy with impartiality in community health workers and emergency disaster relief programmes. He recruited through a stringent selection process and managed operations with exceptional efficiency and discipline.

This transparent and merit-based governance led to remarkable improvements in public welfare. One of the most striking achievements under his leadership was the dramatic increase in child vaccine coverage from 25 to 90%, coupled with a nearly 50% reduction in infant mortality. Jereissati's leadership exemplifies how commitment to transparency and impartiality in public administration can lead to rapid and significant progress in addressing long-standing social challenges (McDonnell 2020).

2.3.6 Empowered Public Servants

Rooted in psychology's self-determination theory, Honig (2024) conceives empowerment as fulfilling an individual's basic psychological needs for autonomy, competence, and relatedness. In practical terms, this translates to a managerial approach that (i) allows autonomy, giving bureaucrats the independence to make decisions and see themselves as influential agents; (ii) cultivates competence, encouraging a sense of skill and capability, bolstering confidence in their abilities to advance their agency's mission; and (iii) creates connections to peers and purpose, enabling bureaucrats to feel valued through their work and interactions with colleagues. This empowerment-oriented management significantly influences organisational behaviour and decision-making processes by fostering a motivated and mission-driven workforce (Perry 2021). Empowerment, as an indispensable cultural attribute, not only improves the effectiveness of public service but also elevates the morale and engagement of those within the organisation, thereby creating a positive ripple effect on the quality of public service delivery.

By allowing autonomy, empowerment enables bureaucrats to function as influential decision-makers, enhancing their sense of agency and ownership in their roles. This autonomy, coupled with a focus on cultivating competence, not only builds confidence in their abilities but also aligns their efforts with the broader mission of the organisation. Moreover, fostering connections to peers and purpose provides a sense of belonging and value, essential for sustained motivation and commitment. Such an empowerment approach ensures that employees are not just functionally capable but also psychologically invested, leading to a workforce that is both effective and efficient. In essence, empowerment, through meeting fundamental human needs for autonomy, competence, and relatedness, creates a robust environment for high performance and the realisation of good governance ideals.

In the heart of Thailand, a transformative shift unfolded in the public sector. Local district heads, distanced from the central directives of Bangkok, found themselves in a managerial void, devoid of traditional tools to enforce compliance. This predicament sparked an unexpected revolution. Unshackled by rigid protocols, these leaders embraced empowerment as their guiding force. They cultivated a culture of inspiration and motivation, replacing authoritative commands with mentorship, care, and appreciation. This nurturing environment bred a sense of ownership and pride among employees, transforming their approach to work. Collaboration flourished, and a new era of trust and harmony dawned between bureaucrats and managers. This empowerment-centric approach, though not foolproof, revealed its strength in fostering a workforce that was not just competent but autonomously driven by a deep-seated mission. What was perceived as a weakness in the Thai bureaucratic fabric emerged as a cornerstone of its development success, illustrating the profound impact of empowerment in reshaping the public sector (Honig 2024).

Identifying key attributes like mission mystique, high-performance expectations, professional integrity, leadership's strategic focus, transparency, and impartiality as fundamental public values, and empowered public servants sets a foundation. These pillars embody the essence of exceptional governance and performance cultures. The crucial question now emerges: How do organisations build such a culture? This inquiry marks a significant transition, guiding us towards actionable strategies for cultivating important attributes in organisational culture.

2.4 Blueprint for Cultivating Good Governance and High Performance

The role of leadership is central for cultivating a culture of good governance and high performance. By making safety a non-negotiable priority in Alcoa Aluminium, CEO Paul O'Neill signalled a broader commitment to employee well-being and operational excellence at Alcoa (Perry 2017). This focus on safety transcended all levels of the organisation, fostering a culture where every employee felt valued and responsible for not just their safety but also the company's success. The result was not just a remarkable improvement in safety records, but also enhanced operational efficiencies, cost savings, and profitability.

Similarly, the anecdote of the NASA janitor telling President Kennedy, "I'm helping to put a man on the moon", exemplifies the profound impact of leadership in instilling a collective sense of purpose (Carton 2018). This narrative ensures that every team member, regardless of their position, feels essential to the organisation's mission, demonstrating the powerful influence of leadership in creating a cohesive sense of purpose. It underscores the importance of leaders in communicating a unifying vision that transcends individual tasks, promoting a shared commitment to overarching goals. It results in driving organisational success through a deeply embedded culture of collaboration and accountability.

Leaders do not just dictate practices, vision, or mission; they live by them. Through consistent communication, they embed a clear vision and set of values into the organisational DNA. Furthermore, they prioritise transparent communication with openness and clarity to foster an atmosphere of trust, driving engagement and facilitating smoother transitions during periods of change. This not only fosters a strong ethical culture but also aligns employees with the organisation's core mission. Clear policies and a focus on performance with accountability ensure that organisational goals are met with integrity.

Furthermore, developing a culture of good governance and high performance within an organisation involves a series of strategic and structural processes. These processes aim to embed ethical standards, accountability, transparency, and a commitment to excellence in every aspect of the organisation. Here is a breakdown of these processes.

2.4.1 *Crafting Culture: The Power of Narrative, Rituals, and Symbolic Action*

In organisations, culture thrives in the hearts of employees, far beyond the confines of paper, pulsating through the actions and beliefs of its employees. This culture shapes an institution's culture, influencing not just how it is perceived externally but, more importantly, how it functions internally. It is sculpted through a blend of narratives, rituals, and symbolic actions, deeply embedding a sense of mission and values within the workforce identity.

Consider the US National Weather Service, for instance. The National Weather Service's guiding principle, "saving lives and livelihoods", is more than a mere slogan; it encapsulates the organisation's fundamental commitment to public safety through timely and accurate weather forecasting. This principle is brought to life through rigorous scientific research, state-of-the-art meteorological practices, and the dedication of its personnel who often work around the clock during severe weather events. This rallying cry not only motivates employees by reminding them of the critical nature of their work, but also fosters public trust and reliance on the National Weather Service for life-saving information (Goodsell 2010, 2011).

Similarly, the Virginia State Police (VSP) operates under the motto "Virginia's Finest". This motto is testament to the Virginia State Police's commitment to excellence, integrity, and service. It is manifested through their rigorous training programmes, the high standards they uphold, and the pride they take in their duty to protect and serve the citizens of Virginia. The symbolic presence of a trooper statue inscribed with this motto at their training academy serves as a constant reminder to current and aspiring troopers of the values they are expected to embody. This motto binds the force together, creating a cohesive culture of professionalism and dedication (Goodsell 2010, 2011).

Leaders play critical roles in employing storytelling as a tool to fuse the concrete with the ethereal, rendering the core values and achievements of an organisation both tangible and relatable. Through their narratives, they breathe life into abstract principles, transforming them into a vivid tapestry of the organisation's ethos. Rituals and ceremonies, held with varying frequency—from daily affirmations to annual celebrations—serve as the lifeblood of these stories, weaving a fabric of unity and unwavering commitment among all members of the organisation.

Symbolic actions, especially those initiated by leaders, play a pivotal role in reinforcing the organisation's core values. A prime example of this is seen in the adoption of the mantra "To Be the Best" by the Mecklenburg County, North Carolina Department of Social Services (Goodsell 2010, 2011). This performance-oriented slogan is not just a call to action; it is a beacon that illuminates and rewards behaviours emblematic of the organisation's values. Such symbolic gestures guide employees' actions, ensuring they are in harmony with the spirit of the organisation. They highlight the virtues of striving for excellence.

Take, for instance, the legendary response of the janitor at NASA to President Kennedy. The janitor's statement transcends a description of his daily tasks, encapsulating the overarching mission of NASA. It vividly illustrates how clear articulation of purpose and values can inspire every individual within an organisation, regardless of their role, to see themselves as integral contributors to a grand vision.

Integrating narratives, rituals, and symbolic actions into an organisation's culture, however, also presents a nuanced challenge, particularly in ensuring these elements authentically resonate across a diverse workforce. This endeavour requires a dynamic approach to cultural integration, one that not only acknowledges the multifaceted nature of the workforce but also fosters a universal sense of belonging and purpose. Without genuine engagement and the allowance for cultural practices to evolve, there is a significant risk that such elements may devolve into empty formalities, losing their intended meaning and impact.

To prevent this degradation of these cultural practices into mere routine, it is imperative to maintain their relevance and authenticity through adaptability and continuous dialogue within the organisation. This entails creating feedback loops to evaluate the effectiveness of these practices and adjusting them to reflect the changing needs and aspirations of the workforce.

This strategic amalgamation of cultural artefacts ensures that an organisation's vision and values transcend aspiration, becoming a lived experience for its members and steering collective efforts towards high performance and good governance. The intentional moulding of organisational culture through narrative, ritual, and symbol forges a potent collective identity, aligning employees with the mission, nurturing a high-performance ethos, and weaving ethical standards into the fabric of everyday operations.

2.4.2 Integrating Learning with Development

Learning and developing within organisations play a pivotal role in sculpting a culture of high performance and good governance. The cultivation of a learning culture is not only about enhancing individual skills but also about embedding a collective ethos that propels both governance standards and performance metrics forward.

Central to embedding a high-performance culture is the strategic deployment of learning and development programmes that not only sharpen the technical skills of the workforce but also imbue them with the organisation's values and strategic vision. This alignment ensures that every member of the organisation is not just a participant but a custodian of the mission, driving towards collective goals with a shared sense of purpose. Moreover, training and development policies, when intertwined with robust corporate governance mechanisms, significantly impact organisational performance (Brahmana et al. 2018).

Targeted learning and development are fundamental in building a culture of integrity and good governance within organisations. By implementing specialised programmes in ethical decision-making, regulatory compliance, and leadership integrity, organisations not only lay the groundwork for ethical practices and transparency but also prepare a cadre of strategic thinkers and ethical stewards. These future leaders, deeply aligned with the organisation's culture, are crucial for navigating the complexities of governance with a moral compass. Such initiatives ensure that the principles of excellence and integrity are not merely communicated but are intricately woven into the organisational fabric, exemplifying the desired cultural traits at all levels. This holistic approach to learning and development transcends traditional training, creating an environment where ethical governance and leadership excellence become the norm, driving the organisation towards sustained success and impact.

The Virginia State Police's comprehensive training regimen for recruits, for instance, underscores the importance of not just technical proficiency but also ethical conduct and values alignment. This rigorous preparation ensures that officers are not only adept in law enforcement techniques but also deeply ingrained with the principles of justice and community service, thereby reinforcing the organisation's dedication to public safety and integrity (Goodsell 2010, 2011).

Furthermore, the agility and innovation required to thrive in an ever-changing environment are also nurtured through learning and development. Emphasising adaptability, creative problem-solving, and embracing change, these initiatives prepare organisations to face external challenges with resilience, ensuring that governance practices are not static but evolve with changing externalities, ensuring sustainability and relevance.

In conclusion, learning and development are the linchpins in the quest for a culture of high performance and robust governance within organisations. By harmonising the development of skills and competencies with the infusion of ethical standards and a visionary outlook, organisations can create an environment where excellence is the norm, governance is beyond reproach, and adaptability and innovation are embedded in the DNA. This holistic approach to learning and development not only empowers individuals to excel in their roles but also ensures that the organisation stands as a beacon of integrity, excellence, and forward-thinking in an ever-evolving global landscape.

2.4.3 Driving Accountability with Performance Management

Performance management systems are essential for organisations striving to achieve good governance and high performance. They provide a clear answer to the fundamental question of "How are we performing?" by enabling organisations to make rational planning enhance decision-making and stimulate organisational learning, thereby improving performance (Leroux and Wright 2010; Meyfroodt and Desmidt 2021). Such systems are vital for managing human capital, with a focus on boosting employee engagement to significantly raise productivity (Gruman and Saks 2011). By setting clear strategic goals and employing performance measurement systems for regular evaluation, these mechanisms align employee efforts with the organisation's strategic objectives, fostering a culture of continuous improvement (Boyne 2001; Meyfroodt and Desmidt 2021).

Accountability mechanisms are crucial for fostering good governance, as they guarantee decision-making processes are transparent, ethical, and mission aligned. Han and Hong (2019) highlight how accountability in staffing, performance evaluation, and compensation significantly boosts organisational performance. Suykens et al. (2022) further argue that employing management tools and performance measurement systems is essential for evolving accountability demands from mere validation to genuine improvement. By implementing such mechanisms, organisations can cultivate a culture that values integrity, deters misconduct, and upholds professional standards, thereby establishing a reputation for trustworthiness and ethical conduct. This strategic approach not only enhances organisational performance but also solidifies a commendable organisational image.

The strategic application of performance management and accountability mechanisms is key to transcending conventional administrative tasks, embedding a culture of excellence and continuous improvement within daily operations. This ensures that organisations not only achieve their strategic objectives but do so with integrity and a commitment to public welfare. Such a dedicated approach to systematic improvement and ethical behaviour is crucial for creating resilient, effective, and ethically sound organisations that stand as models of excellence in the public sector.

2.4.4 *Laying a Foundation for Essential Policies and Frameworks*

Laying the foundation for a culture of high performance and good governance within public organisations is fundamentally anchored in the establishment of robust policies and frameworks. These structures serve as the blueprint for managing resources and responsibilities systematically, equitably, and transparently, facilitating decision-making and implementation through well-defined, predictable procedures. This systematic approach delineates authority, roles, and responsibilities, ensuring accountability and operational efficiency.

Moreover, these policies and frameworks facilitate the consistent application of practices across the organisation, minimising ambiguity and ensuring that all employees, regardless of their role or level, understand their responsibilities and the standards to which they are held. This clarity promotes fairness and equity, which are critical for maintaining high morale and motivation among the workforce.

By embodying key governance principles, policies, and frameworks transition from aspirational to operational, embedding these values in the organisational ethos. For example, governance frameworks like those developed by the World Bank have successfully guided governance reforms, underscoring the necessity of structured approaches to governance (Kulshreshtha 2008).

Moreover, the responsiveness of policies to socio-economic and cultural contexts enhances governance effectiveness, allowing for the adaptation of practices to diverse environments and thereby improving governance outcomes. In parallel, within the domain of organisational performance, policies and frameworks define critical HR management practices that drive high performance, including comprehensive training and feedback mechanisms. These practices cultivate a motivated, skilled workforce essential for achieving organisational goals (Guest 1997).

Furthermore, these guiding structures foster an organisational culture prioritising continuous improvement, innovation, and accountability. Research, such as a study in the Netherlands, demonstrates the positive impact of high-performance work systems and organisational culture on effectiveness, highlighting the strategic importance of policies and frameworks in nurturing a performance-oriented culture (Hartog and Verburg 2004).

In essence, well-conceived policies and frameworks are indispensable for cultivating a culture of excellence within organisations. They not only ensure the alignment of individual and organisational objectives, but also establish a conducive environment for continuous growth, innovation, and high performance. Through thoughtful design and implementation, these guiding principles lay the groundwork for organisations to thrive in pursuit of good governance and high performance.

2.4.5 *Leveraging Communication with Transparency*

Effective communication is the cornerstone of high performance within any organisation. Communication acts as the vital conduit for ideas, feedback, and objectives, enhancing employee engagement and organisational success. It facilitates a seamless exchange of ideas, feedback, and information across all levels, ensuring that every team member is aligned with the organisation's goals and strategies. Studies highlight communication's significant, positive impact on employee performance (Garnett et al. 2008). Furthermore, communication's positive influence has been observed on enhancing teamwork, job satisfaction, and commitment, indicating its nuanced role in organisational dynamics (Rodwell et al. 1998).

Clear communication channels enable employees to understand their roles and responsibilities fully, reducing misunderstandings. Moreover, an environment that encourages open dialogue fosters innovation, as employees feel valued and confident to share their ideas and solutions. This collective intelligence not only drives organisational growth but also enhances job satisfaction and employee engagement, crucial elements for sustaining high performance.

Transparency, on the other hand, is fundamental to embedding good governance within organisations. It involves open access to information regarding the organisation's operations, decisions, and performance, allowing stakeholders to have a comprehensive understanding of its activities. Transparency builds trust between the organisation and its stakeholders, including employees and customers, by making accountability a central aspect of its culture. A culture of openness encourages feedback and dialogue, leading to more democratic and participative decision-making processes. It ensures that decision-making processes are fair, ethical, and aligned with the best interests of all parties involved. In essence, transparency acts as a deterrent against corruption and malpractice, promoting a culture of integrity and ethical behaviour that is indispensable for good governance.

Integrating communication and transparency within an organisation's culture amplifies their impacts, creating a powerful synergy that fosters a high-performance and ethically governed environment. Effective communication ensures that transparency efforts are understood and appreciated, while transparency reinforces the trust and openness necessary for meaningful communication. Together, they ensure that information flows freely and accurately, enabling informed decision-making, fostering a sense of inclusion, and belonging among employees, and building a strong, trusting relationship with external stakeholders. This combination not only enhances organisational performance but also solidifies its reputation for good governance, attracting talent, investment, and loyalty. The integration of communication and transparency is therefore not just a strategic asset but a fundamental pillar for any organisation aspiring to excellence and integrity in today's competitive landscape.

2.5 Conclusion

Bringing together the various threads discussed, high-performance public institutions are pivotal in realising good governance ideals, particularly in countering rent-seeking bureaucracy. Understanding and nurturing these elements is crucial for policymakers, administrators, and civil society in pursuing a more equitable, efficient, and just governance paradigm.

The journey to good governance and high performance in public sector organisations is deeply rooted in cultivating a culture enriched with mission mystique, professional integrity, meritocracy, and empowering leadership. It is through the conscientious integration of these elements that public organisations can transform challenges into opportunities, aligning actions with ethical principles and public values. This transformation is not just an institutional change, but a paradigm shift towards a more equitable, efficient, and just governance system, where public trust is restored, and organisational excellence becomes a norm rather than an exception.

References

Asmawati, S., H. Haron, I. Ismail, and A. Chambers. 2019. Quality of chief integrity officer, ethical climate and the level of ethics and integrity in the Malaysian public sector. *KnE Social Sciences*: 423–458. https://doi.org/10.18502/KSS.V3I22.5065.

Boyne, G. 2001. Planning, performance, and public services. *Public Administration* 79 (1): 73–88. https://doi.org/10.1111/1467-9299.00246.

Brahmana, R.K., R.K. Brahmana, and T.C.F. Ho. 2018. Training and development policy, corporate governance, and firm performance. *Gadjah Mada International Journal of Business* 20 (1): 59–87. https://doi.org/10.22146/GAMAIJB.12995.

Carton, A.M. 2018. "I'm not mopping the floors; I'm putting a man on the moon": How NASA leaders enhanced the meaningfulness of work by changing the meaning of work. *Administrative Science Quarterly* 63 (2): 323–369. https://doi.org/10.1177/0001839217713748.

Eriksen, A. 2015. What is professional integrity? *Etikk i Praksis—Nordic Journal of Applied Ethics* 9 (2): 3–17. https://doi.org/10.5324/eip.v9i2.1836.

Garnett, J.L., J. Marlowe, and S.K. Pandey. 2008. Penetrating the performance predicament: Communication as a mediator or moderator of organizational culture's impact on public organizational performance. *Public Administration Review* 68 (2): 266–281. https://doi.org/10.1111/J.1540-6210.2007.00861.X.

Goodsell, C.T. 2010. *Mission mystique: Belief systems in public agencies*. Washington, DC: CQ Press.

Goodsell, C.T. 2011. Mission mystique: Strength at the institutional center. *The American Review of Public Administration* 41 (5): 475–494. https://doi.org/10.1177/0275074011409566.

Grindle, M.S. 1997. Divergent cultures? When public organizations perform well in developing countries. *World Development* 25 (4): 481–495. https://doi.org/10.1016/S0305-750X(96)00123-4.

Gruman, J.A., and A.M. Saks. 2011. Performance management and employee engagement. *Human Resource Management Review* 21 (2): 123–136. https://doi.org/10.1016/j.hrmr.2010.09.004.

Guest, D.E. 1997. Human resource management and performance: A review and research agenda. *International Journal of Human Resource Management* 8 (3): 263–276. https://doi.org/10.1080/095851997341630.

Han, Y., and S. Hong. 2019. The impact of accountability on organizational performance in the U.S. federal government: The moderating role of autonomy. *Review of Public Personnel Administration* 39 (1): 3–23. https://doi.org/10.1177/0734371X16682816

Hartog, D., and R.M. Verburg. 2004. High performance work systems, organisational culture, and firm effectiveness. *Human Resource Management Journal* 14 (1): 55–78. https://doi.org/10.1111/j.1748-8583.2004.tb00112.x.

Honig, D. 2024. *Mission driven bureaucrats: Empowering people to help government do better*. Oxford: Oxford University Press.

Kali, M. 2020. Characteristics of bureaucracy: Examining the relations between bureaucrats and politicians in Lesotho. *European Journal of Behavioral Sciences* 3 (3): 20–33. https://doi.org/10.33422/ejbs.v3i3.397

Krueger, A.O. 1974. The political economy of the rent-seeking society. *The American Economic Review* 64 (3): 291–303.

Kulshreshtha, P. 2008. Public sector governance reform: The World Bank's framework. *International Journal of Public Sector Management* 21 (5): 556–567. https://doi.org/10.1108/09513550810885831.

Lachance, J.R. 2017. Commentary: Public service motivation: Lessons from NASA's janitor. *Public Administration Review* 77 (4): 542–543. https://doi.org/10.1111/puar.12813.

Lambsdorff, J.G. 2002. Corruption and rent-seeking. *Public Choice* 113 (1–2): 97–125. https://doi.org/10.1023/A:1020320327526.

Leroux, K., and N.S. Wright. 2010. Does performance measurement improve strategic decision making? Findings from a national survey of nonprofit social service agencies. *Nonprofit and Voluntary Sector Quarterly* 39 (4): 571–587. https://doi.org/10.1177/0899764009359942.

McDonnell, E.M. 2020. *Patchwork Leviathan: Pockets of bureaucratic effectiveness in developing states*. Princeton University Press. http://www.jstor.org/stable/j.ctvp2n4hs

Meyer-Sahling, J., and K.S. Mikkelsen. 2016. Civil service laws, merit, politicization, and corruption: The perspective of public officials from five east European countries. *Public Administration* 94 (4): 1105–1123. https://doi.org/10.1111/padm.12276.

Meyfroodt, K., and S. Desmidt. 2021. Can rational planning stimulate cooperative behaviour? How perceived self-efficacy mediates the relationship between strategic plan use, performance information use and strategic voice by local councillors. *Public Management Review* 23 (6): 818–842. https://doi.org/10.1080/14719037.2019.1699949.

Naim, S.J., and A.H.R. Hasan. 2018. Concentration of authority and rent seeking behaviour in bureaucracy: Evidence of ineffective governance in Bangladesh. *Journal of Social and Development Sciences* 9 (1): 19–30. https://doi.org/10.22610/jsds.v9i1.2165.

Naritomi, J., R. Soares, and J. Assunção. 2007. Rent seeking and the unveiling of "de facto" institutions: Development and colonial heritage within Brazil. https://doi.org/10.3386/w13545.

Perry, J.L. 2017. Know your values and be prepared: An interview with Paul H. O'Neill. *Public Administration Review* 77 (1): 131–134. https://doi.org/10.1111/PUAR.12640.

Perry, J.L. 2021. *Managing organizations to sustain passion for public service*. Cambridge: Cambridge University Press.

Pierre-Daniel, G. 2001. Rent-seeking bureaucracies and oversight in a simple growth model. *Journal of Economic Dynamics and Control* 25 (9): 1345–1365. https://doi.org/10.1016/S0165-1889(99)00057-3.

Rodwell, J.J., R. Kienzle, and M.A. Shadur. 1998. The relationships among work-related perceptions, employee attitudes, and employee performance: The integral role of communication. *Human Resource Management* 37 (4): 277–293. https://doi.org/10.1002/(SICI)1099-050X(199823/24)37:3/4.

Sarte, P.-D. 2000. Informality and rent-seeking bureaucracies in a model of long-run growth. *Journal of Monetary Economics* 46 (1): 173–197. https://doi.org/10.1016/S0304-3932(00)00020-9.

Schein, E.H. 1992. *Organizational culture and leadership* (2nd ed.). Jossey-Bass.

Spinesi, L. 2009. Rent-seeking bureaucracies, inequality, and growth. *Journal of Development Economics* 90 (2): 244–257. https://doi.org/10.1016/j.jdeveco.2008.09.009.

Suykens, B., K. Meyfroodt, S. Desmidt, and B. Verschuere. 2022. Does performance-based accountability impact how non-profit directors perceive organizational performance? Insights from rational planning. *Public Management Review* 24 (9): 1355–1382. https://doi.org/10.1080/14719037.2021.1900349.

Tannimalay, S., N. Fareen, A. Rahim, and H.M. Chee. 2021. The effect of person-environment fit on public servant integrity and performance: Investigating the moderating role of public service motivation. *Journal of Governance and Integrity* 5 (1): 185–199. https://doi.org/10.15282/JGI.5.1.2021.7180.

Tullock, G. 1967. The welfare costs of tariffs, monopolies, and theft. *Economic Inquiry* 5 (3): 224–232. https://doi.org/10.1111/J.1465-7295.1967.TB01923.X.

Vasilev, A. 2013. On the cost of rent-seeking by government bureaucrats in a Real-Business-Cycle framework. https://EconPapers.repec.org/RePEc:gla:glaewp:2013_20.

Verhezen, P. 2010. Giving voice in a culture of silence. From a culture of compliance to a culture of integrity. *Journal of Business Ethics* 96 (2): 187–206. https://doi.org/10.1007/s10551-010-0458-5.

Wright, B.E., and S.K. Pandey. 2008. Public service motivation and the assumption of person—Organization fit. *Administration & Society* 40 (5): 502–521. https://doi.org/10.1177/0095399708320187.

CHAPTER 3

Digital Technologies and Legal and Regulatory Frameworks

Christine Leitner and Christian M. Stiefmueller

3.1 The COVID-19 Pandemic and the New Reality

When the COVID-19 pandemic brought entire countries around the globe to a virtual standstill, technology helped us—at least to some extent—to maintain business and social life during lockdowns and crises. In an unexpected turn of events, governments were compelled to embrace digital platforms as a means of sustaining essential public services and maintaining interactions with their citizens. Consequently, both the public and private sectors witnessed a notable surge in the adoption of

C. Leitner (✉) · C. M. Stiefmueller
Centre for Economics and Public Administration Limited (CEPA), London, UK
e-mail: christine.leitner@cepanet.eu

C. M. Stiefmueller
e-mail: christian.stiefmueller@cepanet.eu

A. Baimenov and P. Liverakos (eds.), *Public Administration in the New Reality*, https://doi.org/10.1007/978-981-96-3845-1_3

technology in the aftermath of the pandemic, with an average rise in digitalisation across advanced economies of six percentage points.[1]

More specifically, digital government maturity has increased globally, as evidenced by the findings of the UN 2024 e-Government Survey (United Nations 2024b) with regions around the world adopting technology to enhance government services and foster greater citizen engagement. The UN e-Government Development Index (EGDI) 2024 indicates that the proportion of the population lagging behind in digital government development decreased from 45% in 2022 to 22.4% in 2024 (United Nations 2024a). Significant investments have been made in the development of resilient infrastructure, cloud computing, broadband, and other digital technologies, including machine learning (ML) and artificial intelligence (AI). As indicated by the 2024 UN Survey, the prevailing global megatrends in public administration can be identified as the rapid digitalisation of services, the shift to remote work, the integration of AI, the focus on digital identity and data management, and the utilisation of emerging technologies, such as AI and data analytics, in policymaking. However, the UN Survey also reveals that 1.73 billion people are still "*on the wrong side of the digital divide*".[2]

These developments have had a significant impact on the way public administrations operate today. In many jurisdictions, digitalisation has been 'mainstreamed', and in many cases 'fast-tracked', across a wide range of policy areas, yielding significant benefits. Concurrently, against the background of rising geopolitical tensions, the risks and dependencies associated with these developments have become much more tangible.

3.2 Technology Governance at a Crossroads

In the context of a globalised and interconnected world, there is a growing concern among policymakers regarding the protection of critical infrastructures, the safety and privacy of citizens, and the integrity of democratic institutions and processes. The concept of 'digital sovereignty' is becoming an increasingly prominent concern for governments across

[1] International Monetary Fund (IMF)Blog, How Pandemic Accelerated Digital Transformation in Advanced Economies, 21.03.2023, https://www.imf.org/en/Blogs/Articles/2023/03/21/how-pandemic-accelerated-digital-transformation-in-advanced-economies.

[2] According to the 2024 UN Survey the most affected regions are Africa and Oceania.

the globe. It can be defined as the ability of a national government to make autonomous decisions that affect citizens and businesses within the digital domain, encompassing data, software, standards and protocols, infrastructure, and public services (Nordhaug and Harris 2021). In addition, there are initiatives aimed at ensuring economic security, which encompass the safeguarding of raw materials and energy required for the digital and green transition, critical public infrastructures, and technologies with potential dual-use applications (European Commission 2020a).

The advent of large language models (LLMs) such as Open AI's ChatGPT has intensified the global debate on technology governance, particularly in the context of artificial intelligence. This has led to a growing consensus among stakeholders on the need for technology regulation. However, as articulated by *Bradford*, in the current global battle for technology regulation "*the most influential regions are striving to extend their spheres of influence by steering the global digital marketplace towards their own distinct norms and values*" (Bradford 2023: 27).

Critics of technology regulation claim that overly stringent regulations could stifle innovation and hinder the further development and adoption of emerging technologies, as businesses may have to cope with excessive compliance and administrative burden. Poorly designed regulation might have unintended consequences, for example for competition, by favouring established companies that enjoy the strategic advantages of incumbency and can more easily adapt to regulatory requirements. The evolving regulatory environment is also reinforcing rising protectionist tendencies in many regions of the world, affecting international relations and trade (OECD 2023b).

Concurrently, as the implications of disruptive technologies for the economy and society become more apparent, a notable shift in governance priorities has emerged in many jurisdictions and international fora. This paradigm shift advocates a human-centred approach with a focus on trust, the safety and security of citizens, and the alignment of technology with ethical standards. There is a growing consensus that digitalisation should be based on a set of core values, with a particular focus on the empowerment of individuals, the protection of fundamental rights, and the delivery of safe, efficient, responsive, and accessible public services. The ethical use of technology has become of paramount importance, coupled with equitable governance that seeks to establish a renewed social contract, ensuring a fair distribution of the benefits and costs associated with the digital transformation and in line with the UN Sustainable Development Goals (SDGs).[3]

In the European Union, for instance, European leaders responsible for digital government in the twenty-seven member states adopted the 'Berlin Declaration on Digital Society and Value-based Digital Government' in 2020 based on these principles.[4] In 2022, the EU's top officials signed the 'Declaration on Digital Rights and Principles' to this effect. This reflects their commitment to promote and apply digital rights and principles based on EU values across all EU policy domains.[5]

Section 3.3 will explore some of the key challenges policymakers are facing in recalibrating the role of government and designing effective policy and regulatory frameworks in this fast-changing environment. By way of illustration, a few recent examples from the European Union are provided in Sect. 3.4, taking into consideration relevant international developments. Based on this analysis, the chapter concludes by attempting to draw lessons from the EU approach and identifies potential areas for further research.

3.3 Rebalancing the Role of Government: Key Policy Challenges

This section highlights some of the most critical policy issues that policymakers need to address when (re)designing policy frameworks for technology regulation. It considers the challenges of achieving a balance between the numerous benefits and the inherent risks associated with the rapid adoption and development of technology, while intervening in a timely manner and avoiding any stifling of innovation.

[3] https://www.un.org/sustainabledevelopment/.

[4] Berlin Declaration on Digital Society and Value-based Digital Government 2020. https://digital-strategy.ec.europa.eu/en/news/berlin-declaration-digital-society-and-value-based-digital-government.

[5] European Declaration on Digital Rights and Principles. https://digital-strategy.ec.europa.eu/en/library/european-declaration-digital-rights-and-principles.

3.3.1 Balancing Benefits and Risks in the Digital Age

The benefits of digital transformation are vast and accrue across multiple policy domains, significantly enhancing the effectiveness of public services. Automation, AI, and data analytics streamline processes, reduce costs, and increase productivity across both the public and private sectors. The automation of administrative processes such as permits, benefits, and licensing has reduced inefficiencies and speed up service delivery in many sectors and allowed more personalised and proactive services for citizens and businesses.[6] Digital tools have enhanced transparency in governance and allowed for greater citizen participation and inclusiveness in decision-making processes.[7]

Digitalisation has proven to be crucial in building resilience and ensuring continuity of public sector infrastructures and services, enabling governments to continue providing critical services even during crises. Enhanced digital public infrastructures support stronger cybersecurity measures, protecting sensitive data and critical services from cyber threats. Essential government functions remain operational in times of emergencies, such as armed conflict, pandemics or natural disasters. By way of example, Diia,[8] the Ukraine's Government portal and mobile app, has played "*a crucial role in continuing to provide the public with access to an extended number of digital services, including to internally displaced persons and Ukrainian refugees*" during the ongoing war.[9]

[6] E.g., Dubai and the UAE. https://economymiddleeast.com/news/building-a-digital-capital-lessons-from-dubais-success-story/ and https://u.ae/en/about-the-uae/uae-competitiveness/digital-transformation-in-the-uae.

[7] According to the UN E-Government Survey 2024a, 2024b e-participation is the least advanced among the five sub-indices, even though the global average value has increased by nine percent since 2022. "*Between 81 and 83 percent of countries have national e-government strategies, policies or legislation on cybersecurity, data privacy, and data protection, 78 percent require citizens to use a digital ID when accessing public services, and 76 percent offer public access to legislation on the right of citizens to access government information. The shares are lower for legislation or policies on open government data (63 percent), e-participation (51 percent), protecting the public against misinformation, disinformation, and/or fake news (47 percent), and frontier technologies such as cloud computing (44 percent) and artificial intelligence (42 percent)*" (UN E-Government Survey 2024: 53).

[8] Diia Open Source—Open Source of the Main Government Application, https://opensource.diia.gov.ua/en.html.

[9] European Commission, Staff Working Document, Ukraine Report, SWD (2023) 699 final, 08.11.2023. https://neighbourhood-enlargement.ec.europa.eu/system/files/2023-11/SWD_2023_699%20Ukraine%20report.pdf. The Diia application currently boasts more than 20 million users, every second resident of Ukraine is currently registered. It is

Remote working and the fast development and adoption of digital collaboration tools have changed the way we work. What began often as a temporary fix during the pandemic has, in many instances, matured into new, oftentimes more flexible, and efficient (hybrid) workflows and routines, including in the public sector.[10]

Digital platforms and tools facilitate seamless collaboration between government agencies, improving service delivery and governance. These tools also enable global cooperation on issues like climate action, public health, and disaster response, fostering integrated approaches to shared global challenges. Data analytics and AI provide new opportunities for informed, data-driven decisions, improving the efficiency and precision of policy implementation, particularly in complex domains such as climate change and energy efficiency, optimising resource management, and improving monitoring, all of which help to address climate change and advancing the SDGs.[11]

Digital platforms have expanded access to healthcare services and education, in particular, to under-served communities. Remote Patient Monitoring (RPM) and other 'tele-medicine' applications were trialled at scale during the pandemic and are now deployed to deliver regular care services.[12] Since the pandemic, there has been an unprecedented increase in the use of digital platforms and tools in education, which enabled the continuation of organised instruction during the crisis. The wider use of blended and hybrid learning is likely to continue in the future (OECD 2023a).

available worldwide as open source code, https://eufordigital.eu/building-a-digital-state-ukraines-diia-app-now-boasts-over-20-million-users/.

[10] Global Government Forum, Tip of the Iceberg: Public Sector Leaders on the Shift to Remote Work and What More Is to Come, 20.04.2022. https://www.globalgovernmentforum.com/tip-of-the-iceberg-public-sector-leaders-on-the-shift-to-remote-work-and-what-more-is-to-come/.

[11] See, for example, the UN Global Pulse initiatives, e.g.,https://www.unglobalpulse.org/?s=disaster+management or https://www.unglobalpulse.org/project/using-artificial-intelligence-to-combat-epidemics-in-the-global-south-ai4covid-programme/.

[12] https://transform.england.nhs.uk/covid-19-response/technology-nhs/supporting-the-innovation-collaboratives-to-expand-their-remote-monitoring-plans/.

However, with the rapid technology advances, particularly in areas such as AI/ML, IoT, cloud, and edge computing, policymakers are increasingly confronted with the question on how to address the risks and potential harms posed by the adoption and wider use of these disruptive technologies. The global nature of the Internet presents significant challenges concerning sovereignty, jurisdiction, and law enforcement. National and international legal frameworks, such as the US CLOUD Act,[13] and Section 702 of the Foreign Intelligence Surveillance Act (FISA),[14] as well as 'adequacy decisions' by the European Commission under the General Data Protection Regulation (GDPR), attempt to address cross-border data access and governance issues.[15] The involvement of organised crime and state-sponsored actors in cyberspace further complicates law enforcement efforts, making it difficult to uphold sovereignty while ensuring global cooperation. Cyber threats, including cyberattacks and cybercrime, continue to grow, targeting both public and private entities. Citizens are also increasingly vulnerable to cyber fraud and other forms of online malfeasance. As cybercriminals and state-sponsored actors become more sophisticated, the need for robust cybersecurity measures, international cooperation, and effective law enforcement becomes critical to ensure the safety and security of digital spaces.

The dominance of a few large technology companies and digital platforms has distorted market competition, resulting in a 'weaponisation' of dependencies. These firms hold vast economic and technological power, making it difficult for smaller players to compete on a level playing field.[16] This concentration of power not only affects competition but also enables the spread of disinformation, creating significant public policy challenges related to online service provision and content regulation.

[13] Clarifying Lawful Overseas Use of Data Act (CLOUD Act), 23.03.2018, Pub. L. No. 115–141, 132 Stat. 348 (2018), 18U.S.C. Ch. 119.

[14] Foreign Intelligence Surveillance (FISA) Act, 25.10.1978, Pub. L. No. 95–511, 92 Stat. 1783 (1978), 50 U.S.C. Ch. 36.

[15] See also Sect. 3.4.2.2: Jurisdictional boundaries in the digital sphere below.

[16] On investment, according to the *Financial Times* (02.08.2024), "Big Tech companies have boosted their capital spending by 50 per cent to more than US$ 100 billion this year, as they race to build the infrastructure supporting artificial intelligence, despite growing scepticism from Wall Street about the returns on this unprecedented investment". https://www.ft.com/content/b7037ce1-4319-4a4a-8767-0b1373cec9ce.

The unsupervised collection and aggregation of personal data, particularly by large digital platform operators for commercial purposes, have raised concerns among policymakers and civil rights groups. Regulations such as the GDPR aim to safeguard individuals' privacy, yet the spread of disinformation and misinformation on digital platforms continues to undermine democratic processes and the rule of law. This challenge extends well beyond data privacy, as it affects the integrity of the public discourse and public institutions in their entirety.

In addition, the rapid advancements in data analytics, artificial intelligence, and machine learning are outpacing current regulatory frameworks. The lack of transparency and accountability in the development and deployment of these technologies raises concerns about potential misuse, bias, and ethical violations. Human oversight is essential to ensure that AI and other technologies are utilised responsibly and for the public good. The task of setting out effective, balanced, and universally accepted rules for the collection, aggregation, and processing of data is becoming more pressing by the day in view of the rapid progress in the domain of data analytics and machine learning. The development and implementation of artificial intelligence, in its various guises, rely on processing data at an unprecedented scale and pose new questions of transparency, accountability, and human oversight (Everest-Phillips 2019).

Furthermore, high energy use in data centres, cryptocurrency mining, and emerging technologies like AI, the Internet of Things (IoT), 5G mobile connectivity, and virtual reality contribute to rising carbon footprints and have intensified the struggle for energy sources (including the increased use of nuclear power). Regulators must encourage energy efficiency without stifling innovation, balancing technological growth with sustainability goals.[17]

Finally, as mentioned earlier, the digital divide has widened globally, exacerbating inequality and creating new vulnerabilities. Both domestically and internationally, dependencies on digital infrastructure have been 'weaponised' through tactics such as Internet shutdowns, further

[17] On data centres and energy consumption see, for example, the EU's revised Energy Efficiency Directive (Directive (EU) 2023/1791) of the European Parliament and of the Council, 13.09.2023, which introduces an obligation for the monitoring and reporting of the energy performance of data centres. A European database will collect and publish data, which is relevant for the energy performance and water footprint of data centres with a significant energy consumption. Data centres in the EU account for nearly 2.7% of European electricity usage. It is expected to reach 3.21% by 2030.

deepening exclusion (UNHRC 2022). Policymakers must address this growing digital divide to ensure equitable access to the Internet and digital services for all, especially in marginalised communities.

In the light of these complex challenges, many jurisdictions have stepped up their efforts to regulate cyberspace in recent years. The European Union, for example, adopted a comprehensive package of tech-legislation over the past five years based on the established principles set out in the European Declaration on Rights and Principles in the Digital Age.[18]

3.3.2 Technology Regulation and the 'Pacing Problem'

The process of technology adoption and its interaction with the policy cycle was discussed previously in the context of the 'technology adoption cycle' (*Gartner*) and the policy cycle model initially formulated by *Lasswell* (Leitner and Stiefmueller 2019). In the nascent stages of technological development, the potential applications and associated impacts are often poorly understood or known only to those involved in their creation. Once the impacts of these technologies on individuals and society become more apparent, regulating technological advances may become more complex. Certain choices and approaches may already be entrenched in norms, market positions, or regulations, making change more difficult and costly.

If a government tries to regulate new technology early on, it may be criticised for stifling innovation, being overly bureaucratic and lacking agility. Conversely, introduced at a later stage, regulation could be seen as reactive or inadequate. If introduced too late, there could be a backlash for failing to anticipate and address negative outcomes. The risk here is that once a technology is adopted, it becomes 'locked in' due to institutional inertia and investments that have already been made.

Public trust is critical to the legitimacy of the use of digital technologies in the public sector.[19] Inadequate regulation can undermine this trust.

[18] Renda, A, Europe's Digital Future Is Brighter Than We Think—We Just Need To Fight For It, 04.08.2024. https://www.ceps.eu/europes-digital-future-is-brighter-than-we-think-we-just-need-to-fight-for-it/.

[19] The term 'GovTech' is used frequently to capture the use of digital technologies in the context of public sector modernisation. It emphasises three aspects: a citizen-centric mind-set, universally accessible public services, and a whole-of-government approach to

The Dutch tax authorities' use of a self-learning algorithm is an interesting case in point. The tool was used to create risk profiles to detect childcare benefit fraud. The tool's inherent bias and lack of adequate human oversight caused significant harm to individuals over a number of years. This ultimately forced the Dutch Government to resign in 2019.[20]

The so-called pacing problem, or the 'right' time of intervention, is a significant challenge for public sector decision makers, as illustrated by the 'Collingridge dilemma' (Collingridge 1980).[21] It is crucial in areas where ethical implications are significant, such as the use of surveillance technologies in law enforcement and AI/ML in health care.[22] Regulators must navigate a complex landscape, striving to achieve a balance between proactive governance and adaptive regulation. This includes the use of strategic foresight (UNDP/GCPSE 2018; Montero and Borgo 2023), regulatory sandboxes (UNDESA 2021), iterative policymaking, and collaborative oversight, with the aim of mitigating the inherent risks associated with both early and late interventions.

In this context, *Bradford* notes that the common assumption that "*more stringent regulation of the digital economy compromises innovation and undermines technological progress*" is flawed. She argues, correctly, in our view, that the debate ought to be reframed on the premise that effective regulation can coexist with innovation through broader legal and institutional reforms, rather than being mutually exclusive (Bradford 2024).

3.3.3 Assessing Government Policy

We have highlighted on previous occasions the need to assess the role of government in the technology innovation and adoption process along three dimensions, which reflect the distinct roles played by the state and

digital government transformation. See, e.g., World Bank, GovTech—Putting People First. https://www.worldbank.org/en/programs/govtech.

[20] Politico, Dutch Scandal Serves as a Warning for Europe over Risks of Using AI, 30.03.2022. https://www.politico.eu/article/dutch-scandal-serves-as-a-warning-for-europe-over-risks-of-using-algorithms/.

[21] See also Demos Helsinki, What Is the Collingridge Dilemma and Why Is it Important for Tech Policy, 15.02.2022. https://demoshelsinki.fi/2022/02/15/what-is-the-collingridge-dilemma-tech-policy/.

[22] See also Sect. 3.4.2.6: Safe, transparent, and responsible use of AI/ML below.

its institutions throughout this process, namely as a sponsor, regulator, and user (Leitner and Stiefmueller 2019). This approach may be applied as a way of mapping the policy stance of a jurisdiction with respect to individual technologies or groups of technologies, for instance AI/ML, at both a given point in time and over time. This mapping could be instructive for the purposes of illustrating a jurisdiction's policymaking priorities and drawing cross-jurisdictional comparisons. To operationalise this concept, the three dimensions will have to be characterised more precisely, as by the following criteria:

- ***Innovation support***: In its role as Sponsor/Promoter, government actively supports technological innovation, most visibly through the provision of public funding for research and development, tax credits and/or other financial incentives, but equally through the creation of supporting infrastructure, such as educational and research facilities, and technology parks. In this context, innovation support can be given either directly, to public sector institutions, or indirectly, to the private sector (Mazzucato 2013, 2017).
- ***Intervention***: As a Regulator, government assesses the potential benefits and risks of an emerging technology, its potential development path, and its expected economic and societal impact in its own jurisdiction and at the international level (Leitner and Stiefmueller 2019). Based on this assessment, and its own policy stance and priorities, government will intervene, usually by enacting new legislation/regulation.
- ***Investment***: As a User, government adopts a technology that has matured and is at or near mainstream for its own operational purposes. It does so by committing investment, e.g., into technical infrastructure and equipment, software and other intellectual property, and human skills, i.e., by training and/or hiring resolute personnel.

The terms 'innovation support' and 'investment' are chosen deliberately to describe to commitment of financial and other resources to either research and development prior to commercial maturity ('innovation support') or to build public sector skills and capacities for the public sector's own use ('investment'). For each of these criteria—innovation support, intervention, and investment—suitable quantitative indicators will have to be identified. For innovation support and investment, these metrics could be based on monetary values, i.e., relevant categories of public spending. This presupposes, however, that such data are available at the required level of completeness and granularity. Intervention, in turn, could be reflected by metrics that capture regulatory density.[23] How and to what extent these indicators could be defined in a meaningful, consistent, and reliable way is the subject of ongoing research. In addition, a high degree of standardisation will be required to achieve cross-jurisdictional comparability. Further work will therefore be required to operationalise this framework.

This approach could deliver a 'footprint' to capture in a concise, visual way a jurisdiction's policy stance on innovation and technology adoption. For instance, the three models typified in *Bradford's* analysis would likely yield different, distinctive profiles (Bradford 2023).[24] Moreover, it could be extended over time to chart the evolution of the policy stance along the innovation adoption cycle (Leitner and Stiefmueller 2019). This exercise could provide useful insights on policy development over time in a given context.

3.4 EU Initiatives

This section presents a brief outline of the EU governance approach, with a focus on the most relevant recent policy and regulatory initiatives and their alignment with pertinent international developments.

3.4.1 The 'Rights-Driven' Model and the 'Precautionary Principle'

Among the major global economies, the EU has for some time taken a particularly proactive stance in regulating technology. The EU approach aims at building trust in technology through compliance with laws, which in turn build on political agreements ('soft law') on and codifications of common European rights and values. Individual legislative measures, which address specific technologies and/or applications, are

[23] A technology-enabled approach, which covers the US, Canada and Australia for the time being, is proposed by the QuantGov project at the Mercatus Center, George Mason University, Arlington (VA); see also Al-Ubaydli and McLaughlin (2014).

[24] See also Sect. 3.4.1: The 'rights-driven' model and the 'precautionary' principle below.

embedded into a programmatic framework, which invests EU institutions with a wide-ranging mandate to regulate and sets out general principles based on fundamental and civic rights. This framework is communicated primarily through political declarations by the EU institutions and member-state governments including, in particular, the Berlin Declaration and the European Declaration on Digital Rights and Principles. While these declarations are by themselves not legally binding, they regularly and consistently refer to the EU Treaties, and the European Union Charter of Fundamental Rights of the European Union. In doing so, they assert a legal mandate, and indeed responsibility, of the EU institutions to intervene on behalf of EU citizens and governments to protect their rights under these foundational legal acts. *Bradford* (2023) labelled this approach as a 'rights-driven' model, in contrast to the 'market-driven' model of the US, and the 'state-driven' model of China.

The EU's proactive stance is characterised sometimes with reference to the so-called precautionary principle, although this connection is still debated. The precautionary principle can be traced back to the Appellate Body of the World Trade Organisation (WTO), originally in the context of product safety, and was invoked initially to justify preventive regulatory intervention aimed at protecting human health and natural resources (Bourguignon 2015). It was also explored in depth in a dedicated report more formally by the World Commission on the Ethics of Scientific Knowledge and Technology (COMEST) under the auspices of UNESCO (2005). In 2000, the European Commission issued a communication noting that recourse to the precautionary principle should be considered as a risk management strategy although it must not "*serve as a justification for disguised protectionism*".[25] Since then, the precautionary principle has been incorporated into the EU Treaties (Article 191 TFEU) and further specified in the case law of the Court of Justice of the European Union (CJEU), again primarily in connection with risks to the environment, human, animal, or plant health. While its status as a general principle of EU law is still debated (Scott 2018), it is extended by some authors to the area of privacy and personal data protection (Costa 2012; Pöysti 2024). This argument appears to have gained currency

[25] European Commission, Communication from the Commission on the Precautionary Principle, COM/2000/1 (final), 02.02.2000.

recently with the mainstream adoption of AI/ML and the adoption of the European AI Act.[26]

3.4.2 *Overview of Relevant EU Initiatives*

The Declaration on Digital Rights and Principles marks the latest step so far in the EU's progression towards a codification of general principles to guide the regulation of technology, which are gradually absorbed into formal EU legislation in due course. This section singles out a number of such principles where this process is already well advanced and has produced tangible results in the form of new legislation. It then highlights how the effects of these new rules could radiate beyond the EU and affect non-EU jurisdictions.

3.4.2.1 Privacy and Data Protection

The most prominent example so far, and which has given rise to what *Bradford* has described as the 'Brussels effect' (Bradford 2012), is the General Data Protection Regulation (GDPR) of 2016,[27] which draws on the earlier EU Data Protection Directive (DPD) of 1995,[28] and an extensive body of case law by the Court of Justice of the European Union (CJEU). The protection of EU citizens' privacy and personal data is guaranteed by Articles 7 and 8 of the EU Charter of Fundamental Rights.[29] The 'Declaration on Digital Rights and Principles' enjoins EU member states to protect citizens' personal data, and the confidentiality of their communications and the information on their electronic devices (Principles 17 and 18), and expressly prohibits "*unlawful online surveillance, unlawful pervasive tracking or interception measures directed against EU citizens*".

[26] See also Sect. 3.4.2.6: Safe, transparent, and responsible use of AI/ML below.

[27] Regulation (EU) 2016/679 of the European Parliament and of the Council, 27.04.2016, on the Protection of Natural Persons with regard to the Processing of Personal Data and on the Free Movement of such Data, OJ L 119, 04.05.2016, pp. 1–88.

[28] Directive 95/46/EC of the European Parliament and of the Council, 24.10.1995, on the Protection of Individuals with regard to the Processing of Personal Data and on the Free Movement of such Data, OJ L 281, 23.11.1995, pp. 31–50.

[29] Charter of Fundamental Rights of the European Union, OJ C 326, 26.10.2012, pp. 391–407.

This protection extends beyond its geographical borders and has a major bearing on the legality of data flows between the EU and its major trade partners, especially the US. As a precondition for transferring personal data of EU citizens to a non-EU jurisdiction, Article 45 of the GDPR authorises the European Commission to issue a formal decision on whether that jurisdiction provides "*an adequate level of protection*" ('adequacy decision'). This decision is subject to review by the EU courts and has been challenged successfully already on at least two occasions. In its landmark judgements, *Schrems I* and *Schrems II*, the Court of Justice of the European Union (CJEU) invalidated the Commission's adequacy decisions governing the transfer of personal data between the EU and US, leaving large volumes of international data traffic on a tenuous legal basis.[30]

In the Court's view, the level of protection of personal data afforded to EU citizens under US law did not meet the standard required to uphold their fundamental rights under Articles 7 and 8 of the EU Charter of Fundamental Rigths. In response, several US-domiciled operators of cloud services announced subsequently that they would start applying GDPR-compliant practices in their relationships with customers worldwide.[31] Nonetheless, the most recent adequacy decision,[32] based on a new EU-US Data Privacy Framework, agreed in 2023, which contains further commitments by the US authorities to improve EU citizens' access to legal remedies to address concerns related to their data, is

[30] *Schrems I*: Court of Justice of the European Union, Judgment of the Court, 06.10.2015, Maximillian Schrems vs. Data Protection Commissioner (*Schrems I*) (C-362/14; ECLI:EU:C:2015:650); and *Schrems II:* Court of Justice of the European Union, Judgment of the Court, 16.07.2020, Data Protection Commissioner vs. Facebook Ireland Limited and Maximillian Schrems (*Schrems II*) (C-311/18; ECLI:EU:C:2020:559).

[31] Microsoft Corporation, Microsoft's Commitment to GDPR, Privacy and Putting Customers in Control of Their Own Data, 21.05.2018. https://blogs.microsoft.com/on-the-issues/2018/05/21/microsofts-commitment-to-gdpr-privacy-and-putting-customers-in-control-of-their-own-data/; Meta Corporation, Facebook's Commitment to Data Protection and Privacy in Compliance with the GDPR, 29.01.2018. https://www.facebook.com/business/news/facebooks-commitment-to-data-protection-and-privacy-in-compliance-with-the-gdpr.

[32] Commission Implementing Decision EU 2023/1795, 10.07.2023 pursuant to Regulation (EU) 2016/679 of the European Parliament and of the Council on the Adequate Level of Protection of Personal Data under the EU-US Data Privacy Framework, C/2023/4745 (final), OJ L 231, 20.09.2023, pp. 118–229.

expected to be challenged again by EU civil society organisations on the same grounds.

3.4.2.2 *Jurisdictional Boundaries in the Digital Sphere*

The ongoing legal controversy between the EU and US over personal data protection has also shed light on another, more general issue, the difficulty of drawing jurisdictional borders in the digital sphere. While the EU bases its authority to rule on the legality of data storage and processing in third countries on the universality of fundamental rights, and the EU authorities' responsibility to protect them, the US invoke national security interests to justify similar extra-territorial powers. Two pieces of US legislation, in particular, the 1978 Foreign Intelligence Surveillance Act (FISA),[33] and the 2018 CLOUD Act,[34] authorise US law enforcement authorities to access personal data of non-US citizens for the purposes of electronic surveillance. Section 702 of FISA, introduced in 2008, enables US government agencies to conduct targeted surveillance of foreign persons outside the US with the assistance of electronic communications providers.

The CLOUD Act, a major amendment of the Stored Communications and Electronic Communications Privacy Acts,[35] reasserts the rights of US government agencies to oblige US corporations providing cloud services to disclose electronic data or communications of non-US citizens and/or entities if required for the purposes of US law enforcement, "*regardless of whether regardless of whether such communication, record, or other information is located within or outside of the United States*". It was prompted by and enacted largely in response to the *Microsoft Ireland* case,[36] which had brought the question of extra-territorial law enforcement in the digital sphere to the attention of the US Supreme Court.

The claims staked by the US authorities, with FISA and the CLOUD Act, have caused considerable anxiety in the EU and other jurisdictions

[33] Foreign Intelligence Surveillance (FISA) Act, 25.10.1978, Pub. L. No. 95–511, 92 Stat. 1783 (1978), 50 U.S.C. Ch. 36.

[34] Clarifying Lawful Overseas Use of Data Act (CLOUD Act), 23.03.2018, Pub. L. No. 115–141, 132 Stat. 348 (2018), 18U.S.C. Ch. 119.

[35] Electronic Communications Privacy Act, 21.10.1978 (ECPA), Pub. L. No. 99–508, 100 Stat. 1848 (1986), 18 U.S.C. Ch. 119 and 121.

[36] United States Supreme Court, United States vs. Microsoft Corporation (*Microsoft Ireland*), 584 U.S. 138 (2018), 17.04.2018.

which rely, to a large extent, on cloud infrastructure and services provided by US-domiciled operators, and are therefore concerned about a loss of 'strategic autonomy' and 'digital sovereignty' (European Commission 2020b). Already now, some jurisdictions, such as China and the Russian Federation, have put in place technical and regulatory frameworks that require domestic Internet data traffic to be routed predominantly, if not exclusively, through infrastructure located on their territory and/or operated by domestic service providers.

Along similar lines, albeit less radically, some EU member states have introduced the so-called localisation requirements, often based on a restrictive interpretation of the GDPR (European Commission 2017), which call for the personal data of their nationals to be stored exclusively on servers located in their jurisdiction. These trends could be seen as evidence of a 'splintering' or 'balkanisation' of the global Internet/World Wide Web into national and/or regional compartments, a trend that would jeopardise its unique role as a global information repository, communication channel, and trade route.

The EU faces a particularly complex situation in that it is composed of sovereign nation states with their own national borders. Localisation requirements at the national level will also block data transfers within the EU and thus impede cross-border cooperation and data sharing between member-state public sector entities, as well as the creation of common, pan-European digital infrastructures. Charting a path towards a harmonised interpretation and application of the GDPR across member states still proves challenging, however. In the less contentious area of non-personal data, EU legislators have already imposed on member states a general obligation to facilitate the free flow of data across intra-EU borders and restricted the scope for member states to require localisation.[37] Meanwhile, the EU has tightened its restrictions on transfers of data across its exterior borders with the introduction of the Data Act (European Commission 2020b), which provides safeguards against the unlawful access by third country governments and/or law enforcement agencies to non-personal data stored in the EU.

[37] Regulation (EU) 2018/1807 of the European Parliament and of the Council, 14.11.2018 on a Framework for the Free Flow of Non-Personal Data in the European Union (Free Flow of Non-Personal Data Regulation, FFoD, OJ L303, 28.11.2018).

3.4.2.3 Competition and 'Digital Sovereignty'

Competition between major jurisdictions to assert their sovereignty in the digital sphere is closely correlated with commercial competition between the providers of digital infrastructure and services. In an industry that is characterised, more than any other, by economies of scale and network effects,[38] both fixed or mobile connectivity and essential online services, such as e-mail and instant messaging, office productivity and other software applications, cloud computing and storage—'core platform services' in EU parlance—are provided by a small number of very large corporate entities with considerable economic power.

While infrastructure-based connectivity services, usually provided by traditional tele-communications companies and other network operators, lend themselves to be regulated and supervised at the national level, this does not apply to 'platform services', which can be readily provided and accessed across borders. For a long time, therefore, these entities have not been subject to effective supervision by competition authorities or, when they were, have been able to leverage their considerable economic power with customers to contract with them in jurisdictions that were deemed less strict.

In its 'Declaration on Digital Rights and Principles', EU member states have committed to ensure that "*everyone should be able to effectively and freely choose which online services to use, based on objective, transparent, easily accessible and reliable information*" (Principle 10). In 2022, this commitment was cast into law through the Digital Markets Act (DMA),[39] which mandates the Commission to designate operators of 'core platform services' who meet certain thresholds of size and market dominance as 'gatekeepers', and subject them to specific regulatory obligations. In particular, 'gatekeepers' are required to refrain from applying anti-competitive practices to the detriment of their customers, e.g., by tying or bundling services or denying customers the right to access and re-use their personal data for their own purposes. Gatekeepers are also obliged not to combine and use customers' personal data across multiple services offered on their platform or to automatically sign in customers

[38] On the conceptual basis and impact of network effects see, e.g., Katz and Shapiro (1994).

[39] Regulation (EU) 2022/1925 of the European Parliament and of the Council, 14.09.2022 on Contestable and Fair Markets in the Digital Sector (Digital Markets Act), OJ L 265, 12.10.2022, pp. 1–66.

to other services to combine data. As of September 2024, the European Commission has designated six US and one Chinese provider as 'gatekeepers' under the DMA.[40] So far, however, it has not been implemented consistently across all of the many sub-segments it covers. The most obvious omission is in cloud services, a field where EU customers, including large enterprises and the public sector, largely rely on a handful of global, mainly US-domiciled, private sector providers (Dietrich and Facca 2022).

The impact of the DMA is already being felt. In June 2024, the Commission launched proceedings under the DMA against Apple for failing to allow developers to steer customers to offers outside its proprietary App Store.[41] Only days later, the Commission opened similar proceedings against Meta with regard to the 'pay or consent' model for its Facebook and Instagram services,[42] which had already attracted criticism from the European Data Protection Board (EDPB).[43]

The DMA also further expands the Commission's existing mandate (under Article 102 Treaty on the Functioning of the European Union—TFEU) to combat anti-competitive practices and preserve a level playing field for businesses competing in the Single Market. According to Principle 11 of the 'Declaration on Digital Rights and Principles' "*everyone should have the possibility to compete fairly and innovate in the digital environment. This should also benefit businesses, including SMEs*". The Commission has made active use of its existing mandate for some time: many of its high-profile cases against major software and digital service providers alleging anti-competitive behaviour have attracted global attention and sometimes criticism from the home jurisdictions of companies affected by its decisions. In one of the most recent cases, the Commission

[40] European Commission, Digital Markets Act: Gatekeepers, https://digital-markets-act.ec.europa.eu/gatekeepers_en.

[41] European Commission, Commission Sends Preliminary Findings to Apple and Opens Additional Non-Compliance Investigation against Apple under the Digital Markets Act, Press Release IP/24/3433, 24.06.2024. https://ec.europa.eu/commission/presscorner/detail/en/IP_24_3433.

[42] European Commission, Commission sends Preliminary Findings to Meta over its 'Pay or Consent' Model for Breach of the Digital Markets Act, Press Release IP/24/3582, 01.07.2024. https://ec.europa.eu/commission/presscorner/detail/en/ip_24_3582.

[43] European Data Protection Board (EDPB), Opinion 08/2024 on Valid Consent in the Context of Consent or Pay Models Implemented by Large Online Platforms. 17.04.2024.

found Microsoft culpable of distorting competition in the videoconferencing sector[44] and required the company to unbundle Teams from its Office 365 product range.[45]

Arguably, the DMA is not the only EU initiative inspired by Principle 11. In addition to the established instruments of competition law, recent EU legislation has started to address concerns about the dominance of major digital platform providers, the risk of 'vendor lock-in' due to proprietary applications and data formats, and the 'weaponisation' of such dependencies, on several levels. At the network, infrastructure, and application levels, the Data Act contains new rules to facilitate switching between providers of cloud services and other data-processing services.[46] At the data level, EU legislators are attempting to loosen the hold of digital platform providers on the data collected, stored, and processed on their proprietary systems by promoting 'openness', which includes, in particular, open standards, open-source software, data sharing and data portability.[47]

For the public sector, specifically, the Interoperable Europe Act (IEA) sets out a comprehensive framework for the coordination, assessment and monitoring of public sector interoperability including the development of common standards and solutions for interoperable, EU-wide digital public services infrastructures.[48]

3.4.2.4 *Safety and Security in the Digital Environment*

The 'Declaration on Digital Rights and Principles' requires EU member states to guarantee a protected, safe, and secure digital environment for their citizens. According to Principle 16, "*everyone should have access to*

[44] European Commission, Commission Sends Statement of Objections to Microsoft over Possibly Abusive Tying Practices Regarding Teams, Press Release IP/24/3446, 25.06.2024. https://ec.europa.eu/commission/presscorner/detail/en/ip_24_3446.

[45] Microsoft Corporation, Realigning Global Licensing for Microsoft 365, 01.04.2024. https://www.microsoft.com/en-us/licensing/news/microsoft365-teams-ww.

[46] Regulation (EU) 2023/2854 of the European Parliament and of the Council, 13.12.2023 on Harmonised Rules on Fair Access to and Use of Data (Data Act), OJ L. 2023/2854, 22.12.2023.

[47] European Commission, Open-Source Strategy 2020–23: Think Open, C/2020/7149 final, 21.10.2020.

[48] Regulation (EU) 2024/903 of the European Parliament and of the Council, 13.03.2024 laying down Measures for a High Level of Public Sector Interoperability Across the Union (Interoperable Europe Act), OJ L. 2024/903, 22.03.2024.

digital technologies, products and services that are by design safe, secure, and privacy-protective, resulting in a high level of confidentiality, integrity, availability and authenticity of the information processed". With respect to collective security, EU member states commit to "*countering and holding accountable those that seek to undermine, within the EU, security online and the integrity of the digital environment or that promote violence and hatred through digital means*".

These commitments were embodied, in the Digital Services Act (DSA).[49] The DSA is designed to protect citizens from illegal and harmful online activities, individually and collectively. It addresses, in particular, the dissemination of illegal and harmful content, such as incitement to violence or terrorism, disinformation, defamatory, or other unlawful discriminating content, which violates the fundamental rights of users or groups of users. It imposes obligations on digital intermediaries, such as social media networks, search engines, app stores, marketplaces, and online booking platforms, and sets out a legal framework for the designation of 'very large online platforms' (VLOPs) and 'very large online search engines' (VLOSs). Digital intermediaries are required to monitor the content offered on their platforms and prevent the use of their services for the distribution of illegal goods, services, and content.

While the DSA maintains the general exemption of digital intermediaries from liability for content provided by their users and does not impose a general obligation to monitor that content, it requires them to respond to alerts from users, cooperate with public authorities, and take active steps against illegal content, e.g., by removing it and/or suspending access for users who frequently provide such content. VLOPs and VLOSs are required, in addition, to conduct regular risk assessments to identify potential systemic risks related to their services, e.g., for the integrity of elections and the civic discourse, public security, citizens' fundamental rights, and physical and/or mental well-being. They are obliged to take mitigating action with regard to any identified risks and to cooperate with EU and national authorities.

[49] Regulation (EU) 2022/2065 of the European Parliament and of the Council, 19.10.2022, on a Single Market For Digital Services (Digital Services Act), OJ L. 277, 27.10.2022.

As of September 2024, the European Commission has designated twenty operators of VLOPs and VSOPs.[50] The majority of them belong to global groups headquartered in the US (11) and China (4). So far, the European Commission, which is responsible for supervision and enforcement of the DSA, has initiated proceedings at various stages against four operators.[51] In one case, the Commission has obtained an undertaking from the operator to withdraw a service that has been considered potentially harmful for citizens' physical and mental well-being, especially of minors.[52]

3.4.2.5 Availability of Digital Public Services

At the same time, a significant part of the EU's regulatory effort is directed at promoting the adoption of digital technologies by the public sector. In this respect, the 'Declaration on Digital Rights and Principles' builds on the 'Berlin Declaration' (2020), as well as on the earlier 'Tallinn Declaration' (2017),[53] where EU member states undertook to transition public administrations towards a 'digital by default' approach. Principle 7 of the 'Declaration on Digital Rights and Principles' gives a general commitment to citizens that "*everyone should have online access to key public services in the EU*". This commitment is broken down subsequently into a number of key elements which are considered necessary preconditions for the successful delivery of digital public services. These elements are now in the course of being implemented through EU and member-state legislation.

In Principle 7, EU member states commit to ensure "*that people living in the EU are offered the possibility to use an accessible, voluntary, secure and trusted digital identity that gives access to a broad range of online services*". The EU has been working for some time on a harmonised

[50] European Commission, Shaping Europe's Digital Future: Supervision of the Designated Very Large Online Platforms and Search Engines Under DSA. https://digital-strategy.ec.europa.eu/en/policies/list-designated-vlops-and-vloses.

[51] Ali Express, Meta (Facebook, Instagram), TikTok, and X (formerly Twitter).

[52] Commission Decision, 05.08.2024 relating to a Proceeding under Article 71 of Regulation (EU) 2022/2065: Case DSA.100121 - TikTok Lite Rewards Programme, C/2024/5654 final, 05.08.2024.

[53] Ministerial Declaration on e-Government ('Tallinn Declaration'), 06.10.2017. https://digital-strategy.ec.europa.eu/en/news/ministerial-declaration-egovernment-tallinn-declaration.

secure digital proof of identity that would be usable and accepted in all member states. The first eIDAS Regulation (2014) established a framework whereby EU member states could, initially on a voluntary basis, develop and notify national digital ID schemes based on a common set of criteria which would ensure interoperability.[54] This legislation was amended recently by the new European Digital Identity Framework (EUDI),[55] which came into force in September 2024 and introduced a secure European digital identity wallet.

As a second pillar, alongside the digital ID, Principle 7 enjoins EU member states to ensure "*wide accessibility and re-use of public sector information*". As a first major step, the Open Data Directive (2019) set out a framework for the re-use of certain categories of public sector information, such as geographical, land registry, statistical or legal information, and publicly funded research data ('open data').[56] Access to data was further expanded in 2022 with the introduction of the Digital Governance Act (DGA).[57] The DGA is complementary to the Open Data Directive in that it provides a framework for the re-use of certain categories of public sector information that is not 'open data', but which could be made available under certain legal conditions and/or processed in trusted and secure environments.

The third pillar in Principle 7 tasks EU member states with "*facilitating and supporting seamless, secure and interoperable access across the EU to digital public services designed to meet people's needs in an effective manner, including and in particular digital health and care services, notably access to electronic health records*". This mandate is reflected in the ongoing effort to create 'common European data spaces'. These are secure, trusted environments for data sharing in a number of strategic

[54] Regulation (EU) No 910/2014 of the European Parliament and of the Council, 23.07.2014, on Electronic Identification and Trust Services for Electronic Transactions in the Internal Market (eIDAS Regulation), OJ L 257, 28.08.2014.

[55] Regulation (EU) 2024/1183 of the European Parliament and of the Council Establishing the European Digital Identity Framework, OJ L 2024/1183, 30.04.2024.

[56] Directive (EU) 2019/1024 of the European Parliament and of the Council, 20.06.2019, on Open Data and the Re-use of Public Sector Information (Open Data Directive), OJ L 172, 26.06.2019.

[57] Regulation (EU) 2022/868 of the European Parliament and of the Council, 30.05.2022, on European Data Governance (Data Governance Act), OJ L 152, 03.06.2022.

areas, such as health, agriculture, manufacturing, energy, mobility, financial, public administration, skills, and scientific research. Each common European data space will be based on a dedicated regulatory framework comprising, on the one hand, technical tools, services, and infrastructure for data sharing; and, on the other, data governance mechanisms which govern the access to and processing of such data in accordance with EU law and values, in particular personal data protection, consumer protection legislation, and competition law.[58] Two legislative proposals by the Commission are currently debated by the European co-legislators, the European Health Data Space (EHDS) Regulation in health care,[59] and the Financial Data Access Regulation (FIDA) in financial services.[60] In both cases, policymakers are engaged in intensive dialogue with stakeholders to strike a balance between the expected benefits of data sharing—improving the efficiency and effectiveness of public services, encouraging private sector innovation, and delivering higher-quality outcomes for citizens—with concerns about privacy, data protection, and the potential misuse of data.

3.4.2.6 Safe, Transparent, and Responsible Use of AI/ML

Finally, no review of its regulatory activities in the digital space, however brief, would be complete without addressing the EU's efforts to establish a governance framework for the mainstream adoption of artificial intelligence/machine learning (AI/ML). The centrepiece of this effort, and the one that has attracted the most attention internationally, is the AI Act,[61] which was adopted by the EU co-legislators in July 2024 and will be applicable in full by 2026.

Again, the guiding principles now enshrined in the AI Act were, to a large extent, outlined already in the 'Declaration on Digital Rights and Principles', in particular in Principles 8 and 9. According to Principle 8,

[58] European Commission, Commission Staff Working Document on European Data Spaces, SWD 2022/45 final, 23.02.2022.

[59] Proposal for a Regulation of the European Parliament and of the Council on the European Health Data Space (EHDS), COM/2022/197 final, 03.05.2022.

[60] Proposal for a Regulation of the European Parliament and of the Council on a Framework for Financial Data Access (FIDA), COM/2023/360 final, 28.06.2023.

[61] Regulation (EU) 2024/1689 of the European Parliament and of the Council, 13.06.2024 laying down Harmonised Rules on Artificial Intelligence (Artificial Intelligence Act), OJ L 2024/1689, 12.07.2024.

"*artificial intelligence should serve as a tool for people, with the ultimate aim of increasing human well-being*", while Principle 9 demands that "*everyone should be empowered to benefit from the advantages of algorithmic and artificial intelligence systems [...], while being protected against risks and harm to one's health, safety and fundamental rights*". Consequently, the AI Act applies a risk-based approach: it bans certain uses of AI which are considered incompatible with EU fundamental rights and values outright ('prohibited practices') and designates other as 'high-risk' (Annex III). For high-risk applications, the AI Act requires registration with the competent authorities, a conformity assessment, and, in some instances, a fundamental rights impact assessment (Kwan et al. 2024). The latter is a new feature in EU law and must be performed by public-law entities or private entities providing public services when deploying 'high-risk' AI applications.

As a supporting measure, and to bridge the interim period until the AI Act comes into full effect, the European Commission has invited industry participants to commit to a Voluntary 'Artificial Intelligence (AI) Pact',[62] which was launched in November 2023 and entered into force in August 2024. Signatories of the 'AI Pact' agree to work towards compliance with the requirements of the AI Act already in advance of the legal deadline. So far, more than one hundred organisations, including some of the major global developers and operators of AI/ML technology, have signed the 'AI Pact',[63] while a number of other major platforms, notably Apple, Meta, and TikTok, have not. Apple, in particular, instead announced in June 2024 that it would postpone the market launch in Europe of certain AI/ML-supported services.[64]

Meanwhile, however, the EU courts have issued decisions, based on other legislation already in force that could exert a decisive influence on the deployment of AI-enabled/powered applications, especially

[62] European Commission, AI Pact. Organisations' Commitments, European Artificial Intelligence Office, September 2024. https://ec.europa.eu/newsroom/dae/redirection/document/107430

[63] European Commission, Over a Hundred Companies Sign EU AI Pact Pledges to Drive Trustworthy and Safe AI Development, Press Release IP/24/4864, 25.09.2024. https://ec.europa.eu/commission/presscorner/detail/en/ip_24_4864.

[64] Chee, F.Y., Apple to Delay Launch of AI-Powered Features in Europe, Blames EU Tech Rules, Reuters, 21.06.2024. https://www.reuters.com/technology/artificial-intelligence/apple-delay-launch-ai-powered-features-europe-blames-eu-tech-rules-2024-06-21/.

in connection with automated decision-making, including profiling. In December 2023, the EU Court of Justice (CJEU) issued a decision based on Article 22 of the GDPR that placed strict constraints on the use of algorithms for the automated credit scoring of individuals.[65] Although the case in question did not directly involve the use of AI models, credit scoring is one of the areas of application where AI is expected to be adopted rapidly and widely, and has been designated as a 'high-risk' application in Annex III of the AI Act.

The use of citizens' personal data for the purposes of training AI models has the potential to become yet another divisive issue between major jurisdictions. Meta recently postponed the introduction of AI models on its Facebook and Instagram services in the EU at the request of the Irish data protection authority, which came in response to a complaint from a civil rights advocacy group over the proposed use of customers' personal data to train the platform's AI/ML algorithm.[66] Shortly thereafter, the Irish Data Protection Commission announced an agreement with X (formerly Twitter) in which the latter committed to suspend the processing of EU citizens' personal data for the purpose of training its AI tool,[67] and launched an enquiry against Google regarding its use of personal data for AI/ML model training.[68]

A different, but closely related issue, which could have a bearing on international trade, is the use of intellectual property, including published content subject to/protected by copyright, for AI/ML training. Again, major jurisdictions seem to take different views on the balance to be struck between the protection of intellectual property rights, on the one hand, and the desire to make available large repositories of data to facilitate the development and fine-tuning of AI/ML models. In

[65] Court of Justice of the European Union, Judgment of the Court, 07.12.2023, OQ vs. Land Hessen (Schufa Holding) (C-643/21; ECLI:EU:C:2023: 957).

[66] Data Protection Commission (Ireland), The DPC's Engagement with Meta on AI, 14.06.2024. https://www.dataprotection.ie/en/news-media/latest-news/dpcs-engagement-meta-ai.

[67] Data Protection Commission (Ireland), The DPC Welcomes X's Agreement to Suspend its Processing of Personal Data for the Purpose of Training AI Tool 'Grok', 08.08.2024. https://www.dataprotection.ie/en/news-media/press-releases/dpc-welcomes-xs-agreement-suspend-its-processing-personal-data-purpose-training-ai-tool-grok.

[68] Data Protection Commission (Ireland), Data Protection Commission Launches Inquiry into Google AI Model, 12.09.2024. https://www.dataprotection.ie/en/news-media/press-releases/data-protection-commission-launches-inquiry-google-ai-model.

the EU, the 2019 Digital Single Market (DSM) Directive provided for 'fair use' exceptions from copyright for text and data mining (TDM), which also cover AI/ML.[69] Under the DSM Directive, copyright owners can, however, choose to reserve their rights, an option that has been maintained by the AI Act. The AI Act maintains these exceptions and imposes compliance reporting and disclosure requirements upon developers and users of AI/ML systems. EU member-state courts will be tasked with the practical challenges of implementation, and case law of the CJEU is expected to provide further guidance in due course. It is well conceivable, however, that they could arrive at different conclusions from courts in other jurisdictions, such as the US, where similar cases are being adjudged at present.[70] Harmonisation on the basis of existing international frameworks, such as the Berne Convention and the WIPO Copyright Treaty, both administered by the World Intellectual Property Organisation (WIPO) would appear highly desirable.

3.4.3 Specific Observations on EU Policies

The overview of the EU legal and regulatory framework above provides (i) an overview of the EU's regulatory activity, specifically in the digital domain; and (ii) an illustration of how the 'values-based' (Article 2 TFEU) or 'rights-based' (*Bradford*) approach to regulation in general, and regulating technology in particular, is implemented based on a continuum of fundamental rights, political statements of intent ('soft law'), and related legislation and regulation. The scale and scope of the EU's regulatory initiatives continue to set the pace globally in many respects, most recently with the EU AI Act. As with other technologies before, the stated objective of the EU's approach is to build public trust in emerging technologies through compliance with laws and observing values.

The EU member states' public commitment to digital rights and principles also encourages the public discourse and stakeholder engagement.

[69] Directive (EU) 2019/790 of the European Parliament and of the Council,17.04.2019, on Copyright and Related Rights in the Digital Single Market (DSM Directive), OJ L 130, 17.05.2019.

[70] A potentially significant case is currently pending in the US: *The New York Times Co. vs. Microsoft Corporation, OpenAI Inc. et al.*, Case 1:23-cv-11195, U.S. District Court for the Southern District of New York, 27.12.2023.

Civil-society initiatives for rights-based, 'safe' online spaces, which range from advocacy groups, such as the European Digital Rights Network (EDRi), to specific, single-issue campaigns, are complementary to governments' regulatory efforts. Implicit in this approach is the recognition that regulation of technology should form a robust basis for citizens/civil society to assert their rights without placing excessive restrictions on businesses and the public sector. To strike and continuously recalibrate this balance, a regular dialogue with stakeholders, both structured and informal, is essential.

As mentioned at the beginning, the EU's regulatory effort in the field of technology has led to the deployment of a new generation of regulatory structures and instruments. A number of legislative acts, such as the DGA, the IEA, and the AI Act, involve the creation of dedicated governance structures, which allow for the integration of a broad range of stakeholders into regulatory design and practice. The European AI Board, the Advisory Forum, and the Scientific Panel, all established under the AI Act, provide a formal framework for continuous engagement between public authorities, industry participants and civil society, and for regular exchange with the scientific community. The European Data Innovation Board acts as an advisory body to the Commission for all matters related to the implementation of the DGA and the common European data spaces. The Interoperable Europe Board, established under the IEA, is composed of representatives from EU member states and EU authorities and tasked with facilitating cooperation and the exchange of information on cross-border interoperability of public sector network and information systems.

With a view to regulatory policy instruments, the use of impact assessments is of particular interest in this legislation. There is a distinct progression over time, from the Data Protection Impact Assessment under the GDPR (Article 35 GDPR), to the much broader Risk Assessment required from VLOPs and VLOSs under the DSA (Article 34 DSA) and the Fundamental Rights Impact Assessment (FRIA) of the AI Act (Article 27 AI Act) (Yeung and Bygrave 2021; Wernick 2024). The FRIA requires certain deployers of a high-risk AI system to provide,[71] in particular, (i) a description of the processes in which the system is intended to be used; (ii) time and frequency of its intended use; (iii) individuals

[71] See also Sect. 3.4.2.6: Safe, transparent, and responsible use of AI/ML above.

or groups affected by its use; (iv) potential harm—to their health, safety, or fundamental rights—these individuals may be exposed to; and (v) risk management, governance, and complaint mechanisms.[72] The results of this impact assessment, as well as any identified risks and proposed mitigation measures, must be reported to the relevant supervisory authority, a step which may be critical in turning them from a potentially inconsequential 'box-ticking' exercise into a point of departure for supervisory engagement.

The AI Act also provides an instructive example of how flexibility and iterative policymaking could be incorporated into legislation. Article 7 and Article 97 of the AI Act empower the Commission to adopt delegated acts to amend the list of 'high-risk AI applications' in Annex III of the Act by adding or modifying use cases of high-risk AI systems which fulfil certain criteria set out in the law.

Any analysis of the EU framework, in particular, is complicated by its unique status as a supranational entity and its complex multi-level governance arrangements. Regulatory density indicators would have to be carefully selected and defined in recognition of its specificities, e.g., the co-existence of directly and indirectly applicable EU legislation ('regulations' and 'directives') with member-state legislation.

In many instances, these EU initiatives highlight the tension between market openness and international cooperation, on the one hand, and value-based regulation, on the other. This balance is difficult to achieve already within the EU, which is relatively homogeneous and bound by member states' legal commitment to common values, e.g., through Article 2 TFEU and the 'EU Charter of Fundamental Rights', but still diverse. It becomes much more challenging still when competing socio-political models with different value scales are involved. In this context, global frameworks, such as the UN's recently adopted 'Global Digital Compact',[73] and the ITU/UNDP Digital Acceleration Agenda,[74] could fulfil a vital role as 'common denominators' to guide and encourage convergence.

[72] On potential shortcomings regarding the definition of 'harm' in the AI Act see Stiefmueller (2022).

[73] United Nations Pact for the Future: Global Digital Compact, UN GAOR, 79th Session, UN Doc. A/79/1, 22.09.2024. https://www.un.org/global-digital-compact/en.

[74] ITU/UNDP, SDG Digital Acceleration Agenda, 15.09.2023. https://www.undp.org/publications/sdg-digital-acceleration-agenda.

3.5 Conclusions

The general considerations in Sects. 3.2 and 3.3 above, and our review of relevant initiatives at the European level in Sect. 3.4, lead us to a number of conclusions, which are summarised in the remainder of this section.

A New Social Contract for Digitalisation

It is imperative that approaches to technology policy and regulation are devised in a manner that promotes the principles of transparency, accountability, and fairness in the digital economy. The formulation of a novel social contract for the digital age must be anchored in a set of principles that guarantee digital rights through a human-centric approach to digitalisation, firmly embedded in fundamental rights. At the EU level, the European Declaration on Rights and Principles is an illustrative example of this approach. It will be essential to achieve a balance between these principles and the necessity to safeguard fundamental rights, guarantee security, and promote digital inclusion.

Flexible and Responsive Governance Frameworks and Instruments

In order to accommodate the diversity of approaches, the various levels of digital adoption and maturity, and the rapid technological change, flexible governance structures are required. The EU has been at the frontier of regulatory development, not only in terms of the scope of its regulations but also in terms of the adoption of new structures and instruments. This approach could be characterised, expanding upon the narrower characterisation by Bradford, as a '*3R*' approach to government policy in the digital sphere. This entails a 'rights-based', and 'responsible' use of technology and a 'responsive' approach to regulation. In this context, it is of utmost importance to ensure the involvement of a broad range of (formal and informal) stakeholders.[75]

Furthermore, as discussed in Sect. 3.3.3—assessing government policy—above, there is a need for additional instruments to provide more detailed, evidence-based insights on policy design and choices. Such

[75] For example on "*Extended Multistakeholderism*" Technology Policy: Responsible Design for a Flourishing World, WEF White Paper 08.10.2024, pp. 29–31. https://www.weforum.org/publications/technology-policy-responsible-design-for-a-flourishing-world/.

contributions could inform comparative studies and promote international dialogue. Further work is required to develop suitable analytical frameworks and establish a robust basis for their operationalisation.

Global Cooperation in the Digital Age

The development and application of digital technologies is inherently global and does not respect national borders. Despite geopolitical tensions, enhanced international cooperation, in all its facets, will be indispensable to navigate the complexities of cross-border jurisdiction, law enforcement, and the evolving digital landscape (Baimenov and Liverakos 2019). Left to itself, national legislation with potentially momentous impact on other jurisdictions places courts in an unenviable position. The application of national law invariably becomes highly politicised and forces judges to bear in mind considerations that extend well beyond their formal (legal) remit and responsibility.

Amidst the growing challenges posed by recent crises, the rapid evolution of digital technologies, and mounting budgetary constraints, public administrations at all levels are being compelled to collaborate, streamline their efforts, and secure greater legal certainty in their digital transformation endeavours. International organisations such as the United Nations (UN) and the Organisation for Economic Cooperation and Development (OECD) play a pivotal role in facilitating cross-jurisdictional dialogue and cooperation.[76] With regard to artificial intelligence, as demonstrated by the OECD.AI Policy Observatory,[77] a global governance ecosystem comprised of local, regional, national and international actors as well as non-governmental is emerging, with more than 1,000 AI policy initiatives across 69 countries. Furthermore, numerous other international and regional fora, including the International Telecommunication Union

[76] For example, the recently adopted UN Global Digital Compact aims to establish a framework for global governance of digital technologyand artificial intelligence. https://www.un.org/techenvoy/global-digital-compact.

[77] The OECD AI principles are reflected in a number of AI policies and regulatory approaches (including the EU AI Act) and are considered in the development of (international) standards. https://oecd.ai/en/ai-principles.

(ITU),[78] the World Economic Forum (WEF),[79] the G7,[80] UNESCO,[81] or the International Organization for Standardization (ISO),[82] among others, play an important role in establishing guidelines, frameworks, and standards that facilitate ethical technology usage, equitable access to digital resources, and the protection of individuals in the digital age.

A Roadmap Towards a Global Governance Framework

The global reach and impact of digital technologies require coherent, coordinated, and consistent global regulatory approaches to sustain a rules-based international order in the digital sphere. Regulating cyberspace in a way that balances innovation with ethical responsibility will be key to addressing the pressing issues of the digital age. However, when trying to analyse legal and regulatory frameworks across jurisdictions it is critical to bear in mind the diverse cultural and legal traditions that shape each system.

Enhanced regulatory cooperation will be required to find common ground despite differing national and regional contexts. To ensure such cooperation, it will be necessary to establish: (i) a common starting point anchored in a 'human-centred' approach to digitalisation, reflecting a global consensus on fundamental rights and the SDGs); (ii) shared concepts to map and understand the varying regulatory profiles and trajectories across different jurisdictions (as discussed in Sect. 3.3.3 above); and (iii) new common frameworks (such as, for instance, on

[78] For example, the Digital Regulation Platform is the result of ongoing collaboration between the International Telecommunication Union (ITU) and the World Bank,https://digitalregulation.org/about/.

[79] For example https://www.weforum.org/publications/governance-in-the-age-of-generative-ai/.

[80] For example, the G7 Hiroshima Ministerial Declaration, adopted at the G7 Digital and Tech Ministers' Meeting on 30.04.2023. https://www.digital.go.jp/assets/contents/node/information/field_ref_resources/efdaf817-4962-442d-8b5d-9fa1215cb56a/f65a20b6/20230430_news_g7_results_00.pdf and the Hiroshima AI Process, https://www.mofa.go.jp/files/100573471.pdf.

[81] UNESCO, Recommendation on the Ethics of Artificial Intelligence. https://www.unesco.org/en/articles/recommendation-ethics-artificial-intelligence.

[82] https://www.iso.org/home.html.

AI/ML) or the expansion of existing ones, such as the Global Digital Compact, and the ITU/UNDP SDG Digital Acceleration Agenda.[83]

In the absence of harmonisation, discrepancies, redundancies, and fragmentation between national and international governance and regulatory approaches, as well as between these and regional and local approaches within countries, could impede international interoperability, give rise to or exacerbate risks to human rights and democratic norms, create barriers to trade and investment, and restrict the dissemination of the benefits of technological progress for all.

References

Al-Ubaydli, O., and P. McLaughlin. 2014. Reg-data: A numerical database on industry-specific regulations for all U.S. industries and federal regulations, 1997–2012. George Mason University Mercatus Center Working Paper No. 12–20, 13 November.

Baimenov, A., and P. Liverakos. 2019. Frameworks for international cooperation and partnerships for human and institutional development. In *Public service excellence in the 21st century*, ed. A. Baimenov and P. Liverakos, 324–339. Singapore: Palgrave Macmillan.

Bradford, A. 2012. The Brussels effect. *Northwestern University Law Review* 107 (1): 1–68.

Bradford, A. 2023. *Digital empires. The global battle to regulate technology*. Oxford: Oxford University Press.

Bradford, A. 2024. The false choice between digital regulation and innovation. *Northwestern University Law Review* 119 (2): 377–453.

Bourguignon, D. 2015. The precautionary principle: Definitions, applications, and governance. European Parliament Research Service, EPRS IDA (2015) 573876.

Collingridge, D. 1980. *The social control of technology*. New York: St. Martin's Press.

Costa, L. 2012. Privacy and the precautionary principle. *Computer Law & Security Review* 28 (1): 14–24.

[83] The UN and the OECD recently agreed on closer cooperation on AI policy and governance to support their member states and other stakeholders in their efforts to foster a globally inclusive approach. https://www.oecd.org/en/about/news/press-releases/2024/09/oecd-and-un-announce-next-steps-in-collaboration-on-artificial-intelligence.html#:~:text=Our%20joint%20efforts%20will%20help,AI%20risk%20and%20opportunity%20assessments.

Dietrich, M., and F.M. Facca, eds. 2022. Cloud computing in Europe: Landscape, analysis, adoption challenges and future research and innovation opportunities. H-CLOUD Consortium. https://www.h-cloud.eu/?wpdmdl=4541&ind=1645025986562.

European Commission. 2017. Commission Staff Working Document: Annexes to the Impact Assessment accompanying the Proposal for a Regulation of the European Parliament and of the Council on a Framework for the Free Flow of Non-Personal Data in the European Union (Part 2/2). COM/2017/495 final, 13.09.2017.

European Commission. 2020a. Communication on a European Economic Security Strategy. https://ec.europa.eu/commission/presscorner/api/files/document/print/en/ip_23_3358/IP_23_3358_EN.pdf.

European Commission. 2020b. A new industrial strategy for Europe. COM/2020/102 final, 10.03.2020.

Everest-Phillips, Max. 2019. Big-data driven public service in the twenty-first century: The politics of big data. In *Public service excellence in the 21st century*, ed. A. Baimenov and P. Liverakos, 275–318. Singapore: Palgrave-Macmillan.

Katz, M.L., and C. Shapiro. 1994. Systems competition and network effects. *Journal of Economic Perspectives* 8 (2): 93.

Kwan, S., C.M. Stiefmueller, and C. Leitner. 2024. Exploring regulatory frameworks for AI/ML through different lenses: A comparative approach. *The Human Side of Service Engineering* 143: 23–35. https://doi.org/10.54941/ahfe1005080.

Leitner, C., and C.M. Stiefmueller. 2019. Disruptive technologies and the public sector: The changing dynamics of governance. In *Public service excellence in the 21st century*, ed. A. Baimenov and P. Liverakos, 237–274. Singapore: Palgrave Macmillan.

Mazzucato, M. 2013. *The entrepreneurial state*. London: Anthem Press.

Mazzucato, M. 2017. Mission-oriented innovation policy: Challenges and opportunities. RSA Action and Research Centre, University College London (UCL). https://www.thersa.org/globalassets/pdfs/reports/mission-oriented-policy-innovation-report.pdf

Montero, B., and R. Dal Borgo. 2023. Supporting decision making with strategic foresight: An emerging framework for proactive and prospective governments. OECD Working Papers on Public Governance No. 63. Paris: OECD Publishing. https://doi.org/10.1787/1d78c791-en.

Nordhaug, L., and L. Harris. 2021. Digital public goods: Enablers of digital sovereignty. In *Development Cooperation Report 2021: Shaping a just digital transformation*. Paris: OECD Publishing. https://doi.org/10.1787/c023cb2e-en.

OECD. 2023a. *Shaping digital education: Enabling factors for quality, equity and efficiency*. Paris: OECD Publishing. https://doi.org/10.1787/bac4dc9f-en.

OECD. 2023b. *Key issues in Digital Trade—OECD Global Forum on Trade 2023 "Making Digital Trade Work for all"*. Paris: OECD Publishing. https://www.oecd.org/en/publications/key-issues-in-digital-trade-review_b2a9c4b1-en.html

Pöysti, T. 2024. The precautionary approach design pattern. *Digital Society* 3 (5).

Scott, J. 2018. Legal aspects of the precautionary principle. A British Academy Brexit Briefing, November. https://www.thebritishacademy.ac.uk/documents/309/Legal-Aspects-of-the-Precautionary-Principle.pdf

Stiefmueller, C.M. 2022. The soul of a new machine: Promises and pitfalls of artificial intelligence in Finance. In *The human side of service engineering*, ed. C. Leitner, W. Ganz, C. Bassano, and D. Satterfield, vol. 62, 353–366.

UNDESA. 2021. Sandboxing and experimenting digital technologies for sustainable development. Policy Brief No 123. https://www.un.org/development/desa/dpad/wp-content/uploads/sites/45/publication/PB_123.pdf.

UNDP/GCPSE. 2018. Foresight manual: Empowered futures for the 2030 Agenda. Singapore: Global Centre for Public Service Excellence. https://www.undp.org/sites/g/files/zskgke326/files/publications/UNDP_ForesightManual_2018.pdf.

UNESCO. 2005. The precautionary principle. Report of the World Commission on the Ethics of Scientific Knowledge and Technology (COMEST), United Nations Education and Scientific Organization.

UNHRC. 2022. Internet Shutdowns: trends, causes, legal implications and impacts on a range of human rights. Report of the Office of the United Nations High Commissioner for Human Rights (A/HRC/50/55). https://documents.un.org/doc/undoc/gen/g22/341/55/pdf/g2234155.pdf.

United Nations. 2024a. E-Government Development Index (EGDI). https://publicadministration.un.org/egovkb/en-us/About/Overview/-E-Government-Development-Index.

United Nations. 2024b. E-Government Survey—Accelerating digital transformation for sustainable development. https://publicadministration.un.org/egovkb/en-us/Reports/UN-E-Government-Survey-2024.

Wernick, A. 2024. Impact assessment as a legal design pattern. *Digital Society* 3 (29): 2024.

Yeung, K., and L. Bygrave. 2021. Demystifying the modernized European data protection regime: Cross-disciplinary insights from legal and regulatory governance scholarship. *Regulation & Governance* 16 (2): 137–155.

CHAPTER 4

Policy Coordination Frameworks in the New Reality

Iveta Reinholde, Ieva Daniela Beinarovića, Malvīne Stučka, and Aleksis Jarockis

4.1 Introduction

Any debate on future governance arrangements will unavoidably focus on policy coordination frameworks to effectively manage the accomplishment of goals and objectives set. As most policy domains are interlinked, and a policy initiative undertaken in one policy area indeed affects another, it is essential to establish policy coordination mechanisms that are capable of reacting to challenges of the new reality going beyond the national boundaries. Policy coordination is no longer an issue of national importance alone. Even though national, regional, and local governments in a country are still the key players, complex problems like climate change and migration require multilevel policy coordination at the multilateral level (Bevir 2009).

Even though the term *new reality* has become common among politicians, policy analysts, and the public, it still includes both the complexities

I. Reinholde (✉) · I. D. Beinarovića · M. Stučka · A. Jarockis
Department of Social Sciences, University of Latvia, Riga, Latvia
e-mail: Iveta.reinholde@lu.lv

A. Baimenov and P. Liverakos (eds.), *Public Administration in the New Reality*, https://doi.org/10.1007/978-981-96-3845-1_4

and wickedness of policy issues, which require many resources and efforts to search for solutions. The multiple actors involved in this process are inter-dependent and independent; thus, observing their coordination efforts, behavioural patterns, and approaches may reveal the real policy coordination game. This chapter explains the policy coordination challenges in the light of wicked problems through three case studies: communication of EU funds, lessons learned after catastrophic events, and emergency laws passed outside ordinary parliamentary procedures.

The new reality is a widely used term to describe our times' complex and interconnected challenges. Even though the term *new reality* is not widely used in the academic literature, it contains the same ideas that were incorporated in the term *wicked problems*, which refers to the problems the world faced during and after the COVID-19 pandemic. However, climate change, technological disruptions, energy crises, and economic uncertainties are, in fact, wicked problems as well.

The debate on the nature of wicked problems started in the 1970s, right after the oil crises of that decade. There were feelings that planning, rational arguments, and negotiations were the key instruments for the "marketability" of solutions (Rittel and Weber 1973: 158). However, the public administration as a system and a structure was perceived as a source of problems, suffering, of gross misunderstanding and even of maltreatment (Rittel and Weber 1973: 158). Despite the warnings from four decades ago, governance today has a somewhat romantic view on policymaking, and that following all of the steps in the policy cycle with a strong focus on planning can help to overcome any problems that arise.

Furthermore, ignoring the wicked problems worsens the situation—the well-established planning system helps when there is stability, and when facing wicked problems, the planning system fails. According to Rittel and Weber (1973), wicked problems can be identified in all policy domains, and they do not have explicitly defined features that make them easy to recognise in the avalanche of issues faced daily by policymakers.[1] Since Rittel and Weber, the term wicked problem has been

[1] Essentially, Horst Rittel was a founding father for the modern understanding of wicked problems (Ferguson 2019), and Rittel and Weber (1973: 161–167) outlined ten features of these problems: (1) there is no definitive formulation of a wicked problem; (2) wicked problems have no stopping rule; (3) solutions to wicked problems are not true or false but good–evil; (4) there is no immediate and ultimate test of a solution to a wicked problem; (5) every solution to a wicked problem is a "one-shot operation"; (6) wicked problems do not have an enumerable (or an exhaustively desirable) set of potential solutions, nor

widely used in both science and practice. Meanwhile, Rittel and Weber do not speak about policy coordination among stakeholders to resolve the wicked problems. Indirectly, but assuming that every wicked problem is unique, Rittel and Weber recognised that due to uniqueness, all policy coordination instruments and attempts to resolve wicked problems will fail. Acknowledging the wicked problems seems akin to opening Pandora's box, where an avalanche of difficulties contests any attempts to undertake complex issues (Andersson and Törnberg 2018). The COVID-19 pandemic and governmental reactions to cope with it qualify the perception that it was a wicked problem.

4.2 Revisiting Policy Coordination

During the COVID-19 pandemic, the public requested more policy coordination, practical solutions, and quick results. Policy coordination is the only instrument to address these challenges in a multi-dimensional manner. Despite the implied uniqueness of every wicked problem, the academic debated on the link between policy coordination and wicked problems has been long enough to grasp the key factors that might serve as a coordination framework for tackling wicked problems.

Policy coordination becomes crucial when decisions involving two or more institutions or bodies are inter-dependent, with each potentially having different interests, positions, and strategic visions. Government coordination mechanisms at both national and local levels can offer strategic, technical, and methodological assistance and expertise to line ministries in addressing routine tasks as well as wicked problems. Effective policy coordination enhances information flow between government departments and fosters increased communication across levels of governance (Peters 2018).

Academic literature has underscored duplications, contradictions, and displacement, highlighting vertical management, evolving demands, and cross-cutting issues as practical reasons to invest time and political

is there a well-described set of permissible operations that may be incorporated into the plan; (7) every wicked problem is essentially unique; (8) every wicked problem can be considered a symptom of another problem; (9) the existence of a discrepancy representing a wicked problem can be explained in numerous ways. The choice of explanation determines the nature of the problem's resolution; and (10) the planner has no right to be wrong.

commitment in developing policy coordination (Peters 2015). Wicked problems such as COVID-19 underscore the necessity for coordination mechanisms, raising questions about the capacity of governmental organisations.

Improved policy coordination is accepted as an essential element in effective responses to many kinds of wicked problems. In the context of discussions on homeland security after 9/11, five different problems related to coordination were highlighted: (1) place-based problems matching the functional systems; (2) ensuring a minimum level of local preparedness wherever the citizens do live; (3) effective coordination depends on routines; (4) capacity of agencies to learn new things when reacting to the new routines; (5) meeting citizens' expectation (Kettl 2003: 256–260).

When it comes to aligning place-based solutions with functional systems, the government may encounter demands for functional, structural, and administrative reforms. Implementing reforms can be challenging, as the government seeks assurance that there is an administrative agency designated to address specific issues. However, this assumes that these agencies are capable of effectively addressing crises or adapting to new conditions, which often proves to be untrue (Hood 1998). Therefore, instead of solely relying on administrative and organisational reforms to address complex problems, it is advisable to prioritise enhanced coordination in decision-making processes (Kettl 2003).

In times of crisis, effective administrative coordination is crucial for ensuring a swift and coordinated response. One of the significant challenges in administrative coordination for crisis response and beyond is the complexity of the disaster management process (Prizzia 2005). This complexity arises due to the involvement of multiple organisations, each with its responsibilities and accountabilities. Furthermore, the limited availability of shared resources adds another layer of complexity to the coordination efforts. Another challenge in administrative coordination for crisis response and beyond is the need for clear communication and information sharing among the various organisations involved. Miscommunication and lack of transparent information flow can lead to delays and confusion, hindering the overall response efforts. Thus, a crisis involves events belonging to the "*un*" category: unexpected, unwanted, unthinkable, and often unmanageable situations (Boin and 'T Hart 2007). In the event of a crisis, there is time pressure for making decisions and explaining them, with an intensive flow of information to be analysed or lack of adequate information. The overload of the system has amplified the emotions and attitudes of society and the government, and events are happening so quickly that designing a constructive plan is complicated. In such situations, well-functioning policy coordination mechanisms and digital solutions serve as a precondition for effective crisis management and allow it to take more control of its fate (Banks 2007). The crisis puts more pressure on agencies; thus, they prefer negative coordination to avoid inter-organisational conflicts (Scharpf 1994) and they stay out of each other's way rather than working closely together.

At its core, any crisis prompts inquiries into the fundamental level of local preparedness to assist citizens during emergencies. Coordination itself presents numerous inherent political, strategic, policy, managerial, and tactical challenges (Christensen et al. 2016). Kettl (2003) which emphasises that coordination (during crises and after) is a process of making and shaping a complex problem, adjusting it to organisational routines by splitting the problem into manageable pieces and then solving it with the said operational routines. Thus, positive policy coordination here becomes crucial as coordination ensures that different organisational departments coordinate simultaneous work towards results (Scharpf 1994).

Managerial coordination is relevant to managing different departments to utilise their specialisation. In addition, leadership direction and a transparent chain of command with hierarchy make the coordination effective (Christensen et al. 2016). Specialisation with specific expertise and knowledge in public administration is essential both during crises and in their aftermath. Administrative specialisation must encompass addressing the needs of citizens during and after crises, as citizens anticipate clear guidance and support (Brunner 2010).

4.3 Multidimensional Challenges and Policy Coordination

The COVID-19 pandemic brought to the forefront of political, public, and media agendas many issues that the academia has been warning about for years: the emergence of a new pandemic (Lee and Fidler 2007), the decreasing capacity of the healthcare sectors all around the developed world (Garrett 2006), and the lack of business continuity planning (Osterholm 2007), including planning and preparedness for the disruptions of various circulations systems due to lack of stockpiling crucial material-technical resources and medications (Elbe et al. 2014). This pandemic required coordination between stakeholders and policymakers from virtually all policy domains on all levels—local, regional, national, and supranational—as anyone and everyone was vulnerable to this new virus.

During the first wave of the pandemic, Latvia's policymakers were immediately faced with the first two problems of coordination outlined by Kettl (2003): dividing work between various institutions and ensuring a minimum level of preparedness and protection for everyone in the country, especially the frontline workers and first responders. Like many other nations worldwide, Latvia did not have stockpiles of personal protective equipment (PPE) and disinfectant, so obtaining these items was high on the priority list. The procurement of said items turned out to require coordination between the Ministries of the Interior, Health, and Defence. Emergency legislation was passed on 12 March 2020, with amendments following on 14 March, allowing a select group of government agencies not to apply the Public Procurement Law provisions (Latvijas Republikas Ministru kabinets 2020). On 20 March, the Cabinet of Ministers issued Cabinet Order No 118 "Regarding the Allocation of Funds from the State Budget Programme Funds for Unforeseen Events", which tasked the State Provision Agency (under the Ministry of the Interior) with conducting the procurement of PPE and disinfectant.

This decision was quickly changed with amendments to Cabinet order No 103 following on 2 April, now tasking the "State Centre for Defence Military Sites and Procurement" (under the Ministry of Defence; henceforth—SCDMSP) with conducting said procurements and taking over the management of crisis-related state material reserves; the National Armed Forces were tasked with providing the required logistical support (Latvijas Republikas Ministru kabinets 2020). Technical specifications for these procurements were prepared by the State Fire and Rescue Service (under the Ministry of the Interior), which in itself is peculiar as per the Civil Protection and Disaster Management Law; the management of a public health emergency falls directly under the Ministry of Health.[2] Thus, one would expect the technical specifications for PPE to come from an agency under the Ministry of Health, for example, the Disease Prevention and

[2] It must also be noted that there is no publicly available information about any memoranda of understanding or cooperation being signed by various agencies and services involved in managing this crisis.

Control Centre, and the procurement of PPE to be carried out by the National Health Service, which carries out routine centralised procurements of medications and medical devices. As such, the evidence indicates that the COVID-19 pandemic was treated more like an issue of homeland security than of public health.

After the goods were procured and received, they first needed to be tested and then further distributed to healthcare institutions, long-term care providers, schools, and other priority institutions. First, ensuring the quality of the procured goods was complicated because Latvia did not have certified facilities for performing the necessary quality testing of PPE, and the facilities abroad were also unavailable due to the global demand for testing the quality of masks and respirators. This challenge was addressed by coordinating and dividing the work with two other government agencies in the quality assurance process—the Health Inspection (under the Ministry of Health) was to assess the quality of medical devices, and the Consumer Rights Protection Centre (under the Ministry of Economics) was to determine the quality of PPE (Latvijas Republikas Valsts kontrole 2021: 22).

Secondly, the absence of a stable and clear list of priority institutions and their needs regarding PPE and disinfectant made procurement and distribution of these goods more complicated. This challenge proved to be more difficult to address, as the "information on the priority needs of institutions continuously changed until the end of the emergency" (Latvijas Republikas Valsts kontrole 2021: 10). The list of priority institutions and the amount of material-technical supplies they would need for a three-month period were only confirmed on 9 June with the Cabinet of Ministers Order No 308 "Provisions on the resources for ensuring epidemiological security required by priority institutions and institutions included in the list of needs"—the same day the state of emergency was lifted (Latvijas Republikas Ministru kabinets 2021).[3]

The distribution of PPE and disinfectant required the SCDMSP to coordinate with both the National Armed Forces and many stakeholders at the local level. The amount of goods and time of delivery had to be agreed upon with every recipient individually and this information

[3] Coordinating the development on various policy documents needed for emergency preparedness, e.g., civil defence plans and material reserve nomenclature, on the national level is a responsibility of the Ministry of the Interior.

then needed to be forwarded to the National Armed Forces for maximally efficient logistics planning. To address the challenge of distributing the procured PPE and disinfectant, the SCDMSP established emergency processes that outlined the rules of engagement—how, where and to whom the information one needs is to be submitted, how the delivery is to be documented, and how defects are to be reported. Ensuring traceability was important not only from the perspective of epidemiological safety but also accountability and good governance, as both the media and the State Audit Office were paying close attention to how emergency funds were spent.

The new reality shaped by the COVID-19 pandemic spotlighted many vulnerabilities of the healthcare system formed over decades of flawed policy coordination, mainly due to inadequate routines and preparedness and a lack of policy learning and change. For example, alarms regarding a critical deficit of healthcare professionals have been sounded in as far as back as 2007.[4] And calls for more funding were voiced regularly. These were pacified with promises from various governments regarding remuneration, education of new healthcare professionals and setting new regulations regarding workloads,[5] which would have required close coordination between the Ministries of Health, Education and Welfare. None of these promises were being fulfilled reaching a breaking point in 2018 when employees *en masse* terminated their employment at the Emergency Medical Services (Delfi 2018). In terms of policy coordination, this would

[4] "Compared to the experience of other countries, where the optimal number of doctors is determined per 10,000 inhabitants (there are no such standards in our legal acts), Latvia currently lacks 634 doctors – according to the data collected by the Ministry of Health in 2005" (Ričika et al. 2007). In 2019, it was estimated that by 2025, state-paid medical services will need to be beefed up with at least 3200 nurses, 168 family doctors, 153 internists, and more than a hundred other medical professionals. These estimates were optimistic as they did not factor in young (and existing) healthcare professionals leaving the country for better opportunities abroad. In 2021, the Latvian Association of Doctors, the Latvian Young Doctors Association, and the Latvian Nurses Association estimated that Latvia loses approximately 200 doctors per year, that Latvia unduly loses 13 people per day, and that (in 2020) it lost ~ 4842.2 potential years of life per 100 thousand inhabitants (aged 0-64) (Jauns.lv 2021).

[5] Unfulfilled promises include, for example, the failure to "increase doctors' wages to 2.5 times the national average by 2009, ensuring that 70 percent of individuals who have acquired education in medicine and healthcare actually work in their profession, and to develop rules on how many patients can be under the care of one doctor and one nurse in a hospital" (Barisa-Sermule 2019).

have meant that the Government of Riga Municipality would have been unable to meet the citizens' expectations for emergency medical help. Emergency steps were taken to mitigate the situation[6]; however, the root cause of the underlying issues remains to be addressed.

Failure to build a reliable learning system and insufficient ability to balance the old with the new (Kettl 2003) contributed both to lack of initial preparedness for a new pandemic and to the challenges confronted with the procurement and distribution of COVID-19 vaccines in 2021. On an international level, there were several warnings leading up to the COVID-19 pandemic that were left unheeded: the 2014/2015 Ebola epidemic in South Africa, the 2015 MERS outbreak in South Korea, the 2009 pandemic influenza H1N1, the 2003 SARS outbreak in southern China, and the 2001 Anthrax attacks in the USA. On a local level, the 2006/2007 influenza season in Latvia highlighted several vulnerabilities that would make managing a new (flu) pandemic very challenging, such as the lack of a stockpile of material-technical resources, medications, and underfunded epidemiological monitoring (Beinaroviča 2021, 2022). Additionally, the 2009 spread of the pandemic influenza virus H1N1 provided an opportunity to analyse whether the vulnerabilities spotlighted by the 2006/2007 influenza season in Latvia were addressed successfully, which was not taken advantage of. Unfortunately, this failure to learn and prepare was acutely felt during the first (discussed above) and second wave of the COVID-19 pandemic.

In terms of balancing the old tasks and functions with the new reality of managing and confining the COVID-19 pandemic during its second wave, the procurement and distribution of COVID-19 vaccines encountered difficulties very early on. In November and December 2020, Latvia's policymakers were presented with opportunities to apply for COVID-19 vaccines under the Advanced Purchase Agreement negotiated by the European Commission. By January 2021, the vaccination rate in Latvia was not meeting expectations, so the Minister of Health issued an

[6] The crisis was resolved by passing an amendment to the Labor Law to allow medical professionals to work more overtime than the law permits, which does not address the underlying issue—lack of human resources, work-life balance, and low professional reputation. Even though this crisis was subverted, another scandal regarding the promised salary increases for medical professionals soon followed. In many cases, the salaries not only did not increase but actually decreased (Beinaroviča 2022: 162).

order to form a special investigation commission comprised of representatives from the Ministries of Health and Justice and the State Chancellery. In their final report, the commission concluded that although no malicious activities were identified and the people involved were qualified and competent, there was a failure to apply the principles of good governance, insufficient risk analysis, and, potentially, flawed communication or withholding of information (Beinarovičа 2021), which led to a lack of vaccines and, consequently, to a slow vaccination rate. Essentially, the Ministry of Health had failed to consider the lessons provided by the procurements of PPE and disinfectant conducted in the spring of 2020 by agencies under the Ministries of Interior and Defence.

Another challenge regarding vaccination against COVID-19 was logistics. Frustration with how this new function was being organised reached a boiling point on 11 March, after a private contractor failed to deliver the medication to several vaccination spots the day before. In the Cabinet of Ministers meeting, the Prime Minister expressed his dissatisfaction with this situation and asked whether vaccine deliveries should be entrusted to the National Armed Forces (TVNET/LETA 2021c). This proposition was supported by the Ministers of Defence, Justice, Foreign Affairs, and the Minister of the Interior. Essentially, the new agency created for the purpose of ensuring effective and efficient distribution of the COVID-19 vaccines—the Vaccination Project Bureau—was failing to meet the expectations of both the government (the Cabinet of Ministers) and the citizens, who were exposed to an unnecessary risk of infection. It must be noted that the Minister of Defence had already expressed readiness to provide logistical support for vaccine distribution in January (TVNET/LETA 2021a). The National Armed Forces had proved efficient and competent in handling complex logistical challenges during the first wave of the pandemic, so by coordinating with the Ministries of Defence and Justice,[7] the Ministry of Health could have ensured safe and reliable deliveries of medications, thus meeting citizens' expectations and mitigating this particular risk.

The frustration with vaccine distribution was further exasperated by the failure of the Ministry of Health and National Health Service in

[7] Although the National Armed Forces did not have access to the refrigeration equipment necessary for transporting the vaccines at low temperatures, these were available to the State Forensic Expertise Office under the Ministry of Justice—enough for up to 100,000 vaccines (TVNET/LETA 2021c).

coordination with private contractors to develop an adequate information technology solution for coordinating mass vaccination. Although almost 1.5 million euros were assigned to completing this task, by March, the dedicated vaccination website still lacked the necessary functionality to ensure effective and efficient IT support for organising vaccine distribution to citizens via the approximately 800 vaccination points in the country (TVNET/LETA 2021b). The National Health Service explained that the information about priority groups had to be compared with other medical registers and that "the work takes place at night and manually, in "Excel" tables" (TVNET/LETA 2021b). This illustrated another failure of building a reliable learning system, as the National Health Service at that point had about nine years of experience operating another IT system used by healthcare professionals—e-Veselība (e-Health)—yet failed to link these two systems in a timely manner.

However, logistics and lack of proper IT solutions were not the only challenges with distributing the COVID-19 vaccine during the second wave of the pandemic. In May, when everyone was eligible to receive the vaccine, an investigative article was published, claiming that "only 55 percent of general practitioners in Latvia, who have a contract with the National Health Service, carry out vaccinations" (Vēbere et al. 2021). Among the reasons for not providing this service, general practitioners mentioned lack of resources as well as the chaotic way the process was organised. Thus, the first four to five months of the vaccination process had already diminished the trust of medical professionals in the government's ability to meet their expectations and provide adequate support in balancing their existing work with the new task of administering the COVID-19 vaccines.

To summarise, during the first and second waves of the COVID-19 pandemic, Latvia's Government encountered all five problems of policy coordination as defined by Kettl: during the first wave of the pandemic, dividing work between various institutions (*Matching place and function*) and ensuring a minimum level of protection (*Defining a floor*) proved to be challenging as dealing with this emergency was largely assigned to the Ministry of Defence and not the Ministry of Health, which would have been the more expected choice. SCDMSP had to establish emergency processes for procuring, stockpiling, and distributing PPE and disinfectant, with logistical support provided by the National Armed Forces. Failures in learning from past experiences (*Building a reliable learning system*), such as previous influenza seasons, warnings about critical lack of healthcare personnel, and the challenges faced during the first wave of the pandemic, contributed to inadequate initial preparedness and response to the COVID-19 pandemic, as well as the procurement of the COVID-19 vaccines during the second wave. Lack of coordination between ministries, government agencies, private contractors, and healthcare providers led to a chaotic and inefficient distribution of the vaccines (*Balancing the old with the new* and *Meeting citizen's expectations in a fragmented system*).

The COVID-19 pandemic exposed many weaknesses in policy coordination in Latvia which need to be addressed now more urgently than ever before. The new geopolitical reality requires a change of paradigm in the public sector: moving away from the sentiment "One country – different ministries", towards a diametrically opposite logic "Different ministries – *ONE country*". The existing, fragmented way of approaching the management of various emergencies and policy issues needs to evolve to a more holistic and agile approach to managing complex problems in a complex world (Gailane 2017).

4.4 Regulatory Agility and Communication as a Policy Coordination Tool

In an era where technological advancements occur at an unprecedented pace, the traditional approaches to regulation have become increasingly insufficient. The concept of regulatory agility emerges as a critical response to this challenge, advocating for frameworks that are not only robust and comprehensive but also flexible and adaptive.

Regulatory agility refers to the authorities taking quick action and adapting swiftly in response to different challenges. This agility is crucial in biotechnology, artificial intelligence, and cybersecurity, where innovations can rapidly outpace existing regulations (Bolislis et al. 2021). In the context of regulatory agility in the legislature, traditional regulatory methods, which are usually slow and strict, struggle to keep up with rapid changes across various fields. This creates a noticeable gap between the pace of change and the regulations that are supposed to manage it. Whatever positive or negative policy coordination is in place, regulations are an integral part of coordination in any policy.

The urgency procedure is primarily used to curtail parliamentary debate. This approach helps fast-track politically sensitive issues, preventing extensive delays and discussions. Regulatory agility is not just a necessity but a strategic imperative in the age of rapid technological advancements. While emergency legislation offers a pathway to achieving this agility, it must be employed judiciously, carefully considering its implications. By embracing flexibility, foresight, and inclusive collaboration, regulators can establish both practical and adaptable frameworks, ensuring that regulation is a facilitator, not a hindrance, to technological progress.

Communication in policy coordination is the second level in the cascade of policy coordination tools designed by Metcalfe (1994). The first level in the Metcalfe's cascade is independent decision-making by the ministries. The next level is communication with other ministries for the purpose of information exchange. Once the agencies exchange the information, they already demark potential conflicting interests that allow them to enter into negative policy coordination—to exchange information to avoid conflicts. However, the new reality of policy coordination depends on communication that builds trust. It is assumed that one of the integral functions of a democratic public administration system is communication since any aspect of public administration is closely related to the communication process and depends on it (Cutlip et al. 2000: 634–667). However, communication may become a wicked problem itself as public administration operates in the public sphere alongside commercial organisations, non-governmental sector organisations, interest groups, and the media (Purvis 2005: 17–40).

During the pandemic-induced crisis, public administration was faced with unprecedented uncertainty and instability when designing crisis strategies. Therefore, the importance of communication in the crisis management strategy chosen became decisive, as the bar of responsibility for public institutions was raised very high during that period. COVID-19 has created specific crisis communication challenges around the world. More than ever, the pandemic has demonstrated how essential digital communication technologies are in today's world. By increasing the role of digital technologies in people's daily lives, the COVID-19 pandemic has caused a rapid breakthrough in digitalisation processes, and we are several years ahead of predicted development. The rapid growth of digitalisation made it possible not only to go on tours of museums and watch theatre performances but also to make Zoom sessions a regular family evening or an everyday activity.

The crisis of trust is a challenge in the modern world and affects almost all countries. The proportion of the world's population dissatisfied with democracy reached 57.5% in 2019, the highest level in the last 25 years, and several researchers link this to economic and political crises (Foa et al. 2020: 42–56). During the COVID-19 pandemic, mistrust of public administration was supplemented by personal and social dimensions of mistrust, such as fear of losing a job, getting sick, concerns about climate change, and cyber security. The general trend is that society trusts government leaders, business leaders, and experts in the health sector less than before. However, in several countries (e.g. Switzerland, Denmark, Norway, the Netherlands, and Luxembourg), the opposite trend is observed—citizens' satisfaction with democracy has increased (Edelman 2021).

Likewise, another challenge that has been directly affected by the global COVID-19 crisis and the accompanying *infodemic* was the relatively low public trust in state institutions (European Commission 2021a: 95; European Commission 2022a; European Commission 2022b; OECD 2022), as well as traditional media.[8] Significant risks were identified for societies with insufficiently high level of public media and information literacy (European Parliament 2022), as well as low public desire and ability to take responsibility, to participate in the socio-economic, social, and political processes of the country's development.

An analysis of the experience of the OECD countries regarding crisis management during the COVID-19 pandemic points to many lessons learnt relevant for the future. For example, coordinating the cooperation of public administration bodies requires the direct support of the highest political and administrative structures adapted to the set tasks with precisely defined mandates of responsibility. In addition, effective crisis management requires pre-established channels of communication for coordination and information exchange. This may turn into a difficult task between different levels of governance. Conversely, to promote trust, which is crucial in crisis management, a more targeted, informed, and coordinated exchange of government information with the public is needed (OECD 2022). In fact, the pandemic experience draws lines with Rittel's assumption *of the marketability* of decisions and public administration as a source of problems (Rittel and Weber 1973: 158). The

[8] According to the World Health Organisation, an infodemic is an "overabundance of information about a problem that makes it difficult to find a solution. It can spread misleading information, misinformation, and rumours during a health emergency. An infodemic can hinder the implementation of effective public health protection measures and create confusion and mistrust among the population".

COVID-19 pandemic required a significant change in habitual behaviour patterns, so communicators were faced with the challenge of developing appropriate messages for the public. In government and institutional communication practice, the concept of strategic communication was primarily understood as message formulation.

It is believed that quality in public administration is not an abstract concept, as it is related to specific things that are essential from the point of view of society. Qualitative public administration possesses the following characteristics: perceptibility, responsiveness, honesty, competence, kindness, reliability, safety, and communication (Bovaird and Loeffler 2003: 35–41). In this context, public administration communication is based on the following principles (McQuail 2005):

- *Information is true, objective, and timely*, that is—the government implements fair and ethical communication, providing comprehensive, objective, and timely information regarding the decisions developed and adopted by the government.
- *Communication is simple, understandable, and constant*, that is—citizens understand the information about government decisions and their impact on their lives.
- *Communication is unified, coordinated, and planned*, that is—communication is a common responsibility of the state administration—not only the head of the communication structural unit or the press secretary, but also the minster, state secretary, and other officials, who may be responsible for it. Continuity is ensured in communication.
- *Communication is based on creating a dialogue*, that is—the government involves the public in making decisions on issues relevant to the public, as well as in the development and implementation of policies and other important legal acts. Communication considers the interests of the public, which are ascertained by regularly conducting public opinion research and consultation on issues relevant to the public.

Another critical factor is the prompt implementation of laws to avoid sanctions from the European Union for missing deadlines on directive implementations. This is another case in which the Parliament may decide that urgent procedures tailored to minimise conflict are appropriate.

Adopting budgets and budget amendments urgently is often used to limit objections from the opposition. This reduces the chances of introducing ungrounded or policy-inconsistent proposals, thereby aiding the country's progress. However, frequent use of the urgency procedure is not a recommended practice. It should be reserved for situations requiring it rather than for political manoeuvring or malicious intents.

When bills are passed urgently but still undergo a thorough examination in committees with sector experts present, they tend to be of high quality, relevant, and unlikely to affect public policy adversely. So, it is essential to collaborate with stakeholders to ensure regulations are informed, balanced, and effective. In addition, the Constitution of the Republic of Latvia allows the public to participate in law-making (Satversmes sapulce 1922). In this way, it is possible to address problems of concern not only to the individual involved or to an association or an institution but also to the larger society because the law applies to a large part of society, if not all.

Emergency policymaking highlights the pitfalls of regulatory agility and emergency legislation. In Latvia's current political system, the Parliament is considered powerful due to its significant authority. The government answers to the Parliament, which monitors and regulates its actions. In this set-up, the Parliament has robust control and oversight over the government.

Typically, Latvian legislation involves a three-reading process for the approval of bills (Latvijas Republikas Saeima 1994). However, contemporary legislative practices in Latvia have shown variations from this standard procedure, with some bills passed through a two-reading process. In general, the urgency procedure is necessary for a Parliament to react quickly. It is also essential that the urgency procedure is clearly defined both in the constitution and in the laws relating to the legislative work of Parliament so that situations do not arise in which it can be adapted as representatives see fit. Of course, where urgency is decided and who decides it is also essential.

Regulatory agility was also important in the organisation of the work of the Cabinet of Ministers to ensure continuity of its work. Before COVID-19, the last face-to-face meeting was held on 19 March and a week later, on 24 March, the Cabinet of Ministers met already remotely via digital means. Meetings of the Cabinet of Ministers were also held remotely in 2021. Normally, Cabinet of Ministers meetings are held once a week in person, but in these circumstances, they were organised remotely twice a week to ensure swift decision-making (Valsts kanceleja 2020, 2021).

The data indicate that from 2019 to 2022, the Cabinet of Ministers experienced a significant increase in both extraordinary sittings and cases dealt with, particularly peaking in 2020 due to the COVID-19 pandemic (Fig. 4.1). This surge in extraordinary sittings in 2020 reflects the urgent and unprecedented challenges posed by the pandemic, necessitating more frequent and urgent decision-making. Despite this, the number of ordinary sittings remained stable, highlighting the Cabinet's consistent routine amidst a growing and complex workload.

Over the 2008–2022 period, the Parliament passed 2534 laws, including approval of the budget and international treaties (Fig. 4.2). Reacting to rapidly changing external conditions, the number of laws adopted under extraordinary proceedings increased dramatically in 2022. In 2020, 90% of laws were subject to amendments after adoption due to COVID-19 and extraordinary conditions. By comparison, only 52% of laws were amended in 2019, while 61% of responding businesses found that fast-changing legislation and policies were problematic when doing business (European Commission 2022b).

Most of the laws adopted as a matter of urgency are budget related. But at the same time, the urgency procedure is also used to reduce the opposition's chances of tabling many proposals and delaying the adoption of a law. The factors that most often influence the urgency of decisions are an unforeseen event, a crisis, the need to coordinate with other countries, controversial issues on politically sensitive topics, and malpractices of the government or Parliament's commissions.

Additionally, urgency can be invoked to minimise parliamentary debates, especially in politically sensitive matters where discussions might be lengthy and heavily media-focused, potentially swaying public opinion against a political group. Thus, not only agencies but also Parliament may opt for negative coordination as a quick solution to avoid conflict and push through faster requirements for legal amendments.

The COVID-19 pandemic also highlighted the gaps and shortcomings in the Latvian public information system, as there were no mechanisms in place to quickly and efficiently communicate information to all people in Latvia. The pandemic also highlighted the problem that the country did not have a crisis communication platform in place, so both a website and a separate crisis hotline had to be set up quickly.

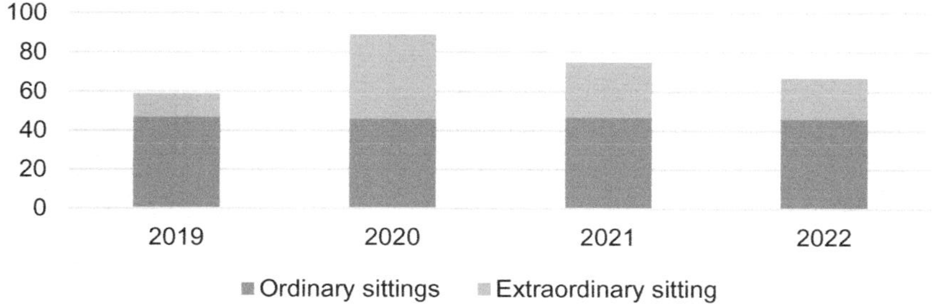

Fig. 4.1 Number of the Cabinet of Ministers sittings (2019–2022) (*Source* Valsts kanceleja [2019, 2020, 2021, 2022])

Fig. 4.2 Number of passed laws through the emergency procedure in Latvia (2008–2022) (*Source* Collected by authors from the database of Saeima)

During COVID-19, chaotic communication between public administration, the government, and the public was frequently observed in Latvia. Government institutions were not prepared to act together, as there had been no training or preparations for coordinating joint actions, and no coordination tools had been developed between the different institutions involved. Therefore, public administration communication did not provide a coherent, official, and competent explanation to members of the public on decisions taken by the Parliament and the Cabinet of Ministers, as there were often diverging views on the appropriate course of action for the ministers themselves.

Given the role of communication coordination in crisis management, communicators were not only observers of government or management group decision-making, but active participants, providing expert opinion on how decisions could potentially be perceived by the public, so that the proposed crisis management solutions were more closely aligned with the current public mood and issues of importance to them, and thus contributed to the effectiveness of government and institutional communication.

In Latvia, the crisis management structure of COVID-19 during the first wave of the pandemic consisted of a Crisis Management Centre, a National Emergency Medical Commission, a Crisis Management Coordination Group, an Economic Stimulus Development Group, and a Business and Employee Support Coordination Group. Members of the Crisis Communication Coordination Group were present at horizontal level in inter-agency and sectoral crisis management groups. Members of the Crisis Communication Group also attended Cabinet of Ministers meetings and other relevant meetings. The members of the Crisis Communication Coordination Group present at these meetings passed on relevant information to the entire Crisis Communication Group, which ensured that communicators from all institutions involved had access to timely and coherent information, as communication is interdisciplinary.

The COVID-19 pandemic affected several sectors and has highlighted the need for interdisciplinary communication management in government communication coordination (CDC 2012). Crisis communication coordination therefore identified a clear need for collaboration between communication specialists from different sectors. As the level of qualification and professionalism of communication specialists varies from one government institution to another, the inter-institutional transfer of knowledge that several communicators have acquired in other important projects—the Latvian Presidency of the Council of the EU, the introduction of the euro in Latvia, etc.—was very important.

Following the COVID-19 pandemic, there is a growing awareness in the Latvian public administration of the importance of communication in a crisis. This was evident during the COVID-19 pandemic, which was a prolonged and widespread crisis affecting almost the whole of society and every sector of activity, so communication (and coordination) with the public is crucial to explain government decisions and to bring about a change in public behaviour.

Given that the COVID-19 pandemic affected several areas and sectors, it demonstrated in practice the need for a comprehensive national defence system, one of the key principles of which is the so-called whole-of-government approach, where each line ministry focuses on its own areas of competence and responsibility, while all sectors are centrally coordinated and harmonised with the common goal of ensuring public safety and all functions essential for the existence of society.

4.5 Conclusions

Policy coordination in the public sector pertains to the alignment of actions and interactions among agencies, officials, and politicians within individual sectoral institutions involved in a specific policy area or the execution of a particular activity or task. The effectiveness and legitimacy of democratic governance in modern states hinge critically on governments' ability to coordinate decision-making and policymaking in an increasingly complex and multifaceted environment influenced by existing challenges and emerging risks. Effective policy coordination often requires intensive collaboration and communication between various government agencies and departments. In Latvia's complex, multi-dimensional policy landscape, there remains a need for systematisation of knowledge and knowledge sharing among policy sectors to effectively manage and implement policy coordination during crises. Knowledge is essential for policymakers across Europe to navigate everyday decision-making, particularly amidst the pressures of crisis management and digitalisation.

Policy coordination is not frozen in time, concepts, and approaches. Every case, policy domain, and policy actor shapes the policy coordination setting in public administration. Based on the case, some preconditions for setting up a policy coordination system are identified. First, whatever policy coordination instrument or coordination structure is designed and applied, communication is the key for everyone to see, accept, and understand the challenges and problems. Communication regarding wicked problems needs to be proactively formed before social groups form their no-evidence-informed opinion. It is insufficient to make decisions, plan, and implement initiatives and projects if no one is aware of them. It is also ineffective to create communication campaigns that are separated from real-life problems and challenges. Decisions, actions, and achieved results need to be linked to the country's strategic goals; however, wicked problems encountered by policymakers illustrate that the achievement of strategic goals via systematic coordination is so complicated that it often leads to policy failure (Head 2022).

Second, all policy coordination tools need to be adaptive to the challenges of wicked problems and poly-crises. Wicked problems can be separated into two categories: ones whose life cycle is long and they return to the administrative agenda on a regular basis (e.g. before elections) and those that are more sporadic; their life cycle is short, but still, they do require attention. Traditionally, legislators react to this with emergency legislation, often with a poor *ex-ante* assessment that, in turn, creates the next round of wicked problems.

Third, evidence is a necessary force for driving decisions. Meanwhile, with wicked problems, there is time pressure to make decisions, or data are controversial, and thus obtaining enough evidence in a timely manner becomes a wicked problem itself.

Fourth, the same mechanisms applied to communication are supposed to be used for data sharing among the actors as they enhance the effectiveness of policy coordination. Communication plays a vital role ensuring policy coordination and explaining quickly changing conditions. If the decision are taken "on the go", their justification and explanation are an essential part of legitimisation.

Fifth, the new reality brings increased uncertainties and risks. Under these conditions, policy coordination frameworks should be built upon robust risk management strategies and mechanisms for building resilience at both national and international levels.

Finally, none of the policy coordination mechanisms outlined above would work if there were no resources and competencies. Thus, funding, training, expertise development, and policy lesson-learning become crucial factors for various stakeholders to effectively carry out their roles and responsibilities and remain accountable.

References

Andersson, C., and P. Törnberg. 2018. Wickedness and the anatomy of complexity. *Futures* 95 (January): 118–138. https://doi.org/10.1016/j.futures.2017.11.001.

Banks, K. 2007. *Crisis communication: A casebook approach*. Mahawh, NJ: Lawrence Erlbaum Associates.

Beinaroviča, I.D. 2021. Policy learning from influenza and the preparedness of the public health sector: 2006/2007 influenza season in Latvia. *Science Open Research*. https://doi.org/10.14293/S2199-1006.1.SOR.2021.0002.v1.

Beinaroviča, I.D. 2022. Rīcībpolitikas mācīšanās un maiņa pēc ārkārtas situācijām Latvijā. Thesis: University of Latvia.

Bevir, M. 2009. *Key concepts in governance*. Los Angeles: Sage.

Boin, A., and P. 'T Hart. 2007. The crisis approach. In *Handbook in Disaster Research*, ed. R.Q. Havidan. New York: Springer.

Bolislis, W.R., M.L. De Lucia, F. Dolz, R. Mo, M. Nagaoka, H. Rodriguez, and T.C. Kühler. 2021. Regulatory agilities during COVID-19: Overview, trends, and opportunities. *Clinical Therapeutics* 43 (1): 124–139.

Bovaird, T., and E. Loeffler. 2003. *Public management and governance*. London: Routledge.

Brunner, R.D. 2010. Adaptive governance as a reform strategy. *Policy Sciences* 43 (4): 301–341.

CDC. 2012. Crisis emergency risk communication, i–440. Centre for Disease Control and Prevention.

Christensen, T., O. Danielsen, P. Lægreid, and L. Rykkja. 2016. Comparing coordination structures for crisis management in six countries. *Public Administration* 94 (2): 316–332.

Cutlip, S., A. Center, and G. Broom. 2000. *Effective public relations*, 634–667. New York: Prentice Hall International.

Delfi. 2018. Ārkārtas situācija NMPD Rīgas reģionālajā centrā turpinās. https://www.delfi.lv/news/national/politics/arkartas-situacija-nmpd-rigas-regionalaja-centra-turpinas.d?id=50593403.

Edelman. 2021. Edelman Trust Barometer 2021. https://www.edelman.com/sites/g/files/aatuss191/files/2021-03/2021%20Edelman%20Trust%20Barometer.pdf.

Elbe, S., A. Roemer-Mahler, and C. Long. 2014. Securing circulation pharmaceutically: Antiviral stockpiling and pandemic preparedness in the European Union. *Security Dialogue*. https://doi.org/10.1177/0967010614530072.

European Commission. 2021a. Standard Eurobarometer 95—Spring 2021. 2532/STD95. https://europa.eu/eurobarometer/surveys/detail/2532.

European Commission. 2021b. Standard Eurobarometer 91—Spring 2019. 2253/STD91. https://europa.eu/eurobarometer/surveys/detail/2253.

European Commission. 2022a. Directorate-General for Communication and Visibility, Rules—European Union Funding Programmes 2021–2027—Guidance for Member States. Publications Office of the European Union. https://data.europa.eu/doi/10.2775/499676.

European Commission. 2022b. Directorate-General for Structural Reform Support, Public Administration and Governance—Latvia. Publications Office of the European Union. https://data.europa.eu/doi/10.2887/344177.

European Council. 2019. A new strategic agenda 2019–2024. https://europa.eu/!UF34Jv.

European Council. 2020. Joint statement of the members of the European Council, 2603.2020. https://europa.eu/!Ff39rq.

European Parliament. 2022. Flash Eurobarometer: News & Media Survey 2022. https://europa.eu/eurobarometer/surveys/detail/2832.

Ferguson, B. 2019. The problem of policy formation. In *Competing for influence: The role of the public service in better government in Australia*, 99–126. ANU Press. http://www.jstor.org/stable/j.ctvp2n3pr.8.

Foa, R.S., A. Klassen, M. Slade, A. Rand, and R. Collins. 2020. The global satisfaction with democracy report 2020. Cambridge: Centre for the Future of Democracy.

Gailane, G. 2017. 10 gadi kopš Reģu ugunsgrēka: Nelegāla būvniecība un 26 bezpalīdzīgu cilvēku nāve—DELFI. http://www.delfi.lv/news/national/criminal/10-gadi-kops-regu-ugunsgreka-nelegala-buvnieciba-un-26-bezpalidzigu-cilveku-nave.d?id=48545013.

Garrett, L. 2006. The next pandemic? *Salud Publica de Mexico* 48 (3): 268–278.

Head, B.W. 2022. *Wicked problems in public policy. Understanding and responding to complex challenges*. Cham: Palgrave Macmillan.

Hood, C. 1998. *The art of the state: Culture, rhetoric, and public management*. Oxford: Oxford University Press.

Jauns. lv. 2021. Mediķi: Cilvēkresursu trūkums medicīnā ir sasniedzis katastrofālu līmeni. Atbildīgi ir politiķi. https://jauns.lv/raksts/par-veselibu/464577-mediki-cilvekresursu-trukums-medicina-ir-sasniedzis-katastrofalu-limeni-atbildigi-ir-politiki.

Kettl, D.F. 2003. Contingent coordination: Practical and theoretical puzzles for homeland security. *American Review of Public Administration* 33 (3): 253–277.

Latvijas Republikas Ministru kabinets. 2020. Latvijas Republikas Ministru kabineta rīkojums Nr. 103 "Par ārkārtējās situācijas izsludināšanu. https://likumi.lv/ta/id/313191-par-arkartejas-situacijas-izsludinasanu.

Latvijas Republikas Ministru kabinets. 2021. Latvijas Republikas Ministru kabineta noteikumi Nr. 308 "Noteikumi par prioritāro institūciju un vajadzību sarakstā iekļautajām institūcijām nepieciešamajiem epidemologiskās drošības

nodrošināšanas resursiem". https://likumi.lv/ta/id/323213-noteikumi-par-prioritaro-instituciju-un-vajadzibu-saraksta-ieklautajam-institucijam-nepiecies amajiem-epidemiologiskas-drosibas.
Latvijas Republikas Saeima. 1994. Saeimas Kārtības rullis. http://likumi.lv/doc.php?id=57517#p54&pd=1.
Latvijas Republikas Valsts kanceleja. 2019. Valsts kancelejas gada pārskats 2019. https://www.mk.gov.lv/lv/media/50/download?attachment.
Latvijas Republikas Valsts kanceleja. 2020. Valsts kancelejas gada pārskats 2020. https://www.mk.gov.lv/lv/media/10565/download?attachment.
Latvijas Republikas Valsts kanceleja. 2021. Valsts kancelejas gada pārskats 2021. https://www.mk.gov.lv/lv/media/14053/download?attachment.
Latvijas Republikas Valsts kanceleja. 2022. Valsts kancelejas gada pārskats 2022. https://www.mk.gov.lv/lv/media/16278/download?attachment.
Latvijas Republikas Valsts kontrole. 2021. Covid-19 izplatības ierobežošanai nepieciešamo resursu nodrošinājums valsts un pašvaldību institūcijās, 44. https://lrvk.gov.lv/lv/getrevisionfile/29564-4Hm_jBBeRAn51QA73DY yUxlsueBKoSXS.pdf.
Lee, K., and D. Fidler. 2007. Avian and pandemic influenza: Progress and problems with global health governance. *Global Public Health* 2 (January 2015): 215–234. https://doi.org/10.1080/17441690601136947.
McQuail, D. 2005. *McQuail's mass communication theory*, 68–72. London: Sage.
Metcalfe, L. 1994. International policy co-ordination and public management reform. *International Review of Administrative Sciences* 60: 271–290.
OECD. 2022. *First lessons from government evaluations of COVID-19 responses: A synthesis*. Paris: OECD Publishing, https://www.oecd.org/coronavirus/policy-responses/first-lessons-from-government-evaluations-of-covid-19-res ponses-a-synthesis-483507d6/.
Osterholm, M.T. 2007. Unprepared for a pandemic. *Foreign Affairs* 86 (2): 47–57.
Peters, B.G. 2015. *Pursuing horizontal management: The politics of public sector coordination*. Lawrence: University Press of Kansas.
Peters, B.G. 2018. The challenge of policy coordination. *Policy Design and Practice* 1 (1): 1–11. https://doi.org/10.1080/25741292.2018.1437946.
Purvis, H. 2005. *Media, politics, and government*. New York: University of Arkansas.
Prizzia, R. 2005. Agency coordination and the role of the media in disaster management in Hawaii. *International Journal of Emergency Management* 2 (4): 292–305.
Ričika, D., A. Ādamsone, and M. Celmiņa. 2007. Mediķu trūks arvien vairāk. Ko darīt? https://www.doctus.lv/raksts/personibas-un-viedokli/veselibas-apr upes-sistema/mediku-truks-arvien-vairak.-ko-darit-daina-murmane-umbrasko-andrejs-spridzans-ints-brunenieks-911/.

Rittel, Horst W.J., and M.M. Webber. 1973. Dilemmas in a general theory of planning. *Policy Sciences* 4 (2): 155–169. http://www.jstor.org/stable/4531523.

Satversmes sapulce. 1922. Satversme. http://likumi.lv/doc.php?id=57980.

Scharpf, F.W. 1994. Games real actors could play: Positive and negative coordination in embedded negotiations. *Journal of Theoretical Politics* 6: 27–53.

CHAPTER 5

Achieving Inter-governmental Performance on Strategic Priorities in the Delivery of Public Services

Aziza Umarova

5.1 Introduction

Many policy areas, such as social policy, span multiple government agencies and require effective collaboration to meet strategic priorities in public service delivery. This is a complex challenge that necessitates a cultural shift within government organisations to facilitate cohesive efforts and achieve established policy objectives. In this context, the exploration of innovative experiences of "deliverology" such CompStat in US cities, Blair's Delivery Unit and its successors in the UK, and the Results Programmes in New Zealand are worth examining; as these approaches are known to be some of the best. Their exploration will elucidate the methodologies employed by each country and trace their evolution over the past two decades, alongside the lessons learned. The analysis will examine the prevalent incentives within various political systems and

A. Umarova (✉)
SmartGov Consulting, Tashkent, Uzbekistan
e-mail: aziza@smartgov.consulting

A. Baimenov and P. Liverakos (eds.), *Public Administration in the New Reality*, https://doi.org/10.1007/978-981-96-3845-1_5

will highlight the necessity of dismantling organisational silos and integrating metrics into a unified dashboard. This dashboard will be designed with accessibility in mind for all stakeholders involved, enabling effective monitoring of policy implementation progress. The analysis will also focus on strategies to align different government agencies in achieving outcomes that are meaningful to citizens, promote resource alignment and collaboration, and incorporate innovative practices to enhance overall effectiveness.

The chapter begins with a discussion of political and bureaucratic considerations and their effect on inter-governmental performance and collaboration. It continues with the presentation of innovative experiences of "deliverology" as practiced in the US, UK, and New Zealand. It then leverages a substantial body of academic literature on public administration in the Soviet Union to analyse the lingering effects of the communist era on contemporary public sector management, particularly emphasising bureaucratic rigidity, and the lack of interagency collaboration. The chapter also explores the motivations of public servants, recognising the constraints and issues specific to the administrative practices in Central Asia, especially in Uzbekistan and Kazakhstan. It concludes by providing strategic directions for the Central Asian region, along with policy recommendations and institutional designs for interagency performance targets and "delivery teams".

5.2 Political Considerations of the Inter-governmental Performance and Collaboration

When a country is confronted with economic stagnation, political unrest, or social inequality, the imperative for change becomes undeniable. Many complex challenges, such as the public health crises or environmental issues, require multifaceted solutions that span across multiple domains. Interagency collaboration promotes a holistic approach to problem-solving and enables the stakeholders with diverse expertise to collaborate, exchange ideas, and develop comprehensive strategies that address various aspects of a problem.

Contemporary social problems cross agency boundaries and require a collective effort by government institutions. Hence, interagency collaboration and coordination become the enabler to achieve a common outcome. In the ongoing dialogue, in the field of public management, about inter-governmental performance these terms are used interchangeably. Blair's Government in the UK popularised them using the term "joined-up government". As far as back 1978, the academic literature considered "*horizontal management as the most difficult challenge in the government*" (Hanf and Scharpf 1978). Furthermore, it was noted that "*almost nothing about the bureaucratic ethos makes it hospitable to interagency collaboration*". This is because collaborative ethos values equality, adaptability, discretion, and results; whereas the bureaucratic ethos venerates hierarchy, stability, personal loyalty, obedience, and procedures. Making the transition from the prevailing ways of doing agency business to a new and more collaborative way requires actors to withdraw at least temporarily from the bureaucratic ethos. "*They must spurn something they may have at least respected if not cherished*" (Bardach 1998).

Additionally, unlike horizontal management, a strict vertical hierarchy in bureaucratic routines is easier to control. Around the world public officials are used to operating in a vertical structure where responsibilities and attribution of the success are linear and clear. This has also been the case even in New Zealand that has long been considered at the forefront of public administration, challenging its public service to re-align itself around achieving ten results, as any attempts to shift towards a horizontal structure require negotiations and increase transactional costs (Scott and Boyd 2022). Conversely, horizontal management requires a longer time horizon and more interpersonal involvement at all levels, than public officials are comfortable with. In an authoritarian system this can have profound consequences for the executives: at best, failure, at worst, sabotaging from different constituents.

5.3 Innovative Experiences of "Deliverology": The US, UK, and New Zealand Cases

The three models presented below—Delivery Unit, CitiStat, and Results Programme—may all be viewed as leadership strategies, since accountability pressures related to the approach of elections make politicians more inclined to demonstrate tangible results. Public scrutiny and political debates motivate political elites to fulfil their stated priorities and objectives, along with plans detailing how the government will monitor, assess, and report the extent of their success (or failure). By contrast, political regimes that do not depend on the electoral cycle, may have moving targets, inadequate data ecosystems and discouraging political disincentives for collaboration. Nonetheless, through this outcome-focused approach, government policies and objectives wield greater influence over the selection of projects funded by the government and the indicators that agencies are mandated to monitor.

Overall, it is crucial for governments to understand the key elements of these models that contributed to their success: how to focus agencies on delivering government results that matter to citizens; how to promote resource alignment and collaboration to achieve these results; and, how to infuse innovation and ensure system capability. This context also underscores the importance of dismantling silos and creating metrics and dashboards to transparently monitor progress, addressing the related challenges in measurement, organisation, and decision-making.

5.3.1 Delivery Unit Model

This model is based on working with data and data analytics. With the help of this new system incorporated into the structure of public administration, the government is able to control the implementation of the most important government orders thanks to the systematic work of a group consisting of several dozen experts and independent consultants maintaining and updating the system.

This model originated in the United Kingdom, where centurial tradition of political parties in the United Kingdom presenting manifestos before General Elections began in the late nineteenth and early twentieth centuries, becoming more formalised after the First World War. One of the earliest examples is the Labour Party's 1906 manifesto, which focused on social and economic reforms. Since then, manifestos have evolved into more comprehensive and professionally produced documents.

In 2001, Tony Blair—frustrated by the lack of progress in meeting the Labour's manifesto commitments during his first term in office, and by the lack of a mechanism to track departmental progress on key priorities—invited renowned educationist and government advisor Michael Barber to lead his new unit in the Cabinet Office, the Delivery Unit. Thus, the Delivery Unit model first appeared in the office of Prime Minister Tony Blair to monitor and drive progress on key policy priorities across various government departments.

By 2016–2017, the Governments of Ghana, Costa Rica, New South Wales (Australia), Pakistan, Peru, Saudi Arabia, and Serbia had established similar structures. For instance, the Prime Minister's Delivery Unit (PMDU) has been operating in Uganda since 2016 and it is involved in the development and implementation of the contracts between agencies and executive branches management. The case of this Unit, as well as other similar cases, i.e., the Malaysian Performance Management Delivery Unit (PEMANDU), the Indonesian President's Delivery Unit for Development Monitoring and Oversight (UKP4), the Chilean *Unidad Presidenciale Gestióndel Cumplimiento*, and a series of units established in Tanzania, South Africa, and Sierra Leone are all well documented in the public management literature and used as teaching material in the field.

However, variations are noted across Units with respect to the professional experience and expertise potential heads of these Units should possess. For instance, for the Malaysian Unit—PEMANDU, it was determined from the very beginning that its head should have extensive experience in project and performance management and should ideally be an expert in the field of reform and transformation, given the state of the public sector in the country. In contrast, the head of the Delivery Unit in the UK should typically possess experience in using data and statistics to improve government performance, e.g., Michael Barber, an academic possessing such skills (World Bank 2017).

When piloting a Delivery Unit, regular reporting is important. Thus, ministers must report monthly to the President or Prime Ministers (depending on the system in place) on achieving KPIs in the presence of the Delivery Unit management. The Delivery Unit will not work if it does not help departments in their transformation, and also if it does not assign roles and determines the responsibility of each government department in the implementation of common tasks.

5.3.2 *CitiStat Model*

The CitiStat approach is unique due to its emphasis on the data-driven management, regular accountability sessions, cross-departmental collaboration, and a strong focus on results. By continuously monitoring real-time data, departments can rapidly adjust and improve services, fostering a culture of accountability and transparency.

Unlike the Delivery Unit, the CitiStat system originated in the police's CompStat, when the New York Police Department was addressing the challenges, it faced in the 1990s. This system, which is still in place today, tracks and collates data on virtually every crime category, from murder to theft to drug trafficking. By paying attention to the numbers and closely monitoring performance, the Department can identify trends and allocate limited resources more effectively. Police workforce is deployed based on the latest pattern of criminal activities to prevent crime. From 1993 to 1998, New York's homicide rate plummeted by 67% and reported robberies dropped by 54%, well above the national average.[1] Since then, this system has been replicated in dozens of cities, such as Baltimore, Syracuse, San Francisco, Miami, etc.

Transitioning from police departments to municipal administrations, CitiStat evolved into a sophisticated *data-driven management system* aimed at real-time monitoring and enhancing the performance of city services. Essentially, the CitiStat framework ensures the efficient administration of urban services. The heads of various city departments convene bi-weekly at City Hall to discuss progress and performance metrics derived from CitiStat data, responding to inquiries from senior officials, including the mayor.

Following a history of budget deficits, meticulous spending tracking enabled city officials to identify and address inefficiencies. The capability to collect and analyse substantial data volumes has enhanced the precision of government operations. Notably, the CitiStat approach instituted a continuous review process, ensuring that data remains integral to daily decision-making. By evaluating data bi-weekly, the CitiStat process guarantees that critical information reaches key decision-makers promptly, facilitating immediate corrective actions.

CitiStat's methodology necessitates a comprehensive and robust data infrastructure, ensuring that data is systematically organised to facilitate the assessment of issues and performance metrics. This involves presenting data through various visual aids, such as charts and graphs that depict trends, and maps that illustrate geographic distributions, all of which are reviewed regularly at CitiStat meetings. These presentations enable decision-makers to grasp the complexities of the issues at hand swiftly and effectively, thereby allowing for prompt and informed decision-making.

[1] PolitiFact | How much credit does Giuliani deserve for fighting crime? https://www.politifact.com/article/2007/sep/01/how-much-credit-giuliani-due-fighting-crime/.

Furthermore, CitiStat emphasises the importance of addressing data gaps by striving to quantify as many facets of government performance as possible. This quantification is critical for creating a detailed and accurate picture of government operations, ultimately leading to more effective governance and accountability (Fig. 5.1).

Three considerations are critical to the effectiveness of the approach for policymakers. First, there must be oversight and coordination to ensure that data collection is complete and consistent from department to department. Second, there must be independent review to ensure that issues are brought to the attention of senior management. And third, expectations must be set to motivate departments to perform better. Above all, success depends on the commitment and participation of the senior political leadership.

5.3.3 New Zealand's "Results Programme"

The "Results Programme" is an initiative designed to enhance the performance and effectiveness of New Zealand's government agencies in delivering services and achieving desired outcomes. This programme underscores the nation's commitment to better outcomes for its citizens through effective governance, performance management, and public sector reform. It is a crucial component of ongoing efforts to modernise the public sector, ensuring that government services are responsive, efficient, and accountable to the needs of New Zealanders.

Leadership accountability plays a pivotal role in the programme's success. Leaders of various ministries are collectively responsible for the delivery outcomes. New Zealand has explored various approaches to foster accountability for **collaborative work**. These approaches include appointing a group leader responsible for motivating colleagues and evaluating individual contributions. Through trial and error, New Zealand has adopted a "blind" collective responsibility approach, where a small number of leaders are held accountable for finding solutions to issues affecting multiple agencies. Except for the requirement that all agencies draft and submit an initial action plan, the New Zealand government typically allows each set of agencies to determine the best method to achieve their goals.

The Cabinet—a committee of senior ministers—selected ten problems that were important to the public and public servants alike (listed in Table 5.1). The responsibility for each problem spanned across several

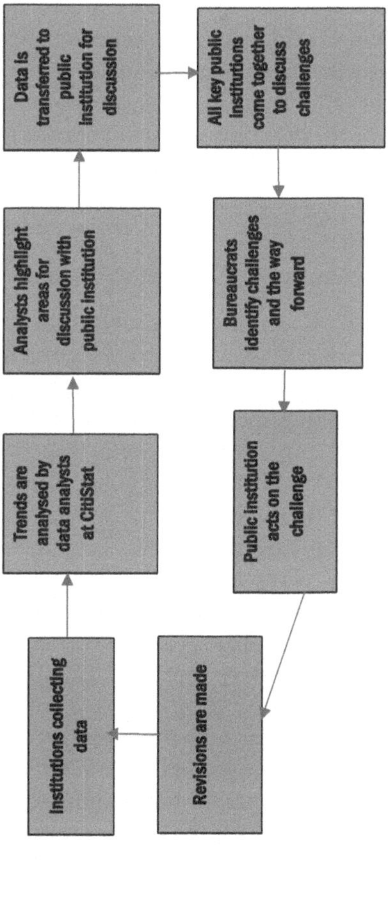

Fig. 5.1 CitiStat processes

agencies and would likely require those agencies to work together if their efforts were to be successful. Work to address these ten problems is collectively known as the "Better Public Services Results Programme".

Based on the observations of the implementation efforts undertaken by the New Zealand Government and its public service when addressing these ten problems, experts organised its thirteen practice insights (Table 5.2).

Unlike in some other countries where meeting targets is often viewed as a minimum requirement and exceeding targets is seen as positive, in New Zealand, progress is typically assessed in relation to the initial baseline rather than rigid targets. Even a significant improvement that narrowly misses the target is cause for celebration rather than criticism. At the conclusion of each six-month reporting period, New Zealand emphasises the achievement of incremental changes and their impact on the lives of New Zealanders, highlighting successes in human terms. This approach proves highly motivating for public servants. To sum up, providing updates on the advancements should involve showcasing trend data, typically presented as line graphs, illustrating progress over time.

Table 5.1 The ten results of New Zealand

Result #1	Reduce the number of people continuously receiving Jobseeker Support benefits for more than 12 months
Result #2	Increase participation in early childhood education
Result #3	Increase infant immunisation rates and reduce the incidence of rheumatic fever
Result #4	Reduce the number of assaults on children
Result #5	Increase the proportion of 18-year-olds with high school diploma or equivalent qualification
Result #6	Increase the proportion of 25- to 34-year-olds with advanced trade qualifications, diplomas, and degrees
Result #7	Reduce the rates of total crime, violent crime, and youth crime
Result #8	Reduce the criminal re-offending rate
Result #9	New Zealand businesses have a one-stop online shop for all government advice and support they need to run and grow their business
Result #10	New Zealanders can complete their transactions with government easily in a digital environment

Table 5.2 Insights on addressing crosscutting problems using interagency performance targets

Selecting results
- Focus on a few problems
- Involve other agencies in selecting problems to be addressed
- Build on existing relationships when selecting results to pursue
- Measure intermediate outcomes
- Align results, targets, and measures
- Commit publicly

Designing accountability
- Hold leaders collectively responsible
- Get started and learn by doing

Managing collaboration
- Start simply
- Limit group size
- Signal shared responsibility

Reporting on progress
- Report on trends
- Share success stories

To further integrate data and performance management within New Zealand's public sector, the role of the Government Chief Data Steward was established. This position is responsible for guiding nationwide data policy. New Zealand's commitment to policy accountability is exemplified by Stats NZ's quarterly dashboard, which highlights key achievements.[2] This framework is designed to enhance transparency and effectiveness by leveraging data for informed decision-making across governmental functions. The implementation of such roles and frameworks underscores the importance of data in driving more efficient and accountable public administration.

To conclude, high-quality data ensures accurate and reliable decision-making, while strong institutions provide the necessary integrity and transparency to prevent corruption and data manipulation. Together, they form the foundation for effective policy implementation and accountability, enabling countries to address issues proactively and achieve sustainable outcomes.

[2] Stats NZ. 2019. Data Leadership Quarterly Dashboard, New Zealand Government. https://www.data.govt.nz/about/government-chief-data-steward-gcds/data-dashboard.

Notably, countries with successful delivery models often exhibit high levels of integrity and low levels of corruption. In the absence of such ethical standards, data manipulation and inaccuracies can lead to distorted representations of reality, causing decision-makers to base their judgments on flawed information. It is, therefore, essential to identify and systematically address data gaps to prevent the oversight of critical issues and persistent under-performance. Although addressing these gaps may incur additional costs, these expenditures should be viewed as a long-term investment in the effectiveness and reliability of policy implementation.

Furthermore, data dashboards serve a purpose beyond merely displaying performance metrics. Effective use of dashboards involves comprehensive analysis, regular follow-up meetings, and established feedback loops. Without these elements, there is a risk that leaders, in their pursuit of innovation, may merely replicate superficial features of accountability tools without fully understanding or implementing their underlying principles. This can undermine the true potential of dashboards to enhance transparency and performance monitoring.

5.4 Path Dependence: Vertical Control Problem, Firemen, Target Setting, and Quality of Data

While comparing different political systems, it is evident that historical paths countries follow influence present-day challenges and organisational structures. This section builds on the theory of path dependence and how it critically influences the political processes. In this context, path dependency in the post-Soviet Union states refers to the enduring presence of institutional structures, administrative practices, and policies established during the Soviet era, influencing governance in the region. This persistence is largely attributed to the bureaucratic inertia, where administrative frameworks like centralised decision-making, hierarchical structures, and a focus on command and control that remain largely unchanged. Indeed, a substantial body of academic literature explores the principles of political economy in post-Communist societies, particularly examining the role of single-party rule from their Communist past, influenced by various contextual factors. Historically, lower-level decision-makers in these societies have operated under top-down command structures, focusing on fulfilling directives and reporting back. The expansion of state authority often integrated previously autonomous entities, establishing a centralised apparatus to enforce central directives (Rutland 1985).

According to the Soviet studies literature, when policy priorities faced perceived breakdowns in implementation, the response often involved a flurry of new policy initiatives, the activation of responsible bodies, and the creation of new institutions. When form is more important than content, bureaucratic churn mirrors the Soviet system, where social actors navigate evolving interactions, institutional frameworks, and regulatory rules (Zaleski 1971).

Economic activities in this context were marked by short-term actions and reactive responses. This short-term focus is apparent in the vertical control mechanisms centred on regional authorities. In Soviet studies literature, regional public administration, akin to "*obkoms*" (regional highest level of the Communist Party of the Soviet Union) at the local level, is often depicted as "firemen", primarily reactionary, tasked with implementing directives from above and monitored closely by organisational departments like the "*orgotdel*" (department dealing with personnel), responsible for overseeing the apparatus's performance (Rutland 1992). Yet Rutland convincingly reveals that control in USSR was always a political issue, lack of a clear model of operation together with the phenomenon of multiple control agencies (Rutland 1985). Control implies a traditional hierarchical structure where authority and decision-making flow from the top down.

The analysis of the Soviet planning system has extensively discussed the inefficiencies in incentive structures, particularly focusing *on the failure of target setting*. Scholars argue that the Soviet planning process resembled an iterative game between central planners and subordinate managers, marked by a prevalent culture of manipulating targets to meet expectations (Nove 1991; Bevan and Hood 2006). Furthermore, discussions on targets underscore how the manipulation and control of data played a critical role in maintaining political power.

Political elites frequently benefited from the patrimonial capitalism, maintaining substantial control over the state resources and policies. Hierarchical frameworks allowed for effective control, with superiors directing subordinates with relative ease, while horizontal collaboration among equals required negotiation and consensus-building, posing challenges to centralised control.

Institutionalised fragmentation within the government restricted access to data, with different agencies or departments having limited access to specific information types. This arrangement allowed the regime to control the flow of information, ensuring that only trusted individuals had access to crucial data, thereby reinforcing centralised control and limiting transparency within the government apparatus.

The fragmentation of data often mirrors institutional fragmentation within the governments. Elite groups did manipulate data to align with their interests, using it strategically to maintain power and control. Simultaneously, they restricted access to information that could potentially expose internal vulnerabilities or dissent, thereby safeguarding their positions of authority. This manipulation of data not only influenced policy outcomes but also reinforced centralised control by limiting transparency and accountability within the governing apparatus.

In authoritarian regimes lacking independent oversight or checks and balances, governmental entities prioritise allegiance to the ruling regime over holistic governance approaches, leading to isolated decision-making and limited information exchange. Different factions within these regimes fiercely guard their data reservoirs, resulting in compartmentalised information and hindered collaboration.

The dissolution of the Soviet Union accelerated during *perestroika*, a period of attempted economic and political restructuring. Simultaneously, the advent of the New Public Management (NPM) doctrine sought to prioritise measurable performance metrics and outcomes (Pallott 1999). This shift marked a significant departure from the traditional Soviet methodologies, underscoring the inter-dependence of short- and long-term objectives and highlighting the imperative of achieving one to facilitate the attainment of the other (Scott 2019; Ketti 2000). Nonetheless, the entrenched interests and power dynamics inherent within the prevailing political and economic frameworks frequently obstructed a genuine commitment to these reforms. This resulted in a complex milieu characterised by inertia and resistance to change, despite the external pressures advocating for systemic transformation.

5.5 Central Asia

In a preceding section, the inherently political nature of control within the USSR was examined, and which was characterised by ambiguous operational models and a proliferation of oversight agencies. This dynamic is also evident in Central Asia, indicating significant path dependency within governance structures. A salient feature of the public administration in Central Asia is the highly centralised decision-making process concentrated within the Presidential administration, coupled with the persistent governmental fragmentation and a lack of a cohesive whole-of-government approach.[3] Despite widespread recognition that Communist legacies have influenced post-Soviet reform trajectories, these legacies have endured in Central Asia (Baimenov and Liverakos 2022).

Central Asian states, despite numerous reform attempts, have retained key Soviet-era public management practices, such as "manual management", "*fishka*" (direct tasking), and appointments based on personal loyalty rather than institutional merit. This persistence of Soviet-era practices has often been met with resistance to change, as political and economic influences become increasingly intertwined, shaping political structures, and exacerbating social inequality.

The prevailing paradigm tends to emphasise short-term thinking and the influence of elite groups, which can sometimes make long-term and medium-term planning in national development strategies more challenging. This environment perpetuates entrenched path dependencies in the political system, characterised by excessive oversight and bureaucratic procedures. The theoretical and empirical importance of addressing control mechanisms within "patrimonial capitalism" is underscored by Norman and Lindahl (2006), who highlight the need for critical examination and potential reform of systems where political elites disproportionately benefit from the state resources and power, thus shaping policy outcomes and impeding broader developmental goals that necessitate sustained, strategic planning.

Additionally, such regimes often grapple with insufficient resources to meet state mandates while also catering to the demands of ruling elites. Ultimately, countries failing on the inter-governmental performance on strategic priorities in the delivery of public services are those with a deeply rooted patterns of public resource utilisation that is indispensable from the ***principal-agent relationships***. This implies structuring incentives so

[3] According to the Policy Framework on Sound Public Governance (OECD 2020), a whole-of-government strategy can more easily handle complex strategic goals when it is able to coordinate activities across policy domains and administrative silos. This is why the ability to develop and organise behind a shared future vision is crucial to this process. This strategy is becoming more and more important in a complex and uncertain policy environment where governments face a range of interrelated and unforeseen issues. Efforts can be more efficiently integrated and directed towards persuasive policy solutions that proactively and effectively address the complex nature of these challenges by creating a shared vision.

that "agents" who are placed in control over resources will perform obligations as promised. Robinson (2011) asserts that adequate resources are vital for maintaining basic welfare and security, which are essential for societal stability and effective governance. Disagreements over economic policies can undermine the political foundations of regimes based on patrimonial capitalism. Although state capture and resource shortages may be temporarily alleviated by external factors—such as high commodity prices or foreign borrowing—without substantial improvements in state capacity, particularly in implementing growth-oriented policies, these conditions are likely to hinder long-term development prospects for nations dependent on such authoritarian systems.

Despite pursuing divergent paths during the 1990s and 2000s, the distinctions between Kazakhstan and Uzbekistan have become increasingly blurred. This convergence is attributed to similarities in institutional quality, systems of checks and balances, and overarching bureaucratic culture. In both Kazakhstan and Uzbekistan, which inherited a legacy from the Soviet era, there is a notable tendency towards functional duplication, resulting in parallel structures within the executive branch. This phenomenon manifests in the co-existence of entities such as the Cabinet of Ministers and Presidential Administrations, echoing the historical configurations of the Central Committee of the Communist Party and the Council of Ministers. Additionally, the manipulation of targets has persisted over time, reflecting continuity in administrative practices. Conversely, scholarly discussions on contemporary Central Asia often underscore the pervasive role of informal networks and patronage, which continue to play a significant role in shaping the political and administrative frameworks of both Kazakhstan and Uzbekistan. This observation is supported by the work of Wedel (2003) and Hale (2005, 2014), who detail the enduring impact of entrenched patronage systems on the governance structures within these countries.

Kazakhstan has introduced several ambitious development strategies, starting with "Kazakhstan 2030" in 1997 and followed by "Kazakhstan 2050" in 2012. In comparison, Uzbekistan did not have long-term national development plans until 2016, when it adopted its first Uzbekistan's Development Strategy 2017–2021. This was later succeeded by the "Uzbekistan Development Strategy 2022–2026" and "Uzbekistan-2030". Furthermore, both nations have recently introduced new reform agendas: "*Yangi Uzbekistan*" (New Uzbekistan) in 2021 and "*Jana*

Kazakhstan" (New Kazakhstan) in 2022, respectively. While these developments are promising, challenges persist in effectively operationalising these visionary plans.

In both Kazakhstan and Uzbekistan, strategic decisions are formally sanctioned by the President, leaving minimal scope for error or evaluative feedback. It is customary for ministries to produce numerous Presidential Decrees to address an array of urgent issues, often at the expense of comprehensive, long-term planning. This approach complicates the monitoring of programme outcomes and the management of allocated budgets, leading to a reliance on reactive measures akin to those employed by "firemen", and a neglect of evidence-based methodologies in policy design and evaluation. Consequently, the disparity between regulatory mandates and their practical execution—where policies are frequently abandoned or altered due to implementation challenges—raises concerns about the bureaucracy's capacity to effectively execute the declared reform agendas.

The predictability of policies and the establishment of a stable civil service could significantly enhance the alignment of long-term national strategies with the strategic planning documents, state budgets, annual state programmes, and comprehensive socio-economic development plans. Such alignment would represent a substantial advancement in addressing the fragmented approach to strategic planning and policy formulation, where varying levels of governmental commitment and adherence to long-term strategies can undermine coherence. Resources would be concentrated and directed more precisely to areas of greatest need, allowing for swift adjustments in response to changing circumstances. Furthermore, enhanced responsiveness would be achieved as agencies and departments are incentivised to improve performance, thereby fostering a more streamlined and effective governance framework.

Central Asian government agencies seem to approach development objectives in a mechanistic manner, often failing to address the practical challenges that emerge in implementation. This tendency may be attributed to a lack of decentralisation in decision-making processes. Additionally, frequent ministerial rotations in both Kazakhstan and Uzbekistan contribute to a climate of caution among public sector executives. These individuals are frequently constrained by political considerations and ongoing elite reshuffling, which diminishes the incentives for bold and proactive measures. Consequently, the drive for rapid and visible success is weak, as such achievements could provoke unnecessary competition and jealousy within the political landscape.

Uzbekistan's and Kazakhstan's public service structures adhere to a hierarchical paradigm inherited from the Soviet era. Within governmental structures, various departments and institutions are tasked with distinct domains and responsibilities, rather than focusing on inter-governmental performance. In both countries, the civil service has become increasingly politicised, largely due to the pervasive influence of patronage in hiring practices, promotions, and career advancements. Consequently, appointments and career progression within the civil service are frequently driven by political considerations rather than professional qualifications or merit. This politicisation undermines the effectiveness of the civil service, as career trajectories and organisational roles are shaped more by political objectives than by expertise or performance.

And in all this, data management plays a crucial role. Without data being openly shared across government agencies, data remains susceptible to speculation. Typically, census data serves as the foundation for strategic planning, monitoring progress towards Sustainable Development Goals (SDGs), and national development objectives. However, Uzbekistan has not conducted a census since 1989, resulting in a significant gap in the availability of accurate and representative statistics for the nation. However, the National Statistics Agency has completed all necessary preparations for the census, which is scheduled to take place in 2025–2026.[4]

In Central Asia, linking data to budget expenditures presents significant challenges due to the silo-based nature of the policy cycle and budget negotiations, wherein individual ministers independently negotiate their draft budgets with the Ministry of Finance. This approach is marked by a lack of transparency, as it frequently leads to other ministries being uninformed about strategic plans and outcomes, thereby perpetuating institutional fragmentation. In contrast, the Singaporean

[4] The World Bank's Statistical Performance Indicators (SPI) provide framework for assessing the performance of statistical systems and the efforts to improve them. World Bank evaluation indicates that Uzbekistan statistical performance indicators scoring 70.6. Kazakhstan scores better, with 78.2. https://www.worldbank.org/en/programs/statistical-performance-indicators.

government has implemented a comprehensive national strategic framework centred on shared outcomes, ensuring that all ministers are involved in budget allocation discussions.

The politicisation of the civil service and the opacity in data and financial management underscore that countries with defined electoral cycles often experience considerable pressure on politicians to deliver tangible results. This pressure can lead to a focus on short-term achievements rather than long-term strategic goals. In contrast, regimes without obvious electoral pressure may be more prone to initiating a multitude of initiatives without the same level of immediate accountability. This environment of frequent shifts in priorities complicates inter-government cooperation and impedes the achievement of targets. Consequently, it is imperative to prioritise specific outcomes, implement rigorous project management strategies, and leverage data effectively to ensure the successful execution of government initiatives. These components are crucial for overcoming the challenges posed by the politicisation and shifting priorities that can otherwise undermine the effectiveness of the public administration.

To address challenges stemming from the politicisation of civil service, opaque data management, and shifting priorities, governments should focus on selecting and declaring a small number of strategic priorities aligned with the national goals and the SDGs. Enhancing data utilisation through improved collection, analysis, and sharing across agencies is crucial for transparency and evidence-based policymaking. Implementing a centralised dashboard can track multiple performance indicators, enabling decision-makers to visualise trends, analyse data relationships, and enhance accountability. Promoting interagency cooperation through structured mechanisms fosters collaboration and coherence in policy implementation and budgeting, facilitating effective delivery of public services and policies.

5.5.1 *Experimentation with the Delivery Units*

Despite the systemic challenges faced by both countries, Kazakhstan and Uzbekistan have taken steps to establish Delivery Units, a concept not yet adopted widely in Central Asia. Kazakhstan began exploring this idea in 2015 and revisited it in 2017, leading to the establishment of the National Project Office within the Office of E-government in April 2023, aimed at advancing digital transformation. Similarly, Uzbekistan established its National Agency for Project Implementation in 2017 and later, in 2023, established a Delivery Unit under the Agency for Strategic Reforms under the President. This Delivery Unit focuses primarily on promotion of data-driven policymaking and "deep dive" into the domain of public health, education, and water. To enhance project tracking and address implementation challenges, both countries are developing new government dashboards to monitor key performance indicators and collect transactional performance metrics.

In Uzbekistan, the Delivery Unit conducted a comprehensive assessment of all public-school infrastructure in 2024. The survey involved fifty-five questions directed at school administrators, with schools pinpointed on a map. The findings, such as only 12% of schools being connected to sewage systems and 53% having access to centralised drinking water pipes, were met with surprise and triggered immediate action. This data facilitated the allocation of funds from the Uzbekistan Vision 2030 Fund to support the national reform agenda and advancement of the SDGs. Additionally, collaboration with the Ministry of Economy and Finance was initiated to co-design evidence-based public investment programmes for the coming years, with plans to use this data to evaluate state programmes' implementation.

In Kazakhstan, the Digital Family Card (DFC) represents an innovative solution launched to improve people's well-being through digital technologies and data-driven decision-making. The DFC identifies vulnerabilities, targets specific population segments, and proactively delivers comprehensive public services to vulnerable groups nationwide. It ensures direct provision of social protection measures like benefits, pensions, and newborn care support, bypassing traditional bureaucratic barriers. This approach aims to ensure equitable access to social benefits for all families, irrespective of their circumstances or location.

Within a bureaucratic system, acknowledging and celebrating small victories is important. However, the challenge lies in extending these incremental successes across the entire system to improve inter-governmental performance. The following steps could be critical to promote collaboration, transparency, and data-driven decision-making across the government agencies, facilitating improved efficiency and outcomes in public service delivery even in contexts with historical path dependencies and data limitations.

- Establish a spectrum of societal outcomes, where achieving one outcome necessitates interagency cooperation;
- Develop a comprehensive dashboard featuring key performance indicators that capture the attention of the entire government. Use progress bars to track performance in priority areas, enabling agencies to observe the impact of their actions and adjust strategies as needed. This fosters momentum and encourages further collaboration;
- Build a data-driven workforce focused on collecting, managing, analysing, and visualising statistical and other data.
- Improve collaboration and communication among stakeholders to enable data-driven decision-making.
- Hire and empower a team dedicated to fostering a data-driven culture across government departments;
- Implement a bias towards action by changing bureaucratic norms between ministries and departments;
- Ensure prompt issue resolution and timely, complete reporting. Foster new communication methods with ministers, including joint reporting to the informal ministerial groups;
- Reward positive ministerial behaviour that supports collaborative efforts;
- Ensure public involvement in monitoring and evaluating the implementation of selected indicators;
- Draft and enact a Public Data Governance Law affirming integrity of data as a priority for every government agency and create a shared data lake to pool together across the government;
- Launch a Data Governance Board responsible for monitoring progress on dashboards and other platforms. Task the board with addressing issues and setting annual priorities. Empower board members to investigate specific data questions and build data analysis capacity;
- Assign members of the Delivery Unit to collaborate with co-leads from the partner agencies. Together, these co-leads will innovate and implement practical uses of data, driving forward creative solutions to government challenges.

5.6 Conclusion

Countries, particularly those in the former Soviet Union, began from varied starting points, contending with political and economic challenges rooted in their historical trajectories. Instead of advocating for comprehensive systemic overhaul, the establishment of a Delivery Unit within the existing framework can effectively facilitate change. This unit would focus on prioritising data and performance metrics, ensuring enhanced interagency collaboration to achieve societal outcomes. It would be responsible for securing essential funding, offering technical support, and developing data-driven policies while fostering cooperation among diverse government agencies. This includes establishing mechanisms for tracking and reporting, and equipping government entities and personnel with necessary resources. Transitioning to a data-driven decision-making framework that emphasises outcomes is crucial for improving the effectiveness of critical programmes and ultimately benefiting the public.

The need to dismantle organisational silos and integrate metrics into a cohesive dashboard is also evident, as it fosters transparency, aligns decision-making processes, and resolves measurement tensions. Implementing such a dashboard facilitates clearer progress tracking and more informed decision-making, which can be adapted to various political contexts, thereby improving overall governance and policy implementation.

Ultimately, success in public sector data management depends on bolstering the capabilities of government agencies. This requires personnel skilled in implementing and independently analysing data, alongside training for government officials in technology and statistical data analysis to meet evolving demands. Addressing gaps in data availability is essential for a comprehensive understanding of outcome achievement. Reliable data and rigorous analysis are fundamental to effective policymaking.

References

Baimenov, Alikhan, and Panos Liverakos. 2022. 30 years of transformation: A comparative assessment. In *Public service evolution in the 15-post-Soviet republics*, ed. A. Baimenov and P. Liverakos, 1–49. Singapore: Palgrave Macmillan.

Bardach, Eugene. 1998. *Getting agencies to work together: The practice and theory of managerial craftmanship*, 19–51. Washington, DC: Brookings Institution Press.

Bevan, Gwyn, and Christopher Hood. 2006. *What's measured is what matters: Targets and gaming in the English public health care system*. London: Wiley. https://doi.org/10.1111/j.1467-9299.2006.00600.x.

Hale, H.E. 2005. Regime cycles: Democracy, autocracy, and revolution in post-Soviet Eurasia. *World Politics* 58: 1.

Hale, H.E. 2014. *Patronal politics. Eurasian regime dynamics in comparative perspective*. Cambridge: Cambridge University Press.

Hanf, Kenneth, and Fritz Wilhelm Scharpf. 1978. *Interorganisational policy making: Limits to coordination and central control*. London: Sage.

Ketti, Donald F. 2000. *The global management revolution: A report on the transformation of governance*. Washington, DC: Brookings Institute.

Norman, Graham A., and Folke Lindahl. 2006. *The political economy of transition in Eurasia: Democratisation and economic liberalisation in a global economy*. La Salle: Michigan State University Press.

Nove, A. 1991. *The economics of feasible socialism revisited*. London: Routledge. https://doi.org/10.4324/9780203168813.

OECD. 2020. Policy Framework on Sound Public Governance. Paris: OECD Publishing. https://www.oecd.org/en/publications/2020/12/policy-framework-on-sound-public-governance_931b05fc.html.

Pallott, J. 1999. Beyond NPM: Developing strategic capacity. *Financial Accountability & Management* 15 (3–4): 419–426.

Robinson, Neil. 2011. Russian patrimonial capitalism and the international financial crisis. *Journal of Communist Studies and Transition Politics* 27 (3–4): 434–455. https://doi.org/10.1080/13523279.2011.595155.

Rutland, Peter. 1985. *The myth of the plan: Lessons of soviet planning experience*. London and Melbourne: Hutchinson.

Rutland, Peter. 1992. *The politics of economic stagnation in the Soviet Union: The role of local party organs in economic management*. Cambridge: Cambridge University Press.

Scott, R. 2019. Service, citizenship, and the public interest: New Public Service and our Public Service Reforms. SSC Discussion Paper. https://www.publicservice.govt.nz/assets/Service-Citizenship-and-the-Public-Interest-New-Public-Service-and-our-public-service-reforms.pdf.

Scott, R., and R. Boyd. 2022. *Targeting commitment: Interagency performance in New Zealand*. Wellington: Public Service Commission (Te Kawa Mataaho).

Wedel, J. 2003. Clans, cliques and captured states: Rethinking transition in Central and Eastern Europe and the former Soviet Union. *Journal of International Development, 15*, 427–440.

World Bank Group. 2017. *Driving performance from the center: Malaysia's experience with PEMANDU Open Knowledge Repository* (worldbank.org).
Zaleski, Eugene. 1971. *Planning for economic growth in the Soviet Union 1918–1932*. Chapel Hill, NC: The University of North Carolina Press.

CHAPTER 6

The Appeal and Challenges of Behavioural Public Policy: A View from Central Asia

Saltanat Janenova

6.1 Introduction

There has been a growing surge in behavioural studies across various policy areas around the world in recent years.[1] Debates leading to the rise of behavioural public policy and contributions from cognitive psychology, sociology, behavioural economics, neurosciences, and other behavioural sciences are reshaping public policy interventions. For example, to promote public health, to encourage making savings for retirement, or to increase tax collection.

The behavioural economics and public policy literature argues that since all problems and policies have to be framed in some way, governments should take seriously the idea of *choice of architecture* and seek to structure their policies in ways that nudge people towards the better

[1] See Baggio et al. (2021) and Straßheim and Beck (2019), for an overview.

S. Janenova (✉)
School for Policy Studies, University of Bristol, Bristol, UK
e-mail: saltanat.janenova@bristol.ac.uk; saltanat.janenova@nu.edu.kz

National Analytical Centre, Nazarbayev University, Astana, Kazakhstan

A. Baimenov and P. Liverakos (eds.), *Public Administration in the New Reality*, https://doi.org/10.1007/978-981-96-3845-1_6

choices. Nudges are the most prominent subtype of behavioural change: the rearrangement of fruit and vegetables in cafeterias to focus our attention on healthy options; graphic warnings on cigarette packages; messages to stop people from using too many paper towels or urging them to switch off the light when they leave the office—these and other interventions have become part of everyday life (Thaler and Sunstein 2008).

The first nudge unit, the Behavioural Insights Team (BIT), was established in 2010 under David Cameron's coalition government in the UK within the Cabinet Office. It has since become a quasi-privatised company with more than 150 employees that consults and tests policy innovations for the UK government and abroad. The BIT serves as a model for many other behavioural insights teams worldwide: in Australia, France, Germany, Japan, the Netherlands, Singapore, and the USA, which all have recently created nudge units (OECD 2019). Similar behavioural policy units were established within the World Bank (WB), the United Nations (UN), the Organisation for Economic Cooperation and Development (OECD), and the European Commission (EC).

Lately, policymakers and government officials from the post-Soviet Eurasia region have shown a rising interest in behavioural insights and have attempted to experiment with some behavioural policies (Astana Civil Service Hub 2023). However, limited knowledge and understanding exists about how the governments in the Eurasia region have been transferring and adapting some ideas of behavioural insights from the Western democratic context into their own setting.

The chapter aims to fill in this knowledge gap by addressing two questions: (1) In what ways have the governments in the post-Soviet Eurasia region experimented with behavioural insights? And (2) What are the challenges and ethical considerations related to application of behavioural policies in the Eurasia? In this context, the chapter will consider examples of early behavioural interventions introduced by two governments in Central Asia—Kazakhstan and Uzbekistan; a sub-set of the Eurasia region—aimed at changing the behavioural and social norms of citizens for tackling corruption and improving public health policy.

These research objectives have confronted several challenges. The first is concerned with how one could accurately identify and recognise 'behavioural' policies if behavioural insights are not publicly acknowledged by the policymakers in Central Asia.[2] Irrespective of this, although the use of behavioural public policy has not been formally acknowledged in this region, policymakers in Central Asia have de facto experimented with ideas from behavioural insights. The second challenge is related to the limited data on public responses to the behavioural interventions due to the closed context of Central Asia; characterised by limited public access to data, low citizen engagement in the policymaking process, and weak bureaucratic capacity (Knox and Janenova 2023a). However, in such closed environments, social media provides a relatively safe platform for citizens to express their voices and opinions (Imamova 2015; Knox and Janenova 2020; Nair et al. 2019), so selected 'behavioural style' interventions were juxtaposed with social media commentary on these policies to gather insights of the public's response to the newly introduced changes.

Using vignettes from the two countries—Kazakhstan and Uzbekistan—this study provides a critical analysis of the 'behavioural style' policies launched by the Central Asian governments and the public's response to these interventions, while at the same time it identifies context-specific challenges. The selection of 'behavioural style' policies was based on content analysis of legislation from 2020 to 2023, policy reports, and media articles. Two 'behavioural style' policies have been selected for the use of vignettes in this chapter: the anti-corruption messaging campaign in Kazakhstan and preventing iodine deficiency in Uzbekistan.

6.2 Behavioural Public Policy: Global Perspective

This section focuses on reviewing the development of behavioural public policy across the globe and on criticism of behavioural insights by scholars and practitioners through fast growing academic literature that encompasses knowledge and evidence on behavioural insights applications across Asia—including China, Japan, Singapore, and South Korea—Australia, Canada, Europe, and the USA.

[2] The term 'behavioural' policies did not show up in the web-based search of government bodies and legislation of the case study countries.

The studies of Sanders et al. (2018), Straßheim (2020), Whitehead et al. (2014) examined the rise and spread of behavioural public policy across the globe through a review of international practices and challenges. Many government bodies and international organisations have created behavioural teams and research units to co-design policy interventions, and experiment, as well as to examine the impact of behavioural policies on shaping public attitudes and behaviour (Della Vigna and Linos2022; Halpern 2016).

Baggio et al. (2021) analyse the application of behavioural insights in the policymaking of the European Commission and call for a rigorous methodological approach to avoid abuse and misapplication of behavioural insights, more exploratory and in-house research, and more active collaboration with private sector and academia. Gopalan and Pirog (2017), in a review of behavioural policies in the United States, outline a framework for further integrating behavioural insights into the various stages of policy analysis and policy design. Mukherjee and Giest (2020) define BITs as 'unique knowledge brokers' mediating the use of behavioural insights for policymaking, which influence the content of policy instruments, the level of political support, and their structural diversity in different political departments. Furthermore, some general lessons for behavioural public policy are proposed by shifting focus from individual behaviour to collective action and institutional, cultural, and discursive dynamics (Howlett and Leong 2022; Straßheim 2020).

Moreover, Sunstein et al. (2017) provide reports on nationally representative surveys in eight diverse countries, investigating what people actually think about nudges and nudging. The study covers Australia, Brazil, Canada, China, Japan, Russia, South Africa, and South Korea.[3] Their main conclusion is that while citizens generally approve of health and safety nudges, the different nations fall into three distinct categories: (i) a group of nations, mostly liberal democracies, where strong majorities approve of nudges if they are seen to fit with the interests and values of most citizens and do not have illicit purposes; (ii) a group of nations

[3] The South Korean government launched the proactive administration initiative in 2017 which has been widely implemented in the public sector through a behavioural approach. The South Korean administration established a new principle of protecting public officials, who practice proactive administration and of rewarding excellent results that exempts public officials from audit inspections or disciplinary actions for the results of proactive service and ensures that their achievements are rewarded through special promotion and similar measures (Kim 2022).

where overwhelming majorities approve of nearly all nudges; and (iii) a group of nations that usually show majority approval, but reduced approval rates.

Conversely, besides the potential benefits and the new tools for policymaking offered by behavioural insights, scholars, and practitioners also express criticism of applications of behavioural policies. Straßheim (2020) argues that failures and side-effects of behavioural strategies are the outcome of methodological and conceptual shortcomings of an undersocialised perspective and raises concerns over mechanisms leading to collective failures. In a similar vein, Dunlop and Radaelli (2015) identify different types of bias in the policymaking process in their study on behavioural insights applications in the impact assessment of EU policy proposals.

A recent report by the BIT (2018) suggests that elected and unelected officials are themselves influenced by the same heuristics and biases that they try to address (Hallsworth et al. 2018). Several academic scholars (Bellé et al. 2018; Bovens and Hard 2016; Sheffer et al. 2018) share a consensus on the argument about multiplicity of decision-making biases in the following way:

- Politicians and civil servants choose risky policies depending on how problems are presented (framing effects);
- Independently of their importance, certain issues and solutions are more salient than others to policy actors, leading to overreactions and the neglect of less visible but potentially more challenging problems (attention and salience);
- Professionals in governments have a tendency both to perceive and interpret evidence in line with existing views (confirmation bias);
- In groups, people tend to self-censor and conform to the group-majority view, while the arguments of other groups are rejected (group reinforcement and inter-group opposition);
- The more people are in favour of a policy, the more they assume that others have similar views (illusion of similarity);
- Decision-makers might overestimate the likelihood of future success and their ability to control outcomes (optimism bias and illusion of control).

The BIT (Hallsworth et al. 2018: 11–12) suggests strategies to overcome these biases, such as transparency about the evidence base used, the building of networks to access expert advice and insight, the assembling of teams that are cognitively diverse, or the integration of experimental trials into policy execution 'wherever possible'. And, Sunstein (2017) discusses various reasons for low effectiveness of some nudges: strong antecedent preferences on the part of choosers; successful 'counter nudges' which persuade people to choose in a different way than expected; some nudges produce confusion in the target audience; some nudges have only short-term effects; some nudges are based on an inaccurate understanding of what kinds of choice architecture will move people in particular contexts; and some nudges produce compensating behaviour, resulting in zero net effect.

Based on their extensive work experience in the UK BIT, Sanders et al. (2018) identify two clusters of issues related both to the challenges and opportunities of behavioural public policy. The first cluster concerns current challenges: the long-term effects of interventions; repeated exposure effects; problems with proxy measures; spillovers and general equilibrium effects and unintended consequences; cultural variation; 'reverse impact'; and the replication crisis. The second cluster concerns opportunities: influencing the behaviour of government itself; scaling interventions; social diffusion; and nudging organisations.

6.3 Behavioural Public Policy Vignettes in Central Asia

Two countries from Central Asia were chosen to provide examples of early behavioural interventions in different policy areas—anti-corruption and public health—introduced by the governments of Kazakhstan and Uzbekistan respectively to influence the behaviour and social norms of citizens.

Kazakhstan considers itself a leader in public administration reforms in Central Asia, having implemented civil service and anti-corruption reforms, and has demonstrated noteworthy progress in the digitalisation of public service delivery (Baimenov et al. 2022). In the aftermath of January 2022 public protests, Kazakhstan has introduced a series of policy reforms in moving towards the 'Listening State' and 'Just Kazakhstan' with a priority focus on anti-corruption (Janenova and Kurmanov 2025). Equally, the President of Uzbekistan, Shavkat

Mirziyoyev, appears committed to an ambitious agenda of economic and political reform through economic modernisation and increasing political openness. Uzbekistan has embarked on governance, anti-corruption, and economic reforms designed to strengthen the strategic positioning of the country, although facing bureaucratic resistance and slow progress of implementation (Umarova 2022).

The secondary research, which formed the substance of the vignettes, was collected in the English and Russian languages from state and international media sources, and social media outlets. Despite censorship for public criticism on the government policies in Central Asia, social media provide a valuable source of the citizen's views and opinions on selected policies. Increasingly, the use of social media presents an important research tool for scholars examining policy issues in the closed context of Central Asia (Brian et al. 2012; Freedman and Shafer 2012; Imamova 2015; Lewis 2016).

6.3.1 Kazakhstan: Anti-Corruption Messaging

Kazakhstan has introduced several anti-corruption reforms since gaining independence in 1991, and it has gradually improved its ranking in the Corruption Perception Index (CPI) by moving from 140th position in 2013 to 93rd position among 180 countries in 2023 (Transparency International 2023). Still, the Council of Europe's Group of States against Corruption (GRECO) in its 2022 report on Kazakhstan raised concerns of endemic corruption in Kazakhstan entrenched in different sectors, institutions, public and private spheres. It identified several reasons for high-level of corruption including lack of reliable information, a flawed anti-corruption framework, lack of responsiveness in policymaking, and state control of the media (GRECO 2022). In addition, the National Anti-Corruption Report identifies the most corrupt policy sectors in Kazakhstan such as construction, healthcare, education, and culture (Agency for Anti-Corruption 2023). Consequently, an anti-corruption campaign has become a key priority for the government in order to restore social justice and gain domestic and international legitimacy.

The first vignette provides an analysis of a behavioural experiment conducted by the Anti-Corruption Agency in Kazakhstan. In April 2023, an anti-corruption messaging campaign was launched as a pilot project in two regions: the capital Astana and the regional centre of South Kazakhstan—Shymkent.[4] Kazakhstani citizens received two SMS messages on their mobile phones in Kazakh and Russian languages. The first message said: "*Receiving or giving a bribe or being an intermediary in bribery is a CRIME*". The second message continued: "*REMEMBER - honest business is under the protection of the state and obstruction of legitimate business activities is a serious crime*". The words 'crime' and 'remember' were written with the use of capital letters in the original SMS messages.

The Anti-Corruption Agency made a public response in the following way:

> We tried to convey to everyone once again that taking and receiving bribes or committing other corrupt offenses is prohibited. This entails liability established by law. This is one of the pilot projects aimed at implementing awareness-raising work.[5]

The pilot project was addressed both to government officials and citizens. Telephone numbers for SMS messaging were selected randomly. This messaging campaign provoked a surge in immediate public reaction. Kazakhstani citizens shared memes through social media:

> They've been 'bombing' us since the morning! It's a sinful thing that I even began to suspect myself of something. (Facebook post, April 2023)

> It didn't come to me! I told my colleagues that decent people don't receive such SMS. (Facebook post, April 2023)

> I didn't take the bribe with me. I left it at home in a safe place. (Facebook post, April 2023)

[4] Liter.kz. Kazakhstanis are receiving warnings from the Anti-corruption Agency en masse [Предупреждения от Антикора массово получают казахстанцы], 12.04.2023. https://liter.kz/preduprezhdeniia-ot-antikora-massovo-poluchaiut-kazakhstantsy-1681287452/.

[5] Tengrinews. Kazakhstanis receive SMS warning from Anti-Corruption Agency [Казахстанцы получают SMS с предупреждением от Антикора], 12.04.2023. https://tengrinews.kz/kazakhstan_news/kazahstantsyi-poluchayut-sms-c-preduprejdeniem-ot-antikora-496220/.

Social media users suggested to the Anti-Corruption Agency to send the messages to the government officials and expressed low trust in the following way:

> Why are you sending it to everyone? You need to call the government officials and the traffic police immediately and tell them about it. You won't make a mistake with the timing, I assure you. (Facebook post, April 2023)

> You need to send these messages to each government body with capital letters! (Facebook post, April 2023)

> Civil servants have read the messages and continued 'to cut the public budget'. (Facebook post, April 2023)

In response to the public criticism the Head of the Anti-Corruption Agency gave an interview to the local media:

> Our goal is to convey to people that corruption offenses entail liability established by law. A certain goal has been achieved. The message was delivered – he [a citizen] thought about it. […] A reasonable person will note this in any case. Even if he laughed or expressed a different opinion.[6]

SMS messaging was one of behavioural policy tools used by the Anti-Corruption Agency to raise information awareness. Other examples include anti-corruption messaging through billboards on the main roads in the large cities, which also attracted mixed public reaction. One of the billboards in Almaty city said: "*Do not feed the animals. 1424 call-centre of the Anti-Cor*". Against the red coloured background of the banner, there was a shadow of a wolf opening his cleft mouth and outstretched hand. The billboard was aimed to appeal to the citizens not to feed the 'animals', i.e., corrupt officials.

Kazakhstani citizens shared memes and pictures with civil servants and policemen appearing with 'animal' faces. A group of civic activists expressed concern that the phrase 'Do not feed the animals' could be misinterpreted by some citizens directly as if the government called on

[6] Ditto.

people not to respect animals, 'our little brothers'.[7] Other examples of confusing messages communicated through anti-corruption billboards include the following text: "*Stop feeding the beast*", or "*These [prison] bars do not suit you*", "*Listen to the voice of reason, not the rustle of banknotes*", "*Do you take bribes now? Your children will give bribes later*".

Despite public criticism, the responsible government agency remained confident in implementing its anti-corruption messaging campaign. As the Deputy Head of the Anti-Corruption Department in Almaty city, Daniyar Taumurat, commented on this:

> We wanted to move away from producing standard banners, they are already losing their relevance and becoming unnoticed [...] This year we will continue to create new trends, new approaches in creating an anti-corruption culture and zero tolerance for corruption among the population [...].[8]

6.3.2 *Uzbekistan: Preventing Iodine Deficiency*

In January 2022, the Strategy for the Development of New Uzbekistan 2022–2026 was adopted focusing on seven key priorities including education, public health, and providing access to clean drinking water.[9] A public health problem which modern Uzbekistan is facing is that of iodine deficiency disorders. Iodine deficiency leads to mental impairment, stunted growth (low height-for-age), thyroid disorders, and stillbirths. Preventing iodine deficiency in Uzbekistan like in many other post-Soviet countries stopped right after the collapse of the Soviet Union (Ismailov and Rashitov 2021), but Uzbekistan has since made several attempts

[7] Press.kz. Anticorruption agency called corrupt officials of Aksu as animals [Антикор назвал коррупционеров Аксу животными], 12.07.2023. https://press.kz/novosti/zhivotnyh-ne-kormit-neobychnyj-bilbord-ot-antikora-zainteresoval-zhitelej-aksu.

[8] Zakon.kz. Listen to the voice of reason, not the rustle of banknotes: how Almaty residents are urged to fight against corruption [Слушай голос разума, а не шелест купюр: как алматинцев призывают бороться против коррупции], 27.01.2023. https://www.zakon.kz/obshestvo/6382727-slushay-golos-razuma-a-ne-shelest-kupyur-kak-almatintsev-prizyvayut-borotsya-protiv-korruptsii.html.

[9] Cabar.Asia. Development Strategy of New Uzbekistan for the period 2022–2026. Interview with Eldor Tulyakov, 14.03.2022. https://cabar.asia/en/development-strategy-of-new-uzbekistan-for-the-period-of-2022-2026-interview-with-eldor-tulyakov.

to address iodine deficiency through salt iodisation and by stimulating regular use of iodine at the national scale.

On 20 September 2023 Uzbekistan launched a national iodine campaign called '*Bright Generation*' to provide all children from three to fifteen years old with an iodine supplement free of charge.[10] Wednesday was declared 'Iodine Day' in schools and kindergartens when children were provided with the iodine supplement 'Antistrumin' produced by the local company 'Samo'. The iodine campaign was a joint initiative between several stakeholders: the Ministry of Health, the Ministry of Pre-school and School Education, the Agency for Strategic Reforms under the President of Uzbekistan, the Agency for Youth Affairs, and the Republican Scientific and Medical Centre for Endocrinology. At the launch of the iodine campaign, key stakeholders declared that:

> Our country has a high level of iodine deficiency. Children with iodine deficiency, on average, have lower levels of intellectual development and have difficulty learning new knowledge and skills. A sufficient amount of iodine in children' bodies allows them to study well and conquer new heights in school, science, and sports.[11]

A dedicated website was created to improve awareness about risks of iodine deficiency and provide information and recommendations for parents on healthy diets.[12] Meanwhile, the Uzbek national media in Uzbekistan shared videos and photos of smiling children taking their iodine supplement administered by the school staff.

A few days after the launch of the iodine campaign, over six hundred children were hospitalised with overdose symptoms across different regions of Uzbekistan.[13] Children showed symptoms of vomiting,

[10] Gazeta.uz. Child iodization programme has been launched in Uzbekistan, [В Узбекистане стартовала программа йодизации детей], 20.09.2023. https://www.gazeta.uz/ru/2023/09/20/iodine/.

[11] Gazeta.uz. Deputy Head of the Ministry for Healthcare: 450 fell sick in Namangan, 143 recovered, [450 детей заболели в Намангане, 143 выздоровели — замглавы Минздрава], 23.09.2023. https://www.gazeta.uz/ru/2023/09/23/children/.

[12] https://yodiching.uz; accessible in Uzbek only.

[13] Gazeta.uz. "We were not warned about the drug" - parents of children who fell ill after taking potassium iodide in Tashkent [«Нас не предупреждали о препарате» — родители детей, заболевших после приёма йодида калия в Ташкенте], 25.09.2023. https://www.gazeta.uz/ru/2023/09/25/antistrumin/.

abdominal pain, diarrhoea, and fever. Parents of the sick children shared posts and video messages through social media, while being confused about the reasons for mass poisoning and appealing to the government to stop the campaign.

> They gave the pill to my child at school. The next day his temperature rose, and he was sent home from school. In his class, several other children had nausea and stomach upset. Doctors said it wasn't because of the pill. (anonymous post, September 2023)

> This is a toxicology centre, but the sick leave of children who took this pill includes a diagnosis of ARVI [acute respiratory viral infection]. Parents complain: "If this is ARVI, why are our children being taken to toxicology? You put in an IV, washed the child's stomach and now write ARVI. (anonymous post, September 2023)

> Please stop giving pills to our children. We are not 'guinea pigs' for your experiments! (anonymous post, September 2023)

On 23 September 2023, the Health Ministry of Uzbekistan banned the distribution of the 'Antistrumin' supplement in schools and kindergartens and opened an investigation of the incident.[14] However, the Ministry of Health did not confirm officially that the reasons of mass poisoning were caused by the prescribed supplement. The Deputy Minister of Health, Elmira Basitkhanova, made a public statement:

> Suspicions of food or drug poisoning have not been confirmed yet. Drug poisoning can be confirmed immediately. Food poisoning can be seen through operational tests. Now our main suspicion is related to an acute respiratory viral infection.[15]

The Head of the Toxicology Unit supported the official statement of the Health Ministry and added 'food poison' as a potential cause for mass hospitalisation of children:

[14] Uzdaily.com. The Ministry of Health bans Antistrumin in schools and kindergartens after mass poisoning, 23.09.2023. https://www.uzdaily.uz/en/post/83462.

[15] Newshub.uz. Basitkhanova denied the mass poisoning of children from iodine [Баситханова опровергла массовое отравление детей от препарата йода], 23.09.2023. https://newshub.uz/archives/22032.

> We see that most children have an acute respiratory viral infection or acute intestinal infection. Analyses show that the patients were mostly food poisoned. Or there is an upset stomach in a state of anaemia or immunodeficiency.[16]

The Republican Scientific Centre for Emergency Medical Care in Tashkent city expressed a different opinion on this incident:

> More than four hundred children contacted us today. Of these, over two hundred were poisoned with iodine: these were children who attend schools and kindergartens. Whether it is Basitkhanova [Deputy Minister of Health] or someone else, we have to tell the truth, all children felt bad after taking this drug. There are also many children who were admitted sick with the flu and other acute respiratory diseases.[17]

Nodirbek Ischanov, an independent Uzbek medical doctor and the country's most popular doctor online, with a YouTube following of 3.7 million subscribers, took a different and influential view. In his video Ischanov explained that dosages of the iodine supplement, which were published by the Health Ministry, were 'colossal' and capable of triggering side-effects. His video received over 1.5 million views and over 12,000 comments by social media users. Doctor Ischanov stated in the video message[18]:

> [...] The tablet and half-tablet intakes recommended by the Ministry of Health for older and younger children equated to 1,000 and 500 milligrams of iodine, respectively. That is several times the doses recommended by the World Health Organisation. So, is this a case of overdoses, rather than problems with the medication's quality? A simple miscalculation, or perhaps a typo, scaled up to affect children across the country?

[16] Ditto.

[17] RFE/RL [Radio Free Europe/Radio Liberty]. Mass poisoning of children in Uzbekistan: What are officials hiding? [Массовое отравление детей в Узбекистане: Что скрывают чиновники?], 28.09.2023. https://rus.ozodlik.org/a/32612189.html.

[18] Ischanov, N. This is why the children were poisoned from iodine, what will happen to them now, who is to blame, why they hid it [Мана нега болалар доридан захарланди, энди уларга нима булади, кимлар айбдор, нега яширди, йод иши], 23.09.2023. https://www.youtube.com/live/mdaqFnSyE-g?si=oh8o1F3Et8h_3Yj8.

Some officials blamed 'hype on social networks' for the increased numbers of young patients visiting hospitals since the campaign against iodine deficiency began, while noting that most of the children did not require serious treatment.

This incident increased scrutiny on the supplement's manufacturer 'Samo' and how the company received the massive procurement contract. According to the investigation conducted by local journalists, the government procurement portal showed that the Health Ministry's procurement arm, O'zmedimpeks, purchased 'Anstrumin' in two batches of over 3.5 million boxes in total, securing the medication at a price of 5500 soms per box in 2022 (US$ 0.45) and 6600 soms per box (US$ 0.54) in 2023 from the 'Samo' company, the only bidder for the contract. Yet, Anstrumin was available from several online pharmacies in the country during this period at a retail price of around 3000 soms per box.[19]

In response to the public concerns over transparency of the procurement contract, the Health Minister of Uzbekistan, Amrillo Inoyatov denied that 'Anstrumin' was available for a cheaper price, at a press conference[20]:

> There are petty, empty conversations circulating on the Internet... No matter what happens, these people will check and give the answer themselves. Don't go too deep into this topic. There are organisations that do this. They study everything openly. [Messages] on social networks that in pharmacies [the price of the drug] is three times lower were published incorrectly and provocatively.

During these critical circumstances, the pharmaceutical company 'Samo' remained silent and avoided any public statements. In November 2023, the Health Minister of Uzbekistan—under pressure of public criticism and on-going investigations by local journalists—acknowledged that

[19] RFE/RL, [Radio Free Europe/Radio Liberty]. Uzbek children's poisonings add to graft concerns triggered by cough-syrup deaths, 27.09.2023. https://www.rferl.org/a/uzbekistan-health-crisis-children-corruption/32613136.html.

[20] Anhor.uz. The Minister of Health advised journalists "not to go deeper" into the topic of "Antistrumin" [Министр здравоохранения посоветовал журналистам «не углубляться» в тему с «Антиструмином»], 27.09.2023. https://anhor.uz/news/antistrumin-inoyatov/.

poisoning of children was caused by an overdose of the iodine supplement 'Antistrumin'.[21]

This is the second case of children mass poisoning with drugs in Uzbekistan which took place within one year. In January 2023, 20 cases of children deaths were recorded in Uzbekistan (and forty-five children's deaths unreported for unknown reasons) after taking the cough syrup 'Doc-1 Max' produced in India.[22] All children developed renal failure. Ethylene glycol, a toxic substance, was found in a batch of this drug in a volume that was three hundred times higher than the norm. The World Health Organization (WHO) warned against the use of Indian cough syrup for children that were linked to deaths in Uzbekistan.[23] A number of Uzbek officials were accused of accepting a bribe of more than US$ 33,000 from the Indian company to get around mandatory testing.[24]

6.4 Discussion

The two examples—anti-corruption messaging in Kazakhstan and preventing iodine deficiency in Uzbekistan—represent early attempts of behavioural interventions introduced by two Central Asian governments with a purpose to influence the behaviour and social norms of citizens in offering/accepting a bribe in the first case and improving iodine level among children in the second case. Neither of these examples can be considered as 'nudges' following the Western methodology, nor they have been stipulated in the legislative framework as 'behavioural'. Yet, it is important to analyse these early interventions by the post-Soviet governments to reflect critically on potential challenges and ethical

[21] Gazeta.uz. Health Minister of Uzbekistan: "Antistrumin poisoning was 100% caused by an overdose" [«Отравление "Антиструмином» на 100% было вызвано передозировкой» — министр здравоохранения Узбекистана], 15.11.2023. https://www.gazeta.uz/ru/2023/11/15/antistrumin/.

[22] BBC. Biotech: India cancels licence of drug maker linked to child deaths in Uzbekistan, 23.03.2023. https://www.bbc.co.uk/news/world-asia-india-65048188.

[23] WHO urges action to protect children from contaminated medicines, 23.01.2023. https://www.who.int/news/item/23-01-2023-who-urges-action-to-protect-children-from-contaminated-medicines.

[24] Reuters. Uzbek court sentences 23 over contaminated cough syrup deaths, 26.02.2024. https://www.reuters.com/world/asia-pacific/uzbek-court-sentences-23-over-contaminated-cough-syrup-deaths-2024-02-26/.

considerations related to the implementation of behavioural public policy in the wider context of the Eurasian space.

Design and implementation of 'behavioural style' policies in Central Asia is quite different from liberal democracies. There are several challenges which are specific to the public administration context of this region. First, collaboration between science and government bodies is under-developed and weak. In most cases, policymakers in Central Asia design and approve policies without analysing research evidence and conducting trial experiments. Policymakers in Central Asia tend to rely on a narrow circle of advisers and government officials whose personal loyalty is valued more than their professionalism and competencies (Knox and Janenova 2023b; O'Connor et al. 2021). As a result, policies are designed on the basis of prior experience and on the subjective, and often biased, assumptions of politicians and civil servants, while neglecting evidence and views of local researchers and experts in the relevant field. Even in cases where government agencies in Central Asia collaborate with think tanks—which most often rely on state funding—these organisations have the tendency to provide supportive evidence required for justifying political decisions.

The anti-corruption messaging and iodine campaign were aimed at bringing positive changes, specifically to improve awareness of corruption risks and to prevent iodine deficiency among children. However, the devil is in the implementation process. In both cases, government bodies in both Kazakhstan and Uzbekistan followed traditional patterns of decision-making in a closed context characterised by lack of consultation with researchers; lack of pilot trials; reliance on biased views of team members who surround policymakers and express their personal loyalty rather than service to the public. In Kazakhstan, the anti-corruption messaging was not systematically tested before its launch on a national scale and it subsequently backfired as it received a negative public reaction. In Uzbekistan reputable medical organisations engaged in the policy design, however, there were no mention of pilot trials of the iodine supplement before administering it on a country-wide scale.

Furthermore, policymakers and government officials in Central Asia lack policy communication skills and tend to shift blame to the 'scapegoats' to avoid public criticism (Nair et al. 2019). In Kazakhstan citizens received confusing anti-corruption messages with no follow-up clear communication. In Uzbekistan multiple stakeholders provided conflicting messages about the reasons for mass poisoning of children, which created a conducive environment for speculation and rumours to be floating around. Senior government officials in both countries attempted to shift blame on social media reaction. Social media in Central Asia, while offering an alternative voice for citizens, is used in malign ways to reinforce control of political officials and to seek international public approbation that closed regimes are becoming more open, transparent, and accountable (Knox and Janenova 2020). In sum, the two vignettes demonstrate low public confidence in the government actions. These early attempts of behavioural interventions backfired with mixed public reaction and unintended results. Concerns can be raised regarding weak bureaucratic capacity in Central Asia in using research evidence in the policymaking.

There is growing concern in the academic literature that anti-corruption awareness-raising efforts may be backfiring instead of encouraging citizens to resist corruption. For example, Cheeseman and Peiffer (2022) found in their study in Lagos, Nigeria that exposure to anti-corruption messages largely fails to discourage the decision to bribe, and in some cases, it makes individuals more willing to pay a bribe. An experiment implemented by Kobis et al. (2019) in South Africa also found that anti-corruption messaging did not influence willingness to bribe. In a survey experiment with over 4000 respondents in Costa Rica, Corbacho et al. (2016) concluded that participants exposed to a message that a growing number of Costa Ricans were practicing corruption were more likely to say they would be willing to bribe a police officer.

Iodine deficiency among children in the low-income countries presents serious public health problems. There is research evidence that iodine supplementation improved perceptual reasoning in mildly iodine-deficient children and that mild iodine deficiency could prevent children from attaining their full intellectual potential (Gordon et al. 2009). In the Western context, introducing public health nudges, such as iodine supplement, are based on the evidence gathered through randomised control trials and rigorous experiments. The governments in Central Asia need to strengthen local research capacity and improve transparency in the state procurement processes in order to introduce public health nudges safely and effectively.

Despite many benefits of behavioural public policy, the potential dangers of an unethical use of behavioural science have contributed to concerns and questions about its use, ranging from accusations of excessive paternalism to suspicions of disguised manipulation (Barton and Grüne-Yanoff 2015; Costa and Halpern 2019; Thaler and Sunstein 2008). A central tenet in the political and ethical criticism has been the claim that nudging works by "manipulating people's choices" (Bovens 2009). Another key criticism is that nudging encourages the abuse of power by technocrats (Farrell and Shalizi 2011; Hansen and Jespersen 2013) and that nudging impairs citizens' autonomy and human ability to make moral choices for themselves (Bovens 2009). These concerns would be of particular relevance to the policymakers operating in a closed context.

In a study on nationally representative surveys in five countries (Belgium, Denmark, Germany, South Korea, and the US), Sunstein and Reisch (2019) investigate whether people in these countries approve of a list of fifteen nudges regarding health, environment, and safety issues. This study confirms correlation between trust in public institutions and approval of nudges. It is important for the governments in the Eurasia not only to ensure effectiveness of behavioural policies, but also to develop them transparently and openly, and with an opportunity for researchers and independent experts to engage and to express their concerns.

Howlett and Leong (2022) argue that policymakers and scholars must be more prepared for wrong answers in the behavioural turn, or that there are no right ones, in their research and practices and build into policies the means to learn and correct mistakes. In order to embrace behavioural insights, the governments in the post-Soviet Eurasia region would need to change themselves first: change the punitive nature of the public sector environment for mistakes and errors; improve public trust; engage actively with local researchers; and design policies based on research evidence.

6.5 Concluding Remarks

Behavioural public policy potentially offers new opportunities to improve effectiveness of public service provision for the governments in the post-Soviet Eurasia. First, behavioural policies can lead to development of an evidence-based policymaking in this region. Evidence orientation in public policy would help in separating effective from ineffective policies based on trial experiments. Second, nudges would potentially provide freedom of choice for businesses and citizens as they significantly change economic incentives. Freedom of choice is particularly important in a closed context where citizens experience many legal restrictions and fines, so the public would be more likely to accept 'good' nudges. Third, behavioural public policy would stimulate inter-disciplinary collaboration between universities, research think tanks, and government bodies. In order to design effective nudges and conduct experiments, researchers and government officials would need to develop local capacity, acquire new skills, and learn to collaborate across professional and organisational boundaries. To summarise, behavioural public policy offers to the Eurasia region the promise of cost-effective, evidence-driven, freedom-preserving, and comparatively popular policies.

The challenges associated with application of behavioural insights in the post-Soviet Eurasia context are closely inter-related with long-term challenges present in the public sector including inadequate bureaucratic capacity, weak collaboration among government agencies and local universities, lack of evidence-based policymaking, limited transparency and public accountability, and ethical considerations. Transfer of behavioural insights which have been successful in the Western democratic context to the post-Soviet region would require careful consideration of the context-specific culture, structure, and ethical norms of public administration system in the Eurasia.

Behavioural public policy is an Anglo-American phenomenon (John 2019) and our literature review has shown that there is path dependence in the diffusion of nudges by the Anglo–American democracies. There is a strong international appeal of behavioural insights to the countries outside the OECD including Central Asian states, as illustrated in this chapter. Behavioural public policy would be attractive for the post-Soviet region as it offers enhancement to the efficiency of policies and evidence-based policymaking, while not challenging the political system. With the growing interest towards nudges and speed of global policy transfer, behavioural public policy is likely to develop in the post-Soviet countries in the coming years.

Acknowledgements An earlier draft of this chapter was presented at the Astana Civil Service Hub Panels during an international conference organised by the Academy of Public Administration under the President of Kazakhstan (Astana, 17–19 May 2023), and at the 31st NISPAcee conference at Caucasus University (Tbilisi, 23–24 May 2024). I thank the organisers of the respective conference panels and their participants for their valuable feedback.

References

Agency for Anti-Corruption of the Republic of Kazakhstan. 2023. National Anti-Corruption Report 2022. https://www.gov.kz/memleket/entities/anticorruption/documents/details/494573?lang=en

Astana Civil Service Hub. 2023. Behavioural public policy: New opportunities and challenges for Kazakhstan and the Eurasia region. UNDP/Astana Civil Service Hub. https://www.astanacivilservicehub.org/uploads/journal_archives/20230808_BPP.pdf

Baggio, M., E. Ciriolo, G. Marandola, and René van Bavel. 2021. The evolution of behaviourally informed policy making in the EU. *Journal of European Public Policy* 28 (5): 658–676. https://doi.org/10.1080/13501763.2021.1912145

Baimenov, A., M. Uteshev, and G. Suleimenova. 2022. Kazakhstan: Progress and its paradoxes. In *Public Service Evolution in the 15 Post-Soviet Countries*, ed. A. Baimenov and P. Liverakos, 199–249. Singapore: Palgrave Macmillan.

Barton, A., and T. Grüne-Yanoff. 2015. From libertarian paternalism to nudging - and beyond. *Review of Philosophy and Psychology* 6 (3): 341–359.

Bellé, N., P. Cantarelli, and P. Belardinelli. 2018. Prospect theory goes public: Experimental evidence on cognitive biases in public policy and management decisions. *Public Administration Review* 78 (6): 828–840. https://doi.org/10.1111/puar.12960.

Bovens, L. 2009. The ethics of nudge. In *Preference change: Approaches from philosophy, economics and psychology*, ed. Mats J. Hansson and Till Grüne-Yanoff, 207–220. Theory and Decision Library A. Dordrecht: Springer.

Bovens, L., and P. Hard. 2016. Revisiting the study of policy failures. *Journal of European Public Policy* 23 (5): 653–666. https://doi.org/10.1080/13501763.2015.1127273

Brian, B., F. Eric, and B. Robin. 2012. Social media, cyber-dissent, and constraints on online political communication in Central Asia. *Central Asia and the Caucasus* 13 (1): 144–152.

Cheeseman, N., and C. Peiffer. 2022. The curse of good intentions: Why anticorruption messaging can encourage bribery. *American Political Science Review* 116 (3): 1081–1095. https://doi.org/10.1017/S0003055421001398

Corbacho, A., D. Gingerich, V. Oliveros, and M. Ruiz-Vega. 2016. Corruption as a self-fulfilling prophecy: Evidence from a survey experiment in Costa Rica. *American Journal of Political Science* 60 (4): 1077–1092. https://doi.org/10.1111/ajps.12244.

Costa, E., and D. Halpern. 2019. The behavioural science of online harm and manipulation, and what to do about it. The Behavioural Insights Team. https://www.bi.team/wp-content/uploads/2019/04/BIT_The-behavioural-science-of-online-harm-and-manipulation-and-what-to-do-about-it_Single.pdf.

Della Vigna, S., and E. Linos. 2022. RCTs to scale: Comprehensive evidence from two nudge units. *Econometrica* 90 (1): 81–116. https://doi.org/10.3982/ECTA18709.

Dunlop, C.A., and C.M. Radaelli. 2015. *Overcoming illusions of control: How to nudge and teach regulatory humility*. Bloomsbury.

Farrell, H., and C. Shalizi. 2011. 'Nudge policies' are another name for coercion, *New Scientist*, 2 November. https://www.newscientist.com/article/mg21228376-500-nudge-policies-are-another-name-for-coercion/

Freedman, E., and R. Shafer. 2012. Advancing a comprehensive research agenda for Central Asian mass media. *Media Asia* 39 (3): 119–126. https://doi.org/10.1080/01296612.2012.11689927.

Gopalan, M., and M.A. Pirog. 2017. Applying behavioral insights in policy analysis: Recent trends in the United States. *Policy Studies Journal* 45 (S1): S82–S114. https://doi.org/10.1111/psj.12202.

Gordon, R.C., M.C. Rose, S.A. Skeaff, A.R. Gray, K.M. Morgan, and T. Ruffman. 2009. Iodine supplementation improves cognition in mildly iodine-deficient children. *The American Journal of Clinical Nutrition* 90 (5): 1264–1271. https://doi.org/10.3945/ajcn.2009.28145.

GRECO. 2022. Evaluation report on Kazakhstan. https://rm.coe.int/joint-first-and-second-evaluation-rounds-evaluation-report-on-kazakhst/1680a6e276.

Hallsworth, M., M. Egan, J. Rutter, and J. McCrae. 2018. Behavioural government: Using behavioural science to improve how governments make decisions. The Behavioural Insights Team. https://wiki.gccollab.ca/images/3/3e/BIT-Behavioural-Government-Report-2018.pdf.

Halpern, D. 2016. *Inside the nudge unit: How small changes can make a big difference*. London: Random House.

Hansen, P., and A. Jespersen. 2013. Nudge and the manipulation of choice: A framework for the responsible use of the nudge approach to behaviour change in public policy. *European Journal of Risk Regulation* 4 (1): 3–28. https://doi.org/10.1017/S1867299X00002762.

Howlett, M., and C. Leong. 2022. What is behavioral in policy studies? How far has the discipline moved beyond traditional utilitarianism? *Journal of Behavioral Public Administration* 5 (1). https://doi.org/10.30636/jbpa.51.292.

Imamova, N. 2015. Social media and online public debate in Central Asia: A journalist's perspective. *Demokratizatsiya: The Journal of Post-Soviet Democratization* 23 (3): 359–376.

Ismailov, S., and M. Rashitov. 2021. Results of epidemiological studies on the prevalence of iodine deficiency disorders in the Republic of Uzbekistan. *International Journal of Endocrinology* 13 (3): 197–201.

Janenova, S., and B. Kurmanov. 2025. Open government in Central Asia: towards a more accountable and participatory government?. In *Research*

Handbook of Open Government, ed. M. Gasco-Hernandez, A. Prasad, R. Gil-Garcia, and T. Pardo. Edward Elgar, 193–205, https://doi.org/10.4337/9781035301652.00021

John, P. 2019. The international appeal of behavioural public policy: Is nudge an Anglo-American phenomenon? *Journal of Chinese Governance* 4 (2): 144–162. https://doi.org/10.1080/23812346.2019.1576264.

Kim, P.S. 2022. A behavioural approach to administrative reform: A case study of promoting proactive administration in South Korea. *Public Administration and Policy: An Asia-Pacific Journal* 25 (3): 310–322. https://doi.org/10.1108/PAP-08-2022-0093.

Knox, C., and S. Janenova. 2020. Depicting public servants in authoritarian regimes. In *The Palgrave handbook of the public servant*, ed. H. Sullivan, H. Dickinson, and H. Henderson, 1411–1428. Cham: Palgrave Macmillan.

Knox, C., and S. Janenova. 2023a. Does bureaucratic performance vary across authoritarian regimes? *Asia Pacific Journal of Public Administration* 45 (1): 16–36. https://doi.org/10.1080/23276665.2022.2026794.

Knox, C., and S. Janenova. 2023b. Party patronage in Kazakhstan. In *Political patronage in Asian bureaucracies*, ed. B.G. Peters, C. Knox, and B.S. Kim, 260–287. Cambridge University Press. https://doi.org/10.1017/9781009208055.014.

Kobis, N., M. Troost, C. Brandt, and I. Soraperra. 2019. Social norms of corruption in the field: Social nudges on posters can help to reduce bribery. *Behavioural Public Policy* (December): 1–28. https://doi.org/10.1017/bpp.2019.37.

Lewis, D. 2016. Central Asia: Contested peace. In *The Palgrave handbook of disciplinary and regional approaches to peace*, 387–397. London: Palgrave Macmillan.

Mukherjee, I., and S. Giest. 2020. Behavioural Insights Teams (BITs) and policy change: An exploration of impact, location, and temporality of policy advice. *Administration & Society* 52 (10): 1538–1561. https://doi.org/10.1177/0095399720918315.

O'Connor, K., C. Knox, and S. Janenova. 2021. Bureaucrats, authoritarianism, and role conceptions. *Review of Public Personnel Administration* 41 (2): 358–383. https://doi.org/10.1177/0734371X19888009.

OECD. 2019. *Delivering better policies through behavioural insights: New approaches*. Paris: OECD Publishing. https://doi.org/10.1787/6c9291e2-en.

Nair, B., S. Janenova, and B. Serikbayeva. 2019. *A primer on policy communication in Kazakhstan*. Singapore: Springer Nature.

Sanders, M., V. Snijders, and M. Hallsworth. 2018. Behavioural science and policy: Where are we now and where are we going? *Behavioural Public Policy* 2 (2): 144–167.

Sheffer, L., P. Loewen, S. Soroka, S. Walgrave, and T. Shaefer. 2018. Select nonrepresentative representatives: An experimental study of the decision making of elected politicians. *American Political Science Review* 112 (2): 302–321. https://doi.org/10.1017/S0003055417000569.

Straßheim, H. 2020. The rise and spread of behavioural public policy: An opportunity for critical research and self-reflection. *International Review of Public Policy* 2: 1. https://doi.org/10.4000/irpp.897.

Straßheim, H., and S. Beck. 2019. *Handbook of Behavioural Change and Public Policy*. Cheltenham: Edward Elgar.

Sunstein, C.R. 2017. Nudges that fail. *Behavioural Public Policy* 1 (1): 4–25.

Sunstein, C.R., and L.A. Reisch. 2019. *Trusting nudges: Toward a bill of rights for nudging*. Abingdon: Routledge.

Sunstein, C.R., L.A. Reisch and J. Rauber. 2017. Behavioral Insights All Over the World? Public Attitudes Toward Nudging in a Multi-Country Study. Available at SSRN, https://doi.org/10.2139/ssrn.2921217.

Thaler, R.H., and C.R. Sunstein. 2008. *Nudge: Improving decisions about health, wealth, and happiness*. New Haven, CT: Yale University Press.

Transparency International. 2023. Corruption Perception Index for Kazakhstan. https://www.transparency.org/en/countries/kazakhstan.

Umarova, A. 2022. Uzbekistan: Long awaited transformation of civil service—Paradigm shift or hot air? In *Public service evolution in the 15 post-Soviet countries: Diversity in transformation*, ed. A. Baimenov and P. Liverakos, 549–572. Singapore: Palgrave Macmillan.

Whitehead, M., R. Jones, R. Howell, R. Lilley, and J. Pykett. 2014. *Nudging all over the world*. ESRC Report. Swindon and Edinburgh: Economic and Social Research Council.

CHAPTER 7

The Future of Work and the Gig Economy: Implications for the Public Sector

Guido Bertucci

7.1 Introduction

During the past five years the labour market in many countries has witnessed dramatic changes, these changes were fuelled by a number of factors. First, the speed of technological advancements, including the more general introduction of artificial intelligence (AI) which has revolutionised the job profiles and the type of jobs available. Second, the entry into the market of younger generations of workers, in particular, generation Z.[1] These workers aspire to more flexible work arrangements, including working hours and a better work-life balance. Third, the *"quiet quitting"* phenomenon, particularly on the part of younger workers seeking the flexibility mentioned above. The term which first was used in Tik Tok describes the attitude of workers who choose to do the bare minimum on their job and do not wish to work above and

[1] People born between 1997 and 2012.

G. Bertucci (✉)
Governance Solutions International, New York, NY, USA
e-mail: guido.bertucci@govsolutionsint.org

A. Baimenov and P. Liverakos (eds.), *Public Administration in the New Reality*, https://doi.org/10.1007/978-981-96-3845-1_7

beyond that minimum. Fourth, the COVID-19 pandemic which forced employers to generalise remote work and which, after the end of the pandemic, morphed into the hybrid work modalities. And fifth, the "*great resignation*" phenomenon which started with the COVID-19 pandemic, but was also prompted by some other reasons, among which are low pay, lack of flexibility in the work arrangements and limited possibility of advancement.

"*For people around the world, the past three years have been filled with upheaval and uncertainty for their lives and livelihoods, with COVID-19, geopolitical and economic shifts, and the rapid advancement of AI and other technologies now risks adding more uncertainty*" said Saadia Zahidi, Managing Director of the World Economic Forum. "*The good news is that there is a clear way forward to ensure resilience. Governments and businesses must invest in supporting the shift to the jobs of the future through the education, re-skilling and social support structures that can ensure individuals are at the heart of the future of work*".[2]

According to a March 2022 Pew Poll, in the U.S. during 2021 53% of employed adults quit or changed their job. A substantial percentage were people between 18 and 30 years old. The growth of the gig economy and of gig work through online platforms which now employ growing numbers of workers.[3]

This chapter endeavours to highlight how the labour market is developing by analysing what type of jobs will be available in the near future, what the labour market has to offer and the attitude of potential employees towards work, including towards the new work modalities. The skill revolution and the challenge of re-skilling will also be reviewed in the chapter, as well as the effects of the gig economy and of the gig work on the labour market and what the consequences and challenges from the policy and management perspective are. Moreover, how Governments are being affected by all the change factors mentioned above will be highlighted, and some measures will be suggested for them to remain relevant in the job market.

[2] https://www.weforum.org/publications/the-future-of-jobs-report-2023/.

[3] https://www.pewresearch.org/short-reads/2022/03/09/majority-of-workers-who-quit-a-job-in-2021-cite-low-pay-no-opportunities-for-advancement-feeling-disrespected/.

7.2 Job Trends

Rapid advances in science and technology as well as shifting priorities in business and in society are changing the type of jobs that will be available in the near future. With the emergence of new jobs, the need for several types of occupations will also be diminishing or altogether disappearing. According to the publication of the World Economic Forum "*The Future of Jobs Report 2023*", quoted above, approximately 23% of jobs are expected to change by 2027. According to the estimates of the 803 companies surveyed for the report, employers anticipate sixty-nine million new jobs to be created and eighty-three million eliminated.

The same report indicates that the advancement in technology and in digitalisation, particularly in the field of big data, cloud computing, artificial intelligence, machine learning and cyber security will be responsible for the fastest job creation. Technology however will contribute to the decline of a number of current jobs, particularly clerical and secretarial. The report also highlights that jobs relating to sustainable growth, environmental protection and green and renewable energy will also be growing. Education and health are other areas in which jobs are expected to grow.

The White Paper "*The Rise of Global Digital Jobs*", published in January 2024 by the World Economic Forum, analyses the extent of the growth of digital jobs and incorporates in the list not only technology-related jobs, but also jobs in different fields that can be performed digitally or remotely.[4] The report estimates that digital jobs will grow from 73 million in 2024 to 92 million in 2030 and that 59% of them will come with higher wages.

The list of digital jobs that could pay higher wages include not only those in the area of technology such as software developers, information security analysts, network and computer systems administrators, operations research analysts, computer science teacher and telecommunication managers but also jobs in other areas that can be performed digitally such as financial advisors, financial managers, lawyers, marketing specialists, accountants and auditors, medical and health services managers.

More specifically, research shows that artificial intelligence (AI) will have a strong impact on jobs. The report "*PwC's 2024 AI Jobs Barometer*", published in May 2024 by Price Waterhouse Cooper analyses how

[4] https://www.weforum.org/publications/the-rise-of-global-digital-jobs/.

AI will affect jobs, skills, wages and productivity and concludes that jobs that require AI specialist skills will grow three and a half times faster than all jobs. These jobs will in some sectors pay 25% higher salaries.[5]

7.3 Workers

In addition to the jobs available, the potential workforce is also changing dramatically. Independent workers are becoming a significant share of the workforce as changing work modalities, and the effects of the gig economy are affecting the availability and the attitude towards work of potential workers.

7.3.1 The New Work Modalities

The COVID-19 pandemic has revolutionised the way employees work by forcing employers to expand dramatically remote work and to introduce new working modalities. The receding of the pandemic has slowly brought back employees to the office, but remote work has become an integral part of the working conditions both in the private and in the public sector. In this context, an overly complex tag of war has developed between employers anxious to have workers return to the office and employees reluctant to do so. For example, the United States Federal Government has been struggling to make staff return to work and so has the United Nations Secretariat. As an acceptable compromise solution, the concept of hybrid work, a blend of office and remote work, has been accepted by a large number of employers and generally welcomed by employees.

The *American Opportunity Survey,* published by McKinsey in June 2022, indicated that a majority of employees surveyed, 58%, mentioned that they welcomed the opportunity to work remotely the whole week or part of the week.[6] Twenty-five percent responded that they could work full time remotely and 23% in that they could work remotely on a partial basis. Hybrid work arrangements are also common in many occupations, with high percentages in the areas of education (50%) and health

[5] https://www.pwc.com/gx/en/issues/artificial-intelligence/ai-jobs-barometer.html.

[6] https://www.mckinsey.com/industries/real-estate/our-insights/americans-are-embracing-flexible-work-and-they-want-more-of-it.

(45%). The Survey also highlighted the fact that younger workers are more inclined to choose remote work than older ones and that 77% of workers in computer-related areas are interested in working remotely.

It seems logical to assume that, unless the public sector is able to offer its employees the hybrid work opportunity, it may not be able to recruit staff and/or retain existing staff. Many agencies in the Federal Administration are developing hybrid work arrangements for their employees under the guidance of the Office for Personnel Management (OPM).[7] On the other hand, however, the United States House of Representatives does not seem to be aware of the changing work environment and keeps questioning the Administration's policy on hybrid and remote work, pressing for total return to work in-person for all federal employees.[8]

The hybrid work modality has revolutionised the concept of "workplace" since this term now means "anywhere the employee works". Workers do not have to work from their office device but can use any device at their disposal. This creates flexibility for the workers but challenges for organisation in which they work due to the need to safeguard confidential and personal data and to ensure cybersecurity.

7.3.2 *Management and Leadership Challenges*

The hybrid work modality presents a number of challenges for management and leadership. First of all, managing a hybrid workforce requires the development of a new management approach which includes in-person and remote guidance and supervision. Consequently, new leadership capabilities would be required. Furthermore, as established work processes and protocols are being disrupted; new ones need to be instituted.

Another challenge is that of developing new criteria for monitoring productivity and compliance on the part of the employees. When employees are not always in the office, it may be difficult to motivate them and to instil a culture of engagement and ownership in the organisation.

[7] https://www.opm.gov/policy-data-oversight/future-of-the-workforce/hybrid-work-environment-toolkit/.

[8] https://www.govexec.com/workforce/2024/04/omb-leader-defends-administrations-approach-telework/396206/

Jacob Morgan, in his blog, stressed the importance of in-person work since its boosts morale, helps to build networks and encourages collaboration.[9] While remote work brings flexibility, it can also generate mental strain and loneliness. In addition, socialising in the office can improve the morale and create opportunity for career development. This is especially important for newly recruited staff or for those early in their career who need in person connections to build their skills. Finally, he stressed that in person-work promotes a healthy environment for collaboration and sharing of ideas.

I will add that for all organisations to be successful, it is important that employees share in and contribute to the development of the organisational culture, and this is best facilitated by in-person presence in the office. The Unites States Surgeon General, in his recently issued "Framework for Workplace Mental Health and Wellbeing", advised federal agencies to better promote workplace social connections to counter the feelings of isolation that telework may induce.[10]

It is clear that the hybrid work modality cannot be eliminated. The challenge for companies and agencies is to find the right balance between remote work and work in the office that on the one hand ensures productivity and on the other gives flexibility to the employees. Different jobs also require a different approach to the issue, as not every position is suitable for hybrid work.

Customisation of work arrangements and of responsibilities therefore is emerging as a trend that goes hand-in-hand with hybrid work. The latest guidelines issued by the United States Office for Personnel Management (OPM) seem to lead in this direction stating that "*Certain work arrangements may not make sense for every agency, function or team, or be appropriate for every position or individual*".[11]

[9] https://greatleadership.substack.com/p/virtual-work-office-in-person (10.05.2023).

[10] https://www.hhs.gov/surgeongeneral/priorities/workplace-well-being/index.html.

[11] https://federalnewsnetwork.com/workforce/2024/08/federal-remote-work-posture-should-not-be-one-size-fits-all-opm-says/.

7.4 The Effects of the Gig Economy

The advent of the gig economy and the related spreading of gig work modalities has enormously affected the nature of work and the attitude of people towards work. According to the Merriam Webster Dictionary, *the gig economy* is "economic activity that involves the use of temporary or freelance workers to perform jobs typically in the service sector". According to the same dictionary a *gig worker is* "a person who works temporary jobs typically in the service sector as an independent contractor or freelancer: a worker in the gig economy".

While the gig economy has been growing for the past 20 years, the COVID-19 pandemic has generated an exponential growth of the phenomenon. *Team stage* summarised in a blog entitled "Gig Economy Statistics: Demographics and Trends in 2024" several gig economy statistics and surveys conducted by a number of organisations.[12] The statistics show that the size of the global gig economy is estimated at USD 3.7 trillion. In the US, the gig economy expands three times faster than the entire US work force. Almost 36% of the workers, or 57.3 million are in the gig economy. It is estimated that 50% of the US workforce will participate in the gig economy by 2027. People aged 18–34 make up 38% of the workers in the gig economy. The proportion of male and female workers is almost equal 52 versus 48%.

The ability to choose working hours and thus devise their own work schedule, the flexible working arrangements, the better balance between work and life and the ability to earn extra income are the main reasons why people choose gig work. Eighty-one percent of independent workers do it by choice; 77% of freelancers work independently in order to be their own boss; 82% are happy to be working on their own; and 53% would not return to traditional jobs. It is also interesting to learn that one in six workers employed in traditional jobs would like to work independently. While most gig workers are employed in a number of sectors, such as the service sector, health, education, trade and manufacturing, it is quite surprising to lean that 14% of the gig economy workers in the U.S. are in the public sector.

The gig economy is spreading globally and the platforms which employ a large number of gig workers are growing in all regions. The *360 Research Report "Gig Economy Market Size in 2023: Share, Latest Trends*

[12] https://teamstage.io/gig-economy-statistics/.

and Forecast 2023 to 2030" enumerates the regions and countries where the gig economy is growing. In North America is growing rapidly in the United States, Canada and Mexico; in Europe in Germany, UK, France, Italy, Russia and Turkey; in Asia and the Pacific in China, Japan, Korea, India, Australia, Indonesia, Thailand, Philippines, Malaysia and Vietnam; in South America in Brazil, Argentina, Columbia; and in the Middle East and Africa in Saudi Arabia, UAE, Egypt, Nigeria and South Africa.[13] However, it also appears that gig work is not only a developed country phenomenon, but it is also becoming a popular source of employment in developing countries.

This is highlighted in the World Bank report "*Working Without Borders*" published in 2023.[14] The report identified 545 online gig work platforms worldwide with workers and customers located in 186 countries. Forty percent of traffic to gig platforms comes from low- and middle-income countries. The data collected by the World Bank reveal that the demand for gig workers has increased in developing countries at a faster rate than in developed countries. One of the explanations for the growth is that gig work provides access to work to young people, women and low-skilled workers in those countries. The report concludes that gig work in developing countries is very much similar to the work in the informal economy, a traditional arrangement in many developing countries.

Governments should capitalise on the opportunity provided by the growth of the gig economy by expanding internet access, enhancing training, particularly in digital skills, and addressing the shortcomings of gig work such as lack of social protection and collective bargaining power.

Despite the positive aspects of gig work such as flexibility, ability to be your own boss and better life-work balance, gig work comes with a number of drawbacks, some of which have been alluded above. They range from non-guaranteed pay, lack of legal protection, limited benefits, limited job security, limited collective bargaining power and uncertainty. On this last point, 2023 research by Zippia reports that 45% of people

[13] Data in this report show how pervasive is the gig work phenomenon. https://www.linkedin.com/pulse/gig-economy-platforms-market-size-research-report-2023-2030-rnape/.

[14] https://www.worldbank.org/en/topic/jobsanddevelopment/publication/online-gig-work-enabled-by-digital-platforms.

in the U.S. for whom gig work was the primary source of income experienced high job anxiety and 28% felt financially insecure.[15] Conversely, only 24% of those holding traditional employment experienced high job anxiety and 20% felt financially insecure.

7.4.1 Policy and Management Challenges

It is evident from the above discussion that the gig economy and the related gig work poses a number of policy and management challenges. Both the World Bank in the report quoted above and the OECD in the report *"Policy Responses to New Forms of Work"* review these challenges.[16] One of the challenges is to determine what is the nature of work being performed by the gig workers and what is their status. Are they employees of a platform or of a client; are they self-employed, independent contractors, entrepreneurs, or service providers? The World Bank Reports indicates that countries around the world give a wide range of treatments in this respect.

Another challenge is to determine what kind of protection should be given to gig workers, in particular, what kind of benefits should gig workers receive, such as medical insurance, unemployment insurance or social security without stifling innovation on the part of the platforms. Access to collective bargaining is a basic right of workers in many countries, but what access should be given to gig workers is a challenge, countries are grappling with. Dealing with these challenges is very much connected with the overarching issue of how to deal with the regulation of platforms.

In order to answer these pressing policy questions, it is essential that countries develop a comprehensive policy framework with respect to gig workers. The OECD report made a number of recommendations which such policy framework should contain. Above all they should determine the correct classification of gig workers to ensure that workers have access to labour rights and social protection. In this connexion, social protection systems should be reviewed and, where necessary, reformed to facilitate access to benefits for gig workers. Countries should also aim to

[15] https://www.zippia.com/advice/gig-economy-statistics/.

[16] https://www.oecd.org/employment/policy-responses-to-new-forms-of-work-0763f1b7-en.htm.

minimise the misclassification of employment in order to avoid tax and social contribution liabilities. The OECD also recommends that all countries should devote greater efforts to ensure adequate working conditions of gig workers, including the number of hours worked.

As governments departments and agencies are also utilising gig workers, countries should consider adapting public employment systems to incorporate new forms of work. While policy actions are being taken by countries to deal with these issues, a careful balance has to be struck between the need to regulate the gig economy and gig work and the need not to discourage the platforms to continue operating. As an example of such regulation, the U.S. Department of Labor (DOL) has introduced new worker classifications to determine which workers should be considered employees and receive employee benefits and protections. The new rule went into effect on 11 March 2024.[17]

In addition, the U.S. Internal Revenue Service (IRS) has established a dedicated site to guide the taxation of gig workers containing also an extensive list of some of the activities that fall in the category, namely: driving a car for booked rides or deliveries; renting out property or part of it; running errands or complete tasks for somebody; selling goods online; renting equipment; providing creative or professional services; providing other temporary, on-demand or freelance work. The IRS is obviously trying to tax all activities that may have escaped its reach while the gig work was expanding exponentially. The same website enumerates some types of digital platforms that provide services through gig work which include ridesharing services, delivery services, crafts and handmade item marketplaces, on-demand labour and repair services and property and space rentals. Many known platforms fit into these categories.[18]

The Government of Australia in the Fair Work Legislative Amendments (Closing Loophole) of 2023 and 2024 also made important changes to the conditions of gig workers.[19] And in April 2024, the European Union (EU), where 45 million people are expected to be gig workers by 2025, adopted the Platform Work Directive, which aims to improve the rights of gig workers by regulating the use of algorithms and data

[17] https://news.bloomberglaw.com/daily-labor-report/labor-department-cements-changes-to-gig-worker-classification.

[18] https://www.irs.gov/businesses/gig-economy-tax-center.

[19] https://www.dewr.gov.au/closing-loopholes.

in decision-making, correcting employment status misclassifications and ensuring human oversight of important decisions.[20]

7.4.2 Some Conclusions on Workers' Attitude Towards Work

It would not be correct to generalise about the attitude of workers towards work, but, in the light of the above analysis, some key conclusions can be reached. Most workers, especially the younger ones, want flexibility in their jobs, including the possibility of working in a hybrid manner. The reason behind it is that they are interested in a better life-work balance. They are also interested in multiple work experiences and in the opportunity to develop their talent and in having better economic opportunities. This may also explain why their level of engagement in their job is declining as it has emerged from the "*quiet quitting*" phenomenon. Furthermore, they believe that independent work can provide such opportunities.

As many employers, particularly in the public sector, have difficulty in filling vacant positions and are struggling to deal with the attitudes of workers mentioned above, human resources management systems need to be quickly updated to take into account the evolution of jobs and of workers.

7.4.3 The Skills Challenge

Because of the changing nature of jobs, the skills required to perform them will dramatically change. According to the *Future of Jobs Report 2023* by the World Economic Forum referenced above, employers estimate that 44% of workers' skills will be disrupted in the next five years, and six in ten workers will need training before 2027. Unfortunately, only half of the workers currently have access to training opportunities.

When analysing the change in jobs, it emerged that the fastest job growth was driven by science, technology and digitisation. The companies surveyed in the report, however, indicated that analytical thinking and creative thinking were on the top of the skills required for the new jobs, reflecting the importance of problem-solving ability. Technological

[20] https://www.consilium.europa.eu/en/policies/platform-work-eu/#new.

literacy was considered important but also were curiosity, motivation, flexibility and leadership; however, the appropriate balance between digital skills and soft skill should be determined by individual organisations on the basis of their jobs' profiles.

The fast-changing skill requirements necessitate an equally rapid strategy to develop the new skills in the potential workforce and in re-skilling the existing one. Forty-five percent of the businesses surveyed considered it important that governments should help fund skill training. The report thus suggests that partnership between the public and the private sector would help to accelerate re-skilling strategies.

In view of the quick and continuous change in skill needs, Gartner has been recommending that organisations should adopt a dynamic skill development approach rather than a reactive approach. A dynamic approach involves anticipating skills shifts as they occur and adapting the skill development strategy accordingly. Gartner concludes that when a dynamic skill development strategy is adopted, employees apply 75% of the skills learned.[21]

The emphasis on skills has prompted a number of companies and organisations to re-visit the traditional job requirements based on education credentials. As an example, the United States Office for Personnel Management (OPM) in April 2024 introduced skill-based hiring for technology jobs.[22] And while companies are focusing on the need to upgrade employees' skills, most employees do not seem to have a sense of urgency about the need to upskill, according to the *"PwC's Global Workforce Hopes and Fears Survey 2023"*.[23]

The survey, which was based on responses by 54,000 workers in forty-six countries, reveals that only 36% of all employees feel that the skills required by their job will significantly change in the next five years. Conversely, 51% of workers with specialist skills believe that the skills required by their job will change significantly and 60% have a clear sense of how the skills required will change.

21 https://www.gartner.com/smarterwithgartner/stop-training-employees-in-skills-theyll-never-use#:~:text=Dynamic%20approach%20delivers,75%25%20of%20new%20skills%20learned.

22 https://www.opm.gov/news/releases/2022/05/release-opm-releases-skills-based-hiring-guidance/.

23 https://www.pwc.com/gx/en/issues/workforce/hopes-and-fears.html?j=389649&sfmc_sub=8902626&l=16_HTML&u=7138384&mid=510000034&jb=5.

These diverging attitudes of employers and employees towards the need to upskill will require major efforts on the part of the leadership of organisations to motivate employees and to inspire their engagement in the process of transformation.

7.5 The Implications for the Public Sector

The public sector has been affected even to a greater extent than the private sector by the changes in the labour market in the past five years. "*The Great Resignation*" induced by the COVID-19 pandemic has been particularly serious for the public sector. A survey of state and local government employees in the United States conducted by the Mission Square Research Institute at the end of 2021 revealed that 52% of the employees surveyed were inclined to leave their jobs. Of these 36% to change their jobs, 33% to retire and 28% to leave the workforce entirely.[24]

The situation has not improved since then. One year later, Catherine Rampell in the Washington Post reported that while the private sector had already recovered a good portion of the jobs lost in the pandemic, the public sector still experienced a serious shortage of public workers, many in education, paramedics and sanitation.[25] In January 2024, the Hawaii Department of Human Resources Development reported that 27% of the positions in the state public agencies were vacant. It also warned that 30% of existing state civil servants were due to retire within five years creating thus an additional challenge for the Hawaiian Public Sector.[26] Additionally, a 2023 Gallup poll found that 50% of U.S. employees were *quiet quitters*, many under age 35. Although there are no statistics specific to the public sector, it seems reasonable to assume that the public sector has not been immune from the *quiet quitting* phenomenon.[27]

The attitude of younger people towards jobs in the public sector is also changing. While in the past younger people were interested in joining the public sector because of job security and benefits, public agencies

[24] https://research.missionsq.org/resources/more-than-half-of-state-and-local-government-employees-contemplating-leaving-their-jobs-due-to-ongoing-covid-19-pandemic.

[25] https://www.washingtonpost.com/opinions/2022/09/12/worker-shortage-public-sector-crisis/.

[26] https://www.civilbeat.org/2024/01/where-are-the-workers-last-month-27-of-state-government-civil-service-positions-were-vacant/.

[27] https://www.gallup.com/workplace/398306/quiet-quitting-real.aspx.

have difficulty in recruiting younger workers. According to an article by Sean Newhouse published in "Workforce" in April 2024, 67% of young workers surveyed by the Partnership for Public Service (PPS), recognised that work in federal agencies was beneficial to their communities, but were not interested in applying for such positions.[28]

In view of these factors, the public sector is faced with a number of challenges. The first challenge is that of retaining existing employees who are retiring in large numbers. The public sector also needs to motivate employees, not only to be able to retain them, but also to reduce or eliminate the *quiet quitting* phenomenon. An analysis of the reasons why employees in the public sector leave their jobs should inspire the strategy to retain them. Several surveys have attempted to identify these reasons. A 2021 survey conducted by the U.S. Merit Principles Protection Board showed that the main reasons employees were quitting their jobs were the lack of opportunity for growth and development, the lack of appreciation for their work and the dissatisfaction with pay.[29]

Given the considerable number of vacant positions in many government offices, the public sector is also faced with the challenge of attracting new employees, especially younger ones. Finally, governments are faced with the need to fill the skill gap generated by the changing nature of many jobs. When it comes to improving the compensation, legislative bodies have the authority to do so. For example, the salaries of the U.S. Federal Government employees have been increased by Congress both in 2023 and in 2024.

However, managerial measures also exist that could be taken to address the other reasons for leaving and also for not being able to attract younger people. Some of the measures suggested by Natalia Brouge in her blog of September 2023 include fostering a positive and inclusive work environment and promoting open communication in the workplace. The formalisation of flexible work arrangements, such as hybrid work, providing opportunity for professional development and recognising and rewarding employees' efforts should also make employment in the public sector more attractive for both existing and potential

[28] https://www.govexec.com/workforce/2024/04/young-people-think-federal-jobs-are-beneficial-dont-want-them/396174/.

[29] https://www.mspb.gov/studies/surveys.htm.

employees.[30] Younger people, particularly *Generation Z*, are very technology savvy, consequently, the possibility of using their knowledge and of improving it on their job is very important. Regretfully many people think that work in the public sector is bureaucratic and boring; it is thus important to rehabilitate the "branding image" of the of public sector work, as Bob Lavigna recommended in January 2022, in order to attract new employees.[31]

Hence, as mentioned earlier, a number of government agencies are revisiting the traditional job requirements based on education credentials by focusing the requirements on skills. Not only the U.S. Federal Government, as reported by Brookings, but also a number of State Governments have introduced skill-based hiring in the hope of widening the pool of potential employees. While the emphasis on skills was initially focused on technology jobs, other occupations are increasingly being included.[32] The public sector needs also to widen the definition of its workforce by including the new work modalities which are gaining ground in the private sector.

In addition to the permanent full-time employees, government agencies are expanding their reliance on contractors, independent contractors and gig workers. A May 2023 article by the Brookings Institute explains how some local governments have started building their own gig platforms for public work. The City of Long Beach, California, for example, has established a platform for workers who are interested in flexible or part-time jobs. These jobs are accessible to people who normally would not qualify for or be interested in permanent positions and provide much needed community services. The interesting aspects of this initiative is that gig workers receive some of the benefits available to permanent staff. Other local authorities are in the process of replicating this experience.[33]

These new arrangements are a useful step to attract workers in the public sector and to make working conditions more flexible; however,

[30] https://hubstaff.com/blog/what-is-quiet-quitting/.

[31] https://elgl.org/government-needs-to-rehabilitate-its-image-to-attract-and-retain-workers/.

[32] https://www.brookings.edu/articles/states-are-leading-the-way-in-tearing-the-paper-ceiling-and-making-good-jobs-available-to-workers-without-degrees/#:~:text=This%20post%20was%20updated%20on,fill%20roles%20in%20state%20government/.

[33] https://www.brookings.edu/articles/to-enhance-community-services-and-empower-workers-local-governments-are-building-their-own-gig-work-platforms/.

one needs to keep in mind that governments must continue to rely on a core workforce that ensures continuity to the business of government, preserves institutional memory and maintains the allegiance of the public servants to the principles of impartiality, equity and integrity.

7.5.1 *The Need to Change Public Sector Human Resources Systems*

For governments to be able to respond promptly to the rapid changes in the labour market and thus attract new employees, they need also to update their human resources systems and their human resources planning. The rigid job classification systems and the related rigid salary scales are an obstacle to capture the variety of contractual arrangements being introduced in the public sector. One feasible option would be the establishment of separate pay scales for different occupations and skill requirements. This would be quite useful when trying to attract people with strong technology skills. Based on its research, McKinsey recommends that governments overhaul their workforce planning by estimating workforce needs in the different areas of work through quantitative and qualitative methods and make the hiring decisions based on those estimates.[34]

Human resources management should also focus on improving the opportunities for growth and development, as the lack of such opportunities was indicated as a reason for leaving the public sector or not joining it. Mobility within and among public agencies should be facilitated by developing more flexible modalities to move from one job to another and devising career paths that incorporate mobility and advancement. Different career paths could be designed for different occupations.

Rewards for creativity and innovation should be incorporated in the career paths to motivate staff to improve service delivery systems and to promote the development of new applications by technologically savvy staff. Such rewards could take the form of merit points the accumulation of which could accelerate advancement.

The generalised training plans now in place in many agencies should be replaced by continuous upgrading of the skills and with measures to respond quickly to rapid changes in the skills requited. This would require

[34] https://www.mckinsey.com/industries/public-sector/our-insights/mission-critical-improving-government-workforce-planning.

the creation of capacity in the organisation to assess and anticipate the skills requirements.

Finally, to create conditions that favour the retention and attraction of staff, organisations should include in their human resources systems specific mechanisms for leadership development with the focus on creating a cadre of forward-looking leaders who foster innovation, promote inclusion and are able to motivate the younger generation.

CHAPTER 8

International Cooperation in the New Reality

Catherine Kardava

8.1 Introduction

Political science is made up of various sub-disciplines, all of which have their roots in politics. One of the main branches of political science, among public policy, political theories and state politics, is international relations. The discipline of international relations is a pedestal for political science, which aims to analyse foreign policy and relations between states, international organisations and non-governmental organisations in the international system. No country exists in a complete vacuum, because for all countries, international relations are crucial for forming alliances, solving cross-border problems and facilitating trade. International relations and diplomacy are even more important in modern times as the

C. Kardava (✉)
Altebridge—International University of Management and Communication, Tbilisi, Georgia
e-mail: e.kardava@yahoo.de

Georgian Parliamentary Research Centre, Tbilisi, Georgia

A. Baimenov and P. Liverakos (eds.), *Public Administration in the New Reality*, https://doi.org/10.1007/978-981-96-3845-1_8

world becomes more connected.[1] International relations are rooted in diplomatic history and have undergone several transformations in recent decades,[2] resulting in a new dynamic academic field that integrates theories, perspectives and methods from related and other disciplines, such as economics, health, education or sociology.

International relations and history are inextricably linked and have been for centuries: "History of the Peloponnesian War" by Thucydides, one of the very earliest and one of the very greatest historical works of all time, is widely regarded as the founding textbook of international relations (Koliopoulos 2010). In practice, the establishment of modern sovereign states as fundamental political units traces back to the Peace of Westphalia of 1648 in Europe, which conventionally marks the beginning of international relations (Drezner 2019). The Peace of Westphalia embodied diplomatic relations and established the concept of sovereignty of states, but the modern perception of the theory of international relations itself was not developed before First World War.

Before international relations was structured as a separate discipline, it was a branch of diplomatic history—"actually, it was indistinguishable from diplomatic history" (Koliopoulos 2010). International relations began to develop as a discipline in its own right after the First World War with the creation of the Chair of International Politics at the University of Aberystwyth, UK. Wars, especially world wars, have a significant impact on the process of structuring international relations and the international system in general.

After the First World War, the main reason for separating international relations from diplomatic history was that the international order was seen in a new prism—diplomatic relations became an insufficient mechanism to combat the ongoing world war, and new rules and discipline were needed to follow the new order of the international system in the world war era. The First World War was followed by the Second World War and the Cold War, which had a decisive effect on the development of the system and order of international relations in the twentieth century. The changes in international politics after the Cold War were more fundamental than the

[1] https://prawo.uni.wroc.pl/sites/default/files/students-resources/THE%20FUNDAMENTAL%20PRINCIPLES%20GOVERNING%20INTERNATIONAL%20RELATIONS.pdf.

[2] See https://books.openbookpublishers.com/10.11647/obp.0074.pdf.

usual major wars: crowning of new hegemons, and constructions of new schemes for maintaining peace and order (Philpott 1999).

Based on the history of nations, as world wars have had a greater impact on international order, it is obvious that "the paramount principle of international order is Peace".[3] After the World Wars and the Cold War, maintaining peace was the main issue of international order. With the end of the Cold War and the acceleration of globalisation,[4] many authors have argued that territoriality as a political organising principle had come to an end. In this new post-territorial world, the state would have at most a supporting and facilitating role, reduced to a "market state" (Bobbitt 2003). International cooperation also seemed to be on its way out. After all, according to one of its most general definitions, international cooperation was (and is): the art and practice of negotiation, communication and representation between sovereign states.

Governments are developing a new form of cooperation that they see as a central strategic element in the process of conducting contemporary international affairs. As societies evolve, new scenarios emerge in international relations that require new methods and new priorities. Diplomatic practice keeps pace with the changing world, evolving as it has to meet new challenges and respond to new sets of national interests throughout history. A key change has been the rebalancing of the relative importance of "hard" and "soft" power (Nye 1990). In other words, traditional methods of coercion based on military or economic power are giving way to more subtle diplomatic arts of persuasion and influence.

This new balance is a product of new circumstances. Complex interdependence, cultural globalisation, empowerment of public opinion, the social media revolution, ideas and information are factors that have exerting pressure on national governments to reshape their foreign policy structures and develop mass diplomacy as their new approach for their diplomatic efforts. Facing this new global environment, governments are coming to see the apparent need to inform and influence foreign

[3] Jimmy Carter, *"BUILDING A JUST WORLD ORDER"*, PRINCIPLES OF INTERNATIONAL ORDER, 2021. https://www.ohchr.org/sites/default/files/documents/issues/intorder/peacesecurity/2022-09-01/submission-international-peace-security-hrc51-cs-alfred-de-zayas.pdf.

[4] https://www.history.com/topics/cold-war/cold-war-history.

audiences as a strategic aspect of their diplomacy and an indispensable condition for pursuing their goals.[5]

It is now appropriate to ask some questions and to consider the potential uses of this new approach to diplomacy by states. How can mass diplomacy complement traditional state-to-state diplomacy? What are the benefits of communicating directly with foreign audiences? Is it possible that mass diplomacy could create a more fruitful international environment, leading to better international footholds and greater ease in achieving national interests? Can mass diplomacy promote specific security, economic and political goals? It is shown that answers of a growing number of governments on most of these questions are affirmative. In an attempt to explain this growing consensus, this chapter seeks to determine, first, the extent to which the task of informing and educating foreign populations can positively influence the international context and, second, how mass diplomacy can help advance specific goals.

Major structural changes in international system over the past three and a half decades have put a major question mark over the Westphalian principle of state sovereignty, which assumes that a state—subject to international recognition—exercises legal, unqualified and exclusive control over a defined territory and population. The end of the Cold War in the late 1980s and the process of deepening globalisation have contributed to profound changes in the global political context. These changes seem to make the world a much smaller and more interconnected place, but one that appears to be fragmented by the erosion of the autonomy of the sovereign states and the rise of intrastate conflicts.

In this new environment, where common challenges—such as food security, accessibility on water and health management—require strong interactions between communities across borders, thus, cooperation has taken a more prominent role in the international system. As time went by, new needs appeared on the agenda. Countries realised that in order to maintain peace, it was essential to strengthen international cooperation with the main "players" of the international order. Exhaustible natural resources, agricultural products and human capital became the most important subjects of international relations between countries—economic cooperation, cultural relations and other types of international cooperation developed a new era of international relations.

[5] The reasons for creating the conditions leading to mass diplomacy will be discussed later in the chapter.

These exchange processes among and between countries brought forward various kinds of diplomacy—economic diplomacy, cultural diplomacy, environmental diplomacy, educational diplomacy, health diplomacy, etc.

International relations, international cooperation and international law are related, but yet they are different terms with different contexts, all belonging to the international system. The international system itself includes all the relations that have components of relations arising outside the state, regardless of whether only states, individuals, international organisations or others participate in it. The international system contains all the contacts and international events from diplomacy to cooperation among the professionals of different countries (Aleksidze 2010: 3). Hence, the aim of this chapter is to also highlight the issues related to international cooperation, to distinguish it from international relations and to present the importance and significance of international cooperation in the modern era.

The contemporary world is passing through a stage of development where progress is hardly achieved within the territory of a single state. Modern society represents a global community. It evolves without boundaries. It is impossible to isolate different policy areas, e.g., the economy and environment protection. Public administration is one such area that could not advance further without active cooperation among countries. Analysis of best practices in and experiences of public administration, the constant discussions and working meetings among governments of different states demonstrate that international cooperation and collaboration play a key role in forming uniform approaches, common principles and values at the international level.

With the creation of the first states on earth, interstate relations were also established and regulated by certain rules of conduct, whose context was shifting and changing in accordance with social changes taking place over time. Modern international relations, as already mentioned, are subject to legal regulation with the formation of international law. Accordingly, the norms regulating relations between states, in the form of international law, are the rules of conduct that states observe when they interact in various spheres of life; but the subject of these relations is not at the level of the natural person—but at the state level cooperating with other states. International cooperation covers a wide range of subjects, including individuals, the private sector and others, and it is not limited to legally regulated relations among states.

8.2 Values of International Relations

The rationale for mass diplomacy is threefold: first, to engage foreign populations in a relationship of trust and empathy; second, to create a favourable international context; and third, to facilitate the achievement of national interests (Pahlavi 2003).

> First: No people on earth can be held, as a people, to be an enemy, for all humanity shares the common hunger for peace, fellowship, and justice. Second: No nation's security and well- being can be lastingly achieved in isolation but only in effective cooperation with fellow nations. Third: Every nation's right to a form of government and an economic system of its own choosing is inalienable. Fourth: Any nation's attempt to dictate to other nations their form of government is indefensible. And fifth: A nation's hope of lasting peace cannot be firmly based upon any race in armaments but rather upon just relations and honest understanding with all other nations.[6]

This speech delivered by President Eisenhower, a month after the death of Joseph Stalin, set out the five principles of international relations that still resonate today and are most relevant in today's era of globalisation. The most significant values of international cooperation stand on the following main directions:

- Promoting successful trade policies between nations;
- Encouraging travel related to business, tourism and immigration, providing people with opportunities to enhance their lives;
- Enhancing cooperation on contemporary global issues including pandemics, terrorism and the environment; and
- Advancing human culture through cultural exchanges, diplomacy and policy development.[7]

[6] Eisenhower, D. D. Presidential Inaugural Address. Washington, D.C., 20.01.1953. The Chance for Peace, Speech delivered before the American Society of Newspaper Editors, Washington, D.C., 15.04.1953.

[7] International Relations EDU, "*The Value of International Relations in a Globalized Society*", What is International Relations? https://www.internationalrelationsedu.org/what-is-international-relations/ and https://en.wikipedia.org/wiki/International_relations.

These values of international cooperation underscore the importance of working together to address common challenges and promote a more just, peaceful and sustainable world indicating that international cooperation is essential to address global challenges and promote the common good, as well as for solid public policymaking and well-developed good governance.

Traditionally, conflict prevention and collective security have also been seen as values of international cooperation. The importance of cooperation was increased significantly after Second World War and is now more valuable than ever. Against the backdrop of the Russia-Ukraine war and the hostilities in the Middle East that began just a few months ago, the role of international cooperation in the process of de-escalating conflicts and establishing security is growing by the day. It is also significant to note the importance of international cooperation in the cyber field as one of the most effective mechanisms to prevent cyberterrorism and cyberattacks. International cooperation fosters diplomacy and collaboration, helping to prevent conflicts between nations and promote peaceful resolutions of disputes. Collaboration enhances global security by addressing common threats such as terrorism, nuclear proliferation and transnational crime.

In addition to the need for security cooperation, it is important to note the positive impact of international cooperation on economic development. Therefore, one of the significant values of international cooperation is considered to be cooperation for trade and sustainable development. International cooperation facilitates trade agreements and economic partnerships, leading to mutual benefits, increase of economic growth and poverty reduction. Cooperation enables exchange of knowledge, technology and expertise, supporting innovation and sustainable development.

Conversely, promotion and protection of human rights on a global scale may be defined as a Universal Value, ensuring that fundamental rights are universally recognised and respected. International cooperation works to reduce inequality and promote social justice, addressing issues such as gender equality, education and access to health care. Global environmental challenges such as climate change require coordinated efforts to reduce greenhouse gas emissions, preserve biodiversity and protect ecosystems. Contemporary challenges in the world underline the need for joint initiatives for the sustainable management of shared resources such as water, forests and fisheries.

COVID-19, a global pandemic, showed the World the importance of international cooperation for addressing challenges such as disease prevention, vaccine distribution and healthcare infrastructure development. It required a collaborative effort for international cooperation between governments and professionals to improve access to essential medicines and healthcare services, particularly in developing countries.

International cooperation has also a vital role in promoting cultural exchange and understanding, fostering an appreciation of diversity and reducing the possibility of cultural misunderstanding. Educational cooperation initiatives help to share knowledge and build bridges between nations. Based on this important value, it is necessary to deepen international cooperation in the direction of sports diplomacy, cultural diplomacy and youth diplomacy. When talking about contributing to a more connected and informed global society diplomacy, it is necessary to mention the importance of cooperation within the framework of international law. In particular, cooperation strengthens international institutions and frameworks and promotes adherence to international law and norms. Cooperation contributes to peaceful conflict resolution through mechanisms such as international courts and arbitration. International cooperation is essential to provide timely and effective humanitarian assistance in response to natural disasters, conflicts and other emergencies. Cooperation addresses the needs of displaced populations and ensures the protection and well-being of refugees.

8.3 International Cooperation and a Variety of Different Types of Diplomacy

In ancient times, diplomacy referred to the conduct of formal (often-bilateral) relations between sovereign governments. By the twentieth century, European diplomatic practices had spread throughout the world, and the definition of diplomacy had expanded to include summits, international conferences, multilateralism, the international efforts of supranational and subnational organisations, the informal diplomacy of non-state actors and the performance of international civil servants.[8]

[8] Diplomacy is defined as the art and practice of negotiating and conducting dialogue through various means between states, groups or people to influence the decisions, events and behaviour of the international system. It is undertaken for the promotion of peace among nations and for the avoidance of a state of war or of violence.

Modern day diplomats—in today's multipolar environment, characterised by a rapid flow of information as well—are often in a position where they must quickly and correctly analyse quite a few and often contradictory pieces of information, make conclusions and properly inform their ministry about a specific situation or problem. Special importance is also attached to public diplomacy, nowadays, which involves clear and transparent communication with all segments of society, including dialogue with civil society organisations. Modern diplomacy is open and transparent diplomacy in contrast to traditional diplomacy, which is secret and covert. Diplomacy has developed into different kinds and types over time necessitated by social changes and progress.

In the international arena, every nation has always been interdependent, even when reaching the highest level of development, it will still be dependent on other nations to realise its interests. Therefore, every state must engage in international relations with other countries/actors in the international system. By engaging in international relations, nations can cooperate, pool resources and share information to address global issues beyond any one country or region. Sovereign states conduct their international relations and interact with each other through their foreign policy, promoting their national interests in their relations with other countries, both bilaterally and multilaterally. In this case, foreign policy becomes an essential part of increasing foreign cooperation in various sectors.

Since all types and forms of international cooperation are based on relations between foreign publics of states, it is important to explain first the means of public diplomacy, considered a pedestal of several types of international cooperation.

Public diplomacy is a state's strategy to communicate directly with foreign publics. It can take the form of press conferences and statements of policymakers. But it is also a professional field in its own right, with dedicated governmental organisations that launch campaigns and exert considerable efforts to provide international media with an image of the country's policies and to target specific audiences. In recent decades, public diplomacy has been widely regarded as the transparent means by which a sovereign country communicates with societies of other countries to inform and influence foreign audiences in order to promote national interests and advance its foreign policy objectives.

Traditionally, public diplomacy is seen as an integral part of state-to-state diplomacy, which represents official relations (typically in private), between official representatives (leaders and diplomats) of sovereign states. Nowadays, public diplomacy includes activities such as educational exchange programmes for scholars and students, visitor programmes, language training, cultural events and exchanges and radio and television broadcasts. Such activities usually focus on improving the image or reputation of the "sending" country in order to shape the broader political environment in the "receiving" country (Nye 2008). Public diplomacy seeks to influence the attitudes of individuals and organisations in a positive way in order to build support for the nation's objectives from foreign countries (Melissen 2006).

The economic interests of states play a key role in the process of establishing specific international relations, and it also influences the policies that countries are implementing at the national level. For this reason, economic diplomacy is one of the oldest forms of international cooperation. ***Economic diplomacy*** deals with international economic issues to increase prosperity, the top priority for states in most regions of the world. In a broad sense, economic diplomacy can be defined as any diplomatic activity that promotes the economic interests of the state. It also includes diplomacy that uses economic resources to achieve a specific foreign policy objective. In a narrower sense, economic diplomacy is concerned with the promotion of exports and inward investment. This is sometimes called commercial diplomacy.[9]

Economic diplomacy includes all the activities of a government to support and promote its economic operators through a network of diplomatic and consular missions, the chamber of commerce network, agencies, state export banks, etc. In order to accomplish this task, each country creates its own model of economic diplomacy, which may protect and ensure its economic growth and development and improve its position in the international environment. All the knowledge, experience and tradition that a country has in its international positioning is summarised in its model (mode) of communication with other stakeholders in the international arena.

Economic diplomacy is a tool of economic foreign policy and the state (diplomats, government officials and employees, etc.), as well as non-state actors (transnational companies, NGOs, trade unions, business lobbies, etc.), who are also included in its realisation. The field in which these actors operate is broad and involves: the national economy,

[9] https://www.diplomacy.edu/topics/economic-diplomacy/.

the international economy (international trade, foreign trade, finance, etc.), international organisations (the UN system, governmental and non-governmental organisations, etc.).

In today's globalised world, where the world's economies are increasingly interlinked and interdependent, the economic instruments of foreign policy are proving to be important levers of influence and control over processes and events. Given the prevailing global economic doctrine of (neo)liberal capitalism—which gained remarkable momentum and global inclusiveness after the fall of the Berlin Wall and the collapse of communist regimes in the early 1990s—all world economies are more or less open and subject to global trends. It is almost as if domestic economic policy cannot be separated from foreign policy because they are intertwined and inseparable (Duby 2016).

Today, economic factors are becoming increasingly important in the foreign policy of all countries. The growing international division of labour, now called globalisation, is increasingly binding national economies into an interdependent whole, and in such an environment one can only operate with the help of economic instruments to defend national interests and the interests of the national economy. In order to successfully defend one's interests in international relations, it is necessary to anticipate certain events and situations and act in time in order to benefit from them and, at the same time, avoid suffering losses and/or damage to the national economy.

With the successful presence of a state in international organisations, at the regional and multilateral levels, at the global level and within the UN system, economic and commercial diplomacy bring states in international relations to promote products and services, increase exports, improve country's branding and contribute to economic and social growth/progress. Thus, both components of economic diplomacy—economic and commercial—work in synergy to position the country in the international environment and contribute to its economic prosperity. The organisational form used by individual countries in this process is called the economic diplomacy model (Hussain 2006).

Since ancient times, societies have influenced the cultures and traditions of other peoples. The main cause of cultural impact was their migration to other countries, wars and conquests, which usually resulted in the introduction of the conqueror's culture into the occupied territories. Nowadays, people have more access to other state's cultures—it is easier to travel abroad or to see world's sightseeing, study foreign languages and get acquainted with each other's cultural traditions online. As the cultural exchange phenomenon still retains its importance and popularity, it is important to explain the characteristics of cultural diplomacy as well.

Cultural diplomacy is the notion that refers to the exchange of art, information, ideas and other elements of culture between nations and their societies to promote and extend mutual comprehension. It helps to build "a foundation of trust" with others, on which decision-makers can base agreements in the areas of politics, business and the military. Cultural diplomacy is used as a tool to end the destructive perceptions made by political authorities. The primary goals of cultural diplomacy are to reduce barriers and promote mutual respect and understanding between nations.[10] Cultural diplomacy is essential for promoting peace and stability throughout the world. Cultural diplomacy, if it is taught and used at all levels, has a unique ability to influence the "global public opinion" and ideology of individuals, communities and nations. Governments of countries are using cultural diplomacy as a tool to achieve certain goals: for example, to promote the culture of a particular country abroad; to strengthen bilateral relations with other countries from around the world; and for achieving their desired political or economic goals with the use of a new form of negotiation—soft power.[11]

The analysis of the legislation of the different countries shows that the so-called use of soft power for diplomatic purposes has been taken to a significant level by different states. For example, French cultural diplomacy is regulated by the Law No 2010/873 (27.07.2010) "On external actions of the State". The law obliges public institutions to promote French culture and extend its influence throughout the world. "Government institutions involved in activities outside France's borders are tasked to promote French culture and influence abroad by organising cultural events, extend cooperation and partnership, and managing necessary arrangements for these activities".[12]

Equally, the Hungarian government has developed a cultural diplomacy strategy. Hungary's cultural diplomacy strategy includes the establishment and expansion of cultural centres, a number of institutions,

[10] https://bestdiplomats.org/cultural-diplomacy/.

[11] "Soft power: The ability to persuade through culture, values, and ideas, as opposed to 'hard power' that conquers or coerces through military force" (Nye 1990).

[12] https://www.legifrance.gouv.fr/loda/id/JORFTEXT000022521532/.

organisations and associations abroad. These organisations are actively involved in the field of cultural diplomacy and try to spread Hungarian culture throughout the world. In the framework of the state's cultural diplomacy strategy, projects have been developed that aim, for example, involvement of Hungarians living abroad, and persons interested in Hungarian culture, in the activities of numerous projects. Frequently, these groups build relationships with each other and with similar groups in other countries based on a common passion. Hungary's cultural diplomacy has achieved significant results in the promotion of Hungarian culture and language through various events and cultural institutions and with the support of the public sector.[13]

The new reality is indivisible from technological attainments. Innovative technologies have become part of our everyday lives, and the use of artificial intelligence has spread across numerous spheres. Accordingly, international cooperation in the field of science is becoming more and more actual. Over the years, a new notion called ***science diplomacy*** has gained a foothold in science and technology policymaking as well as in international affairs of numerous industrialised countries. The concept of science diplomacy was given contemporary significance and currency by a meeting held at Wilton House, United Kingdom, in 2009, sponsored by the Royal Society,[14] and the American Association for the Advancement of Science (AAAS).[15] The most influential outcome of this meeting was the development of a taxonomy of science diplomacy, which is now widely used: *Science in diplomacy*: Science providing advice to inform and support foreign policy objectives; *Diplomacy for science*: Diplomacy that facilitates international scientific cooperation; *Science for diplomacy*: Scientific cooperation that improves international relations (Gluckman et al. 2017).

"Science diplomacy seems to involve explicit attempts to connect the fields of science, politics and economics or, at least, it illustrates a new rhetorical strategy that emphasises innovative policies for building bridges between the drivers of supposedly insular fields, thus educating or at least sensitising actors to seize an allegedly common understanding of

[13] Cultural Diplomacy. The Hungarian Cultural Institute Network. https://culture.hu/en/budapest/culturalinstitutes.

[14] https://royalsociety.org/.

[15] https://www.aaas.org/.

problems and solutions" (Flink and Rueffin 2019). Nowadays there are no international affairs without Science and Technology, and no Science and Technology without internationality. Diplomacy for science includes political activities that should serve scientific purposes, such as providing legal frameworks for cooperation, supporting scientific mobility or guaranteeing intellectual property rights. Science for diplomacy expresses political action "to improve international relations between countries" through science (Flink and Rueffin 2019).

Widening the scope beyond national interests brings us to truly global problems such as climate change, ozone depletion, global biodiversity and marine pollution. On these issues, the focus is often greater on the perceived immediate interest rather than the longer-term implications that extend beyond traditional political timeframes. For example, the challenge of eliciting commitments from countries to reduce greenhouse gas emissions has created tensions over jobs dependent on fossil fuels and the political implications of appearing to neglect various constituencies by pushing "green" policies.

Science diplomacy should be a serious part of every nation's toolkit, whether large or small, developing or rich the country is. However, it cannot be instituted capriciously. Science diplomacy requires a structure that includes not only the promotion of international science, as covered by many science agencies, but also explicit attention to issues at the national, regional and global levels. Science diplomacy is an important generator of soft power (Nye 2004). Science diplomacy is an effective emissary of essential values such as evidence-based learning, openness and sharing. Science diplomacy is increasingly important in addressing many of the planet's most urgent challenges—such as the management of the global commons, failing public health systems and the threat of collapsing ecosystems. It can also be used to enhance one nation's interests with respect to another or to defuse international tensions (Turekian et al. 2012).

"Diplomatic practice is central in laying the groundwork for cooperation among state and non-state actors with an interest in cyberspace. However, diplomatic approaches towards cyberspace are fraught with complicated challenges".[16] Cyberspace is already a reality, with sophisticated networks spanning the entire planet, and it is expanding so rapidly

[16] https://www.internationalaffairs.org.au/australianoutlook/defining-cyber-diplomacy/.

that people and corporations need to take the necessary security precautions. This is challenging because cybersecurity problems differ significantly from traditional security problems in that they are characterised by the dynamics, structures and players in complex networks.

In the early days, a network of multi-stakeholders—decentralised community of civil society organisations, the private sector, the government, academic and research communities and national and international organisations, managed Internet governance. The goal of this model of multi-stakeholder governance, also known as multi-stakeholders or multi-stakeholder initiative, is to bring stakeholders together so that they can participate in discussion, decision-making and the implementation of solutions to common problems or objectives (Kim 2014; Gunduz and Das 2020).

Cyberdiplomacy has the potential to de-escalate conflict and build a force for peace. More than thirty states now have commissioners for cyber foreign policy. Denmark has even appointed a cyberdiplomacy ambassador. Cyberdiplomacy in the broadest sense includes confidence-building measures. It also comprises certain aspects of international norm-building, data protection and freedom of expression, Internet governance and law enforcement under international legal assistance agreements. However, many governments have neither the knowledge nor the resources to maintain basic cybersecurity standards, or even to determine what attacks are being conducted through servers on their territory. Nonetheless, most states express profound reservations about national sovereignty, while presenting the idea of a central global security regulator for cyberspace, making it an unrealistic prospect for the time being. It is more likely that cyberspace and information space will increasingly become subject to national sovereignty.

Cybersecurity is not only a national issue, but also an EU issue (Bendiek 2018). In its cyberdiplomacy, the EU relies on EU's Common Foreign and Security Policy toolbox.[17] Its measures can be divided into preventative, cooperative, stabilising and restrictive, as well as legitimate responses by member states in self-defence. Political measures are agreed in the EU Council with the support of the European External Action

[17] https://www.cyber-diplomacy-toolbox.com/.

Service. In serious cases, malicious cyberactivity could lead to punitive measures and the use of force or armed attack in accordance with international law and the Charter of the United Nations (Bendiek 2018).

Cyberdiplomacy poses numerous challenges for states, many of which are at the intersection of law, policy, politics and technology. These challenges include the reluctance of some states to engage in cyberdiplomacy, the issue of attribution in cyberspace, the rapid pace at which cyberdiplomacy is evolving, political divisions among states, gaps in states' technological capabilities, cyberdiplomacy's overlap with other fields and the difficulty of safeguarding non-state actors' cyber interests.

Currently, private actors and non-state groups, including businesses, political dissidents and minority groups, may enjoy the freedom of an under-regulated cyberspace. This under-regulation, to some, means liberty and safety. However, the "diplomacy" in cyberdiplomacy makes it interstate by its very nature. Negotiations exclusively among states may result in over prioritisation of state-based interests like prosecuting cybercrimes—potentially at the expense of other interests like Internet freedom. Without active collaboration among public and private interests, cyberdiplomacy runs the risk of trampling on the most critical advantages cyberspace poses for non-state actors (Khabbaz 2020).

Energy diplomacy is a complex area of international relations that is closely linked to foreign policy and overall national security. Although there is no exact definition of energy diplomacy, it refers to government-related external activities aimed at ensuring a country's energy security while promoting energy-related business opportunities. A large-scale transformation of the energy system to one predominantly based on clean energy will certainly require the alignment of the interests of multiple parties through multilateral diplomacy. Global energy governance is perhaps the most important form of multilateral diplomacy for large-scale energy system transformation, as it seeks to ensure security of energy supply and demand, economic development, international security, environmental sustainability and good domestic governance at the global level (Van de Graaf and Colgan 2016). Although global energy governance is being pursued by a variety of intergovernmental organisations, clubs, forums, networks, partnerships, multilateral institutions and United Nations entities, the potential for strong governance remains unrealised due to genuinely different interests and fragmentation of the actors involved (Florini and Sovacool 2009).

Regional diplomacy is a conduct of relations between nations that are part of a specific geographical area. Regional diplomacy is now a significant player in world affairs. All states understand the importance and value of neighbourly interaction due to interdependence and globalisation. For the purpose of this book, it is necessary to note the importance of regional diplomacy in Eastern Europe or post-socialist countries. The development of the countries in our region is actually based on regional cooperation and includes important aspects of economic, cultural and social development.

Regions are among these new diplomatic actors. Their appearance as territorially bounded political agents coincided with global dynamics of regional integration. Regions and other subnational entities are granted considerable competences, including in international arena. Their external relations and diplomatic activities are a crucial tool in the hands of these actors, which they use extensively to further expand their influence, domestically or globally. This is a truly global phenomenon, with regions, provinces, cities and other local authorities from all continents "going abroad" (Tavares 2016).

Over the years, subnational diplomacy has become a normalised and typical feature of the international environment (Cornago 2010). Subnational diplomacy can be divided into three clusters of activities: horizontal cooperation, vertical cooperation and promotion of interests (Kaiser 2003). We can add a fourth category—the use of innovative policy instruments. Horizontal cooperation includes all forms of cross-border and interregional cooperation between regions. These often take the form of bilateral or multilateral cooperation with neighbouring regions but can also be found in a European context. Vertical cooperation is the way in which regions participate in and shape the foreign policy of the central or federal State. Germany is a pioneer in the way in which representatives of the state governments of the *Länder* define the foreign policy of the Federal Republic in the *Bundesrat*.

The most striking form of advocacy by subnational entities is their own network of representatives or offices abroad. In addition, subnational entities rely on an entire range of innovative policy instruments such as public diplomacy, informal networking, city diplomacy and an integrated international cultural policy. "Network diplomacy", along with virtual diplomacy and e-diplomacy, is one of the elements of the new diplomatic paradigm, as conceived, *inter alia,* in the concepts of transformational diplomacy and the development of the European External Action Service.

Lacking the diplomatic power that international law grants to "traditional" nation-states, subnational polities have had to resort to other means to go abroad, to communicate and negotiate with international partners and to represent themselves.

One of the most important tools in the hands of subnational entities to overcome their relative weakness in this regard is the development of adherence to a political network. These networks can be formal or informal and have been crucial to the development of subnational diplomacy. Looking at the policy networks in which subnational entities are involved, one is struck by the diverse nature of the frameworks in which they operate. Network diplomacy allows polities at different levels (provinces, regions, subnational entities) to develop structural or ad hoc contacts without the need of physical embassies, although more and more subnational entities are establishing an ever-expanding network of pseudo-diplomatic delegations (Duran 2019).

In the twenty-first century, states have adopted new ways of diplomacy to achieve their national interests. It is believed that education is one of the effective strategies of soft power to advance a country's national interests in the international arena, as has been shown after the collapse of the bipolar international order. A state wishing to improve its international image and integrity and to create the right conditions for its long-term socio-economic growth establishes a range of hard and soft power strategies in its foreign policy.

Soft power strategies and ***education diplomacy*** have begun to play a more prominent role in countries' foreign policies in several ways, and it is expected that this role will continue to grow and expand as an influential soft power tool for promoting diplomatic relations and achieving national interests (Vaxevanidou 2018). In this advanced world, through the provision of educational opportunities for international students, cultural exchange programmes, language education, global education partnerships, internationalisation of higher education through transnational education, educational diplomacy in conflict zones, education for sustainable development, virtual education and distance learning, states can promote peace, tolerance and intercultural understanding, build positive bilateral relations and enhance their soft power.

The Fulbright Programme—sponsored by the US Department of State, is an excellent example of public diplomacy, being furthered through higher education. Regarding its principal goal to foster mutual understanding between people and nations, the programme has always been a mix of government and people-generated soft power. It claims to have involved the largest movement of students and scholars across the world that any programme has ever sponsored. The British Council is another prime example. With its offices around the world, some of which are attached to British embassies, the British Council itself can be described as the UK's international organisation for educational opportunities and cultural relations. Modelled on the Fulbright programme, it offers scholarships for studying in the UK and promotes educational exchange between higher education institutions both, at national and international level. The German Academic Exchange Service plays a similar but less extensive role and, importantly, non-Western countries have followed their diplomatic efforts. China produced the idea of its own brand of educational diplomacy in 2004—Confucius Institutes are designed to promote Chinese language and culture abroad (McGill and Peterson 2014; Hong 2014).

In response to these narrower motivations for engagement, many institutions are developing broader internationalisation strategies to seek collaborations that define them as global institutions. They may wish to pursue a variety of goals through engagement—to enrich their academic programmes, to broaden the knowledge and experience base of their students, to host more diverse range of students and faculties, to provide more opportunities for their faculties to participate in international research networks, and ultimately to develop numerous collaborative activities that benefit both partners. Considering all the sustainable relationships, it is significant to mention the importance of characteristics of the parties and the ethical framework in which they operate. Countries and institutions engaged in educational diplomacy have an obligation to provide the benefits—not only for themselves, but also for their partners. This represents the best spirit of international relations and the internationalisation of higher education. If it done well, it will be a rising tide that lifts all ships.

Historically, ***health diplomacy*** has remained on the edges of international relations. However, from the European Union's regional vaccine initiative to India's delivery of hydroxychloroquine to the United States in April 2020, the COVID-19 pandemic has provided numerous examples of states putting health at the centre of foreign policy, a practice that is likely to continue after the pandemic. States choose from a wide range of options to shape their health diplomacy, from engagement with global intergovernmental organisations such as the World Health Organisation (WHO) to bilateral aid for supporting existing foreign investments.

The increasing pace of pandemics in the twenty-first century has highlighted the challenges states face and choices that they have to make in the process of conducting health diplomacy. The very nature of pandemics requires international cooperation to mitigate them. Nevertheless, pandemics also create opportunities for states to pursue foreign policy goals that are primarily in their national interest rather than serving global health goals (Fazal 2020). Today's health diplomacy involves, more than ever before, a variety of actors, which takes place in different settings, both formal and informal at different levels of authority; and it is worth mentioning that not all of them are government representatives.

Sport diplomacy is using sport to promote diplomacy, peace and understanding. It involves making use of sport to encourage communication and cooperation, bridging gaps between nations, cultures and people. Sports diplomacy can promote environmental protection, gender equality, human rights and social and economic growth. It can also be used to improve diplomatic relations between nations and provide a forum for discussing international issues.[18] Compared to some of the major problems in international relations in the twenty-first century—terrorism, poverty, climate change, etc.—sports diplomacy is a positive phenomenon that should be encouraged. By mapping and reimagining the relationship between sport, international relations and diplomacy, it is conceivable that sports diplomacy could become an important soft power tool (Constantinou et al. 2016).

To sum up, some of the defining characteristics of the twenty-first-century diplomacy in a globalised world operating in a multipolar world within a multi-level and multi-dimensional global governance structure that increasingly is getting to include a regional level too. The twenty-first-century's diplomacy is no longer conducted by traditional, professional diplomats. In the new reality, international cooperation is a challenge for managing relations not only between states, but also relations between states and other actors. Nowadays, international cooperation increasingly involves public diplomacy towards an informed society and quite a few newly established actors both, at internal and external level. Additionally, diplomacy is involved in and contributes to a wide

[18] https://bestdiplomats.org/types-of-diplomacy/.

range of international issues that require global coordination under conditions of interdependence, such as security, health, environment, global finance and climate change, including cooperation in the field of public administration.

8.4 Contemporary Tendencies in Civil Servant's International Cooperation

International cooperation requires the establishment of relations among countries' high representatives, public institutions and civil servants. One of the crucial aspects of diplomacy is **Public Administration**, an integral part of countries' governance systems. Hence, exchange of experience and practices for enhancing public administration also ensures the dissemination of the common principles of Good Governance—another component for maintaining peace in the international system. Therefore, international cooperation in public administration is crucial for addressing global challenges, promoting good governance and fostering sustainable development. By working together, nations can leverage their collective strengths to create more resilient and effective governance systems.

The development of governance through international cooperation in the field of public administration is a significant aspect of global governance (Baimenov and Everest-Phillips 2016). As nations become more interconnected and face increasingly complex challenges that transcend borders, collaboration becomes essential. In recent years, democracies have faced a series of shocks, and challenges for ensuring economic and democratic resilience. Russia's unprovoked war of aggression against Ukraine and the global COVID-19 pandemic has had substantial effects on public welfare in our world. Before the pandemic and the above-mentioned war, many countries had already experienced prolonged periods of social, political and economic distresses, as societies worked through the long tail of effects from the global financial crisis of 2009.

However, as countries fight to emerge from the worst health, economic and social crises in decades and prepare for the current and future environmental challenges, the societies in the OECD countries are evenly split—people who trust their national government and those who do not (OECD 2022), only slightly better than in the aftermath of the global financial crisis. In this regard, international cooperation allows countries to share knowledge, experiences and best practices in public administration, which will assist them in the process of overcoming contemporary challenges. Learning from the successes and failures of other nations can help to improve governance structures and processes.

Modern countries are going through a significant stage of development. Public administration is constantly incurring changes and is directly reflecting all the challenges that are faced by the society of a particular country. Accordingly, cooperation and exchange of views between countries and professionals is necessary in order to jointly address the major challenges of public administration through various collaborative approaches. Collaborative efforts often include capacity-building programmes where countries support each other in strengthening their public administration institutions. This can involve training programmes, technical assistance and the exchange of experts.

To ensure democratic resilience in a multi-crisis environment, governments need to take decisive steps to build long-term trust in public institutions. Trust is a key indicator of how people perceive the quality of, and how they associate with public institutions. Trust in democratic public institutions is driven by two complementary components: competence and values. Competence means having the ability, capacity and judgement required to respond to given mandates. Public institutions must demonstrate competence by being responsive to the needs of the public and dependable in assessing evolving challenges, minimising uncertainties and implementing future-oriented policies. Values are the underlying intentions and principles that guide governments' actions. To be considered as a trusted body, public institutions must demonstrate their values regarding the principle of transparency: provide information, hold consultations, listen and respond to stakeholders and ensure equal opportunities for everyone to effectively participate in the activities of institutions in the context of representative democracy. They must work with integrity, by aligning with ethical values, principles and norms to safeguard the public interest, and with fairness, by improving living conditions for all and providing consistent treatment regardless of people's backgrounds or characteristics (Brezzi et al. 2021).

International cooperation plays a role in developing and promoting global standards and norms for effective public administration. This can include guidelines on transparency, accountability and the rule of law, which contribute to good governance. Collaboration fosters policy coherence among nations. By aligning policies and strategies, countries can address common challenges more effectively and ensure that their actions do not have negative spillover effects on other nations (Baimenov and

Liverakos 2019). Democracies, characterised by checks and balances, are in a competition of ideas with governance models that advocate seemingly faster or easier ways of responding to crises. Governments cannot ensure economic and democratic resilience by relying solely on contingency planning and occasional exceptional responses. Governments need to put in place public governance processes and standards that help to systematically maintain and enhance confidence in institutions in a crisis environment. Acting now is an investment in establishing democratic resilience for the long term and for future generations (OECD 2023).

Many contemporary challenges, such as climate change, migration and cybersecurity, require coordinated efforts across borders. Public administration can be enhanced through international cooperation in addressing these transboundary issues. International cooperation in public administration can contribute to conflict prevention and resolution. By promoting inclusive governance structures and addressing underlying issues, nations can work together to prevent conflicts and build sustainable peace. Democratic governments can use their strengths in international cooperation to improve the way they deal with crises that transcend national borders.

Many of the world's multilateral institutions were created in the aftermath of the Second World War, a crisis that posed existential risks to democratic governance. The Organisation for Economic Co-operation and Development (OECD)—an international organisation with thirty-eight member countries, is one of them. The OECD's mission is to shape policies that promote prosperity, equality, opportunity and well-being, establish evidence-based international standards and find solutions to a range of social, economic and environmental challenges.[19] The OECD collaborates with the representatives from governments, parliaments, other international organisations, business and labour associations, civil society as well as citizens from across the globe. This organisation also helps governments design and implement strategic, evidence-based and innovative policies for strengthening public governance, respond effectively to diverse and disruptive economic, social and environmental challenges and deliver on government's commitments to citizens. The OECD's working fields, particularly the area of public governance, cover issues such as Digital Government, Anti-corruption and Integrity in the

[19] https://www.oecd.org/about/.

Public Sector, Open government, Gender Mainstreaming and Governance and Leadership. Activities aimed at fostering cooperation among member countries include joint discussions, workshops, training sessions, roundtables, research and publications which are intended to share best practices and establish international standards related to the OECD's areas of work. All the above-mentioned fields and services provided by the OECD underline the importance of this organisation in the process of ensuring international cooperation between a wide range of professionals, especially civil servants.

Along with the OECD, it is important to mention the Astana Civil Service Hub (ACSH),[20] a leading regional network and a multilateral institutional platform that promotes and nurtures regional cooperation among civil servants. Its mission is to contribute to civil service effectiveness by supporting the efforts of governments in the region and beyond to build institutional and human capacity. The ACSH engages with three main areas of activity: partnerships and networking, capacity building and peer-to-peer learning and research and knowledge management. It ultimately aims to cultivate a network of policymakers, practitioners and other partners for sharing knowledge and experience on public administration and civil service reform and development in the region, and to provide technical assistance and advisory services to the governments of the participating countries to enhance capacity.[21] The Astana Civil Service Hub supports the participating countries by sharing knowledge and experiences and best practices through training programmes, workshops, conferences, etc. Consequently, the Astana Civil Service Hub is a good example of a network that unites countries and promotes international cooperation among civil services (Baimenov and Liverakos 2019).

Establishing global partnerships between governments, civil society and the private sector can contribute to more inclusive and participatory governance. Collaborative initiatives can leverage diverse perspectives and resources to address complex challenges. International cooperation facilitates the transfer of technology and innovative solutions in public administration. Adopting advanced technologies can improve efficiency, transparency and service delivery. Collaborative efforts often involve mutual monitoring and evaluation mechanisms, where countries assess

[20] https://www.astanacivilservicehub.org/.

[21] https://www.astanacivilservicehub.org/page/mission-goals.

each other's progress in achieving their governance goals. This promotes accountability and encourages continuous improvement.

Furthermore, since implementation of public administration should be based on ethical and commonly recognised values, anti-corruption policy, including cooperation in this direction, plays an important role in the process of implementing Good Governance principles. In this regard, it is important to mention the significance of the Group of States against Corruption (GRECO),[22] which it is the Council of Europe's anti-corruption monitoring body. It was established in 1999 as an enlarged partial agreement by seventeen Council of Europe member states. It is currently composed of fifty member states, with others expressing an interest. Apart from all the European Union (EU) Member States, its members include countries such as Belarus, Switzerland, the UK, the USA and, most recently, Kazakhstan, which joined in 2020.[23]

GRECO's objective is to improve the capacity of its members to fight corruption by monitoring their compliance with the Council of Europe's anti-corruption standards through a dynamic process of mutual evaluation and peer pressure. It helps to identify deficiencies in national anti-corruption policies and to encourage the necessary legislative, institutional and practical reforms. GRECO also provides a platform for the exchange of best practices in the prevention and detection of corruption. Accordingly, considering the objectives of GRECO, this monitoring body proves to be one of the most fruitful working platforms in the framework of international cooperation between civil servants, as it is also open to non-European states.

A key issue in our society, a concern shared by every country, is the integrity of public officials. Given that corruption affects all countries and that certain phenomena transcend national borders, it is essential to take concrete measures and provide solutions at the international level to combat corruption and integrity violations and to promote good governance, transparency and open administration. The Network for Integrity is a network that aims to develop and promote an international culture of integrity in order to strengthen citizens' trust in their governments and

[22] What is GRECO? https://www.coe.int/en/web/greco/about-greco/what-is-greco.

[23] European Parliament. EU cooperation with the Group of States against Corruption (GRECO): How to move towards full membership; p. 1. https://www.europarl.europa.eu/cmsdata/236597/GRECO%20briefing_final.pdf.

civil services.[24] The Network brings together fourteen institutions from Armenia, Croatia, France, Georgia, Greece, Ivory Coast, Latvia, Mexico, Moldova, Peru, Republic of Korea, Romania, Senegal and Ukraine.[25] In order to promote integrity, the network has a number of objectives, including facilitating the exchange of information and best practices among its members. Meetings and interactions also serve to advance the fight against corruption and the promotion of integrity both within the countries represented and, more importantly, at the international level, which underlines the importance of the Network in the process of implementing international cooperation between civil services of the member countries.

To prevent and manage the transnational and cascading crises of the current era, it is important that democratically governed countries adopt governance practices for more effective multilateral engagement. These should include better coordination within government for multilateral affairs, including horizontal and vertical coordination across domestic government agencies working on international policy issues, mechanisms to promote policy coherence and developing the capacity of public officials to think globally (OECD 2022).

Nevertheless, despite the will of public officials to collaborate across countries with each other, there are some contemporary challenges that can only be dealt collectively. For instance, the main drivers for deepening global connections among societies, economies and ecosystems are the dangerous planetary changes triggered by the Anthropocene, e.g., viruses, microplastics in our oceans and forest fires and an unfolding Digital Revolution. These have led to a dizzying increase in the sharing of data, ideas and culture across societies (UNDP 2024).

These considerations lead us to the creation of a twenty-first-century architecture for international cooperation aimed at delivering global public goods. "This includes the planetary public goods required to navigate the Anthropocene - from climate change mitigation to pandemic preparedness to biodiversity preservation - as well as the digital public

[24] The Network. https://networkforintegrity.org/the-network/.

[25] HIGH AUTHORITY FOR TRANSPARENCY IN PUBLIC LIFE, Network for Integrity. https://www.hatvp.fr/en/international-activities/network-for-integrity/.

infrastructure and digital public goods that would enable the Digital Revolution to be harnessed to enable people to flourish in more equitable ways".[26]

References

Aleksidze, Levan. 2010. *Modern International Law*. Tbilisi, Georgia: "Innovation" Publishing House.

Baimenov, A., and M. Everest-Phillips. 2016. A shared perspective on public administration and international development. *Public Administration Review* 2: 2016.

Baimenov, Alikhan, and Panos Liverakos. 2019. Cooperation and partnerships for international development in the era of the SDGs. In *Public service excellence in the 21st century*, ed. A. Baimenov and P. Liverakos, 319–339. Singapore: Palgrave Macmillan.

Bendiek, A. 2018. The EU as a force for peace in international cyber diplomacy (SWP Comment, 19/2018). Berlin: Stiftung Wissenschaft und Politik -SWP-Deutsches Institut für Internationale Politik und Sicherheit. https://nbnresolving.org/urn:nbn:de:0168-ssoar-57428-2.

Bobbitt, Ph. 2003. *The shield of Achilles. War, peace, and the course of history*. New York: Anchor Books.

Brezzi, M., S. Gonzalez, and D. Nauyen. 2021. An updated OECD framework on drivers of trust in public institutions to meet current and future challenges. OECD Working Papers on Public Governance, No 48, OECD Publishing, Paris. https://doi.org/10.1787/b6c5478c-en.

Constantinou, Costas M., Pauline Kerr, and Paul Sharp. 2016. *The handbook of diplomacy*, 618–622. London: SAGE Publications.

Cornago N. 2010. On the normalization of sub-state diplomacy. In D. Criekemans (Ed.), *Regional sub-State diplomacy today*, 11–36. Boston and Leiden: Brill. https://doi.org/10.1163/1871191x-05010102.

Drezner, D.W. 2019. Technological change and international relations. *International Relations* 33 (2): 286–303. https://doi.org/10.1177/0047117819834629.

Duby, Ziro. 2016. Theoretical principles of economic diplomacy. https://ssrn.com/abstract=2710671.

Duran, Manuel. 2019. Regional diplomacy: A piece in the neo-medieval puzzle? Rn. 24. https://doi.org/10.4000/belgeo.32375.

[26] The United Nations Development Programme. *Human Development Report 2023/2024*. pp. V–VI. https://hdr.undp.org/system/files/documents/global-report-document/hdr2023-24reporten.pdf.

Fazal, Tanisha M. 2020. Health diplomacy in pandemical times. *International Organization* 74 (S1, December): E78–E97. https://doi.org/10.1017/S0020818320000326.

Flink, Tim, and Nicolas Rueffin. 2019. The current state of the art of science diplomacy. In *Handbook on science and public policy*, ed. Simon Dagmar, Stefan Khulman, Julia Stamm, and Weert Canzler, 104–121. Edward Elgar Publishing.

Florini A., and B.K. Sovacool. 2009. Who governs energy? The challenges facing global energy governance. *Energy Policy* 37: 5239–5248. https://www.sciencedirect.com/science/article/abs/pii/S0301421509005655.

Gluckman, P.D., V. Turekian, R.W. Grimes, and T. Kishi. 2017. Science diplomacy: A pragmatic perspective from the inside. *Science & Diplomacy* 6 (4) (December).

Gunduz, M.Z., and R. Das. 2020. Cyber-security on smart grid: Threats and potential solutions. *Computational Networks* 169: 107094.

Hong, Yan Natalie. 2014. EU-China education diplomacy: An effective soft power strategy? *European Foreign Affairs Review* 19 (Special Issue): 155–171. https://doi.org/10.54648/eerr2014026.

Hussain, A. 2006. Economic diplomacy and its significance for foreign policy. *Indian Foreign Affairs Journal* 1 (4): 35–45. http://www.jstor.org/stable/45340592.

Kaiser R. 2003. Para-diplomacy and multilevel governance in Europe and North America: Subnational governments in international arenas. *Participation* 27 (1): 17–19, at p. 18

Khabbaz, Dana. 2020. Cyber diplomacy: Benefits, developments, and challenges, p. 5. www.cyber.forum.yale.edu.

Kim, Sangbae. 2014. Cyber security and middle power diplomacy: A network perspective. *The Korean Journal of International Studies* 12 (2) (December): 323–352. https://doi.org/10.14731/kjis.2014.12.12.2.323.

Koliopoulos, Constantinos. 2010. *International Relations and the Study of History*. https://doi.org/10.1093/acrefore/9780190846626.013.242, https://oxfordre.com/internationalstudies/display/10.1093/acrefore/9780190846626.001.0001/acrefore-9780190846626-e-242?d=%2F10.1093%2Facrefore%2F9780190846626.001.0001%2Facrefore-9780190846626-e242&p=emailAevc9BxlihbFQ.

Melissen, Jan. 2006. Public diplomacy between theory and practice. 2006 Madrid Conference on Public Diplomacy. https://www.academia.edu/28678308/Public_Diplomacy_Between_Theory_and_Practice.

Nye, Joseph S., Jr. 2008. Public diplomacy and soft power. *The annals of the American Academy of Political and Social Science*, Vol. 616, Public Diplomacy in a Changing World, 94–109. https://www.jstor.org/stable/25097996.

Nye, Joseph S., Jr. 1990. Soft power. *Foreign Policy* 80: 153–171 (Twentieth Anniversary). https://doi.org/10.2307/1148580.

Nye, J. 2004. *Soft power: The means to success in world politics*. New York: Public Affairs.

OECD. 2023. *Build, reinforce and protect resilience in an era of multiple crisis. Government at a Glance 2023*. Paris: OECD Publishing. https://doi.org/10.1787/128bebb5-en.

OECD. 2022. *Building trust and reinforcing democracy: Preparing the ground for government action, OECD public governance reviews*. Paris: OECD Publishing. https://doi.org/10.1787/76972a4a-en.

Pahlavi, Pierre C. 2003. Cyber-diplomacy: A new strategy of influence. Paper presented to the Canadian Political Science Association General Meeting 2003 Halifax, Nova Scotia (30.05.2003).

McGill, Peterson, and Patti McGill. Peterson. 2014. Diplomacy and education: A changing global landscape. *American Council on Education*. https://doi.org/10.6017/ihe.2014.75.5410.

Philpott, D. 1999. Westphalia, authority, and international society. *Political Studies* 47 (3): 566–589. https://doi.org/10.1111/1467-9248.00217.

Tavares, R. 2016. *Para-diplomacy: Cities and States as global players*. Oxford: Oxford University Press.

Turekian, Vaughan C., Sarah Macindoe, Daryl Copeland, Lloyd S. Davis, Robert G. Patman, and Maria Pozza. 2012. The emergence of science diplomacy. www.academia.edu.

UNDP. (2024). Human Development Report 2023/2024: Breaking the gridlock. Reimagining cooperation in a polarised world. https://hdr.undp.org/system/files/documents/global-report-document/hdr2023-24reporten.pdf

Van de Graaf, T., and J. Colgan. 2016. Global energy governance: A review and research agenda. *Palgrave Communications*. https://doi.org/10.1016/j.esr.2019.100386.

Vaxevanidou, Maria. 2018. Education as public diplomacy: How to build an international image in education. *Journal of Media Critiques* 4 (14): 55–70.

PART II

Practices Across the World

CHAPTER 9

Africa Rising in a Fast-Changing World: Transcending Continental Public Administration Challenges

Geraldine Fraser-Moleketi, Demetrios Argyriades, Joseph Besigye Bazirake, and Nadia Mukadam

9.1 Introduction

Following Africa's liberation movements and decolonisation efforts that proceeded through the 1950s and 60 s, the continent experienced significant shifts and challenges in its governance and service delivery. While diverse colonial and liberation experiences shaped Africa's identity, public sector reforms played a crucial role in navigating the continent's newfound independence. Significantly, liberation movements like the

G. Fraser-Moleketi · J. B. Bazirake (✉) · N. Mukadam
Nelson Mandela University, Gqeberha, South Africa
e-mail: besijoe@gmail.com

N. Mukadam
e-mail: nadia.mukadam@mandela.ac.za

D. Argyriades
New York, NY, USA

A. Baimenov and P. Liverakos (eds.), *Public Administration in the New Reality*, https://doi.org/10.1007/978-981-96-3845-1_9

African National Congress (ANC), established in 1912 in South Africa and others across the continent, including Guinea-Bissau and Algeria, predate the 1960 *Declaration on the Granting of Independence to Colonial Countries and Peoples* by the United Nations. Nonetheless, amidst local and international pressures, independence across African countries has driven them to focus on developing unique paths in public administration.

In this chapter, we engage with the challenges faced by African public administration amidst the continent's steadfast vision for development, democracy and good governance. We examine these challenges by scrutinising historical and contemporary dynamics, drawing on specific examples from various African nations. Despite the lack of homogeneity in colonial and liberation experiences across Africa, we note some generic trends in African public administration, focusing on socioeconomic development in the postcolonial period. Notably, African states, once subject to the hegemony of Northern countries, have now become significant contributors on the global scene, offering independent perspectives on matters of international significance. This chapter thus explores the many ways in which Africa's emergence as an independent force in world affairs intersects with the challenges and opportunities within its public administration endeavours.

9.2 Global Dynamics and Africa's Rise in International Politics

Are we close to the end of an era? Global tectonic changes, reflected in pronouncements of global leaders, as well as current trends, promise as much. Still, voices from our past warn us against the dangers of jumping to conclusions. Notoriously, we, people from the South, have often been known to take our dreams as irrefutable evidence of irreversible trends. The rhetoric of "progress" as destiny has led us to discount the moves of major players on the international chessboard when these did not agree with preconceived ideas about the course of history. Ever since the World War II, we have been trained to think that, at long last, the Era of Imperialism had finally come to an end; that with the United Nations (UN), its Charter and the constellation of international agencies, a new age would surely dawn, establishing relations among nations, large or small, based on equality, peace and justice. It was confidently expected that Decolonisation was only a matter of time, and that *realpolitik* would soon yield to respect for the principles of equity, legality and the spirit of cooperation in a new world environment (Newland and Argyriades 2019).

However, events like the collapse of the USSR and subsequent geopolitical turmoil cast doubt on this narrative. The resurgence of colonial proclivities among some nation states, as well as the reassertion of Western hegemony, hinted at a more complex reality. Indeed, it did appear as if, quite unexpectedly, the old colonial order had been resuscitated, imperialism revived and the United States erected into the world's sole arbiter and ruler. At international meetings, the leading lights of NATO continued, for a while, to invoke the "International Community" as if 194 Member States of the UN could still speak with *one* voice—that of NATO and the US. Then something happened. Russia "invaded" Ukraine, and the "collective West" rallied in support of Ukraine, solemnly censuring Russia and sternly applying *sanctions* in an effort to deter the pursuit of invasion. If the West had expected the "International Community" to do its bidding as usual self-righteously, it was taken by surprise. Other than North America and the European Union, the World remained indifferent to Western condemnations. It staunchly resisted pressures to force the global South to join the Western sanctions. Even more emphatically, US and Western voices advocating "Israel's right to defend itself" against Hamas' invasion, after 7 October 2023, have been met with a deafening silence, clearly demonstrating that the "global South and East" no longer feel the need to follow Western leaders in lock step.

Remarkably, however, recent developments in major parts of Africa have cast a bright new light on the history of the past six decades and the world post-World War II. It has become apparent that after an early euphoria, during the 1940s and 1950s, the old colonial powers made a concerted effort to slow down or to arrest the trends that undermined their hold over their former colonies. They tried to recapture the substance of Empire, albeit in a new form. "Colonialism was dead", or so the world was told. However, it soon dawned that it might be revived under the garb of treaties and alliances by means of infiltration, corruption, interference, subversion and the like. Sadly, technical cooperation devised in post-war years to assist the development process has often been misused to such pernicious ends. This was greatly facilitated when, in the 1990s, multilateral approaches by the United Nations gave way to bilateral programmes pretending to greater efficiency. Now, colonial domination could be perpetuated conveniently under the garb of "nation-building" by maintaining puppet regimes which did their masters' bidding.

Periodic sham elections offered a thin veneer of popular assent, acquiescence and participation. The African continent constantly grappled with narratives that democratic processes are, at times, manipulated by external influences. Whenever elections failed to produce the outcomes that Western puppet-masters have worked for or expected, "regime change", in the garb of "popular uprisings" or military coups, sufficed to stem the tide; all in the name of freedom, democracy of course and human rights. Occasionally, such action entailed the assassination of an incumbent leader. From Lumumba to Gaddafi, the list is very long. For close to six decades, a semblance of democracy and independence served to conceal the fact that economies were stagnant, largely under foreign control and that people lived in poverty, even though the African Continent was blessed with rich mineral and other resources. The July 2023 coup in Niger has served to bring to light that the deposits of uranium, exploited and managed by France, have only minimally availed the people of Niger, most of whom still live in poverty.

To those who remember the juntas of military dictators, who until fairly recently, controlled most of the lands of Central and South America, as well as some countries in Europe and in the Middle East, this development may induce some negative feelings occasioned by the experience of frequent "regime changes", triggered by foreign hegemons, in every part of the world. We should recall, however, that it was thanks to the agency of groups of Army officers intent on freeing their country from foreign domination that, in 1956, the Suez Canal could be nationalised. In looking at West Africa where, in Burkina Faso, Mali, Niger and Guinea, big changes were induced by military coups, we need to recognise that though, as a general principle, civilian rule and democratic processes are certainly preferred, it was often through *proforma* "democracies", that colonial domination could be perpetuated for more than six decades, in several parts of the world. Needless to emphasise that, in large parts of West Africa, in the past three years, one military coup after another has brought to power young officers with one shared goal and message: reclaiming, for their countries, control of their economies and natural wealth. In Senegal, for instance, the recent inauguration of Bassirou Diomaye Faye, Africa's youngest elected president at 44 years old, has pledged to prioritise the national exploitation of Senegal's resources.

He promised to reclaim full control of the country's resources and to implement policies which enhance transparency.

It is evident, in retrospect, that Western Hegemony over the African Continent was not merely economic, diplomatic and political. American, British or French, it did not take the form of just pressures by state agents. Perhaps, even more forcefully, it sought to shape the mindset and institutions of nations and elites. Arguably more than in Asia, millions of people in Africa were, for a century or more, led to consider themselves as beholden to the values, models, languages and doctrines that had been bequeathed by the West. During the 1950s, "sixties" and "seventies", though formally independent, African countries continued for a long while to follow western models, as well as political promptings from Western powers. Not surprisingly, such standards and models were portrayed as universal, science-driven and outcomes of decades of gradual evolution of the world's most advanced nations. The world was neatly divided into the "most advanced", "developed" and "developing".

In recent months, a confluence of events has cast new light on our recent past, leading us now to question a version of our history, which we had come to accept, inviting us to explore it with wholly new perspectives. It has been rightly stated that history—or rather "historical truth"—is mostly established by victors.[1] It is victors who determine how much of what occurred during the World War II or afterwards could be consigned to books and in what form. Regarding World War II, far more is known today about Omaha Beach and the Allies' landing in Normandy than, arguably, the battle of Stalingrad which, even Western historians reluctantly recall as a major turning point in the tide of the War. The world had come to accept a version of the history of "Decolonisation" as the historic accomplishment of benign Western leaders, who boldly took the initiative of granting independence to peoples subjugated for a century or more. Reality is more complex. The British in Kenya and Cyprus, the Portuguese in Mozambique, in Angola and Guinea-Bissau or the French in Madagascar and Algeria fought long rearguard actions trying to keep their respective empires against all of the odds pointing to this endeavour's manifest futility. Later, the French were hailed for not repeating the error that led to Dien Bien Phu by moving, in the sixties,

[1] Attributed to Sir Winston Churchill.

to liberate dependencies that had formed their Empire since the late nineteenth Century. Decolonisation in the late 1940s, the 1950s and 1960s had widely been attributed to the far-sighted wisdom of leading Western statesmen, yielding to the dictates of a new spirit of freedom sweeping the world, notably, after the establishment of the United Nations in 1945.

The struggle for liberation and decolonisation in Africa spans a significant historical timeline, reflecting the continent's enduring quest for self-determination. From the early twentieth century to the present day, numerous liberation movements have emerged, each representing a milestone in the fight against colonial domination. Egypt's nationalist movement, led by the Wafd Party, demanded self-rule. This achieved partial independence in 1922 and, following the Free Officers Movement-led liberation, full sovereignty in 1952. Ghana's independence movement, spearheaded by the Convention People's Party (CPP), led by Kwame Nkrumah, marked an important turning point in 1957 as Ghana became the first sub-Saharan African country to gain independence from colonial rule. Algeria's National Liberation Front (FLN) led the struggle against French colonial rule, ultimately resulting in Algeria's independence in 1962, after eight long years of armed conflict and political mobilisation. For Guinea-Bissau, the African Party for the Independence of Guinea and Cape Verde (PAIGC) played a central role in the armed struggle against Portuguese colonial rule. This led to the country's declaration of independence in 1973. Likewise, it took decades of armed resistance and diplomatic efforts for Namibia's resistance against South African rule, led by the South West Africa People's Organisation (SWAPO), to gain independence in 1990. The African National Congress (ANC) played a pivotal role in the struggle against apartheid in South Africa, employing such strategies as nonviolent resistance, mass mobilisation and armed struggle, ultimately resulting in democratic elections in 1994 and the complete dismantling of apartheid.

The above examples affirm the continent's continued fight for its own liberation. Whether through armed resistance, political activism or diplomatic efforts, these movements demonstrate the agency and resilience of African peoples in challenging colonial domination. It needs to be remembered, on the other hand, that while many African countries have achieved independence from colonial rule, challenges related to governance, economic inequality, social justice and cultural autonomy persist. The struggle for liberation and decolonisation in Africa continues to evolve and become manifest in various forms to the present day.

In retrospect and in light of recent events, the process, which, through the 1960s doubled the membership of the United Nations, may aptly be described as one of "Decolonisation without Emancipation". It took the coups in Guinea, Mali, Burkina Faso and Niger to bring to light the extent to which countries of the Sahel, but not they alone, had for six long decades, remained effectively bound by a web of tight constraints, which limited their freedom and kept their economies subject to that of the former metropolis. The ways this could be accomplished were numerous. Some were institutionalised, like the "*franc CFA*", which effectively annulled any national right to make decisions regarding the finances or economic development. It took a powerful speech, made by the representative of Burkina Faso to the General Assembly of the United Nations in September 2023, to enable all to measure the distance separating proforma independence from real and effective self-determination. That such a speech could not have been pronounced in earlier years casts a stark light on the nature of the leadership—leadership that all too widely afflicted many West African nations in postcolonial days. What past colonial masters were not in a position to institutionalise, they tried to obtain through bribery, extortion and corruption. Sadly, examples abound. Remarkably, it required a major conflagration, like the ongoing War in Ukraine and the ripples it produced in several parts of the world to enable African leaders to reclaim their independence and pre-empt colonial masters, who might have contemplated a violent course of revenge, "regime change" or repression.

In the face of all these challenges, the vision of an "African Renewal through the African Renaissance" championed by President Thabo Mbeki, the essence of which has been the New Partnership for Africa Development (NEPAD) described by Prime Minister Meles Zenawi of Ethiopia: "What NEPAD inherited is a bleak ideological landscape where progressive thinking had to go deep underground and hibernate to survive" (Meles Zenawi, 19 June 2008). NEPAD has been gaining prominence across the Continent since 1999, having been adopted by the African Union (AU) in July 2001. It has articulated long-standing aspirations for collective transformation, economic progress, development, democracy, good governance and lasting peace. This vision materialised in the New Partnership for Africa's Development (NEPAD), originating from the 4th OAU Extraordinary Session in Sirte, Libya. Here, Presidents Abdelaziz Bouteflika and Thabo Mbeki were mandated to engage

Africa's creditors, diplomatically, seeking the complete cancellation of the Continent's external debt.

To be sure, the August 2023 Meeting of the BRICS in Johannesburg will long be remembered as a historic moment that marked the end of an era; that postcolonial dominance, the way that it played out for close to six decades, kept former colonial dependencies firmly within the sphere of past imperial masters. In recent years, there has been growing recognition of the need for all the African countries to assert their sovereignty and pursue development strategies that are aligned with their own best interests and priorities. This has led to the strengthening of regional integration efforts, the advancement of South-South cooperation and the exploration of alternative partnerships beyond traditional Western alliances.

In seeking to challenge the dominance of Western powers and systems, BRICS have now established connections and interactions with Africa, demonstrating a shared historical experience and aspirations towards a more equitable and proper global order. These connections encompass support for liberation movements, diplomatic and economic relations, emphasis on South-South cooperation and calls for reforms in global governance institutions. This underscores Africa's ongoing struggle for liberation and its demands for greater representation and voice in all global decision-making processes.

Increasingly, the forces calling for drastic change are multiplying as, all around the globe, countries demand their freedom from threats to their autonomy, along with the right to choose their friends and partners, or the course they want to follow. A recent major blow to occupation, settler colonialism and apartheid was dealt by none other than South Africa through its influential Foreign Minister, Naledi Pandor, when she called upon the African Union to rescind the observer status that had been extended to Israel. Clearly, *Africa is rising* from its postcolonial slumber of proforma independence, which lasted six decades. Imperial Hegemony which, in one way or another, has been perpetuated by the "collective West", is visibly collapsing as countries of the South increasingly distance themselves from their former hegemons. Manifestly, a new day is dawning for a world no longer subordinated to orders and to models emanating from the West. There can be little doubt that interstate relations in Africa and beyond will henceforth be quite different and, though more unpredictable, arguably more promising than in the past.

9.3 Contextualising African Public Administration Within Global Patterns

Readers in the global South will recall how, routinely, Western leaders—Anthony Blinken, for instance—would presume to express the views of what they liked to term the "International Community" though, in the majority of cases, such references applied to no more than the countries of NATO and close East Asian Allies. Simply, from some Western points of view, the rest of the world did not matter. Even several decades after the sudden implosion of the USSR and the end of the Cold War, the "global West" continued to go about the "business of running the world" as if the world still lived in the aftermath of Empires, with the US and Britain—arguably also France—still determining the merits of countries, large and small and charting the course of history. A change, in this regard, has been slow and incremental. It took earth-shaking changes to bring to light the importance of twin events and trends, which marked the slow decline of the "collective West" and the related rise of sub-Saharan Africa, Asia and Latin America in world affairs. Arguably, "*Africa rising*" has more to do with the prevailing winds of change currently sweeping the World and the spirit of self-confidence these entail and less with any single policy moves, in the West or in the global South.

Public administration, we have argued, plays a crucial role in realising the transformative goals of "African Renewal" by ensuring effective governance and sustainable progress in a dynamically evolving global context. The study of public administration involves examining the management, implementation, policies and effectiveness of government operations (Basheka 2015). It has also been understood as the specific type of administration that supports governmental and other public activities (Gladden 1976, 2019). As both an academic discipline and a practical governing approach, public administration has evolved and been shaped by broad historical contexts, values and needs. While comparative perspectives have been central to assessing public administration practices over time, their focus has been mainly on developed Western and Asian countries (Fitzpatrick et al. 2011). This has left indigenous administration at the periphery of public administration theorisation and its consideration as a distinctly African paradigm without a real corollary in Western theory (Basheka 2015). What is significant to note from the different eras of public administration discussed hereafter is that there were no clear-cut transitions, as each era provided the departure point for the next, often carrying on the character and challenges of its preceding era.

Exploring indigenous systems of public administration, Basheka (2012) also reviews the periodisation of its development into four eras. He identifies the scientific management era (1887–1926) as a foundational period, wherein the field's focus was on bureaucratic hierarchy, specialisation and administrative efficiency (Basheka 2012). This era was the foundation of Western public administration's focus on principles like hierarchy, rationality and specialisation deemed to be universal. This era has been recognised as the birth of Public Administration in the USA. President Woodrow Wilson's article, "*The Study of Administration*" (1887), was a foundational text in its rise as a discipline separate from politics. Within this period, African administration involved consensus-building, checks on power, communal values and specialised bodies overseeing defence, trade, infrastructure, justice, health and education. Both the strengths of public participation and the weaknesses of authoritarianism persisted (Basheka 2015). Despite the pre-colonial traces of vibrant African administration systems within this period, the Continent's indigenous knowledge and practices long remained peripheral in scholarly coverage.

Following Frederick Taylor, the scientific management approach and related "principles" arose and lasted between 1927 and 1937. With these principles came a quest for universal guidelines with a view to standardising administrative practices across diverse contexts (Basheka 2012). Willoughby, in his 1927 work "*Principles of Public Administration*", pioneered the argument that specific scientific principles governing administration not only existed but could also be discovered and applied universally by administrators. It was believed that these "principles" would increase the efficiency and economy of public administration. These principles were expected to be uncovered by scholars, who would then become experts, having learnt how to apply these principles.

As the discipline of public administration advanced, the era of challenge (1938–1947) emerged, marked by the critical examination of preceding concepts and the emergence of human relations approaches. Remarkably, within this period, the Atlantic Charter of 1941 resulted in South Africa in the drafting of the African Claims document, which demanded that South Africans—all South Africans—be granted the same rights and freedoms as those enshrined in the Charter. The United Nations could not enforce these claims as long as apartheid persisted, more so while major Western nations continued to support the South African apartheid regime.

However, the end of World War II in 1945 marked a significant turning point in global history, as the confluence of interests, ideas and circumstances set in motion transformative trends that would reshape the world. Two major developments emerged during this period with far-reaching repercussions: firstly, the concept of the Welfare State responding to demands of those that fought the war and now presented for a redefinition of major government functions. The focus shifted gradually from *warfare* to *welfare* and from imperial expansion to providing service to citizens and the community at large. Secondly, the dismantlement of long-standing empires granted freedom to people around the world. These two movements provided an impetus to the United Nations, established in 1945. It also set the stage for the emergence of Development Administration as a global governance priority. We note that both the principles and the challenge phases in Western theory building marked the same period as the bureaucratisation under colonial rule, which took root in Africa.

In the aftermath of World War II, during the period spanning 1948 to 1970, public administration found itself grappling with an "identity crisis" as it endeavoured to establish its distinct role within the realm of political science (Basheka 2012). During the 15 years that followed World War II, some colonies achieved independence and self-governance, giving rise to aspirations for self-determination and representative government. The impact of these trends became evident in the 1950s and 60s, with the earliest transformation observed in the emancipation of British and Dutch colonies in Asia. In Africa, decolonisation and liberation movements brought freedom to nations like Ghana, where President Nkrumah came to power in 1958. Other countries followed suit, not without a struggle, given the marked reluctance of some colonial powers to relinquish imperial control and to set their peoples free. The former Belgian Congo, where civil war erupted and the United Nations was asked to intervene, was arguably the worst-case scenario. Similarly, Mozambique, Angola and Guinea-Bissau only acceded to freedom after protracted wars. These ended in the wresting of power from the colonial masters and even brought regime change to the metropolis itself.

It was also in the 1950s that the term "development administration" came into use to describe the specific parts of public administration and its modifications to suit the implementation of policies, projects and programmes aimed at improving social and economic conditions (Gant 2006). "Development administration" is a Western-origin concept, used almost exclusively with reference to developing nations in Asia, the Middle East, sub-Saharan Africa and Latin America (Dwivedi 1994). One of the key issues that early commentators on development administration included was its potential to balance politics and administration, particularly in the early independence years, where what might be considered "political" in the West represented a necessary administrative intervention in the newly independent countries (Kasfir 1969). Development administrators were initially perceived as crucial intermediaries, bridging the gap between the developed and developing worlds. Their roles were seen as aligned with the interests and the policies of developing countries.

Change in colonial status across Africa brought about such anticipated improvements as greater personal freedom, social equality, elevated national incomes, enhanced living standards, as well as better prospects. Notably, a generation emerged with growing expectations, advocating rapid transformations in politics, society and the economy. This presented major challenges to newly formed governments and administrative structures (Gant 2006). As a result, the significance of education and training in public administration grew due to citizens' expectations of value for money spent on public services. This trend was particularly pronounced in the developing countries, including those in Africa. Education and training initiatives were generally considered as significant enablers for the establishment of a developmental state in Africa (Kwaku Ohemeng 2014).

Notwithstanding these trends, during the 1970s and 1980s, growing scepticism persisted regarding the concept of Development Administration itself. It was increasingly questioned as a tool for managing progress or economic aid and technical support to developing countries (Afolayan and Ogunsanwo 2017). A noteworthy critique, which gained traction during this period consisted in the notion that Development Administration effectively mirrored Western imperialism in its various aspects, including the economic, administrative, organisational, cultural and ideological inputs. This criticism contended that, both in theory and practice, development administration perpetuated Western-centric values and norms. In light of these concerns, there arose pressing demands to thoroughly examine the value system, as well as cultural relevance underpinning prevailing development ideals, particularly concerning their appropriateness within the African context. Such an inquiry is essential to assess the suitability of these ideals in the specific cultural, socioeconomic and historical milieu of African nations (Afolayan and Ogunsanwo 2017).

Yet, African public administration scholars often hesitate to develop and adapt their discipline in ways that align with the realities of their own communities (Chanie 2013). This reluctance has resulted in Africa being "defined" by outsiders, who lack firsthand experience with the Continent itself (Erasmus 2020).

The 1970s and 1980s provided evidence that the challenges facing public administration in Africa stem from multiple sources. These include the pervasive influence of predatory capitalism on a global scale, as well as fiscal constraints that governments face within the broader crisis of capitalist systems. Farazmand (2012) further notes that an "identity crisis" that had come to define public administration before the 1970s prevented it from achieving a definitive sense of identity and stability as an academic pursuit. Consequently, it was institutionally relegated to departments of political science, business schools, planning and even architecture. We argue, by contrast, that the African Continent is currently grappling with a functional and disciplinary identity crisis in relation to public administration. Farazmand (2012) similarly notes that the absence of clear constitutional validation for public administration as a distinct profession and field of inquiry only accentuates this signal identity crisis. Addressing this crisis requires thoughtful and context-specific approaches that draw on African values, traditions and aspirations, while embracing the need for efficient and effective governance practices. It also involves redefining the African identity in public administration, fostering a sense of ownership and promoting innovative and contextually relevant approaches that resonate with the diverse African realities.

The next shift in the conceptualisation of Public Administration was with the rise of the New Public Management (NPM), between the 1970s and 1990s. This sought to redirect the focus of the discipline, away from questions of values to operational issues and questions of efficiency, economy and effectiveness. During this period, public administration began to incorporate private sector practices and market-based ideas. While Ferlie et al. (2005) took note of shifts in terminology from "public administration" to "New Public Management" (NPM) during the 1980s, they also raised the questions of NPM's endurance, relevance and applicability globally. Nyadera and Dagba (2022), on the other hand, argue that NPM was responsible for a significant trend in developed countries, where civil society structures took over roles once exclusively held by the State.

Such reforms mainly focused on improving effectiveness and reducing state intervention in the economy, enhancing fiscal management, increasing transparency in regulation and fostering merit-based practices in the public service. Nyadera and Dagba (2022) further argue that this has influenced the present state of public administration globally, which now emphasises equitable governance, democratic oversight and rational bureaucratic practices. The legacy of NPM remains evident in the persistence and optimisation of its tools and methodologies that governments across Africa have adopted. The resulting approaches signify a departure from the previously acknowledged limitations of NPM, with an observable shift from prioritising efficiency to elevating effectiveness and moving towards an emerging emphasis on good governance (De Vries and Nemec 2013). This shift presents a trajectory that increasingly considers equity, equality and ethics in governance as significant areas of emphasis for Public Administration.

Significantly, since the late 1990s, the *governance* era has come to the fore, underscoring the importance of collaboration, participation and technology-enabled networks in contemporary public administration paradigms (Basheka 2012). The governance paradigm aligns with contemporary reforms in Africa towards transparency, participation and decentralisation. However, Rubakula (2014) notes that, during the 1990s, while the governance era of public administration was looming globally, many African countries embraced the New Public Management (NPM) model in their administrative frameworks, aiming at increased efficiency and effectiveness in the public sector.

To believe the acolytes of NPM, a reduced public sector would surely represent Africa's road to prosperity, opening up the prospect of governments offloading large segments of their functions, onto the private sector and focusing instead on promoting the 3Es (economy, efficiency and effectiveness). These reforms, Rubakuka argues, faced various challenges, resulting in the partial implementation and mixed outcomes across African nations. The mixed outcomes might be explained by the overlap of paradigms in their application across Africa since the 1990s.

Based on the analysis of these public administration trends, two influential global patterns have been poised to reshape the landscape and dynamics of the field. As described by Farazmand (2012), the first pattern revolves around persistent efforts to spread American administrative models globally, particularly in developing countries, Eastern Europe and China. The second represents a contrasting pattern emerging in response to this phenomenon in many developing and former Soviet bloc nations. This transition is underscored by the shift from a unipolar and bipolar global economic order to a multi-polar one, driven by the ascent of emerging powers, notably China and India and the redistribution of economic power from the Atlantic shores to the Asia–Pacific region. This transformation is reshaping global dominance, competitiveness, governance structures and international relations, as evidenced by the shift from the G7/G8 to the G20 and the increasing importance of the BRICS+ in the global economy (Ignat and Bujancă 2014). Of particular importance is China's active role in advocating multipolarity since 1992 and its collaborative efforts with Russia in forming an alternative global governance structure from 2001 to 2015. This is exemplified by the strengthening of BRICS+ and the establishment of institutions like the New Development Bank and the Contingent Reserve Arrangement. These initiatives highlight China and Russia's pivotal contribution to this evolving international landscape (Andreevich 2019). The emergence of a multi-polar global arrangement, characterised by the presence of multiple major players, has therefore become a defining feature of the contemporary world order.

9.4 The Character of Contemporary African Public Administration

African countries approach public administration mostly in the context of their own unique histories, crises and current circumstances. While precolonial indigenous administration relied on chieftaincies, kinship representation, consensus-based decision-making and ways of constraining despotism, colonial administration imposed a centralised bureaucracy and indirect rule for resource extraction, often neglecting communal practices (Basheka, 2015). Postcolonial administrations were aimed at the Africanisation of the civil service, resulting in problems with corruption and capacity amidst rapid transition.

The contemporary reforms era features democratisation, decentralisation, governance improvements and pressure from external donors. Although the integration of elements of indigenous administration into modern practice has yet to be explored at length, Basheka (2015) considers it a means to strengthen African public administration. As a result, Public administration in Africa exhibits unique characteristics, which, Hyden (2020) argues, are due to the absence of a strong economic production-driven societal structure and the imposition of foreign-created states without deep roots in the economy or society. He argues that these factors lead to governance primarily shaped by political conflicts over resource distribution rather than economic production criteria.

It is important to highlight that, in contemporary times, many African countries share similar goals in their public administration approaches. This is evident in the African Charter for Public Service in Africa, which was adopted during a meeting in Windhoek, Namibia, on 5–6 February 2001. This Charter aims to strengthen public administration systems and to promote good governance. It emphasises the importance of effectively updating administrative structures and using modern communication technologies. Additionally, it calls for adapting to the global economy and creating an environment that encourages growth in the private sector. The Charter also stresses a need to reinforce the basic infrastructure, promote social development, address income disparities, as well as to explore opportunities to promote social solidarity. The Charter recognises the vital role of public services in upholding important values, safeguarding public well-being and fostering sustainable socioeconomic progress. It emphasises that these services must be adaptable and responsive to the needs of the people, while staying transparent, respecting human rights and bolstering democracy (United Nations 2001).

Such additional mechanisms, as the African Governance Architecture (AGA), were developed in 2010 as a mechanism for dialogue among African Union (AU) stakeholders and/or sub-regional organs and institutions to promote good democratic governance in Africa. This mechanism works hand in hand with the African Governance Platform and the African Governance Architecture Secretariat, to enhance governance and public administration capacity on the Continent. Other institutions, which have mandates related to governance, include the New Partnership for Africa's Development (NEPAD), the African Peer Review Mechanism (APRM), the African Governance Architecture, the African Peace and Security Council (APSC), the Pan African Parliament and the AU Advisory Board on Corruption (AU-ABC) (Kariseb and Okoloise 2020). In addition, the African Charter on Values and Principles of Public Service and Administration,[2] adopted by the African Union in 2011, serves as a framework

[2] https://www.peaceau.org/uploads/african-charter-values-principles-public-service-adminstration-en.pdf.

for promoting good governance, professionalism and ethical conduct in public administration across participating countries (Busieka 2018).

However, the AU also adopted the African Charter on the Values and Principles of Decentralisation, Local Governance,[3] and Local Development, emphasising the importance of effective decentralisation, local governance and citizen participation in public administration. Similarly, the *AU Agenda 2063* has been considered as a long-term continental development framework intended to provide a strategic vision for Africa's socioeconomic transformation. It highlights the importance of effective governance, sound public administration and transformative leadership in achieving the goals of Agenda 2063. The framework influences public administration trends by promoting innovation, inclusivity and sustainable development (AU Commission 2014).[4] Such other establishments as the African Association for Public Administration and Management (AAPAM), a professional association that operates across African countries, promote excellence and professionalism in public administration. It organises conferences, seminars and training programmes to facilitate knowledge sharing, networking and capacity building in public administration (Hyden 1997).

Regionally, the East African Community Civil Service Reform Programme, implemented by several East African countries, aims to improve public administration by enhancing civil service systems in efficiency, effectiveness and professionalism. This regional initiative focuses on human resource management, performance management and service delivery reforms. Similarly, the West Africa Institute for Financial and Economic Management (WAIFEM) also acts as a capacity-building framework. It operates in multiple West African countries, providing training and technical assistance in public financial management. It offers budgeting, financial reporting, debt management and public procurement programmes, contributing to improved financial governance and administration. The Southern African Development Community (SADC) Regional Public Sector Training Institutes also play a similar role in several member countries. These include the Lesotho Institute of Public Administration and Management (LIPAM) and the National School of

[3] https://www.uclga.org/wp-content/uploads/2018/01/AFRICAN-CHARTER-ON-THE-VALUES-PRINCIPLES-DECENTRALISATION-EN-Final-2.pdf.

[4] African Union Commission. 2014. Agenda 2063. The Africa we want. Draft Document. http://www.nepad.org/system/files/Agenda%202063%20%20English.pdf.

Government in South Africa. Both offer capacity-building programmes to enhance skills and professionalism in regional public administration.

It remains apparent that African public administration dynamics continue to be shaped by such global forces as the growing adoption of the SDGs that have influenced Africa's development agenda and public administration. African countries, for instance, have aligned their policies, plans and public administration practices with the SDGs, emphasising the need for integrated approaches, multisectoral collaboration and evidence-based decision-making to achieve sustainable growth. Similar approaches have taken on a continental character, where Africa's Agenda 2063, for instance, is closely aligned to the global sustainable development goals in the areas of improving of standards of living, health, education and environmental protection, among others.[5] In the following section, such drivers of African public administration are examined theoretically, as well as in practical terms.

9.5 Public Administration Drivers in Africa: Embracing the New Public Service Theory

Farazmand (2012) argues that the future identity of public administration is expected to encompass five key component elements. These include: its role as a "facilitator" in corporate globalisation; its applications in regulatory administration; in the need to strike a balance between control and public interest; in the imperative for capacity building; and in consideration of efforts of the rapid technological advances that will shape public administration's future. Rubakula (2014) suggests that, in Africa's case, this should transition towards a form of public value management; one that takes into account local contexts before implementing external reforms. Rubakula's approach emphasises such critical elements as market competition, business principles, managerial autonomy, customer choice and performance standards.

However, it is Denhardt and Denhardt's (2000) proposition for a New Public Service (NPS) that this chapter considers for theoretical alignment with the continent's aspirations towards addressing its public administration challenges. NPS has proven compatible with the previously discussed

[5] Agenda 2063 and SDGs Implementation in Africa—APRM. https://au.int/en/agenda2063/sdgs.

governance era of public administration in Africa, contrasting with New Public Management, which views public managers as entrepreneurs moving towards a leaner and increasingly privatised government that adopts business practices and values. In contrast, NPS emphasises democratic citizenship, community engagement, civil society involvement, organisational humanism and discourse theory, placing citizens at the core of public administration's role in the governance system.

Denhardt and Denhardt (2000) outline seven principles for the New Public Service. They propose that public servants should focus on helping people express and fulfil their collective needs rather than trying to control how society works. They emphasise the importance of considering the public interest, encouraging public administrators to collaborate with citizens to shape a shared vision of the common good and avoiding quick solutions based on individual preferences. NPS promotes policy-making through strategic thinking and democratic action, underscoring that effective and responsible policies arise from collaboration.

According to NPS, the relationship between public servants and citizens should be built on the basis of trust and collaboration, with a focus on serving citizens rather than treating them mostly as customers who make demands. As such, accountability in NPS lies in considering a combination of factors, including laws, community values, political norms, professional standards and citizen interests; not just market dynamics. Therefore, NPS stresses the importance of valuing people over just being productive. It entails the belief that public organisations are more likely to succeed when everyone works together and respects one another. Significantly, NPS promotes prioritising citizenship and public service over entrepreneurial goals, arguing that public interest is better served when public servants and citizens contribute meaningfully to society, rather than think as managers, treating public funds as if they were their money (Denhardt and Denhardt 2000).

Similarly, Robinson (2015) notes that, viewed through the lens of democratic theory, the New Public Service model is centred on active and engaged citizenship. Here, citizens are encouraged to transcend self-interest, focusing instead on the wider public interest, while officials play a facilitative role in enhancing citizen engagement for societal problem-solving. Under this paradigm, public managers are urged to acquire skills beyond mere control or steering of society, emphasising brokering, negotiating and collaborative problem-solving with citizens. He notes that the NPS advocates for open, accessible and accountable governments that operate to serve citizens, extending accountability relationships beyond the formal structures to include citizens and communities. By prioritising public interest and citizen-focused public service, the NPS model serves as a corrective to earlier, control-oriented models of public administration. However, Robinson acknowledges that the NPS framework is normative and value-driven, providing an essential corrective but hardly a comprehensive paradigm.

Based on both Farazmand and Rubakula's futuristic submissions on public administration and the premise of the New Public Service theory's alignment with the tenets of the governance era, we outline three crucial areas that play a significant role in driving contemporary Public Administration in Africa. These include: (1) Institutional Adaptation; (2) Governance and Leadership Excellence; and (3) Technology-driven Modernisation.

9.5.1 Institutional Adaptation

Institutional adaptation encompasses both institutional restructuring and sustainability efforts. For institutions to become more adept at serving people *first*, certain adaptations, helping citizens articulate and meet their shared concerns, need to be promoted. Similarly, a focus on public interest, rather than personal choices, requires institutions that are better capacitated towards building a collective notion of the public interest, often through citizen participation. This would also necessitate accountability—beyond value for money but a premise on citizen interests—among other socio-political considerations. We argue that *institutional adaptation* is aligned with the New Public Service theory, as the following examples, drawn across the Continent, indicate. We discuss the instances of institutional adaptation within three approaches: (1) Public Sector Reforms and Efficiency, focusing on improving governmental structures for enhanced effectiveness; (2) Public–Private Partnerships (PPPs), fostering collaboration between the public and private sectors for diverse expertise and resources; and (3) Decentralisation and Local Governance. This involves distributing administrative responsibilities to local levels for tailored responses to regional needs. Arguably, these approaches contribute to making administrative institutions in Africa more responsive, efficient and adaptable. Consideration of institutional adaptation also relates to Farazmand's (2012) remarks pointing to two of the earlier noted aspects of futuristic Public Administration: its role as a "facilitator" in corporate globalisation and its need to strike a balance between control and public interest. This is further expounded below.

9.5.2 Public Sector Reforms and Efficiency

The global drive for public sector reforms and enhanced administrative efficiency has catalysed a wave of initiatives within African countries, all aimed at improving the effectiveness of public administration. These initiatives encompass a spectrum of objectives, including the streamlining of bureaucratic processes, reducing corruption and enhancing service delivery. As governments across Africa grapple with these imperatives, a common thread emerges: a commitment to transforming and bolstering public services through institutional reforms and capacity-building efforts that put the citizen at the front and centre.

An illustrative example of this commitment is found in South Africa's *Batho Pele* ("People first") Programme. It was launched in 1997. This initiative stands out as a noteworthy model of dedication to reform, with its primary goal as the enhancement of public service delivery through such innovative strategies as comprehensive training, active citizen engagement and the rigorous pursuit of service quality improvement. In undertaking these efforts, South Africa aimed to align its public administration with global trends, emphasising citizen-centred governance (Kroukamp 1999). It is crucial to contextualise South Africa's reform efforts within the country's broader historical backdrop. Following the end of *apartheid*, South Africa confronted the formidable task of integrating numerous administrative entities from both the central government and the homelands. This aim was to create a unified and coherent administrative system, while addressing the profound legacies of apartheid and colonialism. Following a constitutional imperative and restructuring, South Africa established a governance system consisting of three spheres: the national, provincial and local government levels. It is worth noting that affirmative action programmes, including training and support initiatives designed to promote diversity have been widely implemented across the country. Franks (2014), however, points out that effectiveness in these programmes has often been hampered by challenges in implementation and monitoring. He notes that, in some cases, *favouritism* appeared to take precedence over competence in appointment decisions.

Another noteworthy example of public sector reform, in the early 2000s, is Rwanda's departure on an Institutional Development and Capacity Building Programme (IDCBP). It signalled a resolute dedication to strengthening public institutions. This multifaceted initiative aimed to elevate transparency levels, foster improved governance practices at all administrative tiers and bolster overall institutional capacity. Manifestly, Rwanda's commitment to these reforms aligned with the broader global movement towards accountable and efficient governance (Murindahabi 2016). Similarly, launched in 2004, Nigeria's Economic Reform and Governance Project (ERGP) epitomised the nation's determination to enhance its public institutions' efficiency, transparency and effectiveness. This project sought to drive sustainable economic growth through the various sectors by implementing comprehensive reforms. Nigeria's approach is aligned with the global discourse on good governance and the imperative of efficient public administration (Okonjo-Iweala and Osafo-Kwaako 2007).

Ethiopia also embarked on a transformative journey with its Civil Service Reform Programme, which was initiated in 1994. This ambitious undertaking aimed to modernise the civil service by introducing merit-based recruitment practices, instituting rigorous performance evaluations and further implementing comprehensive capacity-building measures. In so doing, Ethiopia sought to align its administrative practices with international best practices and the imperative of effective public service delivery (Markos 2013). Similarly, in Cameroon, the National Governance Programme, launched in 2004,[6] aimed to enhance institutional capacity, by fostering transparency and strengthening governance frameworks. This programme targeted such critical sectors as education, health and public finance management, emphasising the pivotal role of good governance in driving development outcomes. The Cameroon case underscores a recognition of governance as a principal component of public administration reform efforts, aligning it with global trends that prioritise transparency and accountability.

It is noted that the interplay between global influences and unique cultural contexts also plays a significant role in institutional reform

[6] AFRICAN DEVELOPMENT FUND: Appraisal report - The national governance program support project, Republic of Cameroon. https://www.afdb.org/fileadmin/uploads/afdb/Documents/Project-and-Operations/Cameroon_-_The_National_Governance_Programme_Support_Project_-_Appraisal_Report.pdf.

trends in different parts of the African Continent. For instance, experiences from Tanzania and Ghana reveal the multifaceted nature of reforms and the need to tailor them to local circumstances, while incorporating international best practices. Tanzania's 1998 Public Service Reform Programme,[7] aimed to enhance public service delivery through a comprehensive strategy. This programme spanned three phases aspiring to establish a systematic process for sustainable performance improvement. Key components included civil service management reforms, improved recruitment processes and performance-based management, with decentralisation and expansion of government entities. It also incorporated private sector participation, the creation of executive agencies, modernisation of information systems and promotion of a meritocratic public service with a strong focus on leadership, ethics and gender mainstreaming. Tanzania's case exemplifies the incorporation of global best practices into local reform initiatives, while also recognising the need for multifaceted approaches to improved public service delivery.

In Ghana, as outlined by the IMF,[8] the 2003 Public Sector Reform Programme sought to enhance the efficiency and effectiveness of the public sector. The programme introduced performance management and training measures, reflecting a global trend towards greater accountability and capacity building. However, a critical perspective emerges when considering Ghana's cultural context. Haruna (2003) argues that the reform efforts, influenced by Anglo-American values, may not have fully resonated with Ghana's distinct cultural landscape, which is characterised by a unique form of localism. Haruna suggests an alternative approach; one that emphasises community-oriented reform, starting from the grassroots and striking a balance between national bureaucratic needs and the intricacies of local conditions. This perspective underscores the importance of cultural sensitivity in shaping public administration reforms.

African countries, accordingly, have recognised the value of indigenous knowledge systems incorporating them into public administration practices. This trend involves integrating traditional knowledge practices

[7] Tanzania Public Service Reform Program (Phase II), Report No AB3040. https://documents1.worldbank.org/curated/en/505531468312048819/pdf/PIDAppraisal0Stage112JUNE07.pdf.

[8] IMF: Ghana: Joint Staff Assessment of the Poverty Reduction Strategy Paper. https://www.elibrary.imf.org/downloadpdf/journals/002/2003/132/article-A001-en.xml.

and expertise in such areas as agriculture, natural resource management and healthcare. It recognises the importance of local knowledge and community-led approaches in shaping policies and service delivery. One way that local knowledge and practices have been put to use is through the Village Savings and Loans Associations (VSLAs). These are community-based microfinance groups that have gained popularity in several African countries. Such groups have mobilised savings, provided loans and financial services to community members, promoting financial inclusion, entrepreneurship and economic empowerment at the grassroots level. For instance, CARE introduced VSLAs to address financial inclusion for Africa's poorest households, especially women, by promoting a savings-focused microfinance model that helps them build financial assets and skills, while allowing for diversification of income-generating activities and smoothing consumption patterns. VSLAs are thus seen as a crucial step towards achieving financial inclusion in these marginalised communities (Hendricks and Chidiac 2011).

Similarly, Nigeria's urban centres have struggled with the prevalence of symptoms of environmental degradation with refuse dumped in the streets, drainage channels or behind homes, largely due to inadequate government handling of solid waste. Rural communities have maintained cleaner environments through community action groups. These foster communal living and further the potential for similar practices in urban neighbourhoods to address this problem (Ofong 2004). This was similarly applied to Nigeria's Lagos State, where the "Community Waste Management Scheme" engages local communities in waste collection, recycling and disposal activities. This homegrown initiative not only improves waste management but also creates employment opportunities and promotes environmental sustainability (Adewole 2009). In Tanzania, Village Energy Committees have been formed to promote access to clean and affordable energy in rural areas. These committees manage such community-based energy projects as solar panels and biogas digesters, ensuring reliable energy supply and contributing to sustainable development.[9]

African countries continue to exhibit a commitment to improving administrative efficiency through diverse reforms, while aligning their respective practices to global trends and recognising the importance of

[9] Tanzania's SE4ALL, The United Republic of Tanzania, Ministry of Energy and Minerals, December 2015. https://www.se4all-africa.org/fileadmin/uploads/se4all/Documents/Country_IPs/Tanzania_IP_EN_Released.pdf.

local perspectives in achieving sustainable development, as the above-mentioned examples indicate. Part of this commitment has also extended to Public–Private Partnerships, as the discussion that follows shows.

9.5.3 Public–Private Partnerships

An overarching trend in African public administration is the institutional adoption of Public–Private Partnerships (PPPs). Recognising the potential of PPPs, several African countries have laid the legal foundations to facilitate private sector participation in government infrastructure and development projects. PPPs have become pivotal in fostering collaboration between the public and private sectors, with significant implications for the landscape of public administration in African nations. The impact of this global trend is evident in various African countries, where PPPs have been used to harness private sector expertise, resources and investments in order to bridge infrastructure gaps, deliver essential services and drive economic development.

Among notable departures, Kenya's enactment of the Public–Private Partnership Act (2013) exemplifies this trend. Legislation provided the legal framework for fostering PPPs and facilitated private sector engagement in various public ventures. The Nairobi-Mombasa Standard Gauge Railway project is a salient manifestation of Kenya's commitment to this model.[10] Senegal and Nigeria have adopted similar ventures to attract private investments and improve infrastructure development. The Lekki-Epe Expressway project in Nigeria,[11] initiated in 2006, was a pioneer example of how PPPs can be instrumental in upgrading vital transportation arteries, stimulating economic development and alleviating infrastructure deficiencies. Similarly, the Dakar-Diamniadio Toll Highway project in Senegal was launched as a PPP in 2013.[12] It was aimed to enhance transportation infrastructure and to foster economic

[10] The Republic of Kenya, Laws of Kenya. Public-Private Partnership Act. https://cn.invest.go.ke/wp-content/uploads/2018/10/PublicPrivatePartnershipsActNo.15of2013.pdf.

[11] Lekki-Epe Expressway (Nigeria). https://www.trinityllp.com/lekki-epe-expressway-nigeria/.

[12] Implementation Completion and Results Report. https://documents1.worldbank.org/curated/en/156571533572742552/pdf/ICR-P087304-SECPO-08032018.pdf.

growth. Collectively, these cases highlight the role of PPPs in addressing infrastructure challenges and driving economic progress.

Within the discourse on PPPs in Africa, a recurring theme has been their impact on governance and accountability. Wang and Wissenbach (2019) shed light on the impact of patron-client networks within the PPPs, suggesting that they can affect government accountability significantly. They underscore the importance of local participation in promoting transparency and accountability within these collaborative ventures. This argument is intertwined with the broader discussion on governance-and-leadership imperatives in African public administration. South Africa has also embraced this trend with the launch of the Renewable Energy Independent Power Producer Procurement Programme (Eberhard and Naude 2016). It also signifies an emerging concern for sustainability and integration with indigenous knowledge systems, in the discourse on PPPs in African public administration.

Despite potential benefits, PPPs in Africa are not without challenges. The Bujagali Hydropower Plant in Uganda was initiated on a PPP model in 2007. Before it's completion in 2012, it faced a range of issues, including allegations of corruption and severe cost escalations (World Bank 2018). Experience overall, demonstrates the many complexities inherent in implementing PPPs, particularly within the African context. As African nations strive for genuine sustainable development, assessing the long-term viability of PPPs becomes imperative.

All in all, PPPs have helped African countries by tapping local expertise and the adaptability of the private sector to enhance the efficiency initiatives of the public sector. Consequently, PPPs remain pre-eminent interventions in the ongoing efforts towards institutional adaptation throughout the continent. Integration of PPPs can extend to local levels, empowering decentralised entities to collaborate with the private sector for improved service delivery, infrastructure development and overall governance effectiveness, as further elaborated below.

9.5.4 Decentralisation and Local Governance

The global trend towards decentralisation and local governance has exerted a profound influence on all African countries, prompting the devolution of power and authority to local levels. Fundamentally, this approach is rooted in the goal of enhancing citizen participation, improving service delivery and fostering local development by empowering local governments and communities. As Brosio (2002) aptly notes, Africa has demonstrated remarkable institutional creativity in implementing decentralisation. The majority of countries on the Continent have undergone varying degrees of decentralisation, albeit at different paces and levels of progress. It is important to underscore that current decentralisation trends in Africa tend to prioritise rural areas, where tailored institutional solutions are crafted to suit specific political contexts.

Distinct approaches to devolving powers and resources to subnational governments are discernible across various African countries. Thus, Ethiopia and South Africa have embraced federal or quasi-federal systems, whereas Nigeria has maintained its federal framework, while ceding more authority to subnational governments (Brosio 2002). In Senegal,[13] and Tanzania, reforms have been enacted through local development programmes, facilitating the transfer of authority and resources to local governments and village councils, thereby enhancing community-level service delivery (Tidemand and Msami 2010).

In terms of legislation, Kenya's Constitution (2010) established forty-seven counties with devolved powers, forming County Governments responsible for such critical services as healthcare and education. Similarly, the Local Government Acts of Uganda,[14] Mozambique (1997) and Ghana (2016) decentralised authority and resources to local governments, endowing them with decision-making autonomy and responsibility for local service delivery (Otoo and Danquah 2021; Cheeseman et al. 2016; World Bank 2009). In Botswana, Decentralisation is considered to be a national political priority. This has been articulated in both the Constitution and the National Development Plan (Obasi and Lekorwe 2014).

While decentralisation holds significant promise across the African Continent, it necessitates well-defined rules and robust enforcement mechanisms, which can prove challenging in fragile developing countries; a category that encompasses many African nations. The risk of overburdening newly established local institutions and the need for a gradual,

[13] Senegal Local Development Reform Support Programme—Phase I. https://www.afdb.org/fileadmin/uploads/afdb/Documents/Project-and-Operations/SENEGAL-AR-_Local_Development_Reform_Support_Programme_Phase_I__PARDL-I____.pdf.

[14] Uganda Local Governments Act. 1997. https://www.parliament.go.ug/cmis/browser?id=cdd5fd7c-6d22-4075-b8b8-8a69948de738%3B1.0.

closely monitored implementation process are paramount considerations (Brosio 2002). Furthermore, Kasim and Agbola (2017) observe that many reforms tend to culminate in weak decentralisation or deconcentration, primarily due to the central governments' hesitancy directed at the transfer of substantive powers to local authorities. Regrettably, the absence of appropriate institutional structures and powers undermines the socioeconomic and political potential of decentralisation.

Thus, it is essential to recognise that despite receiving international attention, decentralisation often lacks robust empirical evidence to substantiate its purported advantages. Instead, its implementation in Africa is frequently driven by political factors, with diverse interpretations of what decentralisation entails, particularly within the British and French administrative traditions. Notoriously, these have diverse interpretations of decentralisation (Smoke 2003). The result has been a multifaceted landscape, where the merits of decentralisation must be weighed against its complexities, political dimensions and the nuanced perspectives of the various stakeholders. Faguet and Pöschl (2015) advance these arguments, suggesting that success in decentralisation hinges on how it is implemented. While its benefits are achievable but certainly not guaranteed, as Faguet and Pöschl have noted, decentralisation remains a complex process that requires sustained attention to achieve positive outcomes. Therefore, even when decentralisation holds the promise of empowering local entities and enhancing governance, its successful implementation requires a nuanced understanding of the diverse political, historical and administrative contexts within the particular nation that applies it. As such, the ongoing discourse on decentralisation must transcend theoretical discussions. It must focus, instead, on evidence-based evaluations in order to inform effective policies and practices tailored to the complexities of individual countries.

9.6 Governance and Leadership Excellence

The African trajectory in public administration emphasises the critical importance of effective governance and leadership in shaping practices. This includes the integration of indigenous knowledge systems. A focus on governance and leadership excellence aligns with New Public Service principles of Democratic Action and citizen-focused service towards the public interest. Three areas of special interest are considered: (1) Results-Based Management, highlighting the central focus on achieving tangible outcomes and a measurable impact in public administration; (2) Citizen Engagement and Participation, recognising the crucial role of involving the *public* in decision-making processes, thereby cultivating a governance model that is both inclusive and responsive; and (3) emphasis on anti-corruption measures. This discussion is also grounded in Farazmand's (2012) futuristic conceptualisation of public administration as a form of regulatory administration and the necessity to build administrative capacity. Furthermore, it aligns with Rubakula's (2014) perspective on the anticipated African transition towards a form of public value management that carefully considers local contexts before implementing external reforms.

9.6.1 Focus on Results-Based Management

Performance-based management systems have gained prominence across various African nations as a means of enhancing service delivery and public sector accountability. For instance, Kenya's Performance Contracting system, initiated in 2004, introduced performance contracts between the President and government ministries with a view to establishing specific targets and monitoring performance, ultimately aiming to enhance service delivery and accountability in the public sector. The system's effectiveness hinges on such factors as political will, strong leadership, partnership, teamwork and management participation.[15] Similarly, Ethiopia's Plan for Accelerated and Sustained Development to End Poverty (PASDEP[16]), which was implemented from 2005 to 2010, embraced results-based management principles, setting explicit targets and monitoring progress to achieve poverty reduction and development goals (Debela and Hagos 2012). This was followed by the Growth and Transformation Plan (GTP), implemented through multiple phases, since 2010. It utilises results-based management principles to attain development objectives, setting clear targets, monitoring progress and allocating resources accordingly. The GTP highlights ambitious growth and investment targets, necessitating

[15] ACBF (2016). GETTING BETTER PERFORMANCE FROM THE PUBLIC SECTOR: Performance contracting in Kenya. https://elibrary.acbfpact.org/acbf/collect/acbf/index/assoc/HASH9afe/ea5084cd/de43375c/e3.dir/AfCoPCaseStudy023.pdf.

[16] Plan for Accelerated and Sustained Development to End Poverty. https://extranet.who.int/nutrition/gina/en/printpdf/7935.

increased productivity and substantial mobilisation of both domestic and foreign savings (Engeda et al. 2011).

Rwanda's *Imihigo* system was launched in 2006 as part of decentralisation efforts. It also aimed to enhance local service delivery by establishing performance contracts between local governments and central authorities. Inspired by a traditional Rwandan practice, where leaders publicly commit to specific goals, the modern *Imihigo* process integrated this cultural tradition with contemporary planning, monitoring and oversight mechanisms. By 2010, it was evident that the *Imihigo* process had contributed to improved service delivery at the district level, underlining its effectiveness in promoting results-based management and accountability (Scher 2010). This was also an example of how indigenous knowledge systems could be deployed in governance and in the public service.

Liberia's Agenda for Transformation (AfT) was executed between 2013 and 2017. It applied results-based management principles to direct national development priorities and enhance service delivery outcomes. Despite prior economic growth, Liberia faced persistent challenges stemming from the civil war and income inequalities. As a five-year plan and a stepping stone towards the "Liberia's 2030" long-term vision, the AfT aimed to promote prosperity, inclusivity and socioeconomic development, aligning with such international frameworks as the Paris Declaration and the New Deal for Engagement in Fragile States.[17] Similarly, initiated in 2015, Zimbabwe's Results-Based Management System (RBMS) aimed to enhance service delivery and accountability within government ministries and departments, through performance-based planning, monitoring and evaluation. RBM was initially introduced in Zimbabwe in 2005 by the Public Service Commission. It was driven by resource constraints, the desire for improved service quality, demands for infrastructure development from the informal sector and the need for politicians to be more responsive to public demands and expectations. Donor pressure for efficient resource utilisation and changing global dynamics further motivated RBM's adoption, along with a growing emphasis on corporate governance by national and international stakeholders in government organisations (Chilunjika 2016). This is also an illustration of how external forces contribute to the direction of governance reforms.

[17] Republic of Liberia (2013). Republic of Liberia Agenda for Transformation: Steps Towards Liberia Rising 2030. https://faolex.fao.org/docs/pdf/lbr169062.pdf.

Despite prevailing challenges, the implementation of performance contracting holds substantial promise in fostering the transformation of the public sector, while realising enduring development objectives. This potential becomes manifest in its positive influence on employee performance within state corporations.[18] The adoption of performance contracting aligns with the regulatory role of public administration, signalling a transition towards public value management in Africa.

9.6.2 Citizen Engagement and Participation

Citizen Engagement and Participation hold significant relevance in the context of several African nations. This is evidenced by various initiatives aimed at involving citizens in decision-making processes and local development efforts. For instance, the traditional *kgotla* system of popular participation in Botswana provided a framework for actively promoting citizen involvement in policymaking, with national, district and village-level consultative mechanisms in place. Of course, their effectiveness has varied. Thus, citizen participation is intricately tied to decentralisation efforts in Botswana. It allows both traditional and modern governance systems to co-exist (Obasi and Lekorwe 2014).

Tanzania's introduction of Community Development Funds in the late 1990s signifies a concerted effort to empower communities in decision-making and fund management for local development projects. This initiative enhanced citizen engagement and ownership in the development process. Furthermore, the Constituency Development Fund (CDF),[19] sourced from domestic revenue and overseen by Members of Parliament at the constituency level, supplements existing funding mechanisms for local government. A similar approach has been adopted in neighbouring East African countries like Kenya and Uganda. It is driven by concerns regarding the equitable distribution of development funds and infrastructure enhancement, albeit with variations in implementation and outcomes. In Uganda, for instance, the Participatory Budgeting Initiative operates across the various districts, providing an avenue for citizens to take an active part in local budget allocation and decision-making

[18] African Capacity Building Foundation. https://www.acbf-pact.org/sites/default/files/Annual%20Report%202016.pdf.

[19] Constituency Development Fund in Tanzania: the Right Solution? https://www.policyforum-tz.org/sites/default/files/ConstituencyDevelopmentFund_0.pdf.

processes. This approach aligns with global advocacy of participatory budgeting, emphasising the role of stakeholder involvement in budgeting to enhance transparency, accountability and service delivery (Mukokoma 2010).

Launched in 2010, Senegal's National Initiative for Local Development underscores the importance of involving citizens in identifying, planning and executing development projects.[20] This initiative promotes grassroots participation and inclusiveness in the development process, fostering a sense of ownership and community-driven progress. Malawi's Public Sector Reforms was initiated in 2005. It similarly encompassed such citizen engagement strategies as community scorecards and public hearings. These mechanisms aim to bolster citizen participation in service delivery and governance. However, an examination of reform outcomes reveals that they are rooted in the New Public Management model, mostly influenced by donor organisations based in the Northern Hemisphere, and have fallen short of achieving their intended development results. Implementation challenges have been attributed to the leadership of donor organisations lacking the necessary institutional infrastructure. Accordingly, the need for a more comprehensive approach to reform implementation ought to be emphasised (Tambulasi, 2010).

Citizen engagement and participation in Africa provides a premise for the careful consideration of local contexts *before* implementing external reforms, as Rubakula's (2014) pointer, for the necessary direction of African Public service, indicates. It also supports the New public service's notion of engaged public servants, rather than entrepreneurs, who act as though the public money was their own.

9.6.3 Emphasis on Anti-corruption Measures

Corruption in Africa's public services represents a serious challenge. It is exacerbated by the inability to separate politics from public service. Ayee (2012) has noted that public officials are prone to facing political pressures that can divert public resources for private gain. He further notes that administrators themselves engage in political competition for higher salaries and promotions, complicating the issue even more. Significantly,

[20] https://www.afdb.org/fileadmin/uploads/afdb/Documents/Project-and-Operations/SENEGAL-AR-_Local_Development_Reform_Support_Programme_Phase_I__PARDL-I____.pdf.

corruption is kept alive within the African public services by disruptive reforms imposed on African countries. These have weakened state regulatory capacities and created opportunities for personal accumulation, particularly through privatisation and deregulation (Ayee 2012).

Governments across the African Continent have been actively addressing the pervasive issue of corruption through the establishment of specialised institutions, which are dedicated to combating this challenge. For instance, founded in 1994, Botswana's Directorate on Corruption and Economic Crime (DCEC), operates independently. It is primarily tasked with investigating corruption cases, enforcing anti-corruption measures and promoting transparency with integrity in governance (Sebudubudu 2003). Similarly, Ghana made significant strides in its anti-corruption efforts by establishing the Office of the Special Prosecutor (OSP), in 2018. This institution specialises in the investigation and prosecution of corruption-related offences, reinforcing Ghana's commitment to combating corruption (Osei-Amoako 2018).

In Kenya, the Ethics and Anti-Corruption Commission (EACC), which was formed in 2011 under the 2010 Constitution, plays a crucial role in preventing and investigating corruption in both the public and private sectors. However, the EACC has faced challenges and threats to its stability, particularly during periods of progress in politically sensitive cases. While the EACC has a clear mandate for prevention, sensitisation and education, the goal of fighting corruption and its utilisation by Kenyan citizens for the purpose of reporting corrupt incidents remain distant and limited (AfriMAP 2016).

Nigeria established the Economic and Financial Crimes Commission (EFCC) in 2003 in order to combat corruption and financial crimes. Despite its successes in prosecuting corrupt officials, however, concerns have grown regarding its impartiality and adherence to *due process*. It has faced accusations of political manipulation by the presidency, raising questions about its effectiveness in the anti-corruption campaign (Inokoba and Ibegu 2011). The challenges encountered by the EFCC highlight the intricate nature of anti-corruption initiatives, emphasising the need for continuous evaluation and enhancement of institutional frameworks.

Zambia also initiated the Anti-Corruption Commission in 1996. It focused on anti-corruption law enforcement and transparency enhancement within the public administration. However, structural, and operational challenges, as well as political interference and judicial delays, have hampered the prosecution of corruption cases. To address these issues, calls have been made for improved training, transparency, accountability, enactment of procurement regulations, as well as a Freedom-of-Information Act to empower civil society in the anti-corruption fight (Ndulo 2014). Mauritius, through the Independent Commission Against Corruption (ICAC), established in 2002, plays a pivotal role in combating corruption and promoting integrity within its public administration. Mauritius has ratified international anti-corruption agreements and maintains a robust anti-corruption legal framework. Nonetheless, consistent enforcement of these laws remains a challenge.[21]

The focus on anti-corruption measures within Africa's public services speaks to the pressing need for building ***administrative capacity***. One key concern has been that the intertwining of politics and public service, as highlighted by Ayee (2012), creates vulnerabilities that divert public resources for private gain. This contradicts the New Public Service focus on prioritising citizenship and public service, where public servants are treated as citizens dedicated to making meaningful contributions to society. While, as seen above, various African governments have established specialised anti-corruption institutions, such challenges as political interference, judicial delays and the need for consistent enforcement highlight the necessity for continuous capacity-building initiatives in the fight against corruption across the Continent.

9.7 Technology-Driven Modernisation

The rapid advancement of technology presents both opportunities and drivers for public administration trends in Africa. Access to digital infrastructure, the growth of mobile connectivity and the increasing use of e-government solutions are catalysts for improving service delivery, citizen engagement and administrative efficiency. The following discussion explores the ways in which technology is rapidly changing public administration in Africa. It focuses on two main areas: 1) E-Governance development in Africa's public service, and 2) E-Government and Technology-Driven Governance. This discussion is in line with Farazmand's (2012) ideas about technology shaping the future of public administration. Technological advancements are expected to enhance transparency and

[21] Transparency International Anti-Corruption Helpdesk Answer, Mauritius - Overview of corruption and anti-corruption. https://knowledgehub.transparency.org/assets/uploads/helpdesk/Country-Profile-Mauritius-2019.pdf.

accountability, aligning with the principles of the New Public Service (NPS). New technologies offer potential for fostering citizen engagement in the policymaking process, providing for improved public participation and enabling citizen oversight of government activities (Robinson 2015). This aligns with the NPS framework's emphasis on promoting active citizen involvement and strengthening democratic governance.

9.7.1 E-Governance Development in Africa's Public Service

Through the UN's E-Government Development Index (EGDI) tool, the development of e-government at the national level can now be measured. It is based on three components: the Online Service Index (OSI), the Telecommunication Infrastructure Index and the Human Capital Index. The OSI component of the EGDI measures the use of information and communications technology (ICT) by governments for the delivery of public services at the national level.[22]

Use of technology in the public administration systems of Africa has been a topic of interest for several years. However, recent developments and the COVID-19 pandemic have contributed to a renewed interest in this space. According to EGDI (2022), there has been a 3.6% increase in EGDI value, with 30% of African countries in the High EGDI group and 60% in the middle. In terms of e-government development, only four of the 54 countries of Africa have EGDI values above the global average (South Africa, Mauritius, Seychelles and Tunisia). Still, between 2020 and 2022, three African countries, namely Côte d'Ivoire, Rwanda and Zambia, were listed in the high EGDI group, for the first time. Among the sixteen countries in the high EGDI group in Africa, 14 are upper-middle-income or lower-middle-income countries; only Seychelles is a high-income country, and Rwanda is the lone low-income country, included in this group. Rwanda is thus a leader in e-governance among the least developed countries. By prioritising real-time data collection, SMART analytics and inter-agency collaboration, they are able to improve service delivery, reduce costs, prevent corruption and foster innovation. Through digital inclusion initiatives and partnerships with the World Bank and the private sector, Rwanda aims to expand inclusive digital services and empower its population through ICT.

[22] https://publicadministration.un.org/egovkb/en-us/About/Overview/-E-Government-Development-Index.

Challenges in implementing e-government in Africa are systemic. They include such issues as inadequate infrastructure, lack of technical expertise and limited financial resources. However, the potential benefits from e-government in Africa are significant. They include improved service delivery, increased transparency and reduced corruption (Twizeyimana 2023). To fully realise these benefits, African countries would need to prioritise digital transformation and to develop frameworks that support the adoption of digital technologies in public administration.

9.7.2 E-Government and Technology-Driven Governance

Better use of technology and the development of e-government systems have become critical components of public service delivery and governance in several African countries. In 2013, Morocco initiated the "Digital Morocco 2020" strategy, focusing on digitising public services, enhancing administrative procedures and improving access to basic services. It thus positioned itself as a leader in technology for the Middle East and North Africa (MENA) (Zaanoun 2023). The establishment of an "e-government" committee was instrumental in developing and tracking down the progress of e-government initiatives, with such significant achievements as the launch of the National Portal "maroc.ma",[23] in 2006.

In Ghana, an e-Government project was initiated in 2003. It has facilitated electronic public service delivery, emphasising the role of Information and Communication Technologies (ICTs) in enhancing government efficiency and citizen engagement.[24] Ghana's e-Zwich is a biometric smart card payment system that enables citizens to access government services and make payments electronically. The system has been successful in reducing corruption and increasing financial inclusion in Ghana.

Rwanda's "*Irembo*" platform, launched in 2015, is an e-government initiative that serves as a one-stop portal for online public services. It contrives to integrate approximately ninety-six basic government services including passport applications, business registration and land registration. The platform has streamlined trade programmes, facilitated revenue collection and reduced costs by enabling traders to declare goods and

[23] https://www.maroc.ma/en/content/e-governement.

[24] https://iipgh.org/e-government-initiatives-in-ghana/.

services, process tax returns and make payments digitally. It has also simplified business registration processes, making Rwanda attractive to investors and recognised by the World Bank as a "top reformer" on the index of doing business. Rwanda's Irembo system has demonstrated success in improving service delivery, promoting e-commerce and enhancing citizen convenience by leveraging technology to enhance citizen engagement, reduce bureaucracy and improve service delivery (Ruzindan, 2019).

In a very similar way, launched in 2013, Kenya's "Huduma Kenya Initiative" has aimed to streamline government services and to promote efficiency. It has also extended access to essential services, with a focus on inclusivity and partnership with various institutions, including the National Council for Persons with Disabilities (NCPWD) and the Kenya Institute of Special Education (KISE) (Huduma Kenya 2003).[25] In addition, the "Ushahidi" platform in Kenya was developed as a crowdsourcing tool to map and report incidents during the post-election violence of 2008. This innovation has since been used for varying purposes. This included citizen engagement, election monitoring and reporting public service issues (Rotich 2017). Along with Kenya's widespread adoption of such mobile technology as M-Pesa, innovations in e-government and digital financial services have been promoted. The government has leveraged the country's mobile connectivity to launch mobile payment systems, online tax filing and digital identification services (Maake et al. 2015).

In Nigeria, the "Budeshi" platform was developed to promote transparency and citizen engagement in public procurement. The platform provides open data on government contracts, allowing citizens to monitor and scrutinise public spending (Williams-Elegbe 2018). Similarly, South Africa's "*Vulekamali*" initiative leverages technology to enhance public financial management. The online platform provides citizens with access to budget information, enabling transparency and empowering citizens to participate in budgetary decision-making processes (Plantinga and Adams 2021).

To be sure, the implementation of E-Systems has not been without challenges. Challenges in e-government implementation include the limited accessibility for the poor and rural populations and the need

[25] https://www.hudumakenya.go.ke/newsdetails/44.

to strengthen ICT infrastructure, financing programmes, political leadership and communication mechanisms. Nonetheless, as Twinomurinzi and Visser (2004) argue, most governments in developing countries continue to turn to ICT and internet-based models as their channels of choice for citizen-centred service delivery. However, they also highlight a discrepancy in South Africa's e-government system, noting that it does not align with the Batho Pele service delivery philosophy and, therefore, does not deliver as effectively as required.

Nonetheless, the ICT initiatives in African Public Administration underscore the significance of leveraging technology to improve public service quality, transparency and data exchange. They highlight the commitment of these nations to harnessing ICT for administrative efficiency, citizen convenience and, ultimately, the advancement of economic and social inclusion. These e-government endeavours contribute to a broader discourse on the role of technology in governance and of public service enhancement in Africa.

9.8 Conclusions

This chapter, "Africa rising", has been written on a deep understanding that Africa is not homogenous in the development of the State or Public Administration. There is also a recognition that our colonial past has left deep imprints on our present State formations and Public Administration approaches. It is in this vein that we also take into account that countries in conflict or coming out of conflict like Sudan, South Sudan and the DRC—to mention but a few—may, in some instances, be facing a crisis of the state or be a state at war with its people and, in so doing, be a state that is battling to survive, unable to govern effectively.

In this chapter, we have highlighted the complex evolution of public administration in Africa, as well as its interaction with changing global patterns. We argue that, while African public administration has been shaped by historical, colonial and postcolonial influences, it has had both a distinctive character and inherent challenges. While we acknowledge the influence of global trends, particularly in the adoption of Western administrative models and, later, in response to Western-centric values and norms, we note that the key task of African Public Administration has been to rediscover the relevance of its redistributive role ahead of its operational role. Furthermore, this chapter identifies key drivers of public administration reform in Africa. These include institutional adaptation, governance and leadership and technology-driven modernisation. Such drivers aim to give African public administration a continental face and respond to the evolving global landscape. The chapter thus provides valuable insights into the complexities of public administration in Africa and its interaction with global patterns, emphasising the need for a nuanced and context-specific approach to addressing the identity crisis and promoting effective governance on the Continent.

Postscript

In concluding this detailed and comprehensive analysis of administrative change in some fifty-four African countries emerging from centuries of colonial domination, it is apposite to offer a postscript. This reflection attempts to draw some lessons from the admittedly varied experiences of conquest, domination, predation and exploitation that shaped African nations. The colonial era culminated in the well-known "scramble for Africa", which left virtually no corner of the Continent untouched. It took the sad experience of the most disastrous war in the whole of human history, to call seriously into question the merits of colonialism and apartheid which had long been presented as a "civilising mission".

Still, it took some six decades after the establishment of the United Nations in 1945 for the colonial powers, fighting a rearguard action, to yield to the inevitable—thus, ending all attempts to effectively prolong their former hegemony and domination. From the Algerian Revolution through the War in Vietnam and the struggle against Apartheid, it took decades of fighting and enormous sacrifice for Africa to rise beyond decolonisation and proforma independence to real emancipation and self-determination.

The still-ongoing war in the heartland of Ukraine and the onslaught in Gaza-Palestine have brought into sharp relief the many ways and forms in which realpolitik is practiced to perpetuate imperial hegemony—often by circumventing international law, including basic rules and fundamental provisions of the United Nations Charter.

References

Adewole, A.T. 2009. Waste management towards sustainable development in Nigeria: A case study of Lagos state. *International NGO Journal* 4 (4): 173–179.

Afegbua, S.I., and G.L. Ejalonibu. 2015. Emerging issues in public sector reforms in Africa: An assessment of Ghana and Nigeria. *Africa's Public Service Delivery & Performance Review* 3 (3): 95–126.

Afolayan, G.E., and O.A. Ogunsanwo (2017). Development administration in contemporary Africa: An explorative analysis. In *Global perspectives on development administration and cultural change*, 1–28. IGI Global.

African Union Commission. 2014. Agenda 2063. The Africa we want. Draft Document. http://www.nepad.org/system/files/Agenda%202063%20%20English.pdf

AfriMAP, A. (Ed.). 2016. *Effectiveness of anti-corruption agencies in East Africa: Kenya, Tanzania, and Uganda*. African Books Collective.

Agbese, P.O. 2016. Re-examining public administration in Africa. *Turkish Public Administration Annual* 42: 1–13.

Akinola, A.O., and U.O. Uzodike. 2018. Ubuntu and the quest for conflict resolution in Africa. *Journal of Black Studies* 49 (2): 91–113.

Akuupa, M.U., and G. Kornes. 2013. From 'one namibia, one nation 'towards 'unity in diversity'? Shifting representations of culture and nationhood in Namibian Independence Day celebrations, 1990–2010. *Anthropology Southern Africa* 36 (1–2): 34–46.

Akyeampong, E., and A.D.G. Aikins. 2008. Ghana at fifty: Reflections on independence and after. *Transition* 98: 24–34.

Al-Salim, F. 2020. Defining revolution the Egyptian "Revolutions" in 1952 and 2011. *Glocalism* (3).

Andreevich, D.D. 2019. Multi-polar world order: Old myths and new realities. Vestnik RUDN. *International Relations* 19 (3): 404–419.

Andrews, M. (2010). *How far have public financial management reforms come in Africa?* CID Working Paper No 208. Cambridge, M.A: Harvard Center for International Development. https://www.hks.harvard.edu/centers/cid/publications/faculty-working-papers/how-far-have-public-financial-management-reforms-come-africa.

Ayee, J.R. 2012. Improving the effectiveness of the public sector in Africa through the quality of public administration. Rethinking development challenges for public policy: Insights from contemporary Africa, 83–116.

Barnsley, I., and R. Bleiker. 2008. Self-determination: From decolonization to deterritorialization. *Global Change Peace and Security* 20 (2): 121–136.

Basheka, B.C. 2012. The Paradigms of Public Administration Re-Examined: A Reflection. *Journal of Public Administration* 47 (1): 25–67.

Basheka, B.C. 2015. Indigenous Africa's governance architecture: A need for African public administration theory? *Journal of Public Administration* 50 (3): 466–484.

Behr, A.L. (1988). Education in South Africa: origins, issues, and trends, 1652–1988. Academica.

Brizuela-Garcia, E. 2006. The history of Africanisation and the Africanisation of history. *History in Africa* 33: 85–100.

Brosio, G. 2002. Decentralisation in Africa. In *Managing fiscal decentralization*, 337–365. Routledge. https://www.taylorfrancis.com/chapters/edit/10.4324/9780203219997-27/decentralization-africa-giorgio-brosio.

Busieka, M. 2018. The African Charter: An enabler of good governance. *African Journal of Public Affairs* 10 (1): 44–59.

Chanie, P. 2013. *The trajectory of public administration in Africa: Background. Thirty years of public sector reforms in Africa: Selected country experiences.* Kampala: Fountain Publishers.

Cheeseman, N., G. Lynch, and J. Willis. 2016. Decentralisation in Kenya: The governance of governors. *The Journal of Modern African Studies* 54 (1): 1–35.

Chilunjika, A. 2016. Assessing the operationalisation of the results-based management approach in the Ministry of transport, communication, and infrastructural development in Zimbabwe. *Public Policy and Administration Research* 6 (6): 1–12.

Constituency Development Fund in Tanzania: the Right Solution? https://www.policyforum-tz.org/sites/default/files/ConstituencyDevelopmentFund_0.pdf.

Davis, M. 2007. The FLN's strategy for gaining an independent Algeria, 1954–1962. *Ronald E. McNair Program*, 1–13.

De Vries, M., and J. Nemec. 2013. Public sector reform: An overview of recent literature and research on NPM and alternative paths. *International Journal of Public Sector Management* 26 (1): 4–16.

Debela, T., and A. Hagos. 2012. Towards a results-based performance management: Practices and challenges in the Ethiopian public sector. *Journal of Business and Administrative Studies* 4 (1): 79–127.

Denhardt, R.B., and J.V. Denhardt. 2000. The new public service: Serving rather than steering. *Public Administration Review* 60 (6): 549–559.

Du Plessis, P. 2021. Decolonization of education in South Africa: Challenges to decolonize the university curriculum. *South African Journal of Higher Education* 35 (1): 54–69.

Dwivedi, O.P. 1994. *Development administration: From underdevelopment to sustainable development*, 1–41. London: Macmillan Press.

Eberhard, A., and R. Naude. 2016. The South African renewable energy independent power producer procurement programme: A review and lessons learned. *Journal of Energy in Southern Africa* 27 (4): 1–14.

Enaifoghe, A., N.P. Dlamini, N.N. Jili, and R. Mthethwa. 2023. The role of e-government as enabler of good governance for socioeconomic development in South Africa. *International Journal of Social Science Research and Review* 6 (1): 493–508.

Engeda, E., S. Tamru, E. Tsehaye, D. Debowicz, P. Dorosh, and S. Robinson. (2011). Ethiopia's growth and transformation plan: A computable general equilibrium analysis of alternative financing options. IFPRI Discussion Paper No 30.

Erasmus, M.N. 2020. Western ascendency and african capitulation: Antagonism for true public administration epistemology. *Journal of African Foreign Affairs* 7 (2).

Faguet, J.P., and C. Pöschl, eds. 2015. *Is decentralization good for development? Perspectives from academics and policy makers*. USA: Oxford University Press.

Farazmand, A. 2012. The future of public administration: Challenges and opportunities—A critical perspective. *Administration & Society* 44 (4): 487–517.

Farazmand, A., ed. 2023. *Global encyclopaedia of public administration, public policy, and governance*. Springer Nature.

Farouk, A. 2022. E-government in Northern Africa countries: Ranking and performance evaluation through the last three sessions 2016, 2018, 2020. *Journal of Contemporary Business and Economic Studies* 5 (2): 59–73.

Ferlie, E., L.E. Lynn Jr, and C. Pollitt, eds. 2005. *The Oxford handbook of public management*. Oxford University Press.

Fitzpatrick, J., M. Goggin, T. Heikkila, D. Klingner, J. Machado, and C. Martell. 2011. A new look at comparative public administration: Trends in research and an agenda for the future. *Public Administration Review* 71 (6): 821–830.

Franks, P.E. 2014. The crisis of the South African public service. *Journal of the Helen Suzman Foundation* 74 (1): 48–56.

Gant, G.F. 2006, The concept of development administration. In *Comparative public administration (Research in public policy analysis and management, Vol. 15)*, ed. E.E. Otenyo and N.S. Lind, 257–285. Emerald Group Publishing Limited, Bingley. https://doi.org/10.1016/S0732-1317(06)15009-5.

Gladden, E.N. 1976. Toynbee on public administration. *International Review of Administrative Sciences* 42 (4): 338–348.

Gladden, E.N. 2019. *A history of public administration: Volume I: From the earliest times to the eleventh century*. Routledge.

Green, L.J.F. 2016. Beyond South Africa's 'indigenous knowledge'—Science wars. *South African Journal of Science* 108 (7/8).

Hansen, E. 1977. Freedom and revolution in the thought of Frantz Fanon. *Africa Development/afrique Et Developpement* 2 (1): 17–41.

Haque, M.S. 1996. The contextless nature of public administration in Third World countries. *International Review of Administrative Sciences* 62 (3): 315–329.

Haruna, P.F. 2003. Reforming Ghana's public service: Issues and experiences in comparative perspective. *Public Administration Review* 63 (3): 343–354.

Hendricks, L., and S. Chidiac. 2011. Village savings and loans: A pathway to financial inclusion for Africa's poorest households. *Enterprise Development and Microfinance* 22 (2): 134–146.

Huduma Kenya. 2003. Huduma's deliberate partnerships for devolved and enhanced access to public service. Huduma Kenya. https://www.hudumakenya.go.ke/newsdetails/44.

Hyden, G. 1997. Government in the 21st century: Restoring legitimacy to public authority. Paper for the African Association for Public Administration and Management (AAPAM) 19th Annual Roundtable Conference. Gaborone, Botswana, 24–28.

Hyden, G. 2020. African Public Administration. In *Oxford research encyclopedia of politics*.

Ignat, I., and G.V. Bujancă. 2014. Power shifts in the Global Economy. Transition towards a multi-polar world order. *The USV Annals of Economics and Public Administration* 13 (2 [18]): 24–34.

Inokoba, P.K., and W.T. Ibegu. 2011. Economic and financial crime commission (efcc) and political corruption: Implication for the consolidation of democracy in Nigeria. *The Anthropologist* 13 (4): 283–291.

Kariseb, K., and C. Okoloise. 2020. Reflections on the African governance architecture: Trends, challenges and opportunities. *Governance, Human Rights, and Political Transformation in Africa*, 41–68.

Kasim, O.F., and T. Agbola. 2017. Decentralisation and local government reforms in Africa: Challenges, opportunities, and the way forward. *Eastern Africa Social Science Research Review* 33 (1): 89–113.

Keet, A. 2014. Epistemic 'othering' and the decolonization of knowledge. *Africa Insight* 44 (1): 23–37.

Knaus, C.B., T. Mino, and J. Seroto. 2022. Decolonising higher education: Definitions, conceptualisations, epistemologies. In *Decolonising African higher education*, 1–20. Routledge.

Kroukamp, H. 1999. 'Batho Pele': Putting the citizen first in transforming public service delivery in a changing South Africa. *International Review of Administrative Sciences* 65 (3): 327–338.

Kumaga, D. 2011. The challenges of implementing electronic payment systems—The case of Ghana's E-zwich payment system. School of Management, Blekinge Institute of Technology, Unpublished Thesis.

Kuye, J.O. 2020. Revisiting public administration in Africa through Ubuntu lens for enhanced service delivery. *African Journal of Public Affairs* 12 (1): 52–67.

Kwaku Ohemeng, F.L. 2014. Challenges and prospects of public administration education and training in Africa: The case of Ghana. *Journal of Public Affairs Education* 20 (4): 469–486.

Le Grange, L. 2018. Decolonising, Africanising, indigenizing, and internationalizing curriculum studies: Opportunities to (re) imagine the field. *Journal of Education 74*), 4–18 (University of KwaZulu-Natal).

Leaver, C., O. Ozier, P. Serneels, and A. Zeitlin. 2021. Recruitment, effort, and retention effects of performance contracts for civil servants: Experimental evidence from Rwandan primary schools. *American Economic Review* 111 (7): 2213–2246.

Letsekha, T. 2013. Revisiting the debate on the Africanisation of higher education: An appeal for a conceptual shift. *The Independent Journal of Teaching and Learning* 8 (1): 5–18.

Letsekha, T. 2022. Decoloniality and Africanisation as Instruments for Change. *International Journal of African Higher Education* 9 (1): 73–93.

Lobban, R. 1974. Guinea-Bissau: 24 September 1973 and beyond. *Africa Today* 21 (1): 15–24.

Maake, B.M., N.N. Oino, and F.M. Awuor. 2015. M-powering: How mobile money (M-PESA) services promote realization of a digital society in the kenyan government. In *Emerging issues and prospects in African e-government*, 97–107. IGI Global.

Markos, S. 2013. Civil service reform in Ethiopia: Issus, lessons, and future directions. *International Journal of Public Administration* 36 (4): 235–247.

Masango, R.S. 2002. Public participation: A critical ingredient of good governance. *Politeia* 21 (2): 52–65. https://doi.org/10.25159/0256-8845/1417.

Massey, A. 2006. *The Oxford handbook of public management*. Edited by Ewan Ferlie, Laurence E. Lynn, and Christopher Pollitt.

Mawere, M. 2015. Indigenous knowledge and public education in sub-Saharan Africa. *Africa Spectrum* 50 (2): 57–71.

Mawhood, P. 1983. *Local government in the third world: The experience of tropical Africa*. New York: Wiley.

Mazzucato, M., M. Qobo, and R. Kattel. 2021. Building state capacities and dynamic capabilities to drive social and economic development: The case of South Africa. UCL Institute for Innovation and Public Purpose, Working Paper Series (IIPP WP 2021/09).

Mbembe, J. 2016. Decolonizing the university: New directions. *Arts and Humanities in Higher Education* 15 (1): 29–45. https://doi.org/10.1177/1474022215618513.

Minga, K.J. 2021. African discourses on the africanization and decolonization of social and human sciences. *Journal of Black Studies* 52 (1): 50–76.

Mokhutso, R.J. 2021. The impact of African indigenous knowledge system on healthcare system in South Africa: The Covid-19 perspective. *Gender and Behaviour* 19 (1): 17713–17728.

Molokwane, T. 2019. New public management-in Botswana contemporary issues and lessons. *African Journal of Public Affairs* 11 (1): 48–63.

Moodie, G.C. 1994. The state and the liberal universities in South Africa: 1948–1990. *Higher Education* 27 (1): 1–40.
Mukokoma, M. 2010. The 'people's budget' and budget effectiveness: The case of local governments in Uganda. *Journal of Science and Sustainable Development* 3 (1).
Murindahabi, C. 2016. The trajectory of public administration in Rwanda: An appraisal. *Public Policy and Administration* 6 (4): 46–54.
Ndulo, Muna. 2014. Review of the anti-corruption legal framework in Zambia. *Southern African institute for policy and research*. Lusaka.
Kasfir, Nelson. 1969. Development administration in Africa: The balance between politics and administration. *Canadian Journal of African Studies / Revue Canadienne des Études Africaines* 3 (1): 94–103. https://doi.org/10.1080/00083968.1969.10803524.
Nemec, J., and M.S. de Vries. 2012. *Global trends in public sector reform*. Brussels: Larcier.
Newland, C.A., and D. Argyriades. 2019. Reclaiming public space: Drawing lessons from the past, as we confront the future. In *Public service excellence in the 21st century*, ed. A. Baimenov and P. Liverakos, 1–30. Singapore: Palgrave Macmillan.
Nyadera, I.N., and G. Dagba. 2022. Public administration features in developed and developing countries. In *The Palgrave handbook of comparative public administration: Concepts and cases*, 77–100. Singapore: Springer Nature Singapore.
Nzimakwe, T.I. 2014. *Practising Ubuntu and leadership for good governance: The South African and continental dialogue*.
Obasi, I.N., and M.H. Lekorwe. 2014. Citizen engagement in public policy making process in Africa: The case of Botswana. *leadership* 3 (4).
OECD. 2020. *Policy framework on sound public governance baseline features of governments that work well*. Paris: OECD Publishing.
Ofong, I. 2004. Community participation in solid waste management. In *People-centred approaches to water and environmental sanitation*, ed. S. Godfrey, 124–126. Proceedings of the 30th WEDC International Conference, Vientiane, Laos.
Ohemeng, F.L.K. 2010. The new charter system in Ghana: The 'holy grail ' of public service delivery? *International Review of Administrative Sciences* 76 (1): 115–136.
Okonjo-Iweala, N., and P. Osafo-Kwaako. 2007. *Nigeria's economic reforms: Progress and challenges*. Brookings Global Economy and Development Working Paper, The Brookings Institution, Washington, DC 20036 (6).

Osei-Amoako, Y. 2018. Reflections on Ghana's Office of the Special Prosecutor (1). *GhanaWeb* (16.01.2018). https://www.ghanaweb.com/GhanaHomePage/features/Reflections-on-Ghana-s-Office-of-the-special-prosecutor-1-618041#:~:text=The%20process%20of%20approval%20of%20the%20would-be%20first,its%20passage%20by%20Parliament%20on%20November%2014%2C%202017.

Otoo, I., and M. Danquah. 2021. Fiscal decentralization and efficiency of public services delivery by local governments in Ghana. *African Development Review* 33 (3): 411–425.

Pahad, A. 2014. *Insurgent diplomat-civil talks or civil war?* Cape Town: Penguin Random House.

Plantinga, P., and R. Adams. 2021. Rethinking open government as innovation for inclusive development: Open access, data and ICT in South Africa. *African Journal of Science, Technology, Innovation and Development* 13 (3): 315–323.

Reutener, M. 2015. The role of civic participation in the South African budgeting process. Doctoral dissertation, University of Pretoria.

Robinson, M. 2015. From old public administration to the new public service implications for public sector reform in developing countries. UNDP Global Centre for Public Service Excellence. https://www.undp.org/sites/g/files/zskgke326/files/publications/PS-Reform_Paper.pdf.

Rotich, J. 2017. Ushahidi: Empowering citizens through crowdsourcing and digital data collection. Interview with Juliana Rotich. Field Actions Science Reports. *The Journal of Field Actions*, (*Special Issue 16*), 36–38.

Rubakula, G. 2014. The new public management and its challenges in Africa. *Public Policy and Administration Research* 4 (4): 85–96.

Ruzindan, A. 2019. User satisfaction of E-Government platform in Government service delivery process: Case study-Irembo platform. Doctoral dissertation, University of Rwanda.

Scher, D. 2010. *The promise of Imihigo: Decentralized service delivery in Rwanda, 2006–2010*. Princeton: Princeton University Press.

Sebudubudu, D. 2003. Corruption and its control in Botswana. *Botswana Notes & Records* 35 (1): 125–140.

Smoke, P. 2003. Decentralization in Africa: Goals, dimensions, myths, and challenges. *Public Administration and Development: THe International Journal of Management Research and Practice* 23 (1): 7–16.

Tambulasi, R.I. 2010. Critical perspectives on public sector reforms: An introduction. *Reforming the Malawian Public Sector*, 1.

Tidemand, P, and J. Msami. 2010. The impact of local government reforms in Tanzania. 1998–2008. Research on Poverty Alleviation. Special Paper 10/1.

Twinomurinzi, H., and W. Visser. 2004. E-government and public service delivery: Enabling ICT to put "People First"–A case study from South Africa.

Twizeyimana, J.D. 2023. Towards realisation of the public value of e-government: Anticipation-reality gap and critical success factors in the context of Rwanda. *International Journal of Public Sector Performance Management* 11 (1): 123–147.
United Nations. 2001. *African institutes of public administration: New Role, New perspectives*. ST/ESA/PAD/SER.E/33.
van der Westhuizen, J. 2005. *Public sector reform: A comparative perspective on selected countries in Sub-Saharan Africa*. Budapest: Administratio Publica.
Willoughby, W.F. 1927. *Principles of public administration: With special reference to the national and state governments of the United States (No 5)*. Baltimore, MD: The Johns Hopkins Press.
Waghid, Y. 2021. Why the decolonization of higher education without critique is not possible? *South African Journal of Higher Education* 35 (2): 1–3.
Wang, Y., and U. Wissenbach. 2019. Clientelism at work? A case study of Kenyan Standard Gauge Railway project. *Economic History of Developing Regions* 34 (3): 280–299.
Williams-Elegbe, S. 2018. Systemic corruption and public procurement in developing countries: Are there any solutions? *Journal of Public Procurement* 18 (2): 131–147.
World Bank. 2009. Mozambique—Municipal development in Mozambique: Lessons from the First Decade—Synthesis Report. World Bank. License: CC BY 3.0 IGO. http://hdl.handle.net/10986/3101.
World Bank. 2018. Uganda: Bujagali Hydropower Project—Implementation Completion and Results Report (Report No. ICR00004322). The World Bank. https://documents1.worldbank.org/curated/en/546131539715898602/pdf/Bujagali-ICR-Report-10102018.pdf.
World Bank Group. 2019. *National development strategy Croatia 2030*. Policy Note: public administration modernization.
Zaanoun, A. 2023. Morocco: The impact of the digization of public services.
Zeleza, P.T. 2009. African studies and universities since independence. *Transition: An International Review*, 110–135.
Zembylas, M. 2018. Decolonial possibilities in South African higher education: Reconfiguring humanizing pedagogies as/with decolonizing pedagogies. *South African Journal of Education* 38 (4): 1–11.

CHAPTER 10

Public Administration in an Age of Polycrises: Multi-nodal Governance Approaches in Some South East Asian Countries

Alex Brillantes, Karl Emmanuel Villanueva Ruiz, Ainna Shariz Comia, Nelin Estocado Dulpina, Celine Grace Abella, and Reiou Regie Manuel

10.1 Introduction

In most general terms, this chapter addresses a core concern and challenge of contemporary public administration: the polycrisis being confronted by governance today and the appropriate responses of governance institutions to such crises. The notion "polycrisis" has become increasingly

A. Brillantes (✉) · K. E. V. Ruiz · A. S. Comia · N. E. Dulpina · C. G. Abella · R. R. Manuel
UP National College of Public Administration and Governance, NCPAG Building, Quezon City, Philippines
e-mail: abbrillantes@up.edu.ph

K. E. V. Ruiz
e-mail: kvruiz@up.edu.ph

A. Baimenov and P. Liverakos (eds.), *Public Administration in the New Reality*, https://doi.org/10.1007/978-981-96-3845-1_10

used and, we may add, even fashionable, over the past years (Lawrence et al. 2024: 2). This is not inconsistent with the widespread use of other acronyms such as VUCA, BANI, and TUNA used to describe the contemporary global state of affairs in our rapidly changing environment.[1] It also makes a modest attempt to contribute to the ongoing evolution of contemporary frameworks of contemporary public administration and governance, including those encompassed by new public governance and collaborative governance by taking off from the multi-nodal governance platform.

In 2020, Noam Chomsky said that the crises we are now being confronted globally poses an *existential threat* to humanity pointing out that there indeed are grave risks that can pose a great threat to humanity's long-term potential. He pointed out that multiple hazards might derail humanity's future where a cataclysm or a combination could wipe out humans or imprison us in an awful situation. He warned that the world is facing a confluence of three major crises that threaten the survival of humanity: global warming, nuclear war, and deteriorating democracy; along with the looming dominance of artificial intelligence within the context of the fourth industrial revolution and the exponential growth of digitalisation (Chomsky et al. 2020: 86; Polychroniou and Furtado 2023).[2] In sum, polycrises have affected all facets of human life, including human development. The 2024 Human Development Report for the Asia Pacific Region concludes that "the story of human development in Asia

N. E. Dulpina
e-mail: nedulpina@up.edu.ph

C. G. Abella
e-mail: cmabella@up.edu.ph

R. R. Manuel
e-mail: rmanuel1@up.edu.ph

[1] VUCA: Volatile, Uncertain, Complex, Ambiguous; BANI: Brittle, Anxious, Nonlinear, Incomprehensible; and TUNA: Turbulent, Uncertain, Novel, Ambiguous.

[2] In this study, we use the term digitalisation, not digitisation. According to Oentoro (2024), digitisation converts analogue data to digital. These materials can be photographs, videos, music, or text. *Digitisation* makes anything easy to save, access, and share, whereas *digitalisation* is the extensive use of digital technology in many parts of life. Computers for banking and shopping and phones or tablets for reading are examples. Digital products are leveraged to improve performance, revenue, business models, and more.

and the Pacific has been one of long-term progress, but it has also been one of persistent disparity and widespread disruption" (UNDP 2024a: 10).

A very compelling question for us in the discipline of public administration—both in terms of theory and practice—is how to respond to the existential threats pointed out by Chomsky, or to put it in the frame of this book, how has governance responded to these polycrises. More importantly, what are the next steps and where do we go from here within the context of public administration and governance examining the experiences of our selected countries in Southeast Asia, i.e., Indonesia, Philippines, Singapore, Thailand, and Viet Nam.

Drawing from these countries' responses, this essay uses multi-nodal governance as a public administration handle in looking at their experiences in confronting the polycrises. A decentralised and diffused approach to governance where powers and decision-making authorities are distributed and shared among various centres of power—hence "nodes"—is a central feature of the multi-nodal approach to governance. Equally important is the presence of a strong and competent central authority that would prepare comprehensive long- and medium-term national development plans and set the high policy frameworks so that devolved approaches to multiple challenges can be synchronised well, while national ministries supposedly provide direction and lend financial and technical support to localities.

Certainly, all concerned stakeholders at different levels of government at the local, national, regional, and even at the global levels are the nodes of power and governance. Among the stakeholders are the various government agencies themselves, the NGOs, the private sector, community groups, and people's organisations. The abilities of the various nodes to collaborate and coordinate, share accountability, be agile and flexible, and address wicked and complex problems are all imperatives for successful multi-nodal governance. Special attention will be given to the role of subnational governments as frontline institutions "where the rubber hits the road" in the polycrises.

The institutions and the presence of strategies that address various crises including those at the national and local levels, the presence of emergency response plans to natural disasters, pandemics, economic upheavals, etc., in collaboration with businesses, civil society, and NGOs in these countries will be investigated. Equally important would be to examine the ability of governments to mobilise resources to address these challenges. A very critical aspect of multi-nodal response to the polycrises is cross border international cooperation and collaboration considering that crises transcend national borders and require international collaboration including information sharing.

This is where regional institutions like the Association of Southeast Asian Nations (ASEAN) and the South Asian Nations for Regional Cooperation (SAARC) come in, including the appropriate bodies of the United Nations system. Vertical and horizontal cooperation—and communication—is imperative in multi-nodal governance and how these have been observed and operationalised in the various countries down to the local levels will also be considered. Finally, basic to any governance response is the need to monitor and assess the process within the context of continuous improvement given the rapidly changing environment brought about by the polycrisis.

10.2 Overview

The Singapore-based Chandler Institute, in its Good Governance Index Report (2023, 2024), notes that the world is facing unprecedented challenges, interconnected in ways that were unimaginable before. A single incident, such as a stranded shipping vessel, can impact billions of dollars of global trade, while a country's lockdown can affect the production of essential goods worldwide. Several worldwide crises—the COVID-19 pandemic, global warming, and Russia's assault on Ukraine and the Israel-Hamas war—have interconnected in ways that are large, destructive, and unclear, hence turning into *polycrises.* Many leaders believe that a single catastrophe typically induces or exacerbates another, resulting in both distinct and more severe consequences than those caused by different crises individually.[3] Indeed, as Neil deGrasse Tyson,[4] and Desmond Tutu,[5] once said, we are all connected in so many ways, biologically,

[3] Georgieva K., IMF Managing Director in her presentation "*Facing crisis upon crisis: How the world can respond*" at the Annual Meetings of the World Bank and International Monetary Fund. https://www.imf.org/en/News/Articles/2022/04/14/sp041422-curtain-raiser-sm2022.

[4] Neil deGrasse quotations. *Goodreads*. https://www.goodreads.com/author/quotes/12855.Neil_deGrasse_Tyson.

[5] Broad Street. (06.01.2022). *15 Impactful Quotes by Desmond Tut*u. https://bspc.org/15-impactful-quotes-by-desmond-tutu/.

ecologically, socially, and even philosophically. Tutu also added, "what unites us in our own common humanity."[6]

When the COVID-19 outbreak started, it was observed that countries with strong central governance were able to implement actions with tight coordination. They could harness and deploy resources to support national goals. Horizontal and vertical coordination regarding intergovernmental cooperation at all levels has become imperative. Hence, multi-nodal governance can address the multifaceted polycrises, which are complex, and they represent the kind of challenges that demand the expertise of different government agencies and institutions at different levels (Lallana 2020). It is therefore critical to recognise the potential impact of these interconnected and intertwined problems and take immediate, decisive action. If not addressed sooner, the results might be more severe. The role of governance and public administration institutions therefore cannot be overstated.

10.3 Theoretical Foundations of Multi-nodal Governance

A nation-state is portrayed as the beneficent power in Thomas Hobbes' "Leviathan." However, polycentric governance empirical investigations show that this centralised perspective needs to be more customised as de-centred governance models acknowledge that power is diffused across flows, systems, and nodes (Holley and Shearing 2017). Organisational nodes impact events and collaborate with other nodes to achieve their aims. Governance is an outcome of these relationships and certainly not the responsibility of a single institution. Fields like law enforcement, crisis management, digitalisation interconnectedness and interoperability, health care, and intellectual property management have used nodal governance principles to study and enhance governance processes and outcomes (Holley and Shearing 2017).

Central government agencies are centres of network activity. This setup usually refers to an organisation under a unitary state's central government, a federal government, or local governments. These institutions

[6] Schnall, M. (27.12.2021). Wisdom Shared With Me By Desmond Tutu: 'We Are All Connected. What Unites Us Is Our Common Humanity.' *Forbes*. https://www.forbes.com/sites/marianneschnall/2021/12/26/wisdom-shared-with-me-by-desmond-tutu-we-are-all-connected-what-unites-us-is-our-common-humanity/.

administer a multi-network portfolio of systems. This arrangement is conducted so that the national level would lay out the general policy guidelines while the subordinate levels of government are tasked with local-level policy application (Ysa and Esteve 2013). In a hierarchy, many networks rely on central institutions for authority under the law and funding but operate with relative autonomy. The networks give central and local authorities access to additional resources since they can incorporate the business and nonprofit sectors into their cause. Through networks, civil society also becomes accessible. Government agencies define limits for network activities through strategic management. This arrangement offers a balance between national-level control and decentralised flexibility to respond to local conditions (Rhodes 2017).

It is within this context that the following sections draw from the experiences of selected countries in Southeast Asia and discuss how institutions of governance responded to the polycrises triggered by events such as the COVID-19 pandemic and other health emergencies, environmental degradation and climate change, calamities, and even the advent of rapid digitalisation in the midst of the fourth and fifth industrial revolutions.

The common approaches of these selected Southeast Asian states are viewed from the perspective of ***multi-nodal governance arrangements*** aimed at tackling multifaceted challenges; hence, "polycrises." The fourth industrial revolution and digitalisation and misinformation and artificial intelligence may also be seen as polycrises considering the reality of insufficient resources, poor capacities, the digital talent gap not only in the bureaucracy but even among the population itself, the widening digital divide and cybersecurity and massive misinformation and disinformation. However, digitalisation and information technologies may also be seen as an instrument and a governance mechanism to address the crisis.

In addressing the challenges of the polycrises, the experience of public administration and governance systems in the selected Southeast Asian countries ranged from rapid centralisation, to constituting responsible ministries and line departments (e.g., health, defence, interior, social welfare, emergency management, commerce, tourism, etc.), to mobilising subnational institutions and subnational governments, to harnessing private sector, businesses, NGOs, and civil society groups into task forces and similar arrangements—hence "multi-nodal"—with each responsible for the particular sector, but making sure that the efforts are aligned, coordinated, and not moving in disparate directions, hence the imperative of comprehensive national frameworks and plans.

However, the intergovernmental collaboration is where the tension between, among other things, centralisation and decentralisation comes in, especially during crises which warrant quick, decisive action from governments and may not leave much time for coordination. In essence, the responses of Southeast Asian states on polycrises were influenced by the regime type, existing laws, and their experiences in previous crises like the 2003 SARS pandemic (JICA 2015).

These countries' governance structures have used a combination of centralised and decentralised crisis responses. Singapore's centralised and structured COVID-19 reaction included intensive contact tracing and public health measures, whereas Indonesia's decentralised task groups incorporated public–private collaborations. This diversity shows how different government frameworks handle crises (Djalante et al. 2020). The pandemic revealed their crisis response strengths and vulnerabilities, which could be seen as a vital stress test for these governments. Comparing their responses can help prepare for future health, economic, and societal catastrophes (Daly et al. 2020).

The following sections discuss the experience of the selected Southeast Asian countries utilising the multimodal governance paradigm in their responses to the polycrises, divided into four sections each, i.e., environmental challenges, disasters and responses, health and pandemic responses, and digital technologies.

10.4 Kingdom of Thailand

Thailand is an industrial economy-based country situated in Southeast Asia, occupying the Indochina Peninsula and the northern part of the Malay Peninsula (ADB 2015; JICA 2014). Spanning 513,000 sq.km, Thailand is home to a rich tapestry of ethnicities, including Malays, Chinese, Burmese, Vietnamese, Cambodians, and Indians, resulting in a richly diverse cultural landscape (UNESCAP, n.d.).[7]

Thailand is not new in facing the intersecting crises of today. In addressing the challenges posed by polycrises, Thailand has relied on its proven strategies, continuously refining and adapting them with the

[7] United Nations Economic and Social Commission for Asia and the Pacific (UNESCAP) (n.d.). Thailand: General information. https://www.unescap.org/sites/default/files/General_Information_TH.pdf.

changing times.[8] Thailand has implemented strategies to foster a value-driven economy centred on creativity, innovation, and intellectual development that would capture encompassing solutions against the overall impact of complex interactions among crises (Swilling 2013, 2019). This paved the way for Thailand's transition to become an upper-middle-income state in 2011, and its eventual goal of reaching higher-income status by 2032 (ADB 2016; FAOUN 2020). This social and economic growth has played a crucial role in reducing poverty in Thailand.

Although Thailand may not immediately match the pace of widespread technological innovation, it is concentrating on enhancing its services through effective governance and strategic policymaking. This is most evident with Thailand's steady position in the Chandler Good Governance Index (CGGI) for 2024, ranking 54th overall (CIG 2024). Its impressive 37th place in the "Health" Indicator reflects the country's top-notch practices during the pandemic, which significantly uplifted its overall ranking. In 2023, Thailand responded to polycrises by strengthening its public health system, climbing 22 spots in just a year. By inculcating these strategies in every aspect of governance, Thailand is poised to navigate the polycrises of today.

10.4.1 Environmental Challenges

Thailand is particularly susceptible to the effects of climate change, ranking 62nd out of 181 countries in the 2020 ND-GAIN Index.[9] One of the most pressing challenges is the rising ocean levels, largely caused by rising temperatures leading to the thawing of glaciers and ice caps as reported by the Intergovernmental Panel on Climate Change (IPCC).[10] This growing sea level has been foreseen to contribute to more coastal floods, which has led to saline intrusion in some underground water sources, contaminating them and reducing the productivity of coastal farmlands due to increased soil salinity (Bates et al. 2008).[11] Additionally, storm surges, intensified by tropical storms, pose a considerable threat to

[8] Nation Thailand. (10.08.2023). BTS Group expected to earn THB 2.5 billion from divesting its 10.52 percent shareholding in U City. https://www.nationthailand.com/business/corporate/40034983.

[9] https://gain.nd.edu/our-work/country-index/rankings/.

[10] https://www.ipcc.ch/.

[11] Yuthavong, Y. (25.12.2007). Thai strategies to fight climate change. *The Nation*.

coastal areas, altering coastal processes and beach morphology (Anthes et al. 2006; Phantuwongraj et al. 2013). Scientific studies have indicated that climate change contributes to the increased frequency and intensity of tropical storms, leading to more severe floods in coastal and low-lying areas (Dasgupta et al. 2009).

With inter-systemic impact, the consequences of climate change in Thailand extend beyond rising sea levels causing further domino effect (Klose et al. 2021). The country faces heightened risks of natural disasters, such as landslides, which have been linked to increased rainfall intensity. The International Consortium on Landslides reported a significant rise in landslide-associated casualties due to this intensification (Sassa et al. 2023). Furthermore, higher temperatures are causing more frequent instances of heat-related illnesses, including heat cramps, exhaustion, and sunstroke, particularly in industrial and agricultural settings. Research on five locations found that 80% had severe warnings on the heat indices and 20% on the hazard zone, reducing productivity (Langkulsen et al. 2010).

Further anthropogenic disturbances have caused serious environmental instability to the Holocene equilibrium, and by extension, advancing climate change (McKay et al. 2022; Barnosky et al. 2012; Lawrence et al. 2024). Thailand faces significant environmental degradation, particularly in its marine habitats and ecosystems. Coral reefs are suffering from physical damage due to activities such as anchoring tourist boats, trampling by snorkelers and divers, and illegal fishing practices (Flynn and Forrester 2019; Chanrachkij et al. 2010). Marine debris, originating from both land and sea, further exacerbates the situation (Thushari et al. 2017). Urbanisation and an influx of coastal tourists have spurred extensive development in coastal zones, resulting in building roads, ports, hotels, and restaurants. These developments produce high sedimentation loads, which are released into the coasts, harming coral habitats (Briggs and Funge-Smith 1994). Deforestation in watershed and coastal areas leads to erosion, siltation, and increased sedimentation (Richards and Friess 2015).

Additionally, oil spills pose a severe threat to seagrass and mangroves, reducing photosynthesis and damaging trees and organisms within these ecosystems (Agbogidi et al. 2006; Bureau of Ocean Energy Management 2011; Kingston 2002). Solid waste disposal in mangrove areas, including plastic bags and ropes, can harm trees and roots, which serve as nurseries for various marine organisms. The breakdown of marine debris into microplastics further endangers benthic fauna and introduces these pollutants into the food chain, disrupting the entire mangrove ecosystem (Barnes et al. 2009).

In response to the environmental crisis, the Thai government has implemented a comprehensive 20-Year National Strategy (2017–2036), aiming to transform Thailand into a stable, prosperous, and sustainable nation by 2036. This strategy is grounded on the Sufficient Economy Philosophy and encompasses six key areas: (i) enhancing national security; (ii) strengthening competitiveness; (iii) empowering human capital; (iv) promoting social equality; (v) advancing towards a green economy; and (vi) reforming public administration.

To actualise this vision, three major plans were devised: the National Maritime Security Plan (2015–2022), the Environmental Management Plan (2017–2021), and the 12th National Economic and Social Development Plan (2017–2022). The National Maritime Security Plan focuses on protecting maritime interests and promoting sustainable marine resource management (Department of Fisheries 2015). The 12th National Economic and Social Development Plan emphasises sustainable and people-centred development, targeting critical environmental issues like water resource management, waste reduction, greenhouse gas emission cuts, energy conservation, and climate resilience. Lastly, the Environmental Management Plan aims to conserve, restore, and utilise natural resources equitably, fostering a greener society and building up capabilities to address climate change and calamities (Department of Fisheries 2015). Through these strategic frameworks, Thailand sought to address its environmental challenges through an integrated assessment of the interaction of the polycrises (Baum and Barrett 2018).

10.4.2 Disasters and Responses

Thailand faces a variety of natural calamities like flooding, typhoons, droughts, forest fires, landslides, and high temperatures (Nuntatikul 2023). The geographical diversity of the country, thus, results in varying impacts from the conjoined harm brought by these multiple crises of disasters (Lawrence et al. 2022). Landslides caused by severe rainfall are especially common in the north and south, where high and mountainous environments exist (Sujitapan et al. 2024). Conversely, forest fires are more prevalent in the north during the dry season (UNDRR 2020). Storms exhibit regional patterns; localised storms occur between April and October in the north, while the southern regions face storm activity from

March to November (Nuntatikul 2023). This spatial variability underscores the complex nature of disaster risk across Thailand (Nyström et al. 2019).

An intra-systemic impact is most evident in Thailand, with less noticeable but equally significant threats arising from disasters caused by major hazards (Renn et al. 2017; Schweizer 2019). Long-term issues like flooding affected the central flood plains of Thailand, specifically in the Chao Phraya River basin (JICA 2013). This region's extensive river systems make it prone to riverine flooding, exacerbated by the country's complex hydrology (JICA 2013). Landslides are frequently triggered by intense, continuous rainfall, leading to land mass and debris movement in vulnerable mountainous regions. According to the Department of Mineral Resources, landslide risks are heightened in areas with severe soil erosion and reduced vegetation cover, with 54 provinces identified as highly susceptible to landslides (Sujitapan et al. 2024; Nuntatikul 2023).

Droughts in Thailand manifest in two primary periods: from June to September, following a delayed onset of rainfall, and from October to May during the dry season (Fakhruddin and Chivakidakarn 2014). These droughts are increasingly influenced by El Niño conditions, leading to severe water shortages and correlating with forest fires, which often arise between December and May due to human activities such as land clearing (UNDRR 2020). Statistics indicate that about twenty million rai[12] are affected by intense drought conditions, particularly in areas with inadequate irrigation and water reservoirs.[13] Furthermore, regional discrepancies in water demand exacerbate the situation, particularly in northern regions with high off-season rice cultivation and limited irrigation infrastructure (Bank of Thailand 2019).

In response to these challenges, the Thai government has implemented a robust disaster risk management framework (Thanyalakmetha 2022). The Disaster Prevention and Mitigation Act B.E. 2550 (2007) replaced the obsolete 1979 Civil Defence Act and the 1999 Fire Prevention and Suppression Act, providing a comprehensive legal foundation for disaster management (Government of Thailand 2017; Nuntatikul 2023). The

[12] Rai is a traditional unit of area used in Thailand, commonly used to measure land, especially in agricultural contexts. One rai equals 1600 square meters (or approximately 0.395 acres). In terms of disaster management, particularly during natural disasters like floods or storms, the unit of rai is often used to quantify the extent of land affected.

[13] http://irw101.ldd.go.th/index.php/2017-05-23-02-00-40/2017-05-23-02-00-39.

National Disaster Prevention and Mitigation Plan 2021–2027 builds on previous plans to outline a strategic approach for disaster risk management (Nuntatikul 2023). This plan focuses on enhancing disaster risk management capacity, integrating innovation and technology, improving recovery systems, and fostering multi-agency cooperation (Cazeau 2019; Nuntatikul 2023). It also emphasises international collaboration and the development of standards to improve disaster management practices, reflecting a commitment to strengthening Thailand's resilience and response capabilities (Thanyalakmetha 2022; UNDRR 2020). By doing so, Thailand was able to address the natural disaster polycrisis by devising a systemic architecture able to withstand the polycrisis (Gaupp et al. 2019).

10.4.3 Health/Pandemic Response

The COVID-19 pandemic has been a significant global challenge, and Thailand has faced its own set of hurdles in managing the crisis. In response to the escalating situation, the Thai Government swiftly implemented the National Preparedness and Curfew Policies, subsequent to the declaration of an Emergency Decree under the Communicable Disease Act (Tantrakarnapa and Bhopdhornangkul 2020). These measures were designed to harness the country's existing health crisis management infrastructure and ensure a comprehensive response to the pandemic (Triukose et al. 2021).

To coordinate these efforts, Thailand established the Centre for COVID-19 Situation Administration (CCSA), which brought together government officials from multiple sectors to deliver a cohesive yet adaptable response. This whole-of-government approach enabled policy alignment on critical measures like mobility restrictions, enhanced medical facilities, and financial support, while empowering provincial leaders to make localised decisions within the CCSA's framework. This structure allowed Thailand to effectively carry out contact tracing and isolation protocols, contributing to a low mortality rate in the early stages of the pandemic (Rajatanavin et al. 2021).

A review of Thailand's public health response further highlighted nine essential areas: nationwide coordination, community engagement, quick response teams, surveillance and case detection, migrant health, equipped national laboratory systems, community infection control, clinical management, and operational assistance.[14] Each component aimed to bolster the country's preparedness and response capabilities across various sectors (Bengthong et al. 2024).[15] Specifically, for COVID-19, Thailand's greatest strength was its vast reserves of volunteers—one million village health volunteers (VHVs)—who took the frontlines in all of its provinces (Tejativaddhana et al. 2020). Dubbed as the "Thai People's First Doctors," VHVs served as Thailand's first-level health carers in the community, caring for the sick and implementing orders from medical doctors powered by technology (Kaweenuttayanon et al. 2021; Rajatanavin et al. 2021).

Beyond the immediate COVID-19 response, Thailand's broader health management strategies have been shaped by ongoing challenges such as zoonotic diseases and environmental health concerns (Kelly et al. 2020; Tangwangvivat et al. 2024). The establishment of the *Coordinating Unit for One Health* (CUOH) in 2014 was a direct response to these interconnected health issues, necessitating systemic transformations in different institutions (Baum and Barrett 2018; Innes et al. 2022; Lawrence et al. 2024). This initiative, spearheaded by the Ministry of Public Health, fosters government, academic, and civic engagement on cross-human, animal, and ecological issues (Mwangi et al. 2016). The CUOH has been pivotal in creating guidelines, educational materials, and managing resources both domestically and internationally (Tangwangvivat et al. 2024).

Local government organisations have also played a crucial role in strengthening Thailand's health systems (Boonsang and Penpim 2023). Empowered by the National Health Security Act of 2002, these organisations have utilised programmes such as the Provincial Rehabilitation Fund and Community Health Fund (CHF) to support local health initiatives and public health education (Ngowsiri 2020; WHO-Regional Office for the Western Pacific 2015). During the pandemic, these resources were instrumental in conducting screenings, providing care, and supporting community outreach efforts (National Health Security Office 2020;

[14] World Health Organisation (WHO). (19.09.2020). How a strong health system fights a pandemic in Thailand, https://www.who.int/news-room/feature-stories/detail/how-a-strong-health-system-fights-a-pandemic-in-thailand.

[15] https://www.who.int/thailand/emergencies/novel-coronavirus-2019/situation-reports.

WHO-Regional Office for the Western Pacific 2015). This decentralised approach has proven effective in managing health crises and underscores the importance of local involvement in national health strategies (McManus and Sāthāranasuk 2012; Tangcharoensathien et al. 2014).

10.4.4 Digital Technologies

According to the Digital Riser Report of 2020 of the European Centre for Digital Competitiveness,[16] Thailand is one of the most improved countries in terms of enhancing digital ecosystem and digitalisation as a whole and has ranked 2nd among the East Asia and the Pacific region. Within the level of the government, digitalisation efforts have been welcomed and strongly supported by the government. The Ministry of Digital Economy and Society (MDES), formerly under the Ministry of Information and Communication Technology, was established to lead the government in the enhancement, development, and promotion of the digital economy. Alongside MDES, government agencies such as the Office of the National Digital Economy and Society Commission (ONDE) and the Electronic Transactions and Development Agency (ETDA) were also initiated to help build a digital ecosystem that is user friendly both to the government, private sector, and the public. However, these digitalisation efforts were being hindered by several challenges of the public to adopt these digital solutions. According to a study in 2021, the business sector in Thailand has a relatively slow adoption of digital solutions and mechanisms coupled with the relatively low digital capacities and skills among the professionals and graduates of the country. There is also a concern on the high-cost investment on information and communications technology (ICT) infrastructure such as the 5G network.

Due to the digital talent gap and somehow lack of trust of the public in welcoming digital interactions, the government, through the ETDA, has been expanding its efforts to mainstream digital IDs especially with government offices, as well as face verification service (FVS) and digital signature certification for important public documents. As the world also expands digitalisation into embracing artificial intelligence, the Thailand government will also establish the Artificial Intelligence Governance Centre (AIGC), which will develop guidelines on the use of AI

[16] https://digital-competitiveness.eu/.

particularly on health services and finance. The Academy of Digital Transformation by ETDA (ADTE Institute) will likewise help in coping with the digital skills gaps through training workshops and course offerings designed for the public including the vulnerable groups.

In addition to this, the COVID-19 pandemic has indeed expedited the digital transformation of Thailand through various means including public service delivery, communications, and learning modalities, among others. Some of the notable digital transformation efforts introduced during the pandemic were the Thailand Covid-19 Digital Group (TCDG)—a social media avenue for technology firms and virtual service providers to collaborate in utilising technologies as solutions against the pandemic; gathered tech startups to introduce real-time digital medical consultations through the Yothi Medical Innovation District (YMID) under the NIA and the Technology and Innovation-Based Enterprise Development Fund; and other enterprise initiatives that enabled online self-service purchases through mobile telephones, kiosks, and other technical media.

10.5 Socialist Republic of Viet Nam

The Communist Party of Viet Nam (CPV), as the dominant political party in the country,[17] decides on political programmes, strategies, and guidelines, while Party boards at every level (central, provincial/city) make certain that the Party's guidelines and policies are understood and implemented by members and non-members (Socialist Republic of Viet Nam, n.d.-a).[18] The Vietnamese policy style favours implementing policies without social consultation; however, policies result from complex, time-intensive negotiations and representations involving numerous stakeholders. Furthermore, although the CPV maintains a dominant position in policymaking, social concerns and international players are becoming increasingly significant in formulating policies (Croissant 2019). Hence, the collaborative nature of its policy approach towards public affairs affirms the practice of multi-nodal governance.

The National Assembly of Viet Nam acknowledged multiple achievements and shortcomings in implementing its 2011–2015 social and

[17] Socialist Republic of Viet Nam. (n.d.-a). Political System. https://vietnam.gov.vn/political-system-68959.

[18] Viet Nam has 63 provinces and five central government-run cities (Ha Noi, Ho Chi Minh City, Can Tho, Da Nang, and Hai Phong) (Jones and Gu 2012).

economic growth plan,[19] before introducing its 2016–2020 strategy.[20] While living conditions improved, Viet Nam did not become a modern industrialised nation by 2020 (Socialist Republic of Viet Nam, n.d.-b). In July 2021, the National Assembly passed a five-year socio-economic development plan for 2021–2025. It prioritised the protection of the environment and climate change mitigation for a sustainable future for its people (Socialist Republic of Viet Nam, n.d.-c).

Viet Nam became a member of Association of South East Asian Nations (ASEAN) in 1995. Then-Prime Minister Nguyen Xuan Phuc was the Chair of the ASEAN in 2020, the first year of the COVID-19 pandemic. The same year also marked the 25th anniversary of joining the organisation. Under Viet Nam's leadership, online high-level conferences were initiated, like the ASEAN Coordinating Council Working Group on Public Health Emergencies, ASEAN-EU Ministerial Conference, and ASEAN-United States High-Level Interagency Video Conference on Cooperation to Counter COVID-19 (Tran 2020).

10.5.1 Environmental Challenges

Viet Nam consumed 8.2 tons of material footprint per capita in 2019 (ADB, n.d.)[21] and transmitted 3.7 metric tons of carbon dioxide emissions per capita in 2020 (World Bank Group, n.d.). The UNDP Human Development Report 2023/2024 depicted the vulnerability to rising sea levels of the country's 3000 kilometres of coastline (UNDP 2024b). Furthermore, the Global Forest Watch reported that Viet Nam's forest

[19] Socialist Republic of Viet Nam. (n.d.-c). Socio-economic development plan for 2021–2025. https://vietnam.gov.vn/socio-economic-development-plans/socio-economic-development-plan-for-2021-2025-12056314.

[20] Socialist Republic of Viet Nam. (n.d.-b). Socio-economic development plan for 2016–2020 period. https://vietnam.gov.vn/socio-economic-development-plans/socio-economic-development-plan-for-2016-2020-period-12056315.

[21] Material footprint measures the "total amount of raw materials extracted to meet final consumption demands" (UN, n.d.).

area was reduced by 94.2 kha,[22] equivalent to 118 Mt of CO_2 emissions, from 2010 to 2023.[23] A 2018 World Health Organisation study found links of air pollution to 60,000 fatalities from cardiovascular diseases, stroke, lung cancer, chronic obstructive pulmonary disease, and pneumonia (World Health Organisation 2018).

Viet Nam, as an industrialising country, realised the need to twin its progress with the preservation of its environment and natural resources. To address its present environmental concerns, the "National Green Growth Strategy 2021–2030, Vision 2050," was approved by the Prime Minister in the Fall of 2021 aimed at helping Viet Nam restructure its economy that is conducive for prosperity, ecological preservation, and social equity, with a green, carbon-neutral economy that lessens the impact of global warming (USDA FAS and GAIN 2021).

Viet Nam adopts the whole-of-government approach in implementing its environment and climate change initiatives. As an example, the National Council of Sustainable Development, established in 2005 and headed by the Deputy Prime Minister, comprises 50 members from national agencies, businesses, and trade and labour groups. Initiatives and responsibilities are carried out across ministries. Moreover, the national government's policies are implemented by provincial, municipal, and district authorities (ADB 2013).

10.5.2 Disasters and Responses

From 1990 to 2021, 187 incidents of natural disasters were recorded in Viet Nam, which resulted in 13,508 deaths. Highest number of deaths occurred due to river floods and tropical cyclones, 3281 and 7283 deaths, respectively. Flooding, typhoons, and inundation are classified as high risks in the natural disaster risk classifications in Viet Nam (Open Development Vietnam 2021). Thus, the National Steering Committee

[22] Global Forest Watch. Viet Nam. https://www.globalforestwatch.org/dashboards/country/VNM/.

[23] World Bank Group (WBG) (n.d.). CO_2 emissions (metric tons per capita). https://data.worldbank.org/indicator/EN.ATM.CO2E.PC?fbclid=IwY2xjawFR-M5leHRuA2FlbQIxMAABHSdF8xWhCRtOiaBeMXHj15jtpJz9Nf7AfDezxa1GchQjQsjw-1ABpV4wBQ_aem_8QCXFw335_88JOjjOLY1Kw.

for Natural Disaster Prevention and Control was created to oversee emergency responses during calamities.[24]

The Viet Nam government has shown progress in crafting policies and implementing programmes for disaster mitigation and climate change adaptation through the years. To continue progressing, its capacity to store, manage, and analyse data related to disasters should be further enhanced. Building data management capabilities in the Vietnamese public sector is essential for informed policy decisions. Improved public sector data systems would improve inter-agency coordination and provide an extensive overview of disaster impacts, enabling policy learning and better disaster-preparedness efforts.

According to a study by the International Organisation for Migration, data collection is focused on hazard monitoring, specific disaster operations, and loss and damage assessments. Furthermore, data sharing across Viet Nam is limited. Same study pointed out weaknesses in administrative data because of disjointed standards and definitions of data collection among different ministries, limited data sharing, and lack of coordination mechanisms (IOM, n.d.).

10.5.3 Health/Pandemic Response

The indicators for life expectancy and infant mortality have shown evident improvement through the past three decades. The life expectancy in Viet Nam over a period of 30 years (1990–2020) expanded from 70.5 to 75.5 years. Conversely, infant mortality declined from 32.6 per 1000 live births in 1993 to 16.7 in 2020 (World Bank 2024).

The governance of the healthcare system in Viet Nam is decentralised, while the Ministry of Health (MOH) is tasked with developing policies, technical guidelines, and monitoring policy implementation. The healthcare facilities in Viet Nam are public; there are 47 central level hospitals, 419 provincial level hospitals, and 684 district level hospitals. Since 2018, public hospitals have not received direct budget subsidies for their operating cost (WHO, n.d.).

The world witnessed the effectiveness of Viet Nam's national leadership in handling the COVID-19 pandemic crisis. In January 2020, the

[24] National Steering Committee for Natural Disaster Prevention and Control. http://phongchongthientai.mard.gov.vn/en/Pages/tasks-of-the-central-steering-committee-for-natural-disaster-prevention-and-control.aspx.

Government of Viet Nam constituted the National Steering Committee which represented the central command-and-control of the COVID-19 response (Hue 2023). However, a report by the London School of Economics and Political Science (LSE) and Partnership for Health System Sustainability and Resilience (2021) commented on the significant gap in quality and ease of access between large city upper-level healthcare providers and rural primary care institutions (LSE 2021).

People's participation at the community-level to stop the increase of infections was documented. A study focused on the cities of Hanoi, Da Nang, and Ho Chi Minh highlighted the practice of innovative use of mobile apps or websites like Hanoi Smart City, Ho Chi Minh City COVID-19, and Da Nang COVID maps (Nguyen and Malesky 2020 cited in Hue 2023). Local governments and citizens reported to public authorities the violations of stay-at-home orders from the government using these digital applications.

10.5.4 Digital Technologies

The Global Innovation Index 2023 reported that Viet Nam was one of the most impressive innovation climbers of the last decade, climbing to the 46th position in 2023 (World Intellectual Property Organization 2023) from 76th in 2013 (Cornell University et al. 2013). Similarly, Viet Nam was ranked 39th out of 193 countries for artificial intelligence (AI) readiness in 2023, according to a report by the UK-based Oxford Insights.[25]

In 2020, Viet Nam approved its National Digital Transformation Programme aimed at further advancing national economic growth and social development through expansion of the ICT infrastructure. The vision of digital transformation is anchored on digital government, digital economy, and digital society.

Through this, governance will be enabled by digitalisation at every level—national, provincial, and local. Digital technologies can augment public goods provision, improve governance, and bolster public sector transparency and efficiency (Open Development Viet Nam 2021). Viet Nam has set the target for the contribution of the digital economy to 30%

[25] Viet Nam Economy. (16.02.2024). Government ranks 39th in AI readiness. https://en.vneconomy.vn/government-ranks-39th-in-ai-readiness.htm.

of the country's Gross Domestic Product by 2030 (Open Development Viet Nam 2021).

Growth of Viet Nam's digital economy is primarily reliant on e-commerce. A 2023 study conducted by Lenain and Vu for the Organisation for Economic Cooperation and Development (OECD) asserted that the digital economy in Viet Nam has displayed strong growth since the 2010s. Aside from e-commerce, its digital economy also includes financial technology, blockchain, gaming, education technology, and health care (Lenain and Vu 2023).

Viet Nam welcomed foreign direct investments in the manufacture of smartphones and micro-processors. Viet Nam has also encouraged investments in digital unicorns such as VNG, VNPay, and MoMo, and eleven startups like Tiki and Topica Edtech, valued at US$ 100 M (Lenain and Vu 2023).

10.6 Republic of Singapore

Singapore is a developed city-state at the southern tip of the Malay Peninsula. About 5.6 million people live in an area of 734.3 sq.km. Since its founding as a British trade post in 1819, Singapore has been an international commercial centre due to its strategic location along one of the globe's busiest shipping lanes. The country is multicultural, with 74.2% Chinese, 13.7% Malays, and 8.9% Indians.[26] Since its formation in 1965, the People's Action Party has led it via a unitary parliamentary system. The nation's languages are English, Malay, Mandarin, and Tamil, reflecting its diverse culture.[27]

Singapore remained at the top of the Chandler Good Governance Index (CGI) in 2024 (CIG 2024), since it overtook Finland in 2023. In 2022, it was third globally, as well as in 2021, in the index's first edition. The city-state excelled in leadership and foresight, strong institutions, and attractive marketplace.[28]

[26] The World Factbook—2014 Singapore. https://www.cia.gov/the-world-factbook/countries/singapore/.

[27] Nations Online. (n.d.). Singapore. https://www.nationsonline.org/oneworld/singapore.htm.

[28] Yuen-C, T. (26.04.2023). Singapore moves up 2 spots to top world ranking on government effectiveness. *The Straits Times*. https://www.straitstimes.com/singapore/politics/singapore-moves-up-2-spots-to-top-world-ranking-on-government-effectiveness.

It is a prominent example of a progressive state in East Asia. As a developmental state, Singapore has a significant track record of strategically preparing and carrying out comprehensive government-led changes to society and economy in pursuit of its national interests (Chan et al. 2016).[29] Consequently, it addressed the polycrisis stemming from the COVID-19 pandemic with an active and concerted approach that utilised its leadership and emergency management capabilities. It prompted the Ministries of Health, Trade and Industry, and Finance to act collectively. This collaboration benefited corporate and citizen-centred policymaking and execution (CIG 2023).

As ASEAN Chair in 2023, the country fostered regional cooperation and resilience during the polycrisis.[30] It has significant public–private partnerships to promote development and handle multifaceted issues like green energy. The Singapore Green Plan 2030 facilitates equitable growth by investing in economic development (UNESCAP 2023). In essence, the city-state's polycrises response includes decisive governance, a whole-of-government plan of action, maintaining a vibrant economy, regional cooperation, public–private partnerships, and community resilience.

10.6.1 Environmental Challenges

Asian countries with big coastal cities are exposed to environmental challenges like rising sea levels. Flooding, coastal erosion, and water scarcity can affect water supplies. Singapore's water policies and practices, devised to overcome its restricted resource base and attain self-reliance, have been lauded. Although Singapore's strategic context may have fostered progressive policies, it is worth studying how it adapts to climate change so that other polities can learn from it (Bhullar 2013). Singapore, a small, low-lying island state, may be more vulnerable to climate change than many other countries. However, the economy's size and complexity

[29] Developmental States are countries where governments assume a prominent role in both large and small-scale policymaking to promote economic growth and drive social transformation (Cheung, 2008).

[30] Singapore Institute of International Affairs (SIIA). (04.08.2023). 15th ASEAN and Asia Forum: Polycrisis Must Be a Catalyst for Change in ASEAN and Asia. https://www.siiaonline.org/15th-asean-and-asia-forum-polycrisis-must-be-a-catalyst-for-change-in-asean-and-asia/.

afford ample financial and institutional resources for adjustment. Its officials conduct climate change-related research and take into account the associated risks for the city-state. They have implemented policies to reduce emissions of carbon dioxide and prepare for global warming (McGreevy and Chia 2023).

Singapore is projected to have a 7% increase in the average yearly rainfall (Lau et al. 2021). Additionally, the rainfall is likely to be more plentiful and intense during the rainy season, while dry periods will likely be prolonged. Furthermore, there is an anticipation of an increase in the intensity of rain and storms as typhoons in the area become more frequent and severe. Adding to those issues is the impact of a projected sea level increase of 25–76 cm within the next hundred years on a small island country where no land is more than 20 km away from the coastline, and 20% of the land has been reclaimed (Bhullar 2013).

According to its National Climate Change Strategy, Singapore's supply and demand oversight, wastewater and stormwater control, institutional strength, and a conducive policy atmosphere with strong leadership, effective governance frameworks, and competent and focused personnel make the city-state's water management successful. Its stewardship of water reserves and climate change adaptation measures are underpinned by a supportive environment for advancing new technologies and funding (Tortajada 2006).

10.6.2 Disasters and Responses

Southeast Asian countries are susceptible to many emergencies, such as volcanic eruptions, storms, landslides, droughts, and floods. However, Singapore is relatively safe from several possible disasters compared to its neighbouring Southeast Asian countries, resulting in a notably low incidence of disasters (Lin et al. 2021). Singapore ranks 191st out of 191 countries and regions regarding the risk of calamities. Singapore consistently ranks as one of the most secure locations to call home (Mousavizadeh et al. 2016).

Singapore uses a multi-nodal governance approach to coordinate disaster response and management across institutions. The Singapore Civil Defence Force (SCDF) spearheads the national disaster management policy, collaborating with other government departments and CSOs to guarantee a unified and coordinated reaction to emergencies. This structure encompasses early identification and alert systems, disaster response capacities, and outreach efforts to improve public readiness and endurance.[31] Singaporeans recognise and embrace climate change at the organisational, governmental, civil society, public, and educational levels. The National Climate Change Secretariat (NCCS) creates and implements the country's climate change policies. It collaborates closely with several government ministries to coordinate initiatives to solve the challenges brought by climate change (Ho and Seow 2017).

Furthermore, the Building and Construction Authority oversees projects such as elevating coastal roadways in anticipation of rising sea waters.[32] The city-state prioritises public education on the subject. Its NCCS has released several books to educate the public. One such book is the "Climate-Resilient Singapore for a Sustainable Future,"[33] which provides information on climate change's effects (NCCS 2016). Learning about climate change primarily takes place at the secondary school level as part of a geography course. The curriculum addresses climate change as an urgent issue caused by human activity. Students are required to study climate change research, understand the consequences of climate change, and evaluate the various measures to respond to global warming at different levels (Ho and Seow 2017). Simply, its disaster response and recovery system have a multi-nodal governance approach reflected in its intergovernmental cooperation, emphasis on awareness through education, and international collaboration. These elements prepare the government and citizens for dealing with polycrises.

10.6.3 Health/Pandemic Response

Singapore has invested significantly in pandemic management capabilities and infrastructure. It drew lessons from the initial bout with the SARS pandemic. Frequent simulations in public hospitals assessed and improved pandemic response plans. When a multi-ministry group was formed to respond to the COVID-19 epidemic, the teams from the Ministries

[31] Singapore Civil Defence Force (SCDF) (15.10.2023). Singapore. *The ASEAN* [News outlet], https://theaseanmagazine.asean.org/article/singapore/.

[32] Tan, C. (28.01.2016). Nicoll Drive being raised to stave off rising seas. The Straits Times. http://www.straitstimes.com/singapore/transport/nicoll-drive-being-raised-to-stave-off-rising-seas.

[33] https://www.nccs.gov.sg/files/docs/default-source/publications/a-climate-resilient-singapore-for-A-sustainable-future.pdf.

of Manpower (MOM), Communications and Information (MCI), and Trade and Industry (MTI) received explicit regulations and orders from the highest levels of government (Lee et al. 2023). In the past 10–15 years, the city-state has developed digital networks and technical competence to facilitate its Smart Nation initiative. Singapore may use digital tools to respond quickly and accurately while informing the public about its efforts. Pandemics impact health, create public unrest and unstable politics, have financial consequences, and affect food supply, highlighting the importance of a comprehensive government policy (Lee et al. 2023).

Healthier SG (Singapore)—a government programme—increases general practitioners (GPs') activities beyond acute care, including prescriptions, preventive monitoring, and complex drug administration attending to Singapore's older population, rising long-term illness rates, and growing medical expenses. Although crucial in primary care, GPs may struggle to meet increasing demands due to their solitary operations. Healthier SG employs the Healthy 365 app and portable fitness gadgets to encourage lifestyle changes and track health indicators (Foo et al. 2023). Healthier SG relies on GP-government cooperation to meet GPs' operational needs and promote flexibility within the new governance framework. The programme aims to facilitate easy access to medical records by healthcare professionals across the private and public sectors. GPs' strong response to COVID-19 may further boost optimism for Healthier SG if solutions are developed and public trust is maintained (Foo et al. 2023).

10.6.4 Digital Technologies

Singapore's digitalisation is based on infrastructure development projects and the constant discussion of strategic plans (Graham et al. 2018). Singapore's digital transformation has advanced since the 1980s. The city-state has become one of the most technologically advanced countries by implementing various laws, master plans, and initiatives. It is well-positioned for digital transformation. According to the IMD World Competitiveness Centre, the city-state ranks fifth out of 64 nations in digital productivity based on knowledge transfer, industry preparedness, and spending on education (Erh 2023).[34]

The Smart Nation programme is the city-state's response to digitalising society and governance. Singapore scored 35.8 out of 40 across ten key characteristics, including vision, leadership, budget, and innovation, due to continuous investments in digital capabilities, making it an attractive destination for tech firms.[35] The government has increased ICT procurement spending to support digitalisation, setting aside 2.7 billion Singapore dollars for 250 projects to streamline virtual services across sectors and 500 million for public sector AI adoption. Its Emerging Technology Programme will help digitally mature organisations explore 5G, AI, and digital trust technologies.

Digital literacy programmes, such as the National Digital Literacy Programme and the Better Internet Campaign, are important in improving the population's digital skills. These initiatives signal a change in Singapore's approach from simply developing its digital infrastructure—such as broadband networks and access points—to building up digital competencies among all citizens. This strategy ensured that everyone could effectively use digital tools and resources regardless of their technical background (Ng et al. 2022). These programmes proved important during the COVID-19 pandemic in which nationwide lockdown required an accelerated transition to remote work and online learning, meaning that professionals and students had to depend largely on digital technology to perform their daily tasks. The city-state's well-developed internet infrastructure handled the surge in online activity without major issues, ensuring that most users had reliable access (Ng et al. 2022).

In all, Singapore's national agencies target smart city development, local government services, and cyberspace safety, among other policy challenges. In all cases, such centrally managed organisations consolidate government assets to improve policy effectiveness and performance. Centralisation has also emphasised "whole-of-government" operations (Woo 2018). The city-state's governance model coordinates national

[34] IMD World Competitiveness Centre (2023). *IMD World Digital Competitiveness Ranking 2023*. https://www.imd.org/wp-content/uploads/2023/12/Digital_2023.pdf.

[35] Statista (04.2022). Singapore as a Smart Nation: Assessing the Successes and Challenges of Singapore's Journey to become a Smart Nation. https://www.statista.com/study/88115/singapore-as-a-smart-nation/.

and local policymaking and implementation (Woo 2014), where multi-nodal governance can be implemented when national institutions set policy frameworks and local governments implement them. Paradoxically, multi-nodal governance may succeed against polycrises if a strong and competent central authority can facilitate a good decentralisation setup and capacity building for local governments.

10.7 Republic of Indonesia

Indonesia is a Southeast Asian nation, located between the Indian and the Pacific Oceans.[36] The country holds the position as the world's fourth most populated country and the biggest economy in the region (World Bank 2023) making it a critical source of regional stability and progress. Given its strategic location and large, diverse archipelago of hundreds of ethnic groups (Mahbubani and Sng 2017), Indonesia is an important economic and trade partner.[37] Its governance framework is a unitary presidential system with a bicameral legislature and multiparty politics focusing on large coalition-building (Setiawan and Tomsa 2022).

Over the years, Indonesia made significant redirection in its priorities to ensure strong and productive human capital development and steady economic development. In accordance with the income classification status produced by the World Bank in 2023, Indonesia regained its momentum as part of the upper-middle group post-pandemic compared to where it was in the year 2020. Indonesia's efforts are also reflected in the 2024 Chandler Good Governance Index (CGI), ranking 48th overall. In fact, as part of the "Stories of Good Governance Defying the Polycrisis," Indonesia prioritised inclusive growth as a central priority. In a similar vein, the country ranked 65th in the Helping People Rise pillar, moving up two places from 2023.[38] This ranking is evident with Indonesia's comprehensive health, education, and social protection programmes. Its government vowed to further boost the country's human capital and

[36] Indonesia Country Profile | Indonesia | Fact Sheet | U.S. Agency for International Development. (n.d.). U.S. Agency For International Development. https://www.usaid.gov/indonesia/fact-sheets/indonesia-country-profile.

[37] Asia-link Business (n.d.). *Indonesia's Economy*. https://asialinkbusiness.com.au/indonesia/getting-started-in-indonesia/indonesias-economy.

[38] Chandler Good Governance Index 2024 Report. https://chandlergovernmentindex.com/wp-content/uploads/2024-Chandler-Good-Government-Index-Report.pdf.

global competitiveness and wholly respond to polycrises through the pursuance of its development plans.

Just like the other country studies in this chapter, Indonesia approaches socio-economic, health, and polycrises issues through multi-sectoral collaboration, a hallmark of multi-nodal governance. The central government has instructed subnational agencies to collaborate on stunting prevention (Afandi et al. 2023). For instance, West Java public authorities have implemented child-feeding programmes, and a collaborative setup between community leaders and policymakers promotes equitable decision-making and awareness in preventing stunting (Afandi et al. 2023). Similarly, in the Indonesian context, agrarian reform can be more sustainable and effective by including the local population, government, private, and other stakeholders when making choices and giving them resources and support (Brilianto et al. 2024).

10.7.1 Environmental Challenges

Indonesia is the planet's largest archipelago with over 17,000 islands bearing important consequences both for its identity as a nation and for its character as a state (Cribb and Ford 2015). Although Indonesia is home to pristine rainforests and rich coastal and marine areas, it still faces sustained challenges both from natural phenomena and the country's growing population together with inadequate environmental management (World Bank 2014). The country is seen as fragments rather than a whole making it susceptible to environmental challenges that impact the well-being and livelihood of millions.

Some of the top environmental issues in Indonesia are deforestation, increasing forest fires, rising sea levels, and declining fisheries (ADB 2005; Koons 2024). Deforestation has soared due to illegal logging, and permanent forest conversion for agricultural use and mining. Alongside deforestation is the issue of forest fires which increased since 2001 and have caused 10% of the country's forest loss (MacCarthy et al. 2024) due to slash and burn practices. Climate change also contributed to the country's sea level rise, posing risks to the protection of coastal resources and communities. Moreover, with 60% of Indonesia's population living in coastal areas (Latif 2024), there is a high chance of inundation and displacement. Correspondingly, declining fisheries have direct implications on livelihood, food security, and economic growth. Fisheries provide

US$ 26.9 billion (2.6% of GDP), half the nation's protein source, and employment for over seven million people (World Bank 2024).

In response to these pressing issues, the government has taken bold steps in safeguarding the natural environment by investing in infrastructure, technology, capacity-building, and environmental management. Likewise, the government has built on existing plans and programmes towards sustainable and inclusive reforms such as the Climate Resilience Development Policy Nationally Determined Contributions and the National Long-Term Plan 2020–2024 (RPJMN), as well as sectoral programmes like Pro-Klim (Programme Kampung Iklim), which aims to incentivise local climate adoption; and the Resilient Coastal Zone Development Programme (World Bank 2023).

10.7.2 Disasters and Responses

According to the Asian Disaster Reduction Centre (ADRC),[39] Indonesia suffers from major natural hazards such as floods, landslides, droughts, tsunamis, earthquakes, and volcanic eruptions. Geographically, Indonesia lies on the Pacific "Ring of Fire," a disaster-prone area. In 2023, there were around 5400 natural disasters occurring in Indonesia, up from 2952 in 2020 (Siahaan 2024).[40] This archipelagic country has one of the highest disaster rates worldwide. Most notable disasters were the flooding 5 February 2007 in the Southern part of Jakarta affecting around 220,000 people; and the 2004 Indian Ocean Earthquake with a 9.1 magnitude. Disasters with such impact led to human and economic losses.[41]

The prevalence of natural hazards in Indonesia compelled the government to prioritise disaster risk management and strengthen their existing disaster countermeasures in line with the Disaster Management Master Plan for 2020–2044.[42] The Master Plan was formulated using the United

[39] Asian Disaster Reduction Centre (ADRC). https://www.adrc.asia/nationinformation.php?NationCode=360&Lang=en.

[40] Natural disasters in Indonesia. (21.12.2023). Statista. https://www.statista.com/topics/8305/natural-disasters-in-indonesia/#topicOverview.

[41] Indonesia: natural disasters risk index by type 2023 | Statista. (15.09.2023). https://www.statista.com/statistics/920857/indonesia-risk-index-for-natural-disasters/.

[42] See the document in Bahasa Indonesia and news in English: https://setkab.go.id/en/president-jokowi-signs-regulation-on-2020-2044-disaster-management-master-plan/.

Nations Sendai Framework for Disaster Risk Reduction (SFDRR) 2015–2030 where Indonesia has pledged its strong commitment to proactively minimise the impact of disaster risks. As part of the government's support, budget allocation on disaster management had a significant increase in 2020 following the COVID-19 outbreak.

10.7.3 *Health/Pandemic Response*

Indonesia is actively engaged in the process of responding to urgent health needs brought about by natural disasters and different types of diseases. However, the emergence of a global pandemic was definitely not what the country had prepared for. When the COVID-19 pandemic hit in March 2020, Indonesia faced unprecedented challenges especially considering its standing as the fourth most populated country in the world with over 270 million people (Harapan et al. 2023). The country's initial response to crises such as COVID-19 was reactive, with a focus on border control and health monitoring. The government formed a task force fast-response team on 13 March 2020, but it still needed a comprehensive plan for curbing the virus back then. The country issued its first public measure on 27 January 2020, to prevent the rise of infections (Yen et al. 2022).[43]

As a response, the Government of Indonesia used the pandemic influenza contingency plan created in 2019 with the World Health Organisation (WHO) to craft the COVID-19 response plan. As a whole-of-society approach, the contingency plan was used to promote preparedness measures to combat diseases of the same magnitude. The government also implemented the PEN Programme (National Economic Recovery Programme) which sought to improve economic capacities during the pandemic.

Conversely, Indonesia's COVID-19 handling was far from perfect revealing some of its responses as slow and ineffective due to unclear policies, lack of leadership, incoordination and conflicting statements (Hosen and Hammado 2021). Nevertheless, Indonesia addressed the pandemic by implementing suitable measures such as limiting community activities

[43] UN in Indonesia COVID-19 Response Newsletter July 2020. (n.d.). Indonesia. https://indonesia.un.org/en/93065-un-indonesia-covid-19-response-newsletter-july-2020.

and increasing the budget allocation for the health sector, as well as for social protection of the affected citizens (Putera et al. 2022).

10.7.4 Digital Technologies

Indonesia is one of the most rapidly growing digital economies in Southeast Asia (Wijaya 2022). In the 2023 Institute for Management and Development (IMD) World Digital Competitiveness Ranking (WDCR), Indonesia secured the 45th spot moving up six positions from 51st in 2022. According to Communication and Informatics Minister Budi Arie Setiadi, Indonesia's improvement in terms of its digital competitiveness score is proof of the government's commitment to accelerate national digital transformation. Likewise, this notable success is reflective of the country's digital transformation agenda.[44]

To streamline digitalisation, the Government of Indonesia launched the National Artificial Intelligence Strategy (*Strategi Nasional Kecerdasan Artifisial*) 2020–2045. As articulated by the Ministry of Research and Technology and the National Research and Innovation Agency (BRIN), the document outlined five strategic priority areas where AI may have the biggest impact: medical care, administrative reform, schooling, food availability and connectivity, and smart city development. According to its government, AI, IoT, and sophisticated robotics are needed to transform the nation into an innovation-based economy.

Consequently, the Indonesian Ministry of Communications and Informatics (MCI) published the 2021–2024 Digital Roadmap that serves as a strategic blueprint focused on the overall adoption of digital transformation with four primary sectors namely digital infrastructure, digital economy, digital society, and digital administration.[45] Through the roadmap, the government identified various ICT infrastructure initiatives such as the development of a 5G network and the establishment of a National Data Centre and telecommunication monitoring centre.

[44] The State of Indonesia's Digital Economy in 2022 | FULCRUM (23.11.2022). https://fulcrum.sg/the-state-of-indonesias-digital-economy-in-2022/; *Realizing Indonesia's digital transformation ambition: From AI to IoT | IBM Centre for the Business of Government*. https://www.businessofgovernment.org/blog/indonesia-digital-transformation.

[45] Asian Development Blog (n.d.), Indonesia's Digital Transformation: Leave no region behind. https://blogs.adb.org/blog/indonesia-s-digital-transformation-leave-no-region-behind.

There is also a focus on the digital onboarding of more than sixty-four million micro, small, and medium enterprises (MSMEs), encouraging them to “Go Digital and Go Global.”[46] Furthermore, several other programmes identified were the National Movement on Digital Literacy and Digital Talent Scholarship, which both aim to improve digital skills, competitiveness, productivity, and professionalism.

Greater use of digital technologies in Indonesia became very evident when the COVID-19 pandemic was raging, especially in response management. One major response is the creation of Siap Tanggap (SIAP) which means “Ready to Respond,” an online tool that collects, manages, and analyses local data to help communities and governments understand the socio-economic impacts of COVID-19. However, given Indonesia’s vast archipelago, access to technology remains to be a challenge. While Indonesia made significant strides in the adoption of digital technologies, it still lags in capturing its digital potential (Dash et al. 2016). More must be done to ensure equitable access to digital technology and services for all Indonesians, including the most disadvantaged (World Bank 2021b).

10.8 Republic of the Philippines

The Philippines is a constitutional democracy with a unitary presidential system, and its constitution was established in 1987 (Bueno and Salapa 2021). Culturally, the country is split between its Asian and Western heritage, unlike the other nine ASEAN countries which are clearly Asian societies. The archipelago has the longest Western colonial rule. Spain governed the Philippines between 1565 and 1898. After that, from 1898 to 1946, the U.S. occupied the country and helped establish a professional state bureaucracy to prepare it for selfgovernance. In 1946, the Philippine’s political colonialism ceased. Still, mental colonialism went on. Some affluent, well-known Filipinos advocated giving up sovereignty to become the 51st US state years later. Other Southeast Asian people would have opposed it (Mahbubani and Sng 2017).

On the realm of governance, the Philippines’ decentralisation experience is considered one of the most extensive in the developing world, where local authorities have gained considerable political, administrative,

[46] Indonesia: Digital Economy Opportunities (09.12.2021). International Trade Administration. https://www.trade.gov/market-intelligence/indonesia-digital-economy-opportunities.

and fiscal power (Guess 2005). The enactment of the Local Government Code in 1991 granted local autonomy to them despite the strong track record of centralism in its national government (Brillantes 2003; Brillantes and Ruiz 2021; Guess 2005). Disaster management requires dynamic and collaborative approaches to be addressed well. Thus, businesses, the civil society, and government institutions must collaborate to design an effective strategy for better responding during emergencies (Jovita et al. 2018).

For example, the Inter-Agency Task Force for Emerging and Infectious Diseases (IATF-EID) was composed of several national agencies to jointly formulate policies during the pandemic. It applied multi-nodal governance, which was demonstrated through partnerships with the academe for science advice to facilitate informed decision-making amidst a global health emergency (Vallejo and Ong 2021).

10.8.1 Disaster Risk and Response Management

The 2023 World Risk Index (WRI) ranked the Philippines as the country most vulnerable to natural calamities.[47] The research calculates the risk index of 193 UN member nations using twenty-seven parameters that relate disaster susceptibility with social preparation. The country's risk rating went up to 46.86, from 46.82 in 2022, for the highest risk ranking among 193 nations in the survey. Since 2011, it holds the top spot.[48]

In the archipelago, disasters are inevitable. With a socially and economically frail population and a disaster-prone location, calamities are commonplace (Bankoff 2003, cited in Blanco 2015). The Philippines has a strong civil society. When the 2013 Yolanda Typhoon, better known as Haiyan, ravaged the country, governance inadequacies emerged (Howe and Bang 2017).

[47] World Risk Report 2023. Bündnis Entwicklung Hilft, Ruhr-Universität Bochum—Institute for International Law of Peace and Conflict 2023.

https://weltrisikobericht.de/wp-content/uploads/2024/01/WorldRiskReport_2023_english_online.pdf.

[48] BusinessWorld Online (15.10.2023) World Risk Index 2023: Philippines remains the most at-risk country for 13th straight year. https://www.bworldonline.com/infographics/2023/10/16/551668/world-risk-index-2023-philippines-remains-the-most-at-risk-country-for-13th-straight-year/#google_vignette.

Philippine emergency management is mandated under 1978 Presidential Decree 1566. Local government is responsible for disaster preparedness and response under this law. Local governments receive funding from the national government. The presidential directive established the multi-agency National Disaster Coordination Council (NDCC) to facilitate national disaster response. Local Disaster Coordination Councils (DCCs)—provincial, municipal, barangay—perform similar duties. Meanwhile, Republic Act No. 8185 allocates 5% of the intergovernmental grants (formerly Internal Revenue Allotment, now National Tax Allocation) as yearly financial assistance for disaster relief, reconstruction, and other services. Only disaster-affected locations are covered by the Local Calamity Fund (Lupig-Alcid et al. 2004, cited in Espia and Fernandez 2014).

Mayors typically oversee and coordinate institutional responses to local disasters. Provinces need authorisation from the President to access the National Calamity Fund (Hall 2010). The national government creates temporary task groups to handle major disasters, even with local DCCs. There was a task force to handle responses to the 1991 Mount Pinatubo eruption (Espia and Fernandez 2014).

Locally, the *purok* system, as a sub-village-like organisation, also plays a role for emergency management. The storm Haiyan (local name Yolanda), the strongest storm ever recorded, hit on 8 November 2013, proving its relevance (Matthies 2017). Communities, people's groups, NGOs, and government agencies appreciate community-based disaster risk reduction (DRR) that uses existing knowledge, resources, coping mechanisms, and adaptive tactics. These methods helped local populations adjust to calamities (Allen 2003; cited in Matthies 2017).

10.8.2 Environment

In the 2022 Environmental Performance Index (EPI), the Philippines ranked 158th out of 180 countries.[49] The EPI assesses countries using forty performance indicators across eleven categories: air purity, clean drinking water, waste disposal, and good environmental stewardship (the fishing industry, the agricultural sector, water, and so on). These categories encompass climate change performance, environmental health, and

[49] https://epi.yale.edu/epi-results/2022/component/epi.

ecosystem integrity. According to the results of the assessment, the Philippines scored 28.9 points out of 100 making it the fifth lowest among select East and Southeast Asian countries.

Clearly, the Philippines is facing ecological degradation exacerbated by the pressures of population growth and climate crisis. Some of the environmental issues prevalent are sea level rise and different kinds of pollution concerning air, marine, and plastic (Raji 2024). First, in accordance with World Health Organisation standards on environmental capacities, the Philippines struggles on its air quality making it moderately unsafe. Thus, the Department of Environment and Natural Resources (DENR) oversees the implementation of the Clean Air Programme. Second, the World Bank (2023) stated that plastic waste in the Philippines is around a massive 2.7 million tons annually, and negatively, an estimated 20% ends up in the sea.[50] To address this challenge, aside from the Ecological Solid Waste Act of 2000, the DENR introduced the Extended Producer Responsibility (EPR) Act in 2022. Under EPR, companies will have to establish programmes for plastic waste reduction, recovery, and diversion.[51]

Third, marine pollution poses a risk to the Philippines' biodiversity and as a response, the government implemented the National Plan of Action on Marine Litter with the goal of "Zero Waste to Philippine Waters by 2040."[52] Fourth, sea level rise primarily caused by climate change can be mitigated by installing floodgates and drainage connection systems, among others. Indeed, environmental preservation and sustainability should be advanced locally and globally.[53]

[50] Pollution / Philippines | Interactive Country fiches. (n.d.). https://dicf.unepgrid.ch/philippines/pollution.

[51] Intensified environmental protection: clean air. Department of Environment and Natural Resources. https://denr.gov.ph/priority-program/clean-air-program/.

[52] https://seaknowledgebank.net/sites/default/files/2024-04/Jan%202022%20Final%20Philippines%20NPOA-ML%20%281%29.pdf.

[53] Union of Concerned Scientists (24.06.2024). How to protect coastal infrastructure at risk from sea level rise. UNDRR Prevention Web. https://www.preventionweb.net/news/how-protect-coastal-infrastructure-risk-sea-level-rise.

10.8.3 Pandemic Response

The administration of former President Duterte entrusted retired military personnel with important responsibilities in the government's National Task Force Against COVID-19. The civil-military relations under his administration especially in the time of the pandemic are heavily scrutinised by scholars. According to Solomon (2020), former commanders in the government's pandemic response challenged the idea that medical specialists should primarily lead the pandemic response. Instead, two military leaders led it: then-Defence Secretary (Minister) Delfin Lorenzana as chief of the National Task Force against COVID-19 and ex-Interior Secretary, Eduardo Ano, as Vice Chairman for the revival of the Inter-Agency Task Force on Emerging Infectious Diseases (IATF-EID). Solomon (2020) cited Pearce, who stated that these former soldiers are not healthcare professionals; their military and crisis management expertise bolstered COVID-19 health protocols. Dr Tony Leachon, a renowned physician, said the armed forces' role in a pandemic can be used when the public's social conduct has become unmanageable, which results in negative effects. Typically, the Philippine military helped restore peace and order, assessed damage, and distributed humanitarian materials immediately after calamities like Typhoon Yolanda (international name Haiyan) in 2013.

10.8.4 Digital Technologies

The Philippines is the fastest growing country in terms of digitalisation and internet use. As a matter of fact, in the Digital Riser Report of 2020,[54] the Philippines has ranked first in the East Asia and Pacific region and was among the top countries, including France and Saudi Arabia, which showed drastic improvement on the digital landscape particularly in terms of introducing underlying policies that support comprehensive digitalisation strategies. The World Bank and the National Economic and Development Authority (NEDA) of the Philippines report denotes that the pandemic indeed pushed forth for the rise in online transactions due to the long lockdowns imposed by the government. Online transactions and use of digital payments were very rampant during the pandemic and

[54] See report here. https://digital-competitiveness.eu/wp-content/uploads/ESCP_Digital-Riser-Report_2020-1.pdf.

continues to be up to date. Albeit the significant advancement of digitalisation in the country, challenges such as the digital divide, lack of ICT infrastructure, and poor internet connectivity are still very much present, especially in the rural areas.

As a component of the national authorities' thrust to address these issues, the E-Government Master Plan of 2022 has been launched that showcased the roadmap towards strengthening digitalisation efforts and further developing the digital economy.[55] The current administration likewise launched the e-Gov system where it aims to harmonise and create interoperability on the existing online platforms and mechanisms of various government agencies alongside fostering data sharing and data security—including in these efforts both the national and local authorities. To support these reforms, the World Bank also approved the Philippines' First Digital Transformation Development Policy Loan (DPL) worth US$ 600 million that are allocated to the plans of the government that are aimed to foster digital transformation and infrastructure, expand digital financing, and invigorate development of digital services.[56] Aside from the efforts of the government, the private sector, particularly fintech companies, is also seeing the Philippines as a "vast greenfield market" for digital financing to accommodate demands of a huge unbanked population.

10.9 Discussion

As demonstrated by the experiences of the Southeast Asian countries that we looked at have demonstrated various, sometimes unique but contextualised approaches to multi-nodal governance when addressing crises related to the environment, disasters, health, or digital challenges. For instance, in response to COVID-19, Thailand built a Centre for COVID-19 Situation Administration (CCSA), involving government officials from various sectors to coordinate a unified response with some flexibility for the local level. This whole-of-government approach harmonised national policies, while empowering provincial leaders to make localised decisions

[55] https://dict.gov.ph/ictstatistics/wp-content/uploads/2020/03/EGMP-2022.pdf.

[56] https://documents1.worldbank.org/curated/en/099090823143514731/pdf/BOSIB0b80b9cfc058098b2091dce8012d59.pdf.

within the CCSA framework (Rajatanavin et al. 2021). A crucial component of Thailand's success was its extensive network of one million village health volunteers (VHVs), known as the "Thai People's First Doctors," who served as frontline caregivers by providing community-level healthcare, supporting contact tracing, and facilitating isolation efforts under medical guidance (Tejativaddhana et al. 2020). Their role significantly contributed to Thailand's low COVID-19 mortality rate during the pandemic's early stages, underscoring the vital impact of community-based health resources in effective crisis management (Rajatanavin et al. 2021). These strategies enabled the Thai state to implement health measures more effectively, such as contact tracing and isolation, which contributed to a low number of deaths during the initial phases of the pandemic (Rajatanavin et al. 2021).

Indonesia's wide area and diversified population made responding to COVID-19 difficult. The government was decentralised, thus, local authorities implemented health protocols. However, regional policy execution differences caused different results. The Indonesian government struggled to mobilise resources and ensure fair access to medical care, especially in the countryside (Daly et al. 2020).

The Philippines was one of the first ASEAN countries to limit mobility during the pandemic. The responses were coordinated with health and social services, and municipal government. However, logistics and agency communications hampered progress. Due to infrastructure disparities, government digital technologies to improve service delivery vary by region (IMF, n.d.). The Inter-Agency Task Force on Emerging Infectious Diseases (IATF-EID) advised the Philippine government on COVID-19 policy. Cabinet members and government health departments were also included (Vallejo and Ong 2021). Many professionals compiled and evaluated the data. OCTA Research advised the policymakers with facts. Most OCTA members were University of the Philippines and University of Santo Tomas researchers, medical professionals, media experts, legal and political consultants, and independent scientific advisers (Vallejo and Ong 2021).

Singapore responded to COVID-19 with well-coordinated policies from its central agencies, a strong healthcare system and digital infrastructure. Technology helped the government quickly adopt contact tracking and communication regarding public health methods to contain the pandemic. Health, financing, and social programmes were coordinated across ministries to mitigate pandemic effects and aid the economy to recover (Daly et al. 2020). The city-state's Multi-Ministry Task Force (MTF) provided a whole-of-government COVID-19 response after its formation on 22 January 2020. The task force, co-directed by the Ministers for Health, National Development, and Trade and Industry, addressed pandemic issues with members from other agencies. It handled crisis response, health initiatives like safe distance and travel limitations, and community engagement. In early 2023, the MTF switched to monitoring COVID-19 as an endemic disease before shutting down. The Ministry of Health currently manages and maintains the MTF's structure for future needs (Woo 2020). Furthermore, as mentioned earlier, the Healthier SG programme, which utilised digitalisation and overseen by public authorities, was implemented to ensure the well-being of its citizens even during ordinary times.

Viet Nam's COVID-19 response was rapid and coordinated, that included national ministries and local governments. Community participation and timely reaction were key to the government's public health approach. Viet Nam's outbreak experiences helped it manage the pandemic and reduce its financial consequences (Daly et al. 2020). Governance frameworks, socio-economic development, digitisation, and environmental sustainability are intertwined in Viet Nam's political and environmental policies. While the CPV maintains centralised management, policy changes show a growing awareness of environmental integration in economic planning. To build resilience and sustainable development in Viet Nam, disaster management, health equity, and digital transformation must be addressed through multi-nodal governance.

Over and above these, is the key role of digitalisation and the imperative of interconnectedness and interoperability between and among the bodies that may have to communicate and coordinate vertically and horizontally, operating amidst the challenges brought about by the digitalisation gaps and divides, including challenges brought about by artificial intelligence (AI). AI is both a challenge and an opportunity for governance where it offers an unprecedented capacity for productivity. It can swiftly process many things, including voluminous amounts of data which is crucial for effective policy decisions. Hence, multi-nodal governance and polycrises, empowered with new technologies such as AI, are indeed intertwined for good and responsive governance.

10.10 Conclusion

The multi-nodal governance demonstrated by Thailand, Indonesia, the Philippines, Singapore, and Viet Nam in their multi-ministry responses to COVID-19, natural disasters, and the digitalisation of government services is very important. The joint efforts among various ministries, which were guided by central authorities, have played an essential part in effectively responding to complex challenges faced by each country.

Indeed, in this age of polycrises, a multi-nodal approach to governance and public administration is imperative. This includes poly- and intertwined crises ranging from disaster risk reduction, environment and climate change, health crises such as the pandemic, and crises brought about by the inability to cope with the demands of the fourth industrial revolution and digitalisation.

The experience of these Southeast Asian states has demonstrated that governance institutions must be agile and flexible, with national authorities and central coordinating bodies playing lead roles that may even necessitate strong central governance which facilitate quick, decisive action during a rapidly evolving emergency. However, this setup must be balanced by enabling frontline subnational authorities—local governments—within the decentralised framework. After all, as frontline institutions, local governments are key to implementation of centrally driven programmes aligned with long-term development plans.

This contribution to an emerging and enhanced theory on multi-nodal governance is a modest effort to enhance and build upon existing paradigms and approaches to governance. It builds upon and takes off from, earlier works of other authors in the field, including those by scholars like Ansell and Gash (2007) on collaborative governance and Osborne (2010) on new public governance, which illustrates the theoretical alignment of principles regarding multi-nodal governance.

More specifically, their findings are oriented towards cross-sector collaboration and decentralised approaches to local challenges. However, multi-nodal governance *vis-a-vis* polycrises highlights central authorities' equally critical role in coordinating and issuing enabling frameworks to facilitate cooperative responses to VUCA problems while allowing localised action from subordinate levels of governments on the selected Asian countries in this article, thereby offering valuable insights for real-world challenges.

In this way, multi-nodal responses to polycrises need to be central government enabled, locally implemented, and people-centred to facilitate good coordination and prevent resource waste. In the challenges that may appear in the future, humanity's strength lies in its capacities for knowledge creation, collective learning, and cooperative action. And as the experiences of the Southeast Asian countries have shown, a way out of the woods is collaboration and complementation vertically and horizontally, a multi-nodal governance will enable this.

References

Afandi, M.N., E. Tri Anomsari, A. Novira, and S. Sudartini. 2023. Collaborative governance in a mandated setting: Shifting collaboration in stunting interventions at local level. *Development Studies Research* 10 (1): 1–12. https://doi.org/10.1080/21665095.2023.2212868.

Brilianto, D.E., V.H. Mursa, W.S. Sabekti, S. Maria, S. Hutabarat, and G.J. Prakoso. 2024. The implementation of collaborative governance in Indonesia's Agrarian Reform: (Case study of the 2022 Agrarian Reform Task Force). FIG Working Week 2024: Your World, Our World: Resilient Environment and Sustainable Resource Management for all. https://www.fig.net/resources/proceedings/fig_proceedings/fig2024/papers/ts08d/TS08D_brilianto_hutabarat_et_al_12471.pdf.

Agbogidi, O., B. Okonta, and D. Dolor. 2006. Socio–economic and environmental impact of crude oil exploration and production on agricultural production: a case study of Edjeba and Kokori communities in Delta State of Nigeria. *Global Journal of Environmental Sciences* 4 (2). https://doi.org/10.4314/gjes.v4i2.2461.

Allen, K.M. 2003. Meanings and constraints: Processes shaping vulnerability reduction in Philippine National Red Cross Disaster Preparedness Initiatives. [PhD thesis]. School of Social Science, Middlesex University. https://repository.mdx.ac.uk/download/44013b1cb5a2af2afc67bb936171328bdad6cafef410c26090def1dc052b9cab/33364377/Allen-meanings_and_constraints-phd.pdf.

Ansell, C., and A. Gash. 2007. Collaborative governance in theory and practice. *Journal of Public Administration Research and Theory* 18 (4): 543–571. https://doi.org/10.1093/jopart/mum032.

ADB. n.d. Key indicators database. https://kidb.adb.org/?fbclid=IwY2xjawFRDtleHRuA2FlbQIxMAABHcoWLydYHWuia0jasqNrs6ICdn4bhu96rhRQwrjudYzCmJSl4UveHVGWSg_aem_HHy7bTWltpY3TI9ejG3Www.

ADB. 2005. Indonesia: Country environment analysis. https://www.adb.org/sites/default/files/institutional-document/32184/ino-cea-aug2005.pdf.

ADB. 2013. Viet Nam: Environment and climate change assessment. https://www.adb.org/sites/default/files/institutional-document/33916/files/viet-nam-environment-climate-change.pdf.

ADB. 2015. Thailand: Industrialization and economic catch-up. https://www.adb.org/sites/default/files/publication/178077/tha-industrialization-econ-catch.pdf.

ADB. 2016. Thailand: Industrialization and economic catch-up. https://www.adb.org/sites/default/files/publication/27802/tha-2016.pdf.

Anthes, R., R. Corell, G. Holland, J. Hurrell, M. MacCracken, and K. Trenberth. (2006). Hurricanes and global warming: Potential linkages and consequences. *American Meteorology Society* 87(5), 623–628. http://www.jstor.org/stable/26217169.

Bank of Thailand. 2019. Monetary policy report June 2019. https://www.bot.or.th/content/dam/bot/documents/en/news-and-media/news/PressEng_MPR_June2019_24uyt89.pdf.

Bankoff, G. 2003. *Cultures of disaster: Society and natural hazard in the Philippines*. Routledge Curzon Press.

Barnes, D.K.A., F. Galgani, R.C. Thompson, and M. Barlaz. 2009. Accumulation and fragmentation of plastic debris in global environments. *Philosophical Transactions of the Royal Society. Biological Sciences* 364 (1526), 1985–1998. https://doi.org/10.1098/rstb.2008.0205.

Barnosky, A.D., E.A. Hadly, J. Bascompte, E.L. Berlow, J.H. Brown, M. Fortelius, W.M. Getz, J. Harte, A. Hastings, P.A. Marquet, N.D. Martinez, A. Mooers, P. Roopnarine, G. Vermeij, J.W. Williams, R. Gillespie, J. Kitzes, C. Marshall, N. Matzke, and D.P. Mindell. 2012. Approaching a state shift in Earth's biosphere. *Nature* 486 (7401): 52–58. https://doi.org/10.1038/nature11018.

Bates, B.C., Zbigniew Kundzewicz, J. Palutikof, Wu Shaohong, World Meteorological Organisation (WMO), United Nations Environment Programme (UNEP) and Intergovernmental Panel On Climate Change. 2008. Climate change and water [Electronic resource]: IPCC Technical paper VI. IPCC Secretariat.

Baum, S., and A. Barrett. 2018. Towards an Integrated Assessment of Global Catastrophic Risk Towards an Integrated Assessment of Global Catastrophic Risk. In *Proceedings of the First International Colloquium on Catastrophic and Existential Risk*, ed. by B.J. Garrick, 41–62. Garrick Institute for the Risk Sciences. Los Angeles: University of California.

Bengthong, S., Preecha Suvarnathong, Suwimon Ukraisa, Kanchana Boonphak, Rungrueng Kitphati, Juraporn Krates, Wilailuk Ruangrattanatrai, and Worayuth Nak-Ai. 2024. Examining Thailand's public health emergency management response to COVID-19: Insights from health region 9's

pandemic approach. *Journal of System and Management Sciences* 14 (8). https://doi.org/10.33168/jsms.2024.0823.
Bhullar, L. 2013. Climate Change Adaptation and Water Policy: Lessons from Singapore. *Sustainable Development* 21 (3): 152–159. https://doi.org/10.1002/sd.1546.
Blanco, D. V. 2015. Disaster Governance in the Philippines: Issues, Lessons Learned, and Future Directions in the Post-Yolanda Super Typhoon Aftermath. *International Journal of Public Administration* 38 (10): 743–756. https://doi.org/10.1080/01900692.2014.979198.
Boonsang, A., and S. Penpim. 2023. Development strategy for the local health security fund in national health security office region 10, Ubon Ratchathani, Thailand. *Journal of Population Therapeutics and Clinical Pharmacology* 30 (3): e545–e558. https://doi.org/10.47750/jptcp.2023.30.03.058
Briggs, M.R.P., and S.J. Funge-Smith. 1994. A nutrient budget of some intensive marine shrimp ponds in Thailand. *Aquaculture Research* 25 (8): 789–811. https://doi.org/10.1111/j.1365-2109.1994.tb00744.x.
Brillantes, A.B., Jr. (2003). *Innovations and Excellence: Understanding Local Governments in the Philippines.* Centre for Local and Regional Governance, University of the Philippines.
Brillantes, A.B., Jr., and K.E.V. Ruiz. 2021. Aligning the federalism discourse in the Philippines to the Quest for genuine local autonomy. 50 Shades of Federalism. https://50shadesoffederalism.com/case-studies/aligning-the-federalism-discourse-in-the-philippines-to-the-quest-for-genuine-local-autonomy/.
Bueno, D.C., and A. Salapa. 2021. The Philippine administrative system: A review of the past, present, and the future research. *Institutional Multidisciplinary Research and Development Journal* 4: 1–13. https://www.researchgate.net/publication/357899634_The_Philippine_administrative_system_A_review_of_the_past_present_and_the_future_research.
Bureau of Ocean Energy Management. 2011. Social and economic assessment of major oil spill litigation settlement. Final Technical Report. U.S. Department of the Interior.
Cazeau, J.W. 2019. *Review of the integration of disaster risk reduction in the work of the United Nations system in the context of the 2030 Agenda for Sustainable Development*. United Nations. https://www.unjiu.org/sites/www.unjiu.org/files/jiu_rep_2019_3_en.pdf.
Chan, S., H. Lutz, D. Lam, and C. Clark. 2016. *Beyond the developmental state: East Asia's political economies reconsidered.* Singapore: Springer.
Chandler Institute of Governance (CIG). 2023. Good governance in a time of polycrisis, *Governance Matters Magazine*. https://www.chandlerinstitute.org/governance-matters-2023.

Chandler Institute of Governance (CIG). 2024. Chandler good government index 2024 report. https://chandlergovernmentindex.com.
Chanrachkij, I., N. Yasooka, S. Anantapongsuk, P. Petrasatien, and W. Wanchana. 2010. Survey of small-scale fishing gear and practices contributing to sea turtle mortalities along the coast of Rayong Province, Eastern Gulf of Thailand. SEAFDEC Training Department/TD/SP/38.
Cheung, A.B.L. 2008. The story of two administrative states: State capacity in Hong Kong and Singapore. *The Pacific Review* 21 (2): 121–145. https://doi.org/10.1080/09512740801990188.
Chomsky, N., C. Derber, S. Moodliar, and P. Shannon (eds.). 2020. *Internationalism or extinction*. Routledge.
Cornell University, INSEAD, and WIPO. 2013. The global innovation index 2013: The local dynamics of innovation. https://www.wipo.int/edocs/pubdocs/en/economics/gii/gii_2013.pdf.
Cribb, R., and M. Ford. 2015. Indonesia as an archipelago: Managing islands, managing the seas. In *Indonesia beyond the water's edge: Managing an archipelagic state*, ed. by R. Cribb, and M. Ford, 1–27. ISEAS–Yusof Ishak Institute. https://www.cambridge.org/core/books/abs/indonesia-beyond-the-waters-edge/indonesia-as-an-archipelago-managing-islands-managing-the-seas/5EA31A8D8BDA505938E29A9DE72104A6.
Croissant, A. 2019. Viet Nam: The policy styles of a Lame Leviathan. In *Policy styles and policy making: Exploring the linkages*, ed. M. Howlett and J. Tosun, 242–262. Routledge.
Daly, E., K. Das, and R. Yeoh. 2020. *Reimagining emerging ASEAN in the wake of COVID-19*. McKinsey & Company. https://www.mckinsey.com/featured-insights/asia-pacific/reimagining-emerging-asean-in-the-wake-of-covid-19.
Dasgupta, S., B. Laplante, S. Murray, and D. Wheeler. 2009. Sea level rise and storm surges: A comparative analysis of impacts in developing countries. In *Sea-level rise and storm surges: a comparative analysis of impacts in developing countries (English)*. World Bank Group. http://documents.worldbank.org/curated/en/657521468157195342/Sea-level-rise-and-storm-surges-a-comparative-analysis-of-impacts-in-developing-countries.
Dash, K., M. Gryseels, P. Sudhir, and K. Tan. 2016. *Unlocking Indonesia's digital opportunity*. McKinsey & Company. https://www.mckinsey.com/~/media/McKinsey/Locations/Asia/Indonesia/Our%20Insights/Unlocking%20Indonesias%20digital%20opportunity/Unlocking_Indonesias_digital_opportunity.ashx.
Djalante, R., L. Nurhidayah, V.M. Hoang, T.N.P. Nguyen, Y. Mahendradhata, A. Trias, J. Lassa, and M.A. Millerg. 2020. COVID-19 and ASEAN responses: Comparative policy analysis. *Progress in Disaster Science* 8: 1–12. https://doi.org/10.1016/j.pdisas.2020.100129 and https://www.ncbi.nlm.nih.gov/pmc/articles/PMC7577870/.

Department of Fisheries. 2015. *Marine fisheries management plan of Thailand. A national policy for marine fisheries management.* 2015–2019, 1–89. Thai Department of Fisheries.

Erh, J. 2023. Singapore's digital transformation journey. *Journal of Southeast Asian Economies* 40(1): 4–31. https://www.jstor.org/stable/27211223.

Espia, J.P., and P. Fernandez. 2014. Insiders and outsiders: Local government and NGO engagement in disaster response in Guimaras, Philippines. *Disasters* 39 (1): 51–68. https://doi.org/10.1111/disa.12086.

Fakhruddin, S.H.M., and Y. Chivakidakarn. 2014. A case study for early warning and disaster management in Thailand. *International Journal of Disaster Risk Reduction* 9: 159–180. https://doi.org/10.1016/j.ijdrr.2014.04.008.

Flynn, R.L., and G.E. Forrester. (2019). Boat anchoring contributes substantially to coral reef degradation in the British Virgin Islands. *Peer Journal*, 1–17. https://doi.org/10.7717/peerj.7010.

Foo, C.D., H.X. Chia, K.W. Teo, A. Farwin, J. Hashim, G.C.H. Koh, D.B. Matchar, H. Legido-Quigley, and J.C.H. Yap. 2023. Healthier SG: Singapore's multi-year strategy to transform primary healthcare. *The Lancet* 37: 1–3. https://doi.org/10.1016/j.lanwpc.2023.100861.

FAOUN. 2020. Asia and the Pacific regional overview of food security and nutrition 2020: Maternal and child diets at the heart of improving nutrition. https://openknowledge.fao.org/server/api/core/bitstreams/abd3580a-eecc-4a17-8e82-1674a2c1b47a/content.

Gaupp, F., J. Hall, S. Hochrainer-Stigler, and S. Dadson. 2019. Changing risks of simultaneous global breadbasket failure. *Nature Climate Change* 10 (1): 54–57. https://doi.org/10.1038/s41558-019-0600-z.

Government of Thailand. 2017. Thailand: Sendai framework data readiness review report. https://www.preventionweb.net/files/53160_thailandtha.pdf.

Graham, C., E. Kerr, N. Pang, and M.M.J. Fischer. 2018. The internet in Asia through Singapore. *East Asian Science, Technology and Society* 12 (4): 479–494. https://doi.org/10.1215/18752160-7218957.

Guess, G.M. 2005. Comparative Decentralization Lessons from Pakistan, Indonesia, and the Philippines. *Public Administration Review* 65 (2): 217–230. http://www.jstor.org/stable/3542555.

Hall, R.A. 2010. Governance during disasters: Intra-governmental and non-governmental coordination in the 2006 Guimaras Oil Spill. *Philippine Political Science Journal* 31 (54): 117–152. https://doi.org/10.1080/01154451.2010.9723527.

Harapan, B.N., T. Harapan, L. Theodora, and N.A. Anantama. 2023. From archipelago to pandemic battleground: Unveiling Indonesia's COVID-19 crisis. *Journal of Epidemiology and Global Health* 13 (4): 591–603. https://doi.org/10.1007/s44197-023-00148-7.

Ho, L.C., and T. Seow. 2017. Disciplinary boundaries and climate change education: Teachers' conceptions of climate change education in the Philippines and Singapore. *International Research in Geographical and Environmental Education* 26 (3): 240–252. https://doi.org/10.1080/10382046.2017.1330038.

Hosen, N., and N. Hammado. 2021. Indonesia's response to the pandemic. In *Oxford University Press eBooks*, 307–320. https://doi.org/10.1093/oso/9780197553831.003.0021.

Holley, C., and C. Shearing. 2017. A nodal perspective of governance: Advances in nodal governance thinking. In *Regulatory theory: Foundations and applications*, ed. P. Drahos, 163–180. Canberra: Australian National University Press.

Howe, B., and G. Bang. 2017. Nargis and Haiyan: The politics of natural disaster management in Myanmar and the Philippines. *Asian Studies Review* 41 (1): 58–78. https://doi.org/10.1080/10357823.2016.1265484.

Hue, T.H.H. 2023. Policy Responses to COVID-19 within the context of SDGs: Experience from Local Governments in Viet Nam. *Asian Review of Public Administration* 31 (1 & 2): 47–67.

Innes, G.K., A.S. Lambrou, P. Thumrin, Y. Thukngamdee, R. Tangwangvivat, P. Doungngern, K. Noradechanon, P. Netrabukkana, K. Meidenbauer, T. Mehoke, C.D. Heaney, S. Hinjoy, and A.N. Elayadi. 2022. Enhancing global health security in Thailand: Strengths and challenges of initiating a One Health approach to avian influenza surveillance. *One Health* 14: 100397. https://doi.org/10.1016/j.onehlt.2022.100397.

International Monetary Fund (IMF). n.d. Policy responses to Covid-19: Philippines. https://www.imf.org/en/Topics/imf-and-covid19/Policy-Responses-to-COVID-19.

IOM UN Migration. Country Fact sheet: Viet Nam. https://roasiapacific.iom.int/sites/g/files/tmzbdl671/files/documents/2024-06/viet-nam-snapshot-final_updated.pdf.

JICA. 2013. Flood management plan for the Chao Phraya River Basin in the Kingdom of Thailand. In *Flood management plan for the Chao Phraya River Basin in the Kingdom of Thailand*. https://openjicareport.jica.go.jp/pdf/12127205.pdf

JICA. 2014. *The project for the revision of Bangkok master plan on climate change 2013–2023 in the Kingdom of Thailand: Final report*. https://openjicareport.jica.go.jp/pdf/1000023397.pdf.

JICA. 2015. *Natural disaster risk assessment and area business continuity plan formulation for industrial agglomerated areas in the ASEAN region*. Japan International Cooperation Agency (JICA). https://openjicareport.jica.go.jp/pdf/1000023394.pdf.

Jones, S., and J. Gu. 2012. *Viet Nam's regions and key economic zones*. https://vietnam-briefing.com/news/vietnams-regions-key-economic-zones.html/.

Jovita, H.D., A. Nurmandi, D. Mutiarin, and E.P. Purnomo. 2018. Why does network governance fail in managing post-disaster conditions in the Philippines? Jàmbá 10 (1). https://doi.org/10.4102/jamba.v10i1.585.

Kaweenuttayanon, N., R. Pattanarattanamolee, N. Sorncha, and S. Nakahara. 2021. Community surveillance of COVID-19 by village health volunteers, Thailand. *Bulletin of the World Health Organization* 99 (5): 393–397. https://doi.org/10.2471/blt.20.274308.

Kelly, T.R., C. Machalaba, W.B. Karesh, P.Z. Crook, K. Gilardi, J. Nziza, M.M. Uhart, E.A. Robles, K. Saylors, D.O. Joly, C. Monagin, P.M. Mangombo, P.M. Kingebeni, R. Kazwala, D. Wolking, W. Smith, and J.A.K. Mazet. 2020. Implementing One Health approaches to confront emerging and re-emerging zoonotic disease threats: lessons from PREDICT. One Health Outlook 2 (1). https://doi.org/10.1186/s42522-019-0007-9.

Kingston, P.F. 2002. Long-term environmental impact of oil spills. *Spill Science & Technology Bulletin* 7 (1–2): 53–61. https://doi.org/10.1016/s1353-2561(02)00051-8.

Klose, A.K., N. Wunderling, R. Winkelmann, and J.F. Donges. 2021. What do we mean, "tipping cascade"? *Environmental Research Letters* 16 (12): 125011. https://doi.org/10.1088/1748-9326/ac3955.

Koons, E. 2024. Environmental issues in Indonesia: a growing concern. Climate Impacts Tracker Asia. https://www.climateimpactstracker.com/environmental-issues-in-indonesia-a-growing-concern/.

Lallana, E.C. 2020. A network governance approach to disaster resilience in the Philippines: A department of disaster resilience is not the answer. Ideacorp [Policy brief].

Langkulsen, U., N. Vichit-Vadakan, and S. Taptagaporn. 2010. Health impact of climate change on occupational health and productivity in Thailand. Global Health Action 3 (1). https://doi.org/10.3402/gha.v3i0.5607.

Latif, A. 2024. Climate change and radicalization: A case study of Indonesia. *Harvard International Review*. https://hir.harvard.edu/climate-change-and-radicalization-a-case-study-in-indonesia/.

Lau, H.C., S. Ramakrishna, K. Zhang, and M.Z.S. Hameed. 2021. A decarbonization roadmap for Singapore and its energy policy implications. *Energies* 14: 1–23. https://doi.org/10.3390/en14206455.

Lawrence, M., T. Homer-Dixon, S. Janzwood, J. Rockstöm, O. Renn, and J.F. Donges. 2024. Global polycrisis: The causal mechanisms of crisis entanglement. *Global Sustainability* 7 (e6): 1–16. https://doi.org/10.1017/sus.2024.1.

Lawrence, M., S. Janzwood, and T. Homer-Dixon,. 2022. What is a global polycrisis? And how is it different from a systemic risk? Discussion Paper 2022-4.

Version 2.0. Cascade Institute. https://cascadeinstitute.org/technical-paper/what-is-a-global-polycrisis.

Lee, C., J.M. Lee, and Y.P. Liu. 2023. Catalysing innovation and digital transformation in combating the Covid-19 pandemic: Whole-of government collaborations in ICT. *R&D, and Business Digitisation in Singapore, Public Money & Management* 43 (4): 340–348. https://doi.org/10.1080/09540962.2021.1966197.

Lenain, W., and N. Vu. 2023. Unleashing strong, digital and green growth in Viet Nam. https://one.oecd.org/document/ECO/WKP(2023)21/en/pdf.

Lin, Y.C., F. Khan, S.F. Jenkins, and D. Lallemant. 2021. Filling the disaster data gap: Lessons from cataloguing Singapore's past disasters. *International Journal of Disaster Risk Science* 12 (2): 188–204. https://doi.org/10.1007/s13753-021-00331-z.

Lupig-Alcid, M., M.J. Arcilla, C. Dulce, and E. Delgado. 2004. *A study on current disaster management practice and opportunities for strengthening local capacities*. CARE Philippines.

Mahbubani, K., and J. Sng. 2017. *The ASEAN miracle: A catalyst for peace*. Ridge Books.

MacCarthy, J., J. Richter, S. Tyukavina, M. Weisse, and N. Harris. 2024. The latest data confirm forest fires are getting worse. World Resources Institute. https://www.wri.org/insights/global-trends-forest-fires.

Matthies, A. 2017. Community-based disaster risk management in the Philippines: Achievements and challenges of the Purok system. *Austrian Journal of South-East Asian Studies / Österreichische Zeitschrift Für Südostasienwissenschaften* 10 (1): 101–108. https://doi.org/10.14764/10.ASEAS-2017.1-7.

McGreevy, M., and E.S. Chia. 2023. Sustainability transitioning in a developmental state: an analysis of Singapore's climate change mitigation and adaptation policies. *Climate and Development*, 1–17. https://doi.org/10.1080/17565529.2023.2229779.

McKay, D.I.A., A. Staal, J.F. Abrams, R. Winkelmann, B. Sakschewski, S. Loriani, I. Fetzer, S.E. Cornell, J. Rockström, and T.M. Lenton. 2022. Exceeding 1.5 °C global warming could trigger multiple climate tipping points. *Science* 377(6611). https://doi.org/10.1126/science.abn7950.

McManus, J., and I. B. Sathāban Wičhai Rabop Sāthāranasuk. 2012. *Thailand's Universal coverage scheme: Achievements and challenges: An independent assessment of the first 10 years—2010: Synthesis report*. Health Insurance System Research Office. https://www.loc.gov/item/2013341727/.

Mousavizadeh, A., H. Maltby, P. Caruana-Galizia, F. Xue, G. Gernelli, M. Bradley, and P. Coste. 2016. *The Legatum prosperity index*. The Legatum Institute Foundation.

Mwangi, W., P. de Figueiredo, and M.F. Criscitiello. 2016. One health: Addressing global challenges at the Nexus of human, animal, and environmental health. *PLOS Pathogens* 12 (9): e1005731. https://doi.org/10.1371/journal.ppat.1005731.

National Climate Change Secretariat (NCCS). 2016. *A climate-resilient Singapore, for a sustainable future.* Ministry of the Environment and Water Resources and Ministry of National Development. https://www.nccs.gov.sg/files/docs/default-source/publications/a-climate-resilient-singapore-for-a-sustainable-future.pdf.

National Health Security Office. 2020. *Provincial rehabilitation fund reduce barriers and enhance social inclusion of vulnerable populations.* National Health Security Office. https://eng.nhso.go.th/view/1/DescriptionNews/Provincial-Rehabilitation-Fund-reduce-barriers-and-enhance-social-inclusion-of-vulnerable-populations/206/EN-US.

Ng, I.Y.H., S.S. Lim, and N. Pang. 2022. Making universal digital access universal: Lessons from COVID-19 in Singapore. *Universal Access in an Information Society* 22: 1073–1083. https://doi.org/10.1007/s10209-022-00877-9.

Ngowsiri, J. 2020. Enhance the role of local government organizations in Thai health system. National Health Security Office. https://eng.nhso.go.th/view/1/DescriptionNews/Enhance-the-role-of-local-government-organizations-in-Thai-health-system/215/EN-US.

Nguyen, T.M., and E. Malesky. 2020. Reopening Viet Nam: How the country's improving governance helped it weather the COVID-19 pandemic. Brookings Institute. https://www.brookings.edu/articles/reopening-vietnam-how-the-countrys-improving-governance-helped-it-weather-the-covid-19-pandemic/.

Nuntatikul, T. 2023. Thailand country report 2023. Asian Disaster Reduction Center. https://www.adrc.asia/aboutus/vrdata/CR/FY2023_Thailand_CountryReport.pdf.

Nyström, M., J.B. Jouffray, A.V. Norström, B. Crona, P. Søgaard Jørgensen, S.R. Carpenter, Ö. Bodin, V. Galaz, and C. Folke. 2019. Anatomy and resilience of the global production ecosystem. *Nature* 575 (7781): 98–108. https://doi.org/10.1038/s41586-019-1712-3.

Oentoro, A. 2024. Digitisation, digitalisation, and digital transformation explained: What's the difference? *Agility CMS.* https://agilitycms.com/resources/posts/digitization-digitalization-and-digital-transformation-explained.

Open Development Viet Nam. 2021. Disasters. https://vietnam.opendevelopmentmekong.net/topics/disasters/.

Osborne, S.P. 2010. Public governance and public services delivery: a research agenda for the future. In *The new public governance? Emerging perspectives on the theory and practice of public governance*, ed. by S.P. Osborne, 413–428. Routledge.

Phantuwongraj, S., M. Choowong, F. Nanayama, K.I. Hisada, P. Charusiri, V. Chutakositkanon, S. Pailoplee, and A. Chabangbon. 2013. Coastal geomorphic conditions and styles of storm surge wash over deposits from Southern Thailand. *Geomorphology* 192: 43–58. https://doi.org/10.1016/j.geomorph.2013.03.016.

Polychroniou, C., and M. Furtado. 2023. Noam Chomsky: Another world is possible. let's bring it to reality. In *Truthout*. https://truthout.org.

Putera, P.B., I. Widianingsih, S. Ningrum, S. Suryanto, and Y. Rianto. 2022. Overcoming the COVID-19 pandemic in Indonesia: A science, technology, and innovation (STI) policy perspective. *Health Policy and Technology* 11 (3): 100650. https://doi.org/10.1016/j.hlpt.2022.100650.

Rajatanavin, N., T. Tuangratananon, R. Suphanchaimat, and V. Tangcharoensathien. 2021. Responding to the COVID-19 second wave in Thailand by diversifying and adapting lessons from the first wave. *BMJ Global Health* 6 (7): e006178. https://doi.org/10.1136/bmjgh-2021-006178.

Raji, K. 2024. 4 biggest environmental issues in the Philippines in 2024. Earth.Org. https://earth.org/environmental-issues-in-the-philippines/.

Renn, O., K. Lucas, A. Haas, and C. Jaeger. 2017. Things are different today: The challenge of global systemic risks. *Journal of Risk Research* 22 (4): 401–415. https://doi.org/10.1080/13669877.2017.1409252.

Rhodes, R.A.W. 2017. *Network governance and the differentiated polity: Selected essays*. Oxford University Press.

Richards, D.R., and D.A. Friess. 2015. Rates and drivers of mangrove deforestation in Southeast Asia, 2000–2012. *Proceedings of the National Academy of Sciences* 113 (2): 344–349. https://doi.org/10.1073/pnas.1510272113.

Sassa, K., P. Canuti, P. Bobrowsky, and N. Casagli. 2023. International consortium on landslides: From IDNDR, IGCP, UNITWIN, WCDRR 2 & 3 to Kyoto landslide commitment 2020. In *Progress in landslide research and technology*, ed. by K. Sassa, K. Konagai, B. Tiwari, Ž. Arbanas, and S. Sassa, 11–43. Singapore: Springer International Publishing. https://doi.org/10.1007/978-3-031-16898-7%E2%82%82.

Schweizer, P.J. 2019. Systemic risks—Concepts and challenges for risk governance. *Journal of Risk Research* 24 (1): 1–16. https://doi.org/10.1080/13669877.2019.1687574.

Setiawan, K.M.P., and D. Tomsa. 2022. *Politics in contemporary Indonesia: Institutional change, policy challenges and democratic decline*. Routledge.

Siahaan, M. 2024. *Number of natural disasters in Indonesia 2014–2023*. Statista. https://www.statista.com/statistics/954348/indonesia-number-natural-disasters/#statisticContainer.

Solomon, R.D.S. 2020. Assessing civil-military relations and COVID-19 in the Philippines. *Global Scientific Journals* 8, 12. Assessing_Civil_Military_Relations_and_COVID_19_in_the_Philippines.pdf.

Sujitapan, C., J.M. Kendall, J.E. Chambers, and S. Yordkayhun. 2024. Landslide assessment through integrated geoelectrical and seismic methods: A case study in Thungsong site, southern Thailand. *Heliyon* 10 (2): e24660–e24660. https://doi.org/10.1016/j.heliyon.2024.e24660

Swilling, M. 2013. Economic crisis, long waves, and the sustainability transition: An African perspective. *Environmental Innovation and Societal Transitions* 6: 96–115. https://doi.org/10.1016/j.eist.2012.11.001.

Swilling, M. 2019. The age of sustainability. In *Library union catalog of Bavaria, Berlin and Brandenburg (B3Kat Repository)*. University of Illinois Urbana-Champaign. https://doi.org/10.4324/9780429057823.

Tangcharoensathien, V., S. Limwattananon, W. Patcharanarumol, J. Thammatacharee, P. Jongudomsuk, and S. Sirilak. 2014. Achieving universal health coverage goals in Thailand: The vital role of strategic purchasing. *Health Policy and Planning* 30 (9): 1152–1161. https://doi.org/10.1093/heapol/czu120.

Tangwangvivat, R., Rata Rungsitiyakorn, Chiti Hoonaukit, Somruethai Na Nan, K.R. Hooker, Wichan Bhunyakitikorn, Chadaporn Phiancharoen, Papassorn Pinyopornpanish, Sopon Iamsirithaworn, and Anuwat Wiratsudakul. 2024. Collective activities of the Thai Coordinating Unit for One Health (CUOH): Past activities and future directions. *One Health* 18, 100728. https://doi.org/10.1016/j.onehlt.2024.100728.

Tantrakarnapa, K., and B. Bhopdhornangkul. 2020. Challenging the spread of COVID-19 in Thailand. *One Health* 11: 100173. https://doi.org/10.1016/j.onehlt.2020.100173.

Tejativaddhana, P., W. Suriyawongpaisal, V. Kasemsup, and T. Suksaroj. 2020. The roles of village health volunteers: COVID-19 prevention and control in Thailand. *Asia Pacific Journal of Health Management* 15 (3): 18–22. https://doi.org/10.24083/apjhm.v15i3.477.

Thanyalakmetha, S. 2022. Thailand country report 2022. Asian Disaster Reduction Centre. https://www.adrc.asia/aboutus/vrdata/CR/FY2022_THA_cr.pdf.

The London School of Economics and Political Science (LSE) and Partnership for Health System Sustainability and Resilience. 2021. Sustainability and resilience in the Vietnamese health system. https://www3.weforum.org/docs/WEF_PHSSR_Vietnam_Report.pdf.

Thushari, G.G.N., S. Chavanich, and A. Yakupitiyage. 2017. Coastal debris analysis in beaches of Chonburi Province, eastern of Thailand as implications for coastal conservation. *Marine Pollution Bulletin* 116 (1–2): 121–129. https://doi.org/10.1016/j.marpolbul.2016.12.056.

Tortajada, C. 2006. Water management in Singapore. *International Journal of Water Resources Development* 22 (2): 227–240. https://doi.org/10.1080/07900620600691944.

Tran, B. 2020. Viet Nam leads ASEAN through COVID-19. East Asia Forum. https://eastasiaforum.org/2020/06/01/vietnam-leads-asean-through-covid-19/.

Triukose, S., S. Nitinawarat, P. Satian, A. Somboonsavatdee, P. Chotikarn, T. Thammasanya, N. Wanlapakorn, N. Sudhinaraset, P. Boonyamalik, B. Kakhong, and Y. Poovorawan. 2021. Effects of public health interventions on the epidemiological spread during the first wave of the COVID-19 outbreak in Thailand. *PLoS ONE* 16 (2): e0246274. https://doi.org/10.1371/journal.pone.0246274.

United Nations Development Programme (UNDP). 2024a. 2024 regional human development report making our future: New directions for human development in Asia and the Pacific. https://www.undp.org/asia-pacific/publications/making-our-future-new-directions-human-development-asia-and-pacific.

UNDP. 2024b. Human development report 2023/2024. https://hdr.undp.org/system/files/documents/global-report-document/hdr2023-24reporten.pdf.

UNDRR. 2020. Disaster risk reduction in Thailand: Status report 2020. United Nations Office for Disaster Risk Reduction (UNDRR), Regional Office for Asia and the Pacific. https://www.undrr.org/media/48642/download?startDownload=20240825.

United States Department of Agriculture Foreign Agricultural Service and Global Agricultural Information Network. (USDA FAS and GAIN). 2021. Viet Nam issues green growth strategy 2021–2030 vision to 2050. https://apps.fas.usda.gov/newgainapi/api/Report/DownloadReportByFileName?fileName=Vietnam%20Issues%20Green%20Growth%20Strategy%202021-2030%20Vision%20to%202050%20_Hanoi_Vietnam_11-02-2021.pdf.

United Nations Economic and Social Commission for Asia and the Pacific (UNESCAP). 2023. Nexus thinking is key to sustainable development in the era of polycrisis. https://www.unescap.org/op-ed/nexus-thinking-key-sustainable-development-era-polycrisis.

Vallejo, B.M., Jr., and R.A. Ong. 2021. Emerging independent government science advice in the Philippines in a time of crisis. *Science & Engineering Journal* 14 (2): 212–216. https://scienggj.org/2021/SciEnggJ%202021-vol14-no02-p212-216-Vallejo%20and%20Ong.pdf.

WHO Regional Office for the Western Pacific. 2015. The Kingdom of Thailand health system review. *Health Systems in Transition* 5 (5). WHO Regional Office for the Western Pacific. https://iris.who.int/handle/10665/208216.

World Intellectual Property Organisation (WIPO). 2023. Global innovation index 2023. https://www.wipo.int/edocs/pubdocs/en/wipo-pub-2000-2023/vn.pdf.

Wijaya, A. 2022. Is Indonesia the next global digital hub? Pacific Telecommunications Council. https://www.ptc.org/2022/12/is-indonesia-the-next-global-digital-hub/.

Woo, J.J. 2014. Singapore's policy style: Statutory boards as policymaking units. *Journal of Asian Public Policy* 8 (2): 120–133. https://doi.org/10.1080/17516234.2014.922152.

Woo, J.J. 2018. Singapore's policy style: gradations of developmentalism. In *Policy styles and policy making: exploring the linkages*, ed. by M. Howlett and J. Tosun, 312–329. Routledge.

Woo, J.J. 2020. Pandemic, politics, and pandemonium: political capacity and Singapore's response to the Covid-19 crisis. *Policy Design and Practice*, 1–17. https://doi.org/10.1080/25741292.2020.1835212.

World Bank. 2014. *World Bank and environment in Indonesia*. Washington D.C.: World Bank. https://www.worldbank.org/en/country/indonesia/brief/world-bank-and-environment-in-indonesia.

World Bank. 2021a. Market Study for Philippines: Plastics Circularity Opportunities and Barriers. (March 21). https://www.worldbank.org/en/country/philippines/publication/market-studyfor-philippines-plastics-circularity-opportunities-and-barriers-report-landing-page.

World Bank. 2021b. Beyond Unicorns: Harnessing Digital Technologies for Inclusion in Indonesia. (July 29). https://openknowledge.worldbank.org/bitstream/handle/10986/36018/162061.pdf?sequence=5&isAllowed=y.

World Bank. 2023. Indonesia; Country Climate and Development Report. https://www.worldbank.org/en/country/indonesia/publication/indonesia-country-climate-and-development-report.

World Bank. 2024. The World Bank in Viet Nam. https://www.worldbank.org/en/country/vietnam/overview.

World Health Organisation. 2018. More than 60,000 deaths in Viet Nam each year linked to air pollution. https://www.who.int/vietnam/news/detail/02-05-2018-more-than-60-000-deaths-in-viet-nam-each-year-linked-to-air-pollution.

World Health Organisation. 2024. Building back better: Strengthening Indonesia's preparedness and resilience to emerging threats. WHO. https://www.who.int/indonesia/news/detail/04-03-2024-building-back-better--strengthening-indonesia-s-preparedness-and-resilience-to-emerging-threats.

World Health Organisation. n.d. Hospitals. https://www.who.int/vietnam/health-topics/hospitals.

World Intellectual Property Organisation. 2023. Global innovation index 2023. https://www.wipo.int/edocs/pubdocs/en/wipo-pub-2000-2023/vn.pdf.

Yen, W.-T., L.-Y. Liu, and E. WonTestriono. 2022. The imperative of state capacity in public health crisis: Asia's early COVID-19 policy responses. *Governance* 35 (3): 777–798. https://doi.org/10.1111/gove.12695.

Ysa, T., and M. Esteve. 2013. *Networks never walk alone: The governance of network portfolios*. Paper to the Global Governance Club, Netherlands Institute for Advanced Study in the Humanities and Social Science (NIAS), Wassenaar, The Netherlands, (29.05 to 01.06.2013).

CHAPTER 11

When the Four Horsemen of Apocalypse Get Schengen Visa: European Public Administrations and Governance in the Era of Pandemic, War and Permanent Crisis

Emilia Sičáková Beblavá and Miroslav Beblavý

11.1 Changes of Public Administration Versus Crises

The literature on the state, often defined as the "public bureaucracy or administrative apparatus as a coherent totality and as an institutionalised legal order" (Benjamin and Duvall 1985) and various other sources, examines the degree of congruence between the state and its environment (Krasner 1984). In this context, one stream of literature explores

E. S. Beblavá (✉) · M. Beblavý
Bratislava, Slovakia
e-mail: emilia.beblava@fses.uniba.sk

M. Beblavý
e-mail: miroslav.beblavy@zhiva.sk

A. Baimenov and P. Liverakos (eds.), *Public Administration in the New Reality*, https://doi.org/10.1007/978-981-96-3845-1_11

the extent to which the state responds to the needs of society (Besley and Burgess 2001) and adapts itself accordingly.[1]

European public administrations have undergone numerous changes initiated by governments (Kuhlmann and Wollmann 2019; Pollitt and Bouckaert 2011) for a multitude of reasons. Typically, the literature discusses various internal and external factors driving these changes. In this context, the role of trust (Leibrecht and Pitlik 2015; Bouckaert 2012), the individual characteristics of political leaders (Kettl 2015; Dreher et al. 2009), bureaucratic entrepreneurship (Mintrom and Norman 2009), and external shocks or crises (Randma-Liiv and Kickert 2017; Blondin and Boin 2020) are often highlighted.

Regarding crises, Skowronek (1982) defines them as "sporadic, disruptive events that suddenly challenge a state's capacity to maintain control and alter the boundaries defining the legitimate use of coercion." There is no unified theory of crisis management, and according to Nolte et al. (2020), crisis management in public administration is complex, especially in transboundary situations like mass refugee influxes. On the one hand, rapid responses are required; on the other hand, issues of legitimacy are at stake (Angelis 2017; Christensen et al. 2016). Crises thus present political leaders with challenging agendas central to the political order, compelling them to respond (Jabko and Sheingate 2018). Crisis management typically transcends administrative levels, sectors, and ministerial domains and is characterised by uniqueness, ambiguity, complexity, and high uncertainty (Christensen et al. 2016). Addressing crises may necessitate changes in bureaucrats' problem-solving approaches, fostering dynamic thinking, adaptation, and cooperation between public administration officials and external stakeholders (Janssen and Van der Voort 2020; Ansell et al. 2010). Peters et al. (2011) delve into the relationship between crises and changes in public administration. According to them, a crisis can serve as clear evidence that the existing patterns of public administration are ineffective and in need of new approaches (Peters et al. 2011).

The occurrence of a crisis with a low probability but a simultaneous high impact presents a formidable challenge in terms of management (Christensen et al. 2016; Pearson and Clair 1998). Nonetheless, crises

[1] https://commission.europa.eu/document/download/b2e60d06-37c6-4943-820f-d82ec197d966_en?filename=white_paper_on_the_future_of_europe_en.pdf.

also offer opportunities for learning, change, and administrative adaptation (Andrews et al. 2013). In this context, various theoretical approaches can be employed to elucidate the role of crises in state development.

One school of thought argues that crises serve as catalysts for a state's institutional development, leading to the creation of new institutional forms, structures, powers, and processes. External shocks, whether economic or social crises, are seen as windows of opportunity for institutional change because they signal to voters that maintaining the status quo is no longer a viable option (Ahlquist et al. 2020; Heinemann and Grigoriadis 2016). Crises can disrupt the interest coalitions that had previously resisted change (Tompson 2010). Randma-Liiv and Kickert (2017) suggest that a crisis can open a window of opportunity for changes that were previously deemed impossible or postponed.

On the other hand, historical institutionalists, as exemplified by Fioretos et al. (2016), emphasise the path dependency of government decisions and the notion of a "critical juncture." This critical juncture represents a moment when it becomes possible to diverge from the original path of incremental development and initiate substantial changes, resulting in a new equilibrium (Vis et al. 2011). Additionally, an ideational perspective highlights the role of ideas and their transformative capacity under extreme conditions (Hannah et al. 2022; Béland and Cox 2011). According to Kickert and van der Meer (2011), the nature and extent of administrative change can vary and depend on the existing institutional settings.

There exists another strand of literature that adopts a more sceptical view regarding the facilitation of change by crises (Boin and Rhinard 2023; Peters et al. 2011; Blondin and Boin 2020). This perspective is rooted in arguments related to time pressure, the political context, the availability of financial and human resources, and the organisational climate during fiscal stress (Randma-Liiv and Kickert 2017).

Numerous studies have delved into the impact of crises on sociopolitical and administrative systems. These studies predominantly examine the financial aspects, particularly the politics of austerity and fiscal consolidation (Kickert et al. 2015; Hood et al. 2014; Peters and Pierre 2010). Research from a policy perspective has primarily concentrated on coherence, complementarity, and coordination, as exemplified by Blondin and Boin (2020). Governance-oriented research, on the other hand, has underscored the significance of both formal and informal arrangements, such as joined-up government, coordinated networks (Scott and Merton

2022; Jordan and Schout 2006), and collaborative policy regimes (Zhong et al. 2022; Howlett and Saguin 2018). Additionally, a body of literature explores the connection between ideas and crises in policy and administration. Ideational studies point towards novel approaches for crisis scholars to approach coherence in coordination among crisis actors, network information, and public communication (Hannah et al. 2022).

In this chapter, we examine the changes that European public administrations have undergone since 2008 in response to four crises. In essence, we explore how European public administration structures adapted to unforeseen shifts in domestic and international environments. This chapter thus contributes to the existing body of literature related to state development, shedding light on the notion that institutional change can manifest as episodic and dramatic rather than a continuous and incremental process.

11.2 How We Approach the Topic

We delve into how European public administration structures underwent significant transformations in reaction to unforeseen and substantial shifts in both domestic and international contexts. Our analysis adopts a multi-level administrative perspective within the European Union, focusing on governing and organisational structures (including mechanisms of vertical and horizontal coordination and public bodies) at various levels—local governments, regional governments, central governments, and the EU itself. The utilisation of multi-level governance structures and coordination mechanisms, grounded in principles of territoriality and functionality (Kuhlmann 2015), is considered pivotal to the process and outcomes of crisis management.

While European public administrations confront a multitude of long-term challenges, such as the green transition, demographic shifts, technological advancements, skills shortages, and mounting fiscal pressures (Petmesidou and Guillén 2022; European Commission 2021), our primary focus in this chapter centres on crises and external shocks. Specifically, we concentrate on the changes that were instigated in response to the Eurozone economic and financial crisis, the migration crisis, the COVID-19 pandemic, and the conflict in Ukraine (including the associated energy crisis) spanning from 2008 to early 2023. Thus, our examination hones on the adjustments made to European public administrations as a direct response to these external shocks.

In the context of this chapter, we define "change" as a deliberate policy response, encompassing authoritative actions taken by public sector organisations (Nordlinger 1981; Geertz 1980; Pollitt and Bouckaert 2011). These actions aim to alter the structures, tasks, actors, and processes within existing public administrations, thereby challenging the prevailing *status quo*. Our approach sets itself apart from general crisis management studies by honing on administrative characteristics, organisational features, and key actors—elements that hold significant sway in governing during turbulent periods. As such, we delve into the following dimensions in line with the European Commission's framework:

- **Organisational structures**: In this aspect, we scrutinise both temporary and enduring changes in organisational structures of European public administration structures. We also consider alterations brought about by mergers of European public organisations and the creation of novel structures.
- **Competencies and tasks/authorities**: External crises can serve as opportunities for policy changes by redefining institutional roles, transforming pre-existing rules and norms, and introducing new conceptual frameworks (Ahlquist et al. 2020). Our investigation explores the novel competencies and tasks assigned to European public administrations in response to the external shocks under consideration.
- **Processes (within existing competencies)**: We examine the processes that were adopted in connection with the discussed crises, particularly those within the purview of existing competencies.
- **Changes in human resource management**: As managers and bureaucrats play pivotal roles within European public administrations, we also delve into changes related to human resource management, considering them as essential actors in this context.

By delving into these dimensions, we aim to provide a comprehensive understanding of how European public administrations have adapted and responded to the external shocks discussed. To pinpoint specific changes within European public administrations, we employ two distinct methodological approaches. In the cases of the economic/financial crisis, migration crisis, and the COVID-19 pandemic, we conduct a comprehensive literature survey. Drawing from existing research, we identify main changes initiated in response to these external shocks within European public administrations.

However, in the case of the Ukraine war, which began in February 2022, there is a lack of available research. Consequently, we conducted several interviews to identify the principal changes occurring in European public administrations. Additionally, we delve into formal policy materials issued by relevant EU institutions and by selected countries to augment our understanding.

Furthermore, we investigate organisational changes at the central level of EU Member States by examining alterations in the labelling of organisational structures of key central governing bodies, namely ministries. Existing literature suggests that changes in the labelling of public bodies can signify heightened political attention from the leadership to specific policy issues of importance (Mortensen and Green-Pedersen 2015; Hamnond 1993; Yesilkagit et al. 2022).

11.3 The Eurozone Crisis

The Eurozone crisis unfolded as a multi-year debt crisis within the European Union, commencing in 2009 and reaching its zenith between 2010 and 2012. Its origins trace back to the initial phase in 2008, characterised by a banking crisis that witnessed the collapse of banks and other financial institutions. In response, various governments implemented diverse support and rescue measures to safeguard these financial institutions.

According to Randma-Liiv and Kickert (2017), the 2008 global crisis impacted European countries to varying extents. Southern Europe, Eastern Europe, and the British Isles were among the hardest-hit regions, while continental Western European countries experienced milder effects, and the Nordic countries were relatively unscathed by the crisis (Kickert et al. 2015; Darvas 2010). Consequently, several nations, including Greece, Hungary, Iceland, Ireland, Italy, and Spain, sought financial assistance from the European Commission, the International Monetary Fund, and the European Central Bank, collectively known as the Troika. Greece, Ireland, and Portugal required bailouts in 2010, with Greece receiving a second bailout in 2012 (Copelovitch et al. 2016). Spanish banks received a bailout in 2012, and Cyprus was similarly bailed out by the European Commission, the International Monetary Fund, and the European Central Bank in 2013.

Bakir et al. (2021) contend that the Eurozone crisis primarily resulted from disparities in macroeconomic structures, fiscal impropriety, and financial integration within fragmented regulatory and supervisory governance frameworks. Governance and public administration failures are also examined in this context. These include issues related to vertical and horizontal coordination within government, the problematic regulation of financial institutions, and shortcomings in principal-agent relationships (Pollitt 2010; Peters et al. 2011; Green 2012; Lodge and Hood 2012; Potter 2012). A segment of the existing literature suggests that the fiscal crisis heightened the perception of the need for reforms in public administration.[2]

At the EU level, the following principal changes were introduced in response to the crisis discussed below. As for **the changes in competencies and structural changes,** the EU initiated emergency funding programmes in response to the financial crisis. One of these programmes, the European Financial Stability Facility (EFSF), was introduced in early 2010 and extended to countries such as Ireland, Portugal, and Greece. Subsequently, the European Financial Stability Mechanism (EFSM) was also established. The funding for these programmes was obtained through the issuance of EFSF bonds and various debt instruments on capital markets. These mechanisms effectively facilitated indirect redistributions of funds among EU Member States, functioning as a type of fiscal transfer. It is important to note that these transfers were of a temporary nature, and specific conditions were attached to all the financial assistance programmes as part of the overall framework.

In 2012,[3] the European Stability Mechanism (ESM) was established as a response to the financial crisis. This institution was created with the purpose of addressing financial challenges within the EU. Unlike its predecessors, the ESM is a permanent institution and operates as a multilateral fund responsible for extending loans to Member States facing financial difficulties. Importantly, these loans are provided only when the stability of the Eurozone is at risk, as outlined in the work of Jabko and Luhman (2020).

[2] See, for example, Pollitt (2010), Tompson (2010), Peters et al. (2011), Vis et al. (2011), and Green (2012).

[3] https://www.esm.europa.eu/about-us/history.

EU leaders reached a consensus that the ESM should function as an intergovernmental institution and should only be activated as a measure of last resort, aimed at safeguarding the integrity of the Eurozone. It is worth noting that horizontal transfers are utilised, and no direct EU resources are involved in this process. However, EU institutions play a regulatory, coordinating, or facilitating role in managing these transfers, as discussed by Bremer et al. (2020).

Additional change in competencies and organisational setting is the formation of the Structural Reform Support Programme (SRSS) to assist member states in formulating and executing institutional, administrative, and structural reforms. Its primary objective is to enhance the efficiency and effectiveness of Member States in utilising available EU funds for such purposes. In June 2015, the SRSS was inaugurated, consolidating the EU's structural reform expertise into a unified organisational unit. This centralised approach replaced the earlier practice of establishing various ad hoc Task Forces for the same purpose.[4]

In response to financial crises new competencies were vested in the European Central Bank in 2014 to oversee a Banking Union—a comprehensive framework of policies and institutions designed to shift responsibility for banking policy from the national to the EU level in various EU Member States.[5] Simultaneously, new legal crisis instruments, known as the European Semester and the Six-Pack, were introduced.

The European Semester focuses on enhancing, harmonising, and centralising the coordination of national budgets and economic policies. It empowers the European Commission to scrutinise Member States' budgets and evaluate whether the proposed national budgetary plans align with the criteria outlined in the "Six Pack" regulations. As the calendar year ends and the "Semester cycle" commences, the Commission releases its Annual Growth Survey and Alert Mechanism Report. The latter identifies Member States warranting an in-depth review due to potential imbalances that could disrupt the smooth operation of their economies. These reviews may trigger the Macroeconomic Imbalances Procedure (MIP) integrated into the European Semester. If the imbalances are deemed excessive, the Excessive Imbalance Procedure is

[4] https://www.google.com/url?q=https://www.consilium.europa.eu/en/policies/structural-support-programme/&sa=D&source=docs&ust=1692798604720968&usg=AOvVaw1zRsm6SsdrLmgs0k2NVYC2.

[5] https://www.ecb.europa.eu/press/pr/date/2014/html/pr141104.en.html.

initiated. Conversely, if the imbalances are not classified as excessive, the "preventive arm" of the MIP is activated, and the Commission's recommended policy responses are integrated into the Country Specific Recommendations (Pantazatou 2015).

In the area of **changes in decision-making and coordination processes** a temporary coalition comprising the European Commission, the European Central Bank, and the International Monetary Fund named The Troika was created.[6] Its formation was prompted by the need to confront the financial difficulties encountered by specific EU Member States amid the European debt crisis. The Troika assumed responsibility for coordinating and implementing multilateral responses to these national crises.

Regarding the response of **public administrations in EU Member States** to the financial Eurozone crisis, it is important to note the EU Treaty of Maastricht, which imposes limits on budget deficits and state debt for certain EU countries. Many European nations faced pressure from the EU to adhere to these deficit ceilings. The fiscal crisis emerged when government budget deficits exceeded acceptable levels, leading governments to initiate budget consolidation measures and implement austerity policies (Kickert 2012; Posner and Blöndal 2012).

External conditionality, coupled with specific policy instruments like Memoranda of Understanding (MoU) under financial assistance programmes, prompted several changes in public administrations. Kickert et al. (2015) conducted a comparative analysis of consolidation measures in fourteen European countries during the period from 2008 to 2012. Their findings reveal that the consolidation efforts undertaken by European public administrations largely followed a similar pattern. Below are some illustrative examples.

Changes in human resource management were implemented in various forms across EU public administrations affected by the crises. Almost universally, measures such as hiring freezes and pay freezes were put into effect. Examples of these measures include horizontal pay cuts, wage reductions, layoffs, recruitment freezes, and partial replacement of retiring employees. Reductions in fixed term/temporary positions were also prevalent, often accompanied by the initiation of special mobility

[6] https://www.europarl.europa.eu/doceo/document/A-7-2014-0149_EN.html.

schemes. However, more drastic cutback measures were only implemented in a limited number of countries. These measures were primarily applied in European nations that received bailouts and faced immediate cuts in public sector salaries and employment. For instance, Greece introduced cuts in the number of public servants,[7] while Estonia implemented freezes or reductions in public sector wages and enacted a new Public Service Act in 2012. This act led to a quarter of civil servants losing their civil service status and becoming employed under the Labour Law (Randma-Liiv and Kickert 2017). In Lithuania, the anti-crisis measures package involved reductions in public sector wages, civil service salaries, and various social benefits (Nakrošis et al. 2015).

A comparison of public employment during the Eurozone crises and in 2021 indicates that most EU countries have returned to pre-crisis levels of public employment. According to Eurostat, it took eight years for the total employment rate to recover to its pre-recession level after the 2008 financial crisis.[8] OECD data suggests that the share of government employment in the EU has remained relatively stable. Among the Member States for which data is available, the most significant declines between 2007 and 2021 were observed in Lithuania, Greece, and Italy.[9]

In addition to changes in human resource management, **changes in organisational settings** were introduced. Several countries established new organisations to address their fiscal challenges. One example is the creation of independent authorities tasked with monitoring public finances, commonly known as fiscal councils. A noteworthy illustration is the Council for Budgetary Responsibility in Slovakia, established through a constitutional change in 2011. During the period from 2007 to 2014, the number of countries with such institutions nearly quadrupled, increasing from 6 to 19.[10] Another example involves improved asset management. For instance, in 2009, the Irish government established

[7] https://www.eurofound.europa.eu/publications/article/2016/greece-reducing-the-number-of-public-servants-latest-developments.

[8] https://ec.europa.eu/eurostat/cache/digpub/european_economy/bloc-4d.html?lang=en.

[9] https://stats.oecd.org/index.aspx?queryid=107595.

[10] https://www.ecb.europa.eu/pub/pdf/other/mb201406_focus08.en.pdf.

the National Asset Management Agency to enhance its management of assets.[11]

Several countries also established specialised structures or bodies to plan, coordinate, and oversee administrative reforms. For example, Italy created the Reform Delivery Unit (RDU) and Independent Commission for the Evaluation, Transparency, and Integrity of Government (CIVIT).[12] In 2009, Lithuania re-established the governmental "Sunset" Commission, assigning it the responsibility of streamlining bureaucracy, eliminating duplicate functions in public administration, and enhancing efficiency (Rauleckas et al. 2016).

Some governments undertook reorganisations to curtail budget expenditures. In Lithuania, the government initiated comprehensive organisational reforms that impacted ministries and various agencies, resulting in widespread restructuring (Rauleckas et al. 2016). In the UK, the Public Bodies Reform plan, launched in 2010, aimed to restructure approximately five hundred Arm's Length Bodies through measures like abolishing, merging, or significantly reforming these agencies.[13] In Spain, government restructuring efforts involved eliminating duplicated entities at both the regional and central levels.[14]

Centralisation was also traced in the [re-]organisation of the administrative systems (Di Mascio and Natalini 2016), the decision-making process (Kickert et al. 2013) and the autonomy of local government (Nunes Silva 2017).

In regard to **changes of administrative processes** new budgetary tools and more stringent rules and procedures were implemented in budgetary and financial management. Expenditure monitoring at all government levels became more centralised, and enhanced control mechanisms were introduced. Southern European Eurozone members that received bailout funds were mandated to adhere to austerity measures as a condition for the loans they received (Darvas 2010; Bakir et al. 2021).

Methods for simplifying procedures and public procurement were also implemented. For instance, the UK developed the Operational Efficiency

[11] https://www.nama.ie/about-us.

[12] https://joinup.ec.europa.eu/sites/default/files/document/2014-12/Modernising%20the%20Public%20Administration%20-%20A%20Study%20on%20Italy.pdf.

[13] https://www.gov.uk/government/publications/public-bodies-reform-reports.

[14] https://www.lamoncloa.gob.es/lang/en/espana/stpv/spaintoday2015/transparency/Paginas/index.aspx.

Program for IT reforms and collaborative procurement. In Lithuania, the central government introduced centralisation of procurement functions (Kickert et al. 2015). Additionally, many governments enhanced their e-government initiatives, such as the Italian government with its e-Gov 2012 Plan (OECD 2010).

Our research on **changes related to the labels of central public administration** units reveals that in June 2011, Greece established a separate Ministry of Administrative Reform and Electronic Governance. However, this change was temporary. In January 2015, the Greek Ministry of Interior, which had been formed in 2011, merged with the Ministry of Public Order and Citizen Protection to create the Ministry of the Interior and Administrative Reorganisation. In 2016, a separate Ministry of Administrative Reorganisation was established, and the Ministry of the Interior reverted to its original name for the third time in a decade. Furthermore, a separate Ministry of Citizen Protection was re-established on August 29, 2018. Ultimately, the Ministry of Administrative Reorganisation was absorbed back into the Ministry of the Interior on 9 July 2019 (Table 11.1).

Table 11.1 Types of changes to European public administrations due to Eurozone crisis

Type of changes		*Governing level*	
		EU	*Country level*
Organisational/structural	New temporary structure	X	X
	New permanent structure	X	X
	Restructuring/mergers		X
	Change of the ministry name		X
Competencies	Temporary	X	
	Permanent	X	
Processes	Temporary	X	X
	Permanent		X
Actors–human management changes	Flexibility increase		
	Freezing/cuts		X
	Capacity building		

Source Authors

11.4 The Migration Crisis

In 2015 and 2016, a significant influx of people from war-torn and crisis-ridden regions, such as the Syrian Arab Republic, Afghanistan, and Iraq, sought asylum in European Union countries, including Germany (with 441,900 first-time asylum claims in 2015 and 722,400 in 2016),[15] Italy, and Sweden (UNHCR 2016, 2017). During this period, there were more than 1.8 million irregular border crossings at the EU's external borders, with nearly half (885,386) of these crossings occurring on the Eastern Mediterranean route from Turkey to Greece.[16] Countries like Hungary, located on the EU's eastern border, were also heavily impacted by irregular migration.[17]

Destination states such as Germany, Austria, France, Belgium, and Sweden unilaterally suspended the Schengen agreement on borderless travel and reintroduced border controls (Biermann et al. 2019; Zaun 2020). Many European governments, therefore, found themselves inexperienced in managing refugees and confronted with an unprecedented situation in public administration.

Within the EU, two main regulations pertain to this issue: the Schengen Area, which constitutes an area without internal borders, and the Dublin Convention, which governs the registration of asylum seekers upon their entry into EU territory. In response to the migration crises, various changes have been implemented at the **EU administration level**, as outlined below.

In regard to **changes in competencies** FRONTEX—The European Border and Coast Guard Agency, headquartered in Warsaw—has to be mentioned. It was established in 2004 to enhance the efforts of national authorities and coordinate the implementation of Schengen rules. Originally, its role focused on coordination, training, and assistance. However, in 2016, significant structural changes were introduced to expand its operational powers. FRONTEX is now responsible for monitoring migratory

[15] The German public administration received over 1.1 million applications for asylum in 2015 and 2016, a great many a number more applications than received in other EU countries, such as Italy (ranking second in the EU with over 200,000 applications in the two years) or France (ranking third in the EU with slightly over 150,000 applications) (UNHCR 2016, 2017).

[16] https://www.frontex.europa.eu/media-centre/news/news-release/frontex-publishes-risk-analysis-for-2017-CpJiC8.

[17] https://www.cfr.org/backgrounder/europes-migration-crisis.

flows, assessing risks, identifying potential new threats, and highlighting vulnerabilities in the EU's external borders. This expansion has led to increases in human resources, financial resources, and the geographical coverage of FRONTEX (Niemann and Speyer 2018).

A new coordination mechanism known as the Western Balkans Contact Group was established in October 2015.[18] This weekly coordination meeting, presided over by the Secretariat-General, has consistently convened high-level participants from various entities, including DG ECHO, DG HOME, DG NEAR, DG DEVCO, EEAS, and the offices of the European Commission President.

As for the changes in **organisational setting** the European Union Regional Task Force (EURTF) was established in 2015, consisting of offices located in distressed border areas. These offices were set up to facilitate information exchange and enhance coordination among EU agencies involved in managing the migration crisis.[19] Specifically, they were situated in Catania, Italy, and Piraeus, Greece. As part of this initiative, a permanent staff member from DG HOME was stationed at the EURTF in Catania, with another team from DG HOME located in Piraeus.[20]

In addition, changes were introduced to strengthen **human management skills** and learning has taken place in areas such as information collection and sharing, coordination, leadership, and resourcing (Pannia et al. 2018).

In 2015, the Dublin Convention system ceased to be effective as many **EU Member States** struggled to process the overwhelming number of asylum applications. Even the most refugee-friendly states responded by closing their borders (Jabko and Luhman 2020). As a result, this migration crisis prompted select member states to make financial adaptations, prioritise development assistance policies, and redefine asylum policies (Bech et al. 2017). Furthermore, the reactions of these countries to the migration crisis also had an impact on their public administrations.

Several **changes in competencies** were introduced. The example is re-nationalisation of policies as some EU Member States have pursued the re-nationalisation of policies related to border controls and other

[18] https://ec.europa.eu/commission/presscorner/detail/en/IP_15_5904.

[19] https://ebcgday.eu/files/user_files/debates/2016/Hotspots_interagency_response_to_migratory_pressure.pdf.

[20] https://frontex.europa.eu/media-centre/news/news-release/frontex-to-restructure-its-office-in-greece-ShsH5z.

measures to protect or assert their national interests. Under Schengen and Dublin agreements, states retained the right to unilaterally reintroduce border controls and to return asylum seekers to the first entry country.

Changes in **organisational settings i**n response to migration crises in EU Member States administrations taken place as well. The hotspot approach was introduced by the European Commission in May 2015 as part of a broader policy initiative known as the "European Agenda on Migration."[21] It aimed to manage irregular maritime arrivals, involving activities such as fingerprinting, registration, debriefing, and organising returns. Member States had the flexibility to determine the specific characteristics of the hotspots, and both Greece and Italy implemented them. This approach emphasises inter-agency collaboration, with national experts deployed and operating under the coordination of a specific agency to provide operational assistance to national administrations.

Several countries established detention centres and refugee camps in response to the migration crisis. For instance, Hungary set up a detention centre in Roszke, near its border with Serbia,[22] during the 2015 migration crisis. Another example is the refugee camp in Traiskirchen, Austria.[23]

In some countries, new structures were established to coordinate migration-related efforts. For example, in Great Britain, the Home Office formed the Community Cohesion Unit to coordinate new policy measures at the local level. This committee was later relocated to the Department of Communities and Local Government (Scholten 2016).

Migration crises also led to collaboration with local civil society organisations (NGOs). NGOs played a crucial supplementary role in responding to migration crises, including in Sweden. During the peak of the 2015 crisis, the Swedish Migration Board initiated partnerships with local NGOs and charities (Bevelander and Hellström 2019; Nilsson et al. 2023) (Table 11.2).

[21] https://academic.oup.com/jrs/article-abstract/33/2/469/5626240?login=false.

[22] https://www.hrw.org/news/2015/09/11/hungary-abysmal-conditions-border-detention.

[23] https://eu.usatoday.com/story/news/world/2015/10/12/austria-migrants-globalpost/73806236/.

Table 11.2 Types of changes to European public administrations due to migration crises

Type of changes		*Governing level*	
		EU	*Country level*
Organisational/structural	New temporary structure	X	X
	New permanent structure		
	Restructuring/mergers		
	Change of the ministry name		
Competencies	Temporary		X
	Permanent	X	
Processes	Temporary		X
	Permanent		
Actors–human management changes	Flexibility increase		
	Freezing/cuts		
	Capacity building	X	X

Source Authors

11.5 The COVID Pandemic

The COVID-19 pandemic began with an outbreak in the Chinese city of Wuhan in December 2019. Just a few months later, in March 2020, the World Health Organisation declared the spread of the virus a pandemic. To slow its spread, various measures were implemented, including mask-wearing, physical distancing, frequent handwashing, and, in some regions, lockdowns or stay-at-home orders. Several COVID-19 vaccines were developed, and following rigorous testing, a global vaccination campaign was launched to protect people from the virus. While grappling with the pandemic, scientists identified new variants of the virus. Within a matter of months, COVID-19 affected almost all countries, prompting European governments and public administrations to take measures to address this unprecedented situation.

At all levels of **European public administrations**, changes in work modalities were implemented in response to the COVID-19 pandemic. According to OECD (2023), the impact of the COVID-19 crisis was particularly significant on internal processes, especially those requiring digitalisation, such as communication and **human resource management** (HRM). Valenza et al. (2022) note that daily administrative routines of almost all EU institutions were disrupted, necessitating adjustments and adaptations to new working conditions. EU institutions restructured their internal work processes, accelerating digitalisation and teleworking. ICT infrastructure and services were upgraded to enable more employees to work remotely. Teleworking initiatives began in March 2020, and in July 2021, the Administrative Committee adopted a decision to establish a homeworking scheme, allowing managers to authorise staff to work from home. This introduced a new working modality known as hybrid working. Permanent working stations (private or semi-private offices) were replaced by flexible, mobile ones, facilitated by the provision of laptops to all employees. The pandemic prompted a general rethinking of workspace design in all EU institutions based on the so-called 3Bs: behaviour, bricks, and bytes.

Similar changes were implemented at the central, regional, and local levels in all EU countries. Many public administration employees received equipment and training in information and communication technologies (ICT). For example, the Spanish Government introduced Telework Legislation (Royal Decree Law 28/2020) for this purpose, and specific regulations and software were made available to facilitate virtual document checking and contribute to addressing undeclared and under-declared work in the new context. Germany also saw a significant shift of services to mobile phones and the internet. Moreover, new phone lines were established to replace counselling and advice on social services. For instance, Madrid Salud in Spain launched a 24/7 Emergency Telephone hotline for citizens. Additionally, in the Lubuskie Voivodship Office in Poland, boxes were placed in front of the office to allow citizens to submit paper applications. A computer was also provided at the entrance for citizens to create their electronic signatures (OECD 2023).

To adapt to this new work modality, often referred to as the "new normal," **training programmes** were initiated to enhance staff skills in managing people in hybrid working settings, effectively overseeing teams from home, and coordinating activities at both the EU and national levels (Valenza et al. 2022). For instance, Belgium expanded its online training offerings, transformed in-person training for online accessibility, and expedited certain training programmes (OECD 2022).

The shift to remote work also prompted numerous European public administrations to revise their hiring processes. This included the implementation of remote interviews via videoconference for all recruitment procedures, ensuring that candidates from across the EU had equal access to participation. One example of this adaptation is the introduction of a new IT tool, Apply4EP, by the EP, which manages online applications and facilitates written and oral tests conducted through remote participation. Many EU Member States also expedited and streamlined their recruitment processes (OECD 2023).

At the level of **EU institutions,** numerous additional changes have been implemented in response to the COVID-19 pandemic. Drawing from Valenza et al. (2022), here are some examples.

In regard to **changes in human resource management** several additional flexibility measures were introduced, including extended maternity leaves during the lockdowns, new rules for time-recording that allow for up to 2 hours per day for childcare (ECA), a 50 per cent reduction in work time for families with disabled children with no loss of income when facilities were closed (EP). Additionally, staff members needing to take care of direct relatives were granted the option to work part-time outside their place of employment.

Measures were also introduced to support employees with stress management. All EU institutions enhanced their support for the physical and mental well-being of staff, expanding the scope of existing medical and social internal services. New competencies were introduced in this context, combining support for mental health with medical assistance. These services were customised to individual needs and included helplines, support groups, webinars on well-being and mindfulness, among other. Information was also disseminated to staff on coping with teleworking and maintaining a work-life balance to prevent burnouts. Some institutions, such as the EC, EEAS, and ECA, conducted "pulse" surveys to regularly assess staff well-being during the crisis (Quaglio et al. 2023).

As for **changes in organisational settings** changes to the European institutional infrastructure were introduced under the European Health Union initiative, with the Commission establishing a new authority known as the Health Emergency Preparedness and Response Authority (HERA). HERA was integrated into the European Directorate-General for Health and Food Safety (SANTE) and commenced operations in

January 2022.[24] Its primary mission is to proactively identify, rapidly respond to, and effectively manage health emergencies.[25]

New coordination mechanisms were established in this context as well. In March 2020, the Commission formed an inter-institutional group within the CPQS (*Comité préparatoire pour les questions statutaires*) to facilitate the exchange of information and coordination among institutions in response to the COVID-19 pandemic. Chaired by the Commission, this group comprised representatives from various EU institutions and bodies. Over the course of 2020, they convened forty-eight times, demonstrating the effectiveness of their cooperation in sharing information, best practices, and aligning measures across institutions. Additionally, regular ad hoc exchanges were organised at the service level (Valenza et al. 2022).

In the area of **competencies** several **changes** were introduced. The European Centre for Disease Prevention and Control (ECDC) assumed a monitoring role in response to the pandemic threat (Deruelle and Engeli 2021). While this health agency has existed since 2005, Deruelle and Engeli (2021) note that COVID-19 prompted a functional transformation within the ECDC.[26] Its role shifted from coordinating risk assessments to overseeing risk management. In November 2020, a series of initiatives were proposed, leading to expanded mandates for both the EMA and the ECDC. The extended EMA mandate was officially approved in January 2022.[27]

Numerous actions have been taken to coordinate the response to the COVID-19 outbreak. These measures include the establishment of the EU Digital COVID Certificate and the EU Vaccines Strategy. The European Commission created a vaccine procurement task force to enhance vaccine production capacity within the EU. This task force served as a central hub for manufacturers seeking support and aimed to identify and

[24] https://commission.europa.eu/about-european-commission/departments-and-executive-agencies/health-emergency-preparedness-and-response-authority_en.

[25] https://commission.europa.eu/about-european-commission/departments-and-executive-agencies/health-emergency-preparedness-and-response-authority_en.

[26] https://www.ecdc.europa.eu/en/about-ecdc.

[27] https://www.europarl.europa.eu/legislative-train/spotlight-C19/file-ema-mandate-extension.

resolve production bottlenecks and supply chain issues.[28] In June 2020, the European Commission approved an agreement for the EU to procure COVID-19 vaccines on behalf of member states. The agreement also involved negotiations regarding terms and conditions, all geared towards ensuring a swift and equitable distribution. This initiative marked the union's inaugural collective vaccination programme.

To mitigate the socio-economic impact of COVID-19, the EU bolstered its competencies in economic and social aid. This involved enhancing the fiscal capacity of the European Union through the common programme known as SURE (the temporary Support to mitigate Unemployment Risks in an Emergency).[29,30] SURE's primary responsibility was to provide financial aid of up to one hundred billion Euro through loans offered on favourable terms by the EU to Member States facing economic challenges. While this loan was primarily intended to safeguard jobs within member states, it could also be utilised for health-related measures in the workplace.

Additionally, the EU committed 2,018 trillion Euro to "rebuilding post-COVID Europe" and introduced a comprehensive EU-wide recovery plan designed to address technological and environmental challenges on the horizon. This plan placed particular emphasis on the climate and digital transition, with a focus on research and innovation.[31] At the heart of this strategy was the Recovery and Resilience Facility (RRF), serving as a temporary mechanism within NextGeneration EU—the European Union's recovery strategy fund following crises. The European Commission utilised the RRF to raise funds by borrowing from capital markets, and the facility became operational in February 2021.[32]

In reaction to COVID-19 crises also **changes in processes** were introduced. Here example are changes in voting and other procedures as well as new formal and informal inter-institutional dialogue were enforced. For instance, distance checks have replaced on-the-spot checks for ECA

[28] https://commission.europa.eu/strategy-and-policy/coronavirus-response/public-health/eu-vaccines-strategy_en.

[29] https://economy-finance.ec.europa.eu/eu-financial-assistance/sure_en.

[30] The availability of the SURE instrument ended on 31 December 2022.

[31] https://commission.europa.eu/strategy-and-policy/recovery-plan-europe_en.

[32] https://commission.europa.eu/business-economy-euro/economic-recovery/recovery-and-resilience-facility_en.

auditors. ECA auditing was conducted remotely, using videoconferencing tools as well as secure data and document sharing.

In response to the COVID-19 pandemic, various changes were introduced in **European public administrations.** In this regard, several **changes in organisational settings** were introduced. The onset of the COVID-19 pandemic necessitated swift and foundational political decisions regarding public behaviour, particularly in areas such as lockdowns and vaccination campaigns. These decisions were not only political but also scientific, requiring expertise in epidemiology, public health, and even behavioural psychology. Unlike traditional approaches that might relegate expert consultation to the periphery, the COVID-19 pandemic integrated scientific expertise into decision-making on an accelerated timeline. Countries worldwide established special task forces composed of politicians, administrators, and various experts for this purpose (Bouckaert 2012).

For instance, Italy formed two task forces under the Ministry of Justice, one to manage the COVID-19 situation in prisons and the other to address the emergency's impact on the judicial system.[33] France established a "Scientific Council" comprised of prominent scientists and experts to provide guidance and advice to the government on pandemic-related decisions (Telford et al. 2021). In the Netherlands, a centralised national coordination platform for patient distribution was created (Moorkamp et al. 2020). Many countries introduced coordination by expertise, involving health experts alongside politicians and administrators.

In Italy, the National Health Institute (NHI) serves as the official governmental advisor on health policy. In February 2019, a new committee, the Technical-Scientific Committee (TSC), was established. Initially consisting of seven members holding top organisational positions in governmental and health institutions, the TSC expanded to twenty-five members in the subsequent months, incorporating experts from various medical fields. The TSC played a key role in advising the Department of Civil Protection and served as the primary governmental advisor during the COVID-19 outbreak (Capano 2020).

In several EU countries, new managerial structures and mechanisms were established to guide and coordinate actions during the COVID-19

[33] https://emergenze.protezionecivile.gov.it/en/health/coronavirus/technical-scientific-committee-covid-19-official-reports/.

pandemic. These included daily briefing meetings and weekly horizontal meetings involving top management. Examples of countries implementing such measures include Belgium and Croatia (OECD 2023).

New partnerships were also forged with non-governmental actors, including NGOs, academia, and private companies, both at the same level and across different levels of government. For instance, the City of Thessaloniki established partnerships with private hotel companies, the Greek National Tourism Organisation, and the Ministry of Tourism. Local government also collaborated with NGOs to ensure that homeless shelters remained open (OECD 2023).

As for th**e changes in competencies** the Italian government serves as an example, appointing the Chief of the Department of Civil Protection as a commissioner to oversee the management of the emergency. A second commissioner was also appointed with the specific responsibility of strengthening the healthcare infrastructure (Capano 2020).

In this chapter, our primary focus is on exploring European public administration structures. However, it is crucial to acknowledge that not all public employees in the EU Member States were able to work remotely. This includes those involved in healthcare provision, testing and contact tracing, enforcement agencies, as well as various aspects of policy and prison operations, among others (Janssen and Van der Voort 2020) (Table 11.3).

11.6 War in Ukraine

In February 2022, Russia initiated an invasion of Ukraine, prompting a response from the European Union. In March 2022, for the first time, the Council invoked the Temporary Protection Directive (Council Directive 2001/55/EC).[34] This directive granted all individuals displaced from Ukraine the right to reside in the EU for up to three years. They were also entitled to access employment, healthcare, social assistance, housing, and the freedom to move freely within the EU. As of May 31, 2023, more than four million non-EU citizens who had fled Ukraine due to

[34] https://www.europarl.europa.eu/RegData/etudes/ATAG/2023/739365/EPRS_ATA(2023)739365_EN.pdf.

Table 11.3 Types of changes to European public administrations due to COVID-19 pandemic

Type of changes		*Governing level*	
		EU	*Country level*
Organisational/structural	New temporary structure	X	X
	New permanent structure	X	
	Restructuring/mergers		
	Change of the ministry name		
Competencies	Temporary	X	X
	Permanent	X	
Processes	Temporary	X	X
	Permanent		
Actors–human management changes	Flexibility increase	X	X
	Freezing/cuts		
	Capacity building	X	X

Source Authors

the Russian invasion on February 24, 2022, held temporary protection statuses in EU countries.[35]

Beyond the humanitarian and economic aid challenges, EU Member States faced two additional significant challenges related to the conflict in Ukraine: defence aid and the energy crisis. Defence policy in the EU is highly decentralised, with most member states being part of NATO. However, the war in Ukraine necessitated a response in terms of providing defence aid to Ukraine. Additionally, European public administrations had to address the energy challenge as Russia was a major exporter of oil, natural gas, and coal to the European Union. Notably, according to Eurostat, in 2020, the European Union imported 46 per cent of natural gas from Russia, which accounted for 41 per cent of the EU's gross available energy derived from natural gas.[36]

In response to this external shock, the European Union implemented numerous changes to its administration. In regard to **changes in competencies and organisational changes** coordination was strengthened.

[35] https://ec.europa.eu/eurostat/web/products-eurostat-news/w/ddn-20230707-1.

[36] https://ec.europa.eu/eurostat/web/products-eurostat-news/-/ddn-20220328-2.

According to Hamilton (2023), this war led to the unprecedented provision of lethal military assistance by the EU, as the EU serves as a funding and coordination platform for integrated military and security policy in relation to Ukraine. Although the European Peace Facility ('EPF') was originally established in March 2021 for use in Sahel peacekeeping operations. Fiott (2023) argues that due to the war in Ukraine, the EPF has been strategically employed in this context. It is important to note that the structure of the EPF does not involve the EC directly providing weapons. Instead, lethal military assistance provided under the EPF is collectively decided upon by the Ministries of Defence at the EU Council and then implemented by these Ministries themselves.

The European Commission (EC) also introduced the Ukraine Facility to facilitate recovery, reconstruction, and modernisation within the country.[37] This initiative aims to foster key reforms in Ukraine's EU accession process while demonstrating the EU's unwavering commitment to supporting Ukraine amid Russia's persistent aggression and its journey towards EU membership.[38]

In June 2022, the European Commission adopted FAST–CARE (Flexible Assistance for Territories) with the objective of enhancing assistance to EU Member States in response to the displacement caused by the Ukraine crisis. This programme is designed to improve the accessibility and flexibility of cohesion policy funds and incorporates new provisions to ensure cohesion policy investments are as efficient as possible. FAST–CARE builds upon the support previously offered through Cohesion's Action for Refugees in Europe (CARE).[39]

Also in January 2023, the EU initiated the Donor Coordination Platform to enhance the coordination among international donors and financial organisations, ensuring that support is coherent, transparent, and accountable. The Secretariat of the Donor Coordination Platform for Ukraine, which includes the G7 + UA, was established. This Secretariat operates in both a Brussels office hosted by the European Commission

[37] https://neighbourhood-enlargement.ec.europa.eu/system/files/2023-6/COM_2023_338_1_EN_ACT_part1_v6.pdf.

[38] https://www.google.com/url?q=https://eu-solidarity-ukraine.ec.europa.eu/eu-assistance-ukraine/recovery-and-reconstruction-ukraine_en&sa=D&source=docs&ust=1694653464508712&usg=AOvVaw0j9_eBQtDpURhlH64lFmu5.

[39] https://ecre.org/eu-ukraine-response-commission-proposes-to-give-30-per-cent-of-cohesion-funds-for-ukraine-response-to-local-authorities-and-civil-society/.

and a Kyiv office hosted by the Government of Ukraine. The Platform is expected to collaborate closely with Ukrainian authorities to identify, prioritise, and sequence strategic needs within the recovery process.[40]

Several **changes occurred in the organisational setting** as well. Before the war in Ukraine, the European Council handled sanctions towards Russia. However, since February 2022, the Committee of Permanent Representatives in the European Union (COREPER) has been responsible for making decisions on these matters, signifying a change in the institutional design of the European Commission.

In March 2022, the European Union Agency for Criminal Justice Cooperation (Eurojust) provided support for the establishment of a joint investigation team (JIT) to investigate alleged core international crimes committed in Ukraine. Initially, the JIT was established between Ukraine, Lithuania, and Poland, followed by the participation of Estonia, Latvia, Slovakia, and Romania, along with cooperation from the International Criminal Court (ICC), and a Memorandum of Understanding with the United States.[41] The JIT's primary purpose is to facilitate investigations and prosecutions while promoting the exchange of information among the involved parties.

The EU also established the EU Freeze and Seize Task Force to ensure the effective implementation of EU sanctions against listed Russian and Belarusian oligarchs throughout the EU. Its inaugural meeting took place in March 2022. This task force coordinates actions among EU Member States, Eurojust, Europol, and other agencies to seize and, where permitted by national law, confiscate assets owned by Russian and Belarusian oligarchs.[42]

In addition, The European Union Military Assistance Mission in support of Ukraine (EUMAM Ukraine) was established in 2023 with the objective of strengthening the military capabilities of the Ukrainian Armed Forces. The mission's goal is to enable the Ukrainian Armed Forces to effectively protect Ukraine's territorial integrity and sovereignty. As for the changes in competencies the Defence Innovations Scheme (EUDIS) is an initiative led by the European Commission, launched in

[40] https://coordinationplatformukraine.com/.

[41] https://www.eurojust.europa.eu/joint-investigation-team-alleged-crimes-committed-ukraine.

[42] https://ec.europa.eu/commission/presscorner/detail/en/IP_22_1828.

May 2022,[43] with a budget of two billion Euro allocated over a five-year period. EUDIS primarily targets small and medium-sized enterprises (SMEs), encompassing start-ups and other unconventional contributors in the defence sector. The programme supports start-ups and innovators through various means, including hackathons, business coaching, and growth-oriented activities.[44]

Changes in procurement processes were also introduced. The European Commission proposed the Regulation for the Reinforcement of the European Defence Industry through the Common Procurement Act (EDIRPA), which was published in July 2022. EDIRPA establishes a short-term instrument aimed at strengthening the European defence industry through common procurement until December 31, 2025. This instrument will be financed with a budget of three hundred million Euro.

Under EDIRPA, joint purchases must involve at least three member states and should be open to the participation of members of the European Free Trade Association who are also part of the European Economic Area (associated countries).[45] The European Commission has set the ambition to invest 500 million Euro over the period of 2022 to 2024 in joint defence projects.

EDIRPA has access to a total budget of five hundred million Euro to incentivise actions addressing urgent and critical defence product needs, carried out by a consortium of at least three EU Member States. However, it is important to note that EDIRPA is intended as a short-term measure that will pave the way for the creation of the European Defence Investment Programme (EDIP). A longer-term European Defence Investment Programme (EDIP) has been established, with more substantial funding to support joint procurement, including through a value-added tax waiver. The negotiation for EDIP is scheduled for 2023, with plans for it to be launched in 2024.[46]

Countries in close proximity to the Ukrainian frontlines experienced one of the most significant humanitarian displacements on the continent since World War II, as millions of Ukrainians fled the conflict. As of June

[43] https://ec.europa.eu/commission/presscorner/detail/en/IP_22_3283.

[44] https://eudis.europa.eu/about_en.

[45] https://www.europarl.europa.eu/news/en/press-room/20230911IPR04908/meps-vote-to-strengthen-eu-defence-industry-through-common-procurement.

[46] https://www.eesc.europa.eu/en/our-work/opinions-information-reports/opinions/european-defence-investment-programme.

30, 2023, nearly 4.07 million non-EU citizens who had escaped Ukraine due to the Russian invasion on February 24, 2022, were granted temporary protection status in EU countries. The primary EU nations hosting beneficiaries of temporary protection from Ukraine included Germany (1,133,420 individuals, constituting 28 per cent of the total), Poland (977,740, or 24 per cent), and Czechia (349,140, which is 9 per cent of the total).[47] **European public administrations** were thus compelled to respond to this crisis. In this instance, we will predominantly focus on Poland, which, over an extended period, had to manage the largest influx of Ukrainian refugees.

There were several **changes in organisational settings** introduced. For instance, both Czechia and Poland established governmental roles focused on aiding the reconstruction efforts in Ukraine. In Czechia, the Government Commissioner, Tomáš Kopečný, is responsible for coordinating assistance from both state and non-state entities during the Russian aggression. His role also extends to overseeing this coordination during the post-war period.[48] In Poland, Jadwiga Emilewicz assumed the position of Government Delegate for Polish-Ukrainian Development Cooperation and Secretary of State in the Ministry of Funds and Regional Policy. In this capacity, she has worked diligently to strengthen bilateral ties and foster increased collaboration between the two countries.[49]

In addition, in Poland, the Ministry of the Interior and Administration has designated a government plenipotentiary to oversee the coordination of activities conducted by all organisations assisting refugees across various domains. Additionally, each provincial governor (*voivod*) has appointed their own coordinator or plenipotentiary for this purpose.

Furthermore, in March 2022, the Minister of Health appointed a plenipotentiary specifically tasked with facilitating the transfer and continuation of treatment for Ukrainian patients residing in Poland due to the ongoing armed conflict in Ukraine. One of the key responsibilities of

[47] https://ec.europa.eu/eurostat/web/products-eurostat-news/w/ddn-20230809-1.

[48] https://www.google.com/url?q=https://www.vlada.cz/cz/ppov/zmocnenci_vlady/vladni-zmocnenec-pro-rekonstrukci-ukrajiny-202266/&sa=D&source=docs&ust=1694653464512544&usg=AOvVaw0TeKZl0xz5d7vZq6apagIp.

[49] https://www.google.com/url?q=https://bnn.network/breaking-news/jadwiga-emilewicz-appointed-as-polish-government-delegate-for-polish-ukrainian-development-cooperation-and-secretary-of-state/&sa=D&source=docs&ust=1694653464512641&usg=AOvVaw140tXWHHiYFjuf7wy4FWrz.

this role is to coordinate cooperation between Poland and the European Union regarding the transfer of Ukrainian patients residing in Poland for extended medical treatment in another EU Member State (Uścińska 2023).

Thirty-six reception points have been established, also in Poland, to provide various forms of assistance to refugees. At these points, refugees can take a break, access meals, receive medical care and psychological counselling, submit applications for international aid, complete necessary documentation to obtain residency rights, obtain referrals to Ukrainian refugee centres, and obtain information about transportation options to other cities in Poland (Ociepa-Kicińska and Gorzałczyńska-Koczkodaj 2022; Wojtasz 2022).

Shelters were established in major cities, with one of the largest being the Ptak Warsaw in the Warsaw Expo Centre, capable of accommodating up to 20,000 people. However, many refugees chose to remain near the border to remain close to their homes and properties. These shelters took various forms, including collective and private accommodations.[50]

In regard to the **changes in competencies,** additional tasks were carried out by the Social Insurance Institution (ZUS) in Poland (Uścińska 2023). Among other initiatives ZUS has launched a helpline in Ukrainian. In response to war in Ukraine the Polish government established the Aid Fund,[51] which provides financing for all activities and projects necessary to help and integrate Ukrainian refugees.

Changes were also adopted in **competencies and related processes**. The example is the possibility for a voivodeship governor to issue mandatory orders to specified entities—such as self-government bodies, self-government legal persons, or self-government organisational units without legal personality—was introduced. The mandatory orders are issued in the form of immediately enforceable administrative decisions that do not have to be substantiated or even issued in writing (they may be given orally or take the form of a written note or sent by email). Tasks covered by mandatory orders fall within the scope of state government administration for which local administrative units (LAUs) receive

[50] https://www.acaps.org/fileadmin/Data_Product/Main_media/20220525_acaps_briefing_note_poland_ukraine_refugees.pdf.

[51] https://www.en.bgk.pl/funds/aid-fund/.

Table 11.4 Types of changes to European public administrations due to war in Ukraine

Type of changes		*Governing level*	
		EU	*Country level*
Organisational/structural	New temporary structure	X	X
	New permanent structure		
	Restructuring/mergers		
	Change of the ministry name		X
Competencies	Temporary	X	X
	Permanent	X	
Processes	Temporary	X	X
	Permanent	X	
Actors–human management changes	Flexibility increase		
	Freezing/cuts		
	Capacity building		X

Source Authors

funding, and in case they complete them earlier, they are reimbursed the cost (Ociepa-Kicińska and Gorzałczyńska-Koczkodaj 2022).

Also, amendments have been made to the Polish Public Procurement Law that enabled specific kinds of aid for refugees to be bought without applying this act. Public health tasks were thus outsourced without the need to hold a bidding contest.

In addition, our research on **changes related to labels of central public administration units** shows that in Italy the name of the Ministry of Ecological Transition was changed in 2022 to the Ministry of the Environment and Energy Security[52] (Table 11.4).

11.7 Conclusion: Navigating Unprecedented Challenges in the Era of the "Four Horsemen"

The European Union and its Member States have faced an intense barrage of external crises over the past fifteen years, a succession of calamities that, borrowing from apocalyptic imagery, could well be called the

[52] https://www.italianpost.news/meloni-government-ministries-change-name-the-decree/.

"Four Horsemen": economic instability, pandemic, war, and large-scale migrations. These crises, often global in nature, presented unprecedented challenges to the European public administrations and governance structures. Yet, as Jean Monnet opined in 1976,

> *People only accept change when they are faced with necessity, and only recognise necessity when a crisis is upon them.*

While these crises have exerted pressure on the European systems, they have also acted as catalysts for transformative change.

Following Monnet's framework, we note that the crises have had a creative effect on administrative and governance mechanisms. Particularly at the EU level, there has been greater innovation compared to member states. The EU has evolved from a norm-setting apparatus to an executive actor with direct operational engagement. Collective purchases of vaccines or potential shared bids for energy resources and military support for Ukraine have become new responsibilities. This illustrates that the crises have propelled the EU towards deeper integration, altering its administrative and organisational DNA in ways hitherto unthinkable.

The challenges brought on by these crises have led to reforms that delicately balance the strengthening of EU governance and the concerns of national sovereignty. Notable examples can be found in the responses to the Eurozone and migration crises, which have resulted in reforms that incorporate and recognise national sovereignty while enhancing the EU's governance structures. Such a nuanced approach is indicative of the EU's evolving role in an increasingly multipolar world, where it acts both independently and in coordination with other multilateral organisations like the IMF, WHO, and NATO.

Even though this has not been analysed in the chapter, it is also worth noting the last of the horsemen—war in Ukraine—restarted the long-dormant EU enlargement process, which had in the past proven to be the most transformative of all EU policies.

While the EU has tended towards transformative changes, member states have been characterised by more adaptation than creation. However, the Eurozone crisis did trigger some of the most far-reaching organisational changes at the national level, including the establishment of new ministries and revisions to existing governance protocols. Yet, many of these changes at the national level were often temporary and reactive, making it unclear whether they represent enduring shifts in administrative practice.

We can only speculate that the nation states, with their longer political and administrative histories, are more stable units able to absorb challenges of this magnitude with smaller organisational changes. Indeed, these nation states had, unlike the European Union, themselves gone through wars, epidemics, and bankruptcies before.

Crucially, the multilayered nature of the EU, with its complex decision-making procedures and inherent difficulties of collective action, highlights the indispensable role of coordination and collaboration. Lessons from organisational theory reveal that governance structures and coordination mechanisms are pivotal for effectively addressing and solving complex problems like the crises under examination. The necessity of cross-organisational collaboration is especially pronounced in the policy area of crisis management, a field that requires agile and synchronised action across different tiers of governance.

As the European Union and its Member States navigated crises of unprecedented complexity and scale, the integration of specialised knowledge into politically salient decisions has become a focal point. The COVID-19 pandemic offers an illuminating case study in this regard. Decisions about lockdown measures, vaccination campaigns, and border controls required a nuanced understanding of epidemiological models, public health strategies, and economic projections. This highly specialised knowledge had to be synthesised and harmonised with broader policy objectives and political considerations. Policymakers faced the intricate task of balancing the scientific advice with economic imperatives and social tolerance for restrictions, frequently creating new bodies to achieve this objective.

The integration of such specialised knowledge is not just confined to public health crises; it also extends to managing economic meltdowns, responding to security threats, and crafting policies on migration. This trend marks a shift towards decision-making frameworks that are inherently interdisciplinary and require robust systems for the assimilation of expert knowledge. The challenge lies in ensuring that this specialised knowledge is not just tokenistically included but substantively influences the policy outcomes.

Parallel to these developments is the growing concern over a crisis of transparency in decision-making processes. During times of severe crisis, there is often an urgency to act, and this urgency can sometimes undermine the normal procedures for transparent governance. For example, the procurement of vaccines during the early stages of the COVID-19 pandemic saw a wave of expedited contracts that bypassed standard transparency protocols. In another instance, emergency measures enacted to respond to migration flows or security threats have occasionally been implemented without public scrutiny or parliamentary oversight.

These situations create a dilemma: On the one hand, rapid action is needed to mitigate the impact of the crisis; on the other, the lack of transparency can undermine public trust and democratic accountability. The frequent emergence of such transparency crises indicates a need to strike a more effective balance between urgency and openness. This calls for improved mechanisms that not only allow for swift action in times of crises but also maintain the fidelity of transparent, accountable governance.

As we navigate the complexities and uncertainties of a world increasingly shaped by crises, the European public administrations and governance structures find themselves at a critical juncture. While the "Four Horsemen" have laid bare vulnerabilities, they have also offered transformative potential. The past fifteen years serve as both a testament to the resilience of the European systems and a call to action for further innovation, collaboration, and strategic planning. For the EU and its Member States, the adage "***never let a good crisis go to waste***" may indeed capture the essence of their evolving governance in a world marked by permanent crisis. Future scholarship would do well to monitor these changes in the long term to assess their durability and effectiveness in enhancing the problem-solving capacities of both the EU and its constituent nations. A particular salient question is under what circumstances do such crises lead to not just permanent, but also constructive innovations (in sense of institution building) and when do they lead to more paralysis, discord, or even institutional destruction.

Acknowledgements We would like to thank Ester Ziffová, Alexander Duleba and Vladimír Bilčík for their valuable comments.

References

Ahlquist, J., M. Copelovitch, and S. Walter. 2020. The political consequences of external economic shocks: Evidence from Poland. *American Journal of Political Science* 64 (4): 904–920.

Andrews, R., G. Boyne, Larry O'Toole, K. Meier, and R. Walker. 2013. Managing migration? EU enlargement, local government capacity and performance in England. *Public Administration* 91 (1): 174–194.

Angelis, G.D. 2017. Political legitimacy and crisis management in the economic and monetary union: A model of democratic governance. *European Politics and Society* 18 (3): 363–381.

Ansell, C., A. Boin, and A. Keller. 2010. Managing transboundary crises: Identifying the building blocks of an effective response system. *Journal of Contingencies and Crisis Management* 18 (4): 195–207.

Bakir, C., M.K. Coban, and S. Akgunay. 2021. The European Union financial crisis: A critical analysis. In *Oxford research encyclopaedia of politics.*

Bech, E.C., K. Borevi, and P. Mouritsen. 2017. A 'civic turn' in Scandinavian family migration policies? Comparing Denmark, Norway, and Sweden. *Comparative Migration Studies* 5: 1–24.

Béland, D., and R.H. Cox, eds. 2011. *Ideas and politics in social science research.* New York: Oxford University Press.

Benjamin, R., and R. Duvall. 1985. The capitalist state in context. *The Democratic State*, 19–57.

Besley, T., and R. Burgess. 2001. Political agency, government responsiveness and the role of the media. *European Economic Review* 45: 629–640. https://doi.org/10.1016/S0014-2921)0)00133-7.

Bevelander, P., and Anders Hellström. 2019. Pro- and anti-migrant mobilisations in polarised Sweden. In *The refugee reception crisis in Europe: Polarised opinions and mobilisations*, ed. A. Rea, M. Martiniello, A. Mazzola, and B. Meuleman, 75–94. Éditions de l'Université de Bruxelles.

Biermann, F., N. Guérin, S. Jagdhuber, B. Rittberger, and M. Weiss. 2019. Political (non-) reform in the euro crisis and the refugee crisis: A liberal intergovernmentalist explanation. *Journal of European Public Policy* 26 (2): 246–266.

Blondin, D., and A. Boin. 2020. Cooperation in the face of transboundary crisis: A framework for analysis. *Perspectives on Public Management and Governance* 3 (3): 197–209.

Boin, A., and M. Rhinard. 2023. Crisis management performance and the European Union: The case of COVID-19. *Journal of European Public Policy* 30 (4): 655–675.

Bouckaert, G. 2012. *Trust and public administration.*

Bremer, B., P. Genschel, and M. Jachtenfuchs. 2020. Juncker's curse? Identity, interest, and public support for the integration of core state powers. *Journal of Common Market Studies* 58 (1): 56–75.

Capano, G. 2020. Policy design and state capacity in the COVID-19 emergency in Italy: If you are not prepared for the (un) expected, you can be only what you already are. *Policy and Society* 39 (3): 326–344.

Christensen, T., P. Lægreid, and L.H. Rykkja. 2016. Organizing for crisis management: Building governance capacity and legitimacy. *Public Administration Review* 76 (6): 887–897.

Copelovitch, M., J. Frieden, and S. Walter. 2016. The political economy of the euro crisis. *Comparative Political Studies* 49 (7): 811–840.

Darvas, Z. 2010. The impact of the crisis on budget policy in Central and Eastern Europe. *OECD Journal on Budgeting* 10 (1): 1–42.

Deruelle, T., and I. Engeli. 2021. The COVID-19 crisis and the rise of the European Centre for Disease Prevention and Control (ECDC). *West European Politics* 44 (5–6): 1376–1400.

Di Mascio, F., and A. Natalini. 2016. The reform of the public administration: Centralization and reorganization. *Italian Politics* 31 (1): 155–173.

Dreher, A., M.J. Lamla, S.M. Lein, and F. Somogyi. 2009. The impact of political leaders' profession and education on reforms. *Journal of Comparative Economics* 37 (1): 169–193.

European Commission. 2021. Supporting public administrations in EU member states to deliver reforms and prepare for the future. Commission Staff Working Document, SWD(2021) 25 final.

Fioretos, O., T.G. Falleti, and A. Sheingate. 2016. *The Oxford handbook of historical institutionalism*. Oxford University Press.

Fiott, D. 2023. In every crisis an opportunity? European Union integration in defence and the War on Ukraine. *Journal of European Integration* 45 (3): 447–462.

Geertz, C. 1980. Blurred genres: The refiguration of social thought. *The American Scholar*, 165–179.

Green, R.T. 2012. Plutocracy, bureaucracy, and the end of public trust. *Administration & Society* 44 (1): 109–143.

Hamilton, R. E. 2023. *Tanks a lot (well, actually not that many for Ukraine).*

Hamnond, T.H. 1993. Towards a general theory of hierarchy. *Journal of Public Administration Research and Theory.* 3 (1): 120145.

Hannah, A., E. Baekkeskov, and T. Tubakovic. 2022. Ideas and crisis in policy and administration: Existing links and research frontiers. *Public Administration* 100 (3): 571–584.

Heinemann, F., and T. Grigoriadis. 2016. Origins of reform resistance and the Southern European regime. *Empirica* 43: 661–691.

Hood, C., D. Heald, and R. Himaz. 2014. *When the party's over: The politics of fiscal squeeze in perspective*. Oxford University Press.

Howlett, M.P., and K. Saguin. 2018. Policy capacity for policy integration: Implications for the sustainable development goals. Lee Kuan Yew School of Public Policy Research Paper, pp. 18–26.

Jabko, N., and A. Sheingate. 2018. Practices of dynamic order. *Perspectives on Politics* 16 (2): 312–327.

Jabko, N., and M. Luhman. 2020. Reconfiguring sovereignty: Crisis, politicisation, and European integration. In *The European Union beyond the polycrisis?* 75–93. Routledge.

Janssen, M., and H. Van der Voort. 2020. Agile and adaptive governance in crisis response: Lessons from the COVID-19 pandemic. *International Journal of Information Management* 55: 102180.

Jordan, A., and A. Schout. 2006. *The coordination of the European Union: Exploring the capacities of networked governance*. Oxford University Press.

Kettl, D.F. 2015. *The transformation of governance: Public administration for the twenty-first century*. Jhu Press.

Kickert, W. 2012. State responses to the fiscal crisis in Britain, Germany, and the Netherlands. *Public Management Review* 14 (3): 299–309.

Kickert, W.J., and F.B. Van Der Meer. 2011. Small, slow, and gradual reform: What can historical institutionalism teach us? *International Journal of Public Administration* 34 (8): 475–485.

Kickert, W., T. Randma-Liiv, and R. Savi. 2013. Fiscal consolidation in Europe: A comparative analysis. COCOPS deliverable 7.2. http://www.cocops.eu/wp-content/uploads/2013/10/WP7-trend-report_final.pdf.

Kickert, W.J., T. Randma-Liiv, and R. Savi. 2015. Politics of fiscal consolidation in Europe: A comparative analysis. *International Review of Administrative Sciences* 81 (3): 562–584.

Krasner, S.D. 1984. *Approaches to the state: Alternative conceptions and historical dynamics*.

Kuhlmann, S. 2015. Administrative reforms in the intergovernmental setting: Impacts on multi-level governance from a comparative perspective. In *Multi-level governance: The missing linkages. Bingley: Emerald; Series "critical perspectives on international public sector management"*, ed. by S. E. Ongaro, vol. 4, 183–215. Emerald Publishing Limited. https://doi.org/10.1108/S2045-794420150000004008

Kuhlmann, S., and H. Wollmann. 2019. *Introduction to comparative public administration: Administrative systems and reforms in Europe*. Edward Elgar Publishing.

Leibrecht, M., and H. Pitlik. 2015. Social trust, institutional and political constraints on the executive and deregulation of markets. *European Journal of Political Economy* 39: 249–268.

Lodge, M., and C. Hood. 2012. Into an age of multiple austerities? Public management and public service bargains across OECD countries. *Governance: An International Journal of Policy, Administration, and Institutions* 25 (1): 79–101.

Mintrom, M., and P. Norman. 2009. Policy entrepreneurship and policy change. *Policy Studies Journal* 37 (4): 649–667.

Mortensen, P.B., and C. Green-Pedersen. 2015. Institutional effects of changes in political attention: Explaining organisational changes in the top bureaucracy. *Journal of Public Administration Research and Theory* 25 (1): 165–189.

Moorkamp, M., R. Torenvlied, and E.H. Kramer. 2020. Organisational synthesis in transboundary crises: Three principles for managing centralisation and coordination in the corona virus crisis response. *Journal of Contingencies and Crisis Management* 28 (2): 169–172.

Nakrošis, V., R. Vilpišauskas, and V. Kuokštis. 2015. Fiscal consolidation and structural reforms in Lithuania in the period 2008–2012: From grand ambitions to hectic firefighting. *International Review of Administrative Sciences* 81 (3): 522–540.

Niemann, A., and J. Speyer. 2018. A neo-functionalist perspective on the 'European refugee crisis': The case of the European Border and Coast Guard. *JCMS: Journal of Common Market Studies* 56 (1): 23–43.

Nilsson, M., K. Escobar, and H. Ahl. 2023. Labour market integration of refugees in Sweden–Analysing the interactions of CSOs at different levels. *Journal of Ethnic and Migration Studies*, 1–19.

Nolte, I.M., A.M. Bushnell, and M. Mews. 2020. Public administration entering turbulent times: A study of service quality during the refugee crisis. *International Journal of Public Administration* 43 (16): 1345–1356.

Nordlinger, Eric A. 1981. *On the autonomy of the democratic state*. Harvard University Press.

Nunes Silva, C. 2017. Political and administrative decentralisation in Portugal: Four decades of democratic local government. In *Local government and urban governance in Europe*, ed. by C. Nunes Silva and J. Buček, pp. 9–32. Switzerland: Springer.

Ociepa-Kicińska, E., and M. Gorzałczyńska-Koczkodaj. 2022. Forms of aid provided to refugees of the 2022 Russia-Ukraine war: The case of Poland. *International Journal of Environmental Research and Public Health* 19 (12): 7085.

OECD. 2010. Public governance reviews: MENA/OECD governance programme (No 42601087). https://www.oecd.org/mena/governance/42601087.pdf.

OECD. 2022. Public servants and the coronavirus (COVID-19) pandemic: Emerging responses and initial recommendations. https://www.oecd.org/coronavirus/policy-responses/public-servants-and-the-coronavirus-covid-19-pandemic-emerging-responses-and-initial-recommendations-253b1277/.

OECD. 2023. Supporting public administration in Ukraine (No 8d10bb06-en.pdf). https://www.oecd-ilibrary.org/docserver/8d10bb06-en.pdf?expires=1694075910&id=id&accname=guest&checksum=C0EEFB88D89249207BCCF8AD16C4907E.

Pannia, P., V. Federico, A. Terlizzi, and S. D'Amato. 2018. *Comparative report: Legal and policy framework of migration governance*.

Pantazatou, K. 2015. *Promoting solidarity in crisis times: Building on the EU Budget and the EU Funds*. SSRN.

Pearson, C.M., and J.A. Clair. 1998. Reframing crisis management. *Academy of Management Review* 23 (1): 59–76.

Peters, B.G., and J. Pierre. 2010. Economic crisis, public administration, and governance. *Journal of Policy Studies* 25 (1): 59–71.

Peters, B.G., J. Pierre, and T. Randma-Liiv. 2011. Global financial crisis, public administration and governance: Do new problems require new solutions? *Public Organisation Review* 11: 13–27.

Petmesidou, M., and A.M. Guillén. 2022. Europe's green, digital, and demographic transition: A social policy research perspective. *Transfer: European Review of Labour and Research* 28 (3), 317–332.

Pollitt, C. 2010. Cuts and reforms—Public services as we move into a new era. *Society and Economy* 32 (1): 17–31.

Pollitt, C., and G. Bouckaert. 2011. *Continuity and change in public policy and management*. Edward Elgar Publishing.

Posner, P., and J. Blöndal. 2012. Democracies and deficits: Prospects for fiscal responsibility in democratic nations. *Governance* 25 (1): 11–34.

Potter, M. 2012. Still learning to speak and still not being heard: Public administration and the latest financial crisis. *Administration and Society* 44 (3): 367–373.

Quaglio, G., G. Done, F. Cavallin, M.G. Ojeda, and P. Claes. 2023. Experiences of health professionals in EU institutions during the Covid crisis. *International Journal of Disaster Risk Reduction*, 103810.

Rauleckas, R., V. Nakrošis, R. Šnapštienė, and L. Šarkutė. 2016. The impact of public management reforms in Lithuania: Systemic managerial changes and persisting organisational differences. In *Public administration reforms in Europe: The view from the top*, 105–118

Randma-Liiv, T., and W. Kickert. 2017. The impact of the fiscal crisis on public administration reforms: Comparison of 14 European countries. *Journal of Comparative Policy Analysis: Research and Practice* 19 (2): 155–172.

Scholten, P. 2016. Between national models and multi-level decoupling: The pursuit of multi-level governance in Dutch and UK policies towards migrant incorporation. *Journal of International Migration and Integration* 17: 973–994.

Scott, R. J., and E.R. Merton. 2022. *Contingent collaboration: When to use which models for joined-up government*. Cambridge University Press.
Skowronek, S. 1982. *Building a new American State: The expansion of national administrative capacities*. New York: Cambridge University Press.
Telford, E., I. Ortega-Perez, G. Mellon, B. Lacarra, E. Adjadj, C. Madelaine, and Y. Yazdanpanah. 2021. Chronicles of a pandemic: How France coordinated the scientific research response to COVID-19. *Infectious Diseases Now* 51 (8): 641.
Tompson, W. 2010. Reform beyond the Crisis. In *OECD making reform happen: Lessons from OECD countries*, 11–38. Paris: OECD Publishing.
United Nations High Commissioner for Refugees (UNHCR). 2016. *Global trends: Forced displacement in 2015*. Geneva: UNHCR. www.unhcr.org/statistics/unhcrstats/576408cd7/unhcr-global-trends-2015.html.
United Nations High Commissioner for Refugees (UNHCR). 2017. *Policy on emergency preparedness and response, 2017*. Geneva: UNHCR. www.refworld.org/pdfid/59d4d4c54.pdf.
Uścińska, G. 2023. Polish public institutions activity for refugees from Ukraine, with a special focus on the tasks carried out by ZUS. *Social Insurance. Theory and Practice* 155 (4): 53–65.
Valenza, Allessandro, Dea Hrelja, Pietro Celotti, Caterina Casamassima, Michele Alessandrini, Roland Blomeyer, and Nicolo Francescheli. 2022. *COVID-19 response of EU public administration*. European Commission. https://www.europarl.europa.eu/RegData/etudes/STUD/2022/733411/IPOL_STU(2022)733411_EN.pdf.
Vis, B., K. van Kersbergen, and T. Hylands. 2011. To what extent did the financial crisis intensify the pressure to reform the welfare state? *Social Policy and Administration* 45 (4): 338–353.
Wojtasz, A. 2022. Polish local government aid to refugees from Ukraine on the example of the City of Poznań. *Hapsc Policy Briefs Series* 3 (2): 87–92.
Yesilkagit, K., P. Bezes, and J. Fleischer. 2022. What's in a name? The politics of name changes inside bureaucracy. *Public Administration* 100 (4): 1091–1106.
Zaun, N. 2020. Fence-sitters no more: Southern and Central Eastern European Member States' role in the deadlock of the CEAS reform. *Journal of European Public Policy* 29 (2): 196–217. https://doi.org/10.1080/13501763.2020.1837918.
Zhong, K., Y. Liu, and T. Christensen. 2022. Crisis coordination in centralised regimes: Explaining China's strategy for combatting the COVID-19 pandemic. *International Public Management Journal* 25 (7): 1131–1211.

CHAPTER 12

Transnational Threats in Latin America and the Challenges for Public Administration

Alexander Lopez

12.1 A New Approach of Public Administration Beyond the Nation-State in Latin America

Traditionally, studies of public administration have treated the nation-state as the unit of analysis. However, the state and its public administration does not exist in a vacuum; on the contrary now more than ever they are heavily influenced by international issues. Therefore, public administration in Latin America must adjust traditional practices to facilitate the management of the global processes that, in turn, reshape the world. A good example of the challenges for the Latin American states and their public administration is the so-called transnational threats, that come from a variety of sources, including people, networks, and the physical environment. These include violent extremist organisations, movement of people, cyber connectivity, and disruptive climate change.

A. Lopez (✉)
Latin American Centre for Development Administration (CLAD), Heredia, Costa Rica
e-mail: lopezalex100@gmail.com

A. Baimenov and P. Liverakos (eds.), *Public Administration in the New Reality*, https://doi.org/10.1007/978-981-96-3845-1_12

Two elements that increase the challenge in Latin America public administration is that many countries have some regions where the public administration institutions almost do not exist. This spatially uneven nature of the public administrations has been shown to be consequential for a variety of outcomes of interest, including the emergence of transnational threats such as organised crime. Another factor is that some of these public administrations have been weak in providing public value for the most vulnerable people. An opportunity to join a *mara* (youth gangs prevalent in Central America) or a more structured drug trafficking organisation becomes an attractive option.

The conceptual distance between the sovereign state and the global domain of policymaking and administration is narrowing, challenging the prevailing methodological nationalism. The rise of global policy and transnational administration necessitates new conversations for traditional, often domestically focused, public policy, and public administration studies. The term "transnational" administration suggests that while comparative and development-focused administrative and policy studies are important, an exclusive focus on such state-led acts aligns scholars to a methodological nationalism that is no longer as relevant today as it was some forty years ago. There is reason to believe that the transnational dimension of public administration is growing. Whether it is trade, capital flows, migration, or climate change the world is far more interconnected now than it was in 1945. The importance of transnational issues in our everyday lives becomes more evident with each new crisis or threats rendering comprehensive governance structures necessary to ensure that decisions are made accordingly to this new reality.

It is understood that public administration is responsible for ensuring the proper management of public resources, meeting the needs of society, and establishing a cordial and effective relationship between society and the government. In Latin America these have been undermined by the new transnational threats. While living in a densely interconnected international system, the truth is that States have fallen short in providing public value and quality services to the most vulnerable people, and in maintaining solid social stability and security in each of their processes and territories.

The decision-making capacity of political actors in public management is regulated by the existence of a legal framework and an institutional framework, which "determine the capacities for action and the complexity of organisations and the types of coordination that can take place"

(DEMUCA Foundation 2011: 29). However, these mechanisms have not been sufficiently effective in resolving international security issues that have a direct impact on citizen welfare at all political levels. This has generated a generalised erosion of trust and credibility of the public sector as a manager of social welfare.

12.2 Drug Trafficking: The Weakness of the State vis-à-vis Non-State Actors

Drug trafficking is analysed as a transnational threat that undermines national security and transgresses the international system. "Drug trafficking is a global illicit trade that includes the cultivation, manufacture, distribution and sale of substances that are subject to laws prohibiting their trade" (Garfia 2023).

Latin America is recognised as the world's largest producer of cocaine and its derivatives, specifically the Andean region. The latest report from the United Nations Office on Drugs and Crime (UNODC) states that the region "played an important role in the increase between 2020 and 2021 of cocaine production and distribution in the world, after a slowdown caused by the COVID-19 pandemic".[1] The World Cocaine Report 2023 detailed how "coca cultivation soared 35% from 2020 to 2021, a record high and the steepest year-on-year increase since 2016", the UN explained. It added that "the increase is due to both the expansion of coca bush cultivation and improvements in the process of transforming coca leaf into cocaine hydrochloride".

The cultivation and production of cannabis in Latin America is attributed to Mexico, Bolivia, Colombia, and Paraguay as the main producers in the region. On a smaller scale, other substances such as opium and heroin are produced from the poppy plant, which is grown optimally in countries such as Mexico, Guatemala, Colombia, and Peru thanks to their geographical and climatic conditions.

Regarding the consumption of these substances, the largest scale demands are received from northern countries, e.g., the United States. The United States, to no one's surprise, is considered the world's largest

[1] Sorto, M. (16.03.2023). *América Latina tiene un papel importante en el incremento de producción y distribución de cocaína en el mundo tras la pandemia, indica reporte de la ONU*. CNN. https://cnnespanol.cnn.com/2023/03/16/america-latina-juega-papel-importante-incremento-produccion-distribucion-cocaina-mundo-pandemia-onu-orix/.

drug consumer and is currently undergoing a state of emergency due to the so-called Fentanyl Crisis, "a synthetic analgesic 50 times more potent than heroin" (Matza 2024). In addition, a significant demand comes from the European continent. According to the Cocaine Insights Report, produced by the United Nations Office on Drugs and Organised Crime (UNODC) and EUROPOL, one of the main security issues facing the European Union today is cocaine trafficking (Dudley 2016). "According to recent estimates, some 4.4 million people used cocaine in Western and Central Europe in 2020, making it the second most popular drug in the region after cannabis" (UNODC and EUROPOL 2021).

The main actors in this mega-trend are the criminal groups operating in each of the countries that make up the Latin American region and the other actors with whom commercial dynamics are established, as well as those who regulate and intervene in this illegal activity. In Colombia, for example, the northern valley cartel and FARC are identified; in Brazil, the First Capital Command (PCC) and the Red Command are present; in Peru, the Shining Path and MRTA organisations dominate; and in Mexico, whose organisations are more internationally renowned, the Zetas and the Sinaloa cartel are identified. All of them are dedicated to the production and commercialisation of cocaine to different markets; using land, sea, and some air routes; and using force and repression to dominate vulnerable territories (Mejías 2014: 84).

Regarding the main drug trafficking routes, in the Caribbean area, there is extensive maritime and air trade between Puerto Rico and an entire geographic chain where traffickers of various nationalities converge. In addition, Puerto Rico and the U.S. Virgin Islands are the closest ports to the United States, so the Caribbean area continues to be the one of the most significant routes for transporting drugs from South America to the United States (Arriagada and Hopenhayn 2000: 16).

Colombia, thanks to its geographic and bio-oceanic conditions, serves as a shipper of cocaine and Ecuador and Venezuela also serve as countries that send cocaine by air to Central American countries and Mexico. From these countries, cocaine is sent to the United States by one of three main land routes to avoid the strictest controls by the authorities. These routes are:

The Pacific route that goes to Tijuana on its way to the eastern United States and as far as Vancouver in Canada. The Central route that goes through Zacatecas to Ciudad Juarez and reaches California and the central United States. And the shortest: the Gulf route that goes through

Texas to New York. These are the same routes that migrants follow, who drug traffickers use as mules. They are subjected to the dangers of the disputes between Sinaloa and Jalisco on the central and eastern routes (Villaverde 2021).

Finally, transit regions such as Central America should be considered. "It is estimated that up to 80% of the drugs that travel from the south to the United States transit through the countries of the Northern Triangle" (Guevara 2021). Likewise, due to its geographic conditions, Brazil is considered a high transit country in the area. It "has been exploited as a transit country, given its large Amazonian River network, the size of its territory and, therefore, the availability of poorly controlled transit areas" (Garfia 2023).

12.3 Challenges of Public Administration in the Context of Drug Trafficking as a Mega-trend

In a more in-depth analysis, we consider those drivers that have a direct impact on the implementation of organised crime in the political and social systems of the countries in question. This threat is inserted in national governments due to the governance crises that have been present in Latin America for several decades, particularly in terms of legitimacy, effectiveness, and efficiency. In the case of drug trafficking, it is these criminal groups (DTOs) that provide services and respond to the pressures and demands of populations living on the periphery.

In the first place, the weakness of the state is identified as a determining factor in the little or no protection of vulnerable populations, young people, and women, who live daily with these organisations and experience the consequences of drug trafficking first hand. According to experts, Latin American countries are currently suffering an unprecedented security crisis due to the territorial expansion of the large cartels and the inability of governments to meet the security needs demanded by the population.

Organised illegal drug crime along with prohibitionist policies implemented in the previous century and the declared "war on drugs"; contribute to the increase in murders and violence due to the territorial governance of criminal groups (Viscardi and Tenenbaum 2023: 7). "Globally, criminal gangs with territorial control increased 23% between

2021 and 2023, reports the Global Organised Crime Index". This has led to Latin America being characterised as the most violent region in the world in recent years. On the other hand, it must be considered that this dynamic is immersed in important economic, technological, and globalisation processes.

Regardless of the level of development of organised crime in each Latin American country, the fact is that both for the development of their activities, as well as to achieve "laundering" the origin of their profits, they cannot do without the legal order, even though their nature is illegal. It needs a financial system and economic institutions whose operations are guaranteed by the State, but at the same time there must be enough informality and economic and financial marginality to be able to develop the business in the formal system (Mejías 2014: 89). Latin America is the ideal scenario to conduct these processes in a legal financial system, but with important legal-functional gaps which do not allow these activities to be identified as illicit; and consequently, organised crime is inserted into the national and regional economy.

The third driver goes hand in hand with the previous point. Drug trafficking, being an economic activity nevertheless, it is a source of income for socially vulnerable families; which are also social ghosts in the eyes of governments, as the presence of the government and its institutions, in certain parts of the country, are almost non-existent leaving the vacuum left by public institutions filled by other structures; which in many cases are not strictly national, but transnational. From the cultivation and production to the transportation and commercialisation of these narcotic and psychotropic substances, they generate job opportunities, whose income is higher than that of a formal job. This represents, in the medium and long term, a loss of productivity and schooling in these populations; consequently it constitutes a setback in the region's development.

In Mexico, for example, the drug cartels are positioned in fifth place as the most important generators of employment in the North American country, above important companies such as FEM, Walmart, Manpower, etc. According to a report by Science Magazine, these organisations "recruit 350 to 370 members a week, making them the largest recruiter in the country" (Gallegos 2023).

Based on this, academics and experts question the role and actions of Latin American public administrations to face this transnational threat. What is being done in terms of public policy to combat drug trafficking in

Latin America? Throughout history, all Latin American countries coincide in applying prohibitionist and repressive policies under the so-called War on Drugs. "These are based on the repression of production, interdiction of trafficking and distribution, as well as criminalisation of consumption" (Mejías 2014: 94). However, the results have been deficient and limited.

Several Latin American countries also adhere to international instruments of the United Nations System on international drug control, such as the 1961 Single Convention on Narcotic Drugs, as amended by the 1972 Protocol; the 1972 Convention on Psychotropic Substances; and the 1988 United Nations Convention against Illicit Traffic in Narcotic Drugs and Psychotropic Substances. Countries such as Chile, Colombia, Bolivia, and the Dominican Republic have formulated national plans that coordinate policies, programmes, and measures of a preventive and control nature hand in hand with an integrated information system (Arriagada and Hopenhayn 2000: 29).[2]

Different countries in the region have designed policies or programmes aimed at both supply repression and demand reduction. In the first case, actions are aimed at eradicating illicit crops and drug production centres (in producer countries), developing international cooperation in the control of trafficking and judicial matters, and improving the legal framework for criminalising supply and related crimes such as money laundering. Regarding drug use, governments seek to prevent drug use at an early age, discourage the use of illicit drugs among the most vulnerable sectors of society and reduce the harm caused by drugs (Arriagada and Hopenhayn 2000: 29).

However, despite these efforts, the institutional framework has been undermined by drug trafficking and has had to deal with corruption and the infiltration of drug trafficking into their political systems. "The study of the relationship between politicians, elites and traffickers makes it possible to formulate that the complicity of these agents is conscious and responds to a delegation of central power by the State to formal and de facto powers in the peripheries" (Díaz 2023: 130).

[2] Bolivia's Plan Dignity "which is based on the eradication of surplus and illegal coca crops, and the application of a solid alternative development policy with social investments in infrastructure and financial resources" or Plan Colombia "which faces the problems associated with both the drug economy and social and political violence" (Arriagada and Hopenhayn 2000: 32).

Despite the existence of rules and procedures that are predetermined by the institutional framework and its structures, we see in the case of drug trafficking, moments in which these rules and procedures are violated or omitted by those who are the policymakers. This also means that the behaviour of institutions and the implementation of public policy that has been designed nationally is in many cases influenced by forces operating beyond the national borders (Vallejo and Fergadiotti 2017: 17). Most of these violations begin long before the authorities come to power. They originate through reason understood as will, as explained by Vallejo and Fergadiotti, through extortion and bribes of political campaign payments in exchange for favours between state actors who infringe on their power and criminal organisations that seek certain protection and favour from the authorities to conduct their illicit activities.

A recent example was the trial facing former Honduran President Juan Orlando Hernandez Alvarado in the United States for his ties to drug trafficking. "The former president was accused by U.S. prosecutors of facilitating an international drug trafficking network that moved at least 500 tons of cocaine through Honduras to the United States".[3] In addition to these accusations, he has been accused of "accepting bribes from drug traffickers, including providing protection for drug labs and cocaine shipments".[4]

Colombia is another country with a long history of corruption and infiltration of drug trafficking in its political system. Although in many cases it follows the same pattern of infiltration already explained, in others it is due to the use of force through intimidation or violence; where more than personal enrichment, personal life prevails; such is the case of narcoterrorist attacks.

In a more positive dimension, it is important to mention that the transnational dimension can be also seen in the national policies developed to fight against narcotraffic. Thus, efforts such as the one being undertaken by Costa Rica with the support of the Government of the United States. In view of the considerable number of homicides that are

[3] Soto, M; and Santana, M. (07.02.2024). *Exjefe de la Policía de Honduras, vinculado a expresidente Juan Orlando Hernández, se declara culpable de narcotráfico en EE.UU.* CNN. https://cnnespanol.cnn.com/2024/02/07/exjefe-policia-nacional-honduras-vinculado-expresidente-juan-orlando-hernandez-se-declara-culpable-narcotrafico-ee-uu-orix/.

[4] InSight Crime. (28.06.2024). *Juan Orlando Hernández*. https://insightcrime.org/es/noticias-crimen-organizado-honduras/juan-orlando-hernandez/.

reported daily, the wave of violence and the crisis of insecurity that the country is registering; the fight against drug trafficking has become an urgent issue for national authorities, who have joined forces and generated transnational policies through the U.S. embassy in Costa Rica.

The so-called Joint Patrol Agreement, approved by the Law 7929, "is an international legal instrument—with the status of a treaty—revised and amended by the Constitutional Chamber". This is part of a set of rules or provisions necessary for the conduct of a series of joint operations between the U.S. Armed Forces and the Costa Rican Public Force within the territorial waters of the country in criminal matters. Among the most recent actions that have been generated within the framework of this agreement is to allow U.S. ships with high technology to patrol Costa Rican national waters, as well as to train the personnel of the National Coast Guard.

In conclusion, the incidence of drug trafficking in public policy is growing exponentially and cannot be normalised. Latin American countries must work hard to eradicate all these criminal networks and clean up their institutions. Combating drug trafficking is not an easy task; it will require efforts at the regional level through inter-institutional and intersectoral work, with a network logic to be effective and to meet the needs of all the populations that are vulnerable to this threat.

12.4 Migration as a New Transnational Threat

Migration is understood as the "movement of population to another State or within the territory of the same State" (IOM 2006: 38); as well as a human right, whose objective is centred on the search for better living conditions (Gutiérrez et al. 2020). It generates great concern for national security and the effects it has on the economies of countries; but even more importantly, it requires greater attention from the authorities since it violates the security and human rights of those who decide for different reasons to leave their country of origin.

Migration as a social phenomenon has represented a process of global human transformation and re-definition of international relations. Although it is not a recent phenomenon, the twenty-first century has been characterised by a constant growth of migratory waves throughout the world, and Latin America has been no exception. This region registers the largest migratory flows in the world, presenting a considerable increase compared to previous years. "More than 41 million Latin Americans live outside their country of origin, making the region the one with the largest number of migrants in the world".[5]

The general panorama of migration flows in Latin America points to three general trends. First, the migration flows in South America, which is characterised by receiving international migrants from other regions such as Europe, Asia, or Africa. "By mid-2020, it is estimated that South America has 10.9 million international migrants, and that 21% of this migrant population is of extra-regional origin" (IOM Regional Office for South America 2022).

South America is also recognised for the Venezuelan crisis which has caused one of the major human displacements of today. "As of June 2023, 7.3 million people had left the country, and 6.1 million Venezuelan migrants were residing in other Latin American and Caribbean countries".[6] On the other hand, the Darien Gap—the land border between Panama and Colombia—recorded a total of 501,297 migrants crossing the border by the end of November 2023 (PAHO 2023), which represents a year-on-year increase of more than 86% compared to the previous year (IOM 2023).

The second trend focuses on Central America. This registers a population of at least 3.8 million Central Americans in the United States, of which about 1.9 million were residing there irregularly, representing an increase of 24% since 2010 (Babich and Batalova 2021). As a transit region, the flow of migrants circulating in it, according to the Pan American Health Organisation (PAHO) "has almost tripled between 2022 and 2023" (PAHO 2023). In addition, it is estimated that there are between 200 and 300 thousand Nicaraguan migrants in Costa Rica, the main destination of migrants from that country (Martínez 2020). Moreover, the countries of the Northern Triangle (NT) have a significant migratory flow to the United States.[7] For 2018, the Inter-American Development

[5] Hernández, E. (30.06.2023). *La migración vista como una gran oportunidad para el desarrollo*. El País. https://elpais.com/america/termometro-social/2023-06-30/la-migracion-vista-como-una-gran-oportunidad-para-el-desarrollo.html.

[6] Muñoz, F. (21.07.2023). *Migración en América Latina y el Caribe*. Banco Interamericano de Desarrollo. https://blogs.iadb.org/conocimiento-abierto/es/migracion-america-latina/.

[7] Organización Panamericana de la Salud (OPS). (18.12.2023). *Aumento de la migración en las Américas en 2023: retos para garantizar la salud de las personas*

Bank (IDB) reported that at least three million Central American citizens belonging to the northern triangle, live in the North American country, mostly in an irregular condition. "The stock of migrants represents 23% of the population of El Salvador, eight percent of the population of Honduras and six percent of the population of Guatemala" (Abuelafia 2018).

Finally, a third trend records migration flows from Mexico and the eastern border with the United States. "The International Organisation for Migration (IOM) reported that irregular migration in Mexico increased 62% in the first eight months of 2023 compared to the same period in 2022" (PAHO 2023). Likewise, 22,083 Ecuadorians and 166,748 Venezuelans have been detected between January and November 2022 at the southwest land border of the United States (IOM 2023).

These figures demonstrate the density of the threat faced by Latin American public administrations and the urgency of a joint response that provides optimal conditions to protect these populations from the obstacles derived from governmental action of a dissuasive and punitive nature, the inclemency of the tropical climate and geographical features, and criminal gangs that are settled along the way in an attempt to rob them of the little they can carry with them on their journey. It is imperative to create and implement public policies that prioritise the safety of these populations and their human rights, without affecting the national security interests of the Latin American States.

Whatever the circumstances that give rise to migration and its effects on the countries of origin, transit, or destination, it is certain that human beings have the right to seek better living conditions and greater opportunities for personal and family fulfilment. However, it cannot be ignored that poorly informed migration can lead to dangerous scenarios of vulnerability. Latin America is one of the regions whose demographic, economic, historical, socioeconomic, and political characteristics generate greater vulnerability for the migrant population.

An alert for the public administration is the regional figures which reflect that the population with the highest migration rate are children and adolescents. Along the way, they are constantly vulnerable to being

migrantes y respuesta de la Organización Panamericana de la Salud. https://www.paho.org/es/noticias/18-12-2023-aumento-migracion-americas-2023-retos-para-garantizar-salud-personas-migrantes#:~:text=La%20din%C3%A1mica%20de%20la%20migraci%C3%B3n,el%20mismo%20periodo%20de%202022.

detained, are exposed to human trafficking, run the risk of suffering sexual violence and discrimination, and do not have health services or adequate food conditions, which has serious repercussions on their physical and mental health.

It is also important to consider the smuggling of migrants as one more scenario of vulnerability in the migratory context. Complex drug trafficking networks and criminal organisations use migrants to illicitly transport their shipments and fortify their human trafficking networks. "The United Nations Office on Drugs and Crime (UNODC) notes that by 2018, about 45% of the—globally—identified victims of trafficking were migrants" (Klein 2022).[8] Furthermore, figures indicate that "more than two-thirds of victims in the Americas are trafficked for sexual exploitation, while nearly one-third are trafficked for labour exploitation".[9]

12.5 Migration and the Institutional Capacity of the States

Given these scenarios, it is imperative to look at what Latin American institutions are doing, to analyse the discourses that promote certain ways of dealing with the migration phenomenon, and to critically review the public policies implemented in the region. According to the Sixth State of the Region Report,[10] there is an important share of responsibility of the States in terms of their institutional capacity to manage not only the transit of migratory flows, but also resettlement and mitigation of the vulnerabilities faced by the population (PEN 2021: 397). However, the States of the region are outdated in terms of legislation and poorly prepared in terms of public policies.

One of the biggest problems facing the region, regardless of whether they are developed countries, is the development of policies based on the ideological beliefs of the time and not on the country's vision. For

[8] Savoca, F; Vásquez, M; and Hidalgo, N. (15.11.2022). *Cómo luchamos contra la trata de personas en América Latina y el Caribe?* Banco Interamericano de Desarrollo (BID). https://blogs.iadb.org/igualdad/es/trata-de-personas-en-america-latina/.

[9] Counter Trafficking Data Collaborative (CTDC). https://www.ctdatacollaborative.org/.

[10] https://hdl.handle.net/20.500.12337/8115.

this reason, it is common to see changes in the different administrations regarding such important phenomena as migration. The United States, as the main destination country for Latin American migrants, is no exception. From political figures as particular as Donald Trump to the current President Biden, there has been an evolution of proposals for the benefit of their country, under the umbrella of the discourse of security and national sovereignty; however, humanitarian measures have not been framed with global awareness.

It has not been possible to address migration as a multilevel governance problem, as well as in its multidimensional manner, in Latin America. States should seek a migration management that integrates elements of national security, shared benefits through regular migration, and human rights, as pointed out by Mármora (2010). Consequently, Latin America would be able to "turn international migration into a more orderly, manageable and predictable process" (Neira 2020: 426). The migration phenomenon present in Latin America will continue to represent a major challenge for the Latin American States and other actors in the region. The day that the administrations of developed countries understand that migration is a survival issue and not a problem, will be the moment when they will be able to develop dignified and effective policies. Otherwise, there will be no walls or barbed wire to stop the human desire to survive.

The aforementioned vulnerabilities should be one of the main drivers of alliances and collaboration networks among actors at all political levels, in order to achieve a greater degree of coordination and coherence to achieve an international policy that adjusts to the new migratory reality—causes, consequences and national and regional impacts—that is being experienced at the global level. International cooperation will be a fundamental tool for strengthening the current mechanisms of regional migration governance and for the creation of public policies that, under the premise of shared responsibility, provide adequate attention to the phenomenon in question. In short, it is necessary to migrate towards a new public management that allows for a regeneration of public policies that are adapted to the changing political, economic, and social contexts, currently being experienced due to globalisation; and that are effective in responding to the new mega-trends that concern societies of the twenty-first century.

An example of the need for a transnational approach is found in Central America, more specifically in Costa Rica, where the migration crisis in the Central American region has reached record levels in recent years.

According to official data from the Panamanian Government and the International Organization for Migration, more than 400,000 people crossed the Darien until September 2023. This represents almost double the number registered in all of 2022.[11] The case of Costa Rica attracts special attention due to its dual role in the region as a transit and destination country. As well as the way in which the authorities have dealt with this phenomenon.

During the ministerial meeting of the Los Angeles Declaration on Migration and Protection held on 7 May 2024, in Guatemala, Mr. Arnoldo André, Foreign Minister of the Republic, highlighted Costa Rica's efforts to provide safe, regular, and humanitarian attention to migrants transiting the country and at the same time to the host populations.

However, these efforts have not been sufficient; and it has been the President of the Republic himself, Rodrigo Chaves, who on several occasions has pointed out the inability to address this phenomenon in an individualistic manner. The Costa Rican Government is therefore advocating the generation and implementation of public policies with a transnational approach to provide a more pragmatic and comprehensive response to this problem that plagues the region.

"The Costa Rican President emphasised the need to make joint political decisions from Canada to Ecuador to "avoid disorder and chaos in the region". He also made a latent call to the Government of Colombia to join this transnational initiative and "help identify people who could be accepted in the United States according to U.S. immigration regulations".[12]

This dynamic responds to the versatility of the phenomenon and to the limited and limited capacity of national governments to provide an independent and forceful response. In the specific case of Costa Rica, the country does not have the economic or institutional resources to deal with the high rates of migration registered in the country, which is why it relies on international organisations and urges that this phenomenon be addressed jointly. This will allow for more robust migration governance

[11] France24. (07.10.2023). *Los presidentes de Panamá y Costa Rica se reúnen para abordar la crisis migratoria*. https://www.france24.com/es/am%C3%A9rica-latina/20231007-los-presidentes-de-panam%C3%A1-y-costa-rica-se-re%C3%BAnen-para-abordar-la-crisis-migratoria.

[12] Ibid.

mechanisms and closer cooperation ties with countries such as the United States, whose contribution will make it possible to address migration in its multidimensionality in a safe and regular manner, without burdening this task on countries that have not generated conditions to promote the migration phenomenon directly, and yet have been extremely affected.

12.6 Latin American Vulnerability to Climate Change

Anthropogenic climate change has produced considerable long-term shifts in the world's biophysical stability. The global surface temperature has risen by 1.1 °C between 2011 and 2020 as compared to the period of 1850–1900.[13] As a result, negative impacts and subsequent losses and damages, where vulnerable communities are disproportionately affected, are impossible to eradicate but possible to reduce. Moreover, global greenhouse gas (GHG) emissions keep escalating with unequal historical and ongoing contributions that create future challenges. The current situation forecasts that exceeding the 1.5 °C limit above pre-industrial levels, which is highly probable under the business-as-usual scenario, will have devastating consequences unless significant transformations are made internationally and within state borders (IPCC 2023).

Latin America and the Caribbean (LAC) generate an estimated 7% of GHG emissions, while they represent around 8% of the world's population and 6% of its Gross Domestic Product (GDP). However, the region stands among the most vulnerable territories to climate change. Its contribution to global emissions is minimal, while it suffers many global consequences related to economic activities, ecosystems, and social welfare (Cárdenas and Orozco 2022). Most countries in the region base their economic development on natural resources or ecosystem services; for example, agriculture represents a share of value added of 6.6% compared to OECD countries 1.8% (OECD 2023). Thus, Latin America suffers from direct risks from economic climate-related losses and indirect risks due to impacts on its highly environment-dependent economic activities.

[13] NASA. (12.01.2024). *El análisis de la NASA confirma que 2023 fue el año más cálidoregistrado*. https://www.nasa.gov/news-release/el-analisis-de-la-nasa-confirma-que-2023-fue-el-ano-mas-calido-registrado/#:~:text=En%20general%2C%20la%20Tierra%20fue,mantenimiento%20de%20los%20registros%20modernos.

Climate change has not been central to state affairs in Latin America. It is a reality that until recently, the lack of proper institutionalised mechanisms has made it seem like a peripheral problem rather than a central and cross-cutting issue that has the potential to achieve better and more equitable solutions in traditional areas such as healthcare, education, and the economy. It is no longer just an added value but a necessity due to its increasing impact on every aspect of the traditional nation-state.

"Without concerted climate action, by 2050 over 17 million people in LAC could be forced to move to escape slow onset climate impacts" (World Bank Group 2022). In addition, ECLAC,[14] in 2023, highlighted eight key areas of risks exacerbated by climate change: food insecurity, life and infrastructure, water insecurity, severe health impacts, surpassing infrastructure and public service systems, large-scale changes and biome shifts, ecosystems associated with coral reefs, and socioecological systems in coastal areas.[15] Tourism and poverty are the other two areas Bárcena et al. (2020) emphasised when addressing LAC.

For the above element investing in mitigation efforts like generating electricity through renewable sources, adopting improved agricultural practices, achieving net-zero deforestation rates, promoting e-mobility, or utilising nature-based solutions can stimulate innovation and strengthen economic growth. However, it requires significant structural change. From 2010 to 2019, the world saw a decrease in emissions in relation to GDP (decarbonisation) at an average rate of 0.9% per year. To meet the targets set by the Nationally Determined Contributions (NDCs), this rate must increase by 4–5 times, and to achieve the climate goals outlined in the Paris Agreement by 6–8 times (ECLAC 2023).

Moreover, taking early action in adaptation and mitigation can reduce development gaps and boost economies with a benefit–cost ratio ranging from 2:1 to 10:1, which means that for every unit invested, the return can be doubled to ten times. The ratio can sometimes be higher. However, for the Nation-States climate action is often seen as a burden, but in reality, it is highly advantageous in the long run. Failing to take sufficient action to protect the environment will result in negative consequences in every aspect of development. Thus, the region needs to realise the positive impact of early and sufficient mitigation and adaptation measures

[14] https://www.cepal.org/en.

[15] https://repositorio.cepal.org/items/d3aa85f8-ef71-4161-9b08-607efb0c98d4.

and prioritise their comparative advantages in creating and implementing policies of public value.

The United Nations Framework Convention for Climate Change (UNFCCC),[16] while not the first or only existing regime on the matter, has provided a standardised instrument that creates a synergy in the climate-related international agenda. The Conference of the Parts (COP), with its most crucial treaty being the 2015 Paris Agreement,[17] works under its umbrella and, for the most part, sets commitments that the Parties should achieve and abide by to create public policy within borders while accessing international dialogue and cooperation spaces. This makes domestic and foreign policy synergy vital in creating climate-related strategies. First, it sets the foundation for the region to work as a block and achieve international cooperation to reach its determined goals while taking advantage of its strategic strengths. Joint strategies can be highly valuable in regions with vulnerability to climate change.

Climate change and its subsequent effects significantly impact regional and global development. The consequences of climate change are felt in every aspect of state affairs; therefore, climate change should be conceptualised as one of the most important transborder issues that the region is facing.

12.7 Importance of Transnational Public Policy for Dealing with Climate Change

There are two areas in which one can see, precisely, the transnational nature of climate change: International economy and security. In the first case, climate change is intricately linked to the international economy for several reasons. Firstly, the impacts of climate change, such as extreme weather events, sea-level rise, and shifts in agricultural productivity, can disrupt global supply chains, trade routes, and markets, affecting economic activities worldwide. Additionally, efforts to mitigate and adapt to climate change require substantial investments in renewable energy, infrastructure, technology, and sustainable practices, that require international cooperation. Furthermore, international agreements and regulations aimed at addressing climate change, such as emissions

[16] https://unfccc.int/resource/docs/convkp/conveng.pdf.

[17] https://unfccc.int/sites/default/files/english_paris_agreement.pdf.

reduction targets and carbon pricing mechanisms, can influence trade patterns, market dynamics, and investment decisions across borders.

The second area is related to the fact that climate change is increasingly recognised as a significant threat to international security due to its potential to exacerbate existing geopolitical tensions, trigger conflicts, and destabilise regions. For instance, climate change can lead to resource scarcity, such as water and arable land, which can intensify competition among nations and communities. This competition may escalate into conflicts over access to vital resources, particularly in regions already facing political instability. In addition, could have an impact on migration and displacement, thus, rising sea levels, extreme weather events, and other climate-related impacts can force populations to migrate in search of safer living conditions and livelihoods. Large-scale migration can strain host countries, increase social tensions, and even spark conflicts over resources and territory. Finally, climate change could reshape geopolitical dynamics by altering strategic interests, access to resources, and regional power balances. For example, melting ice in the Arctic is opening new shipping routes and access to natural resources, leading to increased competition among Arctic states and other global powers.

In the Latin American context climate change in Latin America is perceived as a transnational issue due to several key factors among them that many countries share vulnerabilities: Many countries in Latin America are highly vulnerable to the impacts of climate change, such as extreme weather events, sea-level rise, and changing precipitation patterns. These impacts do not respect national borders and can have far-reaching consequences that extend beyond individual countries. The above creates cross-border impacts that can exacerbate existing environmental, social, and economic challenges in Latin America, including water scarcity, food insecurity, and natural disasters. These challenges often spill across borders, requiring regional cooperation to address effectively. In addition, Latin America is home to numerous transboundary resources, such as rivers, forests, and marine ecosystems, which are vulnerable to the impacts of climate change. Managing these shared resources sustainably requires cooperation among countries to mitigate risks and ensure their long-term viability.

Finally, as it has been mentioned climate change can drive migration and displacement in Latin America, as people seek refuge from environmental degradation, natural disasters, and livelihood disruptions. This movement of people can strain social, economic, and political systems across borders, necessitating regional approaches to address the root causes and consequences of displacement.

It is important to stress that some of the most important transboundary resources in Latin America include:

a. *Freshwater Rivers*: Several major rivers in Latin America form a transboundary river basin, such as the Amazon, Lempa, Usumacinta, Paraguay-Paraná, and La Plata rivers. These transborder rivers represent in the case of South America more than 40% of the regional territory providing freshwater for drinking, agriculture, industry, and ecosystems to multiple countries.
b. *Forest Ecosystems*: The Amazon rainforest, the largest tropical rainforest in the world, spans multiple countries in South America, including Brazil, Peru, Colombia, and several others. These forests provide critical ecosystem services, such as carbon sequestration, biodiversity conservation, and regulation of the water cycle, which benefit the entire region and the world.
c. *Marine Fisheries*: Latin America is bordered by both the Pacific and the Atlantic Oceans, providing access to valuable marine resources. For instance, the Eastern Tropical Pacific Ocean comprises the waters of Colombia, Costa Rica, Ecuador, and Panama. These valuable waters are characterised by an extraordinary number of endemic, native and migratory species, and are key habitats for whales, tuna, rays, sea turtles and birds, as well as the highest concentrations of sharks in the world. Transboundary fisheries, such as those for tuna, anchovies, and shrimp, support livelihoods and economies in coastal communities across multiple countries.
d. *Mineral Resources*: Latin America is rich in mineral resources, including copper, gold, silver, lithium, and oil, which are often found in transboundary regions. The region has abundant natural resources, and the extractive sectors have often influenced the region's economic development. Nearly 4% of the Gross Domestic Product (GDP) of Latin America and the Caribbean comes from the extractive sector, a figure equivalent to the value generated by agriculture. Mining exports account for close to 50% of total exports in some countries such as Chile and Peru.
e. *Biodiversity Hotspots*: Latin America is home to several biodiversity hotspots, such as the Andes Mountains, the Chocó-Darién region, and the Cerrado savannas, which span multiple countries. These

hotspots harbour unique species and ecosystems of global significance and require coordinated conservation efforts to protect their biodiversity and ecological integrity.

f. *Hydropower Potential*: Latin America has significant hydropower potential, with many rivers suitable for dam construction to generate electricity. Transboundary hydropower projects, such as the Itaipu, have a profound impact on the development of energy national public policy in Brazil and Paraguay. This project has constituted an entity named Itaipu Binational, entity equally owned by the Brazilian Government (through Eletrobras) and the Paraguayan Government (through Ande).

For all the above elements environmental public policy cannot be conceptualised and operationalised only at national level, the transnational dimension is required if countries in Latin America want to be effective and efficient when developing public policy. Thus, cooperation among countries is crucial to sustainably manage these transboundary resources, address common challenges, and promote regional integration and development in Latin America.

In the international arena, Latin American countries have had difficulties in presenting a unified negotiation block at the UNFCCC, being rather dispersed in different alliances, such as BASIC (Brazil, South Africa, India, and China), AOSIS (Alliance of Small Island States), and AILAC (Independent Alliance of Latin America and the Caribbean). Moreover, some countries participate in more than one negotiation block, like Costa Rica's participation in G-77 and China and AILAC. "Taking into consideration the need for financial support for climate action throughout Latin America, this heterogeneity of positions affects the region's overall bargaining power" (Solorio 2024: 6).

The State public value understood as the collective benefits and contributions the state provides to its citizens and society as a whole present an extra complex situation because achieving goals depends on variables that are not wholly under state or border control and, in most cases, must be reached through international technical and financial cooperation. Along with the specific needs come intertwined complexities, such as becoming a regional priority to receive the cooperation flows, which, as time passes, will need to increase. For this reason, transnational public policy as well as a multilevel approach is required when addressing climate-related issues.

Thus, governments are faced with global and transboundary challenges that must be addressed domestically and through the multilateral system simultaneously. This creates another risky disbalance that needs to be managed. To deal with these challenges, governments must design parallel foreign policies that can work with external causes that have immediate and future consequences for the state.

In sum, cooperation among Latin American nations is crucial to mitigate and adapt to climate change because no single country can effectively address it alone. Climate change transcends borders, and its impacts require collective action on a global scale. Collaboration allows for the sharing of resources, expertise, and technologies, making solutions more feasible and effective. Additionally, coordinated efforts can lead to stronger policies, agreements, and initiatives that promote sustainability and resilience worldwide. Coordinated efforts on climate change can lead to stronger policies because they harness the collective knowledge, resources, and political will of multiple nations. When countries work together, they can pool expertise to develop comprehensive and effective policies that address the complex challenges of climate change. Additionally, coordinated action increases the legitimacy and influence of climate policies, making it more likely for them to be adopted and implemented at both national and international levels.

12.8 Concluding Remarks

It is more than evident that, at present, nation-states are in a process of constant and growing global and regional interconnection. The various transnational threats analysed in this chapter show how they transgress governments, the global transformations they bring about and the exponential flows of information. They have led to an erosion of the distinction between domestic and international affairs and an imminent decline of state sovereignty.

These transnational threats also show how the dividing line between internal and external affairs has become blurred, generating uncertainty for the future. This has spawned an increase in the levels of political integration and more multi-bureaucratic decision-making processes, challenging both the sovereignty and legitimacy of the Nation-State. Based on this, it is suggested that the greatest challenge facing the State is that of adapting to a system of exponential changes; where the reflection for the future is a new conceptualisation of nation-states and their functions based on these transformations; as well as a restructuring of power relations in which diverse forces and actors share tangible power and exchange it. Rights and obligations must be questioned, as well as the capacities of States to resolve domestic issues in a holistic manner, so that in multidimensionality and from interdependence they can respond to international mega-trends sharing responsibility with other actors in the system.

In the context of Latin America, the transnational threats studied here have intensified the crisis of governance in Latin America and have eroded confidence in the public sector as a manager of social welfare. They have shown the institutional weaknesses and how the policies and instruments used by the Latin American public administrations have not been efficient in dealing with these problems.

Public administration in Latin America has been coerced to operate in a densely interconnected international system in which national decisions and actions cannot be taken in isolation. International organisations, such as the International Organisation for Migration (IOM) or the United Nations Office on Drugs and Crime, have gained prominence in the region as these threats have developed and national security has been breached. Thus, for instance climate action is a complex issue that requires the involvement of governmental and non-governmental organisations and multilevel governance. To provide an adequate response, all social actors need to participate. This approach ensures efficient decision-making and enables the creation of adaptable mechanisms tailored to specific contexts, subjects, and sectors.

The interconnection between the national and the transnational has also demonstrated a significant reduction in the control of the States in their territories and the lack of presence of the latter in peripheral zones, which has accelerated the exponential growth of these transnational threats. Borders have been taken over by criminal groups and caravans of migrants seeking better development opportunities against all odds. Latin America is the living example of this spatially unequal nature, where the State and its public administration have forgotten some regions, for example, the Darien Gap or the Petén area—border between Mexico and Guatemala—where public institutions are ineffective or completely non-existent.

As a result of the above, it is these groups, through their de facto power, that resolve the demands and pressures exerted by certain sectors of society, which face political and social vulnerability. They take advantage of the absence of the State and its institutional weakness in providing public value to manage protection and economic and labour opportunities.

These threats demonstrate that the system has failed, that States do not have sufficient resources and that their solutions framed in national contexts are inefficient to solve problems that transcend borders. An effective solution transcends the national level and involves international and transnational organisations, as well as civil society groups willing to form a political integration that provides an inter-institutional and multidimensional response that considers the needs and structural and circumstantial characteristics of all the countries in the region.

In short, these threats require joint decision-making processes among the various countries and actors that have an impact on them and suggest an adjustment in traditional practices to facilitate the effective management of global processes that, in turn, reshape the world. Even though this means a re-definition of the powers and capacities of States, as well as their rights and obligations.

References

Abuelafia, E. 2018. *La política migratoria de los EE. UU. y su impacto en el Triángulo Norte de Centroamérica*. Banco Interamericano de Desarrollo (BID). https://publications.iadb.org/publications/spanish/viewer/La-pol%C3%ADtica-migratoria-de-los-EEUU-y-su-impacto-en-el-Tri%C3%A1ngulo-Norte-de-Centroam%C3%A9rica.pdf.

Arriagada, I., and M. Hopenhayn. 2000. *Producción, tráfico y consume de drogas en América Latina*. División de Desarrollo Social de la Comisión Económica para América Latina y el Caribe (CEPAL). https://repositorio.cepal.org/server/api/core/bitstreams/d9fb6959-e5f8-4e8a-b1f7-87d143dcd045/content.

Babich, E., and J. Batalova. 2021. Migration Policy Institute. https://www.migrationpolicy.org/article/inmigrantes-centroamericanos-en-los-estados-unidos-2019.

Bárcena, A., J. Samaniego, W. Peres, and J.E. Alatorre. 2020. *The climate emergency in Latin America and the Caribbean The path ahead—resignation or action?* ECLAC.

Cárdenas, M., and S. Orozco. 2022. *The challenges of climate mitigation in Latin America and the Caribbean: Some proposals for action*. UNDP.

Díaz, V. 2023. Estado paralelo. Narcotráfico y gobierno en Colombia. Centro de Investigaciones sobre América Latina y el Caribe, Universidad

Nacional Autónoma de México. https://polcul.xoc.uam.mx/index.php/polcul/article/view/1527/1481.

Dudley, S. 2016. Cómo el narcotráfico opera y genera corrupción en Centroamérica. *InSight Crime*. https://insightcrime.org/es/noticias/analisis/como-narcotrafico-opera-genera-corrupcion-centroamerica/.

ECLAC. 2023. *The economics of climate change in Latin America and the Caribbean, 2023: Financing needs and policy tools for the transition to low-carbon and climate-resilient economies.*

Fundación DEMUCA. 2011. *Territorialización de Políticas Públicas: Coordinación Interinstitucional Local en Centroamérica y República Dominicana.* Fundación DEMUCA, San José, Costa Rica. https://dhls.hegoa.ehu.eus/uploads/resources/5215/resource_files/Territorializacion.pdf.

Gallegos, C. 2023. *El narco es el quinto generador de empleo en México: supera a Walmart, Pemex y Oxxo, según Science.* El Economista. https://www.eleconomista.es/actualidad/noticias/12460981/09/23/el-narco-es-el-quinto-generador-de-empleo-en-mexico-supera-a-walmart-pemex-y-oxxo-segun-science.html.

Garfia, A. 2023. El tráfico de Drogas en América Latina. Centro Mexicano de Relaciones Internacionales. https://cemeri.org/art/a-trafico-drogas-america-latina-ev.

Guevara, T. 2021. *Es el estrecho corredor de Centroamérica la autopista de las drogas hacia EE.UU.?* Voz de América. https://www.vozdeamerica.com/a/centroamerica_centroamerica-triangulo-norte-drogas-hacia-eeuu/6074903.html.

Gutiérrez, J., J. Romero, S. Arias, and X. Briones. 2020. Migración: Contexto, impacto y desafío. Una reflexión teórica. *Revista de Ciencias Sociales (Ve)* XXVI (2): 299–313.

Intergovernmental Panel on Climate Change (IPCC). 2023. *Sixth assessment report (AR6).*

Klein, M. 2022. *Trata de personas, el monstruo que sigue acechando a las personas migrantes.* Organización Internacional para las Migraciones. https://costarica.iom.int/es/news/trata-de-personas-el-monstruo-que-sigue-acechando-las-personas-migrantes.

Mármora, L. 2010. Modelos de Gobernabilidad Migratoria. La perspectiva política de América del Sur. *REMHU—Revista Interdisciplinar da Mobilidade Humana* 18 (35): 71–92.

Martínez Pizarro, J. 2020. *Asociación Latinoamericana de Población.* https://www.alapop.org/2020/12/migracion-en-centroamerica-fuerte-impacto-de-las-politicas-migratorias-estadounidenses-sobre-una-realidad-compleja/.

Matza, M. 2024. La crisis de fentanilo que lleva a una ciudad de EE.UU. a declarar el estado de emergencia. *BBC News Mundo*. https://www.bbc.com/mundo/articles/czq4djy7l86o.

Mejías, S. 2014. Estado y crimen organizado en América Latina: posibles relaciones y complicidades. *Revista Política y Estrategia No 124*. https://dialnet.unirioja.es/descarga/articulo/5030960.pdf.

Neira, F. 2020. Los discursos, los actores y las prácticas en la atención migratoria en Latinoamérica. *Estudios de Derecho* 77 (169): 243–265. https://www.redalyc.org/journal/6479/647968648010/html/.

Oficina de Naciones Unidas sobre Drogas y Crimen Organizado (UNODC) and EUROPOL. 2021. *Tráfico de cocaína hacia Europa. Evaluación y Perspectivas*. Departamento de Seguridad Nacional. Gobierno de España. https://www.dsn.gob.es/es/actualidad/sala-prensa/informe-unodc-europol-tr%C3%A1fico-coca%C3%ADna-hacia-europa-evaluaci%C3%B3n-perspectivas.

Oficina Regional de la OIM para América del Sur. 2022. *Migraciones Sur-Norte desde Sudamérica. Rutas, Vulnerabilidades y Contextos del Tránsito de Migrantes Extrarregionales*. Informes estratégicos de coyuntura #1. https://robuenosaires.iom.int/sites/g/files/tmzbdl626/files/documents/oim_migraciones-sur-norte-desde-suramerica.pdf.

Organización Internacional para las Migraciones (OIM). 2006. *Glosario sobre migración*. https://www.corteidh.or.cr/sitios/observaciones/11/anexo4.pdf.

Organización Internacional para las Migraciones (OIM). 2022. *El impacto de la violencia contra las mujeres y niñas en el acceso a medios de vida. Contextos de movilidad humana en Centroamérica, México y República Dominicana*. https://kmhub.iom.int/sites/default/files/2022-12/INFOGRAFIAS-MOVILIDAD-HUMANA-FINAL_CCREV_-07082022.pdf.

Organización Internacional para las Migraciones (OIM). 2023. *Tendencias migratorias en las Américas*. https://robuenosaires.iom.int/sites/g/files/tmzbdl626/files/documents/2023-04/Tendencias-Migratorias-en-las-Americas-ESP-Feb-2023.pdf

Organisation for Economic Cooperation and Development (OECD). 2023. *Latin American economic outlook 2023: Investing in sustainable development*.

Programa Estado de la Nación (PEN). 2021. *Sexto Estado de la Región*. Programa Estado de la Nación. Consejo Nacional de Rectores (CONARE). https://repositorio.conare.ac.cr/handle/20.500.12337/8115.

Solorio, I. 2024. The ABCs of governmental climate action challenges in Latin America and the Caribbean. https://doi.org/10.1038/s41558-023-01820-3.

Vallejo, F., and S. Fergadiotti. 2017. *Historia del Narcotráfico en América Latina e implicancias en los Estados. Los casos de Colombia y Perú*. Panel de Estudiantes Historia y Política. Universidad de Concepción, Universidad Academia de Humanismo Cristiano. https://www.congresoalacip2017.org/arquivo/downloadpublic2?q=YToyOntzOjY6InBhcmFtcyI7czozNToiYToxOntzOjEwOiJJRF9BUlFVSVZPIjtzOjQ6IjMxNjciO30iO3M6MToiaCI7czozMjoiOWMxZTNlZGI4OTVjY2EwOTM2MTZkNWE3M2ZjNzY4YWEiO30%3D.

Villaverde, J. 2021. Ecuador y Venezuela, la primera parada de la ruta de la droga hacia EE UU. *La Razón*. https://www.larazon.es/internacional/20211205/7i5r2roxjjd2lp3nj2wcmghxku.html.

Viscardi, N., and G. Tenenbaum. 2023. Violencias, territorios y tráfico de drogas en América Latina. *Revista de Ciencias Sociales* 36 (53). Montevideo. http://www.scielo.edu.uy/pdf/rcs/v36n53/1688-4981-rcs-36-53-7.pdf.

World Bank Group. 2022.. *A roadmap for climate action in Latin America and the Caribbean: 2021–2025.*

CHAPTER 13

Post-COVID-19 Public Administration and Civil Service Development: Select Country Cases from the Caucasus and Central Asia

Bahram Khalilov, Maia Dvalishvili, Darkhan Zhazykbay, Almazbek Akmataliev, Baktybek Shamkeev, Mirzokhid Karshiev, and Gulimzhan Suleimenova

13.1 Introduction

Across the globe, the COVID-19 pandemic along with the macroeconomic crisis caused by it, the digital revolution, rising geopolitical tensions in different parts of the world, climate change, and demographic shifts have all changed the rules of the game (Ansel et al. 2021), and have ushered the start of a new reality. The dynamic and unprecedented

B. Khalilov
Baku, Azerbaijan
e-mail: b.khalilov@dim.gov.az

M. Dvalishvili
Tbilisi, Georgia
e-mail: makodvalishvili@yahoo.com

A. Baimenov and P. Liverakos (eds.), *Public Administration in the New Reality*, https://doi.org/10.1007/978-981-96-3845-1_13

character of this new reality requires innovative solutions, to satisfy the demands and fulfil the expectations of the population that have been growing more rapidly; often exceeding the capacity of the governments to respond to them effectively and in a timely manner.

The lessons learnt from the COVID-19 pandemic have revealed that the ability of governments to deploy new and improved problem-solving tools depends on their fundamental capacity to be innovative, their ability to make decisions under conditions of high uncertainty while, balancing a multitude of different interests guided by each country's social values and norms. This is crucial as evidence indicates that while political programmes, cultural factors and levels of public trust determine the propensity for innovation, the system of power separation, governance models, systemic management, and support systems determine whether any innovative efforts will be undertaken (Kaur et al. 2022).

Conversely, the importance of building close interaction between the government, the people and CSOs has increased in order to understand the nature of their demands and expectations and to find ways to react to them (Fraser et al. 2021). National leaders have begun to realise that public trust in the government is a key condition for effective implementation of government decisions, as trust is not only a social value, but it is also effective administrative capital, building confidence in the rationality of government actions. When there is no (or poor) trust, society becomes sceptical even if "right" decisions are made by the government (Baimenov 2021).

D. Zhazykbay · G. Suleimenova (✉)
Astana, Kazakhstan
e-mail: gulimzhan.suleimenova@undp.org

D. Zhazykbay
e-mail: d.zhazykbay@kyzmet.gov.kz

A. Akmataliev · B. Shamkeev
Bishkek, Kyrgyz Republic
e-mail: aakmataliev59@gmai.com

B. Shamkeev
e-mail: baktybek.shamkeev@gmail.com

M. Karshiev
Helsinki, Finland
e-mail: mirzokhid.karshiev@helsinki.fi

Moreover, the practical implementation of all reform efforts depends on the professionalism of the public officials, who are able to quickly adapt to the new conditions and continue to respond effectively to crises situations in the midst of considerable levels of uncertainty. For this to happen, the challenges of our times highlight that a modern public administration should demonstrate a forward looking, flexible, fulfilling attitude governed by a strong sense of stewardship (OECD 2021; ACSH 2023).

At the start of the COVID-19 pandemic, in 2019, governments began to rethink their approaches, methods and tools to meet the challenges they faced (OECD 2020, 2023; Deloitte 2020). They proceeded with reforms in public administration systems focusing on the digitalisation of public services, and the development of people-centred policies, while supporting innovation initiatives, improving system resilience, and creating a decent and fair government (Deloitte 2024). However, the direction, scope, and depth of changes in public administration systems varied from country to country. Some countries followed the same path with adjustments and revisions to their policies and strategies, while other countries strived for breakthroughs (Cheung 2022).

The characteristics of the political system and institutional environment play a significant role in this regard. In particular, the political system determines the opportunities and restrictions of the administrative system development (Baimenov 2020a, 2020b). Furthermore, Arjen and Hurt (2022) note that the perspectives of such changes depend on the efforts of political actors, and those can have different impacts, causing different outcomes. In this context, the quality of institutions in place is critical as it determines the speed of changes (Juzhong et al. 2010) and the behaviour of both public officials (Manning et al. 2000) and economic agents (North 1990).

The objective of this chapter is to review the reforms of public administration systems of a select group of post-Soviet countries in the post-COVID-19 period. These countries are characterised by developing institutional environments, similar to an extent, at least in their beginnings, since they all shared a common legacy from the Soviet era. The chapter presents the cases of Azerbaijan, Georgia, Kazakhstan, Kyrgyzstan, and Uzbekistan covering two regions. The first two countries are situated in the Caucasus and the remaining three in Central Asia. However, their development trajectories have not been linear over the past 30 years since their independence (Baimenov and Panos 2022). In this regard, it is also interesting to examine whether their transformations are parallel in comparison with countries that are characterised by a developed institutional environment; some of which are described in other chapters of this book.

Each country section of the chapter outlines how recent legislative and institutional changes have impacted on their policy development and implementation, regulatory frameworks, and levels of public engagement, as well as, how digital technologies have affected the delivery of public services, and the business processes of government organisations. Each section also describes the skills and competences public officials require in the twenty-first century, as well as the development pathways public administration needs to follow in this new reality.

13.2 The Case of Azerbaijan

Prior to delving into the issue of public administration in the new reality in the Republic of Azerbaijan and its development direction after the pandemic, it is necessary to touch upon on what has been accomplished since the time the country gained its independence. After the collapse of the former Soviet Union, Azerbaijan was confronted with a most difficult and tragic reality in comparison with other post-Soviet countries. As a result of the aggression of the Republic of Armenia, more than 20% of Azerbaijan's lands were occupied. At the same time, the internal political situation was very tense with centrifugal forces being active in the republic. Despite this situation one of the main priorities of the country from the beginning has been the reform of its public administration system.

A State Commission for the reform of the state administration system was established under the leadership of the great leader, Haydar Aliyev. The Commission's work culminated to the "Civil Service Law" of the Republic of Azerbaijan that was adopted in 2000. This marked the beginning of civil service reforms in the country. The Law envisaged the creation of a completely new civil service system, which was a departure from the norms—those of the former Soviet State—governing relations between the state and public servants. The concepts of "civil service" and "civil servant" appeared for the first time in Azerbaijan, and new legal norms and regulations were to govern relations in the field of civil service.

These novel legal norms in the civil service law, along with the introduction of new concepts faced many difficulties and confronted problems while implementing its provisions. Nevertheless, implementation started with considerable support by the Technical Assistance for the Commonwealth of Independent States (TACIS) Programme,[1] utilising international experience and "good practices" in the process. During this period, the Civil Servants' Registry was founded, and a network of structural department heads dealing directly with personnel in state bodies was created; while at the same time, many trainings, and seminars were conducted, and study visits were organised.

In 2005, the Commission on Civil Service Issues under the President of the Republic of Azerbaijan (the Commission) was established by Decree of the President of Azerbaijan, in accordance with the technical assistance programme recommendations. The Commission was bestowed with wide executive powers to ensure effective policy implementation in the field of civil service, and it was designated as the government body responsible for all civil service matters. The establishment of an institution, specialising in civil service affairs, allowed for the creation of a centrally managed civil service system through competitive, transparent, and objective procedures. Applying such transparent and objective procedures for public service recruitment was apparent in order to eliminate corruption, nepotism, and "telephone rights", and consequently increase citizens' trust in the state bodies and the civil service.

Within a short period of time after, all vacancies in the civil service were open to the public, with job requirements for all positions defined. Furthermore, selection procedures by computer-based examination were instituted, and interviews were conducted involving independent experts and representatives of non-governmental organisations that specialised in the fight against corruption. Along with such other measures as video recordings of the interviews, these actions contributed to the elimination of most of the unpleasant circumstances that prevailed through the past recruitment and selection practices.

The Commission also provided training to civil servants. Thus, it prepared training modules supplemented by many other practical documents, such as manuals. In addition, it also developed several legal acts on performance evaluation, and ethical behaviour of civil servants, as

[1] Implemented by the European Union to help speed up economic reforms in the Commonwealth of Independent States.

well as a civil service code (the Code).[2] For these tasks, the Commission cooperated closely with international organisations such as the United Nations Development Programme (UNDP), the Support for Improvement in Governance and Management (SIGMA) Programme, the European Union (EU), the German Society for International Cooperation (GIZ), the Astana Civil Service Hub (ACSH), etc. In 2016, as part of the [economic] reforms carried out in the Republic, the State Commission on Civil Service Issues under the President of the Republic of Azerbaijan, along with the State Commission for Student Admission, were abolished, and the State Examination Centre, a Legal Entity of Public Law (SEC) was established.

By the time, the COVID-19 pandemic appeared, a civil service system that met new and modern standards had already been established in the Republic of Azerbaijan. More than twenty laws and more than fifty other legal acts related to the civil service were adopted. Furthermore, the classification of state bodies and administrative and auxiliary positions in the civil service, the qualification degrees of civil servants and the rules for granting and depriving them of those degrees were also determined. Moreover, legal norms regarding restrictions related to the civil service, remuneration (salary and pension provisions allowances based on seniority, professional qualification degrees, and exercise of authority), as well as liability of civil servants, awarding of qualification degrees to civil servants, exercise of authority, and additions according to scientific degree were also fully implemented upon adoption.

13.2.1 Post-pandemic Reform Initiatives

In the post-pandemic period, the implementation of civil service reform initiatives is guided by the Action Plan of the "Strategy for the development of the civil service in the Republic of Azerbaijan for 2019–2025" (Strategy), approved by the President of the Republic of Azerbaijan. The Action Plan includes the following initiatives: (i) Institutional reforms in the civil service; (ii) Implementation of a competency model in the civil

[2] The need to prepare a Civil Service Code arose from the fact that a multitude of laws and other legislative acts on the civil service exist, thus making their application in practice more difficult and cumbersome. Considering the many changes in the Civil Service Legislation related to public human resource management reforms—mentioned abov—the draft Code has been revised and its adoption is planned soon.

service; (iii) Continuous professional development of civil servants; (iv) Information provision of civil service and development of electronic civil service; (v) Establishment of a motivational system in the civil service; and (vi) Improvement of normative legal acts on the civil service and assessment and evaluation of their implementation.

Systematic and structural reforms in public administration have included the creation of several new institutions in Azerbaijan. One of them was the establishment of the State Agency for Public Service and Social Innovations (SAPSSI/ASAN Service). At the time of its establishment, in 2012, "ASAN Service" offered citizens about ten services. Nowadays its centres provide more than 360 services of various state bodies and private enterprises. Currently more than 25 "ASAN Service" Centres are operating in different regions of the country as the Government pays a great deal of attention to the creation of new centres in the regions to increase the number and quality of these services provided.[3]

Another was the establishment of the Agency for Sustainable and Operative Social Security (DOST Agency) created by presidential decree in 2018. The Agency's services (about 160) are provided through the "single window" system, and they include pension and social benefits, issuance of references, social insurance, state compulsory insurance payments, adoption, and other relevant electronic services. In order to ensure equal access by disabled persons a sign language translation service was incorporated in the DOST Agency centres.

And yet another, the "DOST Digital Innovation Centre" Limited Liability Company established under the Agency, which is responsible

[3] Other electronic services provided by "ASAN Service" are document delivery and "Mobile ASAN Services". Thanks to this service citizens and legal entities can benefit by receiving services on an order basis with no physical appearance required. The "ASAN Visa" (e-visa) and "ASAN Pay" services are also provided. At the same time, there are a number of mobile services available on "ASAN Service", i.e., "Online Queue", "MyGov", and "ASAN Application" information system. The overall goal of the ASAN Service is to provide high-quality services in the fastest possible way to individuals and legal entities. To date, more than sixty million applications for services have been made to ASAN Service centres. The ASAN Service has also introduced an innovative initiative; the self-service project. A system, through which citizens are informed about the services provided by different state bodies, and they can submit their applications through computers with Internet access at their disposal in the ASAN Service centres premises. Through this system, citizens can also evaluate the quality of electronic services provided and at the same time contribute with their suggestions for the development of the system through the "Idea Bank".

for determining information technology policy, mutual integration of information databases of state and non-state institutions, organising and ensuring the sustainability of electronic services, providing support and development of information systems, ensuring the efficient and reliable operation of information systems, and carrying operations on the improvement of management systems in this field.

Providing electronic services to citizens by state bodies is one of the main priorities of the country. This is reflected in many state strategies adopted in Azerbaijan. The COVID-19 pandemic made the provision of electronic public services even more urgent and prompted the acceleration of the transition to digitalised public service provision. In this context, the "Electronic Government" portal, based on the "single window" principle streamlining the interaction of individuals and legal entities with state authorities more appropriately and in accordance with international experience, is being implemented. This portal creates the conditions for providing information and e-services to all citizens residing in the territory of the Republic of Azerbaijan, legal and physical persons, foreign citizens, and stateless persons by state bodies, utilising state of the art information technology applications.

The "Electronic Government Development Centre" (ECDC), a legal entity of public law established under the ASAN Service, works closely with other state bodies on the formation of the "Electronic Government" as the coordinator of the work done in this field, and for creating the relevant infrastructure. The Centre's activities are mainly focused on electronic government services, e-visa issuance, and digitisation services. In doing this, advanced international practices were investigated, and innovative innovations were applied considering the needs of citizens in order to improve the quality of service, facilitate the use of services, and increase citizen satisfaction.[4]

[4] The Centre organises the exchange of information and provision of services between the information systems and resources of state bodies through the "Electronic Government" portal. At the same time, the Centre not only provides portal management system performance, but also continues to the improvement of activities in this field. These measures are implemented within the framework of the new model of the "Electronic Government", which will include a single electronic cabinet and other functions. Multifaceted measures are also being implemented by the Centre for the development of electronic services, including government to business (G2B) and business to government (B2G).

In addition, the egov.az portal includes two registries—the "Electronic Registry of State Services" and the "Registry of State Information Resources and Systems". To access the portal, citizens can choose one of two methods: "ASAN Visa" or "Electronic Signature". Moreover, a new e-participation service has been activated on the portal in order to evaluate the efficiency of the activities conducted by state institutions. Public services, draft laws for discussion, etc., are available through this new electronic application.

13.2.2 *The Competency Model*

Following the adoption of the Strategy, over three years ago, a competency model is being consistently prepared, thus introducing a comprehensive human resource management (HRM) tool leading to a transparent system of standards for skills and competencies in the public sector human resource management realm. The Strategy envisages the competency model primarily as a tool in selection and performance evaluation procedures, inevitably linked to the application of a competency-based approach to training, as well as a professional development and career promotion system. The State Examination Centre seeks to develop the competency model both through its own efforts,[5] and with the support of international donors, including the on-going SIGMA project "Competency-based model in the civil service". It is clear that competency-based HRM is one of the main axes of the ongoing civil service reform in Azerbaijan, not only in the selection and performance evaluation processes, but also in other HRM processes, including the processes of career/promotion and professional development (Zukauskas et al. 2021).

Professional development is especially important, as it is currently applied poorly in the civil service, and it is not always aligned with the functions of government bodies and civil servants' actual needs for training and professional development. Hence, it is necessary to focus on building capacities at the managerial level and strengthening managerial competencies. Conversely, with regard to the career and career-planning process, it is also worth mentioning that horizontal and vertical career

[5] A list of competencies has been developed, the competency model developed has been validated during a pilot project, and job profiles have been developed for job groups, and submitted to the Cabinet of Ministers of the Republic of Azerbaijan for approval.

development based on skills and abilities is currently limited. It is expected that incorporation of the competency model in this process with clear standards for career development may eventually also lead to positive results in this area.

Thus, the SEC together with the European Union implemented a project (2021–2024) for developing a conceptual competency model to be used for the civil service in Azerbaijan. This competency model will not only determine the formal requirements for civil service positions, but also the necessary competencies for holding these positions, as well as corresponding measurement and evaluation mechanisms. With regard to the transition to the competency-based model in HRM, twelve competences in four clusters and four levels for each were determined, considering civil service duties and their areas of activity (Fig. 13.1) (Zukauskas et al. 2023).

Then, the competencies and levels of professionalism required for holding civil services were defined (Fig. 13.2). In the meantime, the SEC and the HRM units of these government organisations are preparing profiles for other job position considering the functions and tasks of each organisation.

Furthermore, job profiles were prepared for seven functional areas: (i) international cooperation; (ii) internal audit and control; (iii) legal; (iv) public relations; (v) human resources; (vi) clerical work; and (vii) programming and information technologies. Regarding the transition to the competency model, many trainings and seminars were organised in different government organisations. While at the same time, study visits were conducted to observe and learn from international experience in this field.

Eventually, the competency model will be assessed both in the test examination stage—the first stage of recruitment—and in the course of the interviews—the second. The preparation of test tools (analogue and original situational judgement tests tasks, a Likert scale questionnaire, role-playing games, etc.) are currently under development for assessing candidates' behaviour and psychological characteristics, weighing their strengths and weaknesses, and determining and evaluating the competencies necessary for effective work performance in the public service.

Considering that the key role in the transition to the competence model falls to the HRM function of government bodies, and in order to implement personnel policy in accordance with modern requirements, as well as improve the activities of the human resource departments, the

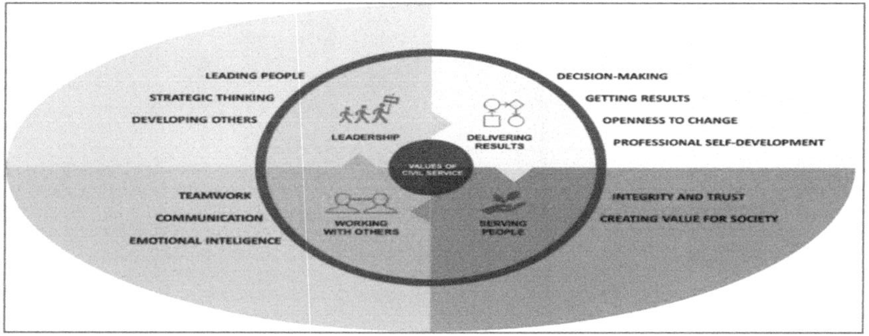

Fig. 13.1 Generic competencies model of the civil service of Azerbaijan

CLUSTER	COMPETENCIES	IA | GROUP | Individual contributor	IB | GROUP | Individual contributor	II GROUP | Managing others	III GROUP | Managing managers	IV GROUP | Managing group of managers	V GROUP | Managing organisation
LEADERSHIP	LEADING PEOPLE			Level 1	Level 2	Level 3	Level 4
	STRATEGIC THINKING			Level	Level 2	Level 3	Level 4
	DEVELOPING OTHERS			Level 1	Level 2	Level 3	Level 4
DELIVERING RESULTS	DECISION-MAKING	Level 1	Level 2	Level 2	Level 3	Level 3	Level 4
	GETTING RESULTS	Level 1	Level 1	Level 2	Level 3	Level 3	Level 4
	PROFESSIONAL SELF-DEVELOPMENT	Level 1	Level 2	Level 2	Level 3	Level 4	Level 4
	OPENNESS TO CHANGE	Level 1	Level 2	Level 2	Level 3	Level 4	
WORKING WITH OTHERS	COMMUNICATION	Level 1	Level 2	Level 2	Level 3	Level 4	Level 4
	TEAMWORK	Level 1	Level 2	Level 2	Level 3	Level 4	
	EMOTIONAL INTELIGENCE	Level 1	Level 1	Level 2	Level 3	Level 4	Level 4
SERVING PEOPLE	CREATING VALUE FOR SOCIETY	Level 1	Level 1	Level 2	Level 3	Level 3	Level 4
	INTEGRITY AND TRUST	Level 1	Level 1	Level 2	Level 3	Level 3	Level 4
	TOTAL COMPETENCIES REQUIRED	9	9	12	12	12	10

Fig. 13.2 Required competency sets and proficiency levels

draft "Model Regulation on the Personnel Bodies of State Agencies" was prepared. The Regulation proposes that human resource departments in government bodies are staffed in proportion to the number of employees in each government body. Furthermore, in order to achieve efficient use of human capital in the civil service, annual work plans for human resource management are employed. Thus, the procedures and rules for forming annual reports based on such plans have also been determined.

To ensure that competencies are managed in the different areas of human resources management, it is essential to cover the different types of competencies required to carry out a function or a category of functions. In this sense, an important distinction needs to be made between generic and technical competencies. Generic competencies are most often covered by a generic competency model, while technical competencies can be organised by specific categories.

The SEC has started to implement a project together with the SIGMA to develop the functional (technical) competencies of civil servants in 2024. As a beneficiary of this project the SEC is interested in SIGMA support for developing a framework of specialised technical skills for the civil service in the central government administration with respect to the types of competencies to be developed, the general approach to adopt, and the clarification of the scope of activities and context (Lazaro and Aitameur 2024) (Fig. 13.3).[6]

In addition, the draft "Rules of Preparation of Civil Servants' Career Plan" was prepared in order to create a conducive environment for the comprehensive professional development of civil servants, for utilising their full potential properly, for promoting them, and for increasing their motivation. The draft contains provisions on preparation for planning the career advancement of civil servants, drawing up the plan, and monitoring of its implementation.

Moreover, the draft "Training Strategy for Civil Servants in the Republic of Azerbaijan 2023–2025" was prepared in order to improve the professional development system for civil servants, by forming a professional and continuous training system that entirely meets the

[6] ***Types of competencies to be developed***: specialised technical skills. ***General approach***: inventory and mapping of the specialised technical skills. ***Scope of the activity***: general framework and contextualised mapping. ***Context for using the specialised technical skills***: priority for recruitment and selection, and possible generalisation to other HR processes (development/training, talent management).

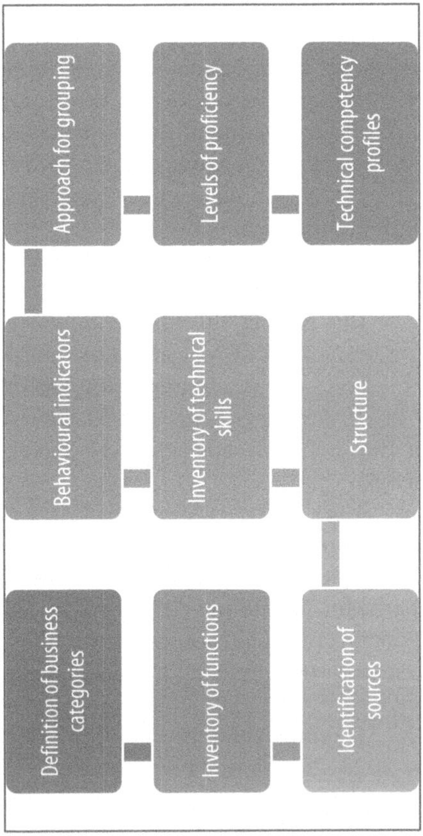

Fig. 13.3 General approach and methodology of the project

training needs of state bodies and of civil servants. Four priority areas of training were determined: (i) Public administration and civil service; (ii) Improvement of competencies: (iii) Performance; and (iv) Civil servants' positions.[7] It is also planned to establish a unified electronic management system for training of civil servants. The main objective is to create a working mechanism for conducting training need analysis for civil servants, and make their trainings systematic, purposeful, and continuous.

13.2.3 Summary

In light of the implementation of the Strategy provisions and the establishment of a competency-based model in HRM, the civil service system in Azerbaijan is on the verge of significant changes. New developments are envisaged for upgrading the civil service admission and performance appraisal processes. Thus, through the adoption of new approaches for the civil service system advancement, a continuous enhancement of public administration is also achieved. The Strategy also emphasises the development of an electronic civil service human resource management information system.

In conclusion, it should be stated that, in the post-pandemic period, not only knowledge and skills, but also competences must be taken into account in the process of recruitment to the civil service. At the same time, IT technologies (artificial intelligence, blockchain, big data) should be accepted and embraced more widely. Another important aspect is the enhancement of civil servants' potential. For this purpose, new training modules congruent with today's requirements should be prepared, and such trainings should be regularly provided. Extensive work is being done in this field in Azerbaijan, but in our opinion, some shortcomings are still present. A single specialised state body responsible for civil service issues, encompassing both defining human resource policy formulation, as well as ensuring its effective implementation, is still lacking.

[7] The first priority area focuses on "Civil Servants' Performance Appraisal" and "Civil Servant's Ethical Code". The second priority area focuses on "Project Management" and "Conflict Management" competence-based training modules. The third priority area is directly linked with practical daily job activities of civil servants. The last priority area mainly focuses on trainings dedicated to Civil Service Admission.

13.3 The Case of Georgia

Nothing in the recent history has had such a large-scale impact on every field of public life as the COVID-19 pandemic and its side effects. The challenges that countries had to overcome continue shaping the direction of their actions and influence their policy priorities, even to date. The pandemic has not only affected the economic and social development indicators of countries, but it has also fundamentally changed the attitude of society about the importance of health systems efficiency, the need for risk management, availability of digital services, and the presence of robust human capital.

The pandemic has highlighted the role and responsibility of public administration for the efficient functioning of a state especially in crisis situations requiring rapid adaptation of all the necessary procedures and processes. The pandemic has changed the agenda of reforms in Georgia, including the on-going civil service reforms. Changes have been introduced considering the future needs for human capital in the Georgian civil service (OECD 2023). It is widely perceived that the post-pandemic public administration in Georgia is becoming more future and risk management oriented, the focus on people and the importance of values in management systems is increasing, digital transformation is becoming an irreversible process, and the demand for data analytics and data-informed decisions is increasing.[8]

Accordingly, conventional attitudes and practices in public administration are changing by focusing more on the need to enhance leadership potential, to develop current and future skills needed and for building a digital world and ensuring the well-being of human capital.[9]

13.3.1 A Changed Paradigm

A study by the Organisation for Economic Cooperation and Development (OECD), countries were basically unprepared for the pandemic

[8] Unfortunately, no large-scale post-COVID-19 pandemic study on public administration trends and implemented changes was conducted in Georgia. This article is based on personal observations during and after the pandemic, professional experience, shared opinions with public administration professionals and others, and communication with people of various professions employed in the civil service; as well as recent scientific articles on the impact of the COVID-19 pandemic on the public administration system.

[9] https://www.sigmaweb.org/publications/principles-public-administration.htm.

(OECD 2023), although "Public sector organisations that used the Common Assessment Framework (CAF) model—reported that their policies and actions resulted in a more efficient response to the COVID-19 crisis. These organisations have demonstrated a strong capacity to adapt institutional arrangements and service delivery models, and introduced novel ways of working, communicating, and interacting with citizens and partners".

Despite the limited use of management assessment models and tools and the lack of concrete evidence highlighting the necessity for digital transformation in Georgia, the country has somehow consistently prioritised the transition of processes into the digital realm long before the Pandemic. In fact, both the electronic document circulation and the electronic signature systems were already operating in the public service for several years prior to the outbreak of the pandemic, which aided towards, the more or less seamless transition of public institutions into remote work modalities. This example serves as a clear demonstration that when a country strategically plans and implements innovative projects, anticipates future challenges, and needs in advance, rather than responding reactively, it can operate and overcome obstacles more efficiently. In sum, as a result of the pandemic, the use of digital technologies in the field of governance has increased and the process of providing digital services has been accelerated (Špaček et al. 2023), while the importance of other public administration reforms seems to have decreased (Dunlop et al. 2020).

However, change, including digital transformation, is only possible in the context of a solid governance system, where people promote innovation, and they have the ability to deal with challenges professionally. For instance, already existing e-services played a crucial role in enabling the transition of public servants to remote work at the initial stage of the pandemic in Georgia. However, the existence of e-services alone does not guarantee long-term efficiency of the system. For a sustainable and forward-looking approach, effective process management and anticipation for future needs depends on the presence of qualified human capital and strong institutional systems (OECD 2023).

In this context, the public administration reform strategy in Georgia pays particular attention to human resources management and recognises the importance of the development of human capital employed in the public sector. The Strategy defines the priorities for reform focusing on public policy planning and coordination, development of civil services and accountability, along with human resources management. However, the document does not include any substantial analysis of the effects of the pandemic and the changed circumstances because of it, which eventually led to reconsidering the reform priorities of the country.

Notwithstanding the lack of such an in-depth analysis, it was made obvious that human resources management in public administration is an area that needs new approaches and adaptation of its existing practices, in line with contemporary reality. The obligation to respond quickly to challenges caused by the pandemic and making decisions independently inevitably shifted to civil servants, since they were working remotely and dealing alone on issues and problems with no detailed instructions put in place; and without traditional means of communication or consultations in place.

The pandemic accentuated the importance of professional and motivated employees in the civil service, who took the first hit on themselves and remained committed to stated goals and objectives despite the risks and obstacles related to their working environment and a rather fluid future. The behaviour of those civil servants, their commitment and dedication for the uninterrupted functioning of the civil service as part of the state mechanism led to the prioritisation of the human resources management reform after the pandemic, by putting even more emphasis on the importance of a human-centric governance system.

13.3.2 The Importance of Leadership in the "New Normal" Reality

All reform initiatives have their own priorities, which are case-specific and based on emerging needs. Thus, rather than constantly responding to emerging challenges, it is necessary to be proactive for reaching a higher level of development and efficiency. Thus, in the midst of a new paradigm characterised by ambiguity, it is important to build a robust system that is always ready to tackle potential threats, while ensuring the continuity and sustainability of the development of the professional civil service system even under conditions of constant change.

Nonetheless, continuity and sustainability require soundness of organisational processes and structured systems that respond to existing needs. Furthermore, no one doubts that embracing digital technologies can enhance efficiency, innovation, and the overall responsiveness level of organisations. This is a major reason why special emphasis is placed on the significance of digital transformation and on electronic systems that enable organisations to move faster and operate efficiently in order to stay competitive in a rapidly evolving landscape. However, it is professional human capital which is identified as the primary asset for an organisation. The skills, knowledge, and creativity of the workforce contribute significantly to an organisation's success and ability to navigate complexities. But revealing the unlimited capabilities of the latter as well as directing it towards common public goals is a managerial responsibility and requires leadership skills.

The integration of well-defined organisational processes, strategic digital transformation, and effective management of human capital are all integral ingredients for an organisation to achieve continuity, sustainability, and contribute to broader public goals. All of those components are equally important, and their simultaneous presence is crucial. However, development of management and leadership abilities are particularly challenging, especially under new conditions and rapidly changing circumstances as general people management and people management in the digital era are somewhat two different terms.

Therefore, changes planned in civil service reform priorities and initiatives ought to also be focused on the reconsideration of leadership competencies, the retention of professionals already in the civil service sector, as well as their well-being and motivation; and of course on the recruitment of professionals from outside the civil service by increasing the attractiveness of the civil service as an employer by improving the existing working environment and conditions (European Parliament 2022). Increasing the attractiveness of the civil service and offering a healthy organisational environment for employees largely depends on the presence of sound managerial skills. Managers' attitudes towards employees, styles of communication and management, and emotional intellect shown by supervisors stimulate the creation of a sound corporate environment and largely influence the retention of employees to the workplace.

The pandemic has proven that rather than focusing on traditional civil service reforms aspects, it is essential that changes need to focus on the growth of a solid human capital that is striving towards excellence, can easily adapt to new environments and changing circumstances, is not afraid of making difficult decisions, and is oriented on achieving tangible results, realising the goals of their organisations. Demonstrating leadership potential is critical for building a strong team. According to observations during the pandemic, teams characterised by high level of trust between managers and employees, and where their work was ongoing under constructive, uninterrupted, and structured communication conditions, proved to position themselves much better in terms of performance and general job satisfaction compared to those teams characterised with lack of trust of and poor communication between employees with their direct supervisors.

In this latter instance, public employees distancing themselves from their place of employment during the pandemic was seen as an opportunity to shift the workload and responsibility towards the management. As a result, the managers and direct supervisors who remained in the office bore full responsibility for fulfilling their obligations, as the pandemic provided an opportunity for less motivated employees to shirk their tasks based on a variety of objective and subjective reasoning, while working from home. Civil servants who failed to grasp the significance of shared goals and their role in the evolving situation adapted poorly. This group of employees resisted to undertake diverse functions, thus posing challenges for managers attempting to reorganise tasks in response to emerging needs. The lack of understanding and reluctance to embrace new responsibilities added complexity to the managerial efforts in adapting to the changing circumstances.

Consequently, in response to such challenges and for the purpose of forming a strong managerial chain, it is essential to plan reform initiatives focusing on strengthening leadership competencies during periods of transition and change, enabling managers to understand their role and responsibility in forming efficient and result-oriented teams, members of which are united around values rather than routine tasks (European Parliament 2022). However, significant effort is required for developing modern, future-oriented, and visionary leadership competencies, as the Georgian administrative culture is deeply rooted in the remnants of Soviet governance. It is particularly difficult to change the control-oriented managerial practices established over the years, especially in the light of the ongoing reforms imposing a heavy burden on a manager in terms of the use of new tools and involvement in human resource management processes, which is often perceived by managers as a routine obligation imposed by the law rather than an important role a manager has to play. In practical terms, this results in a decrease of motivation to fulfil actual managerial and leadership obligations and thus, use of fewer resources for people and teams' management.

13.3.3 Civil Service—An Attractive Employer

Increasing the level of attractiveness of the civil service as an employer was highlighted among the priorities of public administration after the pandemic (European Parliament 2022). This goal, however, does not imply conducting attractive marketing campaigns to improve the image, and attractiveness, of the civil service, but implementation of activities focusing on citizens and their needs, guided by the essential vision, mission, and values of the public sector for the nation. The attractiveness of civil service as a workplace is ensured by practicing fair management approaches, encouraging competency-based leadership, providing continuous personal and professional development opportunities. It is also ensured by putting clear and predictable processes and systems in place and making decisions based on the principles of merit, impartiality, equality, transparency, and legitimacy. The attractiveness of the public service is also positively influenced by offering competitive working conditions, which include flexible work schedules tailored to the needs and interests of employees, the possibility of remote work, fair work and personal life balance, cooperation, a healthy work climate, and an organisational culture based on values.

The conjunction of the above factors increases interest for employment in the civil service among competent individuals in the employment market, including young professionals. The essential attributes and attractiveness features that collectively contribute to the overall appeal of an employment sector can be grouped as follows: (i) Planning, forecasting, and enhancing predictability while maintaining flexibility; (ii) Stability, sustainability, continuous development in consort with innovative and experimental projects; and (iii) Commitment to values associated with the public interest while ensuring the well-being, flexible working conditions, and the personal and work-life balance. This is because Individuals often seek a combination of stability, growth opportunities, an ethical values framework, and a supportive work environment when choosing a career path. The balance between predictability and flexibility, sustainability, and a commitment to well-being can make a sector more appealing to a diverse workforce.

However, the main challenge considering the Georgian, but also the global reality, is the difficulty of concurrently implementing equally important, but at the same time competing features. The first set of features comprises the ability to make long-term plans and predictions that can provide a sense of security and direction for individuals in a public organisation. Yet, despite long-term plans already in place, public organisations should also be adaptable to changes, allowing employees to navigate uncertainties and evolving conditions, as it is expected that sometimes various external and internal factors force organisations to change planned activities and deviate from their set path. Undoubtedly this is challenging, but when plans and priorities must be changed due to changed circumstances, it is necessary for the organisation to be ready to adapt to new environments with minimal losses. Such challenges are also very relevant to managers' ability to respond to emerging needs, considering the expected threats and risks, while preparing employees for potential changes, with suitable and efficient means of communication.

This may sound simple, but it can become rather complicated when it comes to implementation, as stability and clarity are particularly important for civil servants. Fear for the unknown is natural, and sudden and unexpected changes can cause tension, conflicts, discomfort and even chaos among employees; inevitably threatening the effectiveness of organisational processes and services.

The experience from the recent pandemic has clearly shown the significance of proper planning, communications, data analysis and risk management. Consequently, particular emphasis has been placed on data-informed decisions and risk assessment and management during a planning phase. The topic of data analysis is very relevant, data analysis is at the top of the list of future competencies, and public institutions are trying their best to engage personnel with relevant competencies in their workforce (Li et al. 2022). However, after the end of pandemic, risk management is slowly losing its relevance due to unfortunately unclear reasons.

The second group of features refers to job security and a stable work environment as they are some of the crucial factors that attract individuals for employment in a public organisation. Sustainable practices, ongoing learning opportunities and professional growth can enhance long-term attractiveness of employment but at the same timely Inclusion of cutting-edge and experimental initiatives can make the work exciting and dynamic (Schomaker and Michael 2020).

The younger generation—whose involvement is critical for the development of the civil service—does not perceive stability as one of the primary motivators for their decision and aspiration to join the civil service. For young people, interesting work, results achieved, tangible benefits, and opportunities for continuous development are much more attractive. Younger people seem to value more the substance or content of the work and are less willing to be associated with any specific public institution in the long run. Without experimentation, innovation, and constant search for alternatives, development is unimaginable. Therefore, considering the interests of all possible stakeholders is a challenge: to retain the existing human capital in the public service while ensuring stability and sustainability, and to create an attractive environment for the younger generation, by adapting experimental and innovative approaches, taking into account such conditions as finite state resources and bureaucratic rules in place.

Furthermore, the pandemic effectively forced the entire civil service to switch to working remotely, mostly from home, while also taking care of their family obligations. Under such circumstances, the line between professional and personal life was blurred even further. Working hours, workload, and stress increased which emerged as an additional responsibility for the managers, i.e., to take care of the physical and mental health of their employees, along with managing teams under different working modalities. They essentially provided support for their physical and mental well-being, offering flexibility in terms of work hours or other remote work options aimed at improving the work-life balance; an essential condition for overall job satisfaction.

The increased managerial obligations during the pandemic gave rise to another challenge, which is not specific to the Georgian civil service only, but it is rather generic: no matter the circumstances, it is the responsibility of managers to ensure that objectives and results are achieved, while also ensuring work-related satisfaction, and the well-being and the work and life balance of their subordinates, often operating in stressful environments.

Even after the pandemic was over, a flexible work schedule has remained one of the substantial motivators for civil servants, and it is considered a determinant for competitiveness and attractiveness. However, despite the advantages of a hybrid working model—reinforced by the findings of professional studies—public managers are reluctant to continue using flexible work modalities. This is associated with a fear of losing control and letting go of the reins of management, which is ingrained in the conventional managerial culture, as well as to the lack of skills and abilities among managers to effectively manage a team remotely.

Lastly, the civil service is a sector that requires loyalty to public interests by the civil servants. Civil servants are required to adhere to the principles and values of the civil service and to act in favour of the public interest when making decisions, while they often work under stress, as well as work overtime for serving the public interest.

13.4 The Case of Kazakhstan

Following the election of President Tokayev, in 2019, the country identified new priorities for its development. These priorities encompass political reforms, improvements in the socio-economic sphere, and the overhaul of public administration, including the civil service. The COVID-19 pandemic has been one of the triggers for modernising the public administration system, rebooting the state apparatus, and transforming the civil service. All legislative and institutional reforms carried out in the country are systematically aimed at implementing the idea of creating a "Just Kazakhstan".[10] The changes that have occurred over the past five years have irreversibly changed the nature of public relations, expanded political participation of citizens, and set the basis for a constant dialogue between the authorities and the people. At the same time, they led to the adoption of drastic measures to improve the efficiency of public administration and of the civil service.

13.4.1 Political Modernisation

From 2019 to 2021, Kazakhstan embarked on a path towards political modernisation, resulting to the adoption of several packages of political reforms, involving a set of laws, culminating in the constitutional reform of 2022. Initiatives aimed at the consistent democratisation of the country have been implemented. The Constitutional Court was established, the electoral system was changed, a simplified procedure for registering parties was introduced, and direct election of rural akims (governors) came into effect. The "institutional redesign" of public administration allowed for

[10] "Just Kazakhstan" is a concept consolidating the strategic goals for the country's future and constitute the basis of state policy. The following concepts have been identified: "Listening State"; "Strong Presidency—Influential Parliament—Accountable Government"; "Different Opinions—One Nation"; "Law and Order", and "*Adal Azamat*" ("Just Citizen").

an optimal balance between the different branches of government and for a more adaptive system of public administration. In the long term, all changes are aimed at creating a fair, transparent and effective governance system capable of successfully responding to the challenges of our times and ensuring the stable development of Kazakhstan.

13.4.2 Public Administration Reform: "People First"

In 2021, the "Concept for the development of public administration in the Republic of Kazakhstan until 2030: building a human-centric model—people first" was approved by presidential decree. The Concept reflects the principles and values of a new model of public administration, aimed at increasing the efficiency of state planning, strengthening public trust in the state, and involving citizens in management decision-making. In accordance with the provisions of the Concept, changes and amendments were made to the legislative framework governing the civil service, in 2022–2023. These changes laid the groundwork for a civil service that prioritises client-oriented service.

For this purpose, in the Presidential Message "Fair State. One Nation. Prosperous Society"—delivered on 1 September 2022—the strategic goal of the Agency for Civil Service Affairs was defined to become a "full-fledged strategic HR institution". In addition, the HR Institute was created under the auspices of the Academy of Public Administration in the beginning of 2024. Furthermore, aiming at systematising the development of the civil service in the medium term, the "Concept for the Development of the Civil Service of the Republic of Kazakhstan 2024–2029" was developed and approved in 2024. The development of a new law on the civil services is also envisioned in this Concept. It will include the definition of the mission, objectives, and requirement for the new civil service, including the formulation of a service and customer-oriented culture in interacting with citizens.

Moreover, the professionalisation of the civil service will be achieved through the modernisation of the selection system, the introduction of horizontal career advancement, the creation of mechanisms for early professional orientations and the improvement of the compensation system. The Concept also proposes a revision of the hierarchy of civil service positions, expansion of the rotation in key positions, improvement of the social guarantees for civil servants, reconsideration of the disciplinary procedures, and digitalisation of civil service processes utilising artificial intelligence.

13.4.3 De-bureaucratisation of the State Apparatus

To streamline the state apparatus and enhance efficiency while reducing unnecessary bureaucracy, the presidential decree "On measures to de-bureaucratise the activities of the state apparatus" was approved in April 2022. Its initiatives were aimed at simplifying administrative procedures and fostering better interaction between the government and society. Underpinning this Decree, a methodology was developed to outline essential approaches for monitoring and analysing the processes of de-bureaucratisation within the state apparatus. For this purpose, a specialised unit was created in the Agency for Civil Service Affairs responsible for implementing such initiatives and for ensuring effective monitoring of the de-bureaucratisation process.

Furthermore, another new concept was incorporated into the Law "On Public Services"; the term "socially significant service", defined as "a public service provided continuously to satisfy the legitimate interests of society".[11] In this connection, the Agency for Civil Service Affairs, in assessing the quality of public services, also evaluates socially significant services and makes recommendations to improve the quality of their provision.

Moreover, at the initiative of the Agency, the concept of "public service" has been expanded, allowing for the provision of proactive public services online, eliminating the need for the physical presence of citizens. The number of legal acts regulating the provision of public services has been optimised. These measures have made it possible to form a legal framework for the provision of public services and ensure customer

[11] The service model of public services includes individual services and those provided by the state in the interests of the whole society, i.e., socially significant services. Examples of such services include environmental protection, public order, defence, sanitary and epidemiological welfare, and others. To date, these services are still not classified as those provided by the state in the interests of the whole society. There is a lack of list of services, indicators, and criteria for measuring quality, as well as mechanisms for assessing citizens' opinions on activities in this area. For the purpose of ensuring the state apparatus can measure the results of its activities against the needs and expectations of society, measures will be taken to include socially significant services in the Register of State Services.

focus. The active introduction of digital technologies and simplification of procedures have significantly increased the availability and improved the quality of services for citizens and businesses. The level of population satisfaction with the quality of government services has reached a record 81.3%, the highest figure in the last nine years.

13.4.4 Civil Service Reform: Initiatives and New Approaches

At the beginning of 2022, an initiative was put forward by the Head of State, in order to create a system, open to every citizen of Kazakhstan by removing excessive barriers and obstacles to entering the civil service. This set the basis for a significant revision of approaches to personnel policy.

13.4.4.1 New Solutions in the Civil Service Selection System

In response to the contemporary needs of society and the economy, new standard qualification requirements for applicants entering the civil service were developed and implemented. In this context, the Agency for Civil Service Affairs was entrusted with the function of coordinating the process of setting qualification requirements for civil servants. The new requirements consider candidates' total cumulative work experience, both in the public and private sectors. In addition, new education requirements have been established in accordance with the functional area a civil service position belongs to. Since January 2024, the Agency has been entrusted with the function of reviewing and providing recommendations on proposals from government agencies to increase staffing limits. The Agency considers the validity of requests for staff increases, in particular, the availability of internal reserves in the form of permanent vacancies, compliance with standards in respect to the number of managers, and the presence of duplicate functions.

In 2023, an innovative online system for selecting candidates for the civil service was implemented. Pilot testing of the system was carried out throughout 2023 in six government agencies utilising the external portal of the "*E-Qyzmet*" information system.[12] The phased implementation of the new selection system in all government agencies will last until the end of 2025.

[12] The exercise demonstrated the dynamics of the growth of citizens' interest in the public service. The number of applications for vacant positions has increased significantly and the share of candidates from the private and civil sectors accepted has increased.

The new system involves the use of specialised software for conducting competency testing aimed at assessing the professional knowledge, skills, and abilities of applicants. Online testing includes tasks to determine the level of analytical thinking, as well as other competencies necessary for future work in government agencies. The proctoring system ensures objectivity and transparency of the selection process, minimises human factor involvement and corruption risks, and also provides equal opportunities for participation to all candidates, irrespective of their location, round the clock. Moreover, the system allows candidates to track the status of competition stages and receive feedback.

The *"E-Qyzmet"* information system has automated HR processes, freeing HR departments of government agencies from routine work. The system has allowed civil servants to launch HR procedures remotely, which is especially important for employees working in remote regions. In addition, the system helps analyse HR data and provide up-to-date information.

Overall, information technologies contribute to de-bureaucratisation by providing efficiency, transparency, accessibility, and environmental friendliness of the activities of government bodies and the entire state apparatus. The use of big data speeds up query processing and facilitates informed decision-making.

13.4.4.2 No Contest Appointments

In the process of developing and improving recruiting mechanisms for the public service in Kazakhstan, attention was paid not only to improving competitive procedures, but also to developing new methods for selecting candidates for leadership positions in government organisations.

Historically, contest has been the primary and typically the sole method of recruitment for the civil service. The appointments by contest, to one degree or another, ensured objectivity, openness, equal opportunities, and equal chances for all candidates. However, this approach limited the flexibility of government agencies in attracting highly qualified, highly educated, skilled specialists from various sectors of the economy to fill key positions.

The introduction of flexible recruiting methods has provided government leaders with additional tools to find and hire candidates with competencies and skills that meet current requirements. The recruitment process was accelerated and significantly expanded by allowing for no contest recruitment to individual management positions in demand; in agreement with the Agency for Civil Service Affairs. As a result, the implementation of such a flexible recruiting system led to an increase in the share of appointments of individuals originating from the non-governmental sectors, among those appointed to management positions; 26.8% when compared to appointments through the conventional competitive recruitment procedures.

13.4.4.3 Service Contracts

Another step towards increasing the flexibility of hiring personnel is the introduction of the service contract modality into the public administration system. The Government has approved the Rules for attracting contract employees and other issues regulating their activities. The peculiarity of this approach is the ability to hire individuals on a contract basis to carry out specific projects for a limited period, i.e., no more than one year, with the possibility of subsequent extension. However, contract employees hired for public service must meet certain qualification requirements and possess a high level of professionalism and competence.[13]

13.4.4.4 Talent Management

The development and implementation of effective talent management mechanisms aimed at securing the best personnel from the new generation for the country's government bodies are of paramount importance. The appointment to the civil service without contest of the top graduates from higher educational institutions in the country was an innovation under this scheme. It provides non-competitive appointment to government service for university graduates who have demonstrated outstanding academic achievement and leadership qualities during their studies. These graduates were appointed in lower-level positions in regional government organisations to begin their careers in the public service.

[13] In 2023, nine contract employees were hired—eight in the Ministry of Science and Higher Education and one in the Akim' Office in Turkestan. Eight individuals hired by the Ministry were engaged in various projects such as "Automation of ratings of universities in Kazakhstan", "Creation of endowment funds", etc., and the one hired by the Akim's Office was engaged in the "Creation of an agro-industrial industrial zone in Kazygurt and Sairam districts". In 2024, different government agencies hired eighteen contract employees: one by the Anti-Corruption Agency; ten by the Ministry of Science and Higher Education; six by the Ministry of Labour and Social Protection; and one by the Turkistan Regional Administration.

This approach certainly contributes to the dynamic renewal of the civil service workforce by attracting young people. It also encourages students to achieve high results in their studies. For example, without a contest, graduates of the Academy of Public Administration under the President of the Republic of Kazakhstan and other higher educational institutions with educational indicators not lower than GPA 3.33 found jobs in the civil service. From 2023 to date, 236 graduates of the Academy of Public Administration and universities,[14] who were educated through a grant and with high academic performance have been appointed to various civil service positions without contest.

To select talented youth, a tool called "assessment for talented employees" is utilised. Candidates undergo an assessment of their competencies, which is carried out by assessors with international certification and special training. The uniqueness of this project lies in the fact that experienced supervisors accompany the entire process, identifying the participants' personal values, degree of motivation and management competencies.

13.4.4.5 Presidential Youth Personnel Reserve

In 2019, the Presidential Youth Personnel Reserve was established, as a critical element of the strategy to cultivate the leadership skills of personnel in public administration. The Agency for Civil Service Affairs, together with the Academy of Public Administration, and other strategic partners, held three contests—in 2019, 2021, and 2023. As a result, a total of 400 talented young people were selected.[15] The Presidential Youth Personnel Reserve programme is designed to select, train and promote young professionals to leadership positions who demonstrate high academic achievements, leadership qualities, and innovative thinking. The goal of this programme is to prepare talented youth who in the future will work in the strategic directions of development of our state.

The process of selecting candidates for the Reserve is organised with great objectivity and fairness. The programme is open to citizens of the

[14] Twenty of them graduated from the Academy of Public Administration and remaining 216 from different universities. Out of the 20 Academy graduates, nine were appointed to positions at the regional level; three in cities of Republican significance administrations; and eight at the district (city) level. Out of the 216 university graduates, 143 filled vacant positions at the district level and 73 in rural districts.

[15] In fact, the number of interested individuals wishing to take part in the "Presidential Youth Personnel Reserve" competition increased with each intake, e.g., from 13,000 in 2019 to 31,000 in 2023.

Republic of Kazakhstan no older than 35 years of age having completed their higher education and possess at least five years of work experience. Selection includes a series of competitive procedures: testing, assessment of competencies, personal qualities, and interviews with expert commissions. Particular attention is paid to identifying the analytical abilities of candidates and their potential to offer non-standard solutions.

The uniqueness of the project lies in the individual approach to the development of each participant. Young specialists in the Reserve undergo specialised training programmes designed to suit their professional interests and career ambitions. Since the inception of the Reserve programme, a large pool of talented young specialists were trained and included in the Reserve. Many of the specialists in reserve occupy leadership positions in the system of public administration and civil service and are responsible for the implementation of national projects and development programmes.[16]

The concept of talent management was consistently expanded to the regional level with the creation of Regional Youth Talent Reserves throughout the country. The start of this project began in 2024. In the broader context of our state's comprehensive development, establishing a regional personnel reserve will enable more effective consideration of the unique specifics and requirements of each region.

It is worth noting the successfully functioning project "School of Young Civil Servants" for final-year students at Kazakhstani universities. In these schools, young people become familiar with the intricacies of public service and make conscious decisions to become civil servants.

13.4.4.6 Efficiency Mark

In 2023, a new system for the quarterly performance evaluation of Corps "B" employees was introduced. This system allows for evaluating the contribution of each employee to the overall performance of their organisation and determines the size of their bonuses, as it is also linked to their remuneration. The assessment considers and ranks the quality of performance of their official duties, as well as meeting deadlines, taking initiative, demonstrating independent thinking, and work discipline. At

[16] In accordance with the rules of the Presidential Youth Personnel Reserve, persons enrolled in the reserve can be appointed to political government positions, administrative government positions in Corps "A", leadership positions in Corps "B" and category A positions in Corps "B" in the manner prescribed by law.

the same time, assessment of individual managers is carried out using a different method, that of achieving some key target indicators. In this system, individuals must achieve at least three to five tasks set a priori.

This evaluation system is also intricately linked to the promotion mechanism. Employees who demonstrate superior performance for four consecutive quarters are eligible for direct promotion to the next rank position. This stimulates each employee to constant professional growth and improve the quality of their work. Conversely, the new system also allows for measures against employees whose work does not meet established standards. Those who receive unsatisfactory grades for two consecutive quarters are subject to demotion and, in some cases, dismissal.

13.4.4.7 Professional Development and Training of Civil Servants

For an effective public service, a system of continuous professional development and training of public employees is important. In this context, a number of measures have been introduced to unlock the potential and develop the professionalism of civil servants through the introduction of new methods and training programmes.

Every year more than thirty thousand employees undergo retraining and advanced training courses. These programmes are constantly reviewed and updated to remain relevant to changing social and economic realities. Training focuses on professional skills, ethical aspects, including anti-corruption methods, and communication skills enabling them to interact effectively with the public, especially in crisis situations.

To integrate global expertise into the professional development and training realm, partnerships are forged with foreign educational and scientific institutions. Such collaboration enables public employees to engage in internships and exchange programmes, gaining valuable knowledge and skills, including the opportunity to obtain a double-degree at partner universities (e.g., Finland, UAE, USA, etc.), and undergo international internships (Azerbaijan, Bulgaria, Georgia, India, Lithuania, Russia, Switzerland, and UAE).

In collaboration with the Academy of Public Administration under the President of the Republic of Kazakhstan and Nazarbayev University, the training programme "Leader of the New Formation" is implemented annually since 2020. This programme is aimed at developing relevant management competencies needed by modern managers. Of particular note is the successful experience of opening modular master's educational programmes on the job, allowing civil servants to continue working and simultaneously gain new knowledge and skills.

13.4.4.8 Ethics of Civil Servants

In 2022, a new edition of the Code of Ethics for Civil Servants was adopted, focusing on the separation of ethical requirements from other requirements not directly related to official ethics. This allows us to focus on key aspects of ethical behaviour and improve the standards of moral character of employees. New measures have been implemented to combat corruption and enhance ethical standards, such as the rule permitting the dismissal of political employees for "loss of trust" and bolstering the ethics commissioner's authority by placing them directly under the supervision of the head of the government agency.[17]

As part of efforts to strengthen institutional guarantees for protecting civil servants' rights, explanatory comments for the Code of Ethics have been developed to enhance awareness of compliance with ethical standards. Furthermore, to comply with ethical standards while performing official duties, measures were taken to prevent gambling addictions, including the requirement that civil servants refrain from visiting gambling establishments.[18]

13.4.4.9 Changing Work Modalities

Similar to many countries worldwide, Kazakhstan has also adjusted the operational practices of the civil service by implementing remote work and flexible schedules. This transition was not only driven by the desire to preserve the health and well-being of its public employees, but also taking into consideration contemporary trends in human resource management. For instance, maintaining flexible working arrangements post-pandemic has become part of the strategy to increase employee satisfaction and productivity, and also contribute to more efficient use of human resources.

[17] The appointment of a political civil servant to another political position does not relieve him of the obligation to resign for the commission of a corruption crime by a direct subordinate employee at his previous place of work.

[18] In July 2024, amendments and additions were made to some legislative acts of the Republic of Kazakhstan on gambling business issues. Anti-corruption restrictions have been introduced for persons holding responsible government positions and authorized to perform government functions. Dismissal is envisaged for failure to comply with the law. This measure is fully consistent with the petition initiated by public activists.

To regulate and monitor compliance with flexible and remote work modes, the Agency has developed an appropriate procedure. In most cases, flexible working hours are used by employees who are in special life circumstances, for example, parents of preschool and school-age children, parents raising children with disabilities, as well as those who live at a considerable distance from their place of work or need treatment.[19]

13.4.5 Summary

In general, all changes and innovations are aimed at creating a fair and responsive government system that meets the needs of modern society and contributes to its sustainable development. At the centre of all these efforts is the person—both the employee and the citizen to whom the services are provided. Continuing to advance along the path of innovation, enhancing the quality of work within the government, and delivering public services proactively instils confidence that the ongoing development and professionalisation of the civil service will be successful. The future of Fair Kazakhstan will be built on robust and modern foundations of public administration that effectively meet the needs of its people and society.

13.5 The Case of the Kyrgyz Republic

The World Pandemic 2020 was a serious test for all countries, including the Kyrgyz Republic. It had a serious impact on all aspects of social life, sectors of the economy, and on the living standards of the population. A significant role in reducing the negative impact of the pandemic on the country's socio-economic situation was played by the government, which urgently implemented anti-crisis measures. Nevertheless, the health authorities of Kyrgyzstan, as well as other government agencies, were not prepared for the coronavirus crisis. This was particularly evident in the first six months after the March 2020 lockdown in Kyrgyzstan. Despite measures taken by the Government of the Kyrgyz Republic to contain

[19] A survey among civil servants showed that the majority of managers (79%) did not notice a decrease in quality during remote work. This indicates high adaptability to new working conditions and the ability to maintain a high level of efficiency and professionalism even in a crisis situation.

COVID-19, the peak of the disease and human deaths occurred during the summer months of that year (ADB/UNDP 2020).

During this period, the shortcomings of the system of public administration of Kyrgyzstan, and its inability to promptly respond to external and internal challenges became particularly evident. The consequence of this was a decline in the authority of public institutions and the need for fundamental changes in the state governance system. During the pre- and pandemic periods, the Kyrgyz Republic had a parliamentary-presidential form of government defined by the 2020 Constitution. According to its Provisions, the President of the Kyrgyz Republic could be elected for only a one six-year term and had less authority to forming the Government of the country than the *Jogorku Kenesh* (Parliament) of the Kyrgyz Republic. In Parliament only a faction or a coalition of factions constituting a majority could nominate a candidate for the position of Prime Minister. Loss of the parliamentary majority by a faction or coalition of factions entailed the resignation of the Government and a new Prime Minister had to be nominated, and a new Government formed. This led to frequent changes in the composition of the Government, including the Prime Minister.[20]

Such collisions did not contribute to a sustainable performance by the executive branch, significantly affecting the efficiency and effectiveness of decisions made by the Government. These shortcomings of the then prevailing system of state power manifested themselves during the pandemic and the post-pandemic periods. For instance, the health authorities of the republic were not prepared for the pandemic, which caused an increase in the number of infected people and in a number of cases, official health structures were replaced by volunteer associations of citizens and initiatives of private organisations. Furthermore, the coronavirus pandemic, as in other countries, caused a social crisis in Kyrgyzstan, and its restrictive measures caused a contraction of the economy, reduced remittances of migrant workers from Russia, and the closure of many business enterprises.[21]

[20] Article 5, Constitution of the Kyrgyz Republic. Adopted by Referendum on 27.06.2010. https://online.zakon.kz/Document/?doc_id=30778565&pos=4;-106#pos=4;-106.

[21] The pandemic had a serious impact on the economy: exports dropped by 20%, migrant remittances decreased by a quarter, and the budget deficit amounted to almost 6%, (ADB/UNDP 2020).

This situation became a catalyst for change of power. It occurred purely because of the weakness of the previous government, and its inability to effectively solve public problems in a timely manner. Furthermore, its inability to organise and hold fair elections to the parliament of the country also contributed to the decline of its authority among the population.

13.5.1 *The New Constitution and Institutional Changes in the Governance System*

This state of affairs first led to the resignation of the Government of the Kyrgyz Republic, and then to the resignation of President Jeenbekov. In accordance with the 2020 Constitution, the *Jogorku Kenesh* elected Zhaparov as Acting Prime Minister and then as Acting President. In January 2021, Zhaparov was a candidate in the presidential elections, which he won with 79.2% of the vote of those who took part in the elections.[22]

The new political forces that came to power linked the solution of social and economic problems with the strengthening of state institutions and the need for constitutional change in the Kyrgyz Republic. For this purpose, a referendum on the form of government was held in January 2021, in parallel with the presidential election, through which citizens chose a new form of government—a presidential republic.[23] Thus, after several attempts trying different forms of government of other states, ranging from presidential to parliamentary, Kyrgyzstan returned to a presidential one.

[22] AKI-press (2021). Preliminary Voting Results in Kyrgyzstan's Snap Presidential Elections as of 8.00 am of 11 January: Sadyr Zhaparov leads with 79.2% of the votes. https://akipress.com/news:653097:Preliminary_voting_results_in_Kyrgyzstan_s_snap_presidential_elections_as_of_8_00_a_m__of_Jan_11__Sadyr_Japarov_leads_with_79_2__of_votes/?place=main1.

[23] According to official data, 1,394,021 people voted in the referendum, representing 39.12% of the total number of 3,563,574 eligible voters. 84.1% of those voted in favour of the transition to the presidential system, while 11.3% preferred the parliamentary system, and 4.6% of voters voted against both options. Central Election Commission of Kyrgyz Republic: 2021 Referendum Results. https://shailoo.gov.kg/ru/ReferendumReferendum/zakon-naznachenii-referenduma3/.

According to the new Constitution the balance of power between the President of the Kyrgyz Republic and the Parliament changed, with presidential power significantly strengthened. In particular, the President was given the right to determine the structure and composition of the Cabinet of Ministers, as well as to appoint the heads of regional administrations.[24] Furthermore, subject to a plebiscite, the head of state can single-handedly set the date of parliamentary elections or impose a state of emergency, which can be especially crucial in case of pandemics and/or other crises.

Conversely, important changes have also occurred in the organisation and activities of the executive branch. Under the new Constitution, the Government has been replaced by a Cabinet of Ministers headed by the President. He appoints, with the consent of the Jogorku Kenesh, the Chairperson of the Cabinet of Ministers, who is also the Head of the Presidential Administration. In this context, the Jogorku Kenesh of the Kyrgyz Republic still retains considerable powers, including adopting laws, amending, and supplementing the Constitution, approving the republican budget and the implementation report of the Cabinet of Ministers, consenting to the appointment of the Chairman of the Cabinet of Ministers, his deputies and members of the Cabinet of Ministers, and electing or consenting to appointment to a number of state bodies, among other.

In the past, the Jogorku Kenesh members were elected solely on party lists. Consequently, deputies were not directly elected by the people, as they were appointees of their parties. This led to the decrease of the legitimacy of the Parliament from convocation to convocation. According to the new law on the election of deputies to Jogorku Kenesh, its deputies are not elected only from party lists, but also in single-mandate constituencies. The new law also decreased the number of deputies elected from the previous 120 to 90, with 54 of the 90 elected on party lists, and 36 in single-mandate constituencies.[25] All this contributed to raising the level of popular representation in Parliament.

Under the new Constitution, the Constitutional Chamber was removed from the Supreme Court and the Constitutional Court of

[24] The new Constitution was adopted by a popular vote referendum on 11.04.2021. The Constitution specifies that the structure and composition of the Cabinet of Ministers are determined by the President and its activities are ensured by the Presidential Administration.

[25] At the same time, a 30% quota of party lists was retained for women candidates.

the Kyrgyz Republic was established. This was not a novelty: it had been in operation until the adoption of the new Constitution in 2010. The Constitutional Court and the Chamber are called to protect the Constitution of the Kyrgyz Republic, but the Constitutional Chamber was engaged in constitutional control, while the Constitutional Court became the supreme body of judicial power to protect the Basic Law. Amendments to the Constitution were also introduced in the direction of strengthening people's power by establishing such an institution as the People's *Kurultai*.[26] As a deliberative and supervisory public representative assembly, it can give recommendations to the President of the Republic on areas of social development. It is important that the new Constitution endows the People's Kurultai with the right of legislative initiative. With the adoption in 2023 of the Constitutional Law of the Kyrgyz Republic "On the People's Kurultai", this institution was legally enshrined.

13.5.2 Development Priorities

In the post-pandemic period in Kyrgyzstan a new socio-political reality was formed. These conditions required the formulation of a new vision for further development of the state, considering the changes that have occurred in the country, the region, and the world. In this context, the new President of the country Zhaparov, as the head of the state and the executive power outlined the following priority tasks: (i) Modernisation of the entire system of executive power, transformation of the work of the government; (ii) Uncompromising fight against corruption; (iii) New economic policy; and (iv) Digitalisation of public services.

Therefore, one of the first and significant steps of the new Cabinet of Ministers was the development and approval in 2022 of the National Development Programme of the Kyrgyz Republic until 2026.[27] Its relevance lies in the fact that it defines guidelines for public administration reform. The National Programme included a wide range of measures in

[26] The People's Kurultai consists of 700 delegates elected only for the period of its holding. The quota of delegates to the People's Kurultai is determined according to the principle of representation of regional, branch, ethnic, national, and age affiliation.

[27] Decree of the President of the Kyrgyz Republic (No 435, 21.10.2021) "The National Development Programme of the Kyrgyz Republic until 2026". https://cbd.minjust.gov.kg/430700/edition/1096469/ru.

seven priority areas, and its provisions formed the basis for drawing up sectoral and territorial development documents in the Kyrgyz Republic. As a result of the Programme implementation, it is expected that the Kyrgyz Republic will improve its position in key international ratings. It is also planned to achieve considerable progress in the realisation of the UN Sustainable Development Goals until 2030, to which Kyrgyzstan adheres to.

As part of the modernisation of the executive branch, new approaches to human resources policy have been outlined for the post-pandemic period. The President of the Kyrgyz Republic issued two Decrees aimed at ensuring equal access of citizens to state and municipal service, and the formation of a personnel reserve for administrative positions.[28] Along with attracting professionals, the plan is to attract progressive young people, to improve the system of retraining and professional and career development of employees of state and local self-government organisations, and to reduce the risk of corruption in personnel-related issues. Another innovation in personnel policy is that appointments to political state and municipal positions of local authorities will be made from the regional and municipal personnel reserve. Furthermore, the Academy of Public Administration under the President of Kyrgyz Republic (APAP KR) will be responsible for the training of state and municipal personnel reserve together with the State Agency for State and Municipal Service Affairs. Additionally, according to the State Strategy for the Development and Formation of Personnel in the Kyrgyz Republic for 2023–2025,[29] the effective functioning of the state civil service and municipal service as a legal, organisational, and social institution requires enhancement of the legislative framework.

Taking into account the mistakes and lessons learned in public administration during the pandemic and post-pandemic periods, an administrative and territorial reform was initiated. Errors in making operational decisions at the level of territorial administrations to contain the pandemic, corrupt practices in the distribution of humanitarian aid at the regional

[28] "On the new state personnel policy" (29.01.2021) and "On approval of the State Strategy of development and formation of personnel in the Kyrgyz Republic for 2023–2025" (23.02.2023).

[29] Decree of the President of the Kyrgyz Republic (No 17, 23.02.2023) "The State Strategy of development and formation of personnel in the Kyrgyz Republic for 2023–2025". https://cbd.minjust.gov.kg/66-51/edition/1221426/ru.

level, and a sluggish system of state and municipal administration at the regional level required optimisation of the administrative-territorial division. The purpose of the programme is to consolidate rural municipalities, improve their infrastructure and provide services to the population, i.e., the aim is not to reduce the number of municipal employees, which will occur when *aimags* are united, but to create conditions for the provision of quality municipal services to the population and the rational use of natural resources. A Presidential Decree instructs the Cabinet of Ministers to create a system of regional standards for the accessibility of engineering, communications, and social infrastructure for the population in the regions, depending on the size of the population and the type of settlements (urban, rural). It is also planned to introduce a system of state subsidies for local public initiatives aimed at implementing crucial projects for towns and villages to improve their territories and living conditions.

One of the urgent problems negatively affecting the work of public administration, judicial and law enforcement bodies, local self-government bodies, health care and education institutions continues to be the high level of corruption in Kyrgyzstan. As noted, this was particularly evident during the pandemic period, when at the beginning of the pandemic it turned out that there were not enough masks and other medical supplies in the country. At the same time, it turned out to be unknown where four hundred million dollars approximately of borrowed funds from the IMF and a number of countries allocated to combat the consequences of severe quarantine and lockdown were spent on.

In Transparency International's Corruption Perception Index (CPI), Kyrgyzstan is consistently ranked among the 50 most corrupt countries.[30] Taking into account that this is one of the reasons for the inefficiency of the state governance system, the new Kyrgyz authorities declared the fight against corruption as one of their main priorities. The work to eradicate corruption began with unprecedented steps, large-scale arrests of deputies, high-ranking officials and persons associated with the crime bosses. This has yielded tangible results.[31] These measures were supported by the public and delegates of the second People's *Kurultai*.

[30] Corruption Perception Index Report 2021. https://www.transparency.org/en/cpi/2021.

[31] In 2020, they yielded 248 billion soms (USD 2.7 billion), and in 2021 313 billion soms (USD 3.5 billion). Stat KG. 2021. Operative Information. https://www.stat.kg/ru/statistics/finansy/.

The new policy direction in this area is reflected in the Anti-Corruption Strategy adopted in 2023. It emphasises systemic preventive measures, which should help to eradicate not only the causes and conditions, but also all preconditions that give rise to corruption occurrences, as well as minimise administrative barriers to business development and investment attraction and ensure effective protection of the legitimate interests and rights of citizens and entrepreneurs. Thus, the provisions in the law for the prosecution of persons associated with oligarchs and thieves should be seen as the first steps in a long and complex fight against corruption. A comprehensive approach and reforms in the field of justice, strengthening of civil society institutions, as well as raising awareness and the legal culture of the population are also required.

In parallel with the modernisation of the executive branch, a new economic policy was implemented in the post-pandemic period. It manifested itself in the fact that the state began to stimulate the development of the real sector of the economy by defining priorities, creating a reasonable institutional environment, attracting foreign and domestic investors, and financing many important projects while reducing administrative red tape for business. The implementation of major infrastructure projects, such as the construction of the Kambar-Ata-1 Hydro Power Plant (HPP), the construction of the China-Kyrgyzstan-Uzbekistan railroad and others, has begun. A significant event in the economy was the acquisition of the largest gold mine in Kyrgyzstan—"*Kumtor*"—by the state. At the same time, substantial investments were made in the social sphere, e.g., construction of new schools and departmental buildings. However, the main economic task remains the creation of jobs. For this purpose, one hundred large industrial enterprises are to be established in Kyrgyzstan in the coming years.

Overall, positive change is observed in the economy. In 2022, according to the National Statistical Committee, the real growth of the economy amounted to 4.8%. In 2023, Kyrgyzstan's GDP exceeded one trillion soms (USD 1.2 billion) for the first time in its history, and the republic's economy grew by 6% during the same year. The republic's trade turnover with the Commonwealth countries exceeds 5 billion US dollars; a growth rate of almost 30% (Petrov 2023). This positive turn in the economy also allowed for increasing the salaries of state and municipal employees, including teachers, doctors, police, and military personnel, as well as pensions and benefits—from 50 to 100% in 2022–2023.[32]

Given the importance of digitalisation of public services, in the post-pandemic period, a policy decision was made to accelerate the introduction of digital technologies in all spheres of public life. For this purpose, the Ministry of Digital Development was established in 2021. This created the prerequisites for an active policy of wide introduction of information and communication technologies in all sectors and spheres of governance, in the provision of public services. Starting from 2023, one of the deputy heads of ministries and departments, local state administrations and mayors of cities have been vested with the authority to lead the digitalisation efforts as heads of digital development.

Work is currently underway to prepare the National Strategy "Digital Kyrgyzstan 2024–2030". It will include measures to train state and municipal employees in digital competencies. For this purpose, the Academy of Public Administration promotes the improvement of digital competencies of civil servants, and it has introduced a master's programme in Digital Public Administration. Graduates will acquire the necessary competencies in the development, modernisation, implementation, adaptation and use of information systems and technologies in the field of state and municipal administration. The Academy is also working on the creation of a digital educational platform that will allow employees to remotely access educational resources from around the world.

New innovative management tools and technologies are also being introduced into the practice of public administration in Kyrgyzstan. One such example is the implementation of the "Government Accelerators" project, which is a methodology for solving problems and achieving goals within a 100-day period. The first three projects utilising this methodology have been successfully implemented and a decision on its scaling up in the system of state and municipal administration is being prepared.

[32] Stat KG. 2023. The Kyrgyz Republic took 45th place in terms of the SDG for 2023 and is a leader among Central Asian countries.

https://stat.kg/ru/news/kyrgyzskaya-respublika-zanyala-45-e-mesto-po-pokazatelyam-celej-ustojchivogo-razvitiya-za-2023-god-i-lidiruet-sredi-stran-centralnoj-azii/

13.5.3 Summary

A set of institutional measures undertaken by the state in the post-pandemic period has allowed to improve the work of public administration organisations in Kyrgyzstan. This, in turn, has contributed to stimulating the economy, developing infrastructure, supporting the social sector, bringing funds out of the shadow, and attracting foreign and domestic investors. Thanks to the strengthening of state institutions, despite the serious political events in 2020, Kyrgyzstan has adapted its public administration system to cope with new challenges in the face of emergencies and political cataclysms occurring in the modern world.

13.6 The Case of Uzbekistan

Providing a comprehensive overview of Uzbekistan's public administration transformation in the last three years is not feasible given the space limitation. Nevertheless, an attempt is made to outline significant legal and institutional changes and to highlight key trends and patterns to inform readers.

Under President Mirziyoyev's first presidential term (2016–2021), governance reforms' rhetoric focused on mending frayed state-society relations. This goal necessitated opening up public administration, attuned to citizens' needs. The "downshifting" policy (*pastga tushib ishlash*) aimed to empower local officials (district/town and regional) to function as street-level bureaucrats, directly addressing individual and communal concerns raised through "Presidential" and public receptions. Additionally, a new form of local administration such as sectoral management (when a district or city is divided into four quarters (sectors) in which local *hokims* (mayors/governors), prosecutors, heads of local police and tax office are separately responsible to deal with citizen complaints, improve business conditions, etc., have been tried.

Public service centres, built through public–private partnerships and operating under the one-stop-shop principle, have been established in all districts and towns since 2017. This major reform has significantly reduced the administrative burden on citizens, simplifying the process of applying for and receiving state-issued permits, certificates, and other documents.

While initial reforms under President Mirziyoyev enjoyed popular support, they also strained the state budget and faced implementation challenges, such as:

- *High Costs*: The reforms' initial popularity came at a price—the number of central government institutions increased, and the salaries of civil servants were raised—placing a significant additional burden on the state budget (Umarova 2022);
- *Incomplete Frameworks*: In many cases, the legal framework, and regulations necessary for smooth functioning of these new institutions remained incomplete for a prolonged period;
- *Unfulfilled Potential*: Several well-conceived ideas outlined in the President's public administration reform concept note have not materialised;
- *Stalled Participation*: Efforts to enhance public participation in policymaking, another intended reform, encountered resistance from various levels of the state bureaucracy.

The pandemic severely tested the public administration system, demanding agile policymaking and execution amidst immense uncertainty. Furthermore, the state institutions found it easier to mobilise financial and human resources in an old-fashioned way, but harder to engage and build greater trust with the public through collaboration and transparency (Karshiev and Kristiina 2023).

13.6.1 Constitutional Reforms on Local Governance

After securing a second term in the end of 2021, President Mirziyoyev launched a push to reform the Constitution, raising concerns among some analysts that this could be interpreted as a potential move to enable further terms in office. Overshadowed by protests in Karakalpakstan in 2022 regarding the potential change of the sovereign republic's status, the new Constitution finally came into force on 1 May 2023 following a national referendum a day earlier.[33]

[33] The 2023 Constitution of the Republic of Uzbekistan. https://lex.uz/docs/6451070.

The new Constitution has marked a significant rhetorical shift, departing from the "*state as the chief reformer*" principle, championed by President Karimov in the early 1990s to a novel approach, emphasising "*society as the main driver of reforms*". This would imply enhancing the public administration's capacity to translate the public aspirations into policies and programmes that serve the public good, while maintaining impartiality in political decision-making. It also overtly corroborated the secular and social nature of the state in Uzbekistan.

Falling short of earlier calls for elections of the regional *hokims* (heads of local governments), the new Constitution nevertheless entails discontinuing the practice where hokims led both the executive and representative bodies. Consequently, the positions of hokim (head of the executive) and *rais* (chair) of Kengash (Council) are to be separated. As large part of the functions, rights and responsibilities of local governance were jointly shared by executive (*hokim*) and representative (*Kengash*) bodies, their new delineation is worryingly late. The corresponding amendments to the Law on Local State Administration are yet to be introduced, which has resulted in discrepancies in practices on the ground. For example, a quick look at the *E-qaror.gov.uz* website, which publishes decisions of local governments, shows that *Kengash* decisions are currently signed by *hokims*, and chairs (*raises)* of a *Kengash*, and temporary chairs (*rais*es) of the session. Upcoming legislative changes in this regard, while belated, will also demonstrate to what extent the constitutional principle of people as the ultimate powerholder and democratic representation are upheld.

13.6.2 Public Administration Reforms in Central Executive Bodies

The end of 2021 also marked a new attempt to reform the public administration system in Uzbekistan. In contrast to the reforms of 2016–2021, prioritising *effectiveness*—achieving the results with as much resources as required—this time the emphasis has shifted towards *efficiency*—achieving results with as little resources as possible. Major personnel changes in the Presidential Administration had a significant impact on the final document on administrative reforms in December 2022, with the input from a team of foreign consultants, led by former EBRD President Suma Chakrabarti; Advisor to the President of Uzbekistan.[34]

A new wave of administrative reforms that kicked off on 1 January 2023 with a grand reorganisation and unification of many ministries produced an intense debate both within the public administration and the public. "Compact government" was a new motto, which envisaged consolidating ministries, committees, agencies, and inspections into a unified system with 56,466 employees, representing a planned reduction of 17,447 positions.[35] However, following a subsequent personnel reshuffle in the Presidential Administration, the implementation of this reform has slowed considerably. Despite promises, the much-anticipated unified open registry of state functions and their critical reconsideration has yet to be launched, and a substantial number of crucial bylaws and regulations remain unadopted.

13.6.3 Local Self-governance and Participatory Governance

While "*mahallas*" (local self-governing neighbourhood communities) are considered non-governmental organisations in accordance with the existing legislation, the government has tried different options to actively reform the local self-governance system. A separate ministry for mahalla affairs existed in the period 2020–2022 until a new wave of administrative reforms abolished it and transferred some functions to the Ministry of Employment and Poverty Reduction.[36] More recently, mahallas, as the lowest level administrative unit, have been seen as a policy implementation

[34] Decree of the President of the Republic of Uzbekistan (No PF-269, 21.12.2022) "On Measures to Implement New Uzbekistan Administrative Reforms", [Yangi O'zbekiston ma'muriy islohotlarini amalga oshirish chora-tadbirlari to g'risida]. https://lex.uz/docs/-6324756.

[35] Decree of the President of the Republic of Uzbekistan (No PF-14, 25.01.2023) "On priority organisational measures for the efficient activity of the republican executive bodies" [Respublika ijro etuvchi hokimiyat organlari faoliyatini samarali yo 'lga qo 'yishga doir birinchi navbatdagi tashkiliy chora-tadbirlar to 'g'risida]. https://lex.uz/docs/-6369997.

[36] Decree of the President of the Republic of Uzbekistan (No PF-14, 25.01.2023) "On priority organisational measures to efficient activity of republic executive bodies", [Respublika ijro etuvchi hokimiyat organlari faoliyatini samarali yo 'lga qo 'yishga doir birinchi navbatdagi tashkiliy chora-tadbirlar to 'g'risida]. https://lex.uz/docs/-6369997.

arena for social protection, poverty reduction, and small business promotion. The number of civil servants, attached to each of over nine thousand mahallas in the country, has increased up to seven (*mahalla yettiligi*). The newly created non-governmental Association of Mahallas, headed by President Mirziyoyev's protege and former Advisor, has been provided with vast powers, which will oversee allocation and spending of mahalla budget funds.[37] Questions, however, remain over realisation of self-governance principles under a new quasi-state vertical power. While the country's leadership calls for more decentralisation and working towards empowering local democracy in the longer term, we think that the prevalent authoritarian governance model will remain a major impediment towards this end.

Ensuring free and fair public participation in governance necessitates mutual trust, which should be cultivated not only through the public's trust in the government but also through the government and bureaucracy's trust in the public as co-creators. While various initiatives, including public advisory councils, e-petitions, public consultations, and regulatory consultations (such as regulation.gov.uz), have been implemented, they have often failed to gain long-term traction, primarily due to the government's inability to effectively harness citizen input.

In this regard, the participatory budgeting platform (openbudget.uz), initiated by the Government, has demonstrated that citizens are not only willing but also able to actively contribute to decision-making processes. This mechanism effectively addresses the "dictator's dilemma", which arises from information asymmetry in determining public needs at the local level. With 11.7 million citizens participating in the 2024 iteration (more than half of the voting population), the platform has gained significant popularity. While further citizen-centred design improvements are necessary, the enthusiasm shown by the general public for this initiative is promising and is expected to foster increased trust and citizen participation in public decision-making.

[37] Gazeta.uz. Mahalla can carry out any task. Association of mahallas addresses activists [«Makhallya smojet spravitsya s lyuboy zadachey». Assotsiatsiya maxalley obratilas k aktivistam]. https://www.gazeta.uz/ru/2024/01/17/mahallas/.

13.6.4 Civil Service Reform

After years of debate, Uzbekistan finally adopted its long-awaited Civil Service Law in August 2022.[38] This landmark legislation streamlined existing regulations by codifying them into a single document, but more importantly, it established a legal framework for the Civil Service Development Agency (founded in 2019) to implement a comprehensive civil service policy.

However, the law's definition of "civil servant" was narrow, excluding a sizeable number of state employees, including personnel within the parliament, local representative bodies (Kengashes), the judiciary, several ministries (Defence, Interior, Extraordinary Situations) and security entities. The law has stipulated the creation of a State Register of Civil Service Positions, outlining all eligible roles. Unfortunately, as of February 2024, this crucial register remains pending approval and public release. Furthermore, while the Civil Service Law necessitates mandatory income and asset declarations for civil servants, the essential implementing legislation outlining the specifics is still awaiting adoption, which leaves this critical transparency measure ineffective as of now.

The Law has also imposed restrictions on civil servants, prohibiting them from engaging in entrepreneurial activities, founding private companies, opening foreign bank accounts, or owning property outside of Uzbekistan in a push towards preventing conflict of interests. It is expected that the legislation would be developed in the new Law "On preventing conflicts of interests", which was adopted by the Legislative Chamber in 2022 and by the Senate in 2023.[39] Although the new Constitution stipulates that the President shall sign the submitted law within 60 days or must return the law with his/her objections to the Parliament, it was finally signed by the President on 5 June 2024, and it will enter into force in December 2024.[40]

[38] The Law on "The State Civil Service." of the Republic of Uzbekistan. Adopted by the Legislative Chamber on 2 March 2022 and approved by the Senate on 28.05.2022. https://lex.uz/docs/6146009.

[39] Gazeta.uz. Senate approved the law on preventing conflicts of interests [Senat «Manfaatlar to'qnashuvi to'g'risida»gi qonunni ma'qulladi]. https://www.gazeta.uz/uz/2023/06/01/conflict-of-interest/.

[40] BBC News O'zbek. 2024. Uzbekistan: Corruption, Filming the police, conflicts of interests—Interview with Tanzila Norboeva [O'zbekiston: Korruptsiya, IIBni videoga

Civil service recruitment procedures have been significantly simplified and a new Civil Service jobs portal (vacancy.argos.uz) allows centralised and competitive selection for mostly entry-level jobs in the local governments, education facilities and SOEs. Civil servants are divided into three groups: political, management, and auxiliary; with political appointees not subject to competitive selection procedures, as set in the Law. During 2020–2023, a total of 56,000 positions were filled through the portal.[41] However, open competitive selection for senior positions remains an exclusion to the closed selection rule.

At the same time, there is broad consensus within the government, that the required skills and competencies for civil servants are vastly different from those of the available pool. The current system, prioritising loyalty over professionalism, performance over accountability, "rule by law" over "rule of law", discourages strategic review of skills and capacities for the public administrators. The friction of norms and values, emanating from different interpretations of the Weberian ideal bureaucracy, neo-patrimonial nomenklatura, Islamic just governance and post-industrialist networked governance are set to persist.

13.6.5 Strategic Planning and Delivery

Uzbekistan's quest for improved governance through project-based approaches has seen several iterations. The Government has established multiple institutions to guide and coordinate strategic planning and reforms, seeking to enhance delivery outcomes. From 2017 to 2019, the National Agency for Project Management (NAPM) held significant authority in overseeing reforms in the management of SOEs, improving e-governance, and streamlining inter-agency coordination. In 2022, the Government established a new entity, the Agency for Strategic Reforms, indicating a shift in its approach. While the Agency has been tasked with developing and implementing sectoral reforms in relation to "New Uzbekistan" and "Uzbekistan 2030" strategies, its functions, with regard to improving management practices in the bigger SOEs were later called off.

olish, manfaatlar to'qnashuvi—Tanzila Norboeva bilan suhbat]. 26.01.2024. https://www.bbc.com/uzbek/uzbekistan-68103852.

[41] Otabek Khasanov, Blog post, 04.02.2024. https://t.me/otabek_khasanov/1411.

The Government has also established a delivery unit, a specialised team tasked with achieving specific, high-priority goals set by the leadership, employing results-oriented approaches in the social development sector (Agency for Strategic Reforms 2023). The model, based on successful case studies from the UK and elsewhere, seems to be the latest trend in governance reforms in Uzbekistan, as more and more ministries are opening similar units to tackle complex challenges outside traditional bureaucratic structures.

13.6.6 *Anti-corruption*

According to Transparency International's Corruption Perceptions Index, Uzbekistan has been showing slow, but consistent progress in the years 2012–2023 on the perceived levels of public sector corruption. Still, in 2023 it was ranked 121st among 180 countries, sharing the same score of 33 (out of 100) with Angola, Mongolia, and Peru, and being on par with the regional average of sub-Saharan Africa.[42]

Government reforms, by many accounts, led to a decrease in petty corruption (e.g., in police, healthcare, education, and local self-governance bodies) in various degrees. However, there have been numerous reports about conflicts of interest of high-level officials in the government which have not yet been addressed in detail, leading to low trust of society towards the Government's anti-corruption efforts.

In December 2023, Tashkent hosted the Sheikh Tamim bin Hamad Al-Thani International Anti-Corruption Excellence (ACE) Award event, attended by Qatar's Amir and Uzbekistan's President, which coincided with the biggest push in fighting elite corruption. Among the officials, who were arrested on corruption charges that month, were a former minister, hokims of districts, a deputy hokim of a region, and several high-level officials in central agencies.

Criminalisation of defamation and questions over the independence of the judiciary still hinder anti-corruption efforts of civic activists. In a case that received widespread attention, a popular blogger was sentenced to eight years in prison on slander charges in December 2023.[43]

[42] Corruption Perception Index Report 2023. https://www.transparency.org/en/cpi/2023.

[43] Official Information [Расмиий охборот]. https://t.me/AzizAbidov/4387.

13.6.7 *Technological Disruption*

Until recently most of the adopted digital technologies by the Government in Uzbekistan have been seen as facilitating the work of the civil servants, such as internal document-sharing digital platforms, or external web-portals and applications allowing citizen input (public services, e-signatures, petitions, etc.). Oftentimes these technologies were framed as "minimising human discretion" or allowing "fairness" in consideration of citizen appeals.

In 2021–2023 the push towards efficiency meant increased focus on digital tools for public sector modernisation. Accordingly, Uzbekistan moved from Group B to A, joining the list of 69 GovTech leader countries in the World Bank's GovTech Maturity Index 2022 (World Bank 2022). Uzbekistan's portal for digital public services (My.gov.uz) has received praise and the Government is aiming to introduce "digital by default" services, which should be provided in only three steps.[44]

While Blockchain and Artificial Intelligence (AI) technologies appear prominently in the Government's future plans and strategies, e.g., the Digital Uzbekistan 2030 Strategy, they are approached with caution, showing that the Government is also suspicious of their disruptive features. Despite multiple statements since 2017 on using blockchain for trust-based operations where a governmental entity acts as a custodian; a significant working project is yet to materialise. There have been reports that a closed blockchain has been implemented in a civil registry database of the Ministry of Justice,[45] which cannot be independently verified. Furthermore, the Ministry of Digital Development has

[44] Decree of the President of the Republic of Uzbekistan (No PF-76, 24.05.2023) "On Measures for The Effective Organisation of Public Administration in the Field of Digital Technologies Within Framework of Administrative Reforms", *[Ma'muriy islohotlar doirasida raqamli texnologiyalar sohasida davlat boshqaruvini samarali tashkil etish chora-tadbirlari to 'g 'risida]*. https://lex.uz/ru/docs/6472530

[45] @adliyangiliklari. 2022. The Ministry of Justice launched the first project using blockchain technology in the field of public service [Adliya vazirligi tomonidan davlat xizmatlari sohasida blokcheyn texnologiyasi qo 'llanilgan ilk loyiha yo 'lga qo 'yildi]. https://t.me/adliyangiliklari/6711.

established a dedicated AI unit, which is tasked with exploring and identifying opportunities to leverage AI for improved governance and service delivery.[46]

At the same time, there is a growing anxiety in the Uzbek society, for example, over the use of so-called face-recognition cameras (using machine-learning tools with AI capabilities) by the police; and in general, the safe storage and use of personal data, collected and/or generated by a vast governmental organisation. Although the law on personal data was adopted in 2019, the general public is not fully convinced about its fair implementation. While acknowledging problems with ethical, copyright, and other issues related to AI, Uzbekistan has not started active regulation of the sphere. At this moment, it seems that the government is content to be in the receiving end of the global regulatory work.

13.6.8 Challenges

While the efforts to reform Uzbekistan's public administration system have been ongoing for most of the post-independence years and had a new impetus following Mirziyoyev's ascend to power, the administrative culture that stems from the Soviet *nomenklatura* and performative style of governance seems resistant.

Many reform initiatives in Uzbekistan face significant hurdles. Often, progress stalls or even reverses when key proponents leave their positions, leading to lack of continuity and follow-through. Furthermore, some reforms lack robust evidence-based foundations and comprehensive plans for implementation. Instead, they may primarily reflect a performance façade, rather than addressing underlying issues with data-driven solutions. Additionally, intra-nomenklatura competition for resources and influence as well as the entrenched administrative culture can create significant barriers to agility and adaptability. This can be manifested in reforms being cancelled without proper justification or reflection on the reasons for their failure. Moreover, democratic representation principle requires the country's leadership to embrace further transfer of powers and resources towards elected officials in local and regional levels (mahallas and Kengashes), which state bureaucracy may hope to stall.

[46] Structure of the. Ministry of Digital Technologies of the Republic of Uzbekistan. https://digital.uz/en/structure/.

Ensuring the long-term responsiveness of state institutions to popular needs has proven challenging in Uzbekistan. While initial initiatives like the presidential receptions and online portals enjoyed success in 2016–2018, their resource-intensive nature limited wider implementation across the government. Additionally, several participatory mechanisms, including public advisory councils, e-petitions, and consultations, struggled to gain traction without sustained external support and robust public oversight.

Balancing the diverse interests of economic growth, ensuring justice and equality, and environmental sustainability is a delicate governance act. Critics have highlighted the environmental degradation as an example of bad governance, where short-term growthism resulted in reactionary government policies.

13.6.9 Summary

Public administration in Uzbekistan is characterised by a long history of ongoing reform initiatives. The Government is keenly interested in adapting best international practices, as exemplified in the case of delivery units, especially when it meets its current priorities. However, while the past three years have witnessed significant legal and institutional changes, the overall pace and effectiveness remain debatable. Navigating the complex interplay of political dynamics, bureaucratic inertia, and resource constraints has proven difficult. There remains a significant gap between declared principles and their implementation. As demonstrated above, legislative innovation may stay inactive for years due to non-adoption of key bylaws and decisions. Moreover, the personalist authoritarian nature of the state prioritises performance legitimacy, where quick fixes, declarative actions and international rankings drive the reforms momentum. In conclusion, while Uzbekistan's public administration reforms have witnessed positive developments, significant challenges remain. Sustaining momentum, addressing implementation gaps, and fostering a culture of evidence-based governance will be crucial for achieving long-term transformation and inclusive development.

13.7 Conclusion

COVID-19, a pandemic that spread rapidly around the world was also a major challenge for the public administration systems of the countries of Central Asia and the Caucasus. It revealed that the existing development strategies and programmes did not consider such risks as those associated with confronting a pandemic. Nevertheless, it seems that governmental institutions of these countries demonstrated their ability to mobilise rapidly and work effectively under crisis conditions during the pandemic; and they continued to be actively engaged in restoring their national economies by implementing more anti-crisis policies and measures, during the post-pandemic period. And in the midst of these, governments continued to confront other persistent challenges such as climate change, depletion of natural resources, population growth and demographic changes, increasing inequality, and widespread digitalisation including the integration of artificial intelligence across industries. In addition, these challenges have coincided with a transformation of social values caused by the creation of a global communication space through the internet and social networks that led to the emergence and rapid spread of different and novel values depicting a new vision of the world.

In this environment, governments had, and still have, to reconsider their governance approaches to ensure sustainable development and the well-being of their population under conditions of increasing uncertainty, turbulence, and instability. This involves a critical re-evaluation of policies and practices, so actions are formulated, and decisions are made to effectively address these challenges. In other words, governmental institutions need to develop adaptive and responsive policies that can skilfully navigate increasing uncertainty and instability, ensuring the welfare of the populace and advance the objectives of the Sustainable Development Goals (SDG).

In sum, it is crucial for governments to adopt a forward-looking approach by anticipating risks and problems and setting the right priorities. Public officials are encouraged to develop the ability to look ahead, considering not only the immediate objectives of government policy, but also potential risks ahead that may hinder or jeopardise the implementation of their policy objectives. This includes determining the best ways to protect the interests of future generations and ensure intergenerational justice (ACSH 2023). Balancing short- and long-term goals is vital, a lesson reinforced by the pandemic, which shifted the focus to the immediate challenges at the expense of medium- and long-term objectives. Additionally, establishing effective coordination among government organisations and agencies is essential for developing coherent objectives aligned with government priorities, identifying problems effectively, and allocating resources wisely (Baimenov 2020a).

Summarising the reform initiatives focusing on public administration and the civil service implemented in Central Asia and the Caucasus countries in the post-pandemic period; one may observe that the pandemic changed the agenda of the reform direction and priorities. In most cases, the new agenda includes improvements in governance, addressing contemporary challenges—especially in times of high uncertainty—and meeting expectations of citizens. Thus, they have placed their emphasis on improving strategic planning and enhancing risk management in their systems, as well as recognising that citizens are the primary drivers for reform and thus at the forefront of the reform agenda. For this reason, all have generated strategic documents guiding their way forward in public administration and the civil service.

They have also placed considerable emphasis on digitalisation—a process initiated before the pandemic but accelerated during the pandemic—which is still a priority of all countries in the region, although progress in this area seems to vary among them. Azerbaijan and Kazakhstan seem to have advanced much more than the other counties in question. In this respect, the Astana Civil Service Hub, through its joint initiative with the Government of Korea, is contributing to the further development of digital services and the digital transformation of these countries (and beyond).

Another area that the governments of the countries in Central Asia and the Caucasus have focused on is their civil services. In light of this, enhancement of the human resource management function in the civil service has gained considerable momentum across all countries in the region. Azerbaijan has adopted a strategic plan on civil service development and is actively working on creating and implementing a competency framework for civil servants. Georgia has concluded that the quality of leadership is crucial in this new reality, thus attaching significant importance on the development of leadership competencies and enhancing the attractiveness of the civil service as a potential employer. Kazakhstan recently adopted the Concept for Civil Service development, encompassing numerous advanced initiatives, such as universal recruitment.[47] Conversely, Kyrgyzstan and Uzbekistan are also implementing various

[47] In Kazakhstan, following the election of new president, the Government launched extensive reforms to foster a fairer society. These reforms encompass multiple sectors, including politics, public administration, and the civil service, aimed primarily at advancing state democratisation. Key initiatives include fostering a more responsive government,

initiatives for the civil service, aimed at increasing its effectiveness and efficiency.[48,49] An overall conclusion of the analysis demonstrates that the reforms in public administration and civil service undertaken in each of these five countries are characterised by a diversity of initiatives. Despite their differences, all these efforts share common goals: improving the agility, capacity for innovation, efficiency, and transparency of public administration, as well as ensuring a fair distribution of resources and public goods to better meet the needs and expectations of citizens.

References

ACSH. 2023. *Stewardship and public service: An introduction*. Astana: Astana Civil Service Hub. https://www.astanacivilservicehub.org/uploads/research_pdf/research%20project/pdf.

ADB/UNDP. 2020. COVID-19 in the Kyrgyz Republic: Socioeconomic and Vulnerability Impact Assessment and Policy Response. https://kyrgyzstan.un.org/en/87314-covid-19-kyrgyz-republic-socioeconomic-and-vulnerability-impact-assessment-and-policy.

Agency for Strategic Reforms. 2023. "Delivery Unit": A project focused on social reforms. Agency for Strategic Reforms under the President of the Republic of Uzbekistan. https://asr.gov.uz/en/news/7807.

Ansel, Cristopher, Eva Sorensen, and Jacob Torfing. 2021. The Covid-19 pandemic as a game changer for public administration and leadership?

strengthening the rule of law, enhancing parliamentary authority, and increasing governmental transparency. Notably, significant reforms are transforming public administration and the civil service, introducing innovations like the creation of a Presidential Youth Personnel Reserve, the adoption of contract-based employment, and the streamlining of bureaucratic processes, among other measures.

[48] The National Development Programme of the Kyrgyz Republic until 2026 was adopted in 2022. The following development priorities were defined: modernisation of the entire system of executive power, transformation of government performance; combating corruption; new economic policy; and the digitalisation of public services.

[49] Significant changes were made to the Constitution of Uzbekistan in 2023. For the first time, the society was recognised as the main driver of reforms. The priorities in public administration reform have shifted from *effectiveness*—achieving the results with as much resources as required—this time the emphasis has shifted towards *efficiency*—achieving results with as little resources as possible. A new wave of reforms announced in the beginning of 2023 are the establishment of a compact government, according to which the ministries and agencies were reorganised. The reforms are also occurring in the domains of local governance, civil service, strategic planning, combating corruption, and digitalisation.

The need for robust governance responses to turbulent problems. *Public Management Review*. 23 (7): 949–960.
Arjen, Boin, and Paul't Hart. 2022. From crisis to reform? Exploring three post-COVID pathways. *Policy and Society* 41 (1): 13–24. https://doi.org/10.1093/polsoc/puab007.
Baimenov, Alikhan. 2020a. Applying the model of dynamic concentric spheres in the analysis of governance: The case of Kazakhstan. *International Journal of Civil Service Reform and Practice* 5 (2). https://astanahubjournal.org/index.php/ijcsrp/issue/view/27.
Baimenov, Alikhan. 2020b. *О некоторых факторах эффективности государственного управления*. [About Some of the Factors for Public Administration Effectiveness]. *Государственная служба*. 22 (1): 26–32.
Baimenov, Alikhan. 2021. Trust as a factor in improving government efficiency. https://www.undp.org/kazakhstan/blog/trust-factor-improving-government-efficiency.
Baimenov, Alikhan, and Liverakos Panos. 2022. 30 years of transformation: A comparative assessment. In *Public service evolution in the 15 post-Soviet countries: Diversity in transformation*, ed. by A. Baimenov; and P. Liverakos, 1–50. Singapore: Palgrave Macmillan. https://doi.org/10.1007/978-981-16-2462-9.
Cheung, Anthony B. L. 2022. Reflections on public administration and management in a post-NPM, post-COVID-19 and post-Wilsonian world. In Reimagining public sector management. *Critical perspectives on international public sector management*, ed. by J. Diamond and J. Liddle, vol. 7, 15–30. Leeds: Emerald Publishing Limited. https://doi.org/10.1108/S2045-794420220000007003.
Deloitte. 2020. Transforming government post-Covid-19, 32 p.
Deloitte. 2024. Government trends 2024, 120 p.
Dunlop, Claire A., Ongaro Edoardo, and Baker Keith. 2020. Researching COVID-19: A research agenda for public policy and administration scholars. *Public Policy and Administration*. 35 (4): 365–383. https://doi.org/10.1177/0952076720939631.
European Parliament. 2022. *COVID-19 response of EU public administration*. Policy Department for Budgetary Affairs Directorate-General for Internal Policies, PE 733.411—June. European Parliament. https://www.europarl.europa.eu/thinktank/en/document/IPOL_STU(2022)733411.
Fraser, Alasdair, Andrews Donna, and Williamson Tim. 2021. *How officials can do better at delivering services to citizens*. World Bank Blogs. https://blogs.worldbank.org/en/governance/how-officials-can-do-better-delivering-services-citizens.
Juzhong, Zhuang, Emmanuel de Dios, and Anneli Lagman-Martin. 2010. Governance and institutional quality and the links with economic growth and

income inequality: With special reference to developing Asia. Asian Development Bank. No. 193, 63 p. https://www.adb.org/sites/default/files/publication/28404/economics-wp193.pdf.

Karshiev, Mirzokhid, and Kristiina, Silvan. 2023. The COVID-19 pandemic and the performative state in Uzbekistan. In *The politics of the pandemic in Eastern Europe and Eurasia: Blame game and governance*, ed. by M. Zavadskaya. Routledge. https://doi.org/10.4324/9781003364870.

Kaur, Misha, Heather Buisman, Alex Bekker, and Chad McCulloch. 2022. Innovative capacity of government: A systematic framework. OECD Working papers on Public Governance No. 51, 64 p. https://doi.org/10.1787/52389006-en.

Lazaro, Blanca, and Linda Aitameur. 2024. *Approach for the development of functional (technical) competencies of civil servants in the central government administration of Azerbaijan*. SIGMA project by EU and OECD.

Li, Veronica Q. T., Liang Ma, and Xun Wu (2022). COVID-19, policy change, and post-pandemic data governance: a case analysis of contact tracing applications in East Asia, *Policy and Society*, 41 (1):129–142.

Manning, Nick, Mukherjee Ranjana, and Gokcekus Omer. 2000. Public officials and their institutional environment: An analytical model for assessing the impact of institutional changes. Policy Research Working papers. World Bank Group. https://doi.org/10.1596/1813-9450-2427.

North, Douglass C. 1990. *Institutions, institutional change, and economic performance*. Cambridge University Press.https://doi.org/10.1017/CBO9780511808678.

OECD. 2020. The Covid-19 Crisis: A catalyst for government transformation? 29 p. https://www.oecd.org/coronavirus/policy-responses/the-covid-19-crisis-a-catalyst-for-government-transformation-1d0c0788/.

OECD. 2021. Public employment and management 2021. The Future of the Public Service, 136 p. https://doi.org/10.1787/938f0d65-en.

OECD. 2023. More resilient public administrations after COVID-19: Lessons from using the Common Assessment Framework (CAF) 2020. OECD Public Governance Policy Papers, No 29. Paris: OECD Publishing.

Petrov, Artem. 2023. *For the first time in the history of Kyrgyzstan, the volume of GDP exceeded a trillion soms [Впервые в истории Кыргызстана объем ВВП превысил триллион сомов]*. https://rg.ru/2023/12/06/obeshchanie-sderzhano.html.

Schomaker, Rahel M., and W. Bauer Michael. 2020. What drives successful administrative performance during crises? Lessons from refugee migration and the COVID-19 pandemic. *Public Administration Review* 80 (5): 845–850. https://doi.org/10.1111/puar.13280.

Špaček, David, Navrátil Marek, and Špalková Dagmar. 2023. New development: Covid 19 and changes in public administration—What do we know to date?

Public Money & Management 43 (8): 862–866. https://doi.org/10.1080/09540962.2023.2199545.

Umarova, Aziza. 2022. Uzbekistan: Long awaited transformation of civil service—Paradigm shift or hot air? In *Public service evolution in the 15 post-Soviet countries: Diversity in transformation*, ed. by A. Baimenov and P. Liverakos, 1–50. Singapore: Palgrave Macmillan. https://doi.org/10.1007/978-981-16-2462-9.

World Bank. 2022. *WBG GovTech maturity index 2022 update: Trends in public sector digital transformation.* Washington, DC. https://openknowledge.worldbank.org/handle/10986/38499.

Zukauskas, Edvardas, Zakharchenko Eduard, Jakubaityte-Revutiene Kristina, Gulzar Guliyeva, and Vezi Suleyman. 2021. Specific organisation and methodology, "Support to civil service reform in Azerbaijan" EU Technical Assistance Project.

Zukauskas, Edvardas, Zakharchenko Eduard, and Jakubaityte-Revutiene Kristina. 2023. Conceptual framework of competency model, "Support to civil service reform in Azerbaijan" EU technical assistance project.

CHAPTER 14

Public Administrations Reforms in the Western Balkan Countries in the Twenty-First Century: Challenges and Trends

Jahi Jahija

14.1 Introduction

The Western Balkans consist of Albania, Bosnia and Herzegovina, North Macedonia, Montenegro, Kosovo, and Serbia. Over the last two decades, this region has become an indispensable part of the European Union Agenda. Promised the perspective of membership, the countries from the region move towards joining the block at an uneven and uneasy pace. The Union's experience with the Western Balkans is an ambiguous one. On the one hand, the European Union plays a crucial role in the reconstruction, support, and reconciliation of these countries, promotes regionalism and local ownership of cross-border initiatives, provides for security, and promotes western values. On the other hand, the sluggish

J. Jahija (✉)
University of Tetovo, Tetovo, North Macedonia
e-mail: jahi.jahija@unite.edu.mk

A. Baimenov and P. Liverakos (eds.), *Public Administration in the New Reality*, https://doi.org/10.1007/978-981-96-3845-1_14

enlargement paths with unexpected stops and detours, an endless brain-drain, flirting with local autocrats and a growing gap between the Union and the candidate-states trigger frustration and exasperation.

Western Balkan countries applying for membership in the European Union need to reform their public administrations to meet the Copenhagen and Madrid criteria for accession. Most areas of government are covered or affected by the *acquis communautaire*,[1] the entire body of legislation of the European Community. In the various domains of the *acquis*, targets and content of reforms are fairly clear. Candidate countries need to transpose EC legislation into the domestic legal order and then implement and enforce it. Difficulties and delays are mainly linked to the process and pace of implementation due to lack of capacity.

No *acquis communautaire* exists for setting standards of horizontal systems of governance or national public administrations. Targets and orientations for public administration reform in the perspective of EU accession are therefore less distinct. However, over time a general consensus on key components of good governance has emerged among democratic states. These components include the rule of law principles of reliability, predictability, accountability, and transparency, but also technical and managerial competence, organisational capacity, and citizens' participation. Despite the lack of an *acquis communautaire*, this consensus has established principles for public administration shared by EU Member States with different legal traditions and different systems of governance. Over the course of time these principles have been defined and refined through the jurisprudence of national courts and, subsequently, the jurisprudence of the European Court of Justice.

Shared principles of public administration among EU Member States constitute the conditions of a "European Administrative Space" (EAS). The EAS includes a set of common standards for action within public administration, which are defined by law and enforced in practice through procedures and accountability mechanisms. Countries applying for EU membership should take these standards into account when developing their public administrations. Although the EAS does not constitute an agreed part of the *acquis communautaire*, it nevertheless serves as the guide for public administration reforms in candidate countries. In EU

[1] The European Union (EU) *acquis* is the collection of common rights and obligations that constitute the body of EU law and is incorporated into the legal systems of EU Member States.

Member States these standards, together with principles established by the constitution, are usually embedded in, or transmitted by, a set of administrative laws, such as administrative procedures acts, administrative process acts, freedom of information acts and civil service laws.

The extent to which a given candidate country shares these public administration principles and adheres to the standards of the EAS gives an indication of the capacity of its national public administration to effectively implement the *acquis communautaire*, in accordance with the criteria made explicit by the European Council in Copenhagen and Madrid.

The national public administration institutions of EU Member States implement and enforce the *acquis communautaire*. To be able to effectively do the same, the public administration of a candidate country must adhere to the general principles of good governance and meet the administrative standards defined within the EU. Implementation of the *acquis* in an administrative domain is of course a matter of capacity and resources within the relevant sector—but not only that. The general horizontal governance systems of a candidate country must also meet the requirements of the EU, since they are crucial for the reliable functioning of the entire administration, including the areas of the *acquis*. Successful implementation and enforcement are clearly dependent on horizontal governance structures and systems, such as procedures for administrative actions and mechanisms to ensure that the performance of civil servants is in line with EU standards.

The European Commission's approach to public administration reform, including civil service professionalisation, is based on the application of the European Principles of Administration (Nieto-Garrido and Delgado 2007). The concept of the European Administrative Space was developed in the late 1990s by SIGMA on behalf of the European Commission.[2] It considers that public administration at all levels of the European Union system of multi-level governance embodies basic principles such as the rule of law and therefore legal certainty and predictability,

[2] SIGMA —Support for Improvement in Governance and Management in Central and Eastern European Countries is a joint initiative of the OECD and the European Union. The initiative supports public administration reform efforts in thirteen countries in transition and is principally financed by the European Union. See SIGMA Papers No 23 and 27. https://www.oecd-ilibrary.org/governance/preparing-public-administrations-for-the-european-administrative-space_5kml6143zd8p-en and https://www.oecd-ilibrary.org/governance/european-principles-for-public-administration_5kml60zwdr7h-en.

openness and transparency, legal accountability, efficiency, and effectiveness. Each principle includes secondary principles of administration, for instance political neutrality, impartiality, professional integrity, and fair and equal treatment of public administration staff.

These principles describe administrative law principles defined by the European Court of Justice which in fact set public administration standards. Its purpose is threefold: firstly, it aims to define and provide criteria to give direction to public administration reforms in candidate countries; secondly, it provides benchmarks against which progress could be assessed; and thirdly, the ultimate purpose is to assist candidate countries in meeting the Copenhagen and Madrid public administration criteria for EU accession.

In 2014, SIGMA published the *Principles of Public Administration* and set out what good public governance entails in practice and outline the main requirements to be followed by administrations during the European Union (EU) integration process. Good public governance is key for achieving economic growth, competitiveness, and a better quality of life. Democratic governance and the rule of law require capable, accountable, and effective public administrations. In its 2014 and 2018 Enlargement Strategies, the European Commission (EC) highlighted public administration reform (PAR) as one of three "fundamentals first" areas of the EU enlargement process: "*Addressing reforms in the area of rule of law, fundamental rights and good governance remains the most pressing issue for the Western Balkans. It is also the key benchmark against which the prospects of these countries will be judged by the EU*".[3]

14.2 Administrative Law Principles and the European Administrative Space

The national administrations are assessed according to criteria of "legal and administrative capacity to implement the *acquis communautaire*", in fact creating serious difficulties due to diversity of the administrative systems, levels of institutionalisation, and values and resources required by changes.

[3] https://neighbourhood-enlargement.ec.europa.eu/revised-indicative-strategy-papers-2014-2020_en.

The framework of the EU enlargement policy for the Western Balkan states consists of the Stabilisation and Association Process (SAP),[4] which aims for them to get closer to the EU. It has three objectives: (1) stabilisation and transition to market economy; (2) promotion of regional cooperation; and (3) eventual accession to the European Union.

Shared principles of public administration among EU Member States constitute the conditions of a "European Administrative Space" (EAS) (Cardona 2009). The EAS is a metaphor with practical implications for Member States and embodying, *inter alia*, administrative law principles as a set of criteria to be applied by candidate countries in their efforts to attain the administrative capacity required for EU Membership. The EAS represents an evolving process of increasing convergence between national administrative legal orders and administrative practices of Member States. This convergence is influenced by several driving forces, such as economic pressures from individuals and firms, regular and continuous contacts between public officials of Member States and, finally and especially, the jurisprudence of the European Court of Justice.

Traditionally, standards of administrative performance have been defined and refined within the national boundaries of sovereign states (UNDP 2010). They have been the products of national constitutional arrangements, law-making activity of national parliaments, decisions of national administrative authorities and rulings of national courts. Within the EU this process is becoming increasingly supranational, and, for the reason of membership, it is possible to require shared mandatory administrative standards, as defined by the European Court of Justice at the European level and thus across Member States. However, stressing the harmonising potential of public administration standards is not to say that administrative institutions should be homogeneously set up across EU Member States. The important message is that, independently of institutional arrangements, national public administrations must recognise principles and adhere to standards that are shared by EU Member States.

[4] The Stabilisation and Association Process (SAP) is the European Union's policy towards the Western Balkans, established with the aim of eventual EU membership. Western Balkan countries are involved in a progressive partnership with a view of stabilising the region and establishing a free-trade area. https://neighbourhood-enlargement.ec.europa.eu/enlargement-policy/glossary/stabilisation-and-association-process_en.

14.2.1 *Administrative Law Principles*

Although the expression and concepts of administrative law (*Verwaltungsrecht, droit administratif*) differ from one national system to another, it is possible to agree upon a common definition of administrative law as being the set of principles and rules applying to the organisation and management of public administration and to the relations between administration and citizens.[5]

In the field of European Community Law, the European Court of Justice has defined a large number of administrative law principles by making reference to the general legal principles of administrative law common to the Member States, in an ongoing process. Particularly important principles set forth in the jurisprudence of the European Court of Justice, which all Member countries must in turn apply domestically when applying EC Law, are, among others: *the principle of administration through law; the principles of proportionality, legal certainty, protection of legitimate expectations, non-discrimination, the right to a hearing in administrative decision-making procedures, interim relief, fair conditions for access of individuals to administrative courts, non-contractual liability of the public administration*, etc.[6]

If there is an attempt to systematise the main administrative law principles common to western European countries, we could distinguish the following groups: (1) reliability and predictability; legal certainty; (2) openness and transparency; (3) accountability; and (4) efficiency and effectiveness.

- *Reliability and Predictability:* A number of administrative law principles and mechanisms work in favour of the reliability and predictability, also termed as legal certainty or juridical security, of public administration's actions and decisions. All of these principles attempt to eradicate arbitrariness in the conduct of public affairs. The *rule of law—Rechtsstaat; État de droit* - is a multi-sided mechanism

[5] See J. Ziller, *Administrations comparées: les systèmes politico-administratifs de l'Europe des Douze*, Montchrestien, Paris, 1993. See also J. Schwarze, *Europäisches Verwaltungsrecht*, Nomos, Baden-Baden, 1988.

[6] See J. Schwarze, *Europäisches Verwaltungsrecht,* Nomos, Baden-Baden, 1988. English version: *European Administrative Law*, London, 1992.

for reliability and predictability. It assumes the principle of "administration through law". In essence, the rule of law means that public administration ought to discharge its responsibilities according to the law. Public authorities make their decisions by following general rules or principles applied impartially to anyone who comes within their ambit of application. The stress is on the neutrality and generality of such application—the principle of non-discrimination. Public administration should decide according to the rule laid down, and to the interpretative criteria produced by the courts, disregarding any other consideration. The rule of law opposes arbitrary power, cronyism, and other deviations. The rule of law necessitates a strict hierarchy of legal rules enforced by independent courts as well as the principle that a public authority, normally, is not vested with the power to contradict the general rules laid down and made public in a specific regulatory decision.[7]

- *Openness and Transparency:* Openness suggests that the administration is available for outside scrutiny, while transparency suggests that, when examined closely, it can be "seen through" for the purpose of scrutiny and supervision. Openness and transparency allow, on the one hand, anyone affected by an administrative action to know its basis, and on the other, they render outside scrutiny of administrative action by supervisory institutions easier. Openness and transparency are also necessary instruments for the rule of law, equality before the law, and accountability.
- *Accountability:* Generally, accountability means that one person or authority has to explain and justify its actions to another. Thus, in administrative law it means that any administrative body should be answerable for its actions to other administrative, legislative, or judicial authorities. Accountability also requires that no authority should be exempt from scrutiny or review by others. It can be effected through many different mechanisms, including review by the courts, appeal to a superior administrative body, investigation by an ombudsman, inspection by a special board or commission, and scrutiny by a parliamentary committee, among many other. Accountability is instrumental in showing whether principles like the rule of law, openness, transparency, impartiality, and equality before

[7] *Prééminence des actes réglementaires sur les actes individuels d'une même autorité publique*, as It is expressed in French. This doctrine is considered of a French origin.

the law are respected. Accountability is essential to ensure values such as efficiency, effectiveness, reliability, and predictability of public administration.

- *Efficiency and Effectiveness:* One specific dimension of accountability relates to efficiency in the performance of public administration. The recognition of efficiency as an important value for public administration and civil service is relatively recent. Insofar as the state has become the producer of public services, the notion of productivity has entered the public administration. A related value is effectiveness, which basically consists of ensuring that the performance of public administration is successful in achieving the goals and solving the public problems set for it by law and government. It mainly calls for analysing and evaluating the public policies in place, and for assessing how well they are being implemented by public administration and civil servants.

14.2.2 The European Administrative Space

The principles enumerated above can be found in administrative law across all European countries. Although public administrations in European States are old structures, they have continuously adapted to modern conditions including EU Membership, which is itself evolving. Constant contact among public servants of Member States and the Commission, the requirement to develop and implement the *acquis communautaire* at equivalent standards of reliability across the Union, the emergence of a Europe-wide system of administrative justice, and shared basic public administration values and principles, have led to some convergence among national administrations. This has been described as the "European Administrative Space".[8]

All of this demonstrates the emergence of a European Administrative Space, which mainly concerns basic institutional arrangements, processes, common administrative standards, and civil service values (Lucica et al. 2011). This list is far from complete, and there are significant quality differences among the Members. Indeed, the problems raised by these differences among Member States is one of the main reasons why

[8] See SIGMA Paper, No 23, *Preparing Public Administrations for the European Administrative Space*, OECD, Paris, 1998.

institution-building has been given such a high priority in the enlargement process towards Central and Eastern Europe: "*Candidate countries will need to develop their administrations to reach the level of reliability of the European Administrative Space and an acceptable threshold of shared principles, procedures, and administrative structural arrangements. There is a minimum standard of quality and reliability of public administration that candidate countries should attain*".[9]

In the early years, the European Court of Justice case law was influenced by the legal systems of the initial Member States, and particularly by concepts stemming from French administrative law. Yet there has never been a sole French influence on the development of EC law, and the growth of Membership has led to a diversification of the sources of inspiration of the European Court of Justice's legal thinking. This means that the rulings of the Court do not respond particularly to a given national legal background, but that its jurisprudence is rather a composite of influences stemming from virtually all Members of the Union.[10] For example, the "administration through law" principle originated in the French *principe de légalité*as well as in the German concept of *Rechtsstaatlichkeit*, which are more or less close to the British concept of the *rule of law*. It is worth noting that even though these three notions have different national roots, they are nowadays conducive to similar practical effects. The concept of "fair procedure" can be traced back to British and German legal traditions.

14.2.3 Level of Convergence of Administrative Systems

A given administrative system can be assessed by scrutinising the extent to which these principles are actually applied, both in the formal legal arrangements in a country, and also in the daily behaviour of public authorities and civil servants. In this sense, these general administrative law principles serve as standards against which to measure the reliability of public administration, the degree of accountability of civil servants and public authorities, the soundness and practicability of procedures for shaping administrative decisions and for challenging them through appeal and redress.

[9] Ibid.

[10] See J. Schwarze (1992), *European Administrative Law*.

The extent to which different countries share these administrative law principles also gives an orientation as to the degree of compatibility among their administrative systems (Jreisat 2011). In other words, they also serve as preconditions for a closer integration among them on the one hand, and on the other, as measurements of the capacity of public administration institutional arrangements in a given country to implement the formalised *acquis communautaire*.

One of the main elements composing public administration, among others such as appropriate substantive and procedural laws, is the civil service. The behaviour of the civil service is patterned after those administrative law principles as guiding and binding principles. Substantive and procedural administrative laws, shaped against the backdrop of national constitutions and European administrative law, provide the legal institutional framework within which public authorities and civil servants have to behave in Member countries of the EU.

14.3 Administrative Law Principles and Civil Service Standards

The first role of the state in the field of employment is therefore to regulate basic relations between employers and employees. The state has to set minimum standards in order to establish fair working conditions for all employees, as well as to define the minimum rights and obligations of the two parties in the employment relationship.

The state also has the role of the employer. In this second role, as opposed to its first and general role, the state is responsible for ensuring the efficient, professional, and impartial performance of the public administration. This management responsibility creates a need for specific regulations governing state employees: staffing and career management policies, and management systems for selection, recruitment, promotion, and remuneration, all of which aim to guarantee the homogeneity and high quality of the staff and its performance among all branches and levels of government (Peters and Pierre 2004). Closely related to its role as employer, the state also has constitutional responsibilities in running the public administration in accordance with principles enshrined in the constitution and in administrative law. Furthermore, the state has to ensure the performance of the public administration in accordance with Administrative Law Principles and Civil Service Standards.

The modern concept of public administration entails a notion of hierarchical delegation of state powers to individuals operating within the public system. These individuals, the civil servants, are therefore not merely employees of the state but also, to a great extent, holders of state powers. As such, they also have to ensure that constitutional and administrative law principles are actually applied in the daily operation of public administration. Modern, constitutional civil service in a democracy is regarded as possible only when a set of conditions are in place[11]:

- Separation between the public and the private spheres;
- Separation between politics and administration;
- Development of individual accountability of civil servants by overcoming former collegial decision-making processes. This calls for well-educated and skilful public managers;
- Sufficient job protection, stability, and level of pay, and clearly defined rights and duties of civil servants;
- Recruitment and promotion based on merit.

All of these conditions contribute, to a great extent, to defining the nature and values of a modern professional civil service.

14.4 Western Balkan Countries Assessment on Administrative Law Principles and European Administrative Space Standards

The country assessment reports in 2012 for the Western Balkan countries (Albania, Bosnia and Herzegovina, Kosovo, Montenegro, Norh Macedonia, and Sebia) based on Administrative Law principles and the European Administrative Space analyses and takes stock of progress achieved by these countries by 2011, with an aim to also provide inputs into their reform agenda.[12] It focuses on civil service and administrative law, integrity, public expenditure management and control, public

[11] See Raadschelders and Rutgers, "The Evolution of Civil Service Systems", in Bekke, Perry and Toonen (Eds.) *Civil Service Systems in Comparative Perspective*, Indiana University Press, 1996.

[12] See SIGMA Country Assessment Reports 2012/7; Albania Assessment Report 2012. https://ideas.repec.org/s/oec/govaaf.html.

procurement, and policymaking and coordination. The main findings and recommendations for each country are.

14.4.1 Albania

The public administration is heavily politicised and remains fragile. There is intensive rhetoric by the Government regarding the professionalisation of the administration and the implementation of principles regarding fair recruitment, equality of chances and protection of the civil servants, but practice too often contradicts this rhetoric. Changes of ministers are usually accompanied by staff turnover, even in cases where the new minister belongs to the same political party as the preceding one. Polarised politics between Government and Opposition lead to reform deadlock.

The administrative system has the characteristics of a partocratic political regime,[13] in which the state apparatus is seized by partisan interests while the system of checks and balances is very weak, almost non-existent. This includes the dominance of the Parliament by the executive and a de facto lack of parliamentary control over the executive branch. The judiciary is also to a large extent subjected to the political needs of the executive, as it is hardly independent. The civil service has a narrow scope, with large areas of public employment falling outside of it. For these categories, the implementation of principles of professionalism, impartiality, and equality of chances is even more difficult. These non-civil servant officials remain extremely vulnerable to political influence and protection is weak. Civil service training mostly depends on international funds. The Training Institute of Public Administration (TIPA), reporting to the Department of Public Administration (DoPA), is not well supported by the Government. Its budget is not sufficient to support training needs.[14]

Recommendations

- The Government needs to create a climate of cooperation with the opposition, with the aim of setting common and long-term goals that have the support of all of the main political parties. Such a

[13] *Partocracy* is a form of government in which the political parties are the primary basis of rule rather than citizens or individual politicians.

[14] https://ideas.repec.org/p/oec/govaaf/2012-7-en.html.

climate requires political negotiation and compromise in order to build a consensus.

- The adoption of a package of laws, which form the most important structural elements of the state administrative legal framework, is required. The Ministry of Justice will need political support and technical assistance for the implementation of the two new pieces of legislation, namely the Law on Administrative Disputes and the Law on General Administrative Procedures, should the political situation allow for their adoption. The same applies to the DoPA concerning a new Civil Service Law.
- The civil service management system, based in DoPA, needs greater powers and capacities if it is to be respected by politicians and by the institutions employing civil servants. The legal, managerial, and infrastructural capacities of DoPA need to be strengthened so that it is able to exercise oversight and to steer the development of a more professional public administration.
- The civil service oversight bodies, such as the Civil Service Commission, need to be strengthened and their decisions respected by all administrative and political bodies.

A Law on Organisation and Functioning of the State Administration should bring about a new, clearer state organisational policy, which should include amending, where necessary, the current Law on Government and Law on Prefects.

14.4.2 *Bosnia and Herzegovina (BiH)*

Overall, the politico-administrative configuration of the country does not clearly and fully support the meritocratic principle as a basis for the professionalisation of the civil service. BiH State, Federal BiH, and the Respublika Srpska (RS) do not recognise the principle of a professional civil service based on merit in their respective constitutions. In fact, the clauses imposing ethnic representation are inimical to the merit system. Although the right of equal access to public employment is guaranteed to all citizens at all levels, the insistence on ethnic representation clearly favours the main three ethnic groups at the expense of minorities and of the merit system. While ethnic representation is the reality of the *Dayton*

Agreement for BiH,[15] the country would benefit from the development of a modality for balancing the principles of merit and proportional ethnic representativeness.

The status of civil servants, as defined in the existing legislation, is not compatible with prevailing standards in EU Member States. Furthermore, the way in which it is applied prevents the country from developing a professional, politically neutral, and impartial, merit-based civil service. Existing recruitment and promotion mechanisms and practices are not effectively contributing to the professionalism of the civil service. Party politics continues to play a significant role in civil service recruitment and promotion, even though it is often disguised as ethnic representativeness.

Training at all levels of the administration has been traditionally funded since 1995 by foreign donors. The existing authorities and international donors have relied too heavily on training as a sort of panacea to overcome structural problems.[16]

Recommendations

- Administrative legal principles for the organisation and functioning of the public administration and the judiciary at both federal and federated levels would need to be established in the constitution;
- The constitutional model of administration should favour simple structures and decision-making processes, while safeguarding the legal guarantee of individual rights balanced with protection of the public interest.

14.4.3 Kosovo

Patronage, politicisation, and lack of professionalism are still the main characteristics of the civil service system in Kosovo. While waiting for the full implementation of the new Civil Service Law motivation is low, skills are insufficient, and greater efforts are required to implement a service-oriented administrative culture. Limited managerial capacities and lack of delegation of power from the top level are other problems that

[15] The *General Framework Agreement for Peace in Bosnia and Herzegovina*, also known as *the Dayton Agreement* or *the Dayton Accords*, 14.12.1995.

[16] https://ideas.repec.org/p/oec/govaaf/2012-6-en.html.

need to be addressed. The civil service is shifting from a pure position-based to a mixed system blended with career patterns. However, the measures related to career advancement have not been enforced because the government has not yet approved all the necessary regulations, e.g., on performance appraisal. Therefore, the measures concerning vertical promotion cannot be enforced. The same situation applies to horizontal progression in salary steps, which is also due to the non-implementation of the Civil Service Law.

The salary system continues to be unfair, unbalanced, and incoherent. The old salary system based on coefficients and fixed salaries is still in place. The discretionary practice of adding several supplements to the basic salary is continuing. In certain cases, these supplements represent up to two or three times the basic salary, thereby distorting the overall salary system and increasing the difficulties in implementing the new system.[17]

Recommendations

- The Ministry of Public Administration should complete the legislation related to the implementation of the Law on Civil Service and should start as soon as possible the full implementation of the law.

14.4.4 Montenegro

The country's small size may explain some, but not all, of its administrative shortcomings, and in particular those related to the inferior quality of the institutional set-up. Most drawbacks stem from a bureaucracy based on patronage rather than merit, administrative practices disrespecting the rule of law, a political system dominated by a single political party since its inception, and a weak system of checks and balances.

The human resource management system is an area where the lack of respect for the law is particularly obvious. Frequently, ministries and administrative bodies simply disregard legally binding procedures or do not respect the competence of the Human Resources Management Agency (HRMA). Patronage networks, clientelism and politicisation thus dominate recruitment and promotion practices. Furthermore, the lack of statutory cooperation on the part of other administrative bodies is the

[17] https://ideas.repec.org/p/oec/govaaf/2012-4-en.html.

major reason some other efforts of the HRMA to develop the civil service management system, e.g., the completion of a central civil service registry, have failed so far.[18]

Recommendations

- The law is not fully respected. Frequently, public sector institutions do not hesitate to disregard legal provisions or binding procedures if the outcome of their observance would be unwelcome.
- Complaints are widespread that administrative authorities ignore Administrative Court rulings or obligatory decisions of other administrative bodies. The Government should consider providing the legal basis for tasking an appropriate institution, e.g., the Ministry of Interior and Public Administration, with systematically monitoring whether judgements of the Administrative Court are implemented by administrative authorities and publish the findings in an annual report.

14.4.5 North Macedonia

The former Yugoslav Republic has been further backsliding into politicisation and towards lack of respect for the rule of law. The system of democracy is gradually deteriorating, confusion between politics and administration is rife, and the public administration is further becoming de-professionalised. This renders public administration unreliable and unpredictable. Disrespect for the rule of law and the principle of legality is a basic feature of the public governance system. Quite often arbitrariness drives administrative decision-making. In his 2010 Annual Report, the Ombudsman described discrimination on the basis of political affiliation as the "cruellest one", while adding that ethnic and religious discrimination were also practiced.

Reform capacities are low and the willingness to reform in the right direction of democratisation, civil service professionalisation and solidification of a state ruled by law is hardly seen. The few well-intended reforms undertaken so far have been driven mainly from abroad, especially under the auspices of the European Commission, which is pushing

[18] https://ideas.repec.org/p/oec/govaaf/2012-3-en.html.

hard to approximate the country to EU member states' administrative principles and public management standards. The sustainability of these reforms cannot be guaranteed.[19]

Recommendations

- The Government should implement appropriate measures (e.g., awareness raising campaigns) targeted at senior and top-level management personnel of ministries and other administrative bodies in order to develop a culture of managerial accountability in the public administration, so that ministers and other senior staff see themselves as responsible for the legality of administrative actions in their area of authority and are enabled to act accordingly.

14.4.6 Serbia

The merit system in Serbia's civil service is not guaranteed and the professionalism of the state administration is limited. Recruitment to the civil service system is still largely based on political affiliation and patronage. The impartiality mechanism embedded in the recruitment system is not difficult to circumvent as it is relatively weak, and recruitment decisions are still based excessively on discretion. There is persistent confusion between the notion of the public advertisement of vacancies and that of merit-based recruitment. Publicity is necessary, but it is not sufficient to guarantee a merit-based recruitment system.

Accountability, transparency, and predictability in administrative decision-making are weak. Accountability of managers is virtually non-existent as decision-making is limited to political decisions taken by ministers and politicians. There is no widespread practice of delegation of decision-making powers. As such, delegation is not used as a regular management tool. One of the results of this concentration of power in the hands of politicians is the extreme difficulty of implementing laws and policies because excessive political pressure inhibits the development of managerial skills in public administration organisations.[20]

[19] https://ideas.repec.org/p/oec/govaaf/2012-5-en.html.

[20] https://ideas.repec.org/p/oec/govaaf/2012-2-en.html.

Recommendations

- The monitoring of the administration should be streamlined in order to introduce better accountability mechanisms for civil servants, public managers, and administrative bodies. Consideration should be given to the reform of the current administrative inspectorates in the context of designing a better policy for managerial and institutional accountability and improving the quality of services delivered to the public.
- The current organisational policy of the Serbian state and administration should be streamlined in order to reduce its current fragmentation, increase its efficiency, ensure more effectiveness in applying the *acquis communautaire*, and ultimately improve the capacity to govern the country. This streamlining would imply a thorough revision of a package of laws, including the Law on State Administration, Law on Agencies, Law on Ministries, and Law on Public Enterprises. The current fiscal strain argues in favour of the acceleration of these reforms.
- A basic administrative law framework for public administration and for the civil service system is in place. However, it has many shortcomings. A number of crucial reforms remain to be enacted and implemented. These reforms are set out in the "Inter-Sectoral Public Administration Reform Strategy 2009–2013" and in various draft laws, including the Law on Administrative Justice and the Law on General Administrative Procedures.
- The organisation of the central administration lacks coherence and is too fragmented. The current Civil Service Law (CSL), as it is used by politicians, does not promote a merit system. The Law permits dismissals as a result of restructuring. Despite the CSL, individuals are employed in the public service on temporary contracts without a competitive procedure. Individuals so appointed may then become tenured civil servants without undergoing a fair, transparent and competition procedure.

14.5 The Principles of Public Administration

SIGMA developed the Principles of Public Administration in 2014 to support the European Commission's reinforced approach to public administration reform in the EU Enlargement process. The Principles define what good public governance entails in practice and outline the main requirements to be followed during the EU integration process. They also feature a monitoring framework to enable regular analysis of progress made in their application and in setting benchmarks.

The EU *acquis* requirements and guidelines are the core of the Principles, where relevant. In other areas, they are derived from international standards and requirements, as well as good practices in the EU and OECD member countries. As a minimum benchmark of good administration, compliance with these fundamental Principles should be ensured. The extent to which a given candidate country or potential candidate applies these Principles in practice is an indication of the capacity of its national public administration to effectively implement the *acquis*, in accordance with the criteria defined by the European Council in Copenhagen (1993) and Madrid (1995).

The European Commission (EC) has strengthened its focus on public administration reform (PAR) and in cooperation with SIGMA has outlined six key issues of reform for better integrating reform in the enlargement process through Special Groups on PAR and stronger links with accession negotiations (Meyer-Sahling 2012). The Principles specify detailed requirements for a well-functioning public administration in six core areas: (1) Strategic framework for public administration reform; (2) Policy development and coordination; (3) Public service and human resource management; (4) Accountability; (5) Service delivery; and (6) Public financial management.

14.5.1 Strategic Framework for Public Administration Reform

Achieving the necessary standard of public administration requires reforms in many areas of policy and administration. When planned and implemented on a fragmented and ad hoc basis, reforms may not transform the governance system and overall functioning of public administration as expected. Achieving results requires the Government to steer and coordinate the implementation of an overall reform vision and prioritised objectives. It is therefore important to approach public administration reforms sequentially and in a coherently planned way and to compile a reform agenda from a whole-of-government perspective.

Public administration reform (PAR) is one of the most important horizontal reform areas in each country because it provides the framework for implementing other policies. It is therefore equally important for European Union (EU) Member States, candidate countries and potential candidates, as it allows for building a system that provides a sound basis for implementing the EU *acquis communautaire*.

Countries develop at different speeds and exhibit differences in their governance culture and approach to implementation of public administration reforms. However, some Principles are universally applicable in all countries and form the core of the needed public administration reforms. Hence, key requirements such as "reform leadership" and "functioning management systems" are at the heart of PAR policy and are critical in ensuring that strategies are actually implemented and do not remain only on paper.

Key Requirements

- The leadership of public administration reform is established, and the strategic framework provides the basis for implementing prioritised and sequenced reform activities aligned with the Government's financial circumstances.
- Public administration reform management enables guiding and steering reforms, determines the accountability for implementation and ensures the professional administration needed for reform implementation.

14.5.2 Policy Development and Coordination

The preparations for accession and membership need to be underpinned by arrangements and capacities for policy planning, development, coordination, and implementation that:

- Enable consistent policy planning and coordination of government activities, including priority setting in relation to European Union accession and membership issues.

- Create substantive and consistent polices that are affordable, economically efficient, and financially sustainable.
- Include consultation with internal and external stakeholders.
- Ensure that policies are properly implemented, communicated, and monitored.
- Support transposition and implementation of the *acquis communautaire* in all sectors.
- Lay the foundations for operating effectively as an EU Member State.

Key Requirements

- Centre of government institutions fulfil all functions critical to a well-organised, consistent, and competent policymaking system.
- Policy planning is harmonised, aligned with the Government's financial circumstances, and ensures the Government is able to achieve its objectives.
- Government decisions and legislation are transparent, legally compliant, and accessible to the public; the work of the Government is scrutinised by the Parliament.
- Inclusive, evidence-based policy and legislative development enables the achievement of intended policy objectives.

14.5.3 Public Service and Human Resource Management

Public service is one of the key components of public administration. A legally well-designed and managed public service system enables the state to reach an adequate level of professionalism, sustainability, and quality of public service in all parts of its administration and to provide better services to citizens and businesses. Modern, constitutional public service in a democracy is regarded as possible only when a set of conditions is in place:

- Separation between the public and the private spheres.
- Separation between politics and administration.
- Individual accountability of public servants.
- Sufficient job protection, level of pay and stability, and clearly defined rights and obligations of public servants.
- Recruitment and promotion based on merit.

Considering the European administrative law principles, the set of conditions for the public service conducting the core functions of the state, as well as the case law by the ECJ on defining public servants, Sigma applies the narrow scope of public service in these Principles in the area of "human resource management in public service" covering:

- Ministries and administrative bodies reporting directly to the Government, Prime Minister, or ministers, i.e., the civil service strictly speaking.
- Administrations of the Parliament, the President, and the Prime Minister.
- Other administrative bodies at the level of the central administration if they are included in the scope of the public service in terms of the public/civil service law and they exercise public authority conferred by public law and are responsible for safeguarding the general interests of the state or other public bodies.
- Independent constitutional bodies reporting directly to the Parliament.

Key Requirements

- The scope of public service is clearly defined and applied in practice so that the policy and legal framework and institutional set-up for professional public service is in place.
- Professionalism of public service is ensured by good managerial standards and human resource management practices.

14.5.4 Accountability

It is commonly accepted that the organisation of a public administration has a deep impact on its overall performance and, hence, on its democratic legitimacy in relation to citizens' expectations. The search for efficiency, the need for further specialisation, the constitutional/legal context and administrative tradition, the system of control in place, and the political conjuncture all influence the organisational model adopted by each country. As a result, no single pattern exists regarding how public administration is structured and operates in different countries.

However, where accountability (including organisational accountability) is concerned, some conditions are generally deemed necessary to ensure that public administrations perform their functions properly and efficiently:

- *Rationality*: Aiming at efficiency and coherence; avoiding overlaps between public institutions; establishing a balanced system of control.
- *Transparency*: Ensuring clear and simple organisation following common established types.
- *Affordability*: Adapting size and costs to the country's needs and capacities.
- *Accountability*: Each organisation must ensure that each part is internally accountable and that the institution as a whole is externally accountable. This implies accountability to the political, judicial, and social systems, as well as to other independent existing institutions. The cornerstone of accountability is to provide wide access to public information.

Key Requirements

- Proper mechanisms are in place to ensure accountability of state administration bodies, including liability and transparency.[21]

14.5.5 Service Delivery

Good public administration is an essential prerequisite for European Union (EU) competitiveness and growth. A fully functioning national

[21] Key requirements for accountability are governed by five principles: (1) The overall organisation of central government is rational, follows adequate policies and regulations and provides for appropriate internal, political, judicial, social and independent accountability; (2) The right to access public information is enacted in legislation and consistently applied in practice; (3) Functioning mechanisms are in place to protect both the rights of the individual to good administration and the public interest; (4) Fair treatment in administrative disputes is guaranteed by internal administrative appeals and judicial reviews; and (5) Public authorities assume **liability** in cases of wrongdoing and guarantee regress and/ or adequate compensation.

public administration is also a prerequisite for a transparent and effective democratic system. Although no formal *acquis communautaire* exists in this area, the EU enlargement criteria recognise and emphasise the need for candidate countries and potential candidates to build an effective public administration.

The administrative law principles common to all EU countries, setting the standards and inspiring the behaviour of public servants, should be embedded in institutions and administrative procedures at all levels of the administration. They are distinguished as:

- Reliability and predictability (legal certainty).
- Openness and transparency.
- Accountability.
- Efficiency and effectiveness.

Key Requirement

- Administration is citizen-oriented; the quality and accessibility of public services is ensured.

14.6 Western Balkan Countries Assessment on the Principles of Public Administration

SIGMA monitoring reports assess the state of play and progress in improving the quality of national public administrations. Given the geostrategic importance of the Western Balkans to the EU, and the ongoing accession negotiations, SIGMA conducts regular monitoring of the region's countries progress. In 2017, it established a baseline in all areas of public administration. In 2019, monitoring was conducted against selected Principles.[22] The full scope is covered again in the 2021 reports, which compare performance against the 2017 baseline and regional averages.[23] By analysing the long-term perspective, significant changes are identified.

[22] https://www.sigmaweb.org/publications/monitoring-reports.htm.

[23] https://www.sigmaweb.org/publications/Regional-Overview-Western-Balkans-Monitoring-February-2022.pdf.

14.6.1 *State of Play and Regional Trends*

According to the SIGMA Reports, the Western Balkans administrations made further efforts to institutionalise and strengthen the concept of strategic planning of public administration reform (PAR) during 2017–2021. All administrations have used various government planning documents to prepare and implement different complex reforms in all key substantive areas of PAR. Administrations have also established various formal institutional mechanisms for coordination, monitoring, and steering reform implementation. Despite these and other positive developments, the actual implementation of planned reforms across the region has been weak. Further efforts are needed to improve the quality of planning, provide stronger political support, enhance financial sustainability, and improve monitoring to achieve better implementation results. While formal structures of coordination and management of PAR are established in all administrations, additional efforts are needed to make them function more effectively, with more active involvement of all external stakeholders in PAR monitoring and implementation.

The 2021 SIGMA monitoring endeavour in the region coincided with a period of transitioning from old to new strategic frameworks of PAR in many administrations of the Western Balkans. During 2020–2021, most administrations in the region were in the process of renewing, updating, and/or extending various strategies included in their national strategic frameworks of PAR 2020–2021. The process of formal adoption of several key strategic documents in some administrations, including in Kosovo, Montenegro, and Serbia, was not finalised, and completed as of June 2021, the official cut-off date of the SIGMA monitoring exercise. Furthermore, the COVID-19 pandemic, as well as other factors and events, created challenges for some administrations, causing further delays in reform planning, monitoring, and reporting. All of these factors significantly affected the individual administration and regional results of SIGMA's monitoring in the strategic framework of the PAR area.

The overall regional average for the strategic framework of PAR area indicators in 2021 was 1.2, lower than the 2017 average of two. Albania and the Republic of North Macedonia (hereinafter North Macedonia) were the only administrations that had valid and complete strategic frameworks of PAR as of June 2021. North Macedonia is the only administration that had recorded progress in the indicator value since 2017, mainly because its formal strategic planning documents for PAR and public financial management (PFM) areas were approved in 2018; hence, those were not reflected in the baseline figures of 2017. In 2021, at the time of completion of the SIGMA monitoring, Kosovo, Montenegro, and Serbia were still finalising their new strategic frameworks of PAR, which has created gaps in various areas of the strategic framework of PAR, negatively affecting the value of many indicators.

Since 2017, all Western Balkan Administrations have made satisfactory progress in further institutionalising strategic planning and monitoring of reforms in all key substantive policy areas based on formal government planning documents. The overall comprehensiveness and quality of the valid PAR planning documents are assessed to be good and adequate to the existing national standards and requirements. In general, PAR is being prioritised in other government planning documents in most administrations, which is important for securing broad support for PAR and ensuring coherence and alignment between different government planning documents. In all administrations, most of the valid PAR and PFM strategies are supported with detailed action plans. The majority of the planned reform measures included in the valid action plans are assessed to be reform-oriented, which can contribute to major systemic and institutional improvements. Some administrations did not have valid (approved) action plans to support implementation of strategies, which has negatively affected the overall monitoring results. For example, the 2021 Action Plan of the Better Regulation Strategy 2.0 of Kosovo was not available.

Actual implementation of reforms across the region remained low in 2017–2021. Formal mechanisms and structures for monitoring and reporting of PAR are established in all administrations, as envisaged in the relevant strategic planning documents. But weaknesses and gaps exist in the actual implementation of planned reforms and in the effectiveness of performance measurement frameworks, particularly the use of indicators to assess the overall progress towards achievement of policy objectives and outcomes. Overall, PAR reporting in the region is focused mainly on the outputs. Additionally, there is a practice of preparing and adopting annual implementation reports on PAR planning documents quite late in the calendar year, sometimes in July and August. This practice of late preparation, discussion and approval of annual monitoring reports does not help effectively address all implementation challenges and make timely interventions, based on the findings of monitoring, to improve implementation. The monitoring reports have also revealed several instances of not preparing and/or formally discussing implementation monitoring reports among key decision-makers.

The effectiveness of actual implementation of planned reforms is relatively low in all administrations of the region. On average, across all administrations, less than half of annually planned reform activities were fully implemented in 2020. The situation in this regard is unchanged compared to the 2017 monitoring. Weak implementation results can be partly attributed to overly ambitious planning, broader weaknesses and shortcomings in government planning and monitoring systems, and to limited capacities and resource allocation for PAR implementation.

For example, in Albania and North Macedonia, on average only about half of the annually planned measures in the respective PAR planning documents were fully implemented in 2018–2020. Serbia recorded an improvement in implementation of its PAR Strategy in 2020 compared to 2017—61 against 33%—while no results were available about the implementation of the Regulatory Reform Programme. Kosovo and Montenegro had not finalised and published the annual implementation results for their PFM strategies as of June 2021 for them to be considered in the monitoring results.

Since 2017, the indicators measuring evidence-based policymaking, stakeholder engagement and inter-ministerial consultation show greater improvements in many Western Balkan Administrations, mainly due to the adoption of key regulations and of previously missing guidelines, as well as a better and more consistent application of existing tools of regulatory policy management in practice. Nevertheless, all administrations still face major challenges in ensuring fully harmonised and effectively functioning government planning and coordination systems, including planning, monitoring, and reporting on European Union integration (EI) and further strengthening of the quality, relevance, and impact of key regulatory management tools, such as regulatory impact assessment (RIA) and public consultation.

The main centre-of-government (CoG) functions are formally established, but weaknesses remain in implementation and coordination. All Western Balkan Administrations have formally established most of the critical CoG functions necessary for effective policy coordination, communication, and smooth functioning of government decision-making. Different models of CoG are established in the region, and they often involve several government institutions responsible for performing various CoG functions. Coordination of work between and within different CoG institutions, which is essential for effective government policymaking, remains a challenge for all administrations. Compared to 2017, some improvements have been recorded in the availability of central guidelines to support line ministries in their work, but gaps also remain in this area in some administrations. CoG bodies cooperate and coordinate with each other during the preparation of government annual work plans only in Albania and Kosovo. At the same time, coordination within and between the General Secretariats, Offices of the Prime Minister, and/or similar CoG institutions during the review of individual policy proposals remains weak in all Western Balkan Administrations.

No major improvements in the quality of planning or monitoring of government work; gaps and weaknesses exist in EI planning and monitoring in many administrations. Overall, in the region, the quality of government planning has improved slightly since 2017, but major challenges remain in enabling a fully harmonised and an effectively functioning planning system of government work. Administrations face different types of challenges, such as gaps in the methodological frameworks, limited coordination, and central guidance, which result in weak planning and implementation of government work. For example, the share of legislative commitments that are not implemented on time and are thus carried forward from one year to the next remains excessively high for most administrations.

14.6.2 Albania

Albania's performance in the area of policy development and coordination has been strong and has shown improvement. By comparison with other Western Balkan countries, it received the highest value for many indicators, and its overall average value and individual indicator values have risen from 2.6 in 2017 to 3.4 in 2021, the highest in the region. This improvement is largely a recognition of the institutionalisation of Albania's *ex-ante* tools for policy development and the development of new regulations and systems for government planning. However, many challenges have yet to be addressed. Particularly by ensuring systematic implementation of all new processes and tools, the government has laid the foundation for further improvements in areas such as centre-of-government (CoG) coordination, strategic planning, regulatory impact assessment (RIA), and public consultation.[24]

Main Findings

- Key CoG functions are all formally assigned to the Office of the Prime Minister (OPM), and other institutions.
- As for coordination of European integration (EI), the coordination structure established in 2019 functions effectively on the administrative level, but not on the political level.
- Governmental decision-making is not transparent enough. The government publishes its decisions after a session, but the agendas for Government sessions are not announced in advance.
- Overall, the quality and stability of legislation is high.
- A more active approach to monitoring the implementation of *acquis* alignment plans is in place, including weekly reports to the OPM and the Chief Negotiator.
- The Rules of Procedure (RoP) of the Government were amended in 2018 to institutionalise *ex-ante* analysis of regulatory proposals.
- Public consultation on key policies has not been successful in generating comments and feedback from stakeholders and ensuring meaningful input in final policy design.

Recommendations

- The Government should strengthen the capacities of the OPM, as the key CoG institution for conducting all key functions.
- The OPM should ensure that the agendas of the government sessions are published in advance and communicate to the public the key decisions that have been taken, in an easily understandable way.
- The Parliament should introduce the practice of discussing the implementation of key laws and policies on a regular basis.

[24] https://www.sigmaweb.org/publications/Monitoring-Report-2021-Albania.pdf.

- The Government should ensure full enforcement of the RIA methodology across the ministries,[25] including for secondary legislation, by increasing its quality control and oversight, and continuing to provide training for key officials.
- The Government should plan and conduct an evaluation of the new government planning and monitoring system, in particular on the effectiveness and impact of the IPSIS system on the quality of final plans and monitoring reports.[26]
- The Government should finalise the development of the integrated planning system and revise the fragmented medium-term policy planning set-up. This would involve both drafting a new legislative framework for planning and continuing efforts to roll out the IPSIS system.

14.6.3 Bosnia and Herzegovina

Overall, there have been no major changes in the policy development and coordination area in Bosnia and Herzegovina (BiH) since the 2017 SIGMA assessment. As different methodological approaches have been applied, it is not possible to make direct comparisons between the indicator values in the 2017 and 2021 assessments.[27]

Main Findings

- Most of the key centre-of-government (CoG) functions have been established at all administrative levels of government of BiH, with exception of the function of coordinating policy content of proposals before final adoption.
- Government work-planning and monitoring processes, legal drafting and policymaking processes and tools (such as application of regulatory impact assessment and public consultations on new policies)

[25] Regulatory impact assessment (RIA) is a systemic approach to critically assessing the positive and negative effects of proposed and existing regulations and non-regulatory alternatives.

[26] Integrated Planning System Information System is a Government Systemic Platform, which aims to improve the coordination of policies/strategies.

[27] https://www.sigmaweb.org/publications/Monitoring-Report-Bosnia-and-Herzegovina-May-2022.pdf.

are mostly regulated and supported, detailed guidelines on sector strategic planning exist only in the Respublika Srpska (RS) and the Brčko District (BD). There are significant issues with monitoring and reporting practices for key government and policy planning documents at all levels.
- The European integration functions, such as daily coordination, planning and monitoring, and legal harmonisation rules and procedures, are mostly in place from a regulatory perspective. However, current practice shows deviations from regulations, as there it is still not adopted countrywide.
- The legislative branches at all administrative levels have well-defined regulations and procedures for scrutinising the work of the executive level.
- Regulatory impact assessment, as an *ex-ante* tool for policy analysis, is formally established at all levels, but it is not systematically and fully used in practice.

Recommendations

- The Council of Ministers (CoM) of BiH should set up a legal framework for sectoral strategic planning and start implementing it.
- Capacities of the CoG at all administrative levels should be enhanced to provide the necessary guidance and support during implementation of the legal framework for sectoral strategic planning, as well as to conduct final checks and quality control of draft planning documents.
- The CoM of BiH and the governments of the FBIH, the RS and the BD should establish a formal requirement to proactively publish online reports on implementation of key planning documents that include information on progress towards achievement of set objectives and outcomes.
- The CoM of BiH and the governments of the FBIH, the RS and the BD should formally designate an institution (preferably a CoG body) to be in charge of scrutinising the quality of the public consultation process as well as the quality of reporting on this process and its outcomes. Also, a proactive system of informing stakeholders about upcoming consultations should be set up at all levels of government of BiH.

- All administrative levels of BiH should ensure implementation of the existing rules and procedures for conducting *ex-ante* Regulatory Impact Assessment (RIA) on regulatory proposals in line with the existing methodologies, targeting the most significant policy proposals first.
- The CoM of BiH and the governments of the FBIH, the RS and the BD should establish the function of coordination of policy content of proposals heading for approval within their respective CoG institutions, to ensure closer formal and informal coordination in regard to both policy planning and policy development. The respective CoG institutions should have a right to analyse draft proposals and send them back to initiating institutions if the package content is not coherent and consistent with set government priorities and previously announced policies.
- All levels of the BiH administration should ensure systemic monitoring of implementation of sectoral policy planning documents, by setting the quality requirements and reviewing the procedures, and should put in place activities to build the capacities required for these purposes. These monitoring reports should also be proactively published online.
- The ministries of the State level, the FBIH, the RS, and the BD should establish clear internal rules to ensure that policy development and drafting of legislation are well coordinated and that key elements, such as public consultation, are well prepared.

14.6.4 Kosovo

The overall average indicator value for 2021 has decreased compared with the value in 2017 for the policy development and coordination area and is below the regional average. The legal and regulatory frameworks and rules of procedure for planning and policy coordination are largely in place, but both the implementation and the enforcement of procedures are inadequate. Particular attention is required to improve planning with respect to both domestic and European integration (EI)related legislation to reduce the number of acts that are carried forward from one year to the next. While parliamentary elections had a negative impact on policy planning in general, in 2020, the issues identified by the assessment are to a large extent systemic.[28]

Main Findings

- While all key centre-of-government functions for effective policymaking are established and supported by detailed regulations and guidelines, coordination arrangements between the centre-of-government (CoG) institutions are not consistently implemented.
- The EI process needs to be strengthened through more regular coordination meetings at both the senior management level and the political level.
- Strategic planning is hampered by a lack of clarity in the hierarchy of key planning documents and the coordination of planning processes.
- Government transparency is also not sufficient, and the monitoring of the Government's work remains a challenge.
- Adequate parliamentary scrutiny of government policymaking is formally ensured, but in practice the Assembly very rarely discusses the Government's implementation of laws and policies.
- Impact assessments are not used for secondary legislation or for strategies.
- Regulations and procedures for conducting public consultations are in place, and the regularity in publishing draft laws for written public consultation has improved. However, rules are not followed consistently in practice.

Recommendations

- Agendas of government sessions should be published online in advance and all decisions made by the Government should be available online.
- The Government should take steps to strengthen regulatory impact assessment (RIA) and enforce the central quality control more consistently.

[28] https://www.sigmaweb.org/publications/Monitoring-Report-2021-Kosovo.pdf.

- The Government should strengthen central oversight to ensure consistent implementation of the existing rules on public consultation.
- The Government should explore why business confidence in its legislative process has fallen so dramatically.
- The Government should take steps to ensure that the transitional period before new laws take full effect is sufficient for the adoption of the necessary supporting bylaws, to promote full and consistent implementation and increase legal clarity.
- The role of the Assembly in monitoring progress made by the Government should be strengthened.
- The Assembly should start scrutinising the implementation of government policies by requesting that the Government prepare reports on the implementation of key reforms.
- A more structured system of coordination between the Assembly and the Government should be developed, including more systematic government review of draft bills brought by the Assembly and mechanisms to reduce the use of extraordinary procedures.

14.6.5 Montenegro

Montenegro has an average value of 2.7 for policy development and coordination. This is the same as the regional average. However, compared to 2017, the area average has fallen from 3.1. Only the value for the indicator on evidence-based policymaking improved over the period, while the values decreased for six indicators (and remained the same for seven). The challenges with the implementation of central planning documents in 2020 contributed most to the reduction in indicator values, especially in the area of planning for European integration.[29]

Main Findings

- The critical functions for ensuring well-organised policymaking are assigned to the centre of government (CoG) bodies.

[29] https://www.sigmaweb.org/publications/Monitoring-Report-2021-Montenegro.pdf.

- The coordination forums for EI at both the administrative and political levels, established to ensure the smooth running of the accession process, continue to convene only rarely despite significant challenges with the implementation of the planned EI commitments.
- The main positive development in the area of policy planning is the establishment of the regulatory and methodological framework supporting strategic planning 2018.[30]
- Reports on the implementation of central planning documents are publicly available but do not contain any outcome-level data on the achievement of objectives.
- The mandatory bylaws for implementing the laws are not adopted by the time laws take effect, contributing to a lack of legal certainty.
- Access to legislation is hampered by the absence of consolidated versions of legal acts free of charge.

Recommendations

- The Government should ensure alignment between the objectives of policy and fiscal plans.
- The Government should ensure that the EI coordination bodies at the political and administrative levels become fully functional with meetings taking place regularly.
- The Government should strengthen the General Secretariat of the Government (GSG) role by mandating it to return draft legal acts and strategies to the ministries with requests for consideration of adjustments if the substance requires further improvement or is inconsistent with the Government's priorities.
- The Government should follow its legislative plans when submitting drafts to the Parliament. It should request the processing of drafts in urgent procedures only in case of unforeseen circumstances and should not use this possibility for the regular adoption of the state budget.

[30] Article 19 of the Government Decree on Modalities and Procedure of Drafting, Alignment and Monitoring of Implementation of Strategic Documents; adopted on 19.07.2018. Official Gazette 54/2018.

- The Government, under the leadership of the MoFSW should establish quality control over the RIA covering all key impact areas, including economic, environmental, and social impacts.[31]
- The Ministry of Public Administration, Digital Society and Media should establish the internal procedures for ensuring that all draft proposals from all ministries are reviewed prior to their submission to the Government to ensure their compliance with the requirements for public consultation.
- The Government should ensure that all draft laws foresee an adequate transitional period after the adoption of the law and before the law takes full effect, to allow for the timely adoption of all bylaws necessary for the implementation of the law.
- The Government should ensure that all primary and secondary legislation is available online in consolidated format, free of charge.
- The Parliament should increase oversight of the implementation of laws, by establishing a system of reporting on major legislation.
- The line ministries should further engage the officials currently involved exclusively in the EU-related affairs into the domestic policy development in order to use their experience most effectively.

14.6.6 North Macedonia

Overall, compared to 2017, North Macedonia has made some progress in the policy development and coordination area. The average value of the policy development and coordination indicators rose during the assessment period, from 1.8 in 2017 to 2.1 in 2021. However, it is still lower than the regional average of all Western Balkan countries (2.7). The improvement in the indicator value compared to 2017 is primarily due to a more consistent application of the critical tools for evidence-based and participatory policymaking and to some improvement in the transparency of government decision-making. However, major weaknesses and gaps still exist in both the regulatory and the methodological frameworks for government policy development and policy planning and monitoring,

[31] The Ministry of Finance and Social Welfare (MoFSW) is responsible for drafting and monitoring policies for social protection, including economic assistance, disability support and social care services.

including European Union integration planning, as well as in the implementation and enforcement of key procedures and functions required for the effective functioning of the centre of government (CoG).[32]

Main Findings

- Most CoG functions are formally established, but weaknesses and gaps exist in regulations and guidance, as well as in implementation and policy coordination by the CoG institutions.
- The institutional and regulatory framework for European integration coordination was revised and upgraded in 2019 to be better prepared for the EU accession negotiations phase. However, the new coordination mechanisms are not yet fully functional.
- A medium-term government planning system is established, but it has gaps, particularly in the area of sector strategy development and monitoring, and the quality of the planning documents is still weak.
- Some progress is observed in the area of the transparency and legal compliance of government decision-making, largely because the agenda and minutes of the government sessions are now publicly available through a central website.
- North Macedonia has one of the highest rates of processing and adopting laws in shortened or urgent proceedings, which remains a major concern (60% in 2020).
- Some improvements are observed in the area of evidence-based and consultative policymaking compared to 2017, largely due to a more consistent application of the Regulatory Impact Assessment (RIA) process and public consultation rules. However, the quality of RIA reports and their impact on final policy design and decision-making by the Government remain very limited.
- No major changes are recorded in the area of the predictability, consistency, and accessibility of legislation since 2017.

Recommendations

- The Secretary-General (SG) should ensure consistent and full implementation of all assigned CoG functions, including final checks on

[32] https://www.sigmaweb.org/publications/Monitoring-Report-2021-Republic-of-North-Macedonia.pdf.

the content of proposals, to ensure policy coherence and checks on compliance with the RIA and public consultation requirements.

- The Government, in consultation with the Parliament, should review the existing regulations, criteria and practice for approving laws through urgent proceedings with the objective of reducing the number of laws processed through non-standard procedures to a minimum.
- The SG should make sure that the draft agendas of the government sessions are published before the meetings.
- The Secretariat for European Affairs and the Ministry of Finance should ensure the adequate planning, funding, and preparation of translations of the acquis to help achieve evidence-based transposition of EU law.
- The Government should strengthen the mandate and capacity of the Ministry of Information Society and Administration (MISA), as the RIA oversight body, to ensure more effective and consistent quality control of RIAs, including checks on the content and analysis, and ensure regular trainings for ministries to improve the quality of RIAs and the initiation of RIA early in the process.
- The Government should strengthen central oversight and reporting on public consultation by assigning the function to a CoG institution. More consistent checks should be conducted.
- The Government should ensure that all secondary legislation and guidelines required for the effective implementation of primary laws are developed and adopted before the relevant provisions are set to come into effect.
- The Government, in consultation with the Parliament, should develop and implement a programme for preparing official consolidated versions of all primary and secondary legislation. All legislation should be made available free of charge to the public through the Official Gazette website.

14.6.7 Serbia

Serbia is at the level of regional average in the area of policy development and coordination. The average value for this indicator has not changed significantly compared to 2017, increasing slightly from 2.7 to 2.8 in

2021. Improvements were observed in the functioning of centre-of-government (CoG) institutions, the legal framework for policy planning, parliamentary scrutiny over government policymaking, and accessibility of legislation. However, these positive developments were levelled by the worsening of all three indicators related to European integration (EI) and some setbacks in the organisation and procedures for implementable policies and legislation.[33]

Main Findings

- Key CoG functions are formally established by relevant legislation and assigned to responsible bodies but there is still insufficient internal coordination among CoG units.
- New shortcomings were identified in the area of coordination and planning of EI activities. The main weaknesses are related to the outdated National Programme for the Adoption of the *Acquis Communautaire* (NPAA) and the lack of regular reporting on the implementation of the NPAA in 2020 and 2021, which makes operational management of the EU accession process difficult.
- Governmental decision-making is not sufficiently transparent, which reflects both in weak reporting of key central planning documents as well as in lack of openness of decision-making.
- Parliamentary scrutiny over Government policymaking has slightly improved thanks to less use of extraordinary procedures and better scrutiny of policy implementation.
- Evidence-based policymaking, through the Regulatory Impact Assessment (RIA) system, is established and managed, but the quality of analysis does not yet lead to the desired results.
- Public consultation on key policies remains weak.
- The predictability and consistency of legislation remain high.

Recommendations

- The Ministry of European Integration (MEI) should significantly improve EI planning and implementation quality by renewing the NPAA, preparing annual NPAA implementation reports, and

[33] https://www.sigmaweb.org/publications/Monitoring-Report-2021-Serbia.pdf.

deploying a renewed coordination system, also at the administrative level.

- The MEI should prepare regular updates to the multi-year NPAA plan to ensure the EI plan is up-to-date and aligned with other government planning documents, such as the Government Annual Work Programme (GAWP).
- The General Secretariat of the Government (GSG) should prepare and publish the GAWP annual implementation reports on a timely basis.
- The GSG should make Government session agendas public before the sessions and publish all official Government decisions shortly after the respective Government session unless the content is classified as confidential.
- The GSG should set up a senior administrative level coordination and conflict resolution mechanism across ministries prior to the Government sessions to help improve the quality and efficiency of Government decision-making.
- The Government in collaboration with the Parliament should ensure that coordination is functioning in practice and that the Parliament is informed on a timely basis about the actual legislative activities of the Government.
- The Government should ensure that all secondary legislation is adopted by the time the respective law enters into force, at the latest.

14.7 The Way Forward

According to SIGMA, during 2017–2021, the Western Balkan Administrations made further efforts to institutionalise and strengthen the concept of strategic planning of public administration reform (PAR). All administrations have used various government planning documents to prepare and implement different complex reforms in all key substantive areas of PAR. Administrations have also established various formal institutional mechanisms for coordination, monitoring, and steering reform implementation. Despite these and other positive developments, the actual implementation of planned reforms across the region has been weak. Further efforts are needed to improve the quality of planning, provide stronger political support, enhance financial sustainability, and improve monitoring to achieve better implementation results. While formal structures of coordination and management of PAR are established in all administrations, additional efforts are needed to make them function more effectively, with more active involvement of all external stakeholders in PAR monitoring and implementation.

SIGMA in its Regional Overview Monitoring Reports 2022 for the Western Balkan countries gives its recommendations for the steps that need to be taken on public administration reform. Those are:

- All administrations should plan ambitious reforms but be realistic as to what can be achieved in the short-, medium-, and long-term. Additional efforts are needed to ensure timely and full implementation of all planned measures.
- All administrations should ensure regular monitoring and reporting on PAR implementation, focusing more on the outcomes and impacts, and ensuring all external stakeholders are involved. All annual monitoring reports should be prepared and published on time, preferably during the first quarter of the year, to help address implementation challenges.
- Administrations should aim to reduce the reliance of PAR implementation on donor funds and ensure better alignment between the resource estimates in the PAR planning documents and the financial allocations of the area reforms in the state budget.
- All PAR coordination mechanisms, at both the political and administrative levels, should be used more effectively to monitor implementation, address implementation challenges, and exchange best practices, with active participation of external stakeholders.
- Improve the existing mechanisms for coordination and cooperation between the government and the parliament for better legislative planning to reduce the share of laws adopted by shortened procedures, ensure more systematic review by government all draft laws initiated in the legislative branch, and achieve more systematic scrutiny of major policies by the parliament.
- Apply regulations and methodologies for RIA and public consultations more consistently and fully in practice, enhance capacities of line ministries and CoG to improve the quality of policy analysis, and ensure early planning and implementation to increase their use and impact in policy design and final decision-making.
- Legislation and how it is applied to top managers in the civil service should be a subject of wide political consensus and ensure

a high level of their professionalism, stability, responsiveness, and accountability (SIGMA/OECD 1995).

- Public administration should increase efforts to be considered an employer of choice, offering attractive jobs, competitive compensation packages and career perspectives able to attract and retain talented professionals.
- Recruitment and selection procedures should continue to be improved, to ensure the candidates who best fit the job requirements are hired based on experience, knowledge, skills, and competencies to enable them to do their job well.
- While service delivery has improved in the region, it requires political and administrative leadership to maintain sustainable progress and guarantee ownership to initiate and coordinate service delivery improvement initiatives.
- Improve the alignment and integration between financial planning, sector strategies, and overall government policy planning.
- Work with centre-of-government institutions to establish plans to support the implementation of managerial accountability.
- Develop strategies to ensure that the organisation and staffing of internal audit units is developed, in order to enable the efficient and effective delivery of internal audit services in line with international standards.
- Harmonisation of public procurement legislation (including PPPs and concessions) with EU legislation should be completed.
- Transparency of the review process should be enhanced (in particular to improve smart online access to decisions of the review bodies).

14.7.1 EU Report 2023 on Public Administration Reform in Balkan Countries

On November 2023 Directorate-General for Neighbourhood and Enlargement Negotiations published the Report related to Public Administration Reform in Balkan countries. The main findings and recommendation for each of the Western Balkan countries are:

14.7.2 Albania[34]

Albania remains moderately prepared in the area of public administration reform. It made limited progress in delivering on last year's recommendations. A new national strategy for development and European integration for 2023–2030 was adopted in February 2023. Preparations for the new strategies on public administration reform (PAR) and public financial management (PFM) have started but they still have to be adopted. The new 2022–2026 digital agenda was adopted in June 2022. The new 2023–2030 decentralisation strategy was adopted in April 2023. Implementation of the ongoing 2015–2022 PAR, and 2014–2022 PFM strategies continued. The centre of government entities under the Prime Minister's Office has evolved, but the new structure still needs to settle in. A more consistent legislative framework with clear criteria for the creation of subordinated entities still needs to be created. Provisions on merit-based recruitment in the civil service law are not consistently implemented, especially for senior level positions. A salary reform was initiated in 2023, but the reform does not yet fully address the complexity of the salary structure or the limited role of performance. Progress on the implementation of the automated payroll system stalled. Significant efforts were made on digitisation of service delivery through the e-Albania platform. This was accompanied by a closure of front office contact centres in 2022, which raised concerns over access to services to vulnerable and digitally less-apt citizens. A restitution of some contact centres is under consideration, together with other ongoing efforts to improve the user experience of the portal online. Further efforts are needed to ensure equitable access to services for people with limited digital skills or limited access to IT equipment. Increased attention is required to digital security and protection of personal data. The Commission's 2022 recommendations remain mostly valid. In the coming year, Albania should, in particular:

- Put in place a legislative framework that properly regulates the typology and criteria for establishing subordinated bodies and clarifies lines of accountability.
- Adopt and start implementing the new public administration and public financial management strategies and review the effectiveness of the current monitoring structures.

[34] https://neighbourhood-enlargement.ec.europa.eu/albania-report-2023_en.

- Consistently and effectively implement the provisions on merit-based recruitment, promotion, and dismissal in the civil service law at all levels, especially at senior level; continue the reform of the salary system for civil servants and re-initiate the automation of the payroll system.

14.7.3 *Bosnia and Herzegovina*[35]

Bosnia and Herzegovina is at an early stage of preparation and made some progress in public administration reform (PAR). Some positive steps were taken by (i) adopting the PAR coordination arrangement ('common platform'), including a political decision-making body; (ii) implementing the comprehensive and countrywide public finance management strategy, (iii) improving capacity for public consultation at state level and on regulatory impact assessment in the Respublika Srpska entity, (iv) adopting a strategy on human resource management in the Federation entity, (v) improving the professional development and performance appraisal in the Federation entity and at state level, and (vi) adopting a Law on freedom of access to information, aimed at fostering proactive disclosure and transparency. Some five years after adoption, the PAR action plan has been implemented only to a limited extent. Civil service laws are still not harmonised with each other, and merit principles are not enshrined in recruitment procedures. The monitoring of human resources is not effective in detecting irregularities. The political decision-making body included in the "common platform" still needs to become operational to steer reforms effectively. The capacity of entity-level PAR coordinators remains weak. In line with key priority 14 of the Commission Opinion, Bosnia and Herzegovina needs to complete essential steps to improve the overall functioning of the public administration by ensuring a professional and depoliticised civil service and a coordinated, countrywide approach to policymaking. Last year's recommendations were partially implemented. In the coming year, Bosnia and Herzegovina should in particular:

- Adopt and start implementing the revised action plan on the PAR strategic framework 2023- 2027 at each government level, while

[35] https://neighbourhood-enlargement.ec.europa.eu/bosnia-and-herzegovina-report-2023_e.

prioritising activities on digitalisation of services and adopting the outstanding legal framework for sectoral strategic planning at state level.

- Establish a functioning coordination structure with a political decision-making body and upgrade the staffing and skills of PAR coordinators to steer the implementation of public administration reforms across all levels of government.
- Ensure a professional civil service system by amending state and entities' civil service laws in line with merit principles and establishing performance-based monitoring for transparent human resource management at all levels of government to detect irregularities.

14.7.4 Kosovo[36]

Kosovo has some level of preparation and made no progress with regard to public administration reform during the reporting period. Oversight of the implementation of the legislative framework for public administration reform (PAR) across line ministries is still ineffective. This is despite the adoption of a new strategic framework for both PAR and public finance management. New legislation on public officials and salaries was approved by the Assembly using fast track procedures. Both laws were sent for review to the Constitutional Court which ruled some articles of the Law on Public Officials unconstitutional. The amended Law on Public Officials risks creating and exacerbating existing gaps in administrative capacities. Some progress was made with harmonising sectoral laws with the Law on general administrative procedures and in digitalising public services. However, the overall pace of public administration reforms remained insufficient to deliver tangible results in the reporting period. As last year's recommendations have not been sufficiently implemented, they remain broadly valid. In the coming year, Kosovo should:

- Improve the functioning and accountability of the public administration, including through rationalising agencies and introducing performance management in agencies; to that end, strengthen administrative capacities, fill open vacancies regularly and in line with the principle of merit-based recruitments, and amend the new Law

[36] https://neighbourhood-enlargement.ec.europa.eu/kosovo-report-2023_en.

on public officials in line with the principles of a modern public administration.
- Ensure efficient functioning of the new remuneration system by implementing the Law on organisation and functioning of the state administration and independent agencies and to finalise the processes of: (i) regulating the internal organisations of public bodies, (ii) job classification; and (iii) systematising positions at central level according to job descriptions.
- Improve legal certainty, reduce the administrative burdens, and increase the number of e-services in the public administration for businesses and the public.

14.7.5 Montenegro[37]

Montenegro is moderately prepared in the area of public administration reform. Overall, limited progress was made. Implementation of the public administration reform strategy continued, while a new public finance management reform programme was adopted, and its implementation was started. Both strategic documents are linked to the budgetary framework. By contrast, amendments to the civil service legislation adopted in 2021, introducing relaxed qualification requirements and ample discretion of appointing authorities to dismiss heads of administrative authorities, remained in place. Furthermore, the Parliament adopted amendments to the Law on local self-government to harmonise it with the Law on civil service, disregarding last year's recommendation. The relaxed requirements introduced by these amendments are a source of continuing concern for merit-based recruitment, competence, and independence of civil servants. Continued staff changes in the public administration led to further loss of know-how on matters related to the EU accession process and an overall slowing of the pace of reforms. The Parliament has yet to adopt long-awaited amendments to the Law on access to information. Effective lines of accountability within the administration are still to be set up. The 2022 recommendation on adoption and implementation of the strategic framework was met, while other recommendations remain valid. In the coming year, Montenegro should in particular:

[37] https://neighbourhood-enlargement.ec.europa.eu/montenegro-report-2023_en.

- Adopt and implement amendments to the Law on access to information in line with the principles of good public administration and introduce measures to reduce the high number of requests for information and related appeals.
- Amend the Law on civil servants and state employees and the Law on local self-government to ensure that recruitment follows the principles of merit, competence, and transparency.
- Put in place a unified, comprehensive, and transparent system for capital investment planning and management.

14.7.6 North Macedonia[38]

North Macedonia is moderately prepared in the reform of its public administration. Limited progress was made in the reporting period with the adoption of the new public administration reform strategy and the accompanying action plan in July 2023. Despite having started the process 5 years ago, the country still has not adopted the revised legislative framework for human resources management, which includes the revised law on administrative servants and the law on public sector employees and new legal provisions on top level of management. The new framework should improve human resources management across the administration and help ensure merit-based recruitments, promotions, and dismissals at all levels, including senior management. Legislation has not yet taken on board the State Commission for the Prevention of Corruption's recommendations on nepotism, cronyism, and political influence in the recruitment of public sector employees and in the appointment of members of supervisory and management boards. Improvements in accountability in the public administration are undermined by the failure to adopt the new law on state organisation. There are ongoing efforts to improve delivery of services to citizens and businesses. As last year's recommendations were only partially addressed, they remain valid. In the coming period, the country should, in particular:

[38] https://neighbourhood-enlargement.ec.europa.eu/north-macedonia-report-2023_en.

- Adopt and start implementing the revised law on administrative servants, the revised law on public service employees and the legal provisions on top management service.
- Adopt and start implementing the law on state organisation and other related laws in line with the recommendations on the new organisation of state administrative bodies.
- Ensure full implementation of the law on general administrative procedures by completing the digitalisation of institutions' registers and data exchange and simplifying electronic procedures.

14.7.7 Serbia

Serbia is moderately prepared as regards the reform of its public administration (PAR). Overall, there was limited progress in this area, notably through the continued development of e-services, implementation of the e-government policy, and further roll-out of training courses for civil servants. The Commission recommendations from last year are still to be implemented. On human resources management, more than half of senior manager positions are filled on an acting basis. As regards policy development and coordination, no mechanism is yet in place to verify that the Public Policy Secretariat's comments have been incorporated into the final draft versions of laws and policy documents submitted for government approval. On public financial management (PFM), action is still needed to fully implement the recommendation for a single mechanism for prioritising all investments regardless of type and source of financing. There is an urgent need to address these shortcomings. In the coming year, Serbia should in particular:

- Reduce the excessive number of acting positions, and allocate sufficient resources for effective, merit-based recruitment processes.
- Strengthen the mechanism for systematically integrating the opinion of the Public Policy Secretariat in draft laws and policy documents, in line with the Law on the planning system.
- Put in place a unified, comprehensive, and transparent system for capital investment planning and management.

In the same period of EU Report, in November 2023, SIGMA published a revised edition of the Principles of Public Administration.[39] The structure of the 2023 edition of the Principles of Public Administration still follows the six thematic areas set out in the 2014 Enlargement Strategy. To better reflect the content of the Principles, the fourth thematic area, previously called "Accountability", is now "Organisation, accountability and oversight". "Digitalisation" has been added to "Service Delivery". The thematic areas are:

- ***Strategy***: The government ensures a strategic vision and leadership for an agile, innovative, and continuously improving public administration responsive to new challenges.
- ***Policy development and coordination***: The government ensures that policies and budgets are harmonised, effectively planned, coordinated across whole of government, implemented, monitored, and evaluated against clearly defined policy objectives. Ministries develop coherent public policies through an open and participatory process, informed by sound evidence and analysis.
- ***Public service and human resource management***: Public servants act with professionalism, integrity, and neutrality. They are recruited and promoted based on merit and equal opportunities and have the right competencies to deliver their tasks effectively.
- ***Organisation, accountability, and oversight***: The organisation of the public administration is efficient and effective across all levels of government. Public administration bodies are open and transparent and apply clearly defined internal and external accountability mechanisms. Strong oversight bodies protect the rights of citizens and the public interest.
- ***Service delivery and digitalisation***: The public administration places users at the centre and delivers high-quality and easily accessible services online and offline to all people and businesses. Digitalisation enables data-driven decisions, effective and efficient processes, as well as high-quality and accessible services.
- ***Public financial management***: The public administration plans and manages public finances to ensure that they are sustainable and

[39] SIGMA, OECD The Principles of Public Administration revised edition, November 2023.

transparent and allow the delivery of policy objectives. Control, procurement, and oversight arrangements are in place to ensure the economic, efficient, and effective use of public resources shared across all levels of government.

The 32 Principles outline values, behaviours, and outcomes, while the 270 sub-principles provide more detailed guidance on how to achieve these results and ensure adequate administrative capacity. The following prerequisites are crucial for effective implementation of the values stated in each Principle. They are reflected at the level of the monitoring framework rather than repeated in each Principle:

- Adequate legislative framework (both primary and secondary legislation).
- Established institutional and organisational set-up with clearly defined responsibilities, as well as adequate capacities of responsible institutions.
- The right people with the right skills, supported by good management.
- Orientation towards outcomes for citizens and businesses.
- government decisions informed by reliable evidence and data.
- Systematic monitoring and evaluation of performance to create a learning and feedback loop.
- Organisational culture internalising the desired values and behaviour.
- Change management.

14.8 The Strategic Framework for Public Administration Reform

The latest SIGMA monitoring report for the region coincided with a period of transitioning from old to new strategic frameworks of PAR in many administrations of the Western Balkans. During 2020–2021, most administrations in the region were in the process of renewing, updating, and/or extending various strategies included in their national strategic frameworks of PAR 2020–2021.

14.8.1 Albania

The last PAR Strategy of Albania was adopted in 2015 for the period 2015–2020.[40] According to this document, the vision of the Strategy is *"Development of public administration, which provides high quality services for citizens and businesses in a transparent, effective, and efficient way through the use of modern technologies and innovative services and, that complies with the requirements of European integration through impartial, professional and accountable civil servants, part of efficient setups"*.

The Strategy reflects the main directions of the government programme for public administration based on the following objectives: (1) Sustainability and depoliticisation of the administration; (2) Strict implementation of civil service legislation and implementation of transparent competitions and career advancement; (3) Boosting of online services for their modernisation and the fight against corruption; (4) Enhancement of the quality of services through the use of information technology; and (5) Enhancement of the accountability of public officials when performing their duties.

In the area of *Policymaking and Quality of Legislation* the aim of the policy goal was to have policymaking, legislation drafting, monitoring and evaluation systems, which are clearly defined and regulated, linked with government priorities and budget planning in order to enhance efficiency by enabling the government to have analysis-based policies, drafting of qualitative policies and legislation and approximation of legislation to the *acquis*.

In the *Organisation and Functioning of Public Administration* area the aim of the policy goal was to establish efficient and accountable public administration structures and reduce corruption. And in the area of *Civil Service Human Resource Management*, the policy goal was to develop a professional, impartial, independent and merit-based civil service.

14.8.2 Bosnia and Herzegovina

The latest PAR Strategy of Bosnia and Herzegovina is for the period 2018–2022. The shared vision of the Strategy is "*to develop a modern public administration at all four levels of government that will ensure*

[40] Albania Crosscutting Public Administration Reform Strategy 2015–2020.

and respect the principles of the European Administrative Space underlying the functioning of public administration in the European Union and contribute to a successful accession and approximation process, while safeguarding public interest and meeting the needs of citizens and businesses".

The priority areas of the Strategy are:(1) Strengthening public administration capacities through implementation of the principles of the European Administrative Space; (2) Establishment of customer-oriented and transparent public administration; (3) Development of professional and depoliticised and merit-based service system; and (4) Establishment of rational, coherent, efficient, effective, and accountable organisational structure in public administration, at every level of administrative authority.

And the expected results from its implementation are: (1) Public administration operation improved in accordance with the European Administrative Space principles; (2) Simplified service provision procedure in support of economic development; (3) Service quality tailored to users' actual needs, accompanied by adequate level of communication and technology development; (4) Policies and regulations adopted based on assessments of options and evidence, with participation of the public; (5) The principle of competence and performance appraisal affirmed as the main principle of human resource management in public administration; and (6) Transparent and accountable public administration.

14.8.3 Kosovo

The Public Administration Reform Strategy (PARS) 2022–2027 is a strategic document of the Government of the Republic of Kosovo that sets out objectives and guidelines for the development and modernisation of public administration over the next five years. The vision of the PAR Strategy is "*a modern public administration that serves the public interest, meets the needs of citizens and businesses, and successfully completes the EU membership process, supporting democracy and the rule of law*".

The scope of PARS is summarised into four priority areas[41]: (a) Policy Planning and Coordination; (b) Service Delivery; (c) Public Service and Human Resource Management (HRM); and (d) Accountability and transparency. For each priority area, a general medium-term objective

[41] Public Administration Reform Strategy 2022-2027 (Kosovo).

has been set that defines the main direction of reforms. The general and specific objectives of the PARS and their links to the strategic objectives of the NDP are illustrated below:

- *Government effectiveness:* The planning and coordination of results-oriented policies will be among the main priorities of the Government, with the view of ensuring more effective governance through better planning, monitoring, and supervision of the performance of the state administration. For this purpose, further support will be provided for the integration of policy and financial planning through additional measures.
- *Better regulation and service delivery*: The economic development of the country should not be affected by government regulations, therefore barriers and burdens for business should be reviewed, i.e., considered, and therefore lifted or reduced, while new obstacles should be prevented. Taxpayers, citizens, and businesses deserve treatment and services of much higher standards and better protection of their rights against the voluntary or discretionary powers of the administration. The service-oriented administrative culture must evolve from the bureaucratic mindset and attitude.
- *Public Service and HRM:* Professional, impartial, and competent civil and public service employees are necessary to turn the vision of PARS into reality. Building a modern and effective public service system with advanced HRM policies and practices that are effectively implemented in the public sector is among the central goals of the PARS. The modernisation and development of the public service system that started several years ago will continue to its completion. Enhanced HRM policies will improve personnel planning, merit-based recruitment, and promotion processes, including transparency. They will develop competencies of civil servants, support better mobility and performance in the public service and will promote systematic monitoring of employee performance.
- *Accountability and transparency*: The successful completion of reforms aimed at improving the organisation and functioning of the state administration is the main objective in this priority area. Although the earlier reforms provided a good legal basis for streamlining of the state administration, its full implementation and effects are yet to be seen. For this purpose, additional measures will be

taken to ensure that the state administration is organised and developed in accordance with established criteria and standards. In this regard, coordination, and supervisory responsibilities of the relevant institutions—Ministry of Internal Affairs (MIA), and the Office of the Prime Minister (OPM)—must be strengthened and their capacities increased. The process of streamlining of agencies will assume a new dynamic, based on the criteria and improved methodology established by the government, while its implementation will also be monitored by the government. The accountability of agencies (including their management) for their performance will be strengthened by the implementation of the results-oriented performance management system. The system will be promoted, implemented gradually and employees will be supported in developing the required knowledge, skills and techniques through training and capacity development programmes. The implementation of the system may require some internal organisational adjustments in the "parent" ministries and the MIA will facilitate this process. The performance management system will also extend to the ministries within the broader framework of performance management coordinated by the OPM, thus increasing the accountability of the ministries' performance.

The direction and implementation of the PARS will be coordinated at three levels:

- *Political level*—The Council of Ministers for Public Administration Reform (CMPAR), is the main structure responsible at the political level for the strategic direction and supervision of the reform process, including taking corrective measures. The Council meets at least two times a year.
- *PAR Secretariat*—The Department of PAR (DPAR/MIA) which will serve as the secretariat for both CMPAR, as well as for continuous monitoring and reporting.
- *Administrative level*—consisting of two coordination groups responsible for the supervision of implementation, implementation of CMPAR instructions and coordination between institutions on a quarterly basis.

14.8.4 North Macedonia

The PAR Strategy (2023–2030) is directly aimed at achieving its priorities through defined goals that provide a strategic framework for the development of public administration until 2030.[42] Through the four priority areas in which measures are defined to fulfil the general and specific objectives, the PAR Strategy strives to fulfil the vision in four priority areas: (1) Policy Development and Coordination; (2) Public Service and Human Resource Management; (3) Responsibility, Accountability and Transparency; and (4) Service Delivery and Digital Transformation.

- *Policy Development and Coordination:* General objective in this area is an effective, efficient, transparent, inclusive, and evidence-based policy development. In order to achieve the general and specific objectives in this first priority area, measures will be taken to develop and maintain a functional mechanism for alignment of the long-term with the medium-term and annual planning through the improvement of processes and electronic horizontal and vertical connection of organisational units for strategic planning in the state administration bodies with the GS. Also, activities will be undertaken to strengthen the capacities in the GS and those of the employees in the organisational units for strategic planning in the state administration bodies. The policy coordination and decision-making system of the Government of the Republic of North Macedonia (GRNM) will be enhanced by improving the quality of the legal framework (new Rules of Procedure of GRNM) and further digitalisation of the planning and coordination processes and simplification of the work of the GS by upgrading the E-Government system.
- *Public Service and Human Resource Management:* General objective in this area is an expert and professional public administration free from political influence. Priority measures are aimed at building an expert and professional public administration free from political influence. Recruitment planning according to the needs will be ensured by linking the strategic planning with human resource planning in institutions, and recruitment procedures in the public administration will be improved by strengthening the role of the

[42] Public Administration Reform Strategy 2023–2030 with Action Plan 2023–2026 for North Macedonia.

interview based on appropriate competences. Special attention is given to the periodic verification of competences of the already employed staff to ensure adequate distribution of administrative servants according to their performance. In addition, unification of the organisational structure of the administrative service will be carried out in municipalities and in institutions performing activities of public interest (education, health, culture, social and child protection, utility, and other activities).

- *Responsibility, Accountability and Transparency:* General objective in this area is the responsible, accountable, and transparent operation of institutions. To achieve the defined general and specific objectives in this third priority area, special attention is devoted to the reorganisation and optimisation of the state administration, in order to enhance and increase efficiency, as well as to clearly define the lines of responsibility (Mitrvic 2023).
- *Service Delivery and Digital Transformation:* General objective in this area is a digitalised public administration. Priority measures are aimed at building a digital environment for better operation of the administration, i.e., creating channels of electronic communication within the administration, establishing a unified document management system (DMS) in the bodies of the state administration, local self-government, and other public sector institutions.

14.8.5 Montenegro

The vision of the Public Administration Reform Strategy 2022–2026 is a professional public administration,[43] which in a high-quality manner delivers services to end users and has adequate capacity for accession to the European Union. The following values underpin the vision and goals of the Strategy: (1) Equality; (2) Participation and Partnership; (3) Accountable and Efficient Management and Governance; (4) Decision-Making based on Data and Evidence; and (5) Transparency.

This strategic document defines five strategic goals, followed by situation analysis for each of them, challenges identified, and operational objectives and indicators developed, in accordance with the Methodology for Developing Policies, Drafting and Monitoring the Implementation

[43] Public Administration Reform Strategy 2022-2025 for Montenegro.

of Strategic Documents. They are: (1) Citizen-oriented organisation and operation of Public Administration; (2) Citizens and businesses use high-quality services of the public administration; (3) Professional public administration; (4) Transparent and open public administration; and (5) Policy planning with and for citizens.

14.8.6 Serbia

The latest PAR Strategy in Serbia covers the period from 2021 to 2030. According to the Strategy, the public administration reform process will be based on the principles of depoliticisation, professionalisation, development of human resources in the administration and their competencies, modernisation and digitalisation, openness to change and innovations, reliability and predictability (legal certainty), openness, transparency and participation, accountability, efficiency, effectiveness (result-oriented), decentralisation, social accountability, consistency in the application, and the implementation of reforms within a sustainable public finances framework.

The overall objective of the Strategy that must be achieved is further improvement of public administration operations and the quality of formulation of public policies in line with the European Principles of Public Administration; delivering high-quality services to citizens and businesses; as well as a professional public administration which will significantly contribute to economic stability and improvement of the standard of living. The main area of the PAR Strategy are: (1) Public policy planning and coordination; (2) Human resource management; (3) Service delivery; (4) Accountability and transparency; (5) Public financial management; and (6) Local self-government system.

- *Public policy planning and coordination:* In the long-term, the following objective is envisaged: the business environment in Serbia is to be competitive, with a public administration guided by EU Principles of Good Governance, as a result of a well-designed (realistic and fact-based) and widely accepted (transparent, inclusive, well-communicated) process of planning public policy documents and regulations and their consistent implementation. A specific objective of the PAR Strategy on the Public Policy Management and Regulatory Reform Programme is based through four specific objectives: (1) Regulatory reform in the function of improving the business environment and decreasing the burden for citizens and economy; (2) Strengthening capacities and use of instruments for quality planning and monitoring of the implementation of public policies and regulations;(3) Effective policy coordination; and (4) Increasing the level of civil society, businesses, and other stakeholder participation in early phases of public policy and regulation development and monitoring of the effects.

- *Human resource management:* In order to have a citizen-oriented public administration the aim is to ensure further development of the civil service by (1) Attracting and employing staff with the necessary competencies; (2) Promoting and retaining competent and motivated staff who achieve their career goals in an enabling environment; and (3) Innovating the system of professional development and professional exams in public administration based on the analysis of needs for the improvement of competencies, knowledge, skills, and abilities of public administration staff. Under this objective, it is expected that by the end of 2030 state administration will be perceived as a desirable employer who applies transparent procedures, identifies better the staff needed by state administration, who have adequate job competencies, and has more efficient recruitment and selection procedures, including merit-based appointment of senior civil servants.
- *Service delivery:* The focus of reforms in the field of service delivery by 2030 is the establishment of an adaptable public administration that provides integrated user-oriented services in a short period of time, at reasonable costs, especially considering minority and vulnerable social groups. A specific objective in service delivery is that public administration provides services in an efficient and innovative manner matching the needs of end users and enhances their user experience. In order to achieve this specific objective, the implementation of the following measures is envisaged: (1) Development of new and optimisation of existing services tailored for end users; (2) Raising human and technical–technological capacities of public administration for service delivery to end users; and (3) Improving the system of service quality control and quality assurance.
- *Accountability and transparency:* The specific objective in this case is increased level of accountability and transparency at all levels of the government to enable, to a greater extent, a public administration that is accountable for the results, and achieving its goals in

line with principles of "sound management". It should also enable the establishment of a more efficient ethical infrastructure in public administration, with sustainable capacities, as well as reduce the risk of corruption and unethical behaviour to a minimum. Emphasis will also be placed on regular publication of open data and informing the public on all aspects of the work of public administration in order to enable citizens to monitor and influence its work, including reports on the achievement of objectives from public policy documents.

- *Public financial management:* For the next ten years, the objective is for the Republic of Serbia to manage its public finances in a way that ensures fiscal and macroeconomic stability, effective financing of national policy priorities, transparency of public finances and effective control over public spending. Specific objective in this area is to achieve a sustainable budget with a stable public debt to GDP ratio through better financial management and control, the audit process and linking budget planning to Government policies.
- *Local self-government system:* The objective is to build a modern, professional, and efficient local self-government that is capable of providing quality public services to citizens and the economy, to apply the principles of good governance in its work and to improve the quality of life of citizens and contribute to the balanced development of the Republic of Serbia. The specific Objective of the PAR Strategy on Local self-government system reform Programme is based through four specific objectives: (1) Enhanced status and accountability of local self-government; (2) Enhanced financing system that enables adequate and predictable financing of local self-government; (3) Enhanced organisation and capacities of local self-government; and (4) Enhanced quality and accessibility of administrative, utility and services of public institutions of local self-government to all users.

14.9 Conclusions

According to SIGMA/OECD, public administrations of the Western Balkan countries have improved their overall performance since 2017, especially Albania and Serbia On average, the performance of Western Balkan Administrations improved since 2017 in all areas except strategic framework of PAR, where all administrations except North Macedonia were in the process of either establishing, renewing, or extending their PAR strategies in 2020–2021. Albania and Serbia demonstrated the most consistent and substantial improvements across all areas. Albania recorded the highest averages for four areas: policy development and coordination, public service, and human resource management, service delivery and public financial management. Serbia stands out by progressing well overall, especially in service delivery, accountability, and budget management, and having the best-performing external audit system. Kosovo advanced the most in its PFM systems, particularly in strengthening budget management. North Macedonia was the only administration that improved its strategic framework for PAR and made satisfactory progress in public procurement and accountability. Montenegro has the highest average in the area of accountability, but this has not progressed since 2017. Across all areas, Montenegro progressed the most in public service delivery and human resource management.

Laws Improved, but Implementation Remains Weak

Progress was the most pronounced in the quality of regulations and policy documents, and least for indicators that measure implementation practices and outcomes. Across the region, for the public service and HRM area, legislation was strengthened, whereas practice improved by only 1.8 percentage points.[44] Overall progress in the accountability area was largely driven by improvement in the legal framework for "accountability and organisation of central government"; however, this dimension remains the worst in absolute terms across the area because laws are still not implemented consistently. In the PFM area, the quality of the legal framework for public procurement recorded both the highest absolute value (4.4) and best improvement (+1.2) across all 52 composite indicators. On the other hand, the practical, operational support of central public procurement institutions to contracting authorities and economic operators has deteriorated since 2017. Similarly, formal systems for regulatory impact assessment and public consultations have been significantly strengthened, but from a low base, and practices are still inconsistent and in need of improvement. Additionally, despite already good legislation in place, laws are very frequently amended, leading to regulatory instability.

[44] SIGMA/OECD, "Methodological Framework of the Principles of Public Administration" (2019).

A lack of timely adoption of mandatory bylaws impedes implementation efforts. Future gains will not come mainly from improving primary legislation, which in many cases is already comparable with what exists in EU member countries. Rather than legal drafting, it is policy implementation, change management and improvement of organisational culture that are needed to be going forward.

Major Reforms Rarely Succeed Without Sustained Political Leadership and Public Trust

A predictor of overall progress across the public governance domain since 2017 is the level of continued and consistent political direction and leadership. Mature administrations are expected to deliver public services and scheduled reform processes even in the absence of political leadership, so that major reforms will not suffer or falter from neglect. The public administrations that advanced the most overall—Albania and Serbia—benefited from sustained political support and rising levels of public trust. In Kosovo, Montenegro and North Macedonia, several key public governance reforms did not advance when there was no government in place due to a political deadlock. Public administrations in the Western Balkans have space to increase their capability to sustain reform activities during changes in political leadership. Trust in government and public institutions can help sustain positive reform plans. In Kosovo and North Macedonia, trust fell not only in government and parliament but also in the Ombudsperson, the Supreme Audit Institution, and the courts. When trust falls in institutions that are supposed to be politically neutral and should be a factor of stability in periods of political turbulence—such as the Ombudsperson—it reinforces the need to further support capable and independent oversight institutions and the judiciary.

Better Top Management and Managerial Accountability Are Needed in the Western Balkans

Despite overall progress since 2017, it is worrisome that several dimensions related to the quality of top management and managerial accountability showed deterioration. Capable and accountable managers are at the frontline of implementing legislation, transforming policy into action, safeguarding public finances, and ensuring continuity of government operations. "Merit recruitment/dismissal of top civil servants" was the worst-performing dimension of all in 2021 in the public service and the HRM area. The weakest sub-area of PFM in all administrations was internal control and audit. "Functioning of internal control", which provides a measure of managerial accountability, fell on average from 1.2 in 2017 to 0.6 in 2021. Increasing the talent pool and strengthening the competences of existing top managers will require a dedicated focus on attracting the best candidates and developing this group of civil servants, something that has so far been missing. Existing professional development and training resources are rudimentary, are not aimed at top managers, and deteriorated since 2017. Continued progress in public governance in the Western Balkans depends on more professional, competent, responsive, accountable, and stable top management of civil services. Greater managerial accountability is needed, not only to reduce fiduciary risk but also to strengthen trust in the public administration.

14.9.1 New PAR Strategy

As already mentioned, some of the Western Balkan countries already have new PAR Strategies. Those Strategies contain many activities in their Action Plans with the intention to reform their public administrations. But are these activities in accordance with global trends in public administration reform? SIGMA in its revised edition of the Principles of Public Administration, published in November 2023, admits that public administrations today, are expected to be more digital, agile, innovative, and green than in 2014. These new versions reflect the importance of fully embracing the potential of digitalisation, lessons learned during the global COVID-19 pandemic (strengthening agility and resilience of public administration and flexibility of working arrangements), as well as the expectation that public administration contributes to addressing the environmental challenges, including those of climate change and loss of biodiversity.

However, these new PAR Strategies do not reflect new global trends in public administration (Çela et al. 2020). Let us mention some of them that public administration reform policy in the Western Balkan countries should take into consideration, in order their administration to be more compatible with global trends in public administration:

- *Increased Digital Governance:* The complications of the COVID-19 pandemic have ushered in the next generation of government digitalisation. For many public agencies, digital transformation went from "good to have" to "must-have". Governments in Westerns Balkan countries need to speed their digital journey along three important dimensions to accommodate the spike in service demand while working virtually: building a more digitally skilled staff; growing their digital infrastructure; and investing in citizen connection.

- *Improved Data Management:* Within and beyond government, data is becoming increasingly important. Public agencies are developing new ways to maximise the value of the data they have, including sharing it correctly and ethically. The trend towards fluid, dynamic data is transforming how government and its partners in academia, charities and the commercial sector utilise and exchange data around the world.
- *Anticipatory Public Services:* Citizens are increasingly receiving tailored, seamless, and proactive services in their daily lives, and they expect the same from government entities. In order to transform their services and realize this idea of seamless service delivery, governments are pursuing several strategies, such as: Committing to entirely digital services; Constructing infrastructure to enable such seamless services; Establishing proactive services based on life events.
- *Diversity, Equity, and Inclusion:* Another concern related to increased digitisation and data usage is ensuring that government agencies also prioritise diversity, equity, and inclusion. Responsible organisations are now concentrating more on the underlying causes of systemic inequalities and examining how their policies are produced, implemented, and reviewed. Some of the approaches being used are: Accessible design of government services; Co-creation and citizen engagement; Data sovereignty and equity; Equitable access to public goods.
- *Flexible and Remote Workplaces:* Organisations are rethinking how to conduct their missions. The pandemic brought the future of government employment into the present, from remote labour to telemedicine and online classrooms. This direction coincides with the rise of flexible and remote workplaces, including methods for managing a distributed workforce and providing high-quality citizen services remotely.
- *Agile Administration:* The COVID-19 pandemic underlined the importance of rapid, flexible, and mission-driven governance. Government entities must be able to make quick judgments and

move ahead with confidence, especially during emergencies. Policy-making, legislation, procurement, and the workforce are all examples of where this is needed.

- *Rebuilding Government Trust:* In the Western Balkan countries trust in the government has been near historic lows for years. To rebuild government trust there are steps that need to be taken like:
  - Arming citizens with meaningful information (publishing public spending data, allowing citizens to track how their government is spending taxpayer money, report cases of official misconduct and request specific information on spendings);
  - Reaching out to marginalised citizens (inclusion of the most vulnerable in public dialogue and policy priorities is essential to win their trust)
  - Responding to citizen needs (citizens need to feel that government is responsive to their voice);
  - Empowering citizens to follow the money (Enabling citizens to monitor government spending and report the misuse of public funds helps build confidence in public institutions by demonstrating that tax money is being spent wisely);
  - Enlisting citizens in the fight against corruption (Elite capture and grand corruption fuel citizen distrust and apathy, reinforcing the corrosive perception that government does not work for the people. Open government approaches can rebuild citizen trust on Government).

References

Çela, Alba, Spasimir Domaradzki, Balsa Lubarda, Ivana Radić Milosavljević, Ivan Stefanovski, and Naum Trajanovski. 2020. *Western Balkan 2030 trends*. Poland: Res Publica Foundation.

Cardona, Francisco, SIGMA. 2009. *Integrating National Administrations into the European administrative space*. Budva, Montenegro.

Jreisat, Jamil. 2011. *Globalism and comparative public administration*. London: CRC Press Taylor & Francis Group.

Lucica, M., D. Vašiček, and M. Kaštelan. 2011. *European administrative space Balkan realities*. Bucharest: Editura Economica.

Meyer-Sahling, Jan-Hinrik. Civil service professionalisation in the Western Balkans. Sigma Paper No 48. https://one.oecd.org/document/GOV/SIGMA(2012)1/En/pdf.

Mitrvic, Sava. 2023. *Transparency of public administration reform in the Western Balkans: Numerous shortcomings and limited examples of good practice in the region*. Belgrade: WeBER 20.

Nieto-Garrido, Eva, and Isaac Martín Delgado. 2007. *European Administrative Law in the constitutional treaty*. Portland: Hart Publishing.

Peters, B. Guy., and Jon Pierre. 2004. *Politicization of the civil service in comparative perspective*. New York: Routledge.

SIGMA/OECD. 1995. Top management service in central government: Introducing a system for the higher civil service in central and Eastern European countries. SIGMA Paper No 1. https://doi.org/10.1787/5kml6gln4cbq-en.

UNDP. 2010. *Motivating civil servants for reform and performance*. New York.

Index

A. Baimenov and P. Liverakos (eds.), *Public Administration in the New Reality*, https://doi.org/10.1007/978-981-96-3845-1

The manufacturer's authorised representative in the EU is Springer Nature Customer Service Centre GmbH, Europaplatz 3, 69115 Heidelberg, Germany. If you have any concerns regarding our products, please contact ProductSafety@springernature.com

Printed and bound by CPI Group (UK) Ltd, Croydon, CR0 4YY

01/10/2026

02225924-0012